INJUSTICE

GODS AMONG US

VOLUME 2

INJU
GODS A
VOL

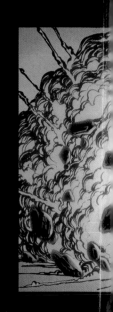

THIS STORY TAKES PLACE BEFORE
THE START OF THE GAME

Tom Taylor
Writer

**Mike S. Miller   Bruno Redondo   Tom Derenick
Kevin Maguire   Neil Googe   Jheremy Raapack
Xermanico   Jonas Trindade**
Artists

**Rosemary Cheetham   Alejandro Sanchez
David Lopez & Santi Casas of Ikari Studio**
Colorists

Wes Abbott
Letterer

STICE

ONG US

E 2

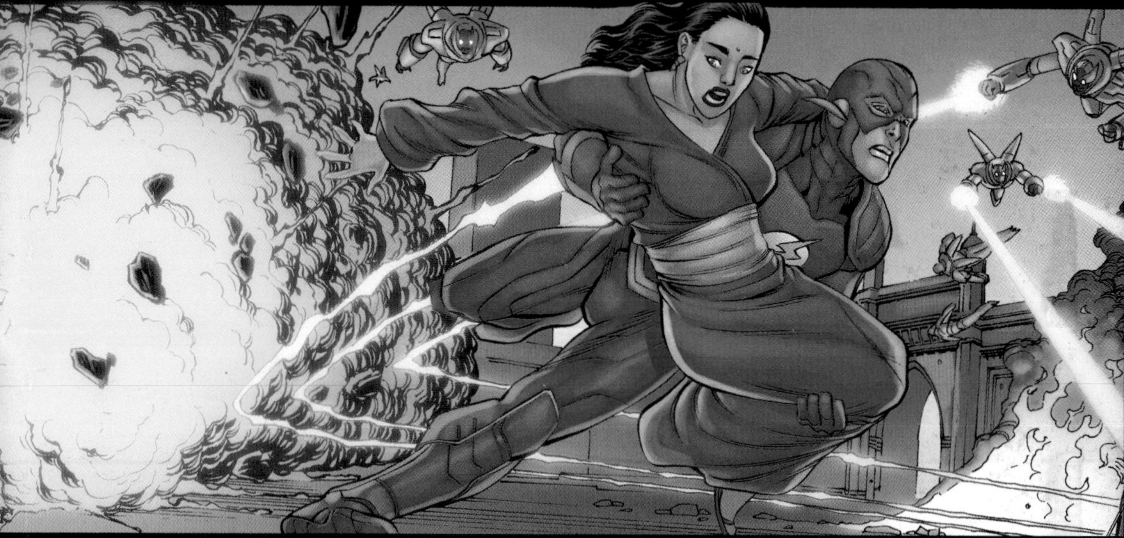

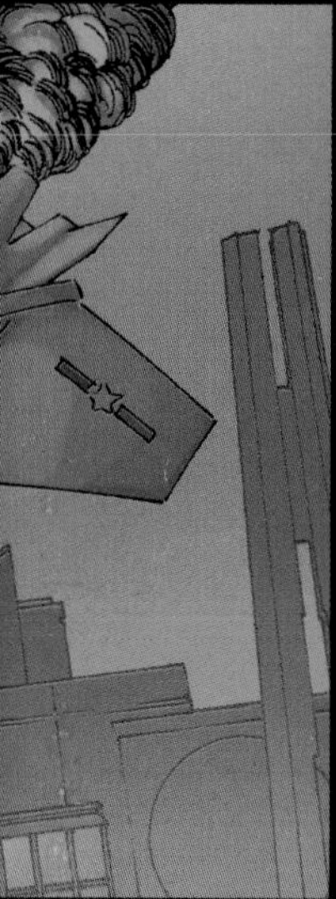

SUPERMAN Created by JERRY SIEGEL and JOE SHUSTER.
By Special Arrangement with the Jerry Siegel Family.

BASED ON THE VIDEOGAME INJUSTICE: GODS AMONG US

Jim Chadwick Editor – Original Series
Aniz Ansari Assistant Editor – Original Series
Rachel Pinnelas Editor
Robbin Brosterman Design Director – Books
Louis Prandi Publication Design

Hank Kanalz Senior VP – Vertigo & Integrated Publishing

Diane Nelson President
Dan DiDio and Jim Lee Co-Publishers
Geoff Johns Chief Creative Officer
John Rood Executive VP – Sales, Marketing & Business
               Development
Amy Genkins Senior VP – Business & Legal Affairs
Nairi Gardiner Senior VP – Finance
Jeff Boison VP – Publishing Planning
Mark Chiarello VP – Art Direction & Design
John Cunningham VP – Marketing
Terri Cunningham VP – Editorial Administration
Alison Gill Senior VP – Manufacturing & Operations
Jay Kogan VP – Business & Legal Affairs, Publishing
Jack Mahan VP – Business Affairs, Talent
Nick Napolitano VP – Manufacturing Administration
Sue Pohja VP – Book Sales
Courtney Simmons Senior VP – Publicity
Bob Wayne Senior VP – Sales

INJUSTICE: GODS AMONG US VOLUME 2

Published by DC Comics. Copyright © 2014 DC Comics. All Rights
Reserved.

Originally published in single magazine form in INJUSTICE: GODS
AMONG US 7-12 and INJUSTICE: GODS AMONG US ANNUAL 1.
Copyright © 2013, 2014 DC Comics. All Rights Reserved.
All characters, their distinctive likenesses and related elements
featured in this publication are trademarks of DC Comics.
The stories, characters and incidents featured in this publication
are entirely fictional. DC Comics does not read or accept
unsolicited ideas, stories or artwork.

DC Comics, 1700 Broadway, New York, NY 10019
A Warner Bros. Entertainment Company.
Printed by RR Donnelley, Salem, VA. USA. 5/23/14. First Printing.
ISBN: 978-1-4012-4601-3

Library of Congress Cataloging-in-Publication Data

Taylor, Tom, 1978- author.
   Injustice : Gods among us, Volume 1 / Tom Taylor, Jheremy
Raapack, Mike S. Miller.
       pages cm
   "Originally published in single magazine form as INJUSTICE Digital
Chapters 1-18."
    ISBN 978-1-4012-4500-9
1. Graphic novels. I. Raapack, Jheremy, illustrator. II. Miller, Mike S,
illustrator. III. Title. IV. Title: Gods among us, Volume 1.
    PN6727.T293I55 2013
    741.5'973—dc23
                                                    2013021242

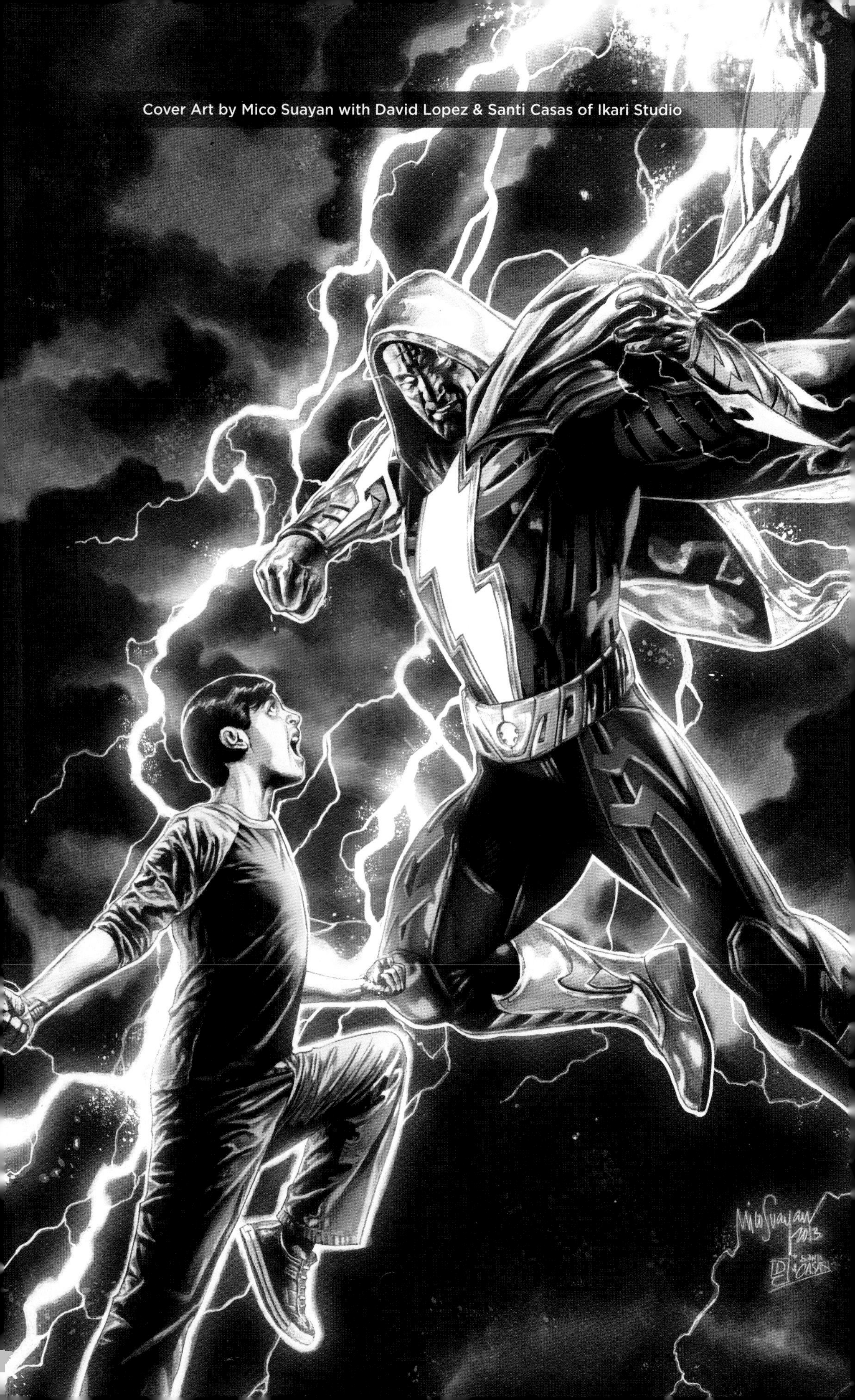

Cover Art by Mico Suayan with David Lopez & Santi Casas of Ikari Studio

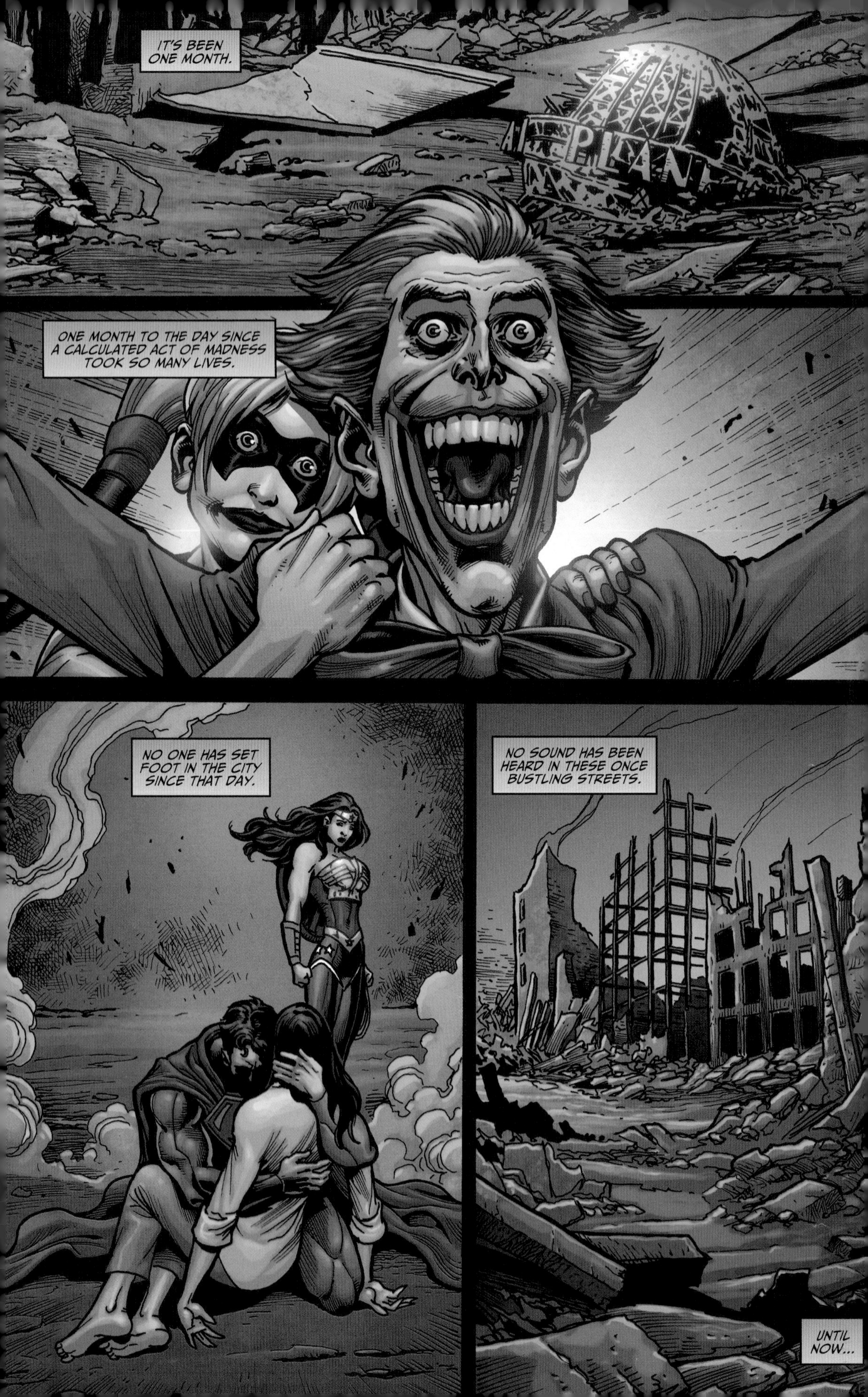
IT'S BEEN ONE MONTH.
ONE MONTH TO THE DAY SINCE A CALCULATED ACT OF MADNESS TOOK SO MANY LIVES.
NO ONE HAS SET FOOT IN THE CITY SINCE THAT DAY.
NO SOUND HAS BEEN HEARD IN THESE ONCE BUSTLING STREETS.
UNTIL NOW...

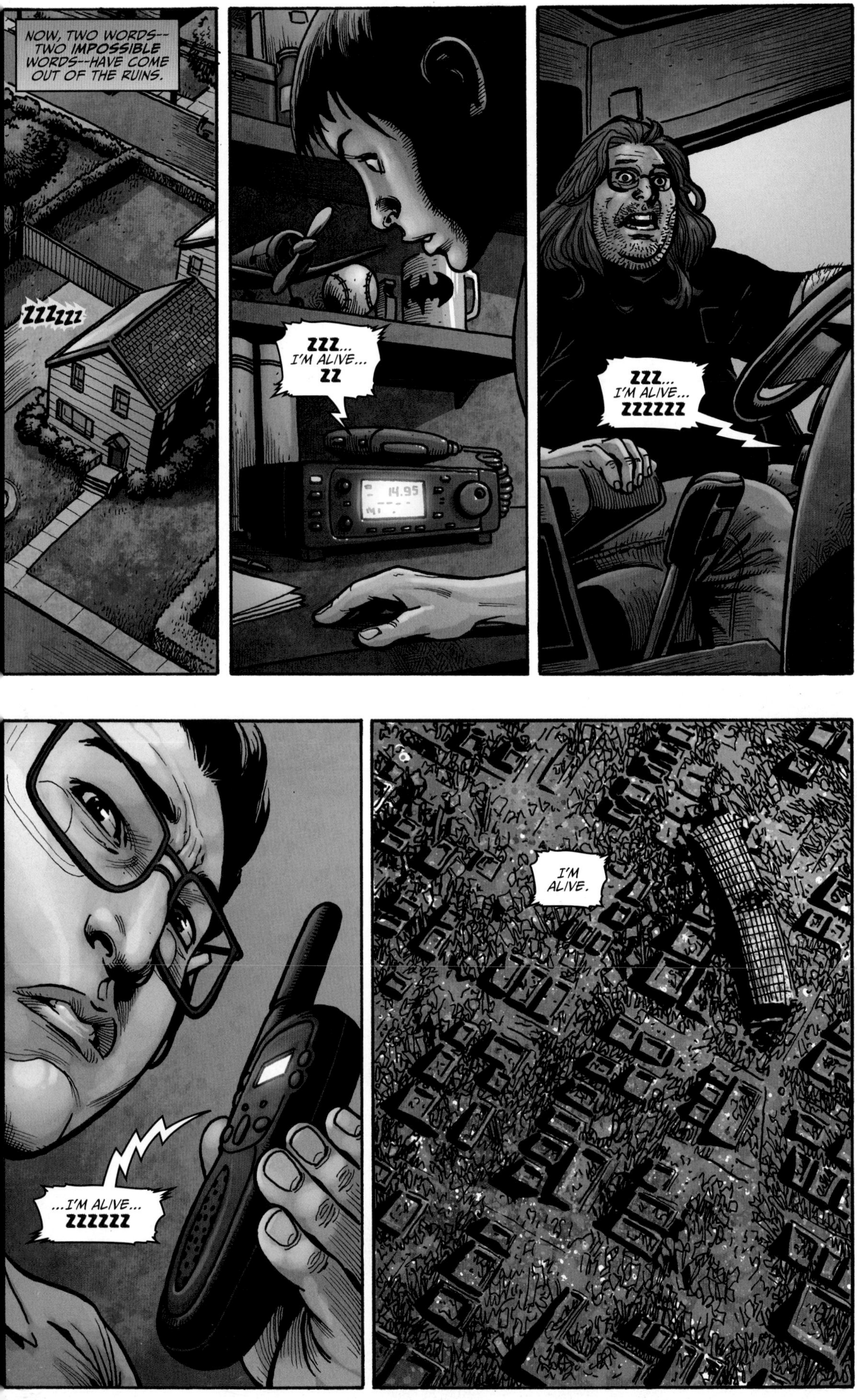
NOW, TWO WORDS--
TWO IMPOSSIBLE WORDS--HAVE COME OUT OF THE RUINS.
ZZZzzz
ZZZ... I'M ALIVE... ZZ
14.95
ZZZ... I'M ALIVE... ZZZZZZ
...I'M ALIVE... ZZZZZZ
I'M ALIVE.

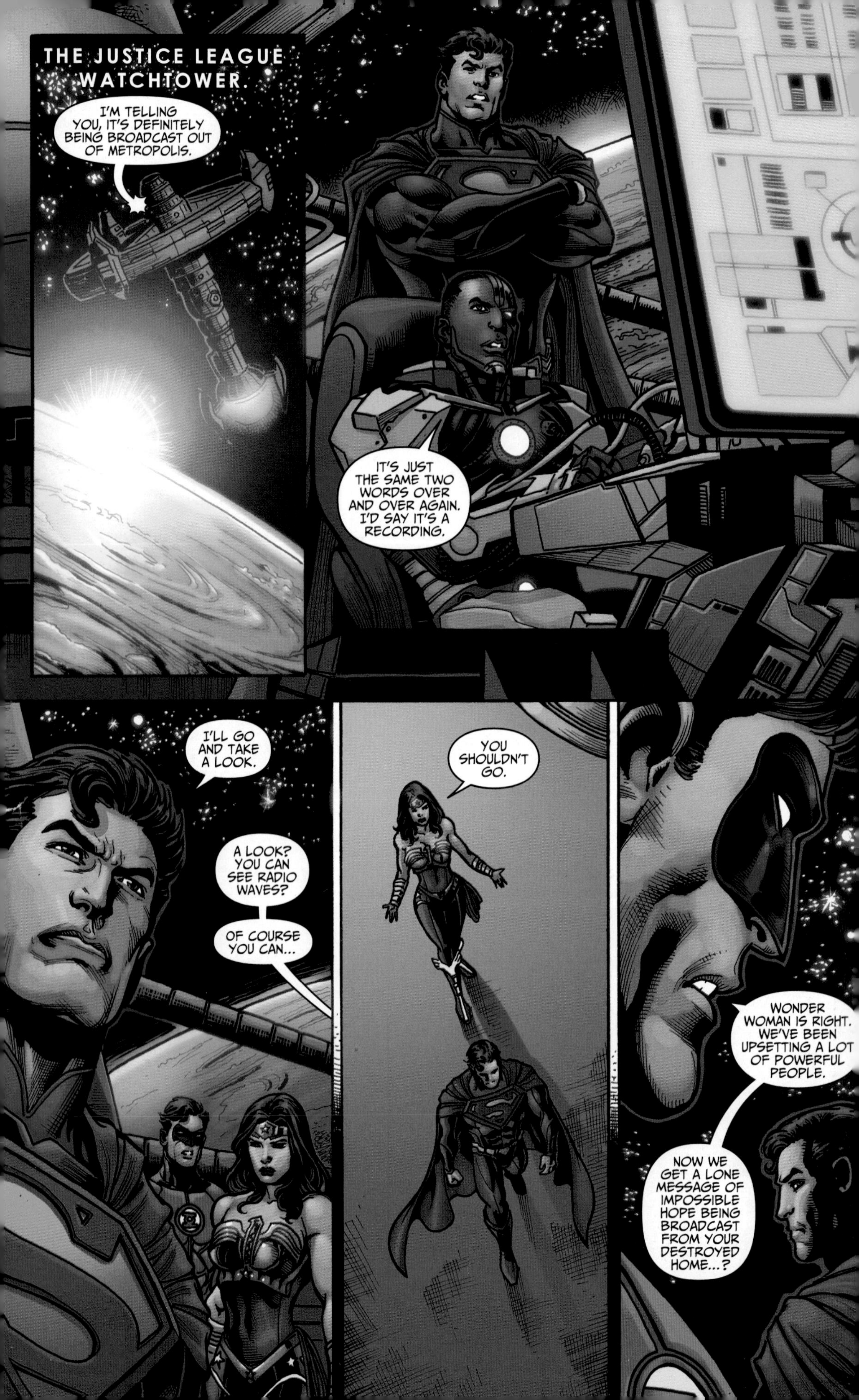
THE JUSTICE LEAGUE WATCHTOWER.
I'M TELLING YOU, IT'S DEFINITELY BEING BROADCAST OUT OF METROPOLIS.
IT'S JUST THE SAME TWO WORDS OVER AND OVER AGAIN. I'D SAY IT'S A RECORDING.
I'LL GO AND TAKE A LOOK.
A LOOK? YOU CAN SEE RADIO WAVES?
OF COURSE YOU CAN...
YOU SHOULDN'T GO.
WONDER WOMAN IS RIGHT. WE'VE BEEN UPSETTING A LOT OF POWERFUL PEOPLE.
NOW WE GET A LONE MESSAGE OF IMPOSSIBLE HOPE BEING BROADCAST FROM YOUR DESTROYED HOME...?

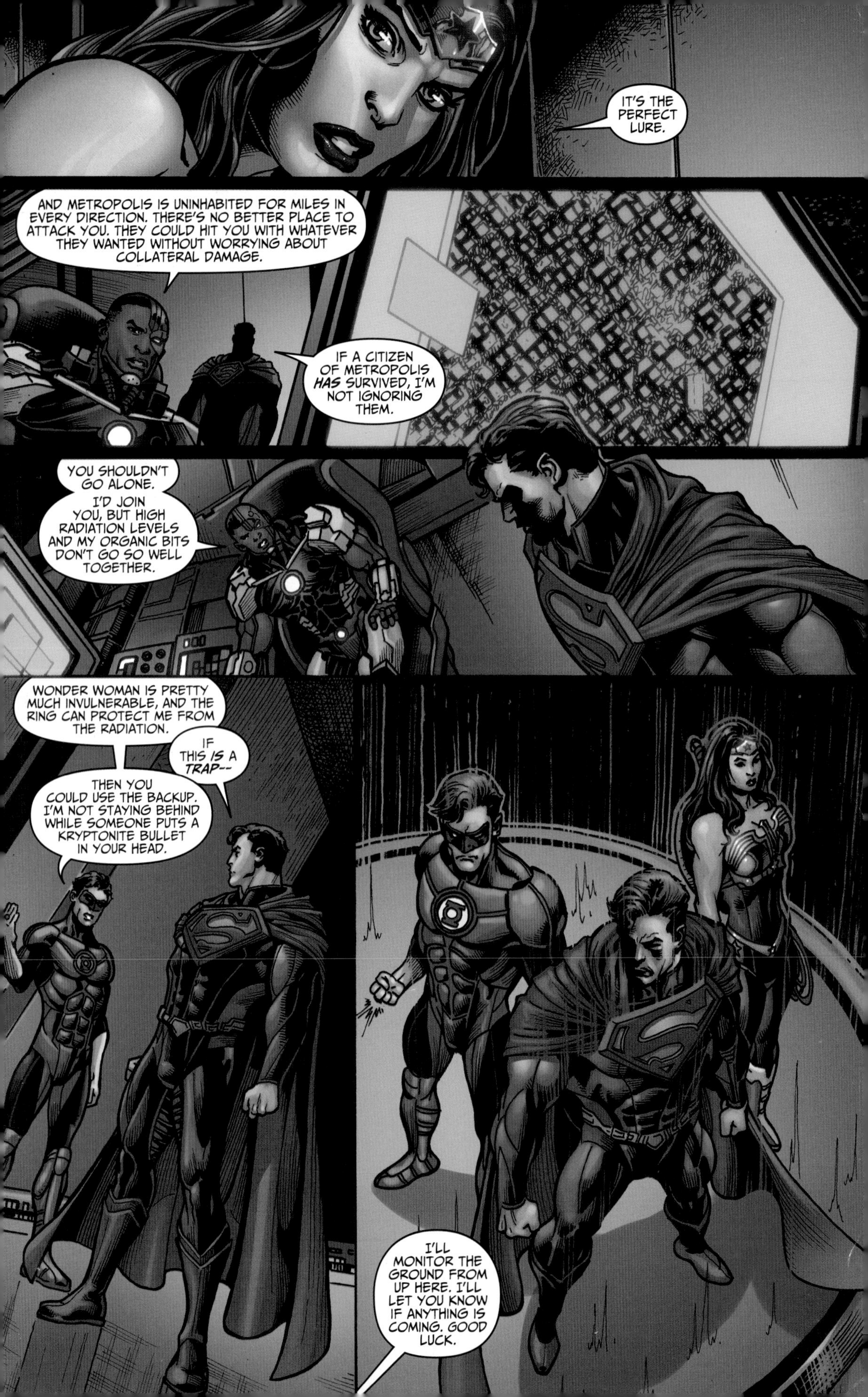
IT'S THE PERFECT LURE.
AND METROPOLIS IS UNINHABITED FOR MILES IN EVERY DIRECTION. THERE'S NO BETTER PLACE TO ATTACK YOU. THEY COULD HIT YOU WITH WHATEVER THEY WANTED WITHOUT WORRYING ABOUT COLLATERAL DAMAGE.
IF A CITIZEN OF METROPOLIS *HAS* SURVIVED, I'M NOT IGNORING THEM.
YOU SHOULDN'T GO ALONE.
I'D JOIN YOU, BUT HIGH RADIATION LEVELS AND MY ORGANIC BITS DON'T GO SO WELL TOGETHER.
WONDER WOMAN IS PRETTY MUCH INVULNERABLE, AND THE RING CAN PROTECT ME FROM THE RADIATION.
IF THIS *IS* A *TRAP--*
THEN YOU COULD USE THE BACKUP. I'M NOT STAYING BEHIND WHILE SOMEONE PUTS A KRYPTONITE BULLET IN YOUR HEAD.
I'LL MONITOR THE GROUND FROM UP HERE. I'LL LET YOU KNOW IF ANYTHING IS COMING. GOOD LUCK.

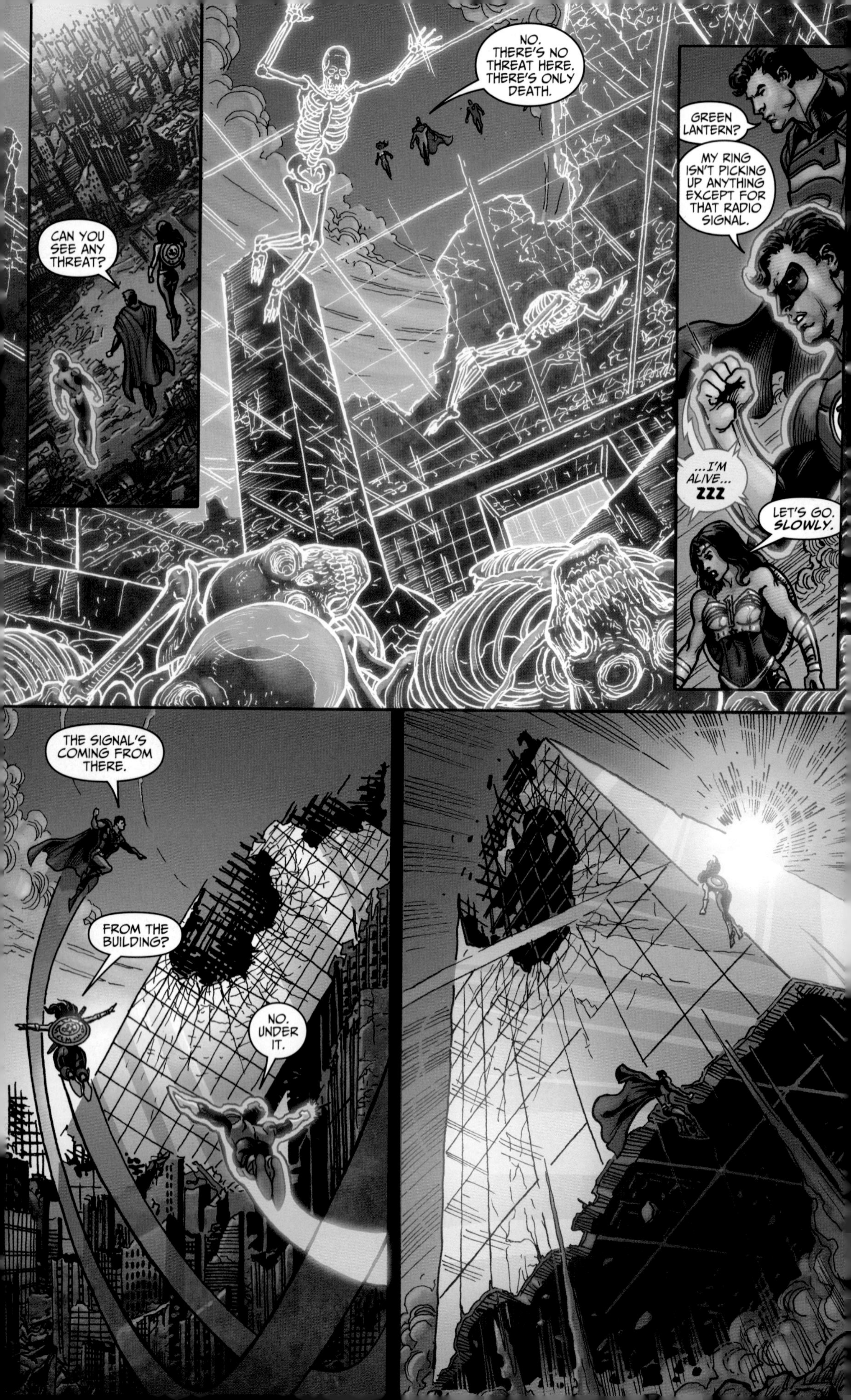
CAN YOU SEE ANY THREAT?
NO. THERE'S NO THREAT HERE. THERE'S ONLY DEATH.
GREEN LANTERN?
MY RING ISN'T PICKING UP ANYTHING EXCEPT FOR THAT RADIO SIGNAL.
...I'M ALIVE... ZZZ
LET'S GO. SLOWLY.
THE SIGNAL'S COMING FROM THERE.
FROM THE BUILDING?
NO. UNDER IT.

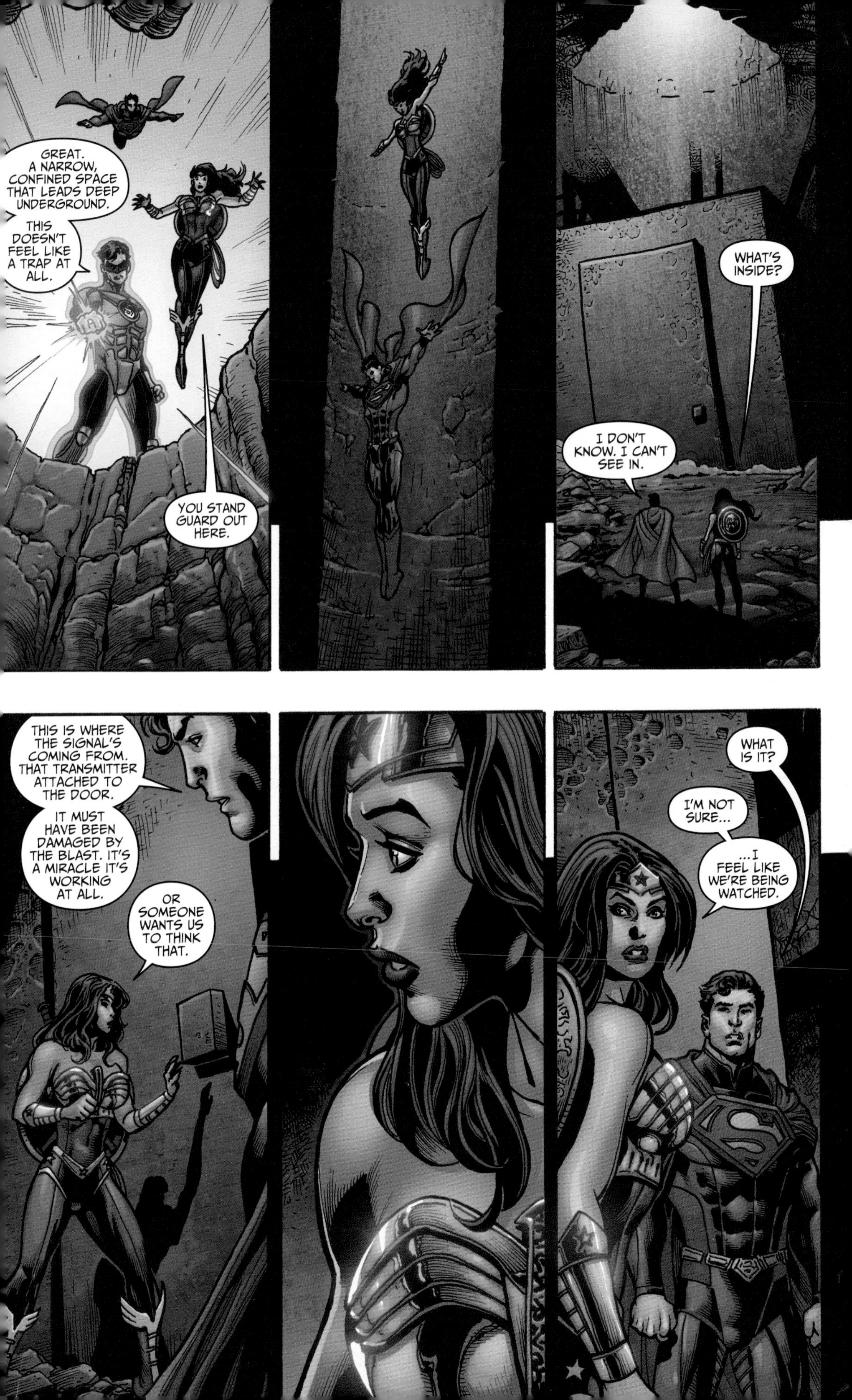
GREAT. A NARROW, CONFINED SPACE THAT LEADS DEEP UNDERGROUND.
THIS DOESN'T FEEL LIKE A TRAP AT ALL.
YOU STAND GUARD OUT HERE.
WHAT'S INSIDE?
I DON'T KNOW. I CAN'T SEE IN.
THIS IS WHERE THE SIGNAL'S COMING FROM. THAT TRANSMITTER ATTACHED TO THE DOOR.
IT MUST HAVE BEEN DAMAGED BY THE BLAST. IT'S A MIRACLE IT'S WORKING AT ALL.
OR SOMEONE WANTS US TO THINK THAT.
WHAT IS IT?
I'M NOT SURE...
...I FEEL LIKE WE'RE BEING WATCHED.

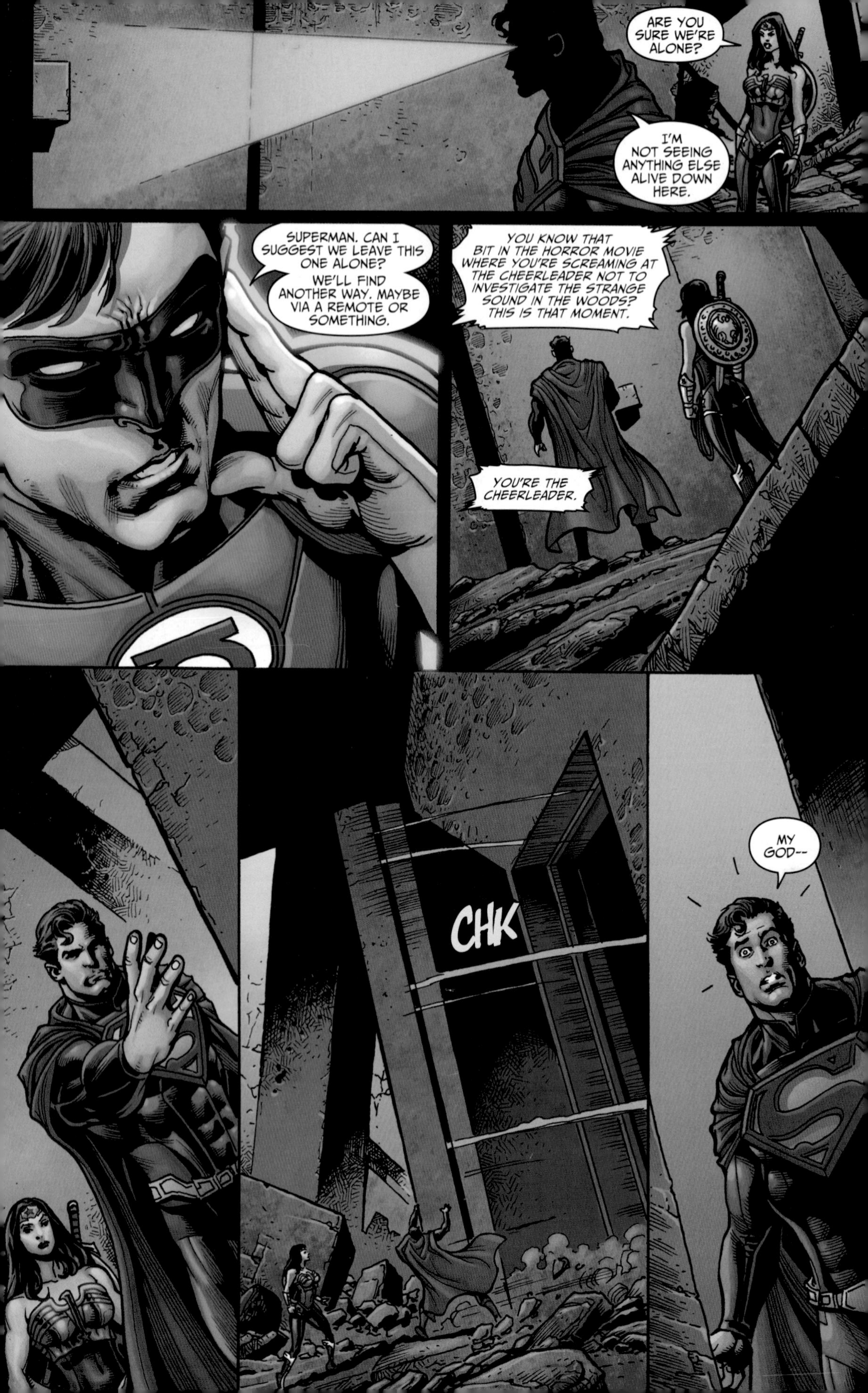
ARE YOU SURE WE'RE ALONE?
I'M NOT SEEING ANYTHING ELSE ALIVE DOWN HERE.
SUPERMAN. CAN I SUGGEST WE LEAVE THIS ONE ALONE?
WE'LL FIND ANOTHER WAY. MAYBE VIA A REMOTE OR SOMETHING.
YOU KNOW THAT BIT IN THE HORROR MOVIE WHERE YOU'RE SCREAMING AT THE CHEERLEADER NOT TO INVESTIGATE THE STRANGE SOUND IN THE WOODS? THIS IS THAT MOMENT.
YOU'RE THE CHEERLEADER.
CHK
MY GOD--

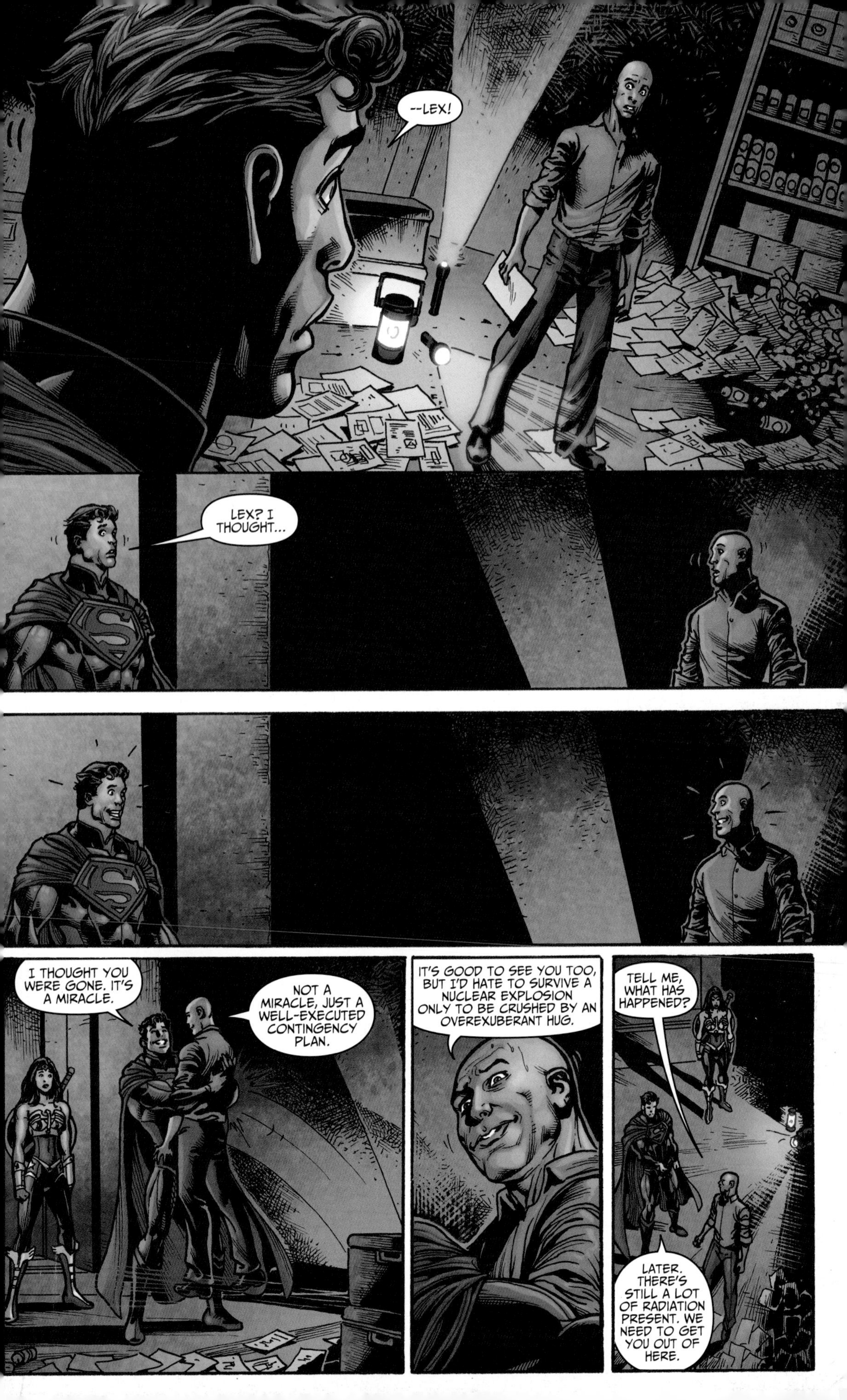
--LEX!
LEX? I THOUGHT...
I THOUGHT YOU WERE GONE. IT'S A MIRACLE.
NOT A MIRACLE, JUST A WELL-EXECUTED CONTINGENCY PLAN.
IT'S GOOD TO SEE YOU TOO, BUT I'D HATE TO SURVIVE A NUCLEAR EXPLOSION ONLY TO BE CRUSHED BY AN OVEREXUBERANT HUG.
TELL ME, WHAT HAS HAPPENED?
LATER. THERE'S STILL A LOT OF RADIATION PRESENT. WE NEED TO GET YOU OUT OF HERE.

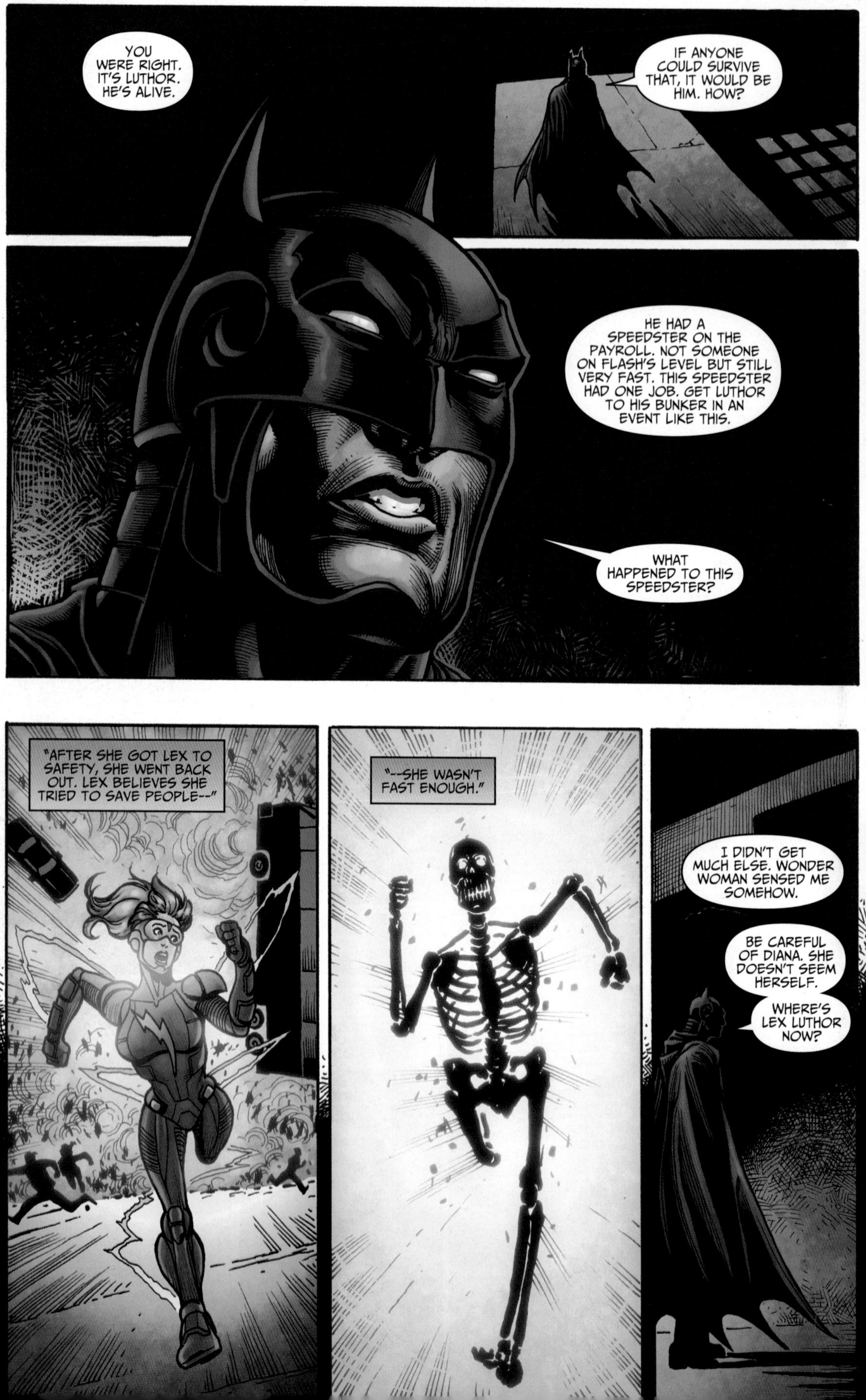
YOU WERE RIGHT. IT'S LUTHOR. HE'S ALIVE.
IF ANYONE COULD SURVIVE THAT, IT WOULD BE HIM. HOW?
HE HAD A SPEEDSTER ON THE PAYROLL. NOT SOMEONE ON FLASH'S LEVEL BUT STILL VERY FAST. THIS SPEEDSTER HAD ONE JOB. GET LUTHOR TO HIS BUNKER IN AN EVENT LIKE THIS.
WHAT HAPPENED TO THIS SPEEDSTER?
"AFTER SHE GOT LEX TO SAFETY, SHE WENT BACK OUT. LEX BELIEVES SHE TRIED TO SAVE PEOPLE--"
"--SHE WASN'T FAST ENOUGH."
I DIDN'T GET MUCH ELSE. WONDER WOMAN SENSED ME SOMEHOW.
BE CAREFUL OF DIANA. SHE DOESN'T SEEM HERSELF.
WHERE'S LEX LUTHOR NOW?

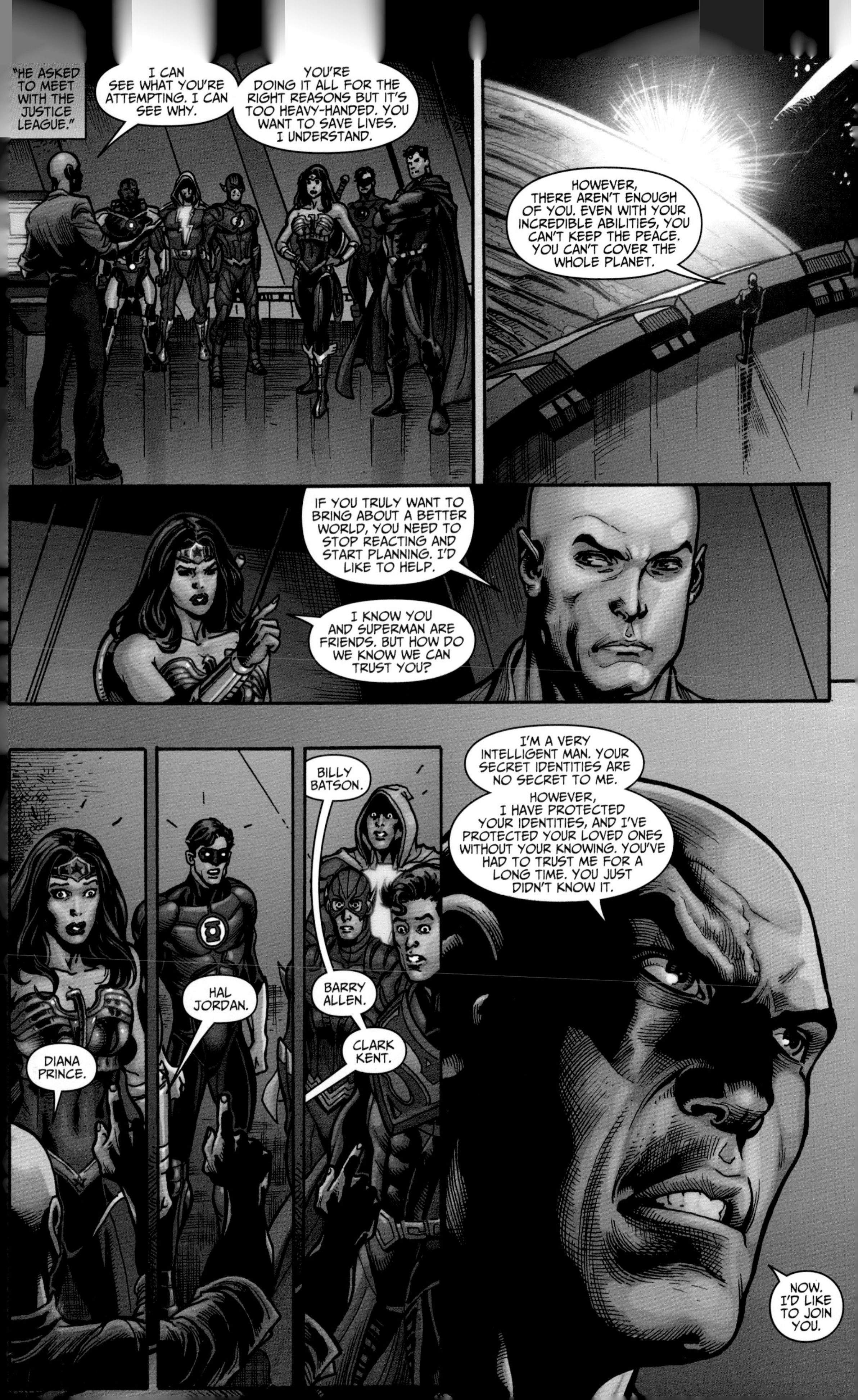
"HE ASKED TO MEET WITH THE JUSTICE LEAGUE."
I CAN SEE WHAT YOU'RE ATTEMPTING. I CAN SEE WHY.
YOU'RE DOING IT ALL FOR THE RIGHT REASONS BUT IT'S TOO HEAVY-HANDED. YOU WANT TO SAVE LIVES. I UNDERSTAND.
HOWEVER, THERE AREN'T ENOUGH OF YOU. EVEN WITH YOUR INCREDIBLE ABILITIES, YOU CAN'T KEEP THE PEACE. YOU CAN'T COVER THE WHOLE PLANET.
IF YOU TRULY WANT TO BRING ABOUT A BETTER WORLD, YOU NEED TO STOP REACTING AND START PLANNING. I'D LIKE TO HELP.
I KNOW YOU AND SUPERMAN ARE FRIENDS. BUT HOW DO WE KNOW WE CAN TRUST YOU?
I'M A VERY INTELLIGENT MAN. YOUR SECRET IDENTITIES ARE NO SECRET TO ME.
HOWEVER, I HAVE PROTECTED YOUR IDENTITIES, AND I'VE PROTECTED YOUR LOVED ONES WITHOUT YOUR KNOWING. YOU'VE HAD TO TRUST ME FOR A LONG TIME. YOU JUST DIDN'T KNOW IT.
DIANA PRINCE.
HAL JORDAN.
BILLY BATSON.
BARRY ALLEN.
CLARK KENT.
NOW. I'D LIKE TO JOIN YOU.

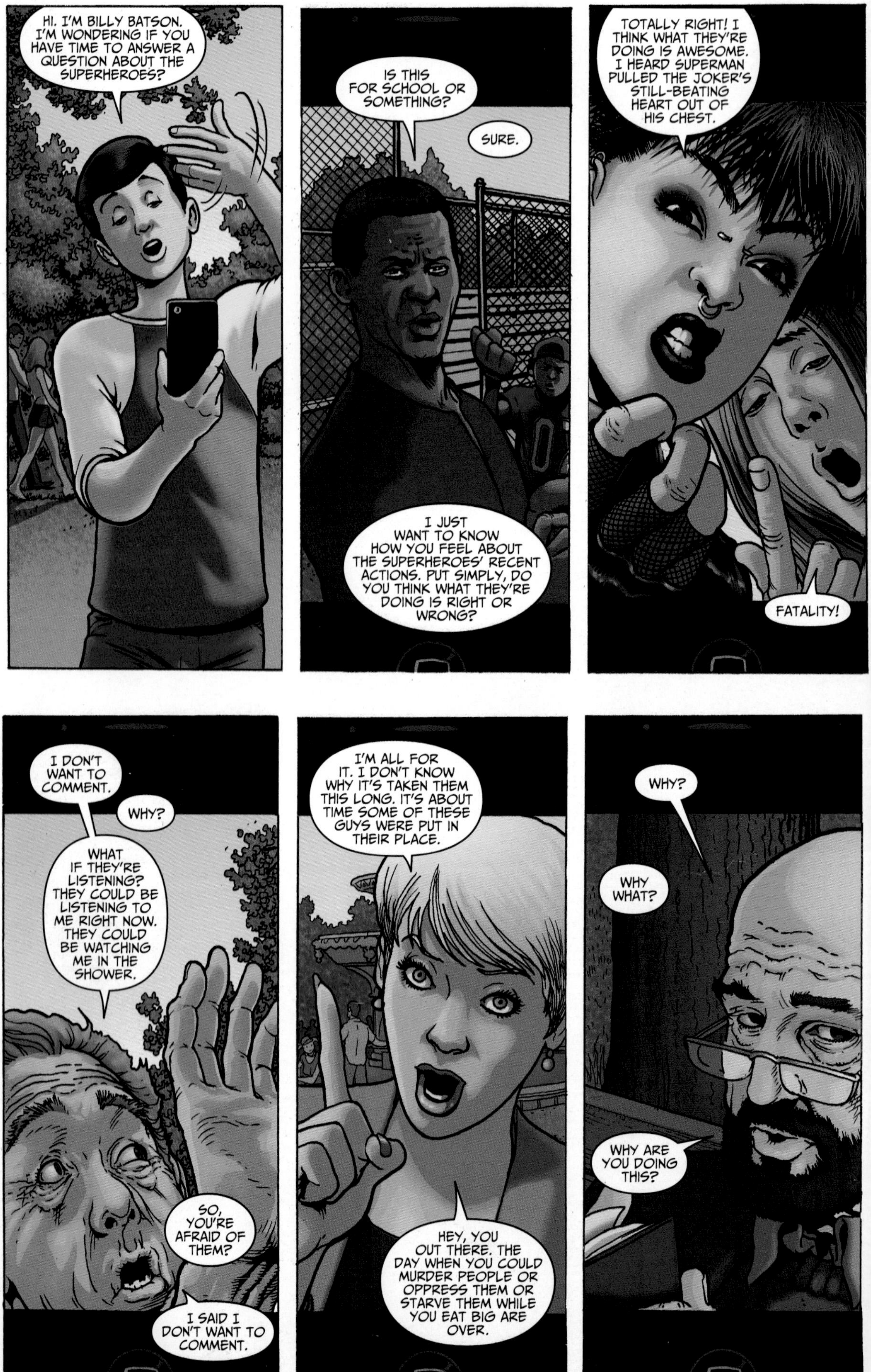
HI. I'M BILLY BATSON. I'M WONDERING IF YOU HAVE TIME TO ANSWER A QUESTION ABOUT THE SUPERHEROES?
IS THIS FOR SCHOOL OR SOMETHING?
SURE.
I JUST WANT TO KNOW HOW YOU FEEL ABOUT THE SUPERHEROES' RECENT ACTIONS. PUT SIMPLY, DO YOU THINK WHAT THEY'RE DOING IS RIGHT OR WRONG?
TOTALLY RIGHT! I THINK WHAT THEY'RE DOING IS AWESOME. I HEARD SUPERMAN PULLED THE JOKER'S STILL-BEATING HEART OUT OF HIS CHEST.
FATALITY!
I DON'T WANT TO COMMENT.
WHY?
WHAT IF THEY'RE LISTENING? THEY COULD BE LISTENING TO ME RIGHT NOW. THEY COULD BE WATCHING ME IN THE SHOWER.
SO, YOU'RE AFRAID OF THEM?
I SAID I DON'T WANT TO COMMENT.
I'M ALL FOR IT. I DON'T KNOW WHY IT'S TAKEN THEM THIS LONG. IT'S ABOUT TIME SOME OF THESE GUYS WERE PUT IN THEIR PLACE.
HEY, YOU OUT THERE. THE DAY WHEN YOU COULD MURDER PEOPLE OR OPPRESS THEM OR STARVE THEM WHILE YOU EAT BIG ARE OVER.
WHY?
WHY WHAT?
WHY ARE YOU DOING THIS?

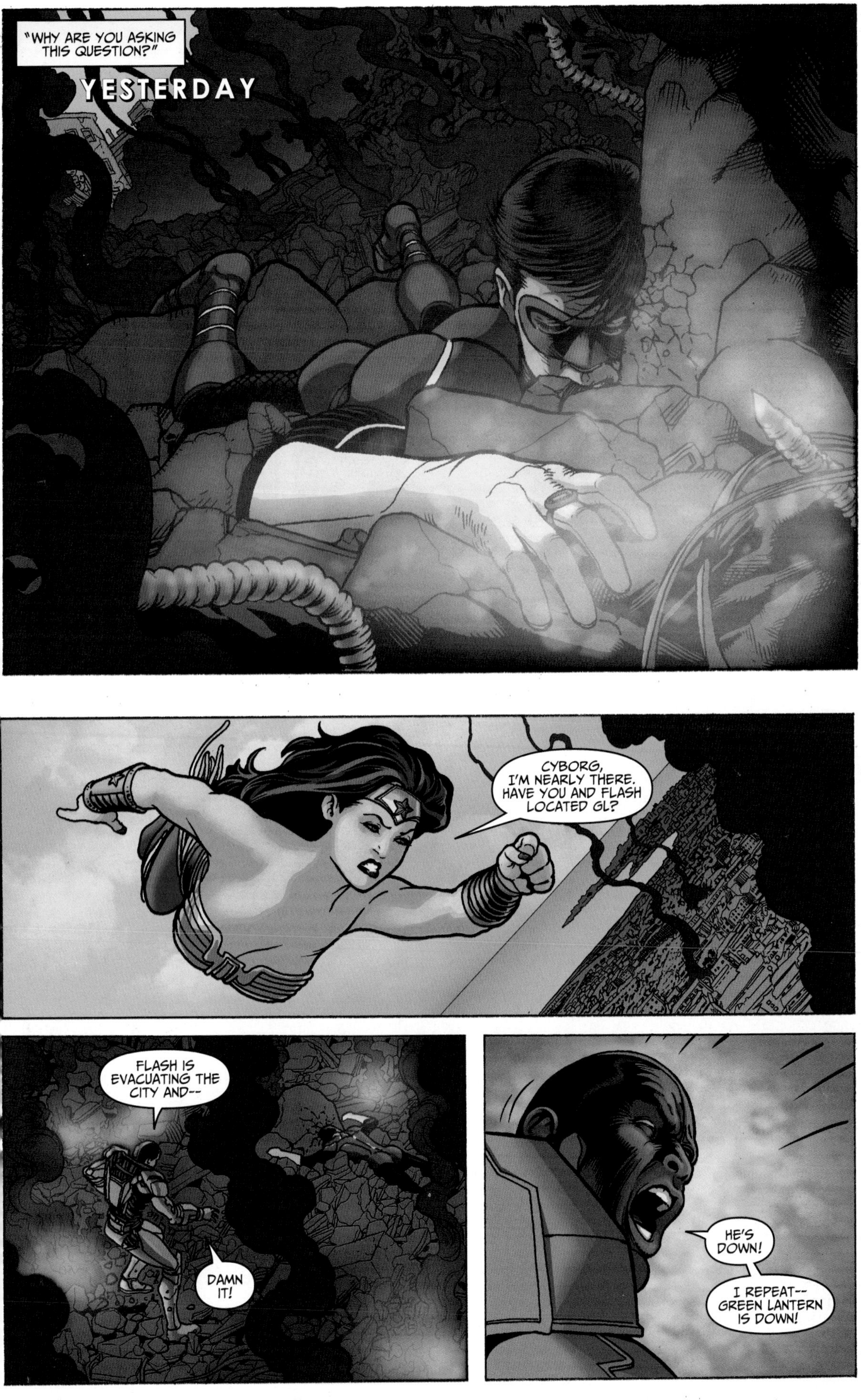
"WHY ARE YOU ASKING THIS QUESTION?"
YESTERDAY
CYBORG, I'M NEARLY THERE. HAVE YOU AND FLASH LOCATED GL?
FLASH IS EVACUATING THE CITY AND--
DAMN IT!
HE'S DOWN!
I REPEAT-- GREEN LANTERN IS DOWN!

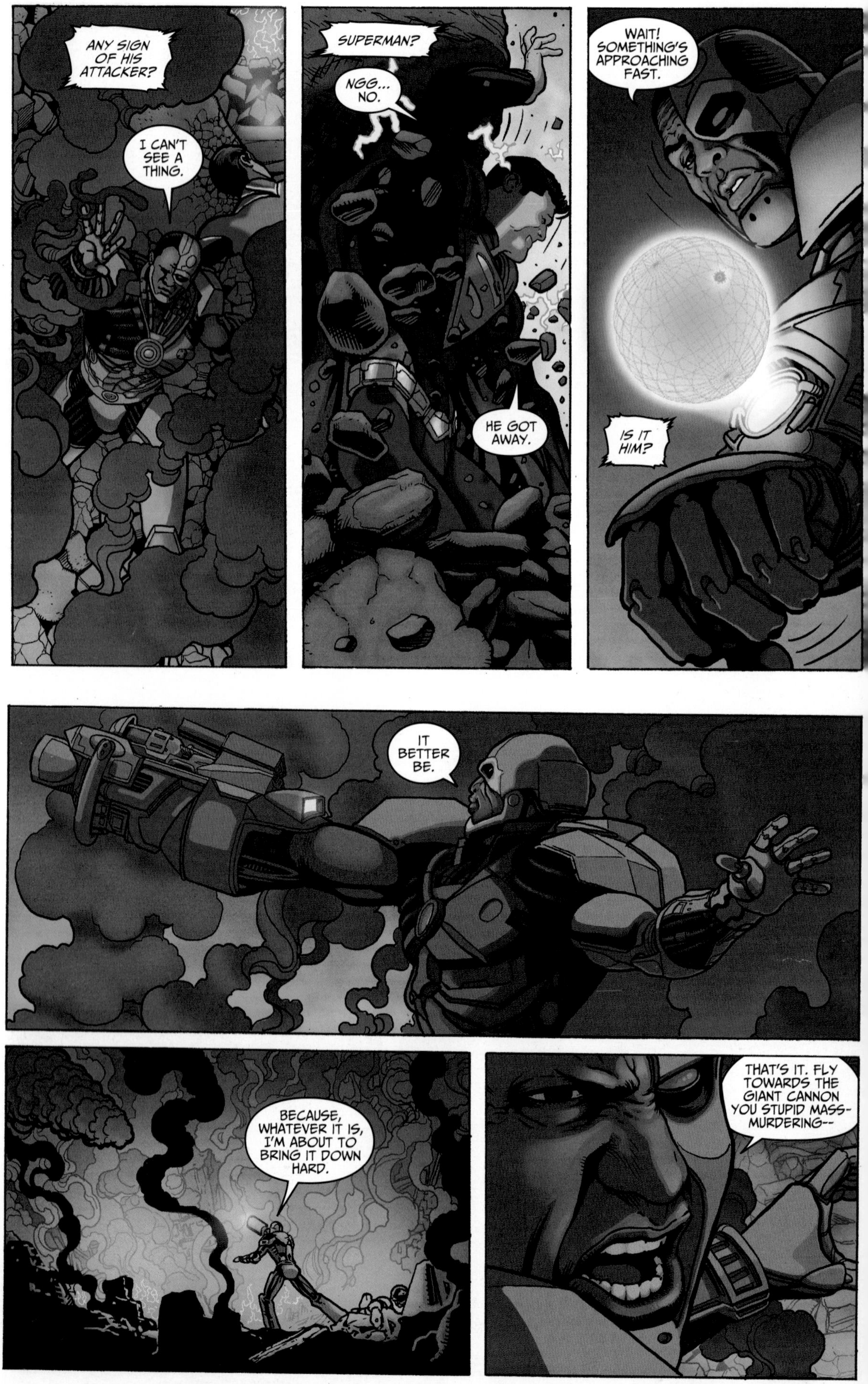
ANY SIGN OF HIS ATTACKER?
I CAN'T SEE A THING.
SUPERMAN?
NGG... NO.
HE GOT AWAY.
WAIT! SOMETHING'S APPROACHING FAST.
IS IT HIM?
IT BETTER BE.
BECAUSE, WHATEVER IT IS, I'M ABOUT TO BRING IT DOWN HARD.
THAT'S IT. FLY TOWARDS THE GIANT CANNON YOU STUPID MASS-MURDERING--

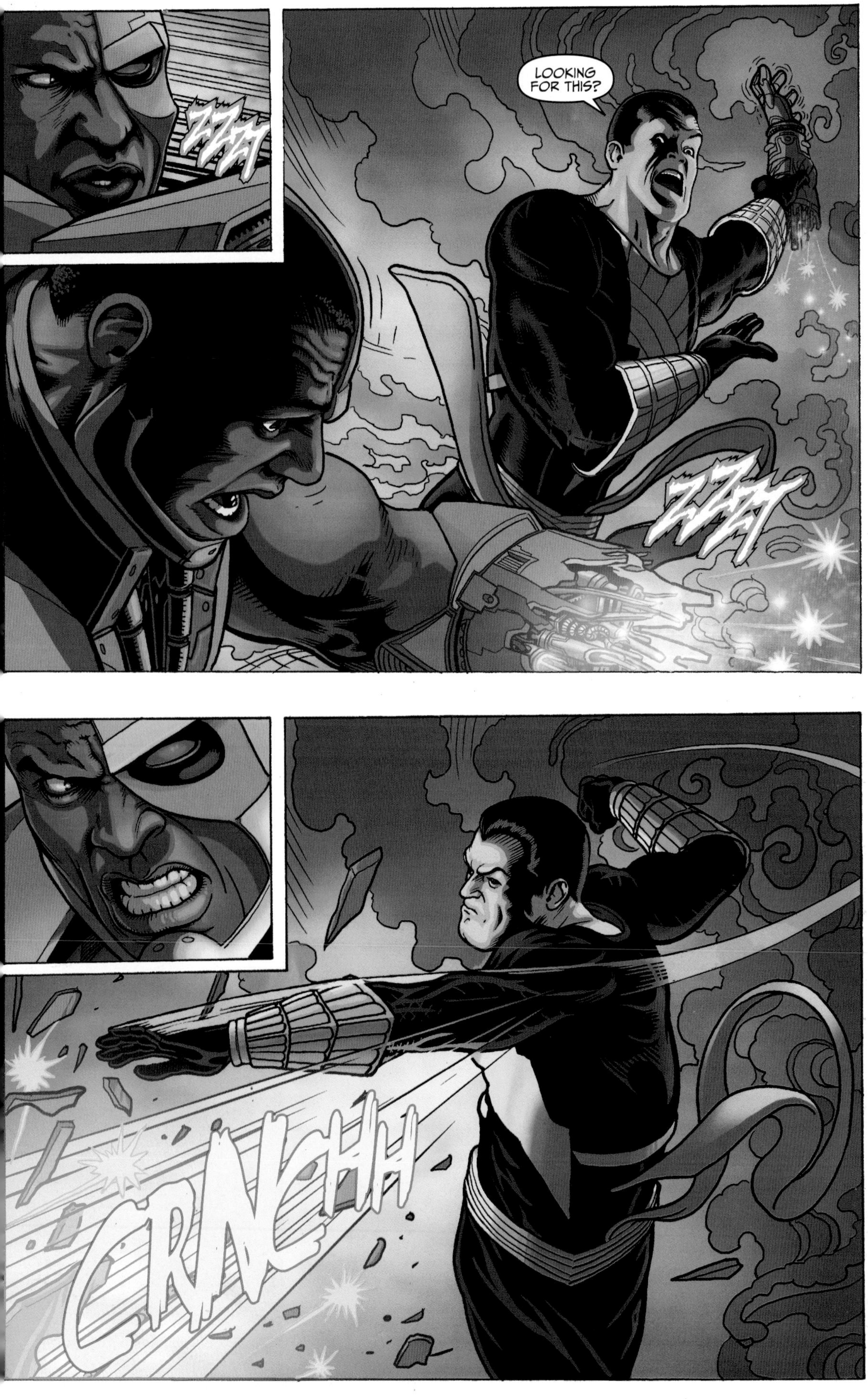
LOOKING FOR THIS?
CRNCHH

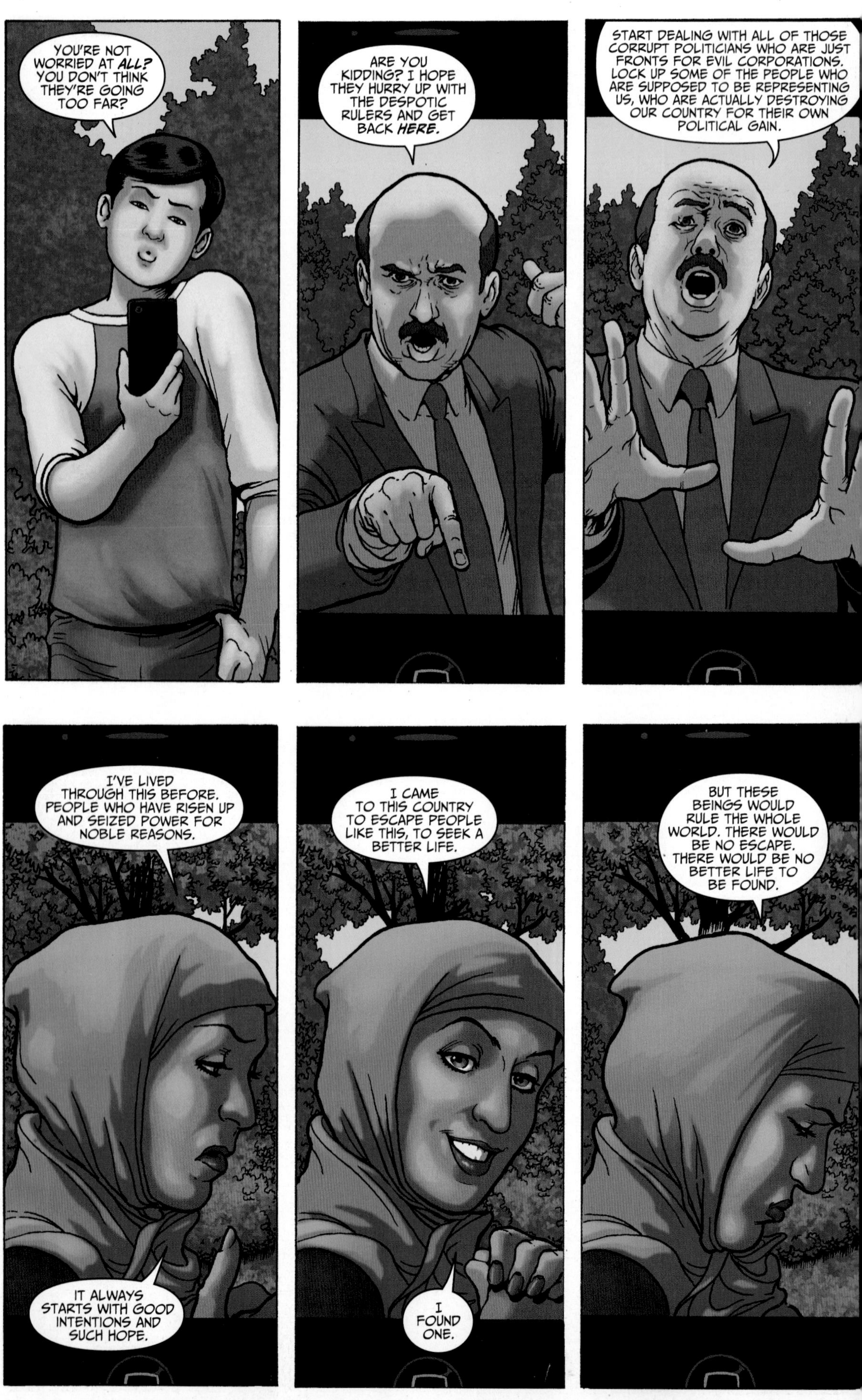
YOU'RE NOT WORRIED AT ALL? YOU DON'T THINK THEY'RE GOING TOO FAR?
ARE YOU KIDDING? I HOPE THEY HURRY UP WITH THE DESPOTIC RULERS AND GET BACK HERE.
START DEALING WITH ALL OF THOSE CORRUPT POLITICIANS WHO ARE JUST FRONTS FOR EVIL CORPORATIONS. LOCK UP SOME OF THE PEOPLE WHO ARE SUPPOSED TO BE REPRESENTING US, WHO ARE ACTUALLY DESTROYING OUR COUNTRY FOR THEIR OWN POLITICAL GAIN.
I'VE LIVED THROUGH THIS BEFORE. PEOPLE WHO HAVE RISEN UP AND SEIZED POWER FOR NOBLE REASONS.
IT ALWAYS STARTS WITH GOOD INTENTIONS AND SUCH HOPE.
I CAME TO THIS COUNTRY TO ESCAPE PEOPLE LIKE THIS, TO SEEK A BETTER LIFE.
I FOUND ONE.
BUT THESE BEINGS WOULD RULE THE WHOLE WORLD. THERE WOULD BE NO ESCAPE. THERE WOULD BE NO BETTER LIFE TO BE FOUND.

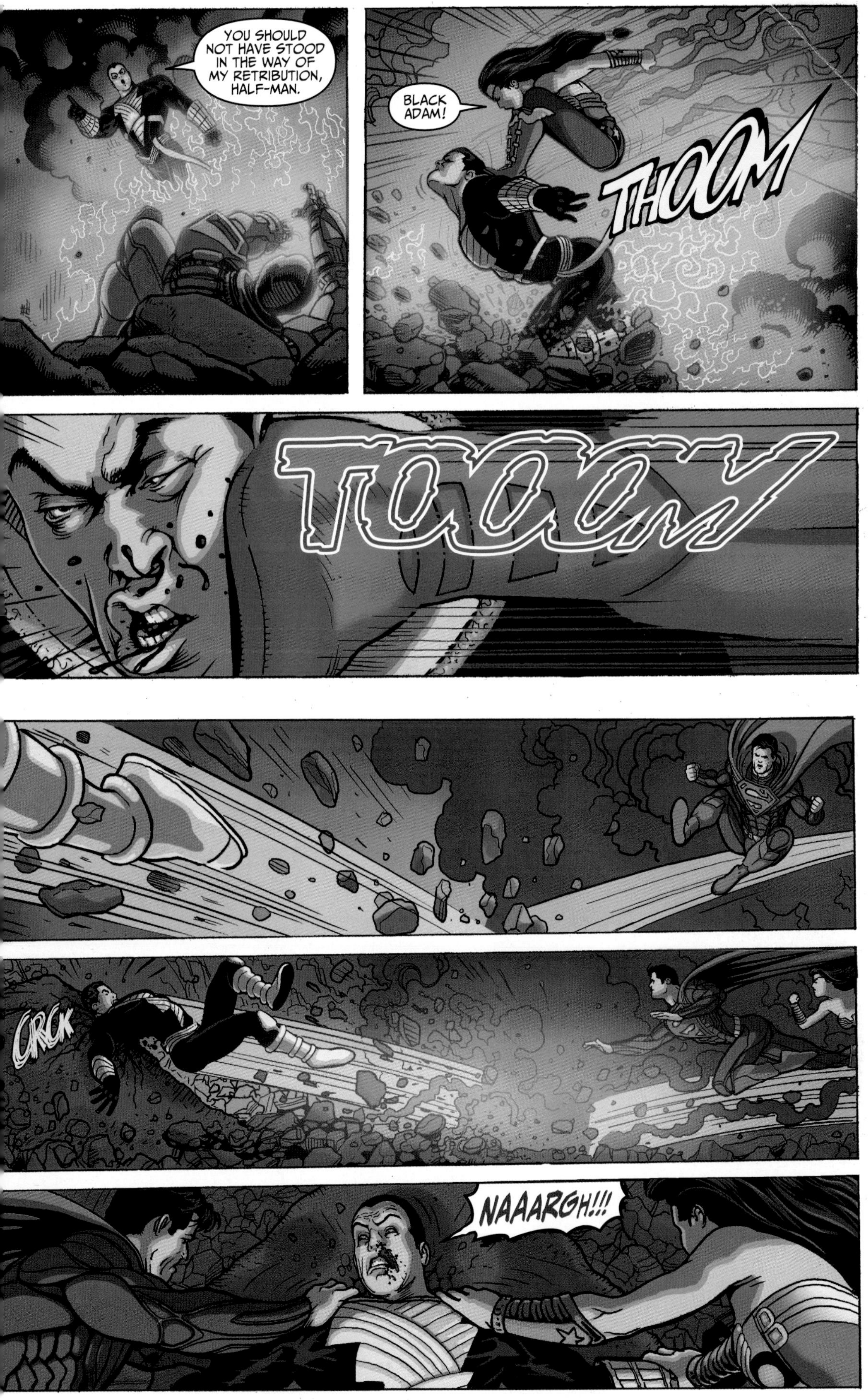
YOU SHOULD NOT HAVE STOOD IN THE WAY OF MY RETRIBUTION, HALF-MAN.
BLACK ADAM!
THOOM
TOOOM
CRCK
NAAARGH!!!

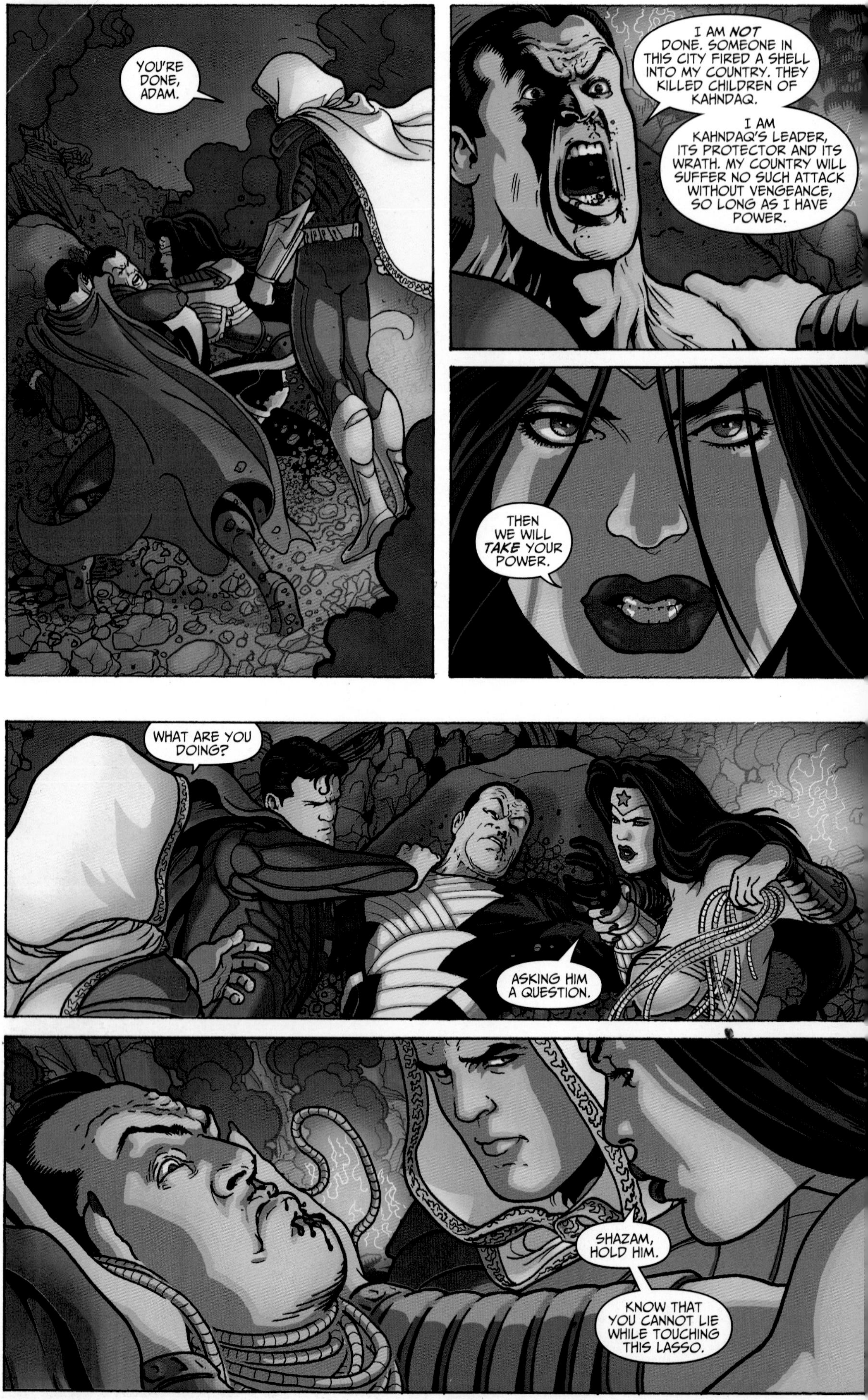
YOU'RE DONE, ADAM.
I AM *NOT* DONE. SOMEONE IN THIS CITY FIRED A SHELL INTO MY COUNTRY. THEY KILLED CHILDREN OF KAHNDAQ.
I AM KAHNDAQ'S LEADER, ITS PROTECTOR AND ITS WRATH. MY COUNTRY WILL SUFFER NO SUCH ATTACK WITHOUT VENGEANCE, SO LONG AS I HAVE POWER.
THEN WE WILL *TAKE* YOUR POWER.
WHAT ARE YOU DOING?
ASKING HIM A QUESTION.
SHAZAM, HOLD HIM.
KNOW THAT YOU CANNOT LIE WHILE TOUCHING THIS LASSO.

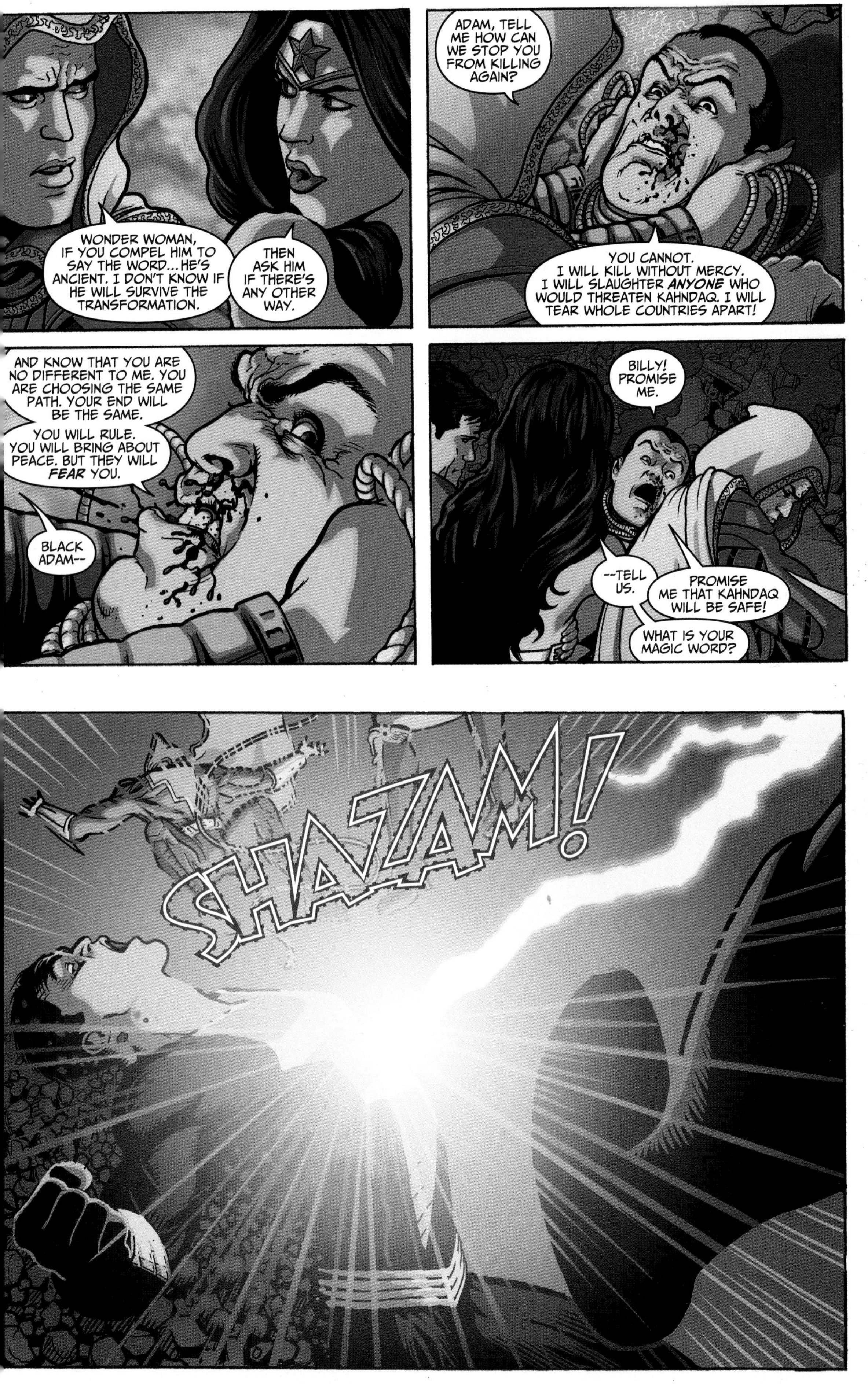
WONDER WOMAN, IF YOU COMPEL HIM TO SAY THE WORD...HE'S ANCIENT. I DON'T KNOW IF HE WILL SURVIVE THE TRANSFORMATION.
THEN ASK HIM IF THERE'S ANY OTHER WAY.
ADAM, TELL ME HOW CAN WE STOP YOU FROM KILLING AGAIN?
YOU CANNOT. I WILL KILL WITHOUT MERCY. I WILL SLAUGHTER *ANYONE* WHO WOULD THREATEN KAHNDAQ. I WILL TEAR WHOLE COUNTRIES APART!
AND KNOW THAT YOU ARE NO DIFFERENT TO ME. YOU ARE CHOOSING THE SAME PATH. YOUR END WILL BE THE SAME.
YOU WILL RULE. YOU WILL BRING ABOUT PEACE. BUT THEY WILL *FEAR* YOU.
BLACK ADAM--
BILLY! PROMISE ME.
--TELL US.
PROMISE ME THAT KAHNDAQ WILL BE SAFE!
WHAT IS YOUR MAGIC WORD?
SHAZAM!

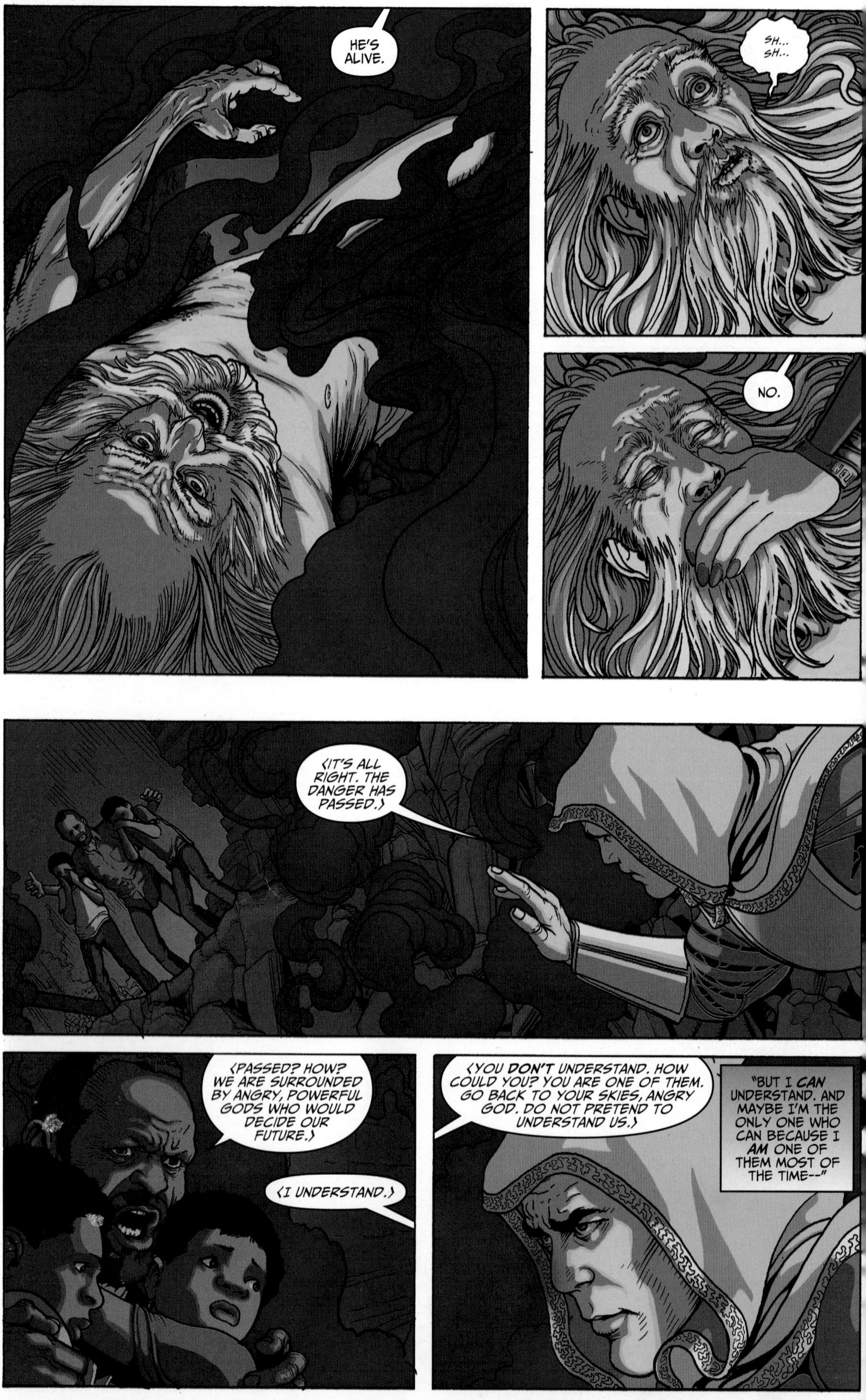
HE'S ALIVE.
SH... SH...
NO.
<IT'S ALL RIGHT. THE DANGER HAS PASSED.>
<PASSED? HOW? WE ARE SURROUNDED BY ANGRY, POWERFUL GODS WHO WOULD DECIDE OUR FUTURE.>
<I UNDERSTAND.>
<YOU DON'T UNDERSTAND. HOW COULD YOU? YOU ARE ONE OF THEM. GO BACK TO YOUR SKIES, ANGRY GOD. DO NOT PRETEND TO UNDERSTAND US.>
"BUT I CAN UNDERSTAND. AND MAYBE I'M THE ONLY ONE WHO CAN BECAUSE I AM ONE OF THEM MOST OF THE TIME--"

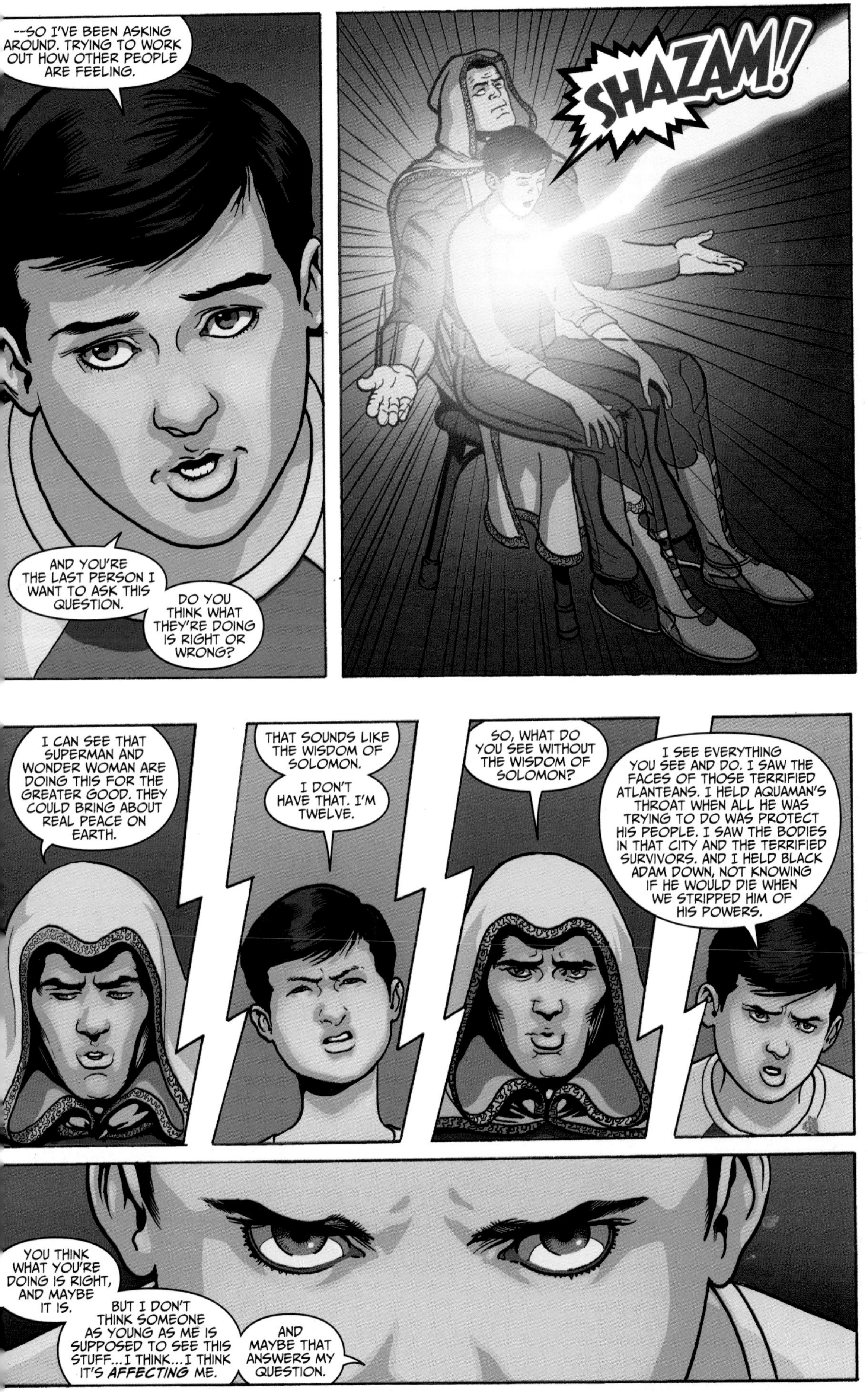
--SO I'VE BEEN ASKING AROUND. TRYING TO WORK OUT HOW OTHER PEOPLE ARE FEELING.
AND YOU'RE THE LAST PERSON I WANT TO ASK THIS QUESTION.
DO YOU THINK WHAT THEY'RE DOING IS RIGHT OR WRONG?
SHAZAM!
I CAN SEE THAT SUPERMAN AND WONDER WOMAN ARE DOING THIS FOR THE GREATER GOOD. THEY COULD BRING ABOUT REAL PEACE ON EARTH.
THAT SOUNDS LIKE THE WISDOM OF SOLOMON.
I DON'T HAVE THAT. I'M TWELVE.
SO, WHAT DO YOU SEE WITHOUT THE WISDOM OF SOLOMON?
I SEE EVERYTHING YOU SEE AND DO. I SAW THE FACES OF THOSE TERRIFIED ATLANTEANS. I HELD AQUAMAN'S THROAT WHEN ALL HE WAS TRYING TO DO WAS PROTECT HIS PEOPLE. I SAW THE BODIES IN THAT CITY AND THE TERRIFIED SURVIVORS. AND I HELD BLACK ADAM DOWN, NOT KNOWING IF HE WOULD DIE WHEN WE STRIPPED HIM OF HIS POWERS.
YOU THINK WHAT YOU'RE DOING IS RIGHT, AND MAYBE IT IS.
BUT I DON'T THINK SOMEONE AS YOUNG AS ME IS SUPPOSED TO SEE THIS STUFF...I THINK...I THINK IT'S *AFFECTING* ME.
AND MAYBE THAT ANSWERS MY QUESTION.

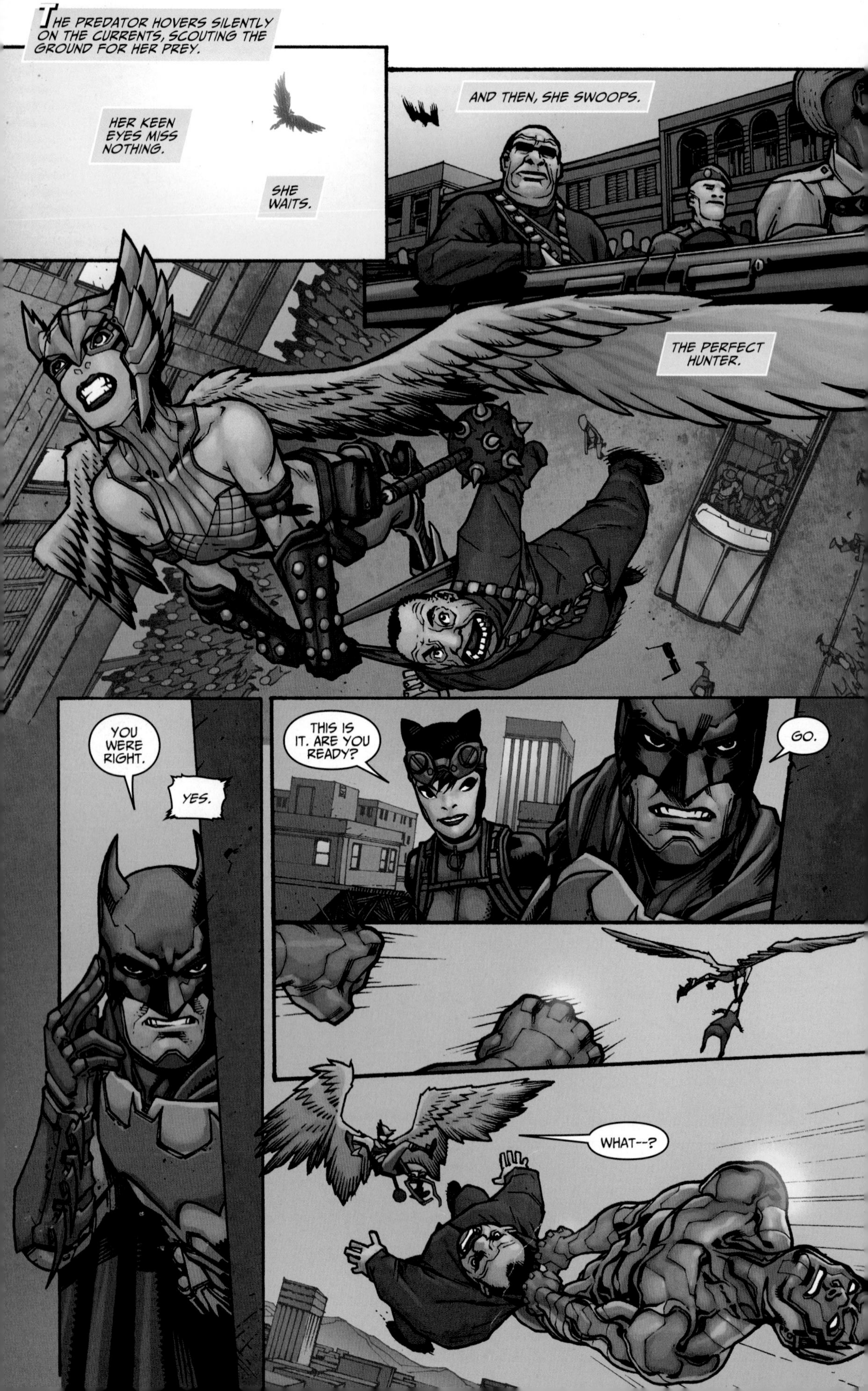
THE PREDATOR HOVERS SILENTLY ON THE CURRENTS, SCOUTING THE GROUND FOR HER PREY.
HER KEEN EYES MISS NOTHING.
SHE WAITS.
AND THEN, SHE SWOOPS.
THE PERFECT HUNTER.
YOU WERE RIGHT.
YES.
THIS IS IT. ARE YOU READY?
GO.
WHAT--?

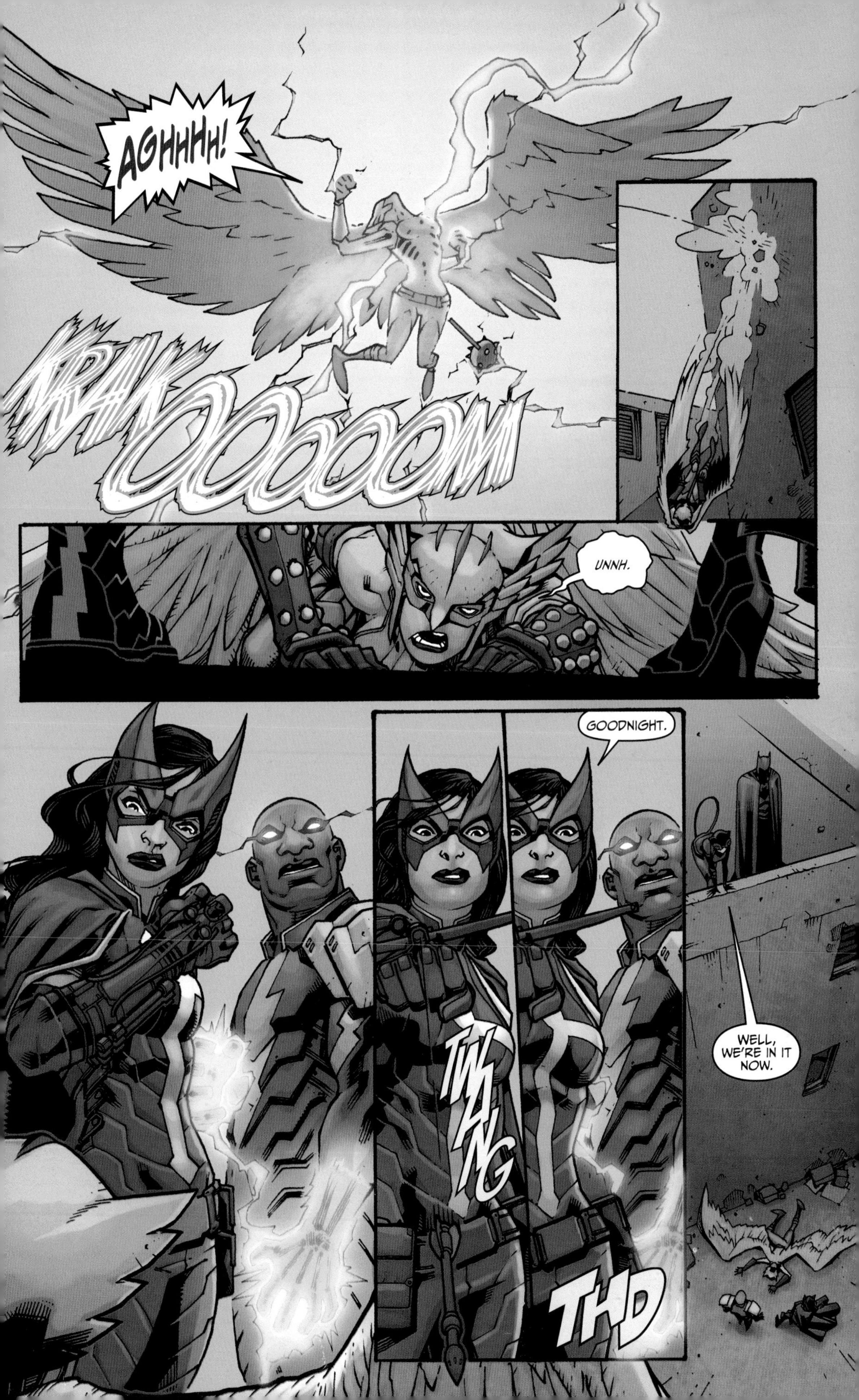
AGHHHH!
KRAKOOOOOOM
UNNH.
GOODNIGHT.
TWANG
THD
WELL, WE'RE IN IT NOW.

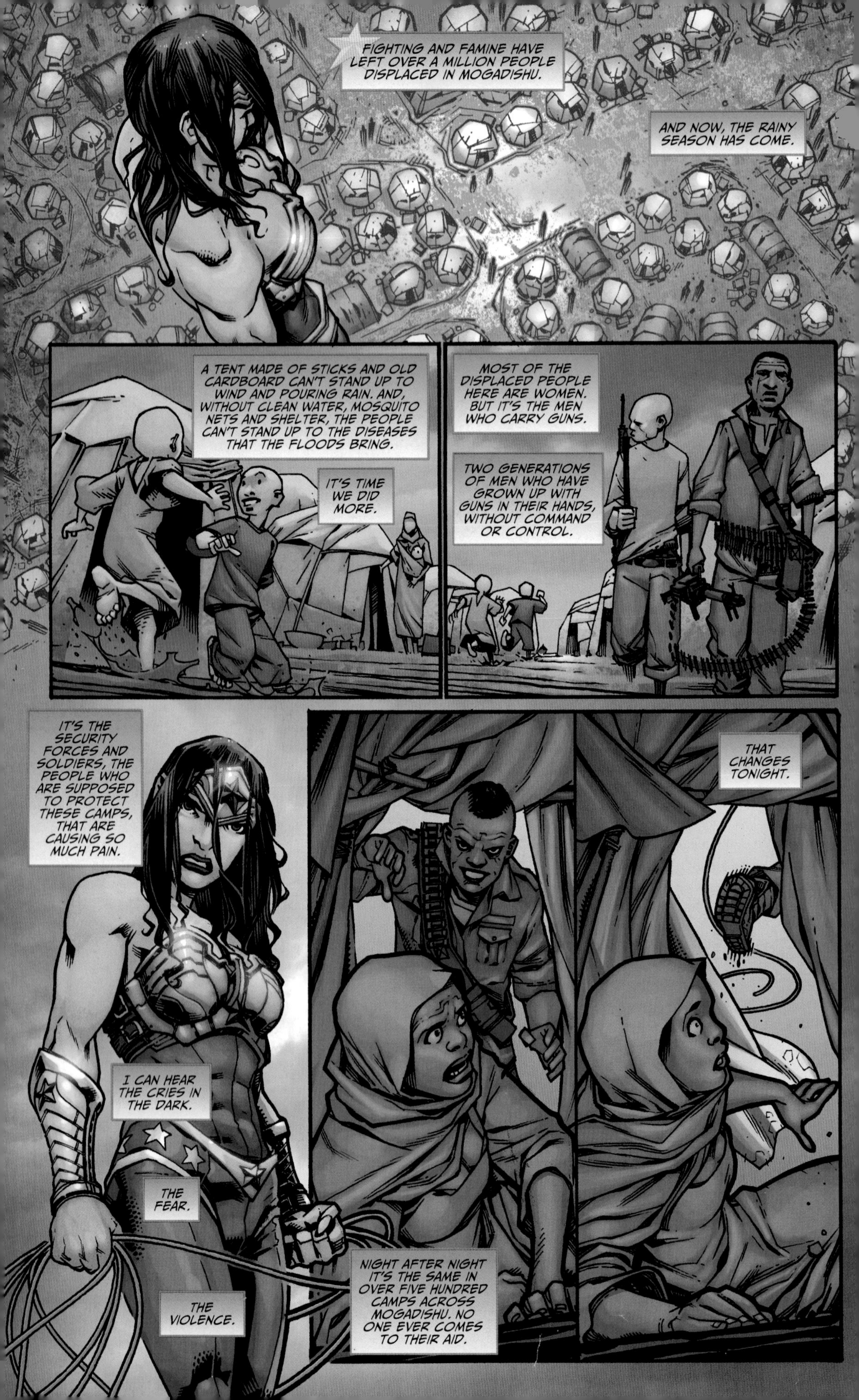
FIGHTING AND FAMINE HAVE LEFT OVER A MILLION PEOPLE DISPLACED IN MOGADISHU.
AND NOW, THE RAINY SEASON HAS COME.
A TENT MADE OF STICKS AND OLD CARDBOARD CAN'T STAND UP TO WIND AND POURING RAIN. AND, WITHOUT CLEAN WATER, MOSQUITO NETS AND SHELTER, THE PEOPLE CAN'T STAND UP TO THE DISEASES THAT THE FLOODS BRING.
IT'S TIME WE DID MORE.
MOST OF THE DISPLACED PEOPLE HERE ARE WOMEN. BUT IT'S THE MEN WHO CARRY GUNS.
TWO GENERATIONS OF MEN WHO HAVE GROWN UP WITH GUNS IN THEIR HANDS, WITHOUT COMMAND OR CONTROL.
IT'S THE SECURITY FORCES AND SOLDIERS, THE PEOPLE WHO ARE SUPPOSED TO PROTECT THESE CAMPS, THAT ARE CAUSING SO MUCH PAIN.
I CAN HEAR THE CRIES IN THE DARK.
THE FEAR.
THE VIOLENCE.
NIGHT AFTER NIGHT IT'S THE SAME IN OVER FIVE HUNDRED CAMPS ACROSS MOGADISHU. NO ONE EVER COMES TO THEIR AID.
THAT CHANGES TONIGHT.

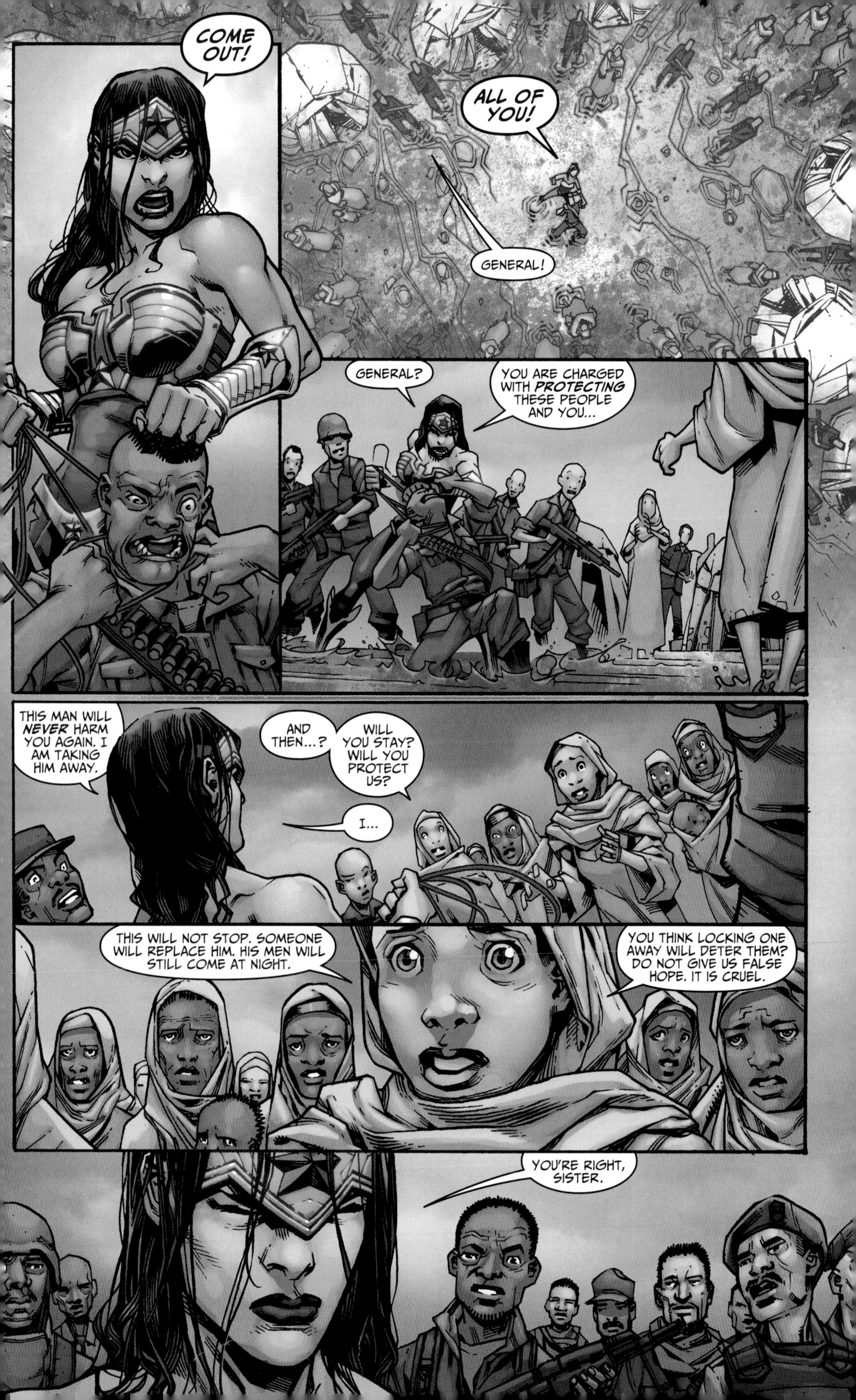
COME OUT!
ALL OF YOU!
GENERAL!
GENERAL?
YOU ARE CHARGED WITH PROTECTING THESE PEOPLE AND YOU...
THIS MAN WILL NEVER HARM YOU AGAIN. I AM TAKING HIM AWAY.
AND THEN...?
WILL YOU STAY? WILL YOU PROTECT US?
I...
THIS WILL NOT STOP. SOMEONE WILL REPLACE HIM. HIS MEN WILL STILL COME AT NIGHT.
YOU THINK LOCKING ONE AWAY WILL DETER THEM? DO NOT GIVE US FALSE HOPE. IT IS CRUEL.
YOU'RE RIGHT, SISTER.

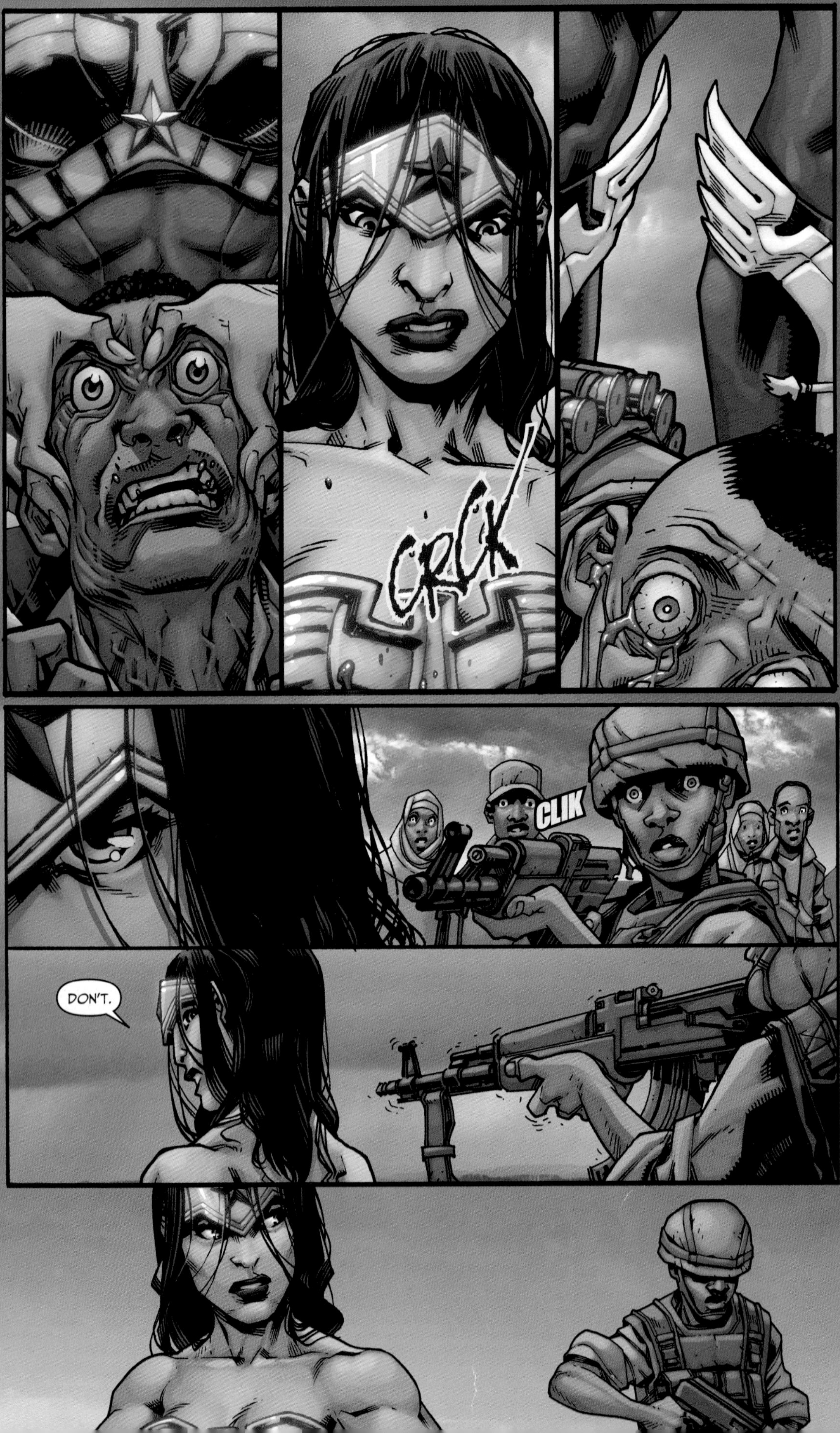
CRCK
CLIK
DON'T.

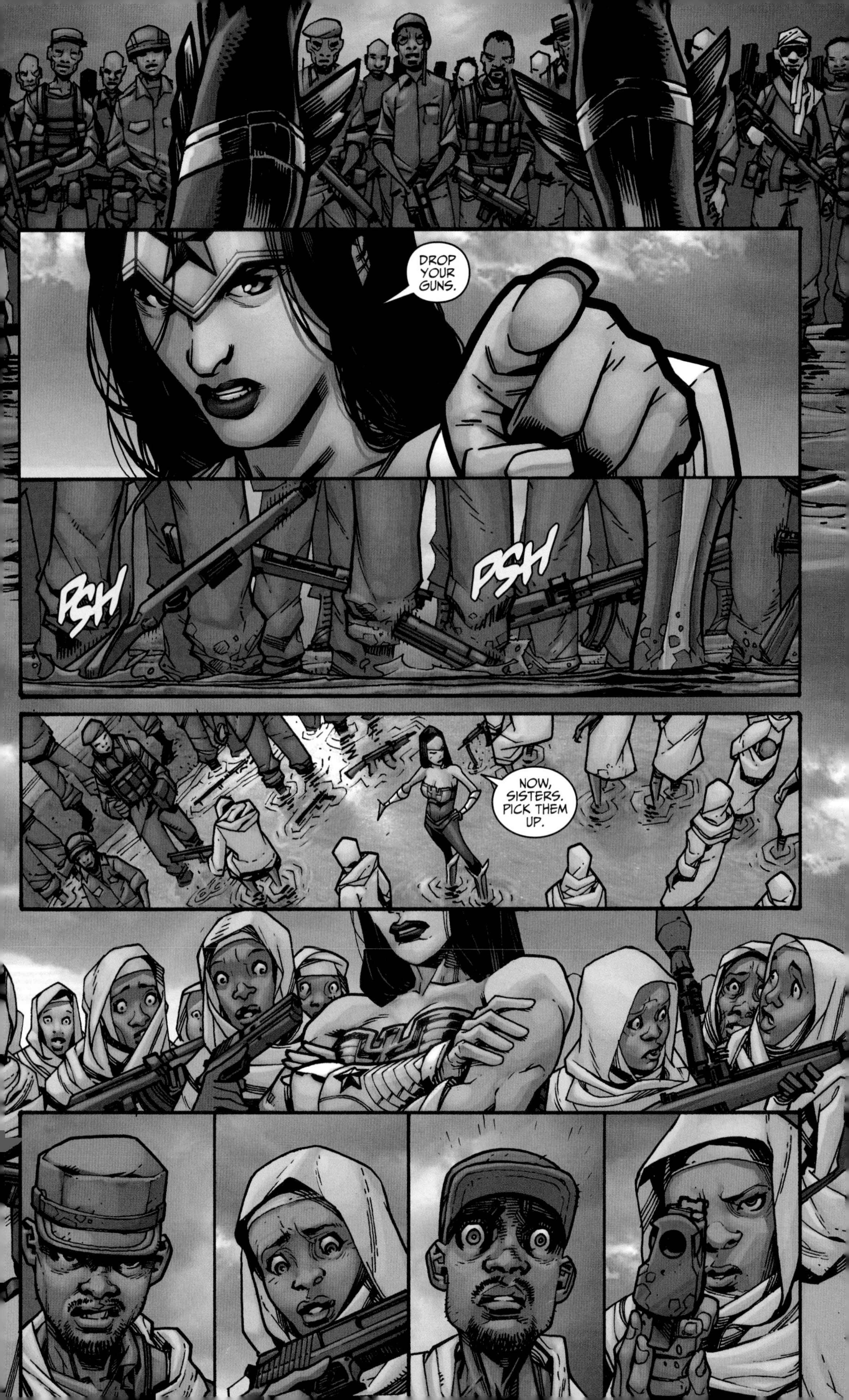
DROP YOUR GUNS.
PSH
PSH
NOW, SISTERS. PICK THEM UP.

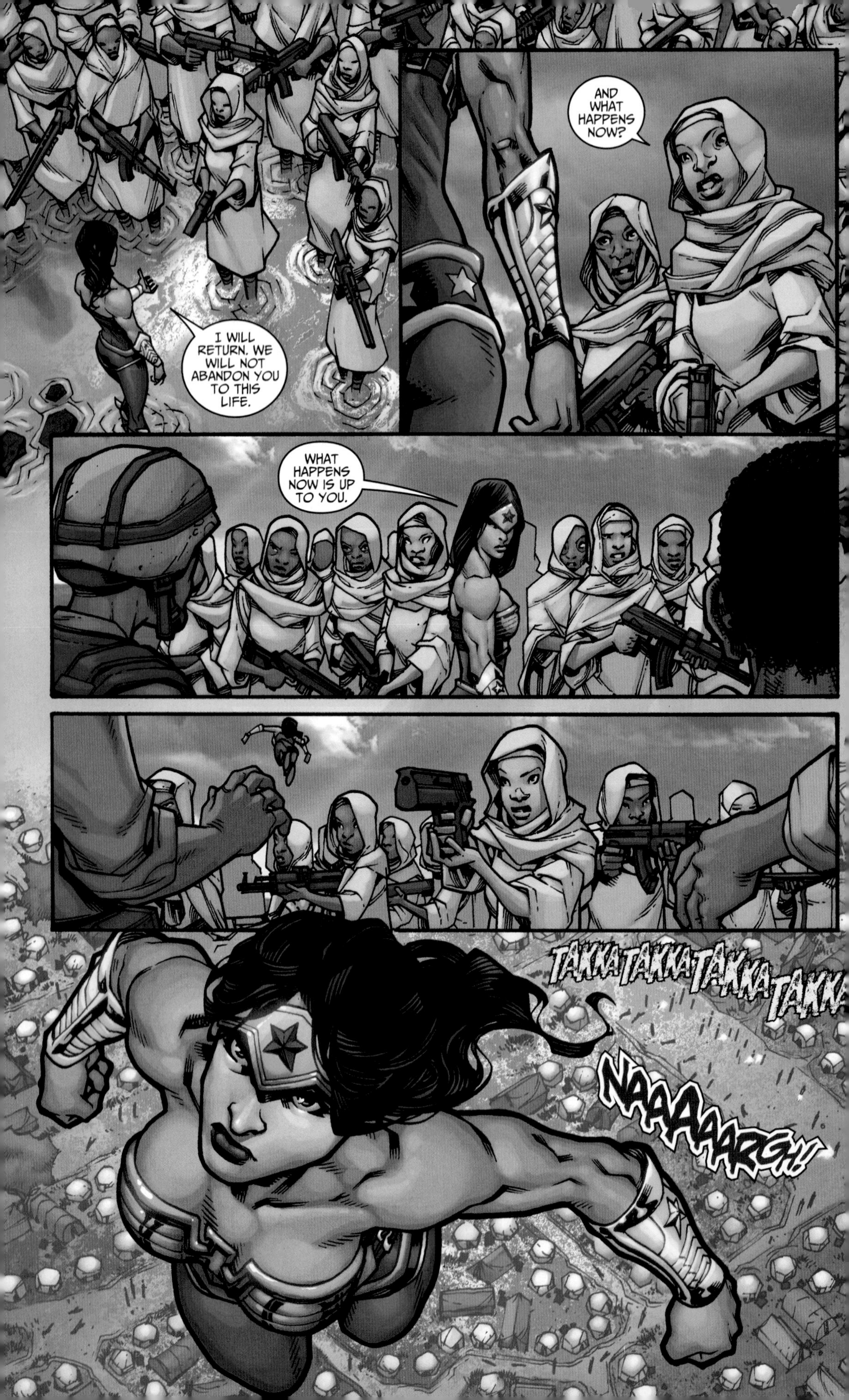
I WILL RETURN. WE WILL NOT ABANDON YOU TO THIS LIFE.
AND WHAT HAPPENS NOW?
WHAT HAPPENS NOW IS UP TO YOU.
TAKKA TAKKA TAKKA TAKKA
NAAAAAARGH!

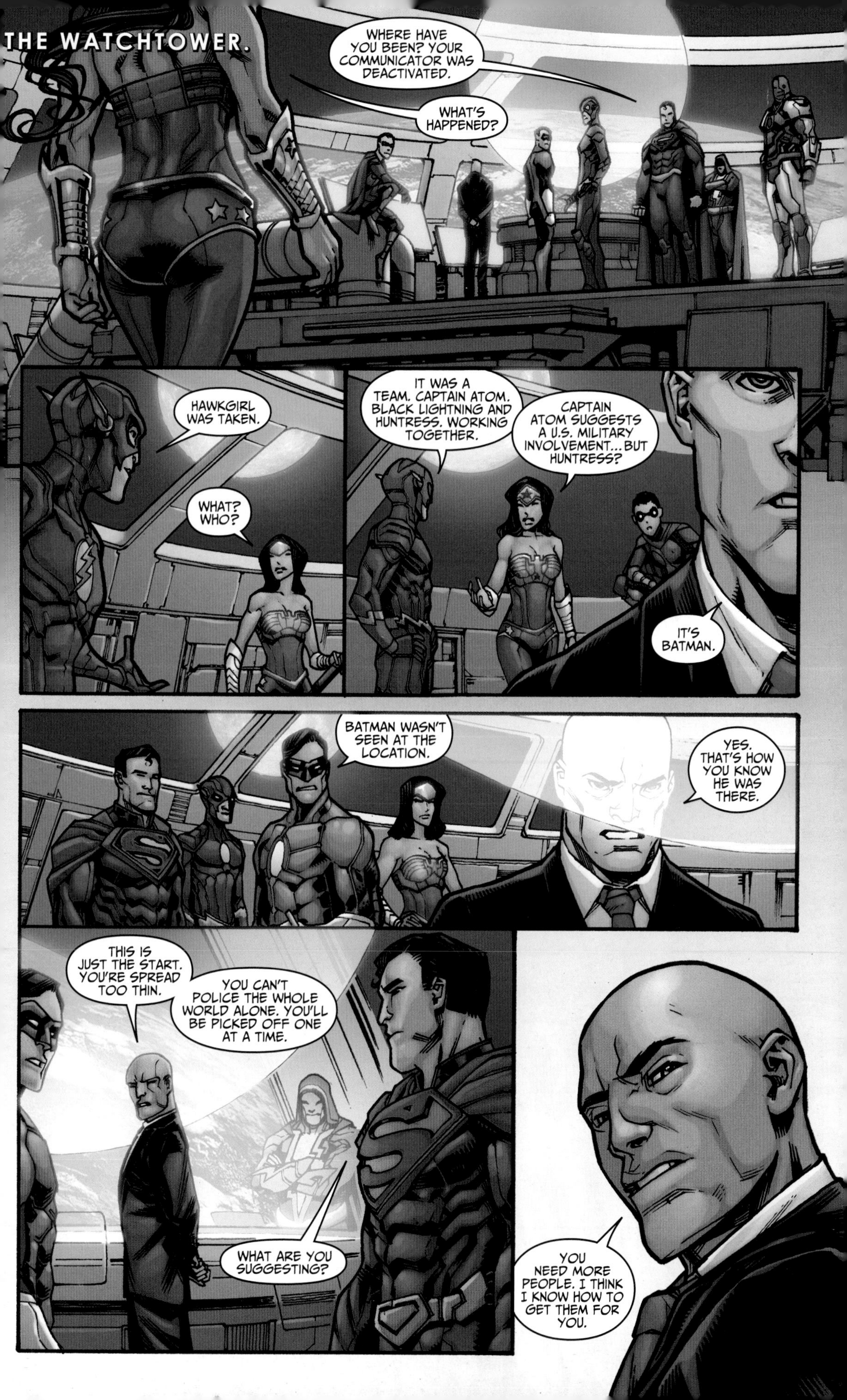
THE WATCHTOWER.
WHERE HAVE YOU BEEN? YOUR COMMUNICATOR WAS DEACTIVATED.
WHAT'S HAPPENED?
HAWKGIRL WAS TAKEN.
WHAT? WHO?
IT WAS A TEAM. CAPTAIN ATOM. BLACK LIGHTNING AND HUNTRESS. WORKING TOGETHER.
CAPTAIN ATOM SUGGESTS A U.S. MILITARY INVOLVEMENT... BUT HUNTRESS?
IT'S BATMAN.
BATMAN WASN'T SEEN AT THE LOCATION.
YES. THAT'S HOW YOU KNOW HE WAS THERE.
THIS IS JUST THE START. YOU'RE SPREAD TOO THIN.
YOU CAN'T POLICE THE WHOLE WORLD ALONE. YOU'LL BE PICKED OFF ONE AT A TIME.
WHAT ARE YOU SUGGESTING?
YOU NEED MORE PEOPLE. I THINK I KNOW HOW TO GET THEM FOR YOU.

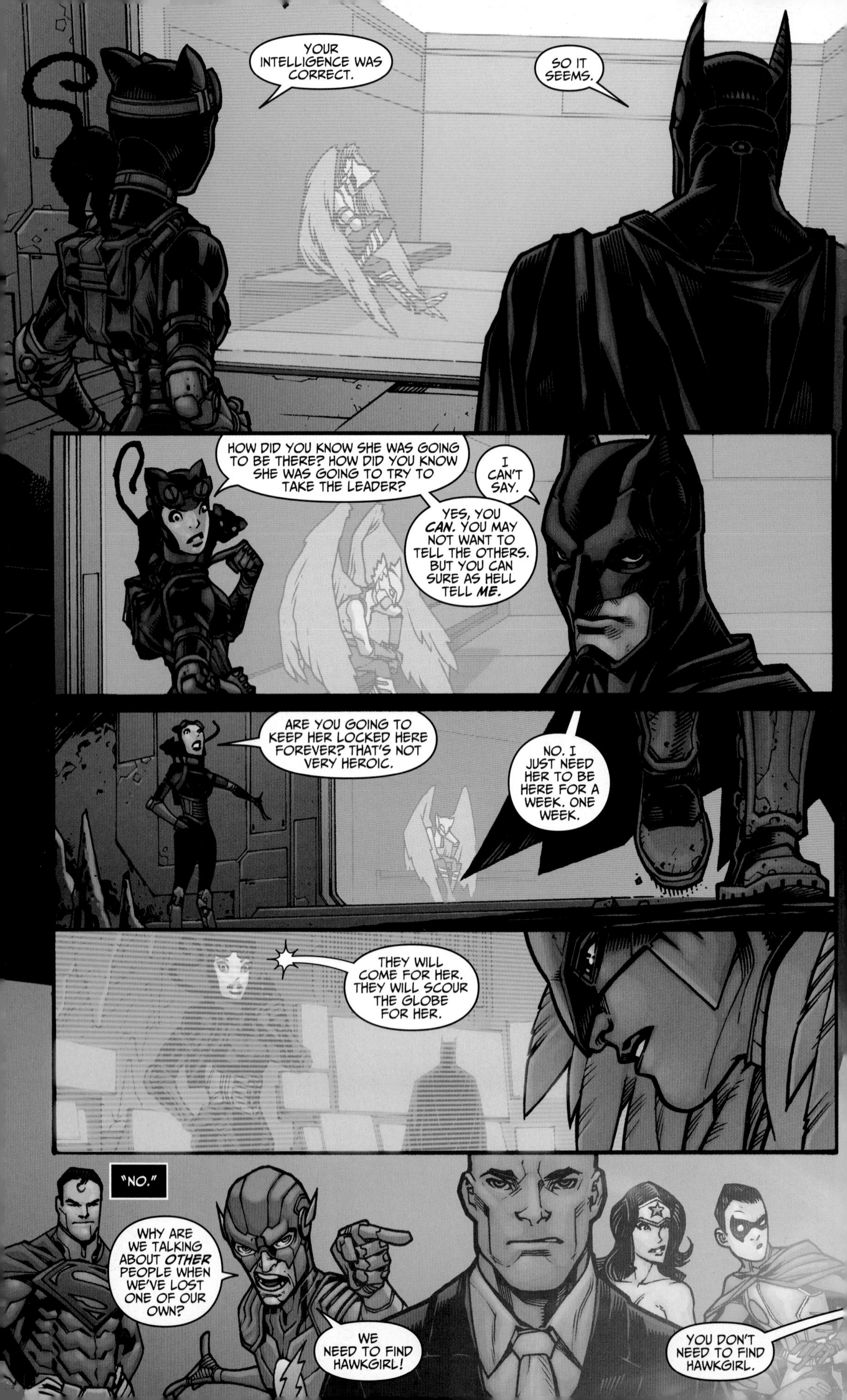
YOUR INTELLIGENCE WAS CORRECT.
SO IT SEEMS.
HOW DID YOU KNOW SHE WAS GOING TO BE THERE? HOW DID YOU KNOW SHE WAS GOING TO TRY TO TAKE THE LEADER?
I CAN'T SAY.
YES, YOU *CAN.* YOU MAY NOT WANT TO TELL THE OTHERS. BUT YOU CAN SURE AS HELL TELL *ME.*
ARE YOU GOING TO KEEP HER LOCKED HERE FOREVER? THAT'S NOT VERY HEROIC.
NO. I JUST NEED HER TO BE HERE FOR A WEEK. ONE WEEK.
THEY WILL COME FOR HER. THEY WILL SCOUR THE GLOBE FOR HER.
"NO."
WHY ARE WE TALKING ABOUT *OTHER* PEOPLE WHEN WE'VE LOST ONE OF OUR OWN?
WE NEED TO FIND HAWKGIRL!
YOU DON'T NEED TO FIND HAWKGIRL.

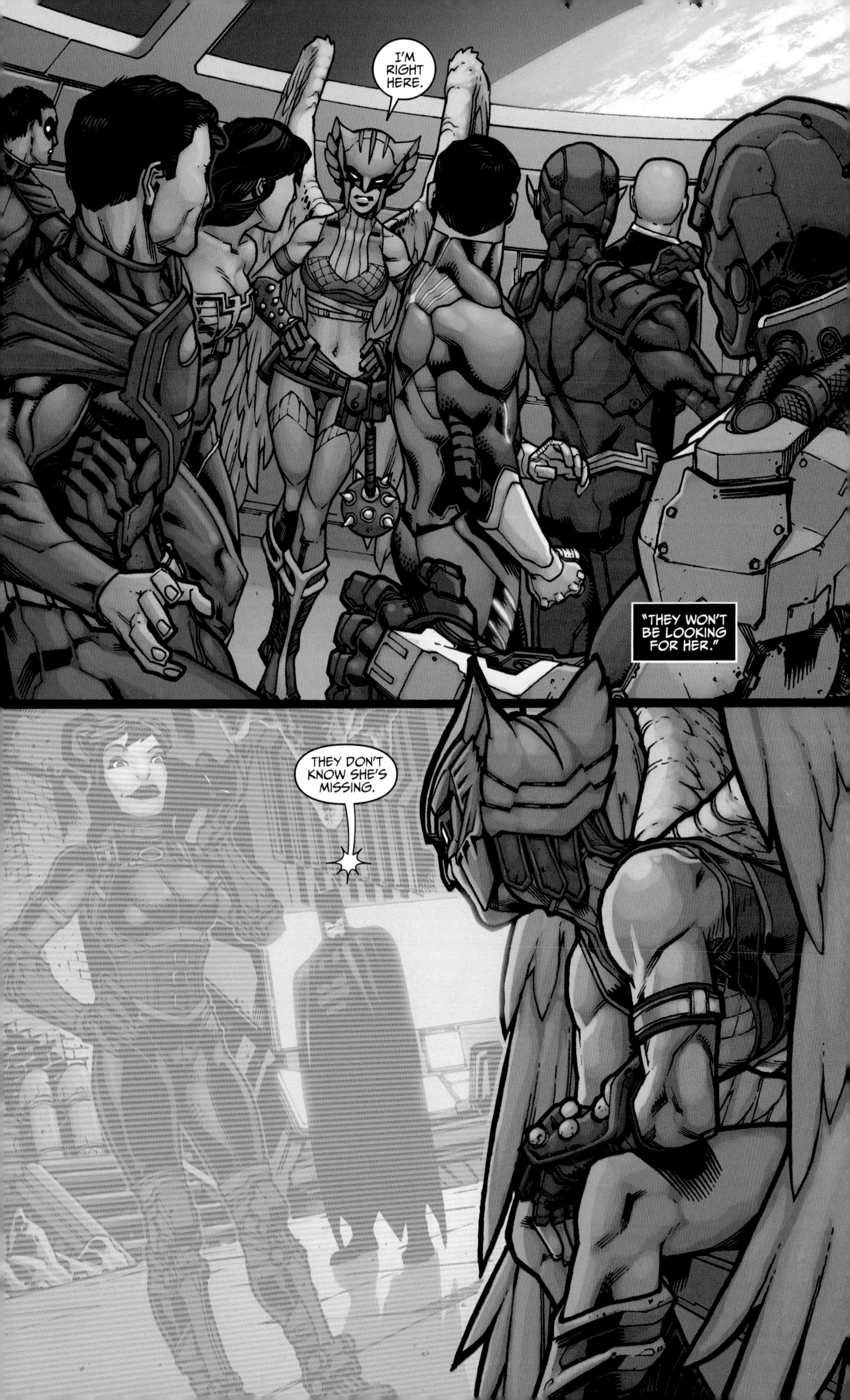
I'M RIGHT HERE.
"THEY WON'T BE LOOKING FOR HER."
THEY DON'T KNOW SHE'S MISSING.

Cover Art by Mico Suayan with David Lopez & Santi Casas of Ikari Studio

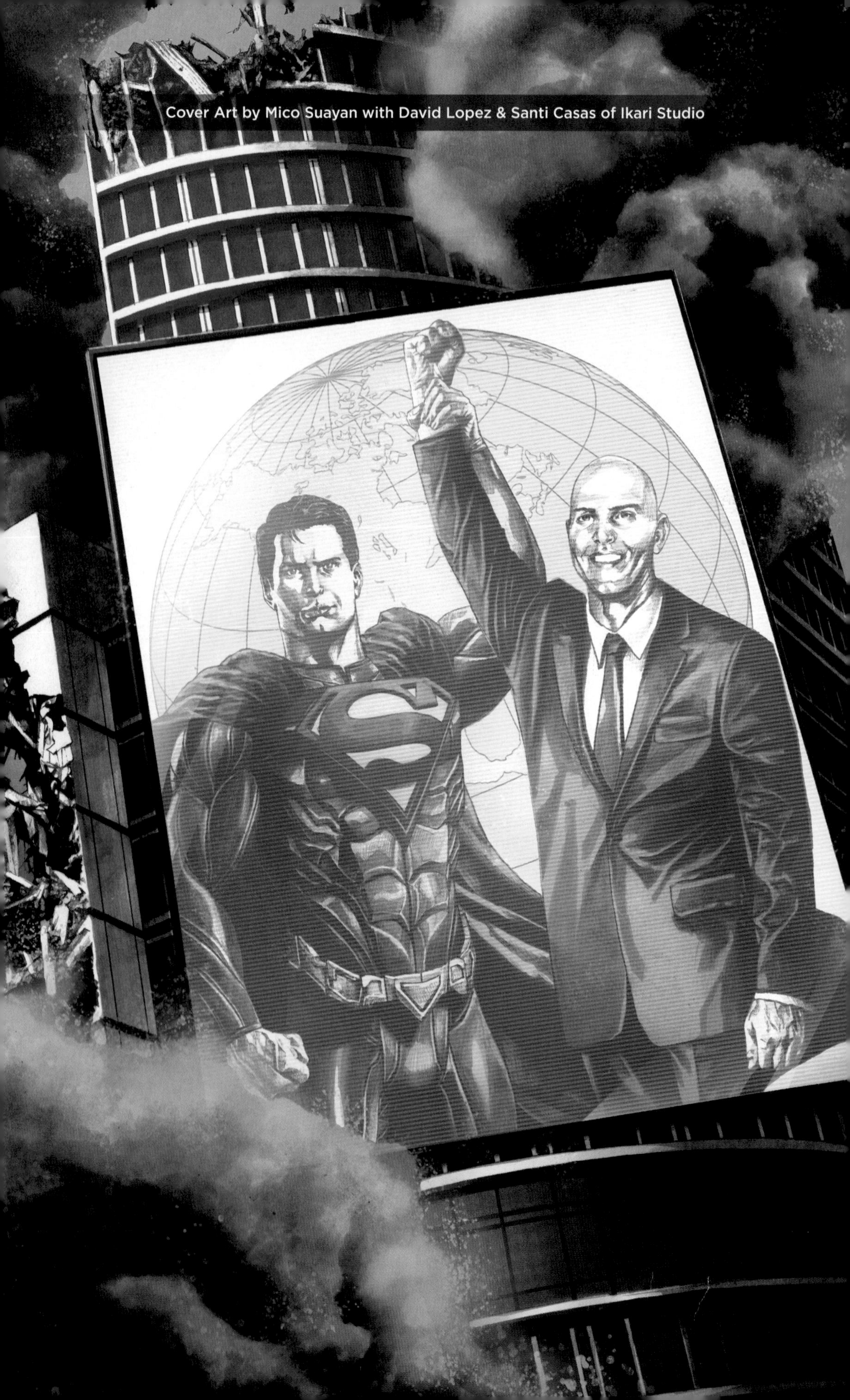

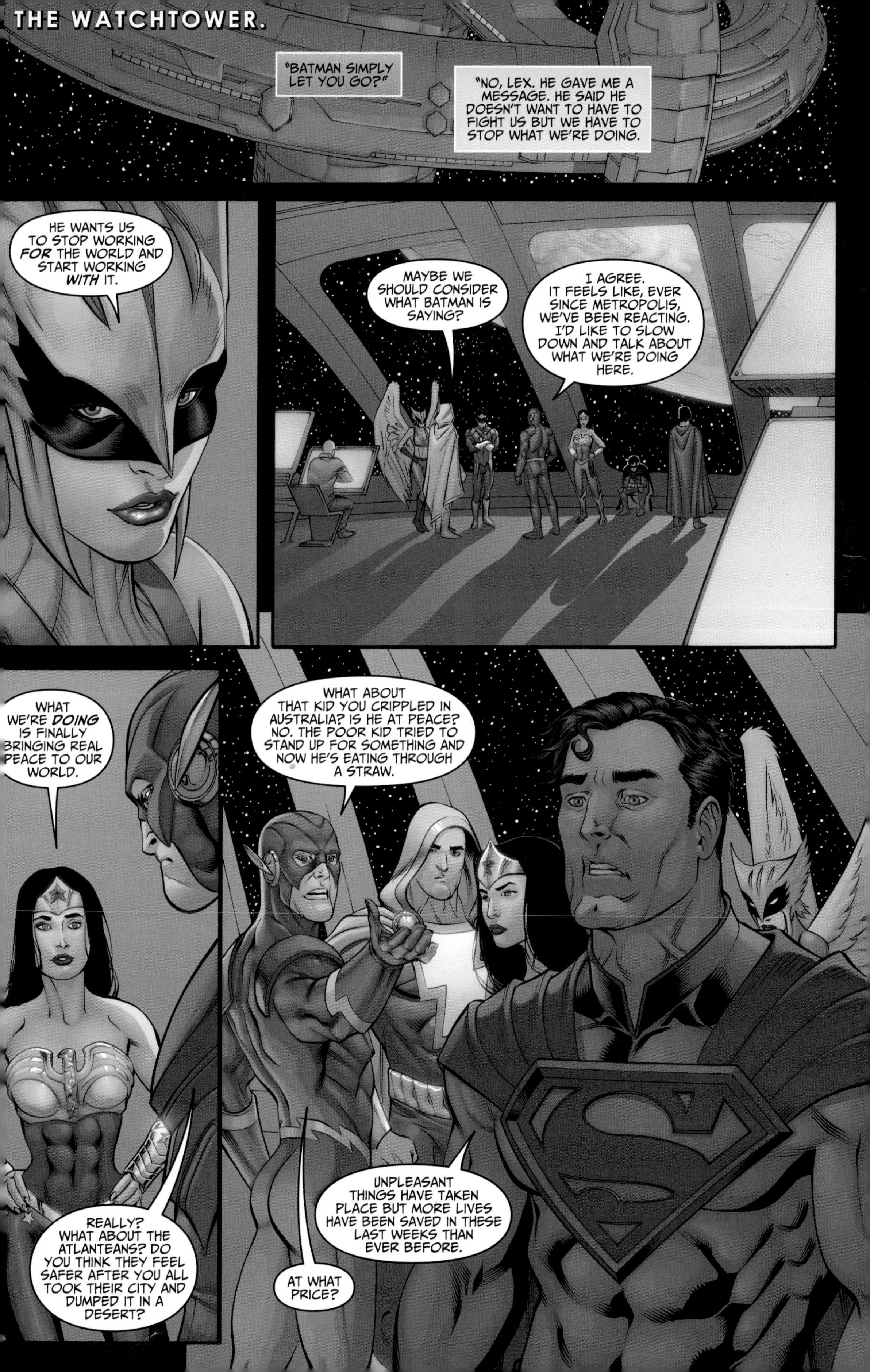

THE WATCHTOWER.
"BATMAN SIMPLY LET YOU GO?"
"NO, LEX. HE GAVE ME A MESSAGE. HE SAID HE DOESN'T WANT TO HAVE TO FIGHT US BUT WE HAVE TO STOP WHAT WE'RE DOING.
HE WANTS US TO STOP WORKING FOR THE WORLD AND START WORKING WITH IT.
MAYBE WE SHOULD CONSIDER WHAT BATMAN IS SAYING?
I AGREE. IT FEELS LIKE, EVER SINCE METROPOLIS, WE'VE BEEN REACTING. I'D LIKE TO SLOW DOWN AND TALK ABOUT WHAT WE'RE DOING HERE.
WHAT WE'RE DOING IS FINALLY BRINGING REAL PEACE TO OUR WORLD.
WHAT ABOUT THAT KID YOU CRIPPLED IN AUSTRALIA? IS HE AT PEACE? NO. THE POOR KID TRIED TO STAND UP FOR SOMETHING AND NOW HE'S EATING THROUGH A STRAW.
UNPLEASANT THINGS HAVE TAKEN PLACE BUT MORE LIVES HAVE BEEN SAVED IN THESE LAST WEEKS THAN EVER BEFORE.
AT WHAT PRICE?
REALLY? WHAT ABOUT THE ATLANTEANS? DO YOU THINK THEY FEEL SAFER AFTER YOU ALL TOOK THEIR CITY AND DUMPED IT IN A DESERT?

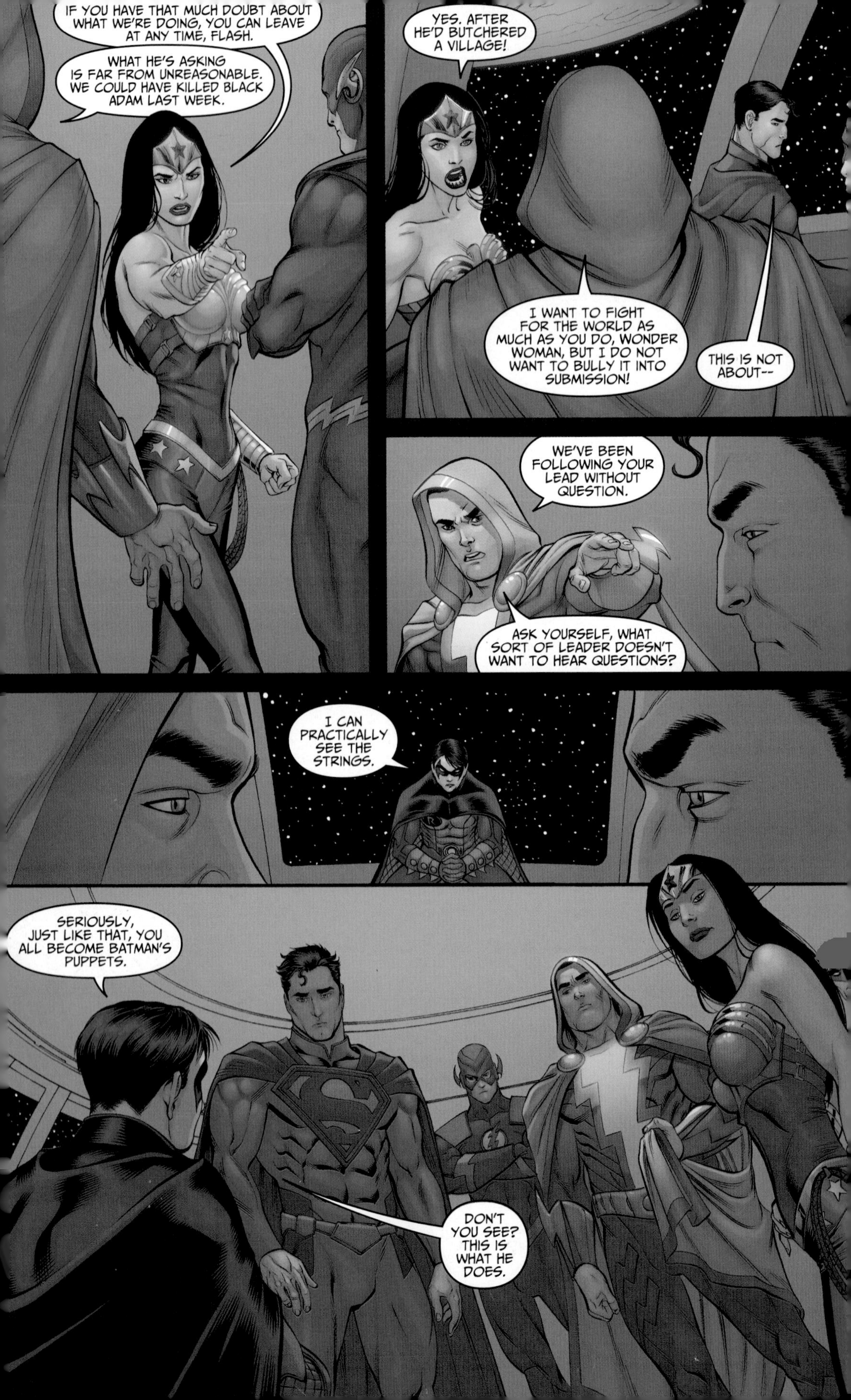
IF YOU HAVE THAT MUCH DOUBT ABOUT WHAT WE'RE DOING, YOU CAN LEAVE AT ANY TIME, FLASH.
WHAT HE'S ASKING IS FAR FROM UNREASONABLE. WE COULD HAVE KILLED BLACK ADAM LAST WEEK.
YES. AFTER HE'D BUTCHERED A VILLAGE!
I WANT TO FIGHT FOR THE WORLD AS MUCH AS YOU DO, WONDER WOMAN, BUT I DO NOT WANT TO BULLY IT INTO SUBMISSION!
THIS IS NOT ABOUT--
WE'VE BEEN FOLLOWING YOUR LEAD WITHOUT QUESTION.
ASK YOURSELF, WHAT SORT OF LEADER DOESN'T WANT TO HEAR QUESTIONS?
I CAN PRACTICALLY SEE THE STRINGS.
SERIOUSLY, JUST LIKE THAT, YOU ALL BECOME BATMAN'S PUPPETS.
DON'T YOU SEE? THIS IS WHAT HE DOES.

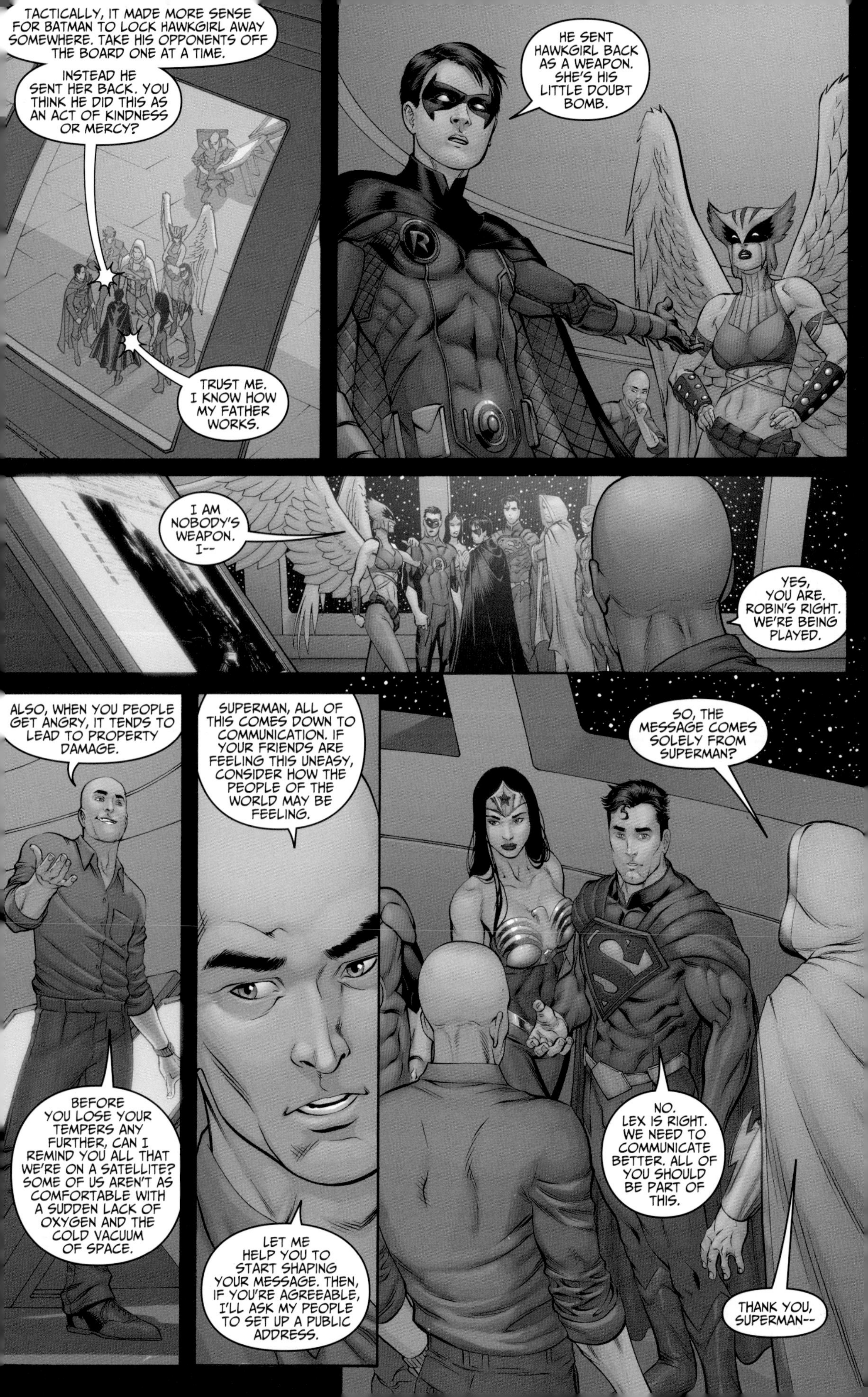
TACTICALLY, IT MADE MORE SENSE FOR BATMAN TO LOCK HAWKGIRL AWAY SOMEWHERE. TAKE HIS OPPONENTS OFF THE BOARD ONE AT A TIME.
INSTEAD HE SENT HER BACK. YOU THINK HE DID THIS AS AN ACT OF KINDNESS OR MERCY?
TRUST ME. I KNOW HOW MY FATHER WORKS.
HE SENT HAWKGIRL BACK AS A WEAPON. SHE'S HIS LITTLE DOUBT BOMB.
I AM NOBODY'S WEAPON. I--
YES, YOU ARE. ROBIN'S RIGHT. WE'RE BEING PLAYED.
ALSO, WHEN YOU PEOPLE GET ANGRY, IT TENDS TO LEAD TO PROPERTY DAMAGE.
BEFORE YOU LOSE YOUR TEMPERS ANY FURTHER, CAN I REMIND YOU ALL THAT WE'RE ON A SATELLITE? SOME OF US AREN'T AS COMFORTABLE WITH A SUDDEN LACK OF OXYGEN AND THE COLD VACUUM OF SPACE.
SUPERMAN, ALL OF THIS COMES DOWN TO COMMUNICATION. IF YOUR FRIENDS ARE FEELING THIS UNEASY, CONSIDER HOW THE PEOPLE OF THE WORLD MAY BE FEELING.
LET ME HELP YOU TO START SHAPING YOUR MESSAGE. THEN, IF YOU'RE AGREEABLE, I'LL ASK MY PEOPLE TO SET UP A PUBLIC ADDRESS.
SO, THE MESSAGE COMES SOLELY FROM SUPERMAN?
NO. LEX IS RIGHT. WE NEED TO COMMUNICATE BETTER. ALL OF YOU SHOULD BE PART OF THIS.
THANK YOU, SUPERMAN--

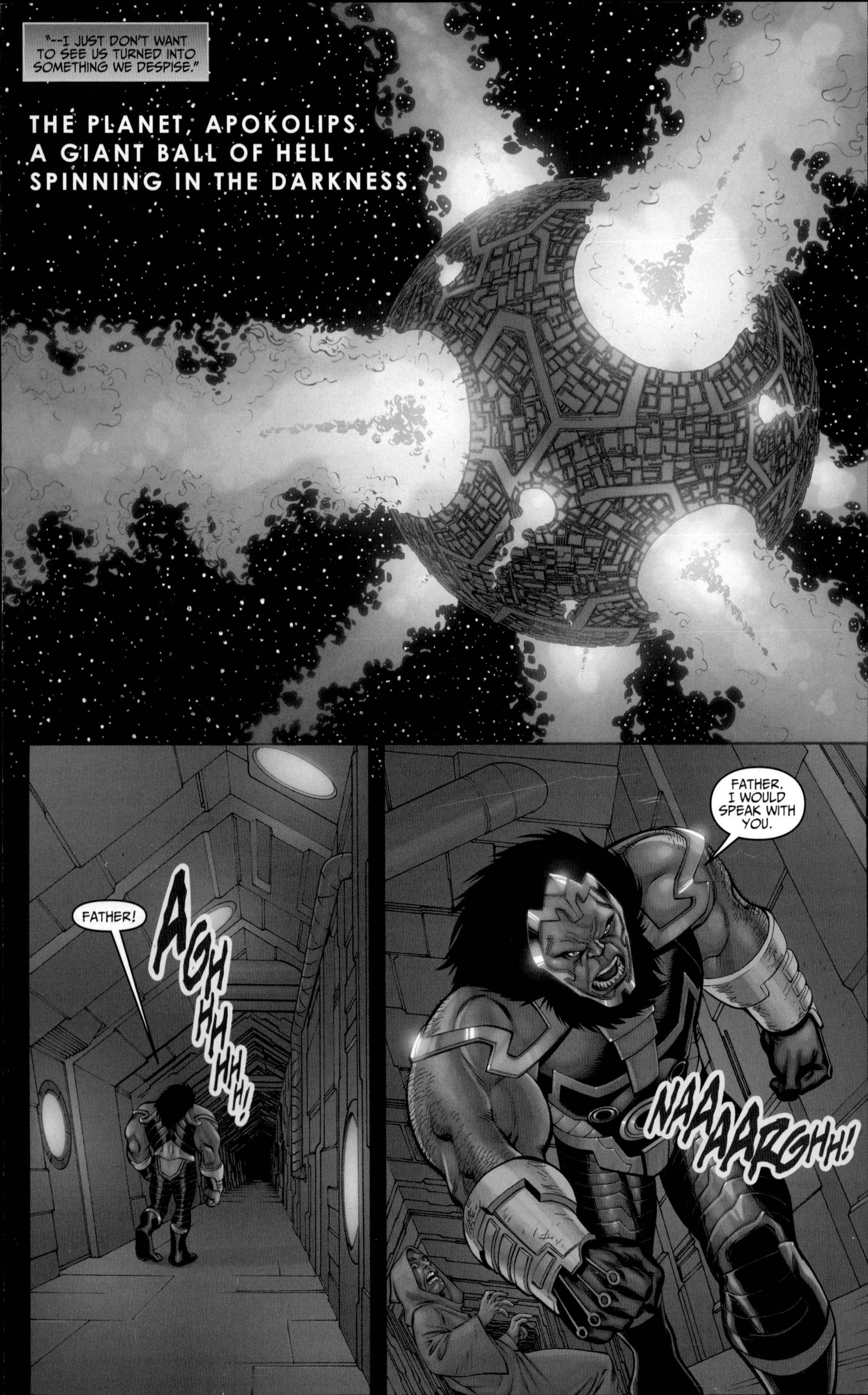
"--I JUST DON'T WANT TO SEE US TURNED INTO SOMETHING WE DESPISE."
THE PLANET, APOKOLIPS. A GIANT BALL OF HELL SPINNING IN THE DARKNESS.
FATHER!
AGHHHHHH!
FATHER. I WOULD SPEAK WITH YOU.
NAAAARGHH!

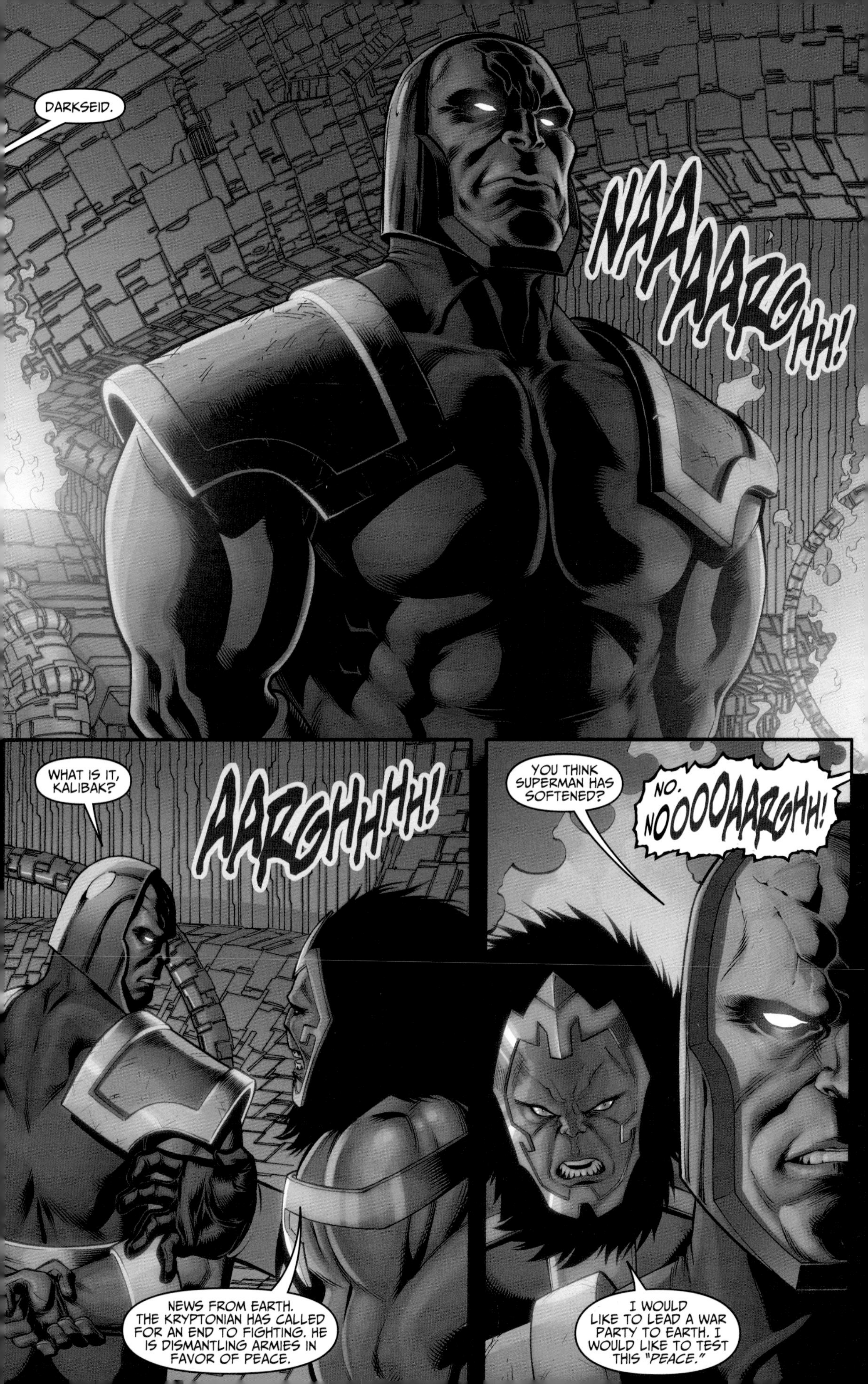
DARKSEID.
NAAAARGHH!
WHAT IS IT, KALIBAK?
AARGHHHH!
NEWS FROM EARTH. THE KRYPTONIAN HAS CALLED FOR AN END TO FIGHTING. HE IS DISMANTLING ARMIES IN FAVOR OF PEACE.
YOU THINK SUPERMAN HAS SOFTENED?
NO. NOOOOAARGHH!
I WOULD LIKE TO LEAD A WAR PARTY TO EARTH. I WOULD LIKE TO TEST THIS "PEACE."

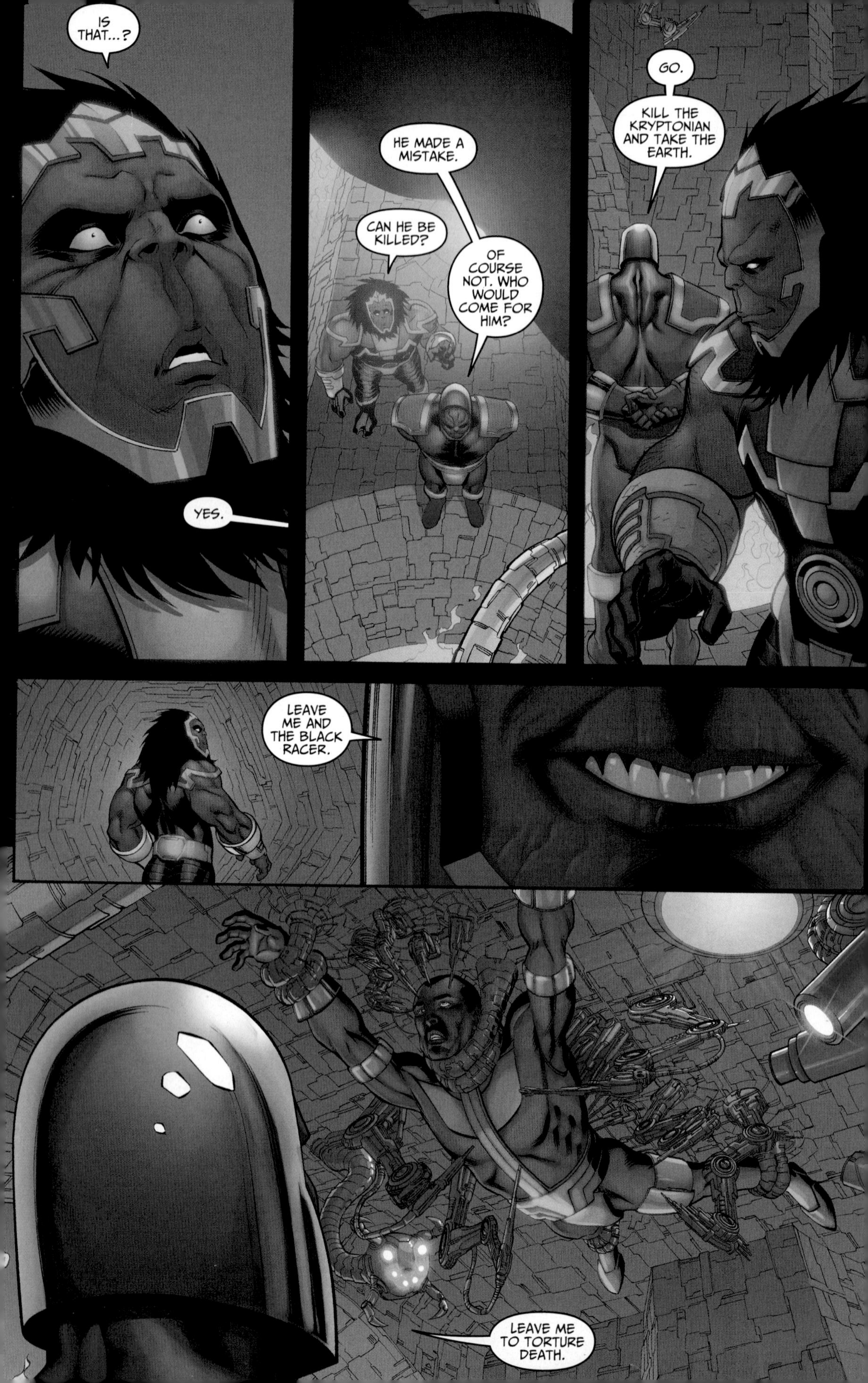
IS THAT...?
YES.
HE MADE A MISTAKE.
CAN HE BE KILLED?
OF COURSE NOT. WHO WOULD COME FOR HIM?
GO.
KILL THE KRYPTONIAN AND TAKE THE EARTH.
LEAVE ME AND THE BLACK RACER.
LEAVE ME TO TORTURE DEATH.

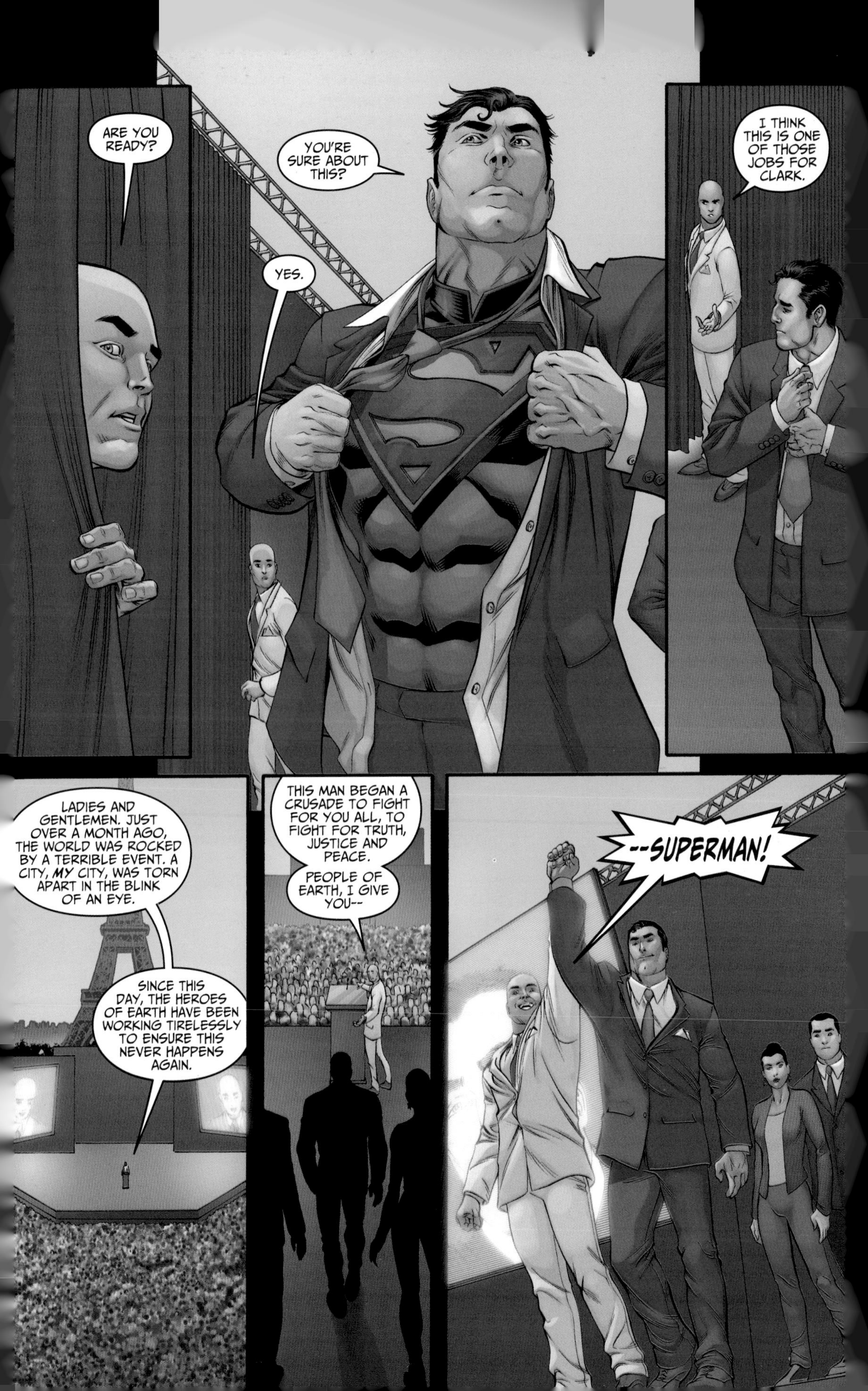
ARE YOU READY?
YOU'RE SURE ABOUT THIS?
YES.
I THINK THIS IS ONE OF THOSE JOBS FOR CLARK.
LADIES AND GENTLEMEN. JUST OVER A MONTH AGO, THE WORLD WAS ROCKED BY A TERRIBLE EVENT. A CITY, MY CITY, WAS TORN APART IN THE BLINK OF AN EYE.
SINCE THIS DAY, THE HEROES OF EARTH HAVE BEEN WORKING TIRELESSLY TO ENSURE THIS NEVER HAPPENS AGAIN.
THIS MAN BEGAN A CRUSADE TO FIGHT FOR YOU ALL, TO FIGHT FOR TRUTH, JUSTICE AND PEACE.
PEOPLE OF EARTH, I GIVE YOU--
--SUPERMAN!

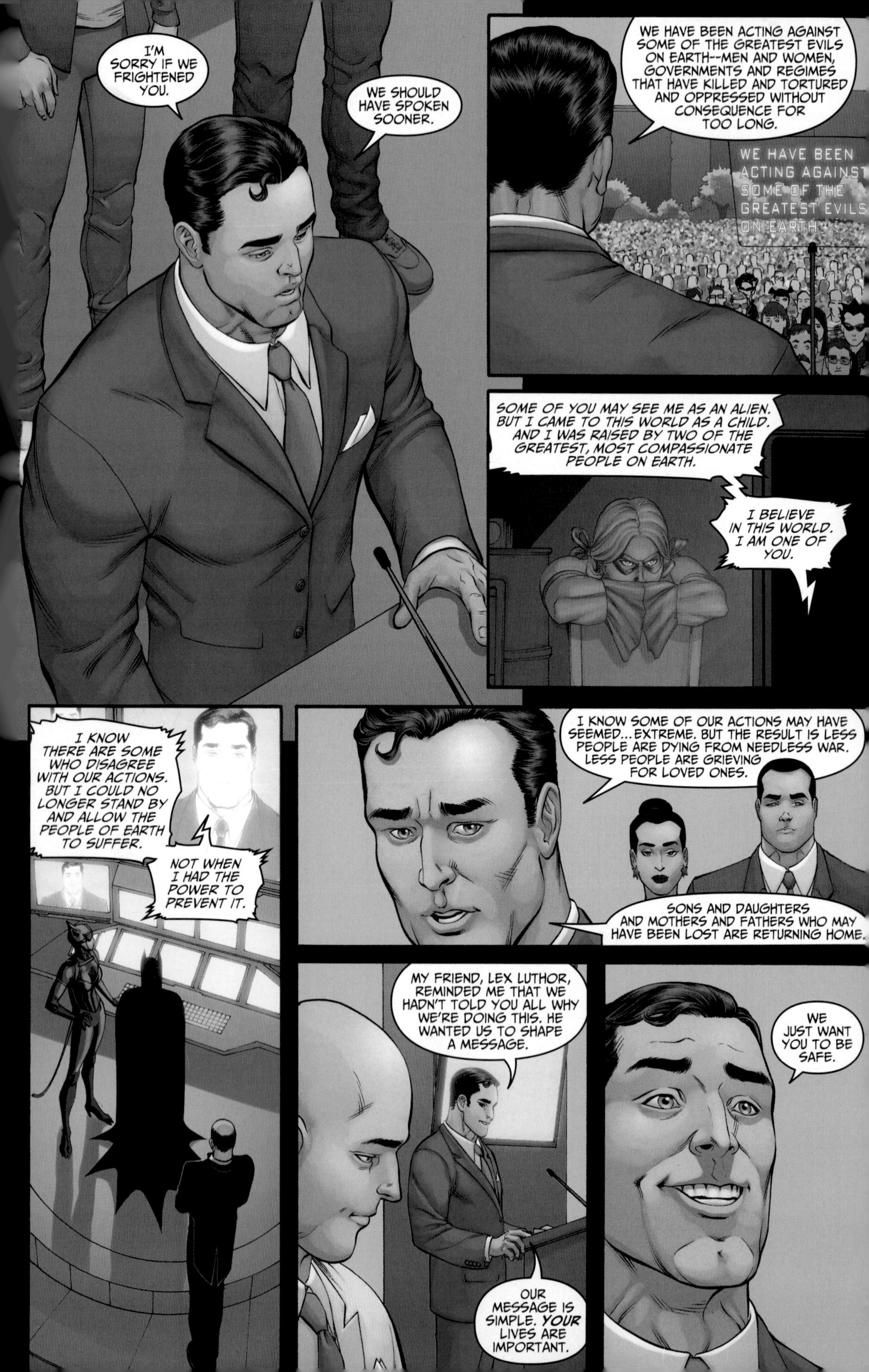
I'M SORRY IF WE FRIGHTENED YOU.
WE SHOULD HAVE SPOKEN SOONER.
WE HAVE BEEN ACTING AGAINST SOME OF THE GREATEST EVILS ON EARTH--MEN AND WOMEN, GOVERNMENTS AND REGIMES THAT HAVE KILLED AND TORTURED AND OPPRESSED WITHOUT CONSEQUENCE FOR TOO LONG.
WE HAVE BEEN ACTING AGAINST SOME OF THE GREATEST EVILS ON EARTH
SOME OF YOU MAY SEE ME AS AN ALIEN. BUT I CAME TO THIS WORLD AS A CHILD. AND I WAS RAISED BY TWO OF THE GREATEST, MOST COMPASSIONATE PEOPLE ON EARTH.
I BELIEVE IN THIS WORLD. I AM ONE OF YOU.
I KNOW THERE ARE SOME WHO DISAGREE WITH OUR ACTIONS. BUT I COULD NO LONGER STAND BY AND ALLOW THE PEOPLE OF EARTH TO SUFFER.
NOT WHEN I HAD THE POWER TO PREVENT IT.
I KNOW SOME OF OUR ACTIONS MAY HAVE SEEMED... EXTREME. BUT THE RESULT IS LESS PEOPLE ARE DYING FROM NEEDLESS WAR. LESS PEOPLE ARE GRIEVING FOR LOVED ONES.
SONS AND DAUGHTERS AND MOTHERS AND FATHERS WHO MAY HAVE BEEN LOST ARE RETURNING HOME.
MY FRIEND, LEX LUTHOR, REMINDED ME THAT WE HADN'T TOLD YOU ALL WHY WE'RE DOING THIS. HE WANTED US TO SHAPE A MESSAGE.
OUR MESSAGE IS SIMPLE. YOUR LIVES ARE IMPORTANT.
WE JUST WANT YOU TO BE SAFE.

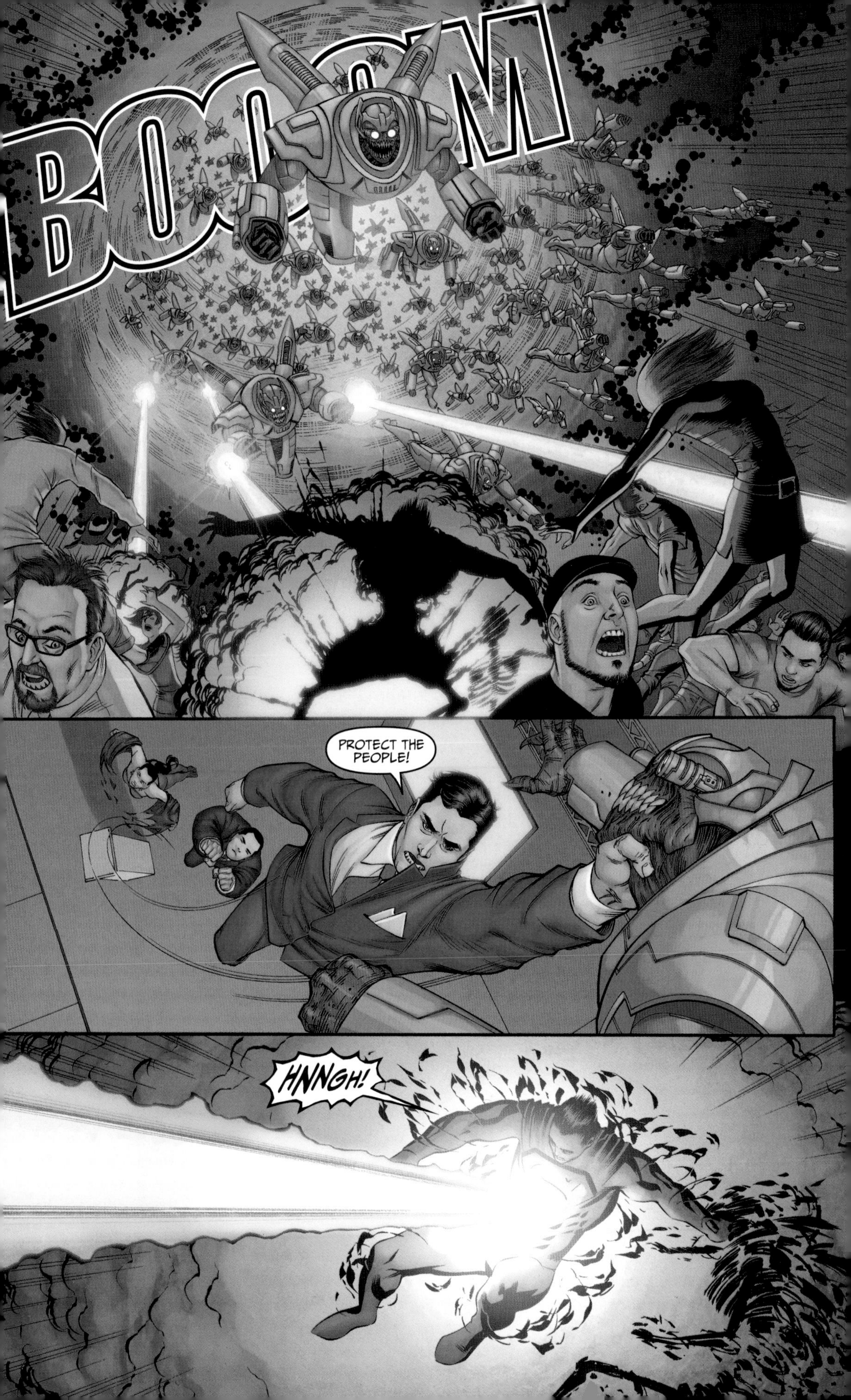
BOOOM
PROTECT THE PEOPLE!
HNNGH!

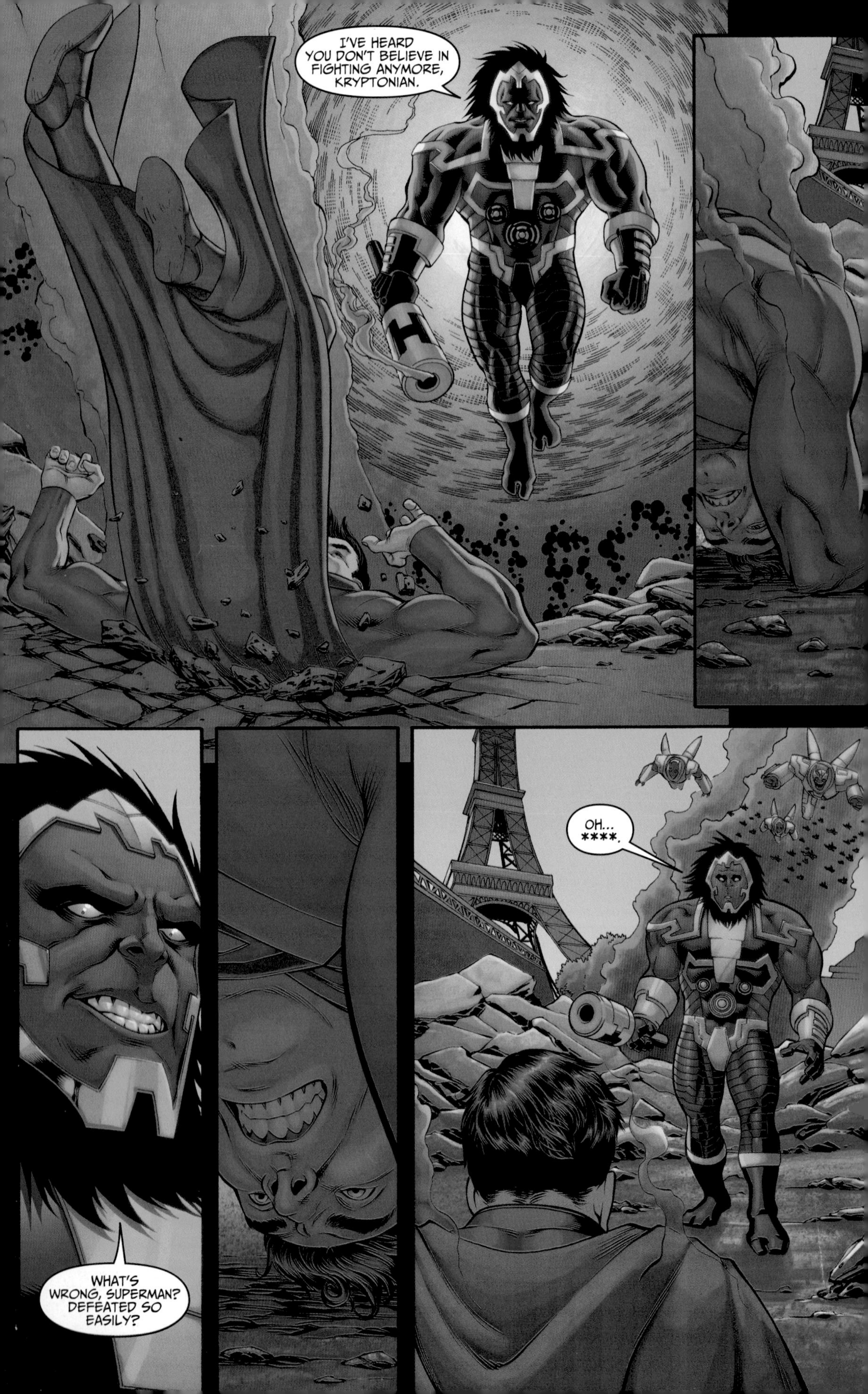
I'VE HEARD YOU DON'T BELIEVE IN FIGHTING ANYMORE, KRYPTONIAN.
WHAT'S WRONG, SUPERMAN? DEFEATED SO EASILY?
OH... ****.

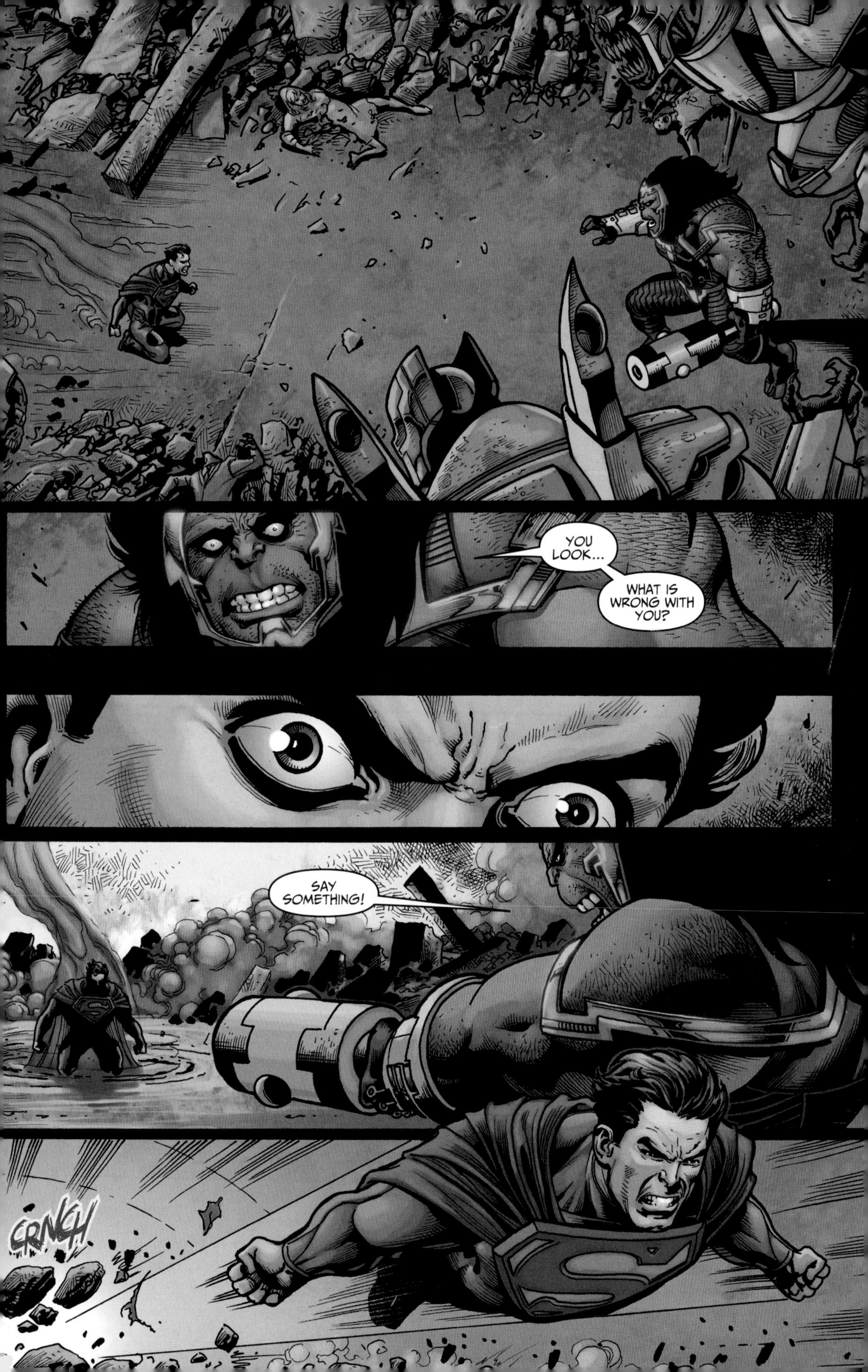
YOU LOOK...
WHAT IS WRONG WITH YOU?
SAY SOMETHING!
CRNCH

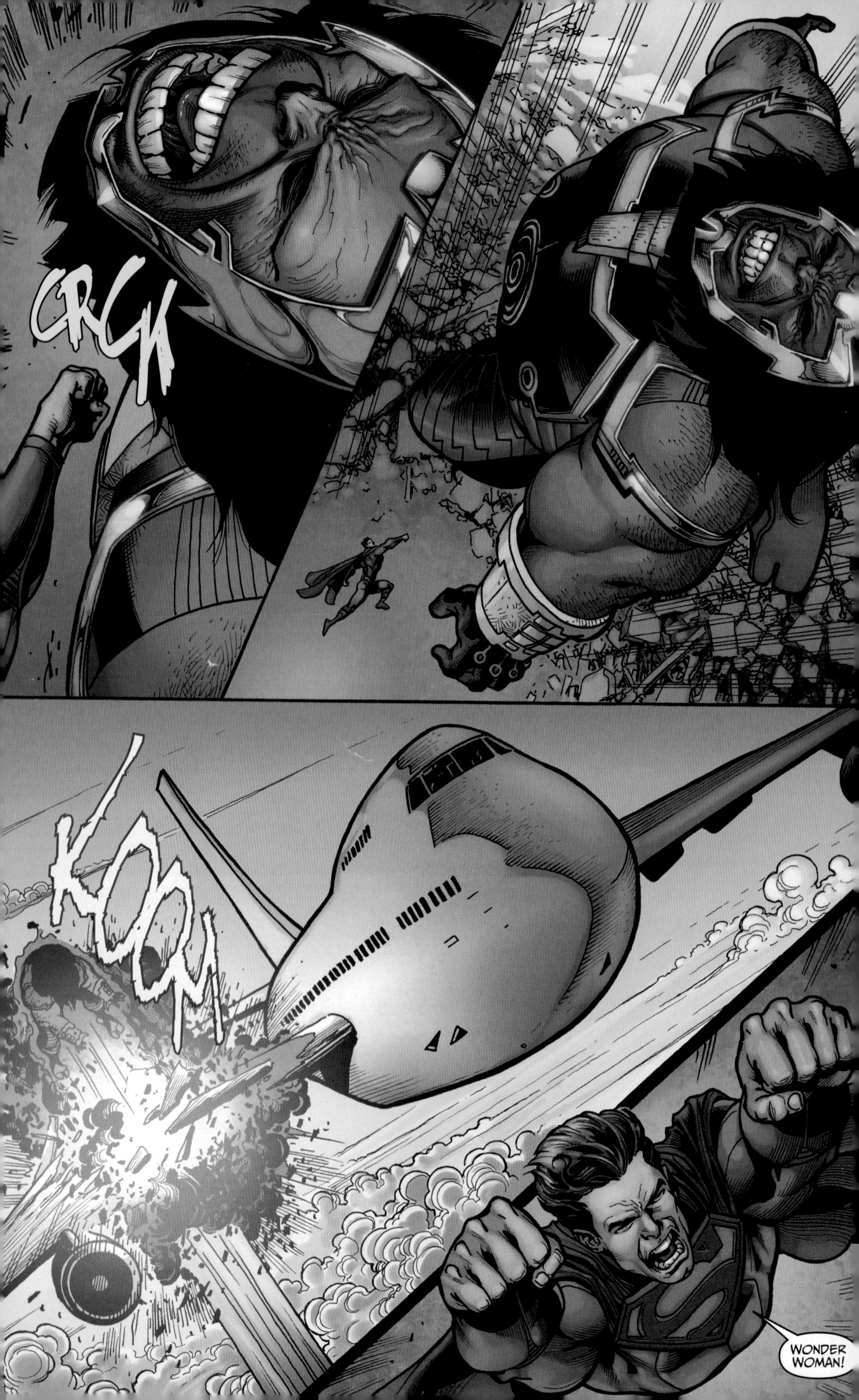
CRCK
KOOM
WONDER WOMAN!

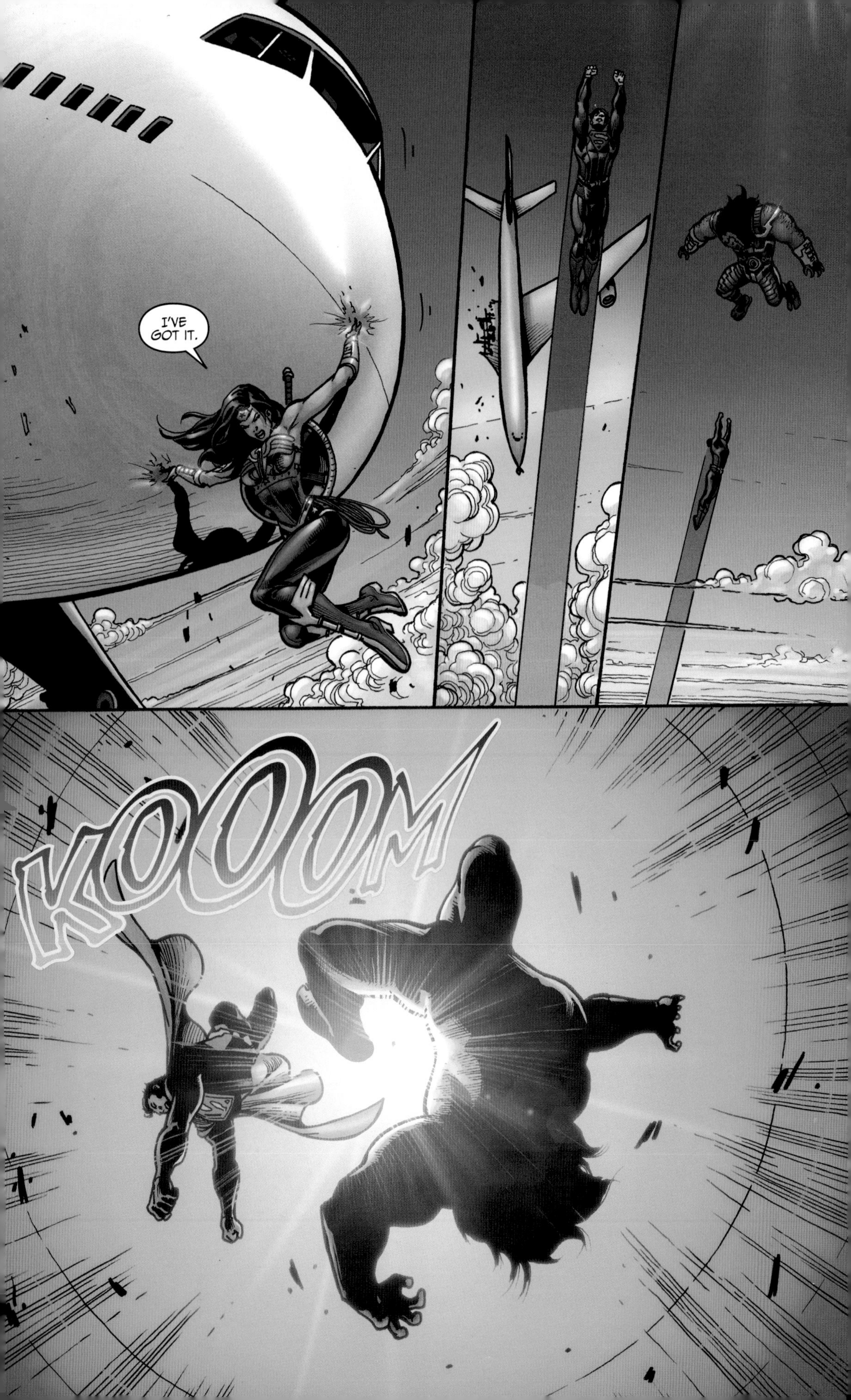
I'VE GOT IT.
KOOOM

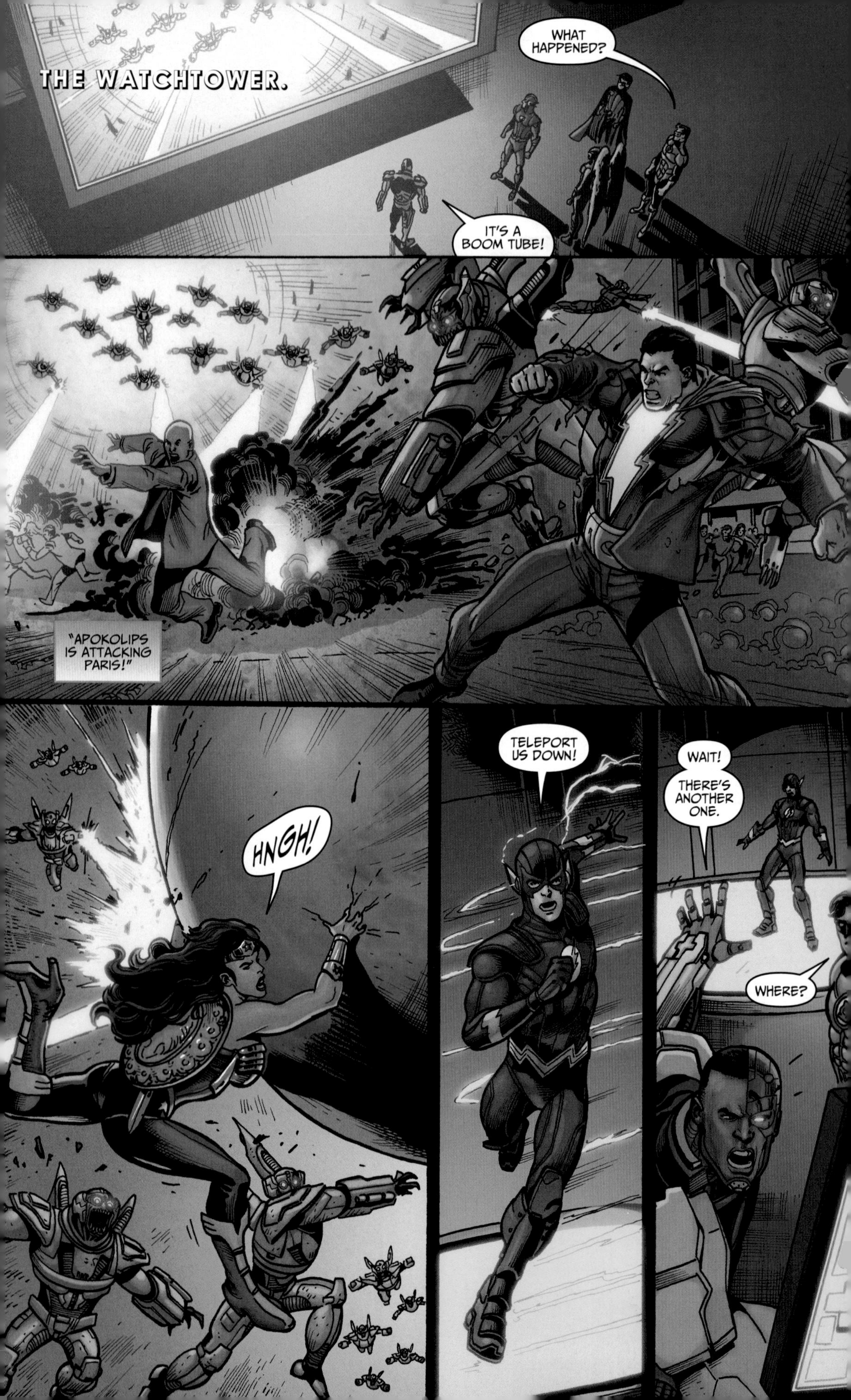
THE WATCHTOWER.
WHAT HAPPENED?
IT'S A BOOM TUBE!
"APOKOLIPS IS ATTACKING PARIS!"
HNGH!
TELEPORT US DOWN!
WAIT!
THERE'S ANOTHER ONE.
WHERE?

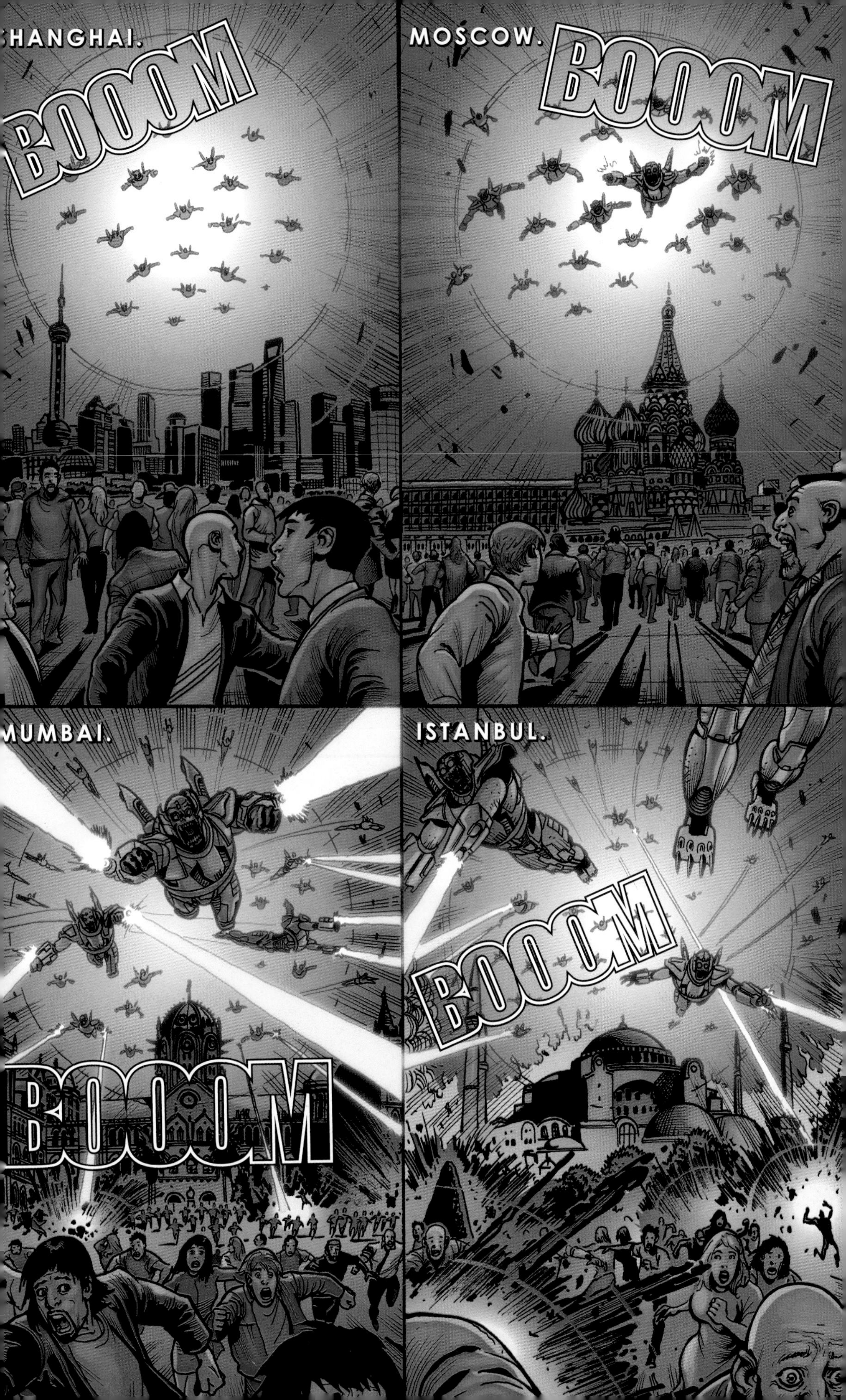
SHANGHAI.
BOOOM
MOSCOW.
BOOOM
MUMBAI.
BOOOM
ISTANBUL.
BOOOM

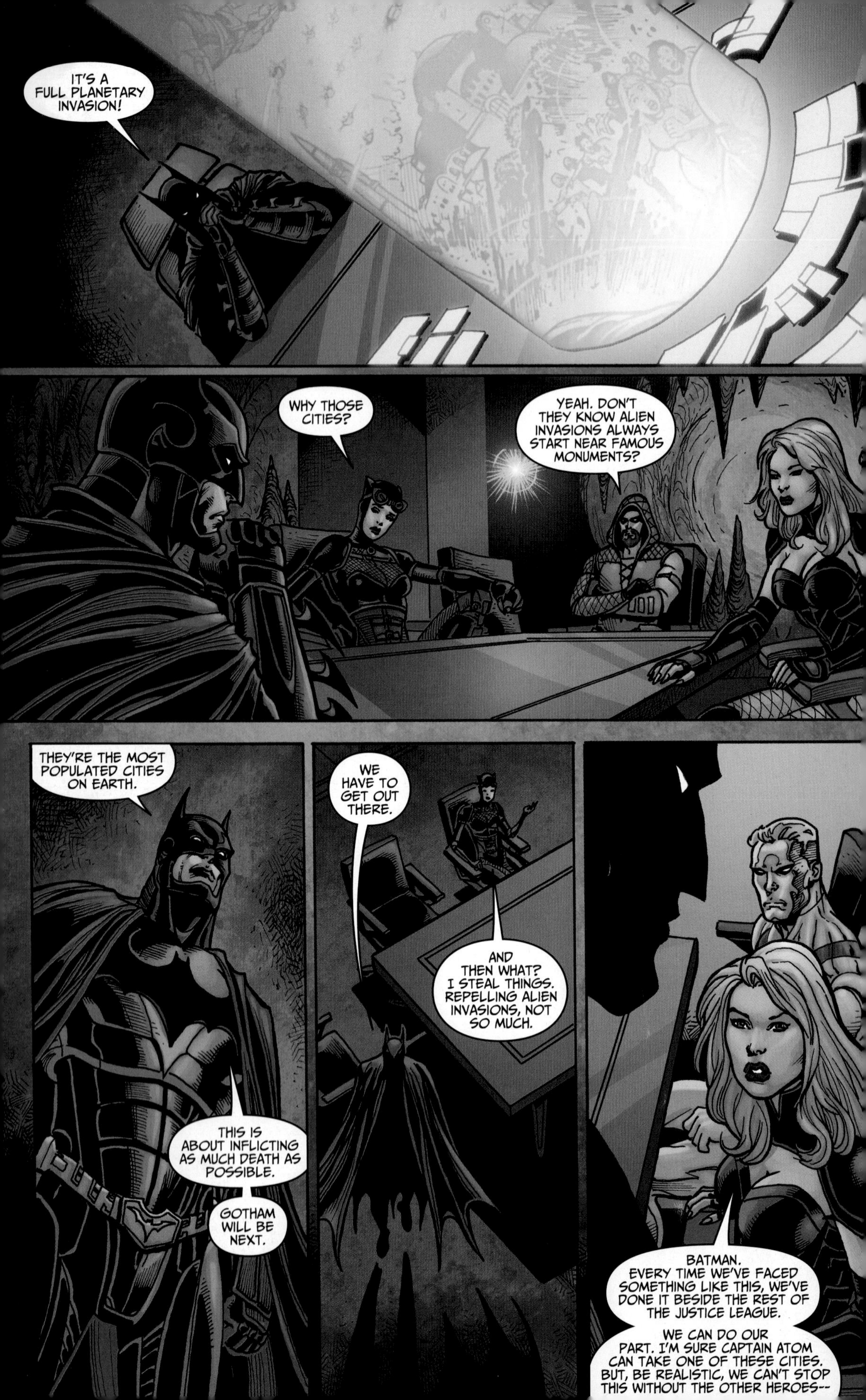
IT'S A FULL PLANETARY INVASION!
WHY THOSE CITIES?
YEAH. DON'T THEY KNOW ALIEN INVASIONS ALWAYS START NEAR FAMOUS MONUMENTS?
THEY'RE THE MOST POPULATED CITIES ON EARTH.
THIS IS ABOUT INFLICTING AS MUCH DEATH AS POSSIBLE.
GOTHAM WILL BE NEXT.
WE HAVE TO GET OUT THERE.
AND THEN WHAT? I STEAL THINGS. REPELLING ALIEN INVASIONS, NOT SO MUCH.
BATMAN. EVERY TIME WE'VE FACED SOMETHING LIKE THIS, WE'VE DONE IT BESIDE THE REST OF THE JUSTICE LEAGUE.
WE CAN DO OUR PART. I'M SURE CAPTAIN ATOM CAN TAKE ONE OF THESE CITIES. BUT, BE REALISTIC, WE CAN'T STOP THIS WITHOUT THE OTHER HEROES--

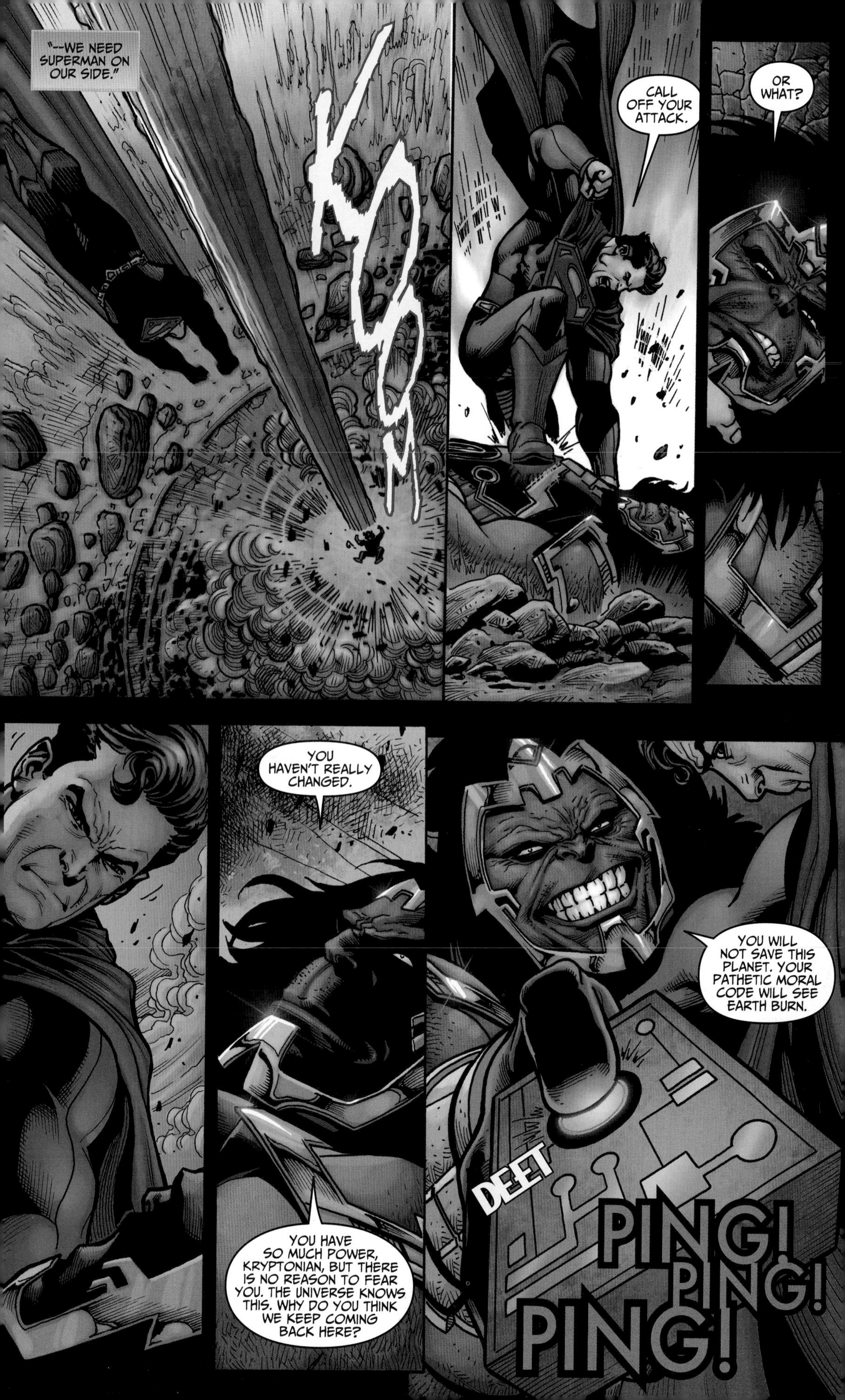
"--WE NEED SUPERMAN ON OUR SIDE."
KSSH
CALL OFF YOUR ATTACK.
OR WHAT?
YOU HAVEN'T REALLY CHANGED.
YOU HAVE SO MUCH POWER, KRYPTONIAN, BUT THERE IS NO REASON TO FEAR YOU. THE UNIVERSE KNOWS THIS. WHY DO YOU THINK WE KEEP COMING BACK HERE?
YOU WILL NOT SAVE THIS PLANET. YOUR PATHETIC MORAL CODE WILL SEE EARTH BURN.
DEET
PING! PING! PING!

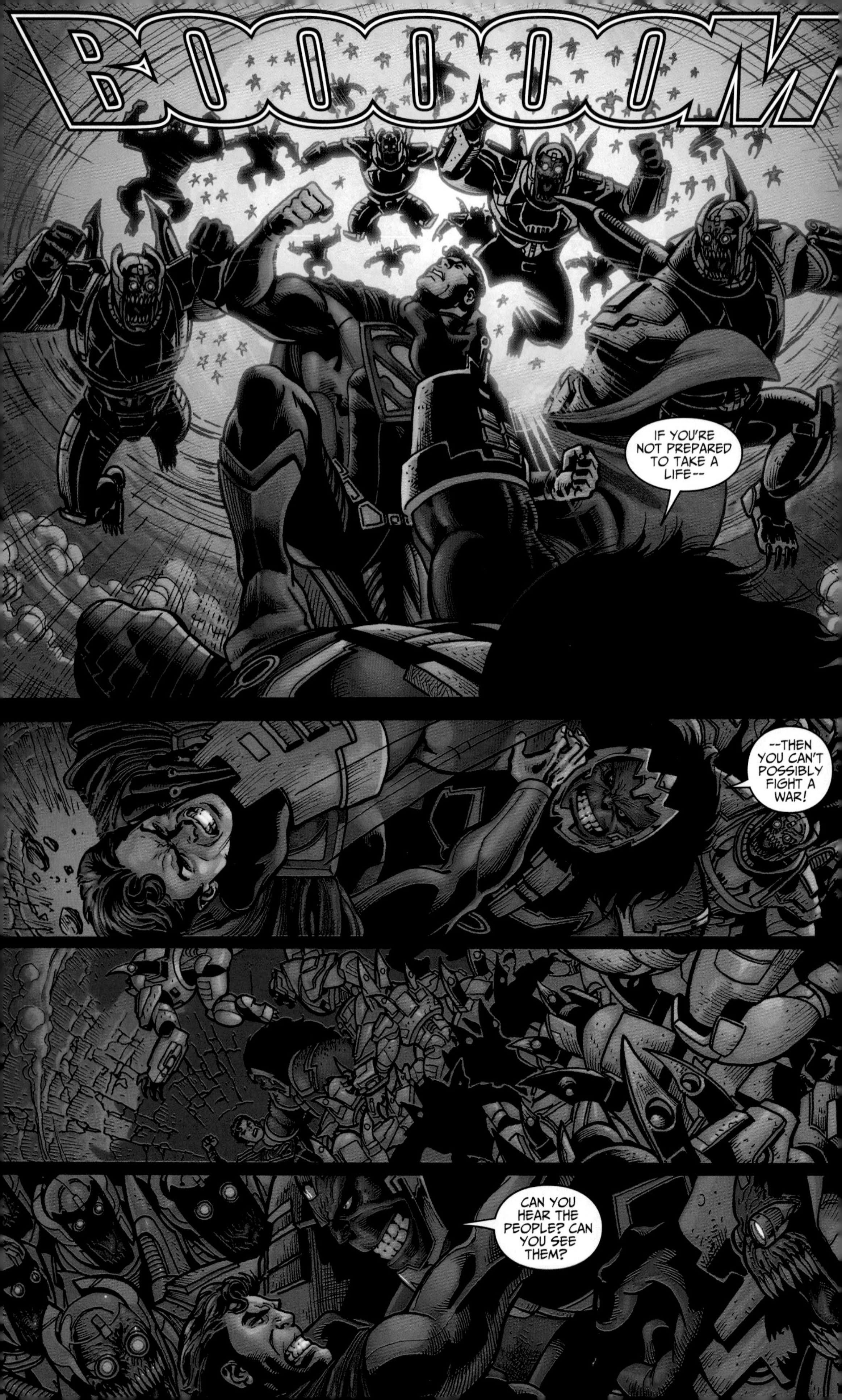
BOOOOOOM
IF YOU'RE NOT PREPARED TO TAKE A LIFE--
--THEN YOU CAN'T POSSIBLY FIGHT A WAR!
CAN YOU HEAR THE PEOPLE? CAN YOU SEE THEM?

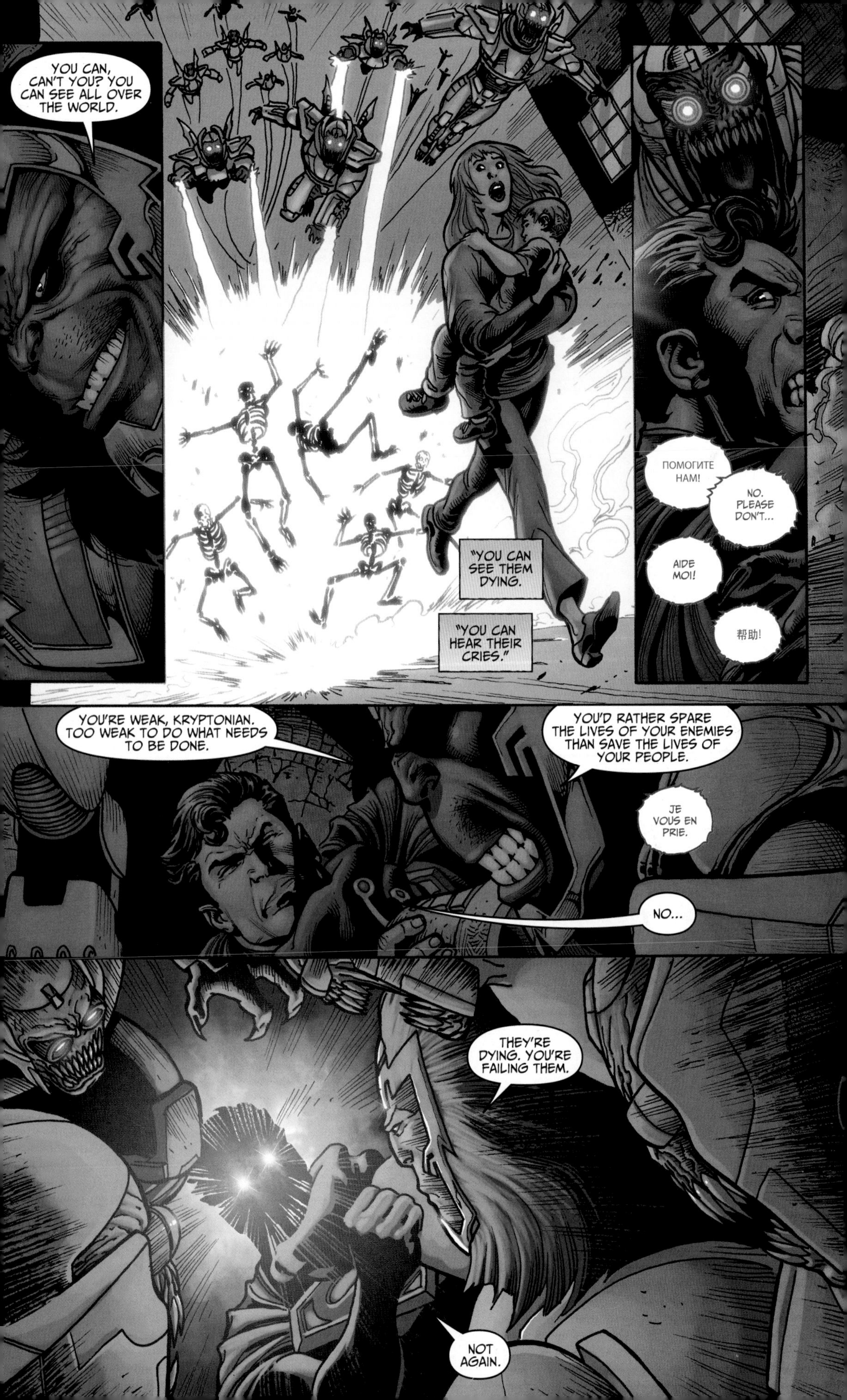
YOU CAN, CAN'T YOU? YOU CAN SEE ALL OVER THE WORLD.
"YOU CAN SEE THEM DYING.
"YOU CAN HEAR THEIR CRIES."
ПОМОГИТЕ НАМ!
NO. PLEASE DON'T...
AIDE MOI!
帮助!
YOU'RE WEAK, KRYPTONIAN. TOO WEAK TO DO WHAT NEEDS TO BE DONE.
YOU'D RATHER SPARE THE LIVES OF YOUR ENEMIES THAN SAVE THE LIVES OF YOUR PEOPLE.
JE VOUS EN PRIE.
NO...
THEY'RE DYING. YOU'RE FAILING THEM.
NOT AGAIN.

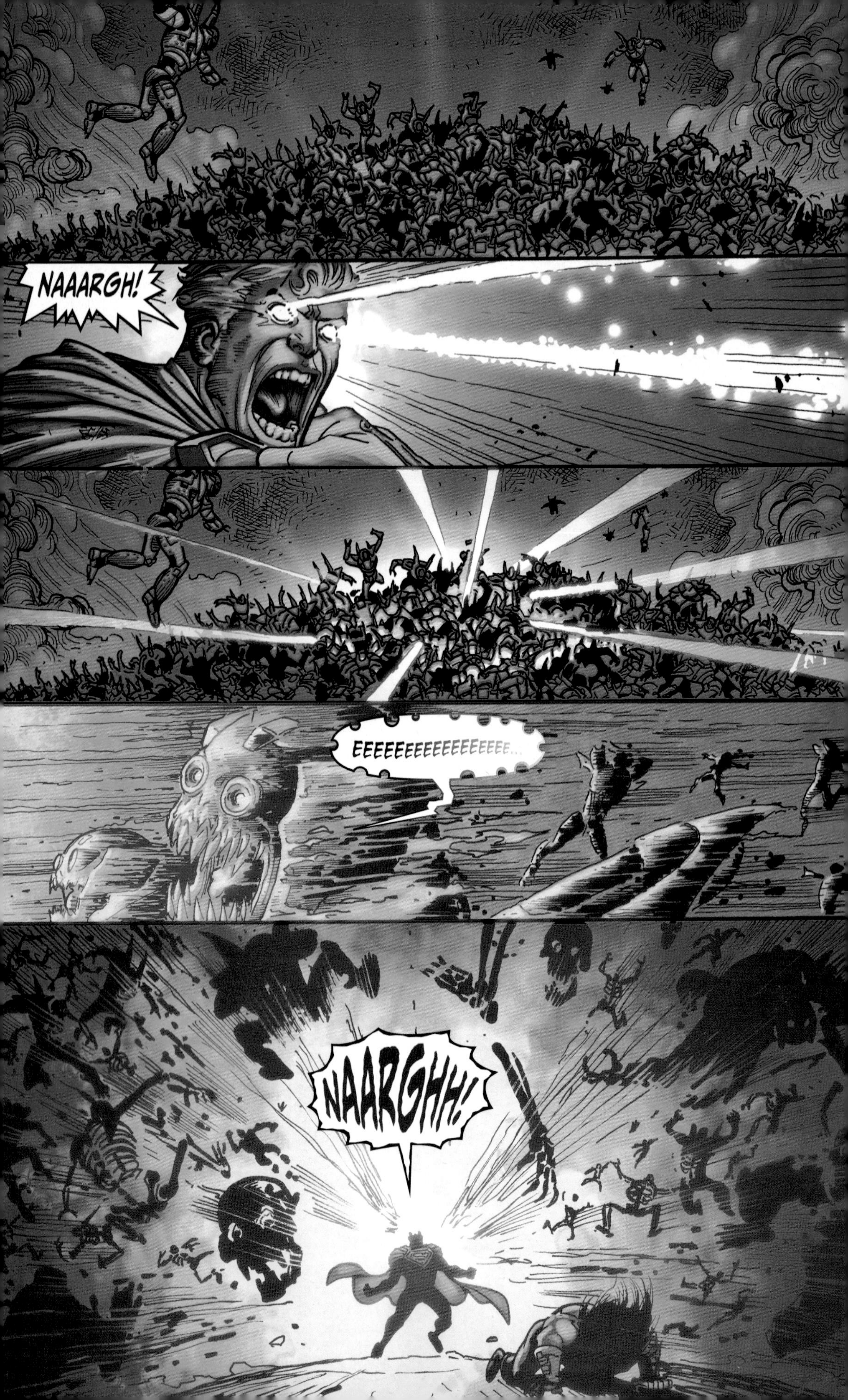
NAAARGH!
EEEEEEEEEEEEEEEE...
NAARGHH!

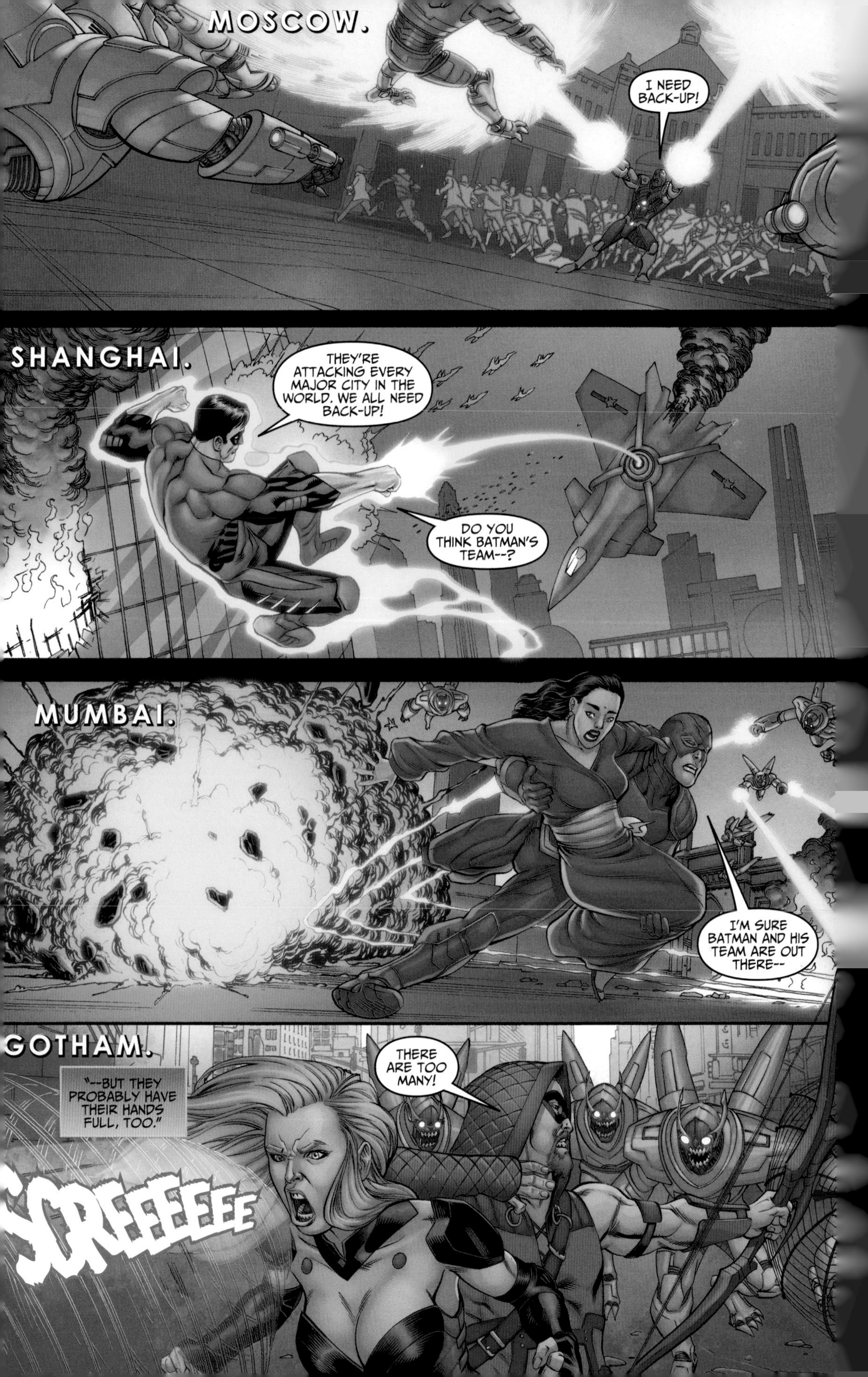
MOSCOW.
I NEED BACK-UP!
SHANGHAI.
THEY'RE ATTACKING EVERY MAJOR CITY IN THE WORLD. WE ALL NEED BACK-UP!
DO YOU THINK BATMAN'S TEAM--?
MUMBAI.
I'M SURE BATMAN AND HIS TEAM ARE OUT THERE--
GOTHAM.
"--BUT THEY PROBABLY HAVE THEIR HANDS FULL, TOO."
THERE ARE TOO MANY!
SCREEEEEEE

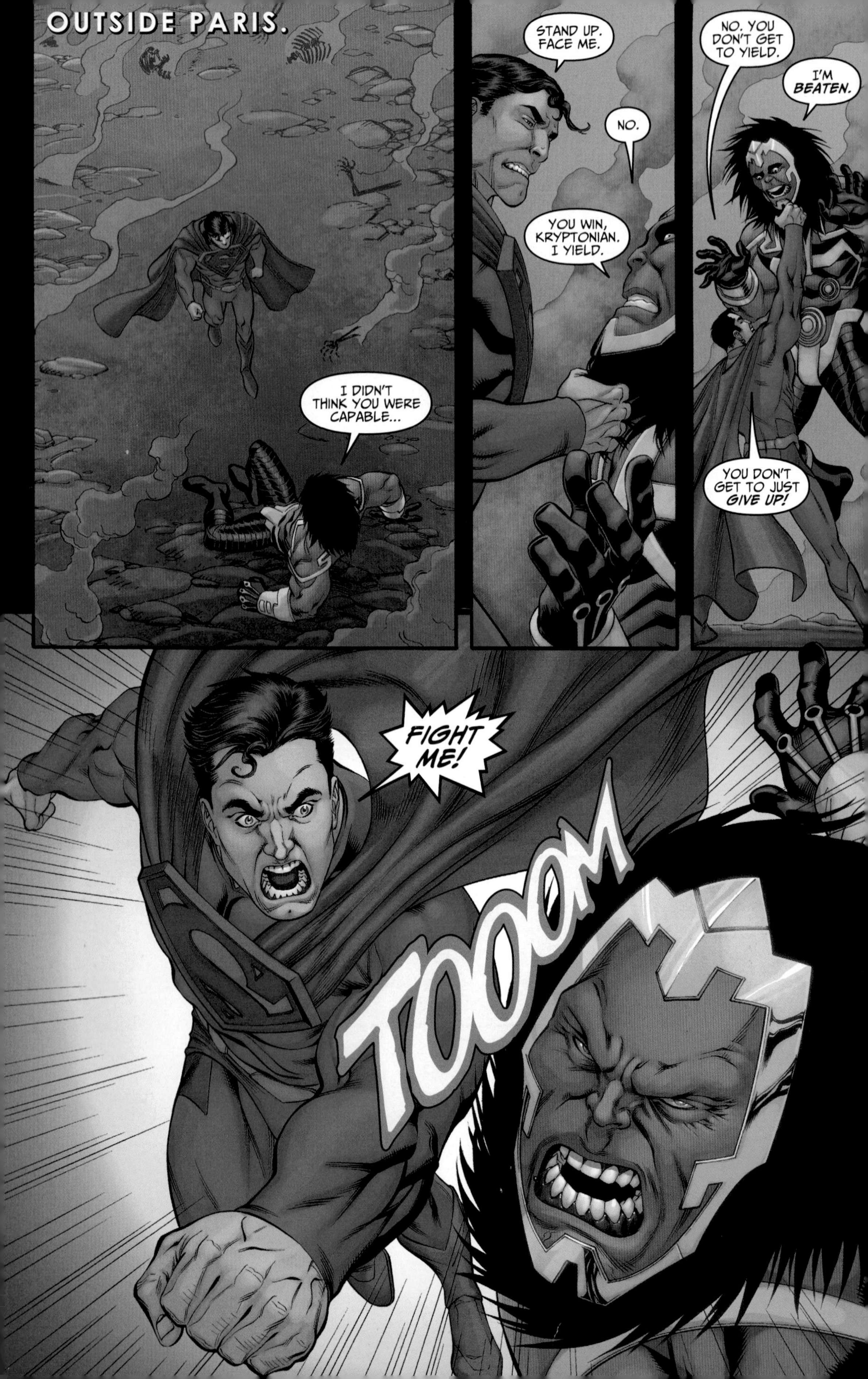
OUTSIDE PARIS.
I DIDN'T THINK YOU WERE CAPABLE...
STAND UP. FACE ME.
NO.
YOU WIN, KRYPTONIAN. I YIELD.
NO. YOU DON'T GET TO YIELD.
I'M BEATEN.
YOU DON'T GET TO JUST GIVE UP!
FIGHT ME!
TOOOM

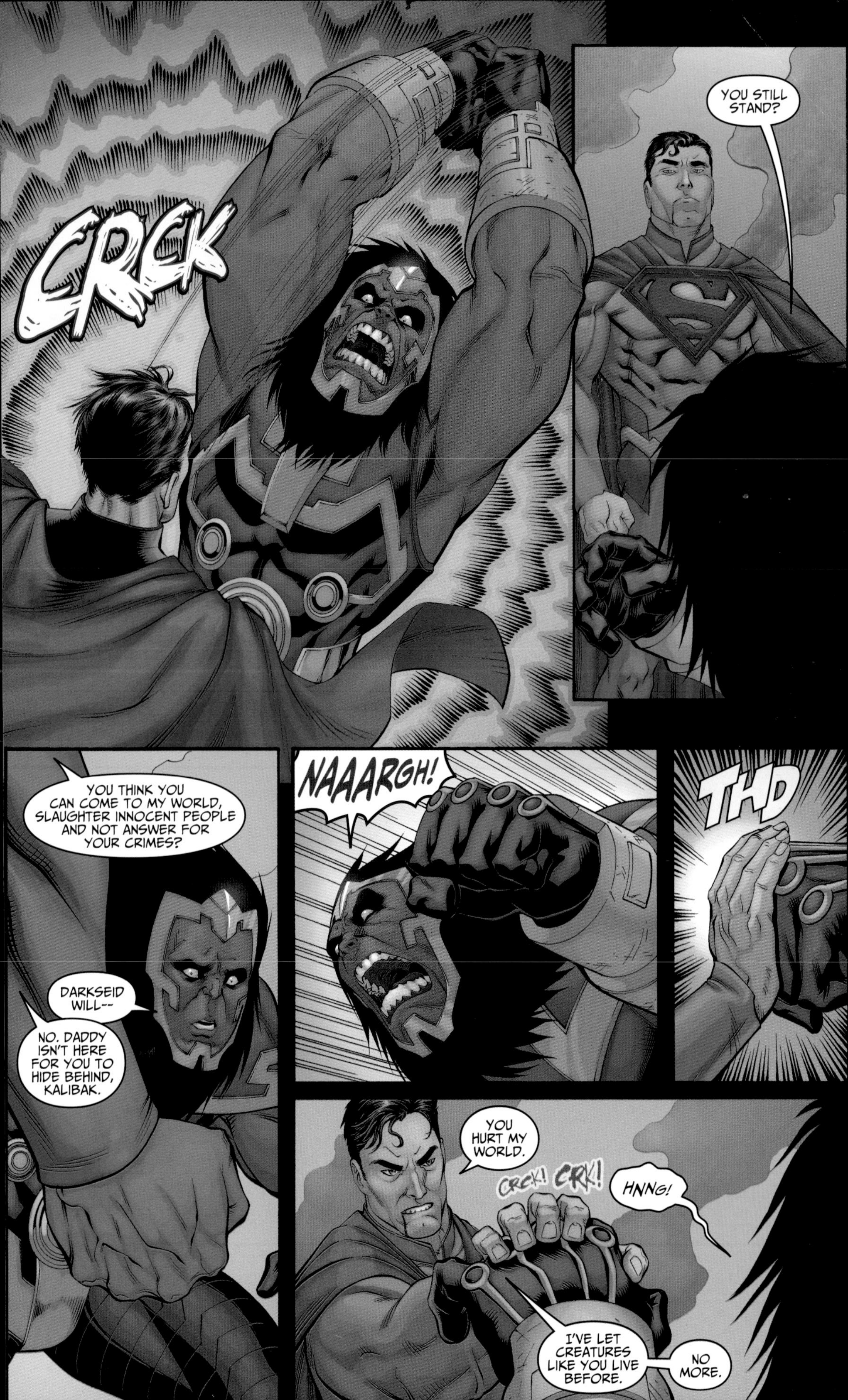
CRCK
YOU STILL STAND?
YOU THINK YOU CAN COME TO MY WORLD, SLAUGHTER INNOCENT PEOPLE AND NOT ANSWER FOR YOUR CRIMES?
DARKSEID WILL--
NO. DADDY ISN'T HERE FOR YOU TO HIDE BEHIND, KALIBAK.
NAAARGH!
THD
YOU HURT MY WORLD.
CRCK! CRK!
HNNG!
I'VE LET CREATURES LIKE YOU LIVE BEFORE.
NO MORE.

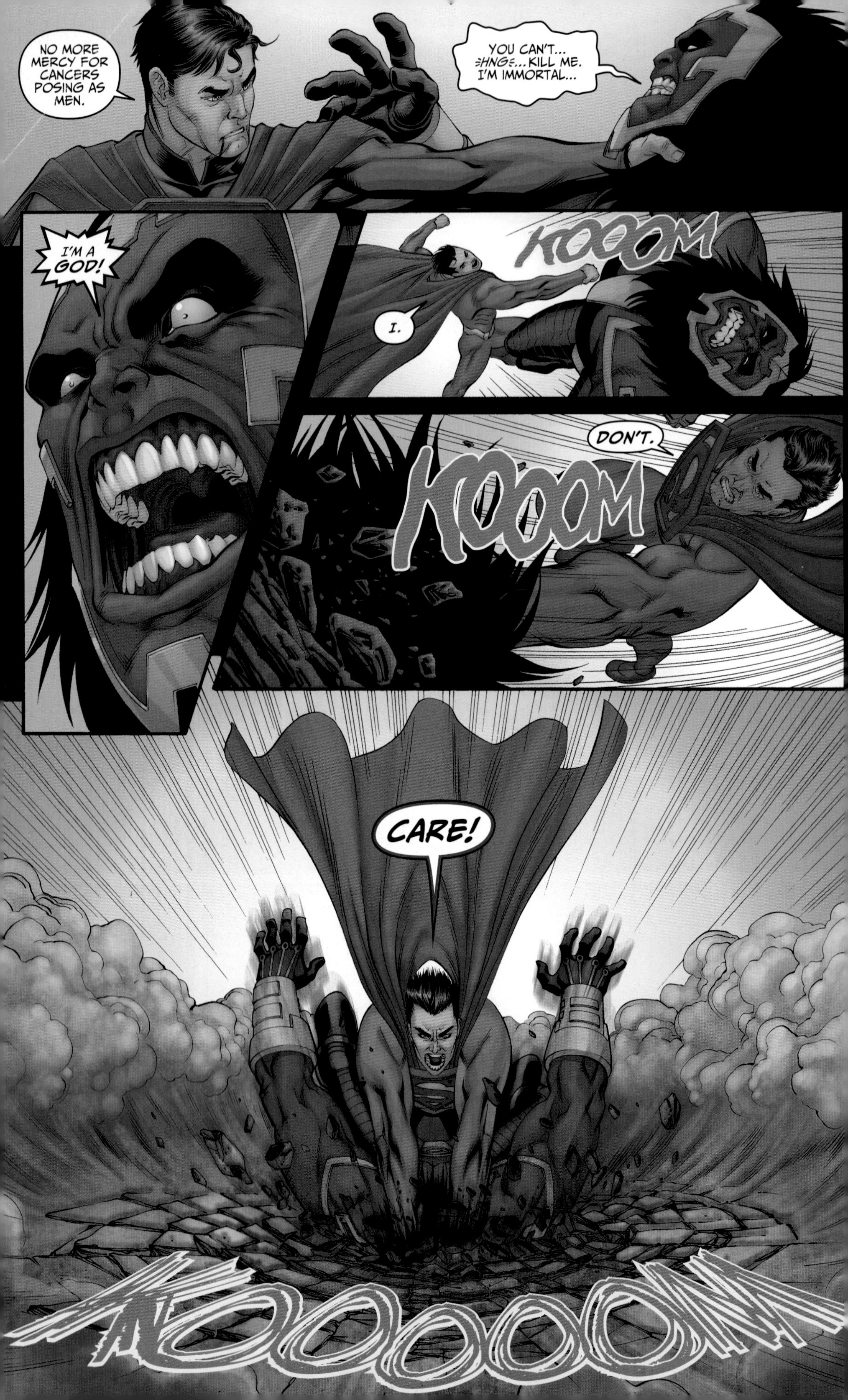
NO MORE MERCY FOR CANCERS POSING AS MEN.
YOU CAN'T... HNG... KILL ME. I'M IMMORTAL...
I'M A GOD!
KOOOM
I.
DON'T.
KOOOM
CARE!
KOOOOOOM

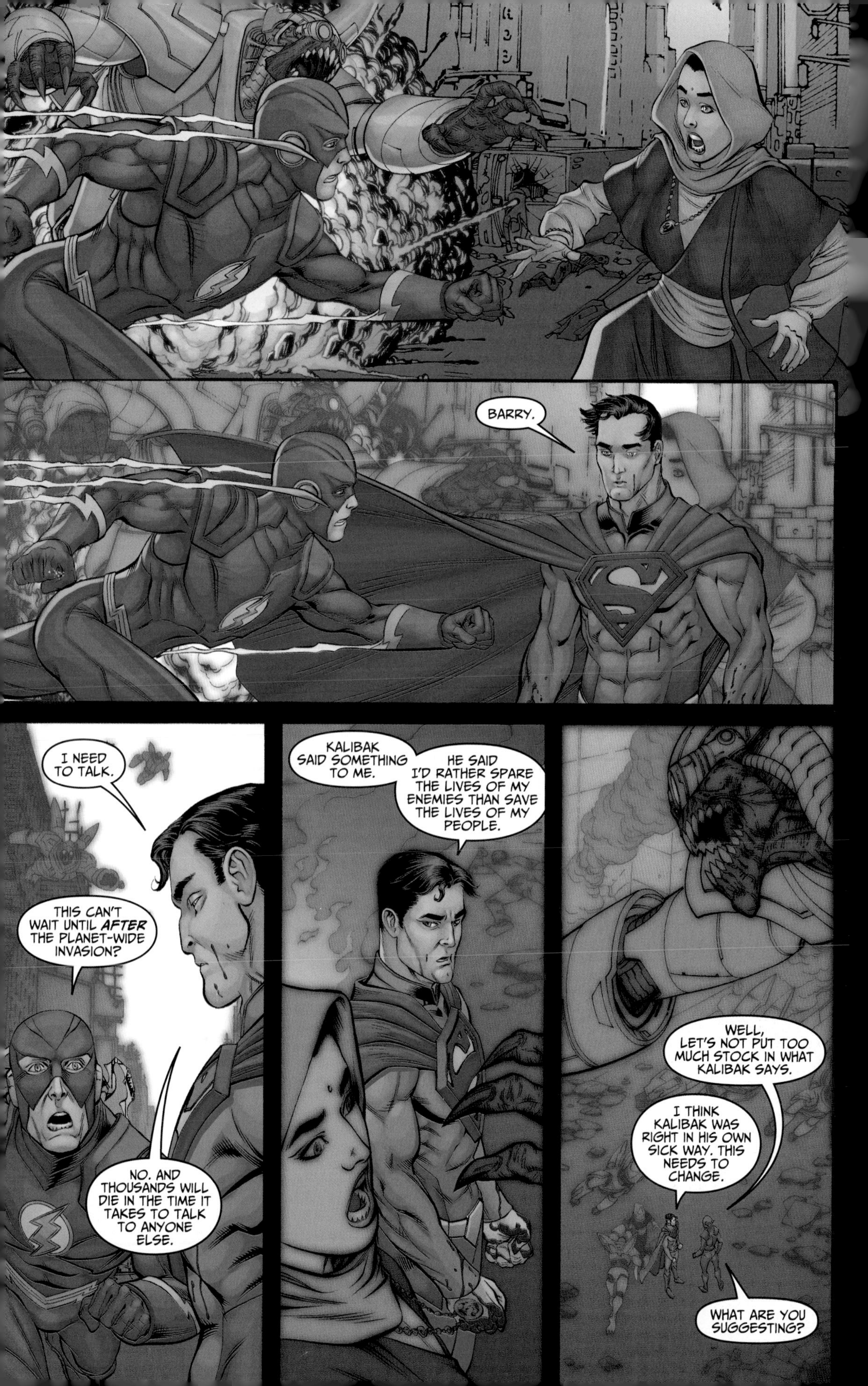
BARRY.
I NEED TO TALK.
THIS CAN'T WAIT UNTIL AFTER THE PLANET-WIDE INVASION?
NO. AND THOUSANDS WILL DIE IN THE TIME IT TAKES TO TALK TO ANYONE ELSE.
KALIBAK SAID SOMETHING TO ME.
HE SAID I'D RATHER SPARE THE LIVES OF MY ENEMIES THAN SAVE THE LIVES OF MY PEOPLE.
WELL, LET'S NOT PUT TOO MUCH STOCK IN WHAT KALIBAK SAYS.
I THINK KALIBAK WAS RIGHT IN HIS OWN SICK WAY. THIS NEEDS TO CHANGE.
WHAT ARE YOU SUGGESTING?

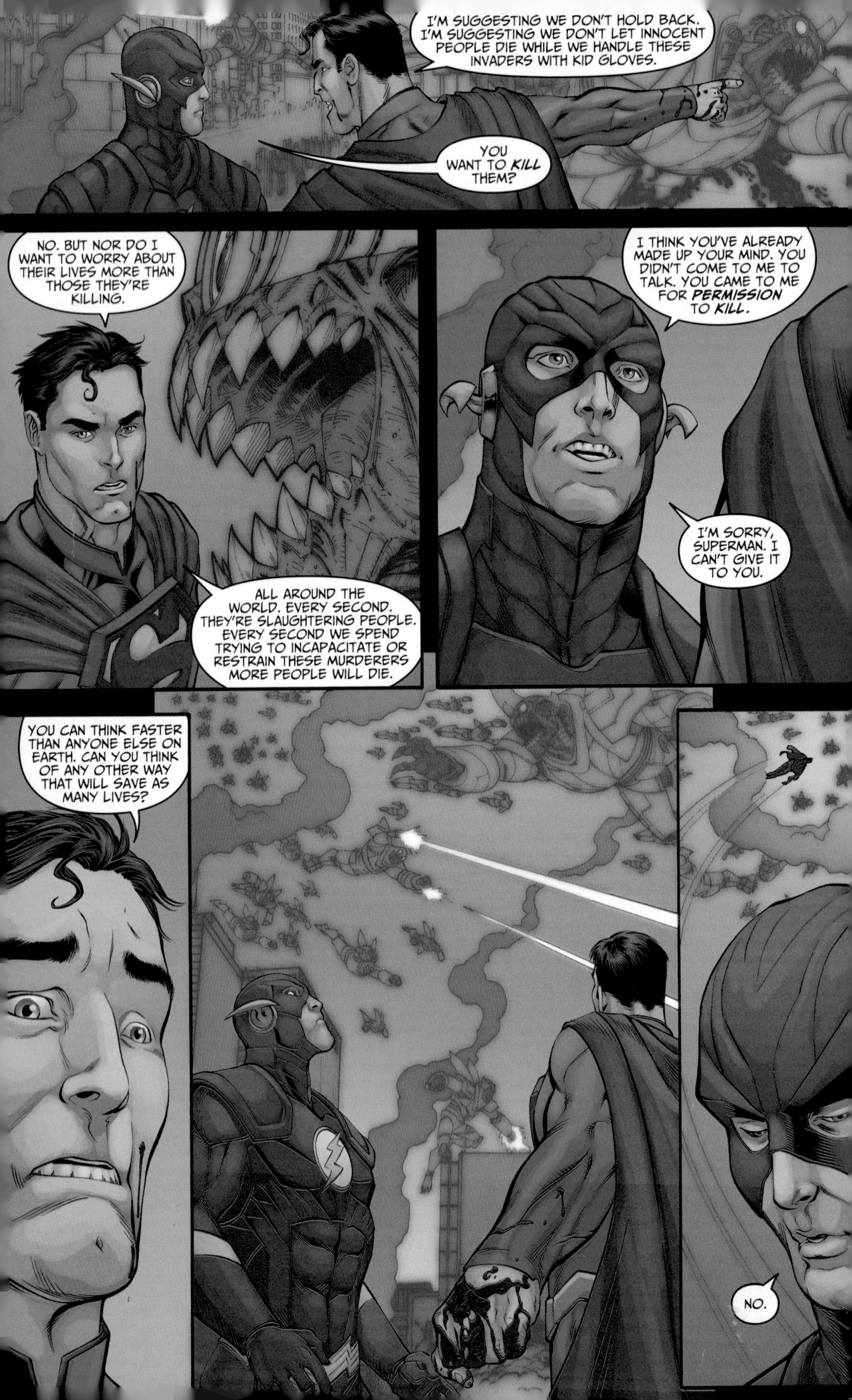
I'M SUGGESTING WE DON'T HOLD BACK. I'M SUGGESTING WE DON'T LET INNOCENT PEOPLE DIE WHILE WE HANDLE THESE INVADERS WITH KID GLOVES.
YOU WANT TO KILL THEM?
NO. BUT NOR DO I WANT TO WORRY ABOUT THEIR LIVES MORE THAN THOSE THEY'RE KILLING.
ALL AROUND THE WORLD. EVERY SECOND. THEY'RE SLAUGHTERING PEOPLE. EVERY SECOND WE SPEND TRYING TO INCAPACITATE OR RESTRAIN THESE MURDERERS MORE PEOPLE WILL DIE.
I THINK YOU'VE ALREADY MADE UP YOUR MIND. YOU DIDN'T COME TO ME TO TALK. YOU CAME TO ME FOR PERMISSION TO KILL.
I'M SORRY, SUPERMAN. I CAN'T GIVE IT TO YOU.
YOU CAN THINK FASTER THAN ANYONE ELSE ON EARTH. CAN YOU THINK OF ANY OTHER WAY THAT WILL SAVE AS MANY LIVES?
NO.

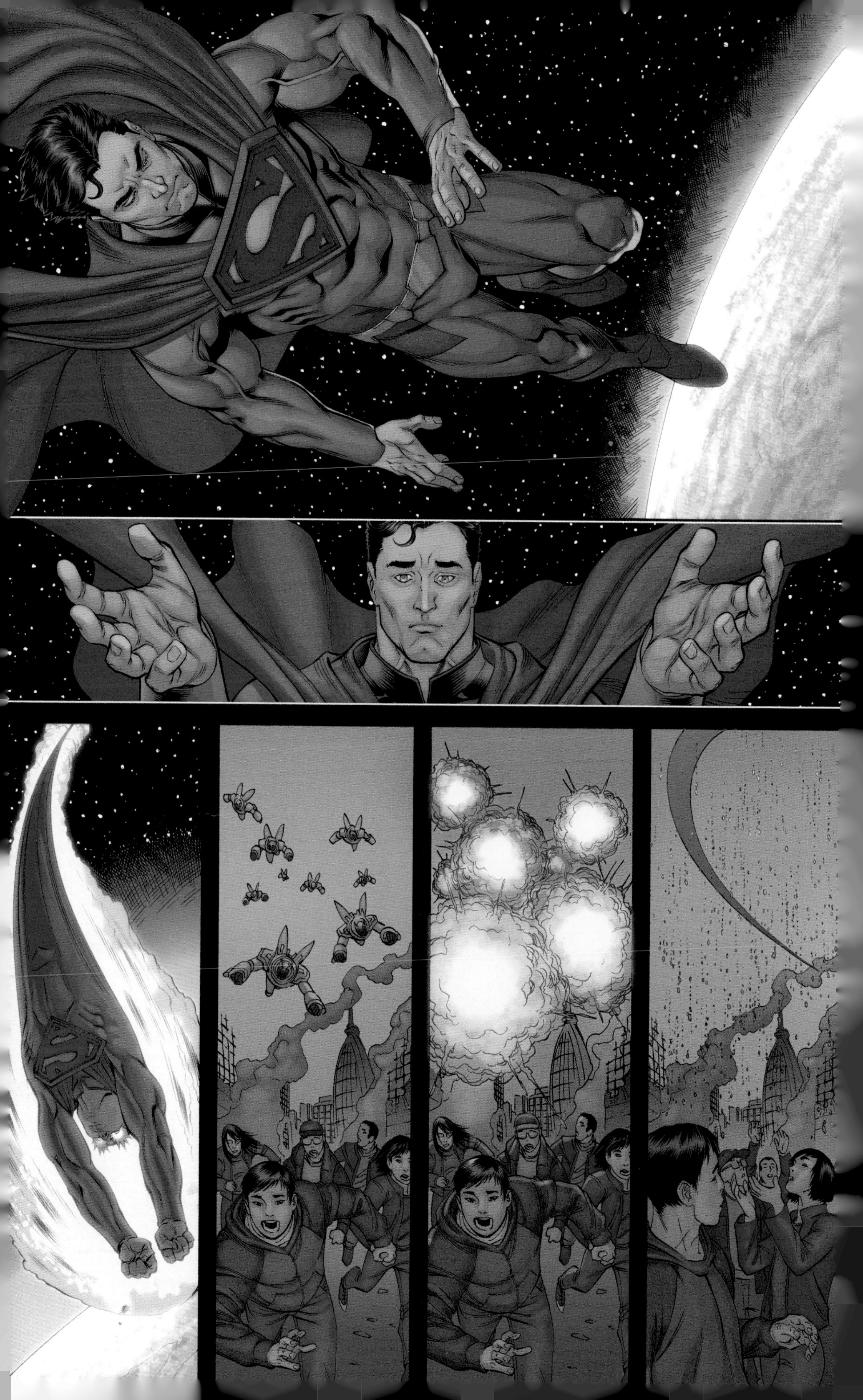

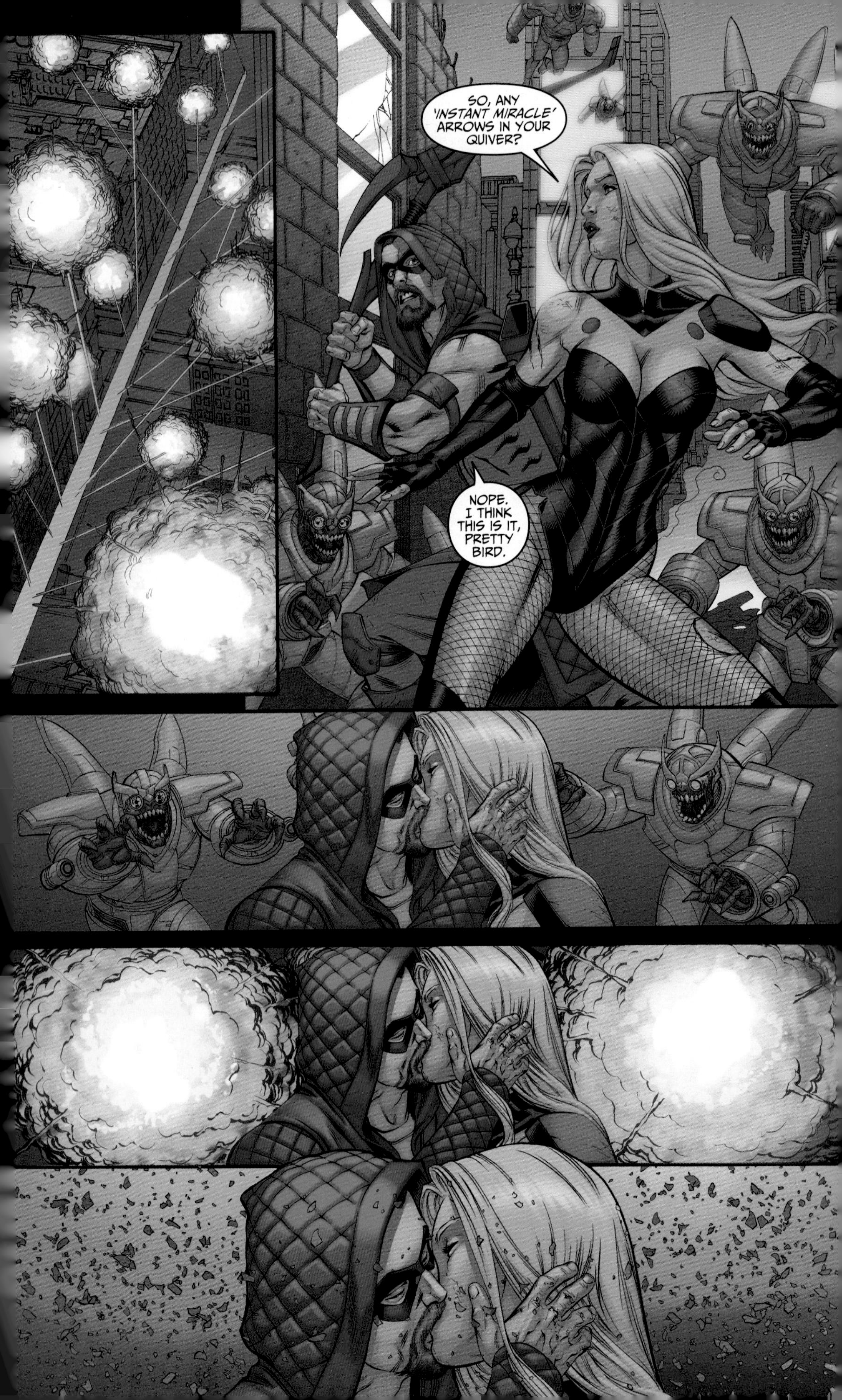
SO, ANY 'INSTANT MIRACLE' ARROWS IN YOUR QUIVER?
NOPE. I THINK THIS IS IT, PRETTY BIRD.

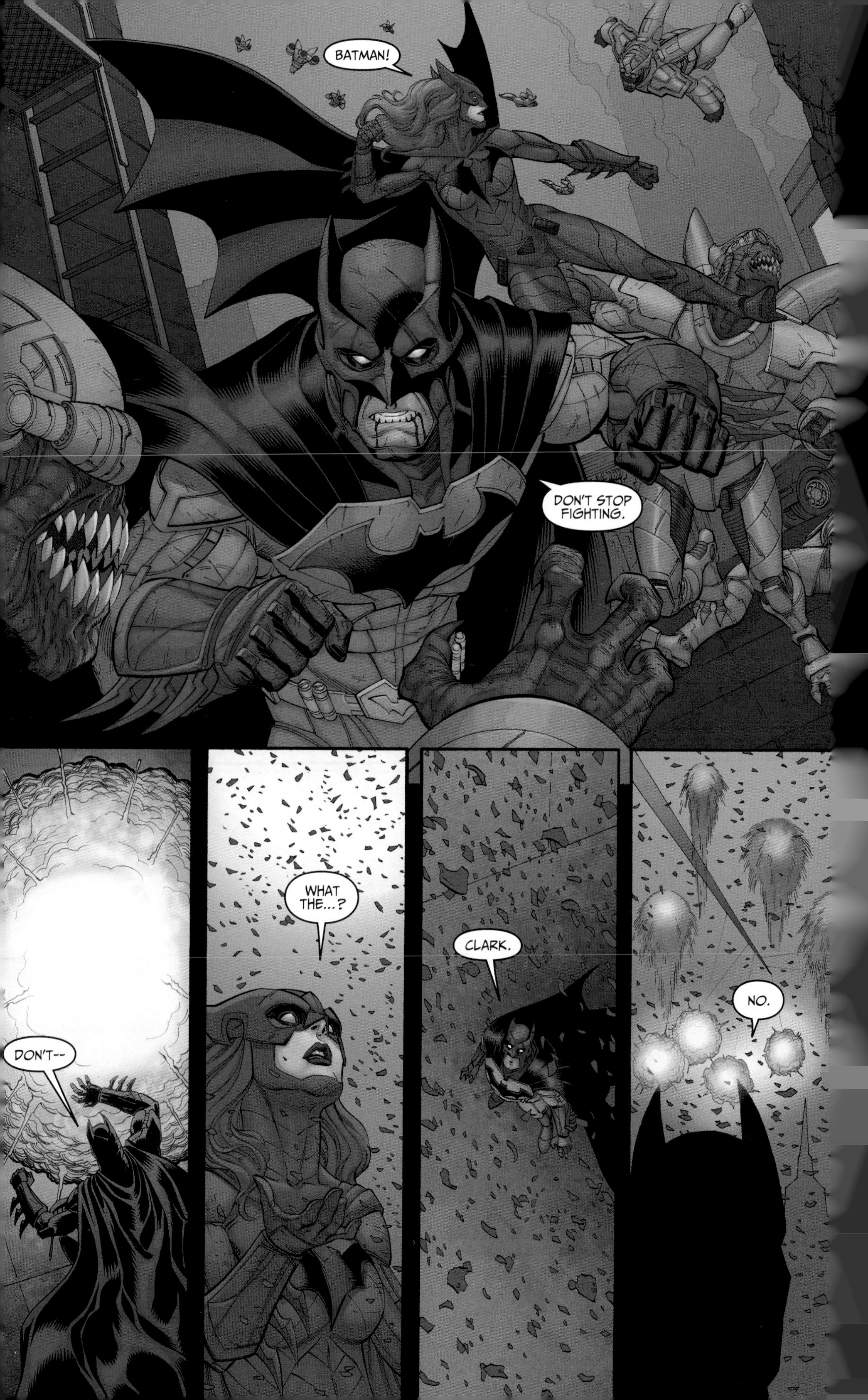
BATMAN!
DON'T STOP FIGHTING.
DON'T--
WHAT THE...?
CLARK.
NO.

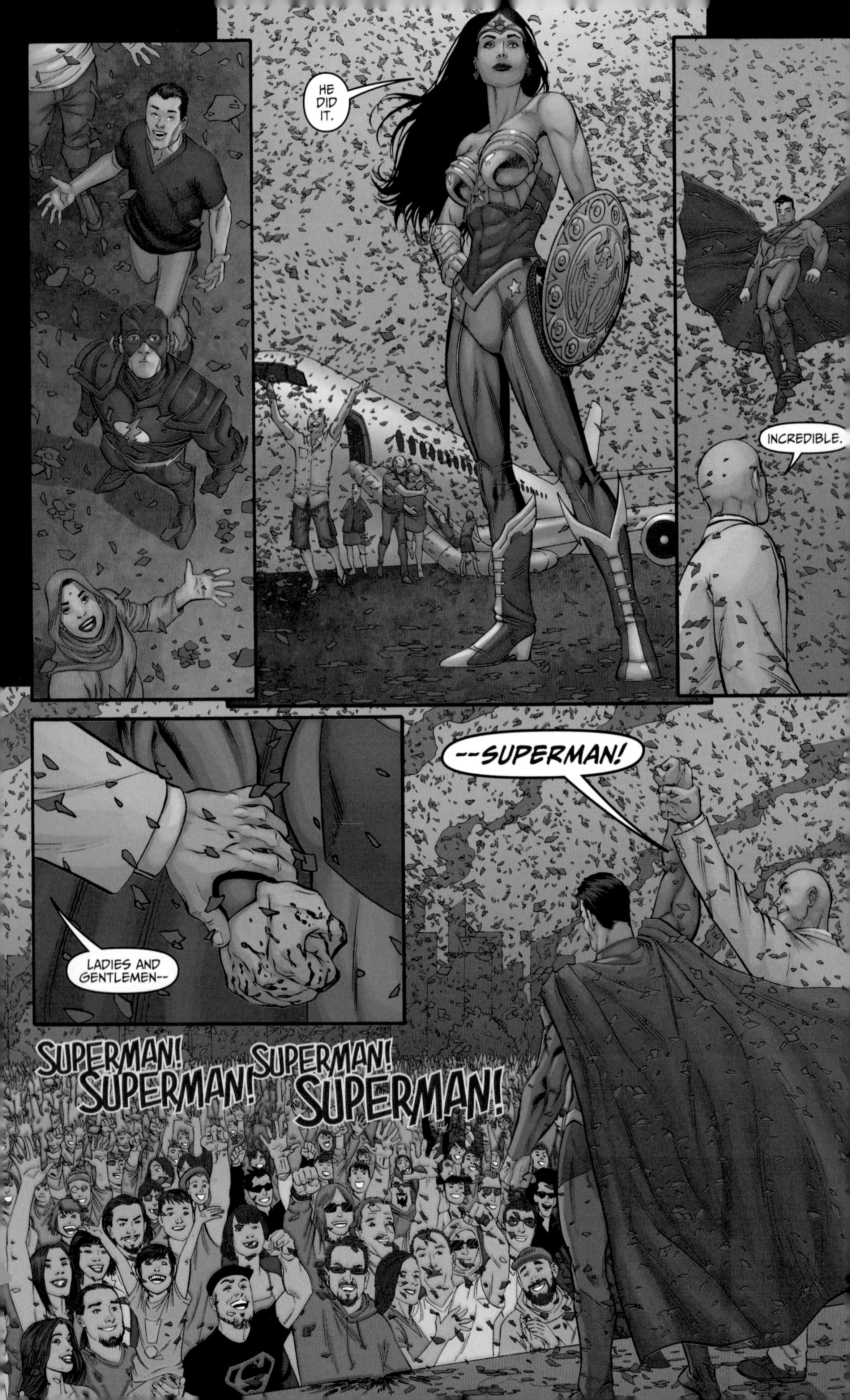
HE DID IT.
INCREDIBLE.
LADIES AND GENTLEMEN--
--SUPERMAN!
SUPERMAN! SUPERMAN! SUPERMAN! SUPERMAN!

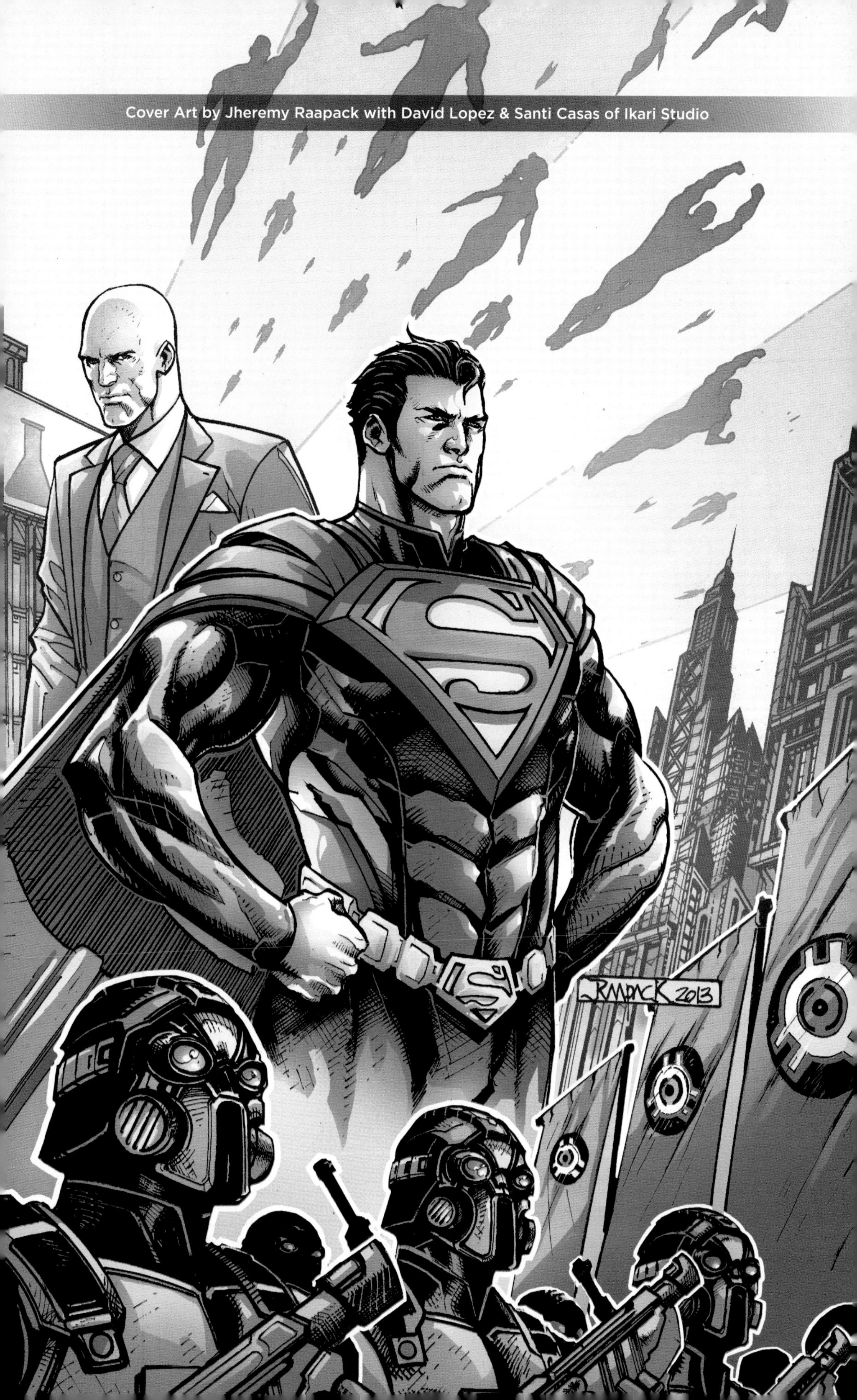
RAAPACK 2013

Cover Art by Jheremy Raapack with David Lopez & Santi Casas of Ikari Studio

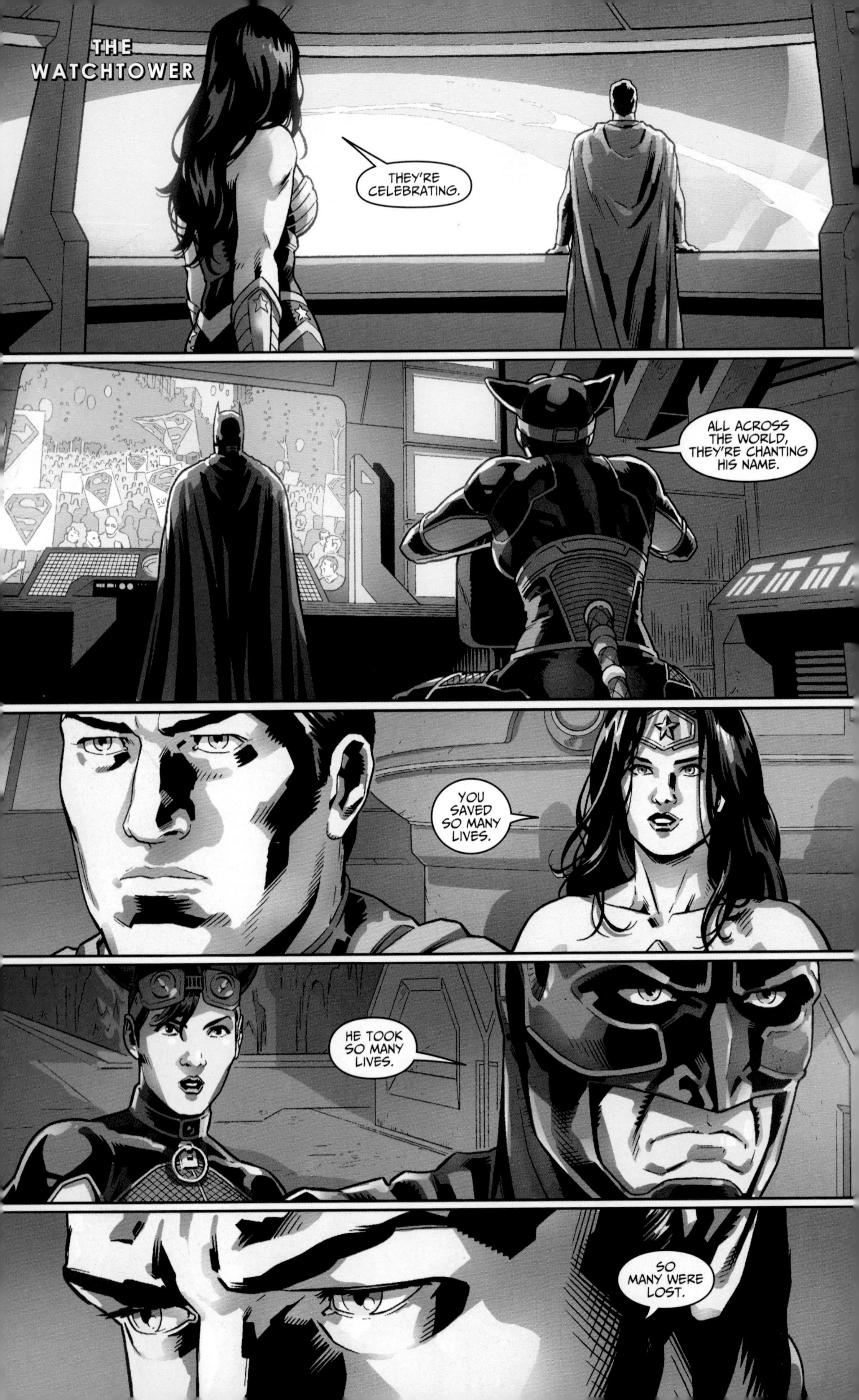
THE WATCHTOWER
THEY'RE CELEBRATING.
ALL ACROSS THE WORLD, THEY'RE CHANTING HIS NAME.
YOU SAVED SO MANY LIVES.
HE TOOK SO MANY LIVES.
SO MANY WERE LOST.

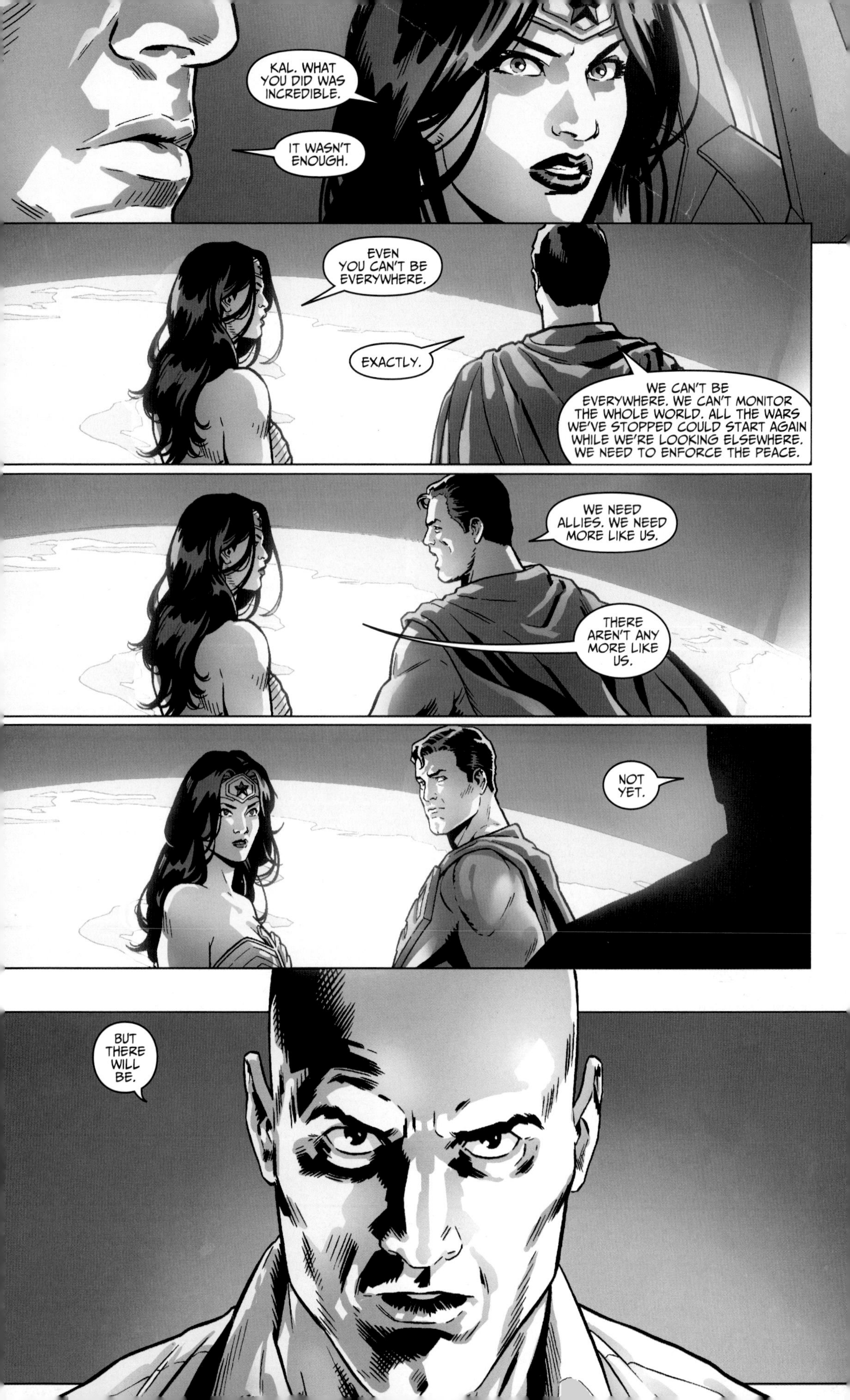
KAL. WHAT YOU DID WAS INCREDIBLE.
IT WASN'T ENOUGH.
EVEN YOU CAN'T BE EVERYWHERE.
EXACTLY.
WE CAN'T BE EVERYWHERE. WE CAN'T MONITOR THE WHOLE WORLD. ALL THE WARS WE'VE STOPPED COULD START AGAIN WHILE WE'RE LOOKING ELSEWHERE. WE NEED TO ENFORCE THE PEACE.
WE NEED ALLIES. WE NEED MORE LIKE US.
THERE AREN'T ANY MORE LIKE US.
NOT YET.
BUT THERE WILL BE.

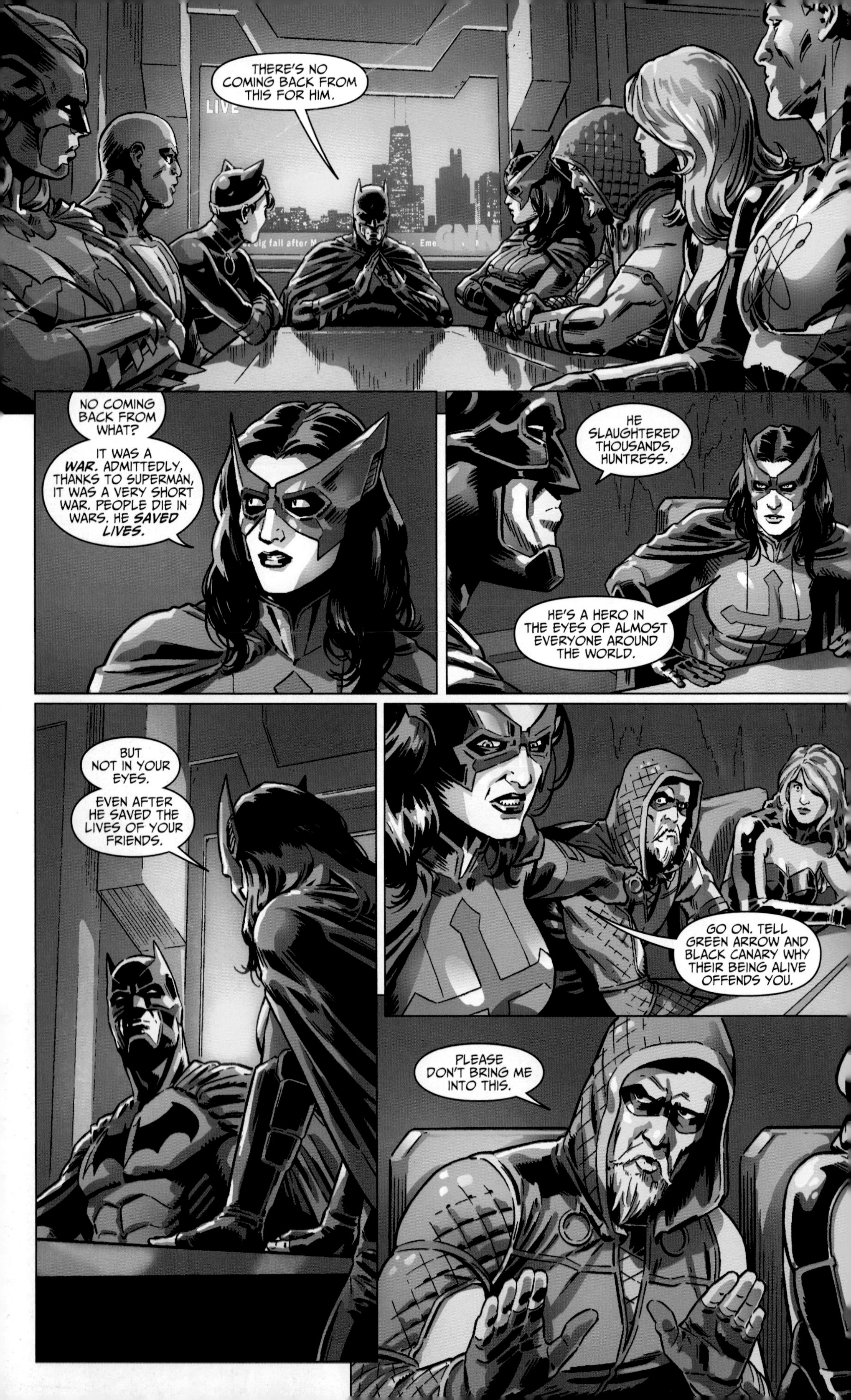

THERE'S NO COMING BACK FROM THIS FOR HIM.
LIVE
CNN
NO COMING BACK FROM WHAT?
IT WAS A WAR. ADMITTEDLY, THANKS TO SUPERMAN, IT WAS A VERY SHORT WAR. PEOPLE DIE IN WARS. HE SAVED LIVES.
HE SLAUGHTERED THOUSANDS, HUNTRESS.
HE'S A HERO IN THE EYES OF ALMOST EVERYONE AROUND THE WORLD.
BUT NOT IN YOUR EYES.
EVEN AFTER HE SAVED THE LIVES OF YOUR FRIENDS.
GO ON. TELL GREEN ARROW AND BLACK CANARY WHY THEIR BEING ALIVE OFFENDS YOU.
PLEASE DON'T BRING ME INTO THIS.

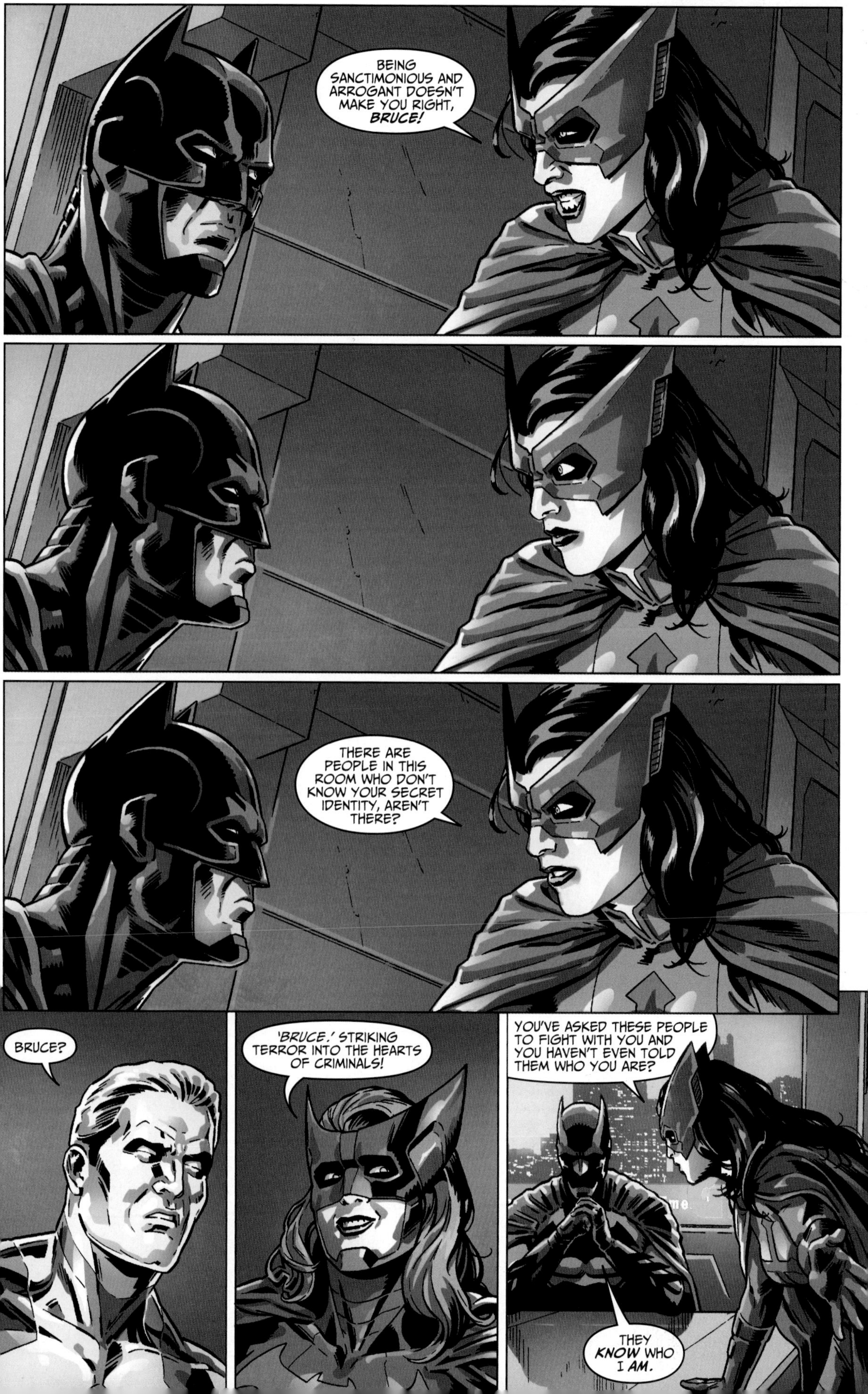

BEING SANCTIMONIOUS AND ARROGANT DOESN'T MAKE YOU RIGHT, *BRUCE!*
THERE ARE PEOPLE IN THIS ROOM WHO DON'T KNOW YOUR SECRET IDENTITY, AREN'T THERE?
BRUCE?
'BRUCE.' STRIKING TERROR INTO THE HEARTS OF CRIMINALS!
YOU'VE ASKED THESE PEOPLE TO FIGHT WITH YOU AND YOU HAVEN'T EVEN TOLD THEM WHO YOU ARE?
THEY *KNOW* WHO I *AM.*

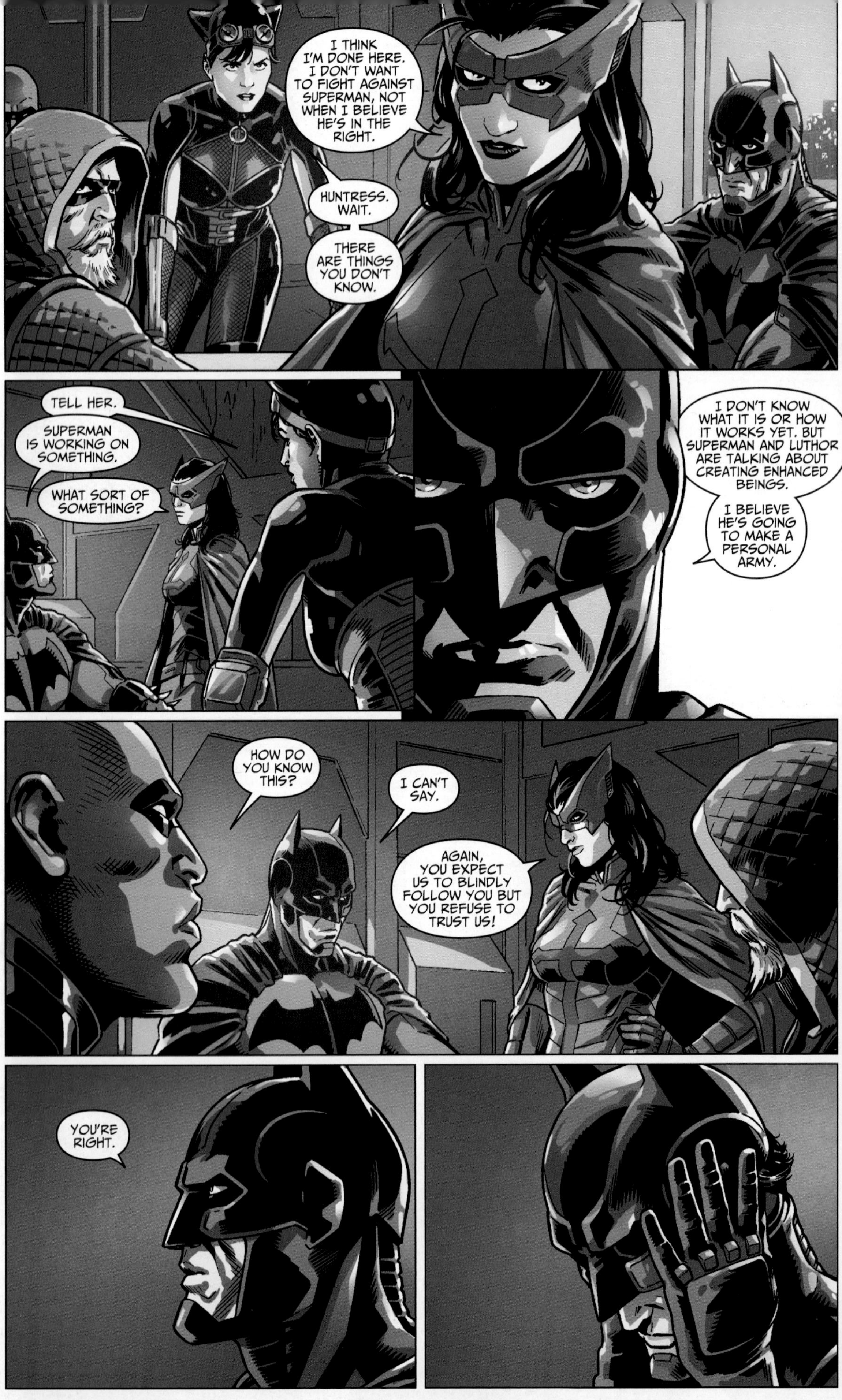
I THINK I'M DONE HERE. I DON'T WANT TO FIGHT AGAINST SUPERMAN, NOT WHEN I BELIEVE HE'S IN THE RIGHT.
HUNTRESS. WAIT.
THERE ARE THINGS YOU DON'T KNOW.
TELL HER.
SUPERMAN IS WORKING ON SOMETHING.
WHAT SORT OF SOMETHING?
I DON'T KNOW WHAT IT IS OR HOW IT WORKS YET. BUT SUPERMAN AND LUTHOR ARE TALKING ABOUT CREATING ENHANCED BEINGS.
I BELIEVE HE'S GOING TO MAKE A PERSONAL ARMY.
HOW DO YOU KNOW THIS?
I CAN'T SAY.
AGAIN, YOU EXPECT US TO BLINDLY FOLLOW YOU BUT YOU REFUSE TO TRUST US!
YOU'RE RIGHT.

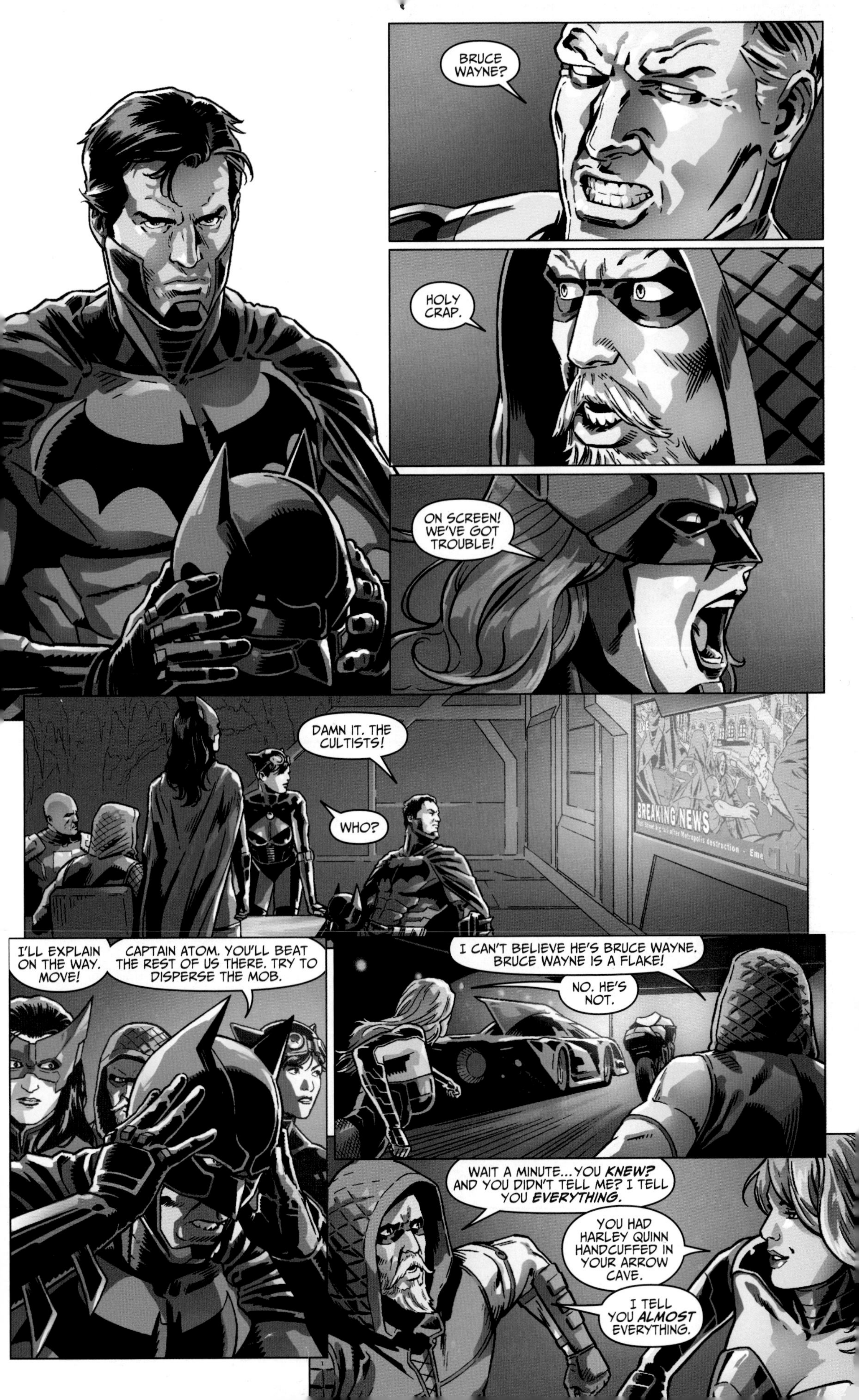
BRUCE WAYNE?
HOLY CRAP.
ON SCREEN! WE'VE GOT TROUBLE!
DAMN IT. THE CULTISTS!
WHO?
BREAKING NEWS
I'LL EXPLAIN ON THE WAY. MOVE!
CAPTAIN ATOM. YOU'LL BEAT THE REST OF US THERE. TRY TO DISPERSE THE MOB.
I CAN'T BELIEVE HE'S BRUCE WAYNE. BRUCE WAYNE IS A FLAKE!
NO. HE'S NOT.
WAIT A MINUTE... YOU *KNEW?* AND YOU DIDN'T TELL ME? I TELL YOU *EVERYTHING.*
YOU HAD HARLEY QUINN HANDCUFFED IN YOUR ARROW CAVE.
I TELL YOU *ALMOST* EVERYTHING.

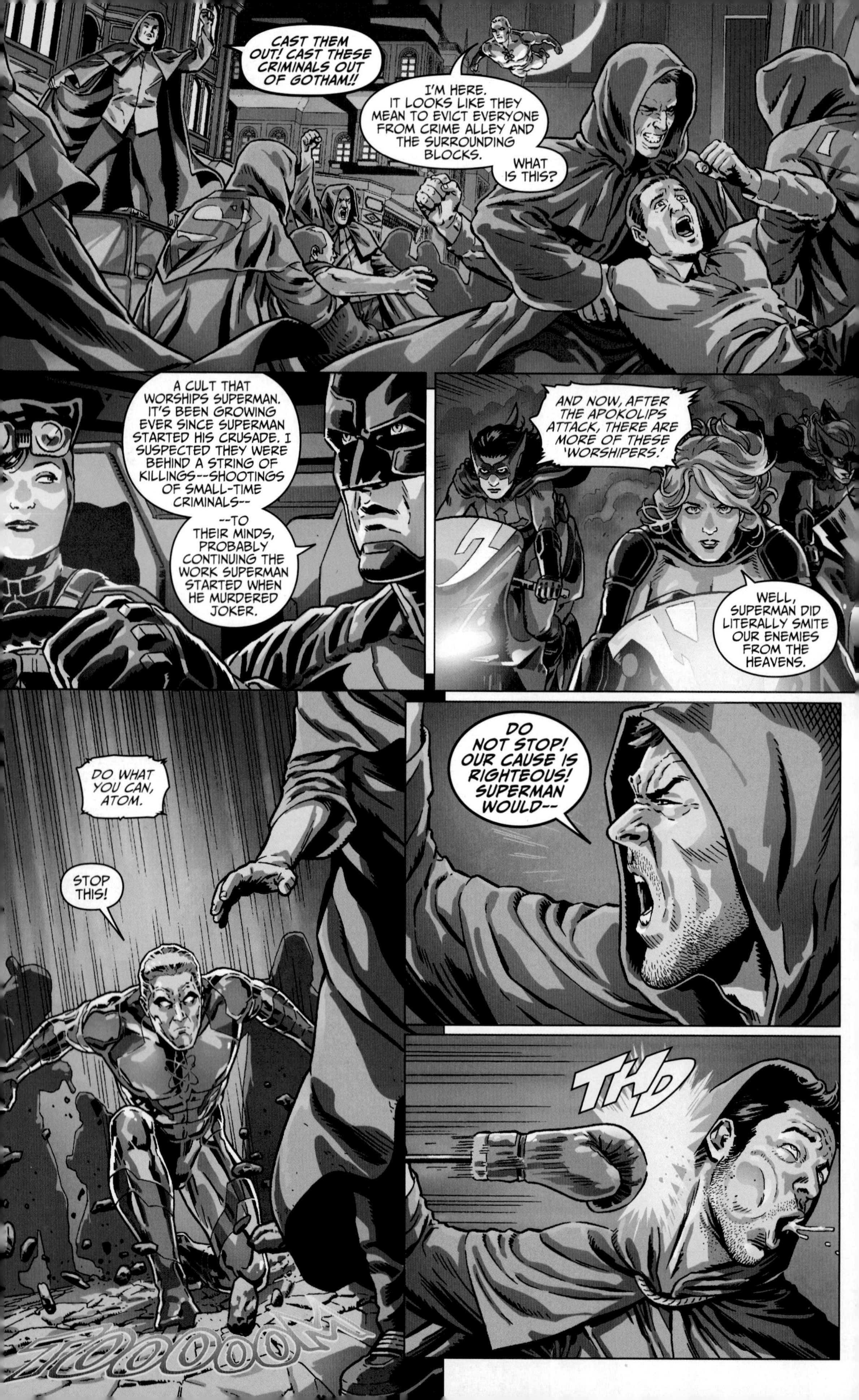
CAST THEM OUT! CAST THESE CRIMINALS OUT OF GOTHAM!!
I'M HERE. IT LOOKS LIKE THEY MEAN TO EVICT EVERYONE FROM CRIME ALLEY AND THE SURROUNDING BLOCKS.
WHAT IS THIS?
A CULT THAT WORSHIPS SUPERMAN. IT'S BEEN GROWING EVER SINCE SUPERMAN STARTED HIS CRUSADE. I SUSPECTED THEY WERE BEHIND A STRING OF KILLINGS--SHOOTINGS OF SMALL-TIME CRIMINALS--
--TO THEIR MINDS, PROBABLY CONTINUING THE WORK SUPERMAN STARTED WHEN HE MURDERED JOKER.
AND NOW, AFTER THE APOKOLIPS ATTACK, THERE ARE MORE OF THESE 'WORSHIPERS.'
WELL, SUPERMAN DID LITERALLY SMITE OUR ENEMIES FROM THE HEAVENS.
DO WHAT YOU CAN, ATOM.
STOP THIS!
FOOOOOM
DO NOT STOP! OUR CAUSE IS RIGHTEOUS! SUPERMAN WOULD--
THD

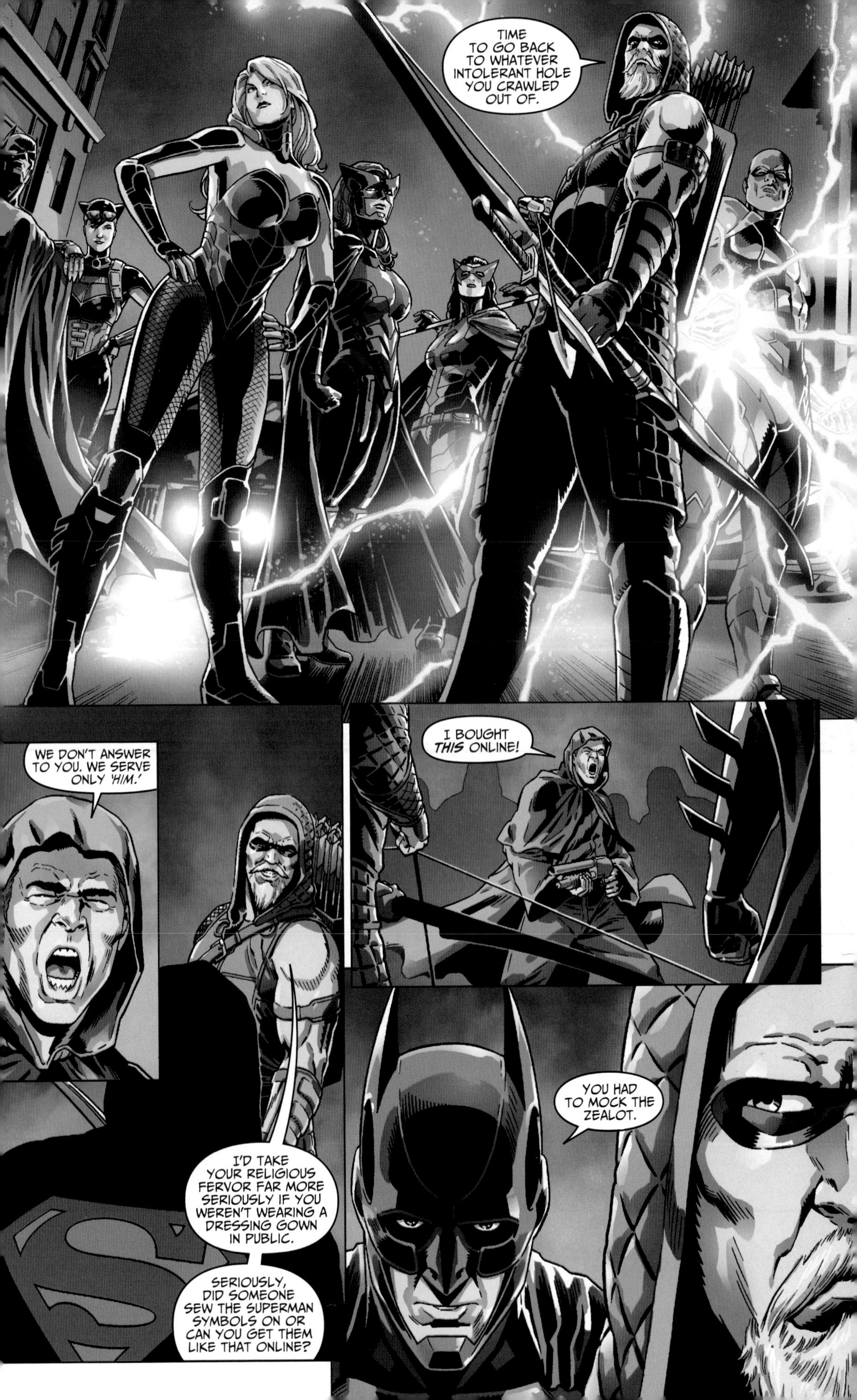
TIME TO GO BACK TO WHATEVER INTOLERANT HOLE YOU CRAWLED OUT OF.
WE DON'T ANSWER TO YOU. WE SERVE ONLY 'HIM.'
I BOUGHT *THIS* ONLINE!
I'D TAKE YOUR RELIGIOUS FERVOR FAR MORE SERIOUSLY IF YOU WEREN'T WEARING A DRESSING GOWN IN PUBLIC.
SERIOUSLY, DID SOMEONE SEW THE SUPERMAN SYMBOLS ON OR CAN YOU GET THEM LIKE THAT ONLINE?
YOU HAD TO MOCK THE ZEALOT.

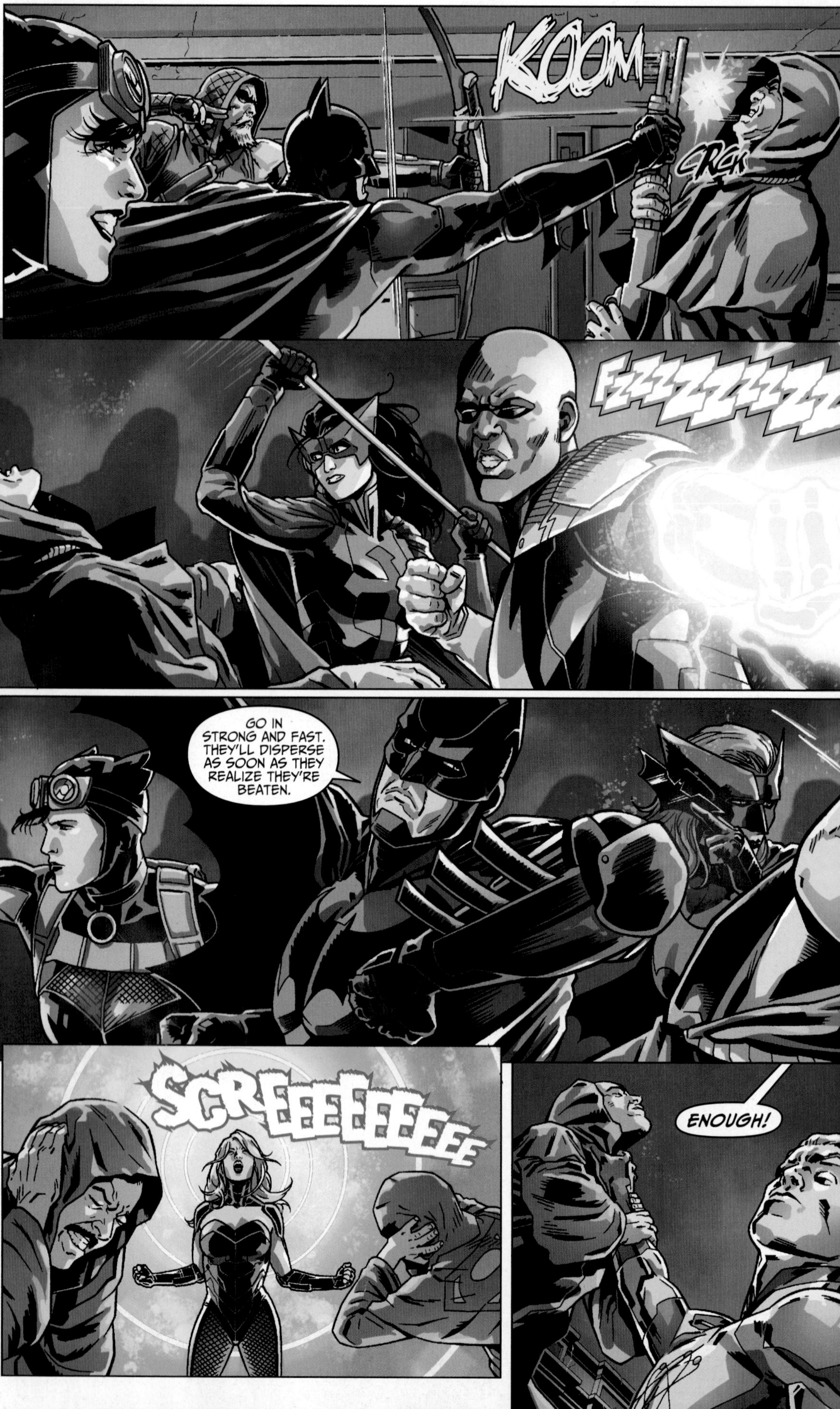
KOOM
CRCK
FZZZZZZZZZ
GO IN STRONG AND FAST. THEY'LL DISPERSE AS SOON AS THEY REALIZE THEY'RE BEATEN.
SCREEEEEEEEEE
ENOUGH!

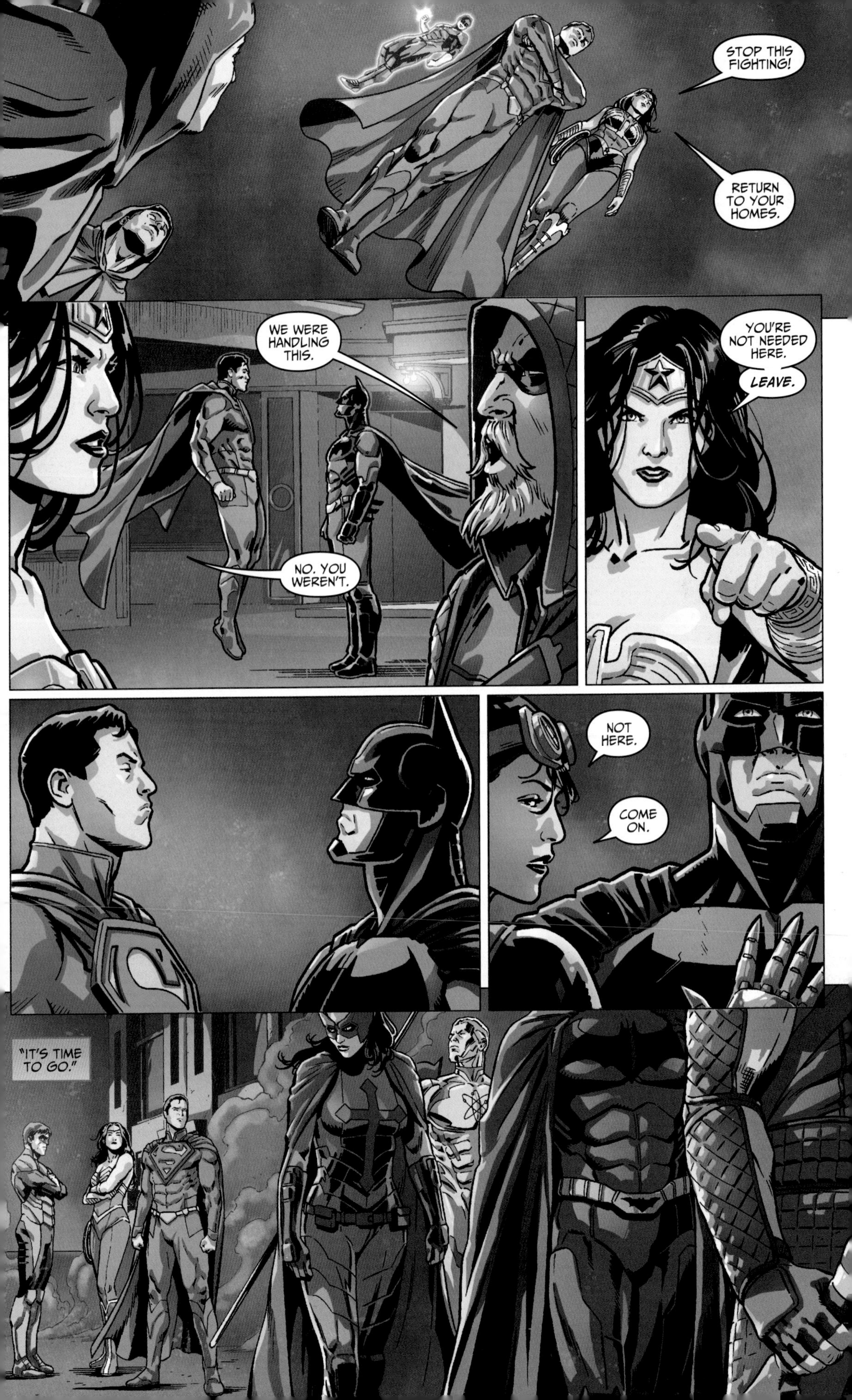
STOP THIS FIGHTING!
RETURN TO YOUR HOMES.
WE WERE HANDLING THIS.
NO. YOU WEREN'T.
YOU'RE NOT NEEDED HERE.
LEAVE.
NOT HERE.
COME ON.
"IT'S TIME TO GO."

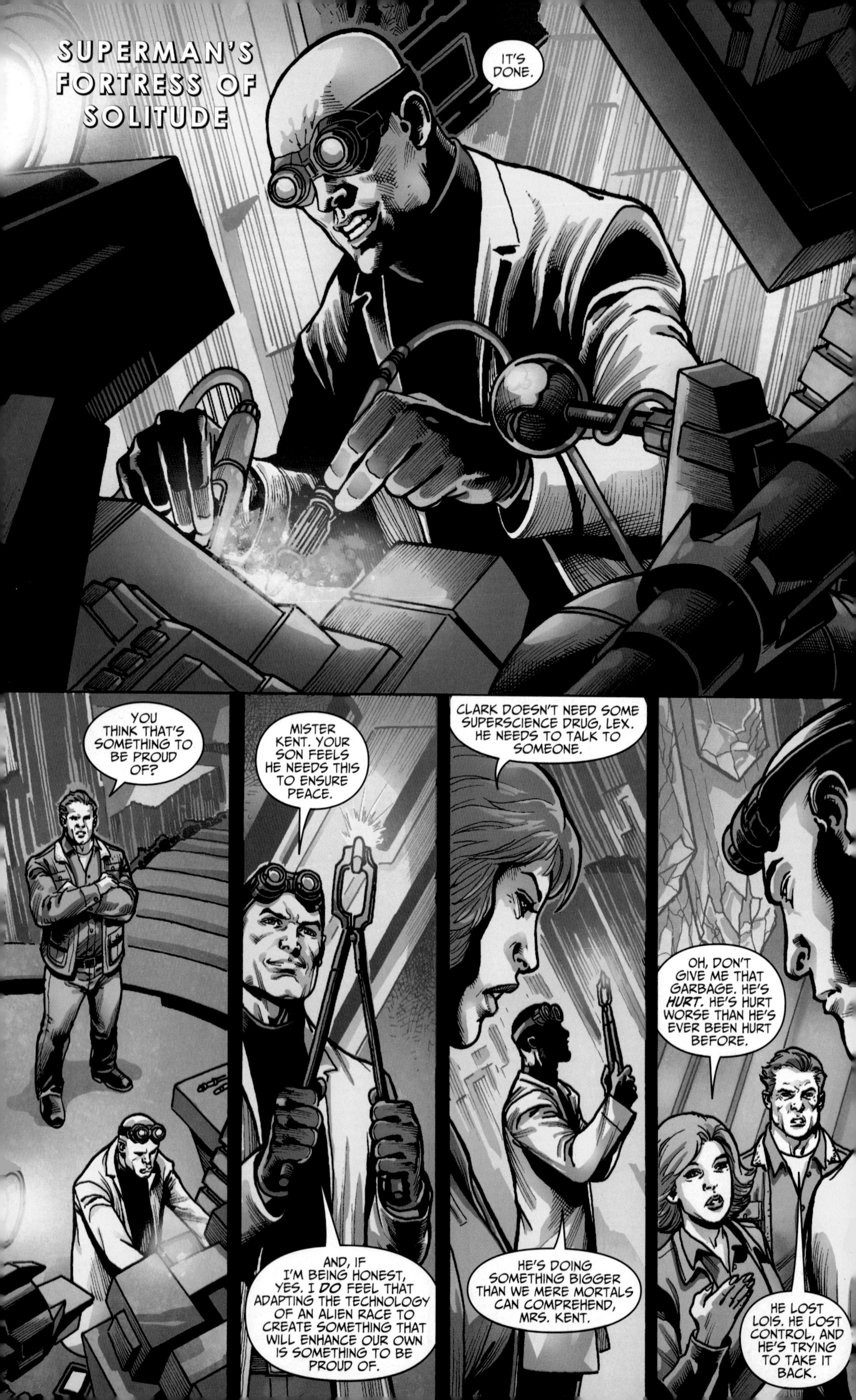
SUPERMAN'S FORTRESS OF SOLITUDE
IT'S DONE.
YOU THINK THAT'S SOMETHING TO BE PROUD OF?
MISTER KENT. YOUR SON FEELS HE NEEDS THIS TO ENSURE PEACE.
AND, IF I'M BEING HONEST, YES. I DO FEEL THAT ADAPTING THE TECHNOLOGY OF AN ALIEN RACE TO CREATE SOMETHING THAT WILL ENHANCE OUR OWN IS SOMETHING TO BE PROUD OF.
CLARK DOESN'T NEED SOME SUPERSCIENCE DRUG, LEX. HE NEEDS TO TALK TO SOMEONE.
HE'S DOING SOMETHING BIGGER THAN WE MERE MORTALS CAN COMPREHEND, MRS. KENT.
OH, DON'T GIVE ME THAT GARBAGE. HE'S HURT. HE'S HURT WORSE THAN HE'S EVER BEEN HURT BEFORE.
HE LOST LOIS. HE LOST CONTROL, AND HE'S TRYING TO TAKE IT BACK.

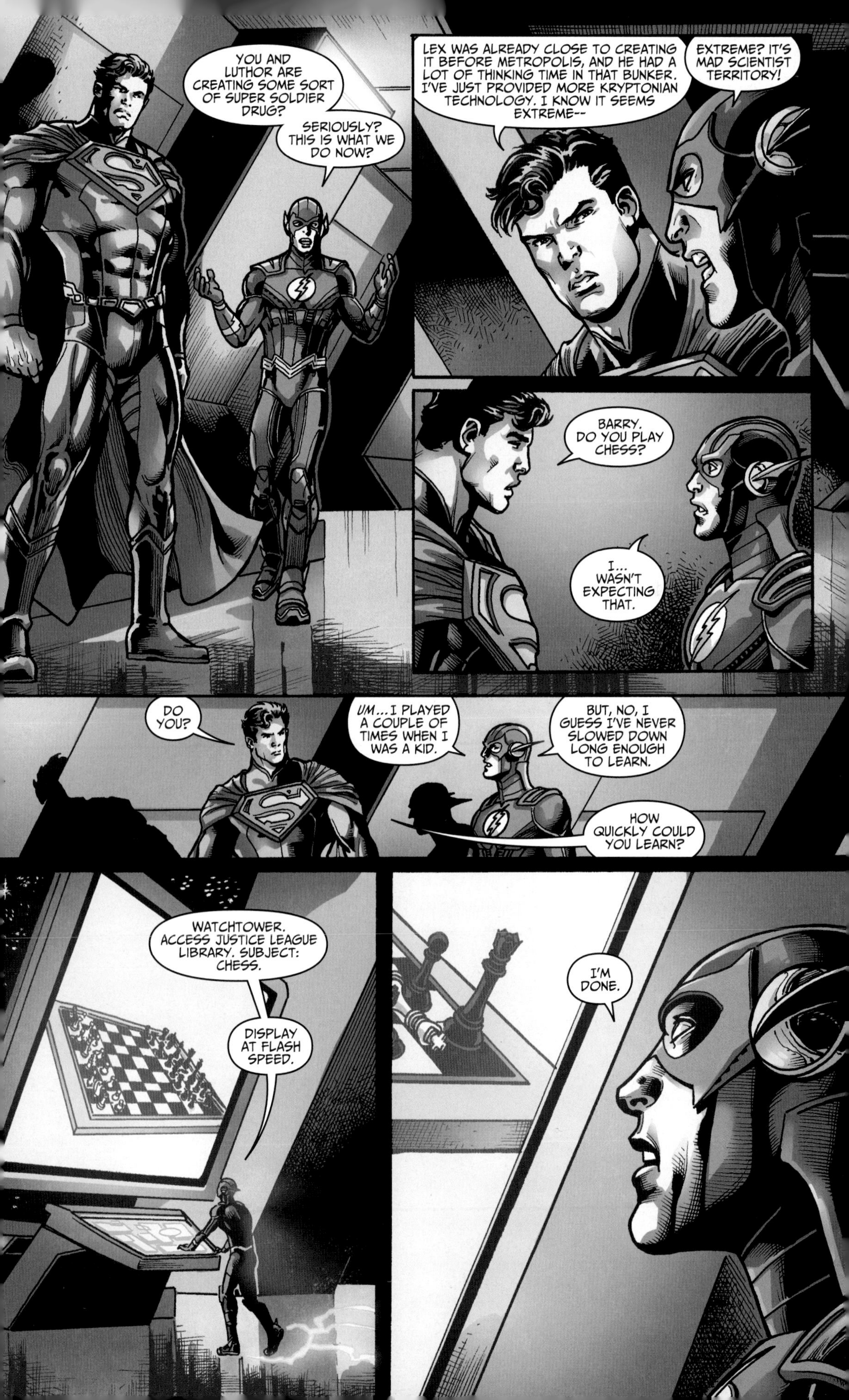
YOU AND LUTHOR ARE CREATING SOME SORT OF SUPER SOLDIER DRUG?
SERIOUSLY? THIS IS WHAT WE DO NOW?
LEX WAS ALREADY CLOSE TO CREATING IT BEFORE METROPOLIS, AND HE HAD A LOT OF THINKING TIME IN THAT BUNKER. I'VE JUST PROVIDED MORE KRYPTONIAN TECHNOLOGY. I KNOW IT SEEMS EXTREME--
EXTREME? IT'S MAD SCIENTIST TERRITORY!
BARRY. DO YOU PLAY CHESS?
I... WASN'T EXPECTING THAT.
DO YOU?
UM... I PLAYED A COUPLE OF TIMES WHEN I WAS A KID.
BUT, NO, I GUESS I'VE NEVER SLOWED DOWN LONG ENOUGH TO LEARN.
HOW QUICKLY COULD YOU LEARN?
WATCHTOWER. ACCESS JUSTICE LEAGUE LIBRARY. SUBJECT: CHESS.
DISPLAY AT FLASH SPEED.
I'M DONE.

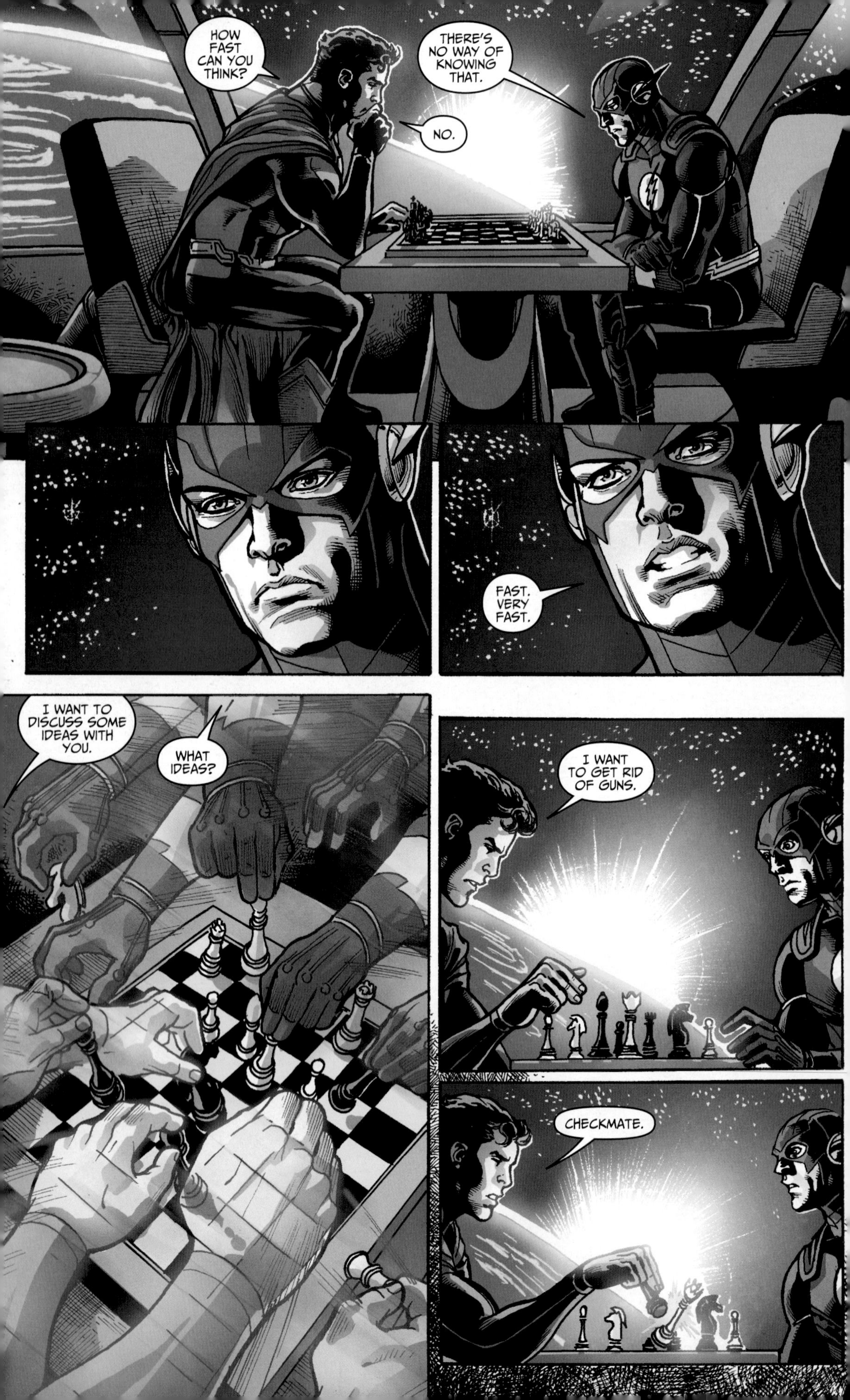
HOW FAST CAN YOU THINK?
THERE'S NO WAY OF KNOWING THAT.
NO.
FAST. VERY FAST.
I WANT TO DISCUSS SOME IDEAS WITH YOU.
WHAT IDEAS?
I WANT TO GET RID OF GUNS.
CHECKMATE.

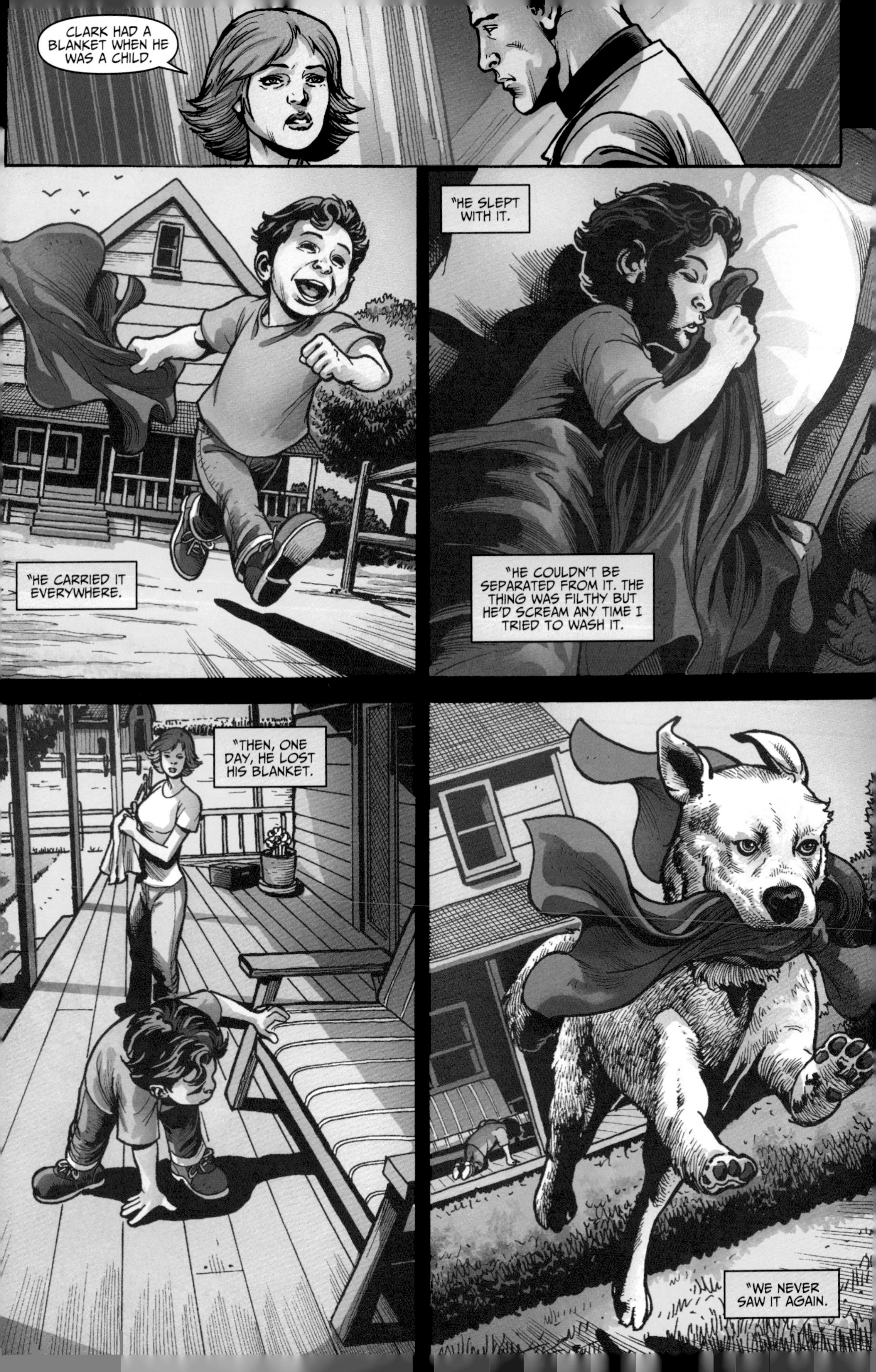
CLARK HAD A BLANKET WHEN HE WAS A CHILD.
"HE CARRIED IT EVERYWHERE.
"HE SLEPT WITH IT.
"HE COULDN'T BE SEPARATED FROM IT. THE THING WAS FILTHY BUT HE'D SCREAM ANY TIME I TRIED TO WASH IT.
"THEN, ONE DAY, HE LOST HIS BLANKET.
"WE NEVER SAW IT AGAIN.

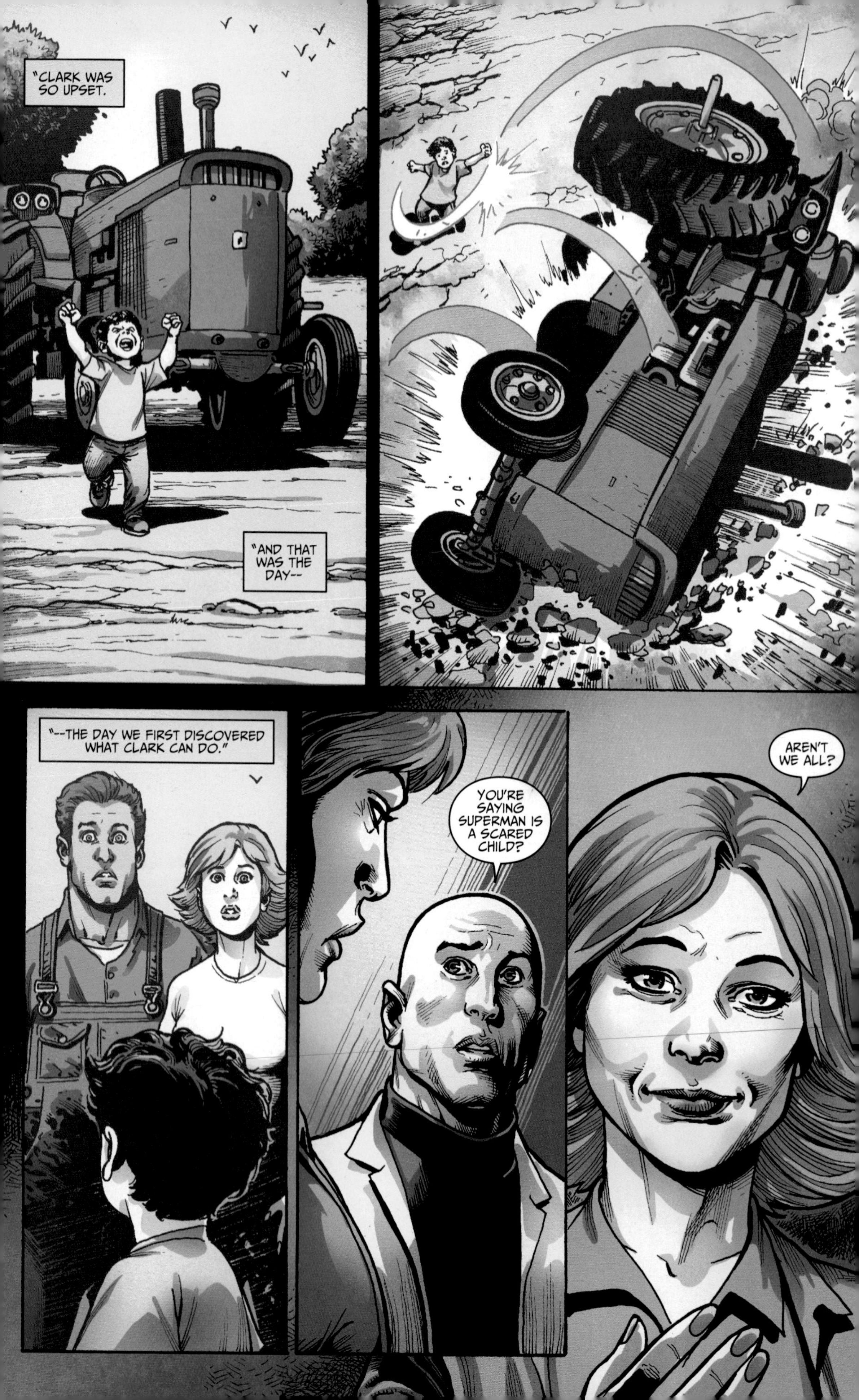
"CLARK WAS SO UPSET.
"AND THAT WAS THE DAY--
"--THE DAY WE FIRST DISCOVERED WHAT CLARK CAN DO."
YOU'RE SAYING SUPERMAN IS A SCARED CHILD?
AREN'T WE ALL?

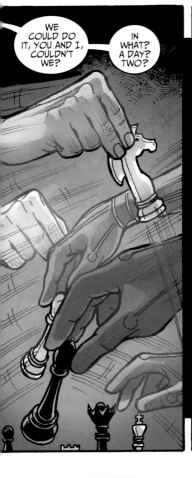

WE COULD DO IT, YOU AND I, COULDN'T WE?

IN WHAT? A DAY? TWO?

WE COULD NEVER GET RID OF ALL GUNS.

NO. BUT MOST. WE COULD DO IT.

YES.

CHECKMATE.

BUT JUST BECAUSE WE CAN DO IT, DOESN'T MEAN WE SHOULD.

UNLESS THEY GIVE UP THEIR GUNS WILLINGLY, THEY WILL RESENT US.

YES. BUT THEY WILL BE ALIVE TO RESENT US.

I KNOW.

THEY WILL RISE AGAINST US.

MAYBE. AND LET THEM COME AT US WITH STICKS.

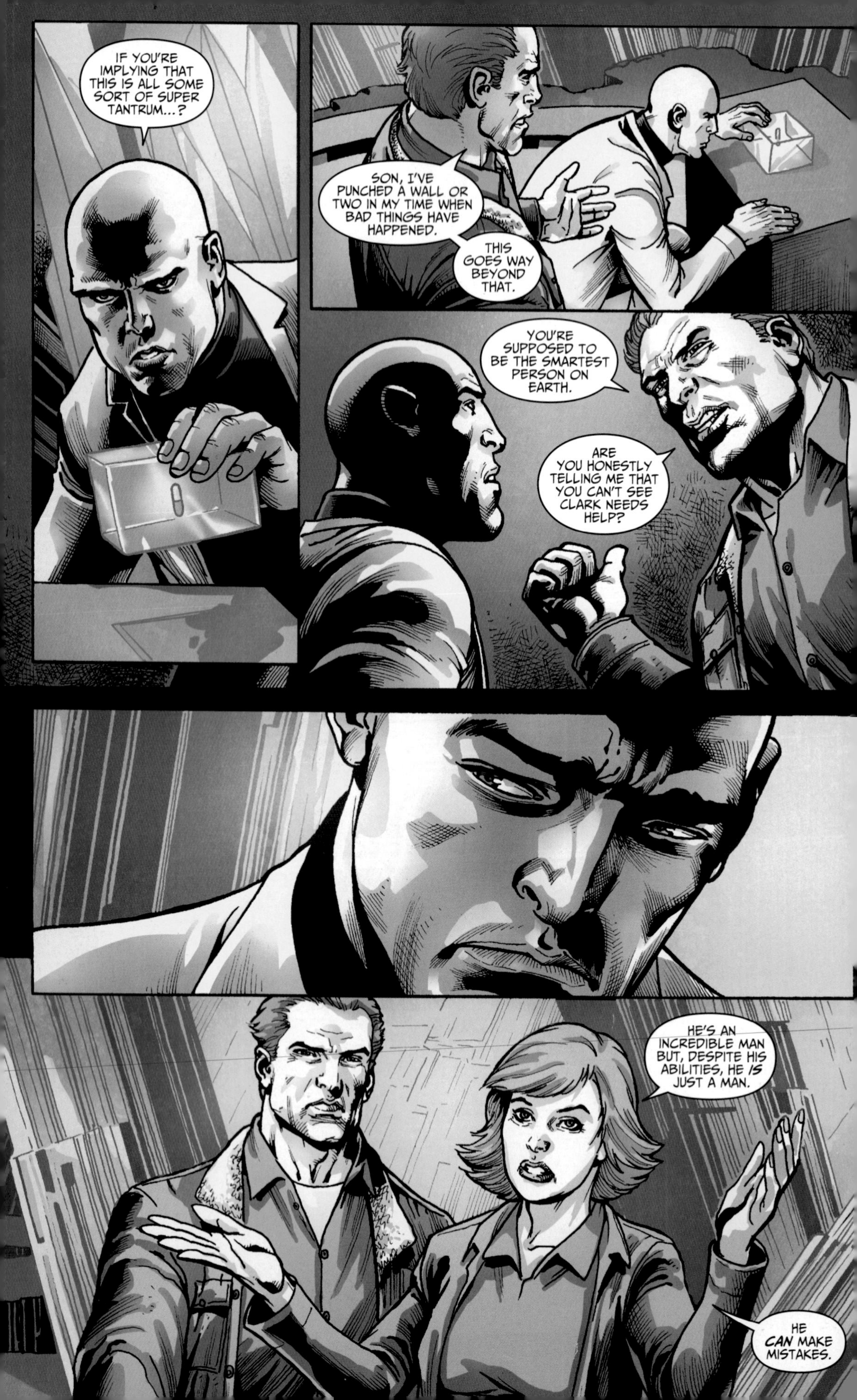
IF YOU'RE IMPLYING THAT THIS IS ALL SOME SORT OF SUPER TANTRUM...?
SON, I'VE PUNCHED A WALL OR TWO IN MY TIME WHEN BAD THINGS HAVE HAPPENED.
THIS GOES WAY BEYOND THAT.
YOU'RE SUPPOSED TO BE THE SMARTEST PERSON ON EARTH.
ARE YOU HONESTLY TELLING ME THAT YOU CAN'T SEE CLARK NEEDS HELP?
HE'S AN INCREDIBLE MAN BUT, DESPITE HIS ABILITIES, HE *IS* JUST A MAN.
HE *CAN* MAKE MISTAKES.

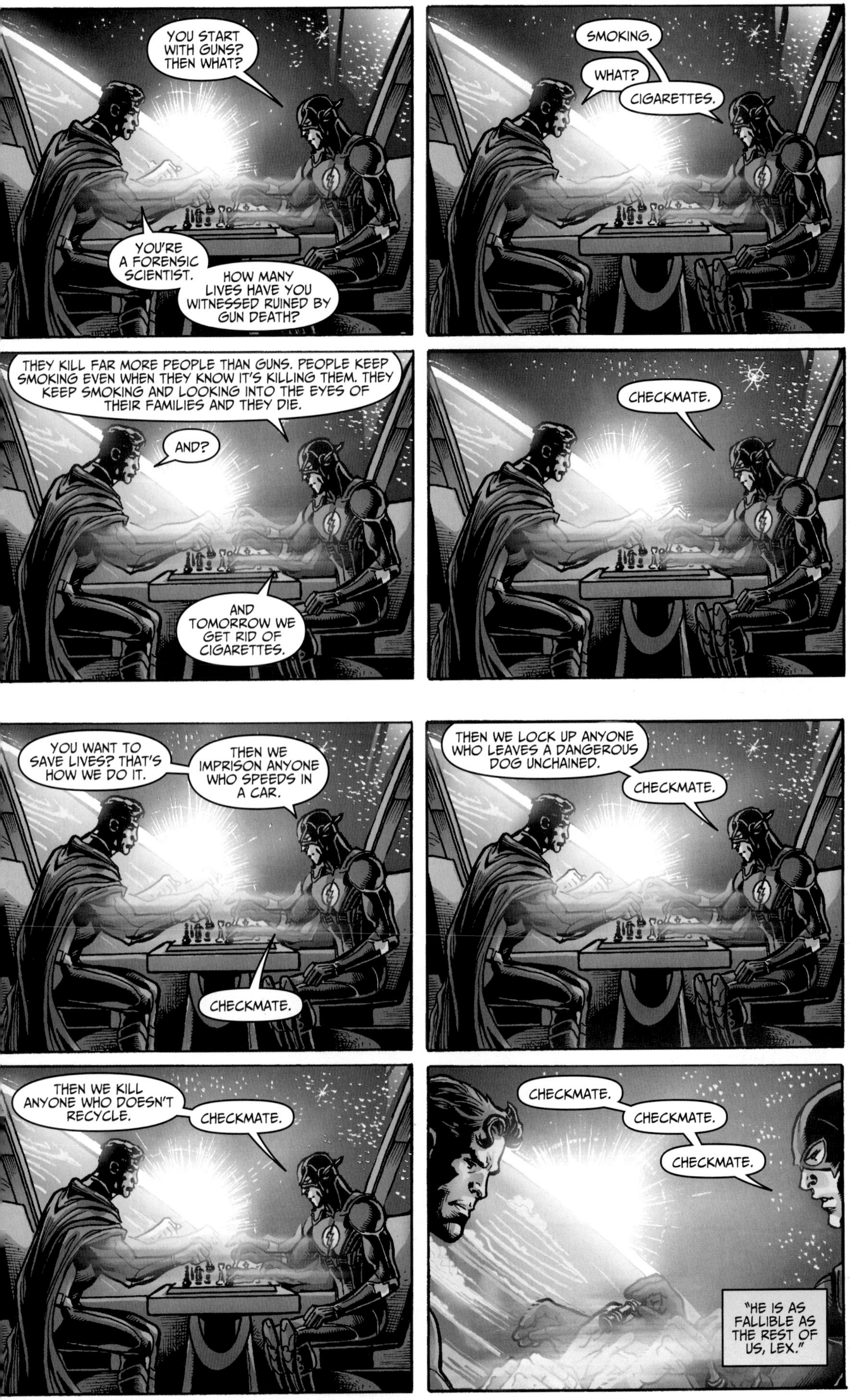
YOU START WITH GUNS? THEN WHAT?
YOU'RE A FORENSIC SCIENTIST.
HOW MANY LIVES HAVE YOU WITNESSED RUINED BY GUN DEATH?
SMOKING.
WHAT?
CIGARETTES.
THEY KILL FAR MORE PEOPLE THAN GUNS. PEOPLE KEEP SMOKING EVEN WHEN THEY KNOW IT'S KILLING THEM. THEY KEEP SMOKING AND LOOKING INTO THE EYES OF THEIR FAMILIES AND THEY DIE.
AND?
AND TOMORROW WE GET RID OF CIGARETTES.
CHECKMATE.
YOU WANT TO SAVE LIVES? THAT'S HOW WE DO IT.
THEN WE IMPRISON ANYONE WHO SPEEDS IN A CAR.
CHECKMATE.
THEN WE LOCK UP ANYONE WHO LEAVES A DANGEROUS DOG UNCHAINED.
CHECKMATE.
THEN WE KILL ANYONE WHO DOESN'T RECYCLE.
CHECKMATE.
CHECKMATE.
CHECKMATE.
CHECKMATE.
"HE IS AS FALLIBLE AS THE REST OF US, LEX."

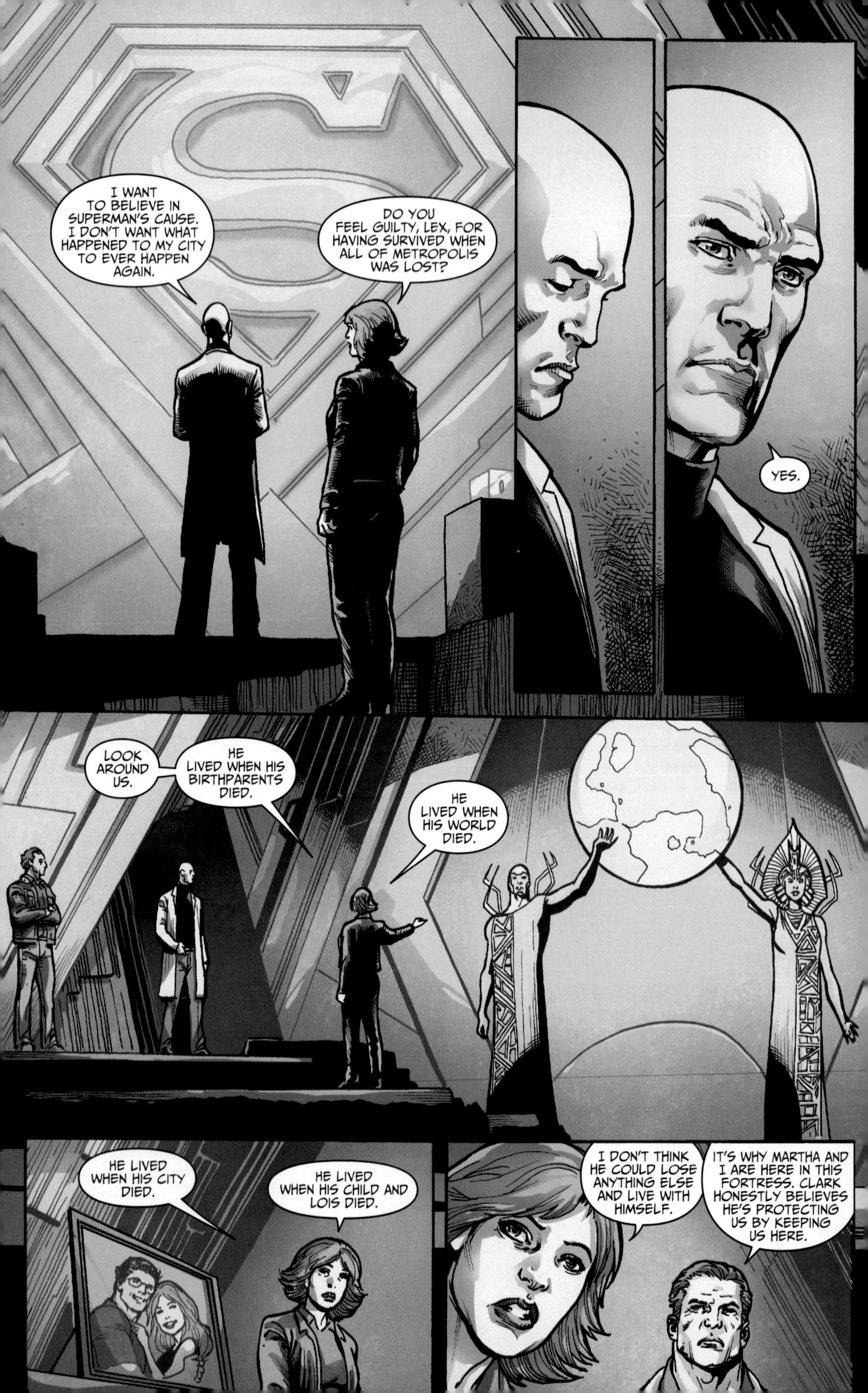
I WANT TO BELIEVE IN SUPERMAN'S CAUSE. I DON'T WANT WHAT HAPPENED TO MY CITY TO EVER HAPPEN AGAIN.
DO YOU FEEL GUILTY, LEX, FOR HAVING SURVIVED WHEN ALL OF METROPOLIS WAS LOST?
YES.
LOOK AROUND US.
HE LIVED WHEN HIS BIRTHPARENTS DIED.
HE LIVED WHEN HIS WORLD DIED.
HE LIVED WHEN HIS CITY DIED.
HE LIVED WHEN HIS CHILD AND LOIS DIED.
I DON'T THINK HE COULD LOSE ANYTHING ELSE AND LIVE WITH HIMSELF.
IT'S WHY MARTHA AND I ARE HERE IN THIS FORTRESS. CLARK HONESTLY BELIEVES HE'S PROTECTING US BY KEEPING US HERE.

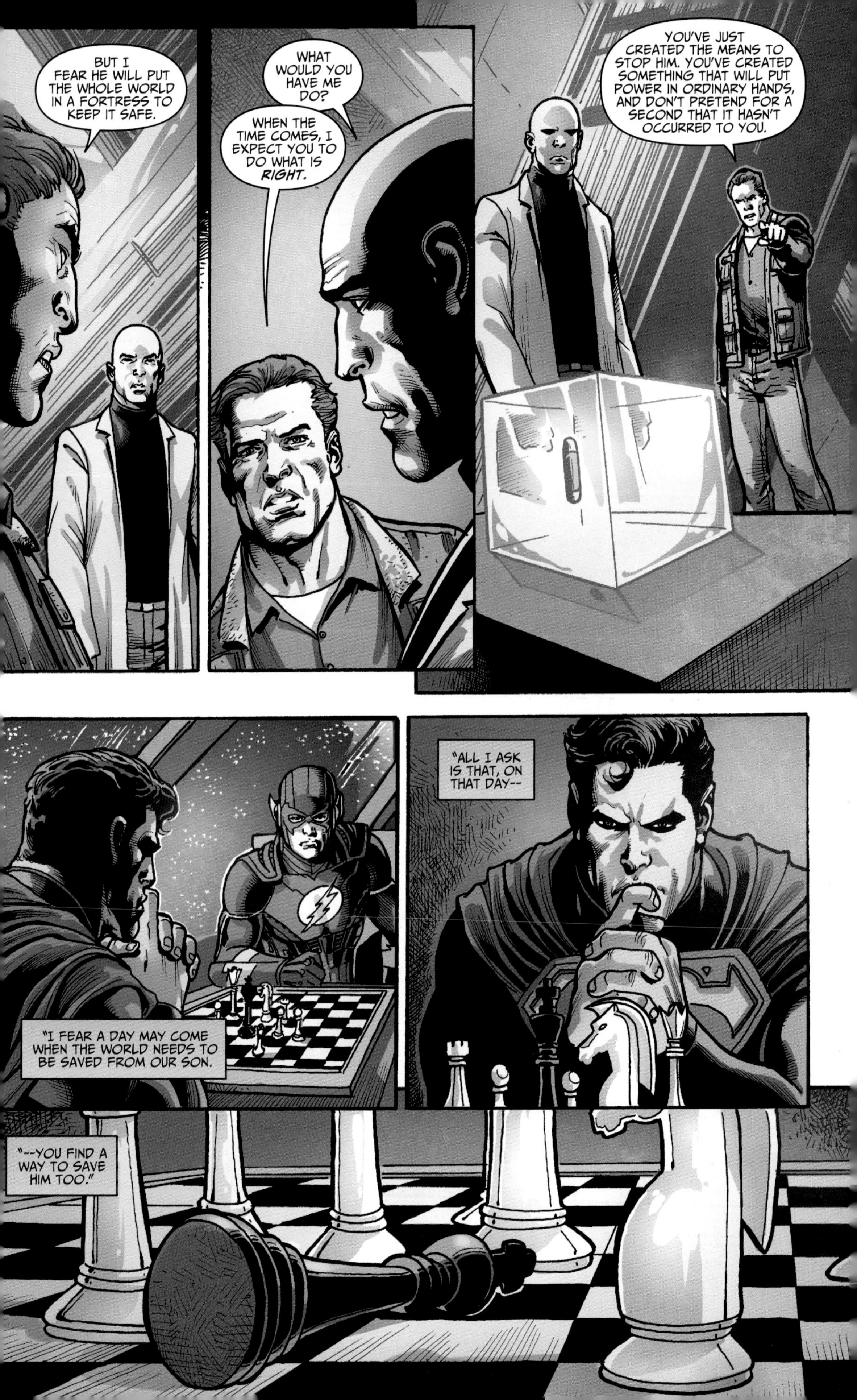
BUT I FEAR HE WILL PUT THE WHOLE WORLD IN A FORTRESS TO KEEP IT SAFE.
WHAT WOULD YOU HAVE ME DO?
WHEN THE TIME COMES, I EXPECT YOU TO DO WHAT IS RIGHT.
YOU'VE JUST CREATED THE MEANS TO STOP HIM. YOU'VE CREATED SOMETHING THAT WILL PUT POWER IN ORDINARY HANDS, AND DON'T PRETEND FOR A SECOND THAT IT HASN'T OCCURRED TO YOU.
"I FEAR A DAY MAY COME WHEN THE WORLD NEEDS TO BE SAVED FROM OUR SON.
"ALL I ASK IS THAT, ON THAT DAY--
"--YOU FIND A WAY TO SAVE HIM TOO."

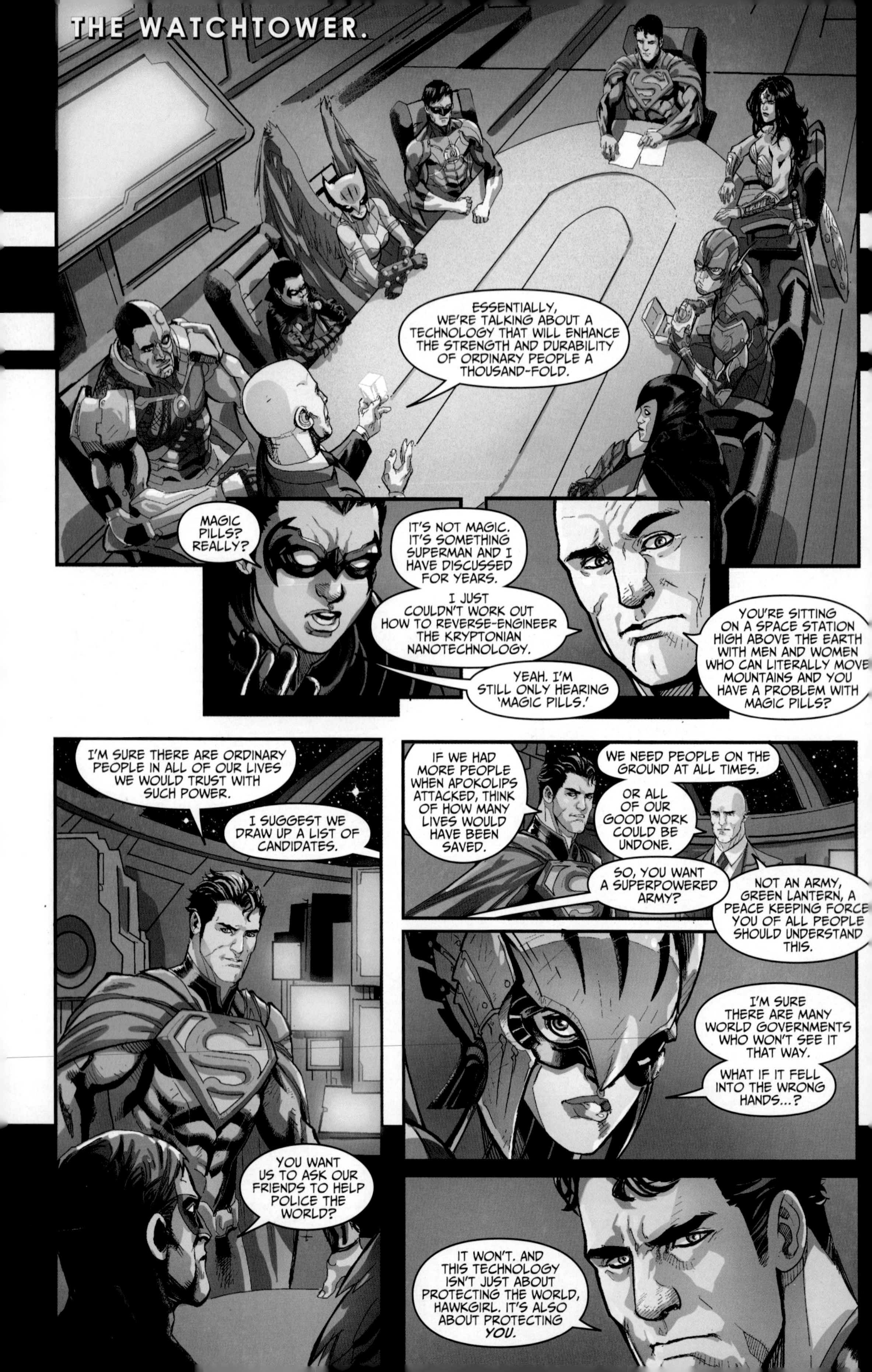
THE WATCHTOWER.
ESSENTIALLY, WE'RE TALKING ABOUT A TECHNOLOGY THAT WILL ENHANCE THE STRENGTH AND DURABILITY OF ORDINARY PEOPLE A THOUSAND-FOLD.
MAGIC PILLS? REALLY?
IT'S NOT MAGIC. IT'S SOMETHING SUPERMAN AND I HAVE DISCUSSED FOR YEARS.
I JUST COULDN'T WORK OUT HOW TO REVERSE-ENGINEER THE KRYPTONIAN NANOTECHNOLOGY.
YEAH. I'M STILL ONLY HEARING 'MAGIC PILLS.'
YOU'RE SITTING ON A SPACE STATION HIGH ABOVE THE EARTH WITH MEN AND WOMEN WHO CAN LITERALLY MOVE MOUNTAINS AND YOU HAVE A PROBLEM WITH MAGIC PILLS?
I'M SURE THERE ARE ORDINARY PEOPLE IN ALL OF OUR LIVES WE WOULD TRUST WITH SUCH POWER.
I SUGGEST WE DRAW UP A LIST OF CANDIDATES.
YOU WANT US TO ASK OUR FRIENDS TO HELP POLICE THE WORLD?
IF WE HAD MORE PEOPLE WHEN APOKOLIPS ATTACKED, THINK OF HOW MANY LIVES WOULD HAVE BEEN SAVED.
WE NEED PEOPLE ON THE GROUND AT ALL TIMES.
OR ALL OF OUR GOOD WORK COULD BE UNDONE.
SO, YOU WANT A SUPERPOWERED ARMY?
NOT AN ARMY, GREEN LANTERN, A PEACE KEEPING FORCE. YOU OF ALL PEOPLE SHOULD UNDERSTAND THIS.
I'M SURE THERE ARE MANY WORLD GOVERNMENTS WHO WON'T SEE IT THAT WAY.
WHAT IF IT FELL INTO THE WRONG HANDS...?
IT WON'T. AND THIS TECHNOLOGY ISN'T JUST ABOUT PROTECTING THE WORLD, HAWKGIRL. IT'S ALSO ABOUT PROTECTING YOU.

"--IT WILL MAKE ALL OF YOU STRONGER."

TK TK

TELEPORTER
DESTINATION: GOTHAM CITY

TELEPORTER
DESTINATION: GOTHAM C

HMM.

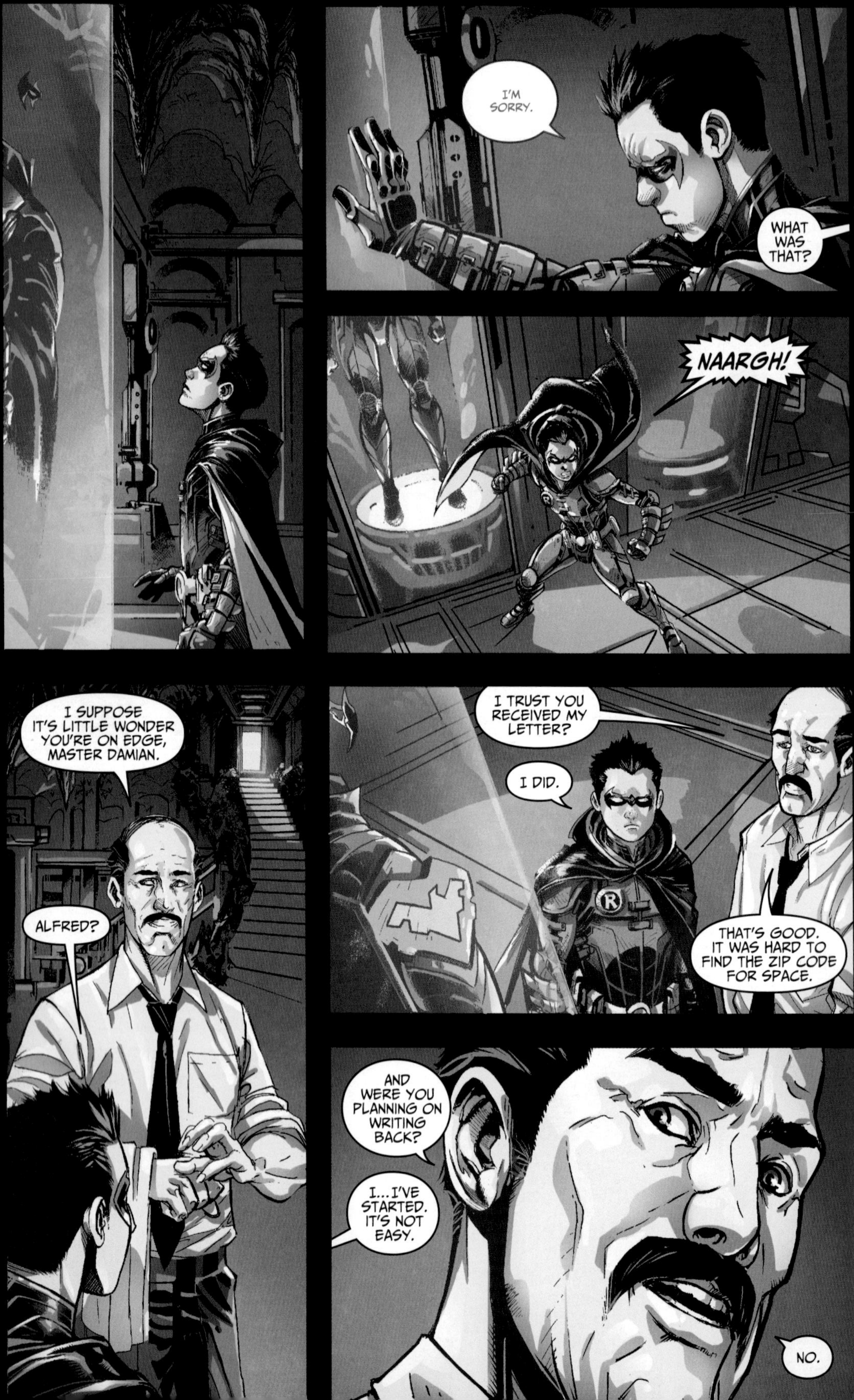
I'M SORRY.
WHAT WAS THAT?
NAARGH!
I SUPPOSE IT'S LITTLE WONDER YOU'RE ON EDGE, MASTER DAMIAN.
ALFRED?
I TRUST YOU RECEIVED MY LETTER?
I DID.
THAT'S GOOD. IT WAS HARD TO FIND THE ZIP CODE FOR SPACE.
AND WERE YOU PLANNING ON WRITING BACK?
I...I'VE STARTED. IT'S NOT EASY.
NO.

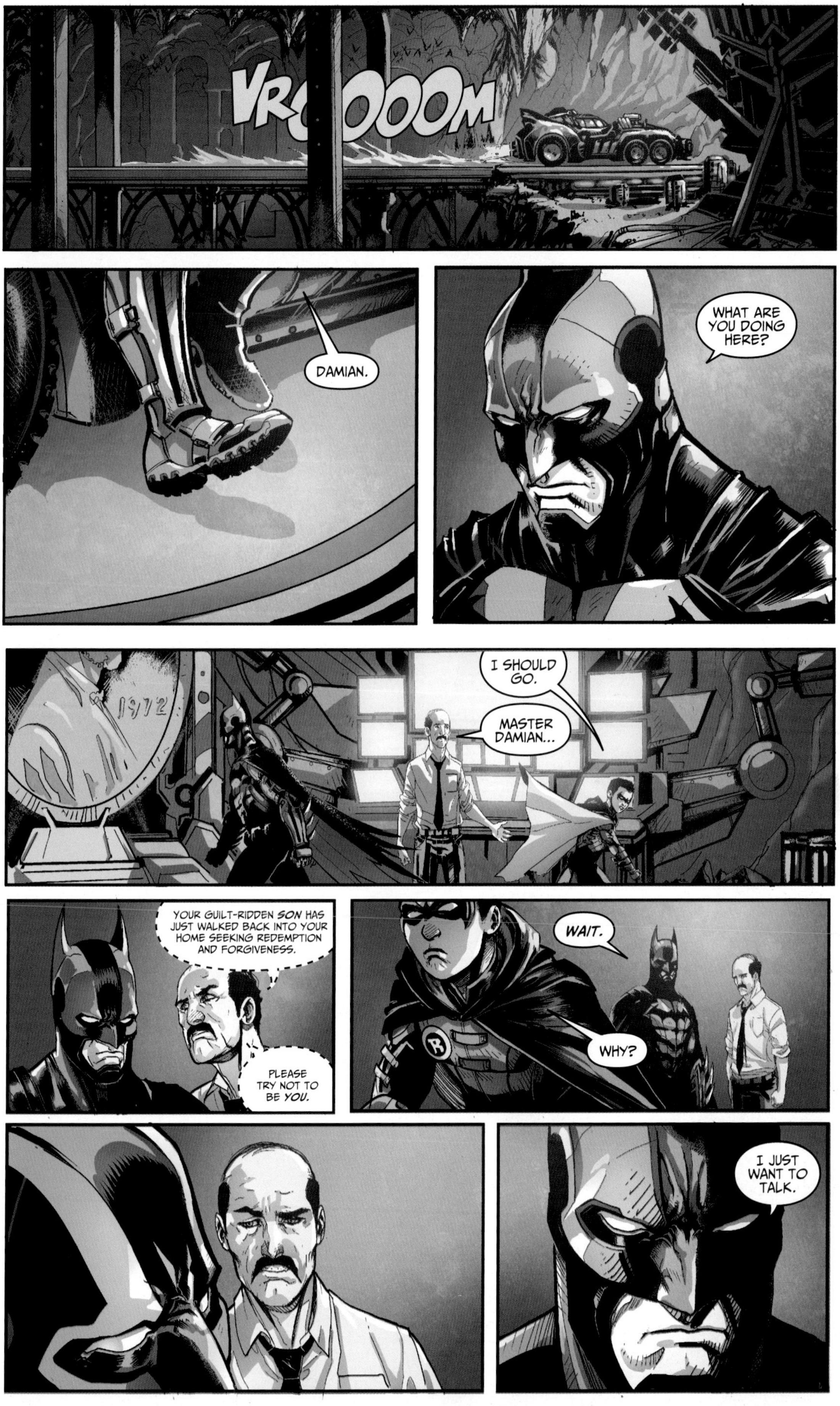
VROOOOM
DAMIAN.
WHAT ARE YOU DOING HERE?
MASTER DAMIAN...
I SHOULD GO.
YOUR GUILT-RIDDEN SON HAS JUST WALKED BACK INTO YOUR HOME SEEKING REDEMPTION AND FORGIVENESS.
PLEASE TRY NOT TO BE YOU.
WAIT.
WHY?
I JUST WANT TO TALK.

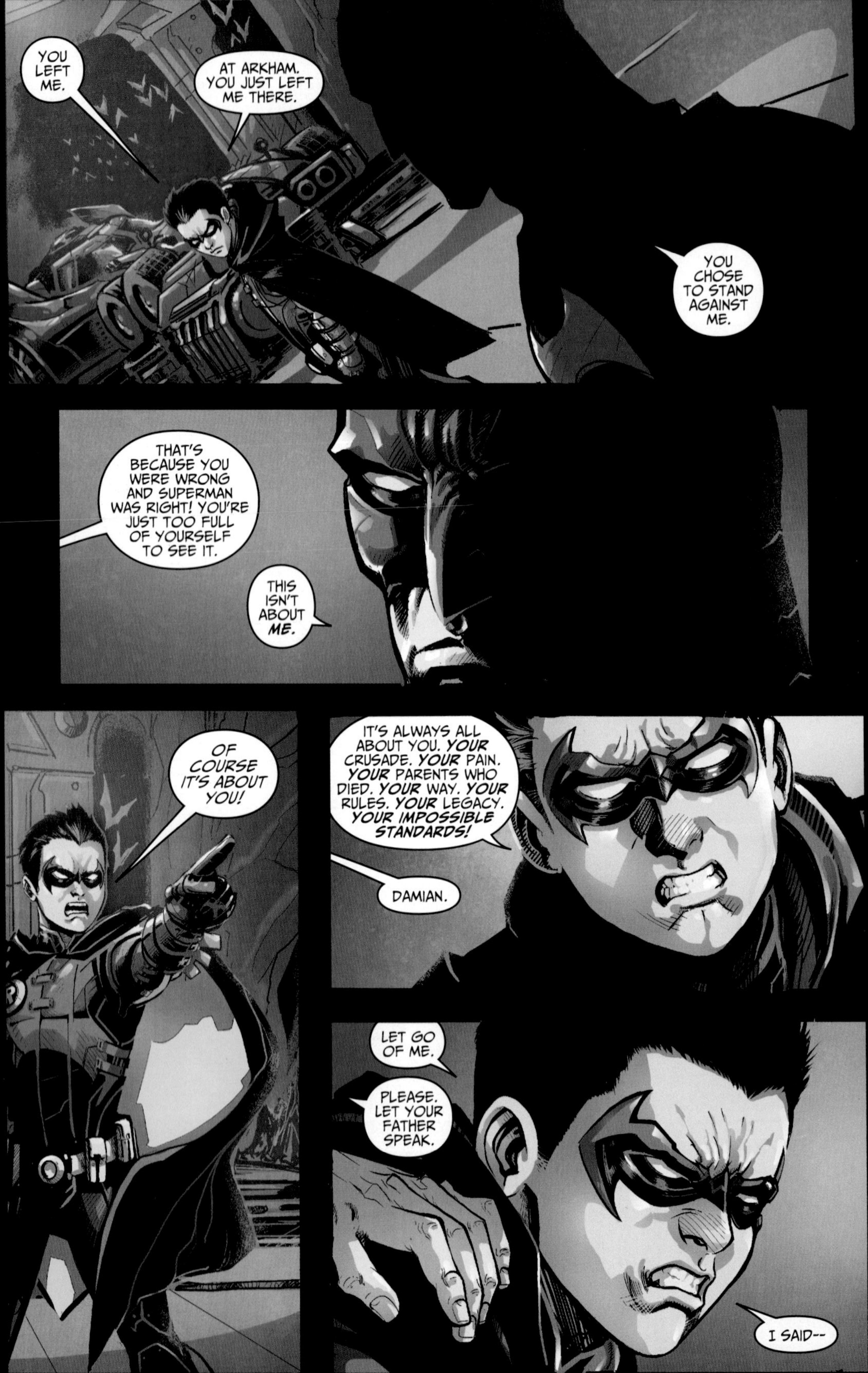
YOU LEFT ME.
AT ARKHAM. YOU JUST LEFT ME THERE.
YOU CHOSE TO STAND AGAINST ME.
THAT'S BECAUSE YOU WERE WRONG AND SUPERMAN WAS RIGHT! YOU'RE JUST TOO FULL OF YOURSELF TO SEE IT.
THIS ISN'T ABOUT *ME.*
OF COURSE IT'S ABOUT YOU!
IT'S ALWAYS ALL ABOUT YOU. ***YOUR*** CRUSADE. ***YOUR*** PAIN. ***YOUR*** PARENTS WHO DIED. ***YOUR*** WAY. ***YOUR*** RULES. ***YOUR*** LEGACY. ***YOUR IMPOSSIBLE STANDARDS!***
DAMIAN.
LET GO OF ME.
PLEASE. LET YOUR FATHER SPEAK.
I SAID--

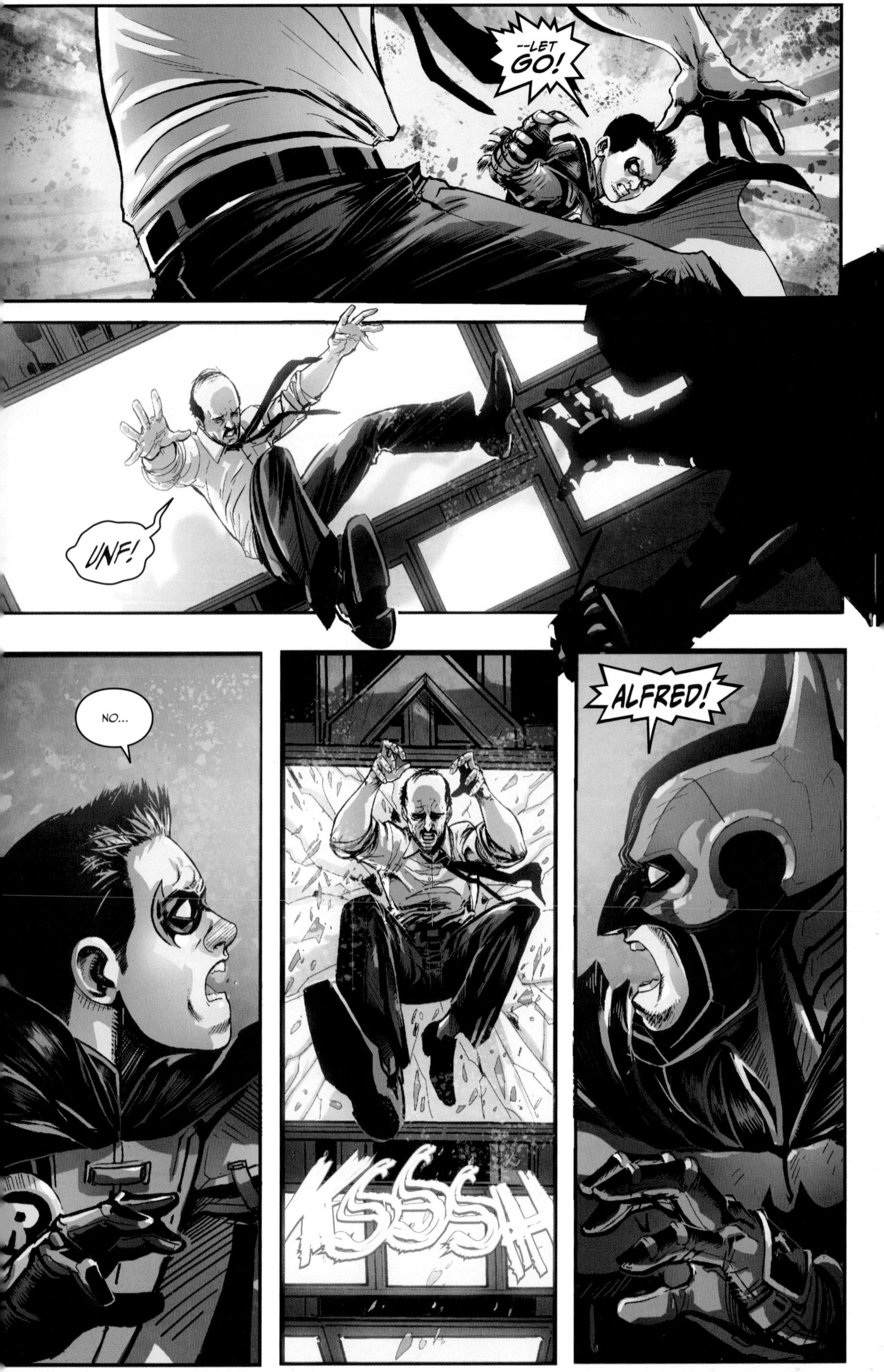
--LET GO!
UNF!
NO...
KSSSH
ALFRED!

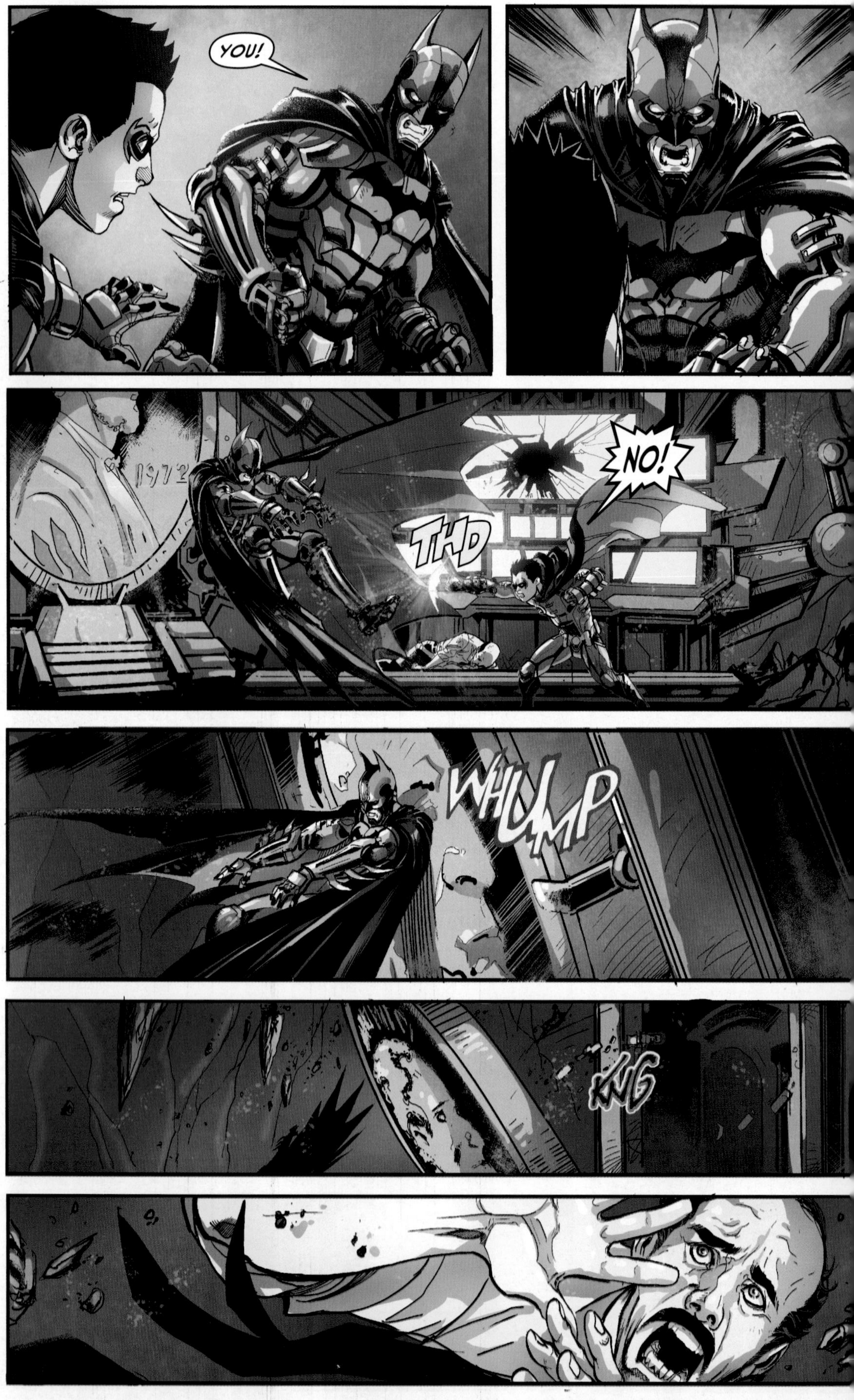
YOU!
NO!
THD
WHUMP
KNG

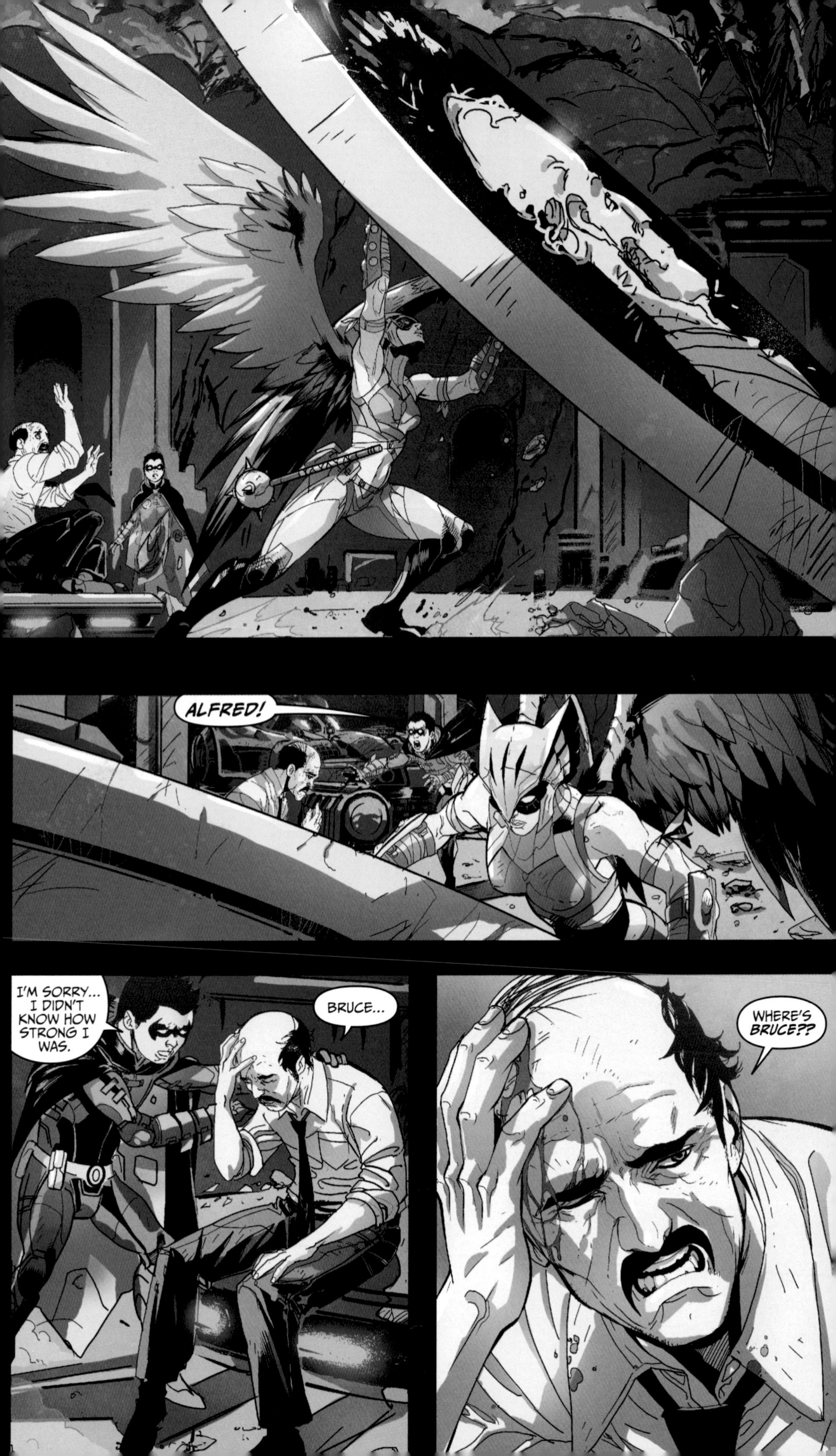
ALFRED!
I'M SORRY... I DIDN'T KNOW HOW STRONG I WAS.
BRUCE...
WHERE'S BRUCE??

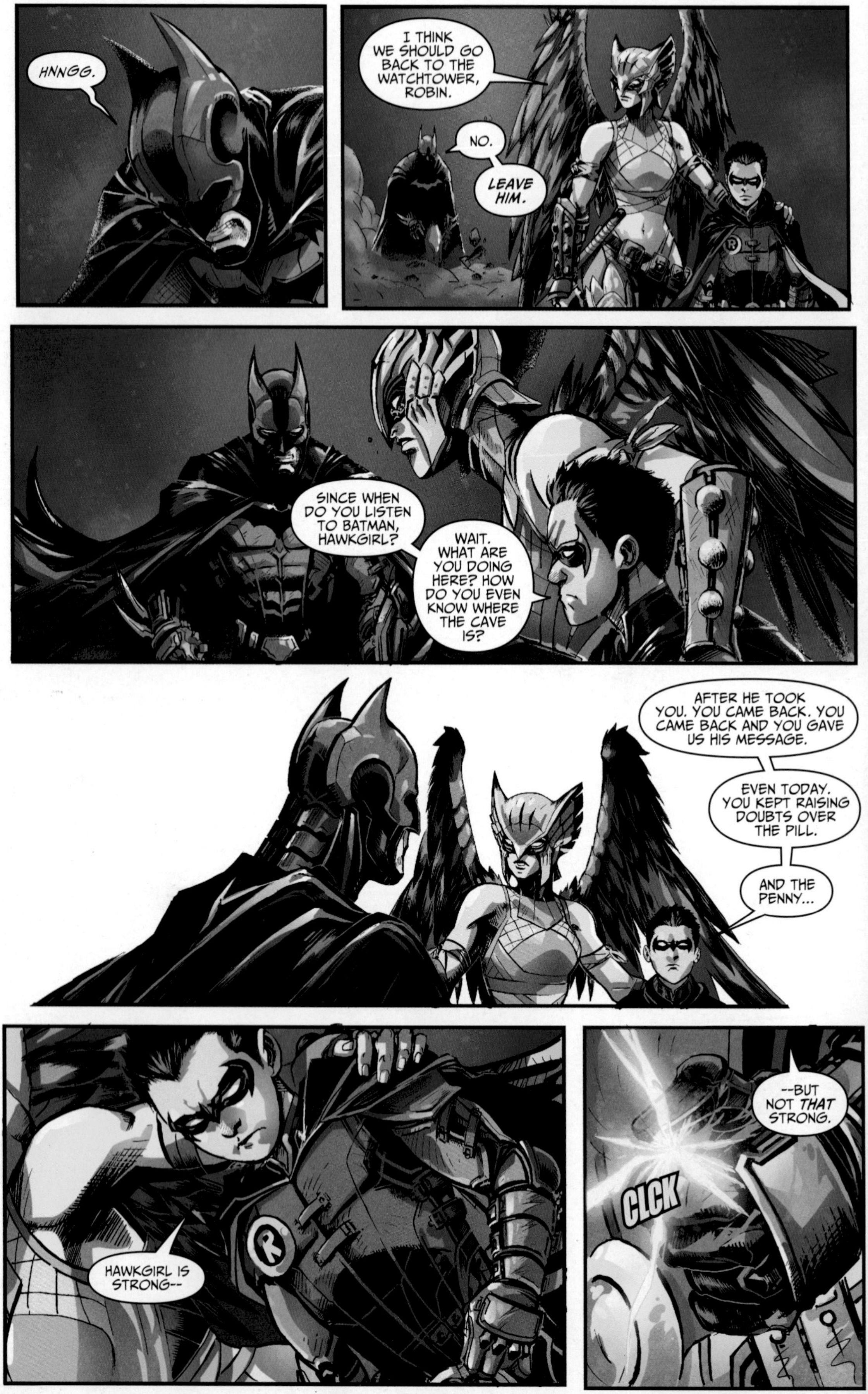
HNNGG.
I THINK WE SHOULD GO BACK TO THE WATCHTOWER, ROBIN.
NO.
LEAVE HIM.
SINCE WHEN DO YOU LISTEN TO BATMAN, HAWKGIRL?
WAIT. WHAT ARE YOU DOING HERE? HOW DO YOU EVEN KNOW WHERE THE CAVE IS?
AFTER HE TOOK YOU. YOU CAME BACK. YOU CAME BACK AND YOU GAVE US HIS MESSAGE.
EVEN TODAY. YOU KEPT RAISING DOUBTS OVER THE PILL.
AND THE PENNY...
HAWKGIRL IS STRONG--
--BUT NOT *THAT* STRONG.
CLCK

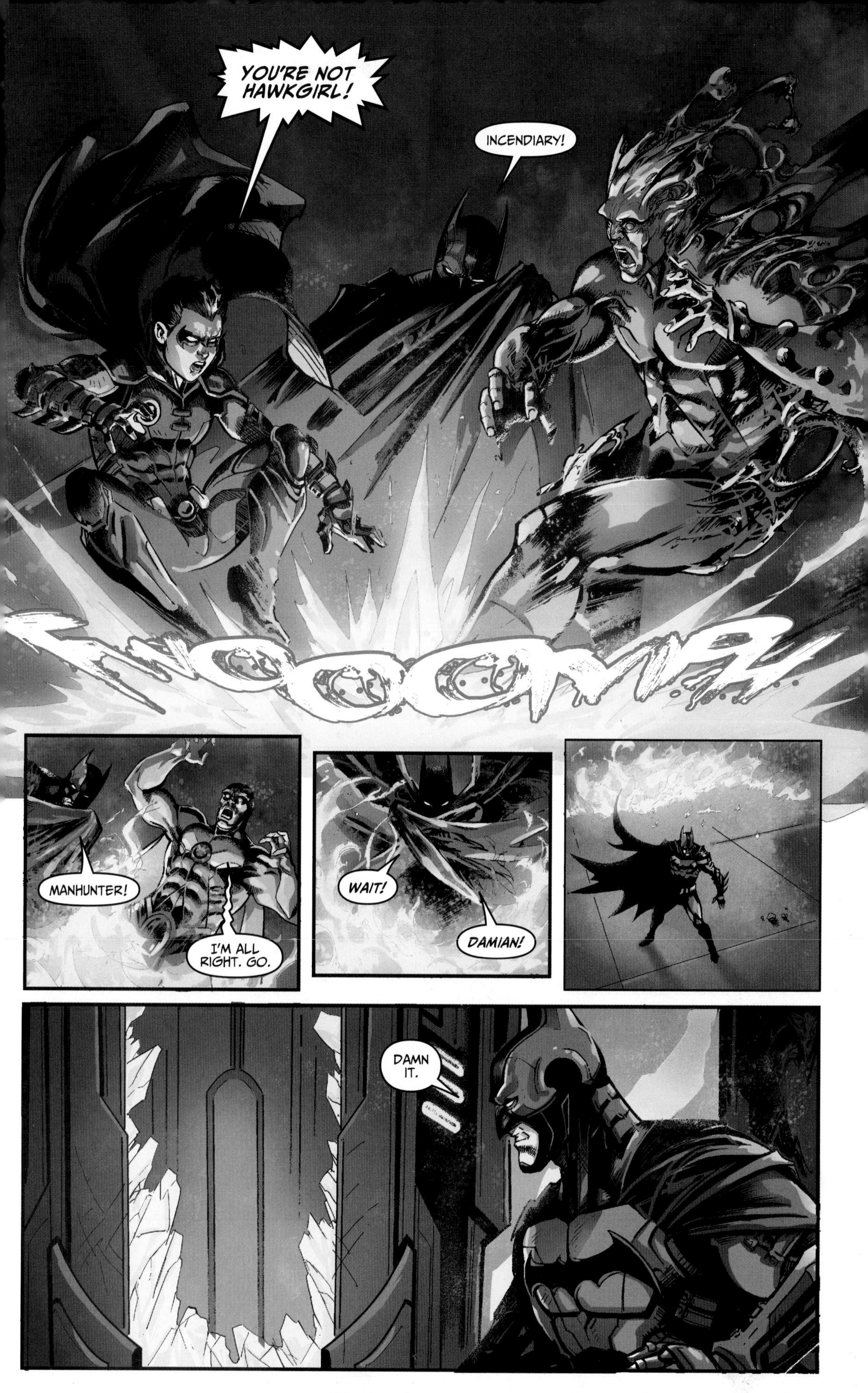
YOU'RE NOT HAWKGIRL!
INCENDIARY!
MANHUNTER!
I'M ALL RIGHT. GO.
WAIT!
DAMIAN!
DAMN IT.

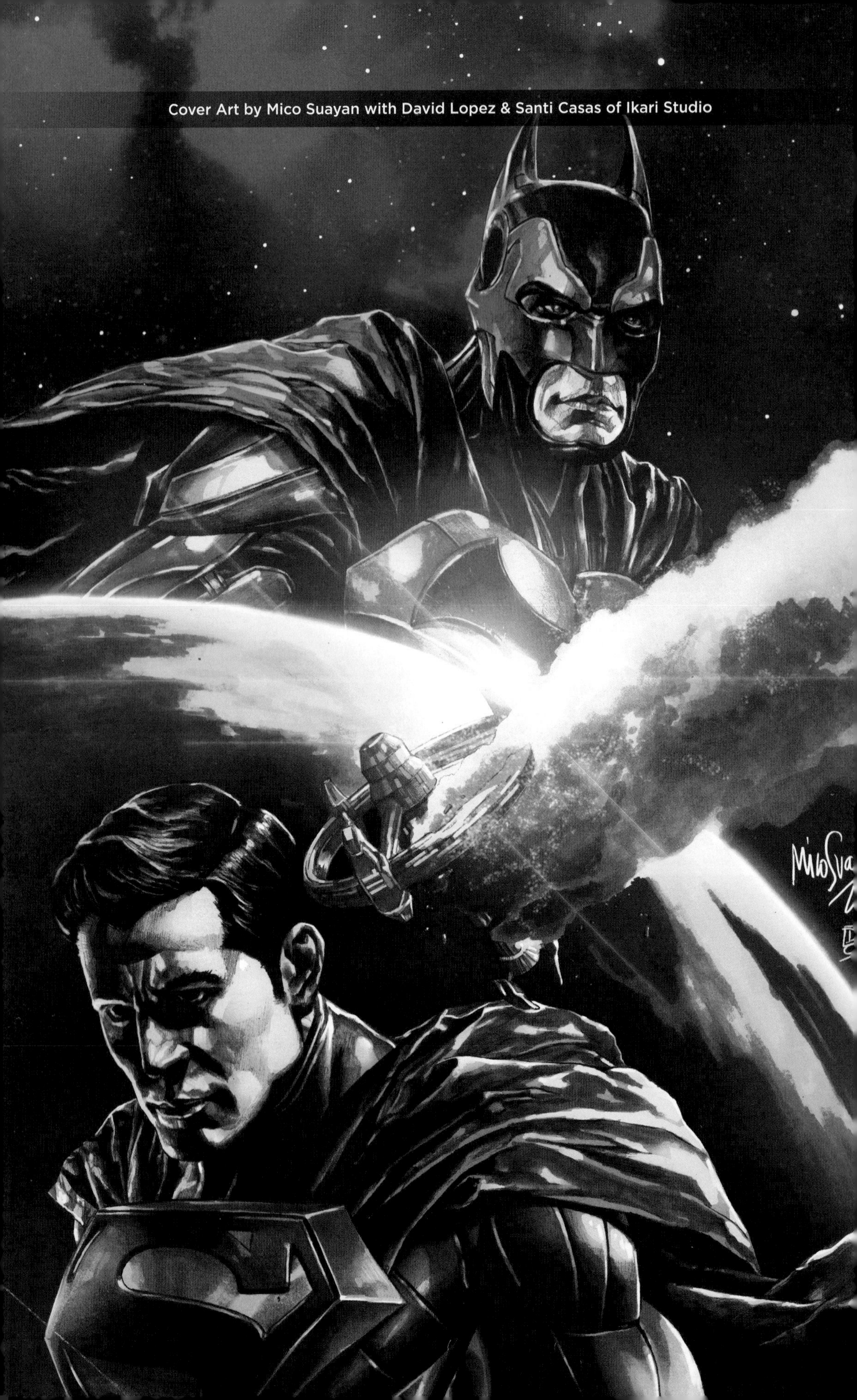
Cover Art by Mico Suayan with David Lopez & Santi Casas of Ikari Studio

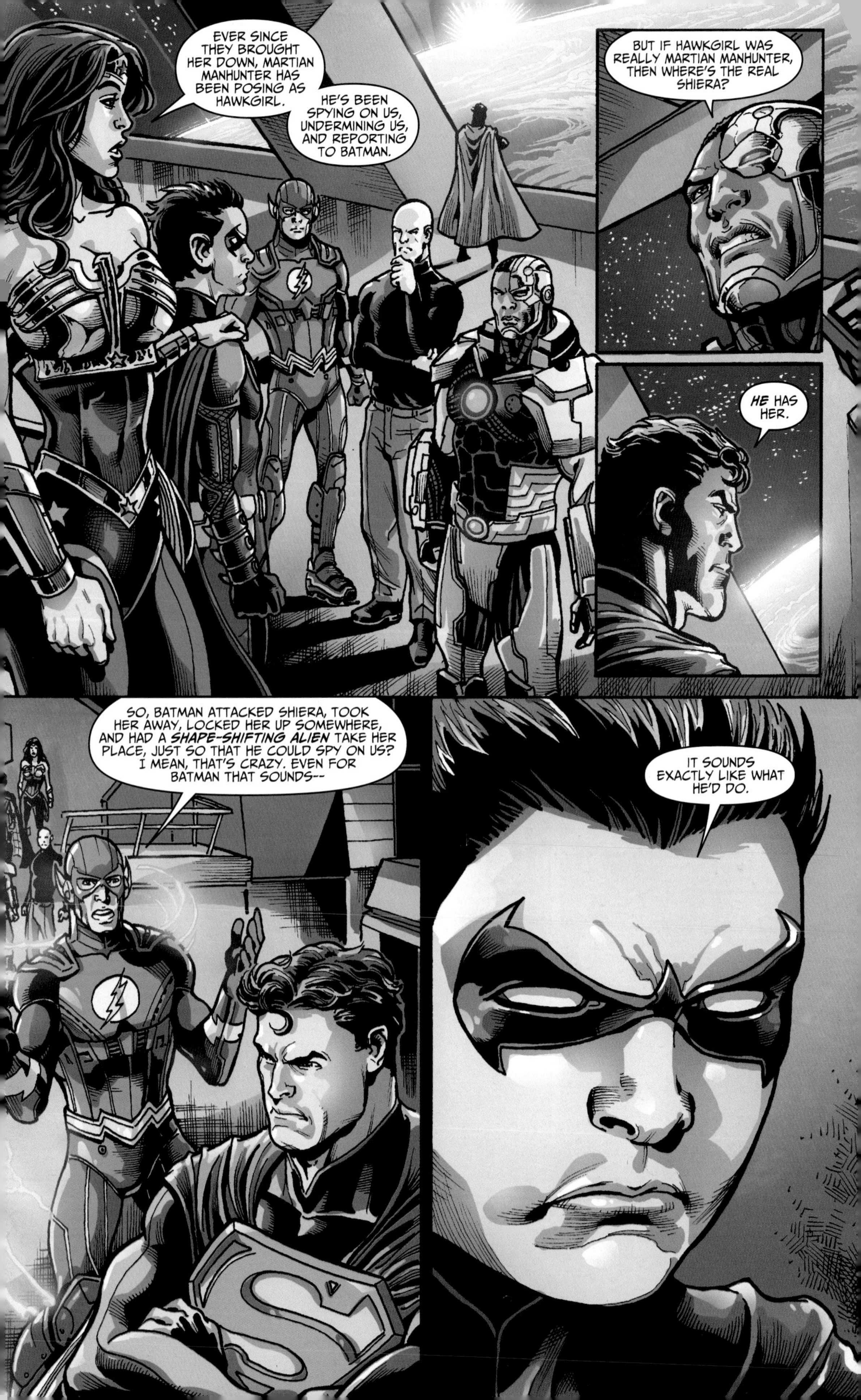
EVER SINCE THEY BROUGHT HER DOWN, MARTIAN MANHUNTER HAS BEEN POSING AS HAWKGIRL.
HE'S BEEN SPYING ON US, UNDERMINING US, AND REPORTING TO BATMAN.
BUT IF HAWKGIRL WAS REALLY MARTIAN MANHUNTER, THEN WHERE'S THE REAL SHIERA?
HE HAS HER.
SO, BATMAN ATTACKED SHIERA, TOOK HER AWAY, LOCKED HER UP SOMEWHERE, AND HAD A SHAPE-SHIFTING ALIEN TAKE HER PLACE, JUST SO THAT HE COULD SPY ON US? I MEAN, THAT'S CRAZY. EVEN FOR BATMAN THAT SOUNDS--
IT SOUNDS EXACTLY LIKE WHAT HE'D DO.

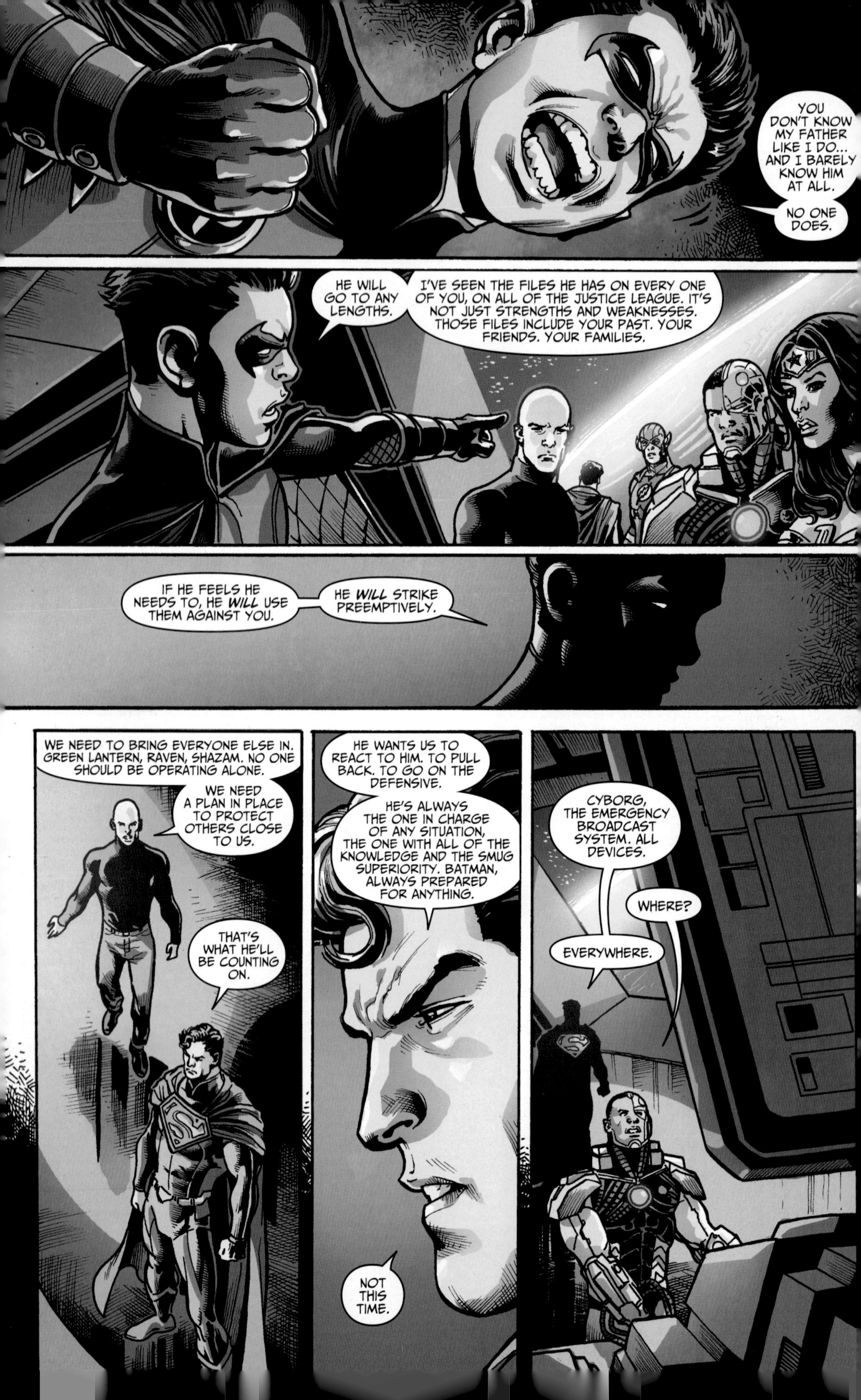

YOU DON'T KNOW MY FATHER LIKE I DO... AND I BARELY KNOW HIM AT ALL.
NO ONE DOES.
HE WILL GO TO ANY LENGTHS.
I'VE SEEN THE FILES HE HAS ON EVERY ONE OF YOU, ON ALL OF THE JUSTICE LEAGUE. IT'S NOT JUST STRENGTHS AND WEAKNESSES. THOSE FILES INCLUDE YOUR PAST. YOUR FRIENDS. YOUR FAMILIES.
IF HE FEELS HE NEEDS TO, HE WILL USE THEM AGAINST YOU.
HE WILL STRIKE PREEMPTIVELY.
WE NEED TO BRING EVERYONE ELSE IN. GREEN LANTERN, RAVEN, SHAZAM. NO ONE SHOULD BE OPERATING ALONE.
WE NEED A PLAN IN PLACE TO PROTECT OTHERS CLOSE TO US.
THAT'S WHAT HE'LL BE COUNTING ON.
HE WANTS US TO REACT TO HIM. TO PULL BACK. TO GO ON THE DEFENSIVE.
HE'S ALWAYS THE ONE IN CHARGE OF ANY SITUATION, THE ONE WITH ALL OF THE KNOWLEDGE AND THE SMUG SUPERIORITY. BATMAN, ALWAYS PREPARED FOR ANYTHING.
NOT THIS TIME.
CYBORG, THE EMERGENCY BROADCAST SYSTEM. ALL DEVICES.
WHERE?
EVERYWHERE.

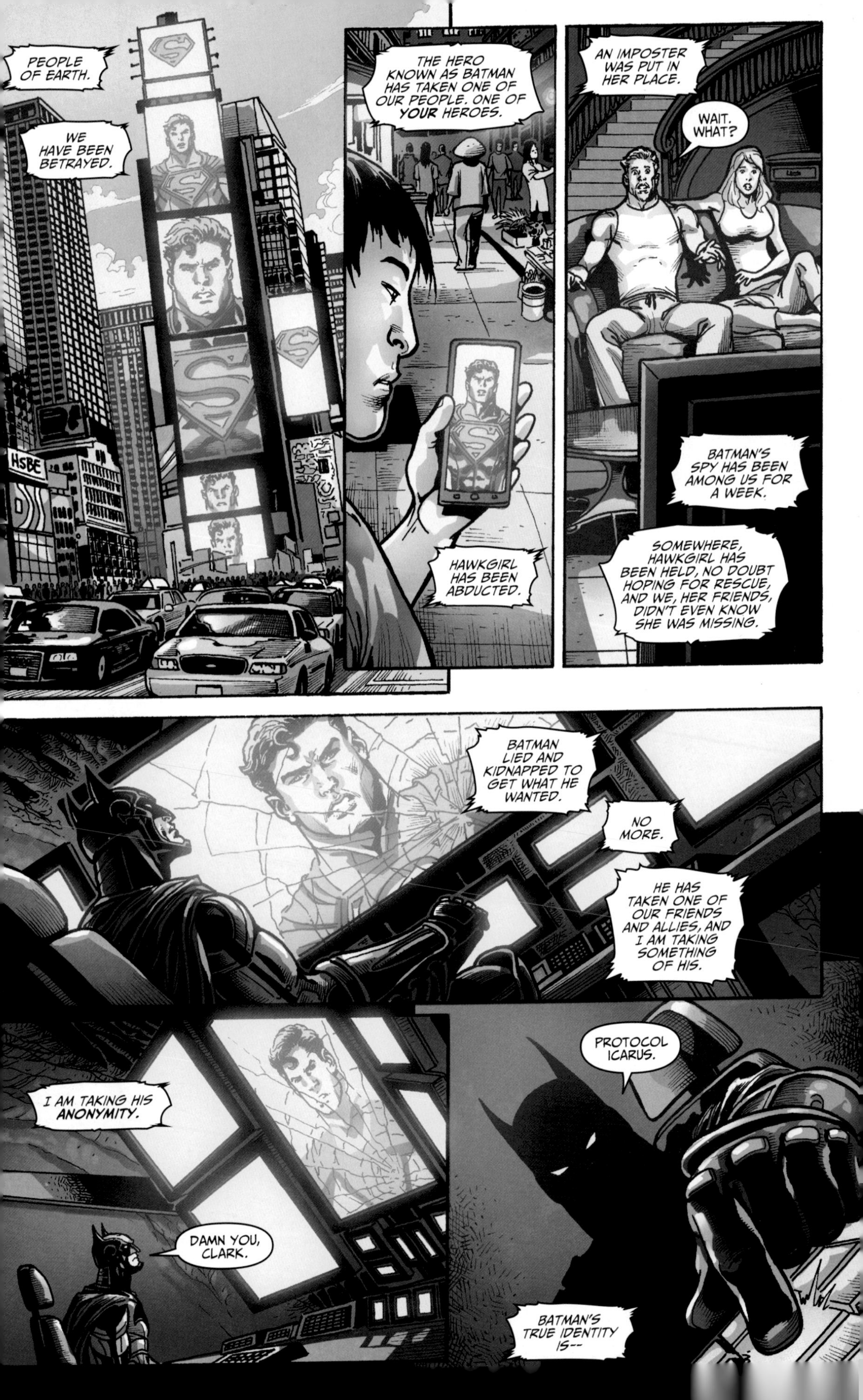
PEOPLE OF EARTH.
WE HAVE BEEN BETRAYED.
THE HERO KNOWN AS BATMAN HAS TAKEN ONE OF OUR PEOPLE. ONE OF YOUR HEROES.
HAWKGIRL HAS BEEN ABDUCTED.
AN IMPOSTER WAS PUT IN HER PLACE.
WAIT. WHAT?
BATMAN'S SPY HAS BEEN AMONG US FOR A WEEK.
SOMEWHERE, HAWKGIRL HAS BEEN HELD, NO DOUBT HOPING FOR RESCUE, AND WE, HER FRIENDS, DIDN'T EVEN KNOW SHE WAS MISSING.
BATMAN LIED AND KIDNAPPED TO GET WHAT HE WANTED.
NO MORE.
HE HAS TAKEN ONE OF OUR FRIENDS AND ALLIES, AND I AM TAKING SOMETHING OF HIS.
I AM TAKING HIS ANONYMITY.
DAMN YOU, CLARK.
PROTOCOL ICARUS.
BATMAN'S TRUE IDENTITY IS--

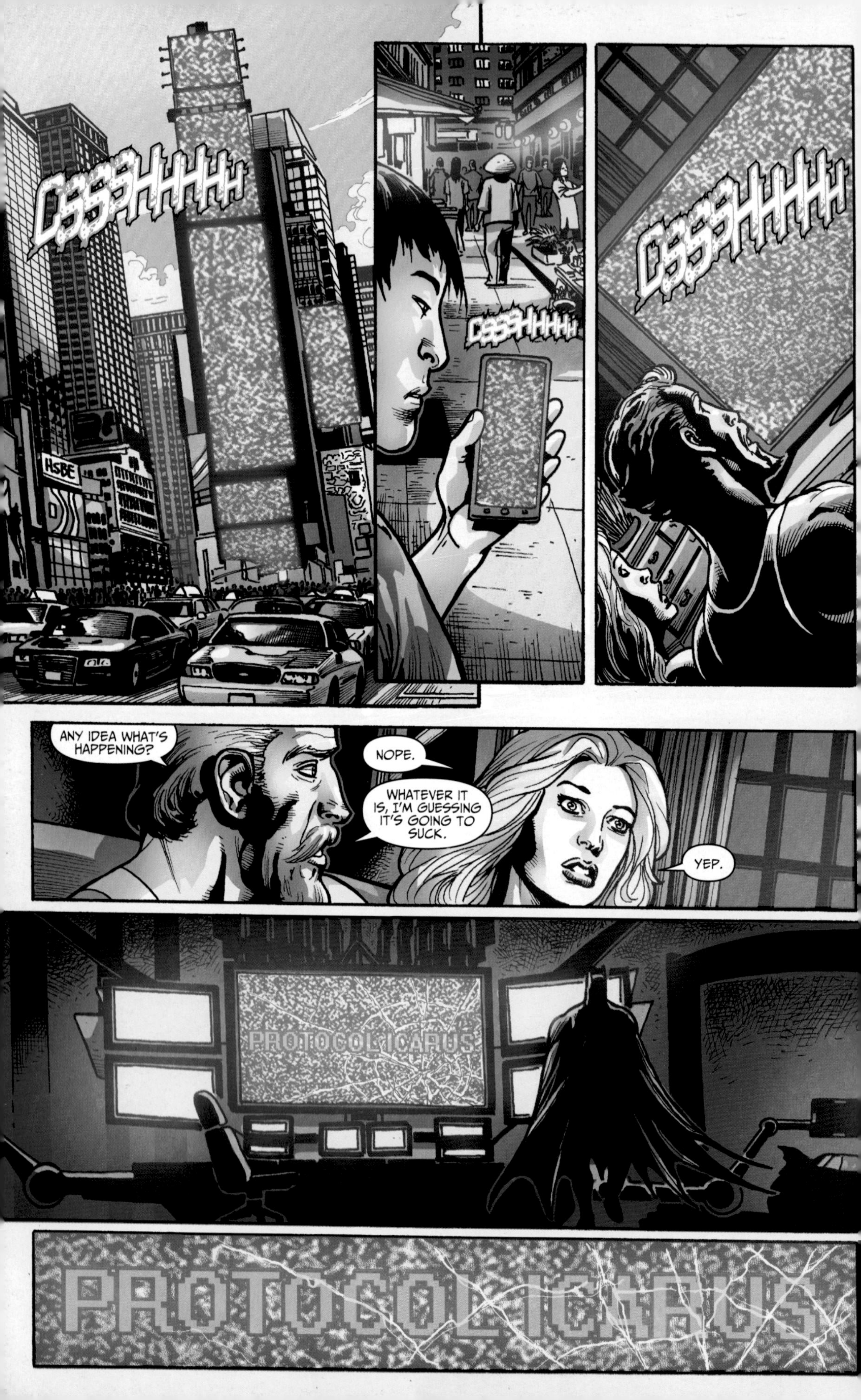
CSSSHHHHH
CSSSHHHHH
CSSSHHHHH
ANY IDEA WHAT'S HAPPENING?
NOPE.
WHATEVER IT IS, I'M GUESSING IT'S GOING TO SUCK.
YEP.
PROTOCOL ICARUS
PROTOCOL ICARUS

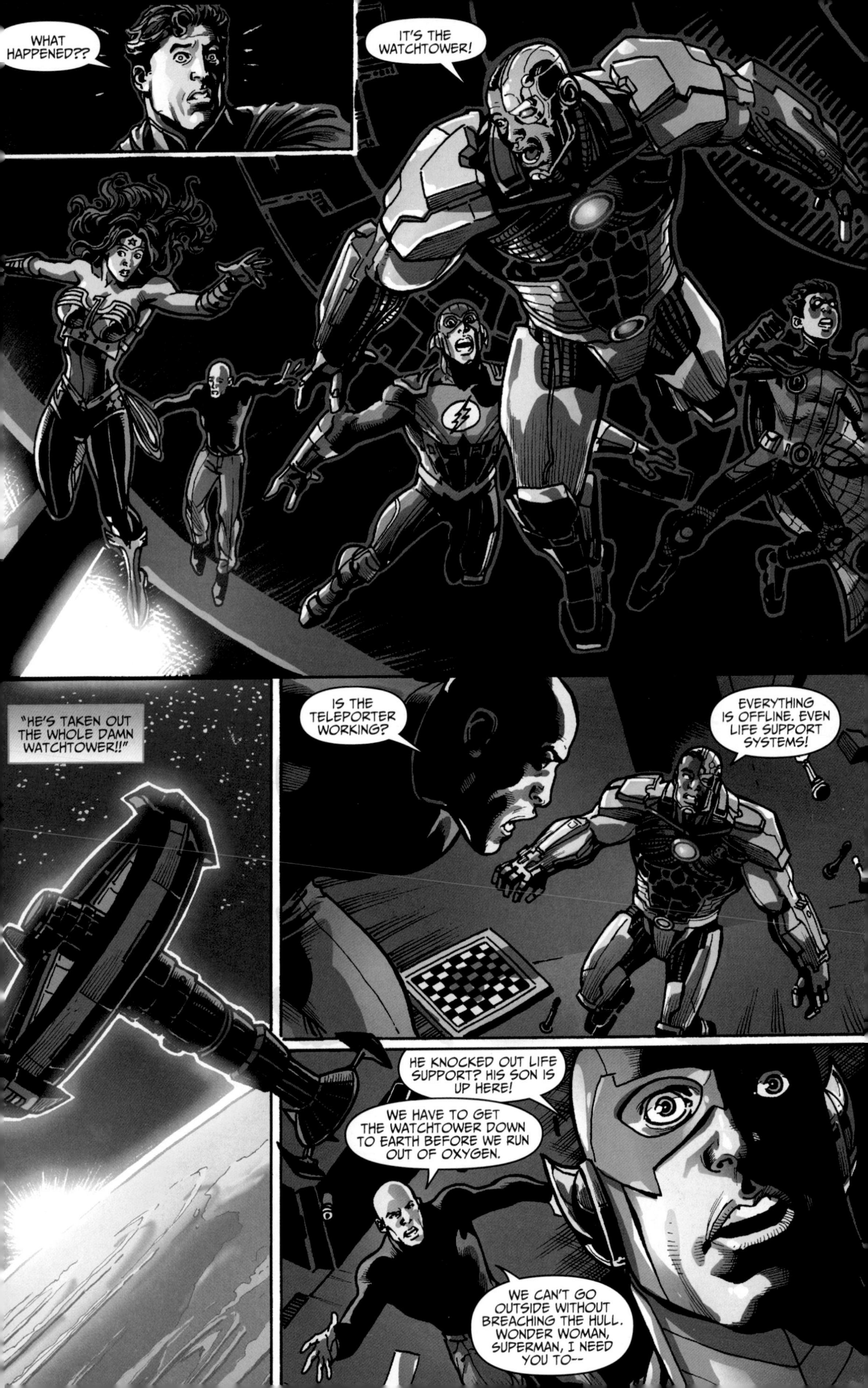
WHAT HAPPENED??
IT'S THE WATCHTOWER!
"HE'S TAKEN OUT THE WHOLE DAMN WATCHTOWER!!"
IS THE TELEPORTER WORKING?
EVERYTHING IS OFFLINE. EVEN LIFE SUPPORT SYSTEMS!
HE KNOCKED OUT LIFE SUPPORT? HIS SON IS UP HERE!
WE HAVE TO GET THE WATCHTOWER DOWN TO EARTH BEFORE WE RUN OUT OF OXYGEN.
WE CAN'T GO OUTSIDE WITHOUT BREACHING THE HULL. WONDER WOMAN, SUPERMAN, I NEED YOU TO--

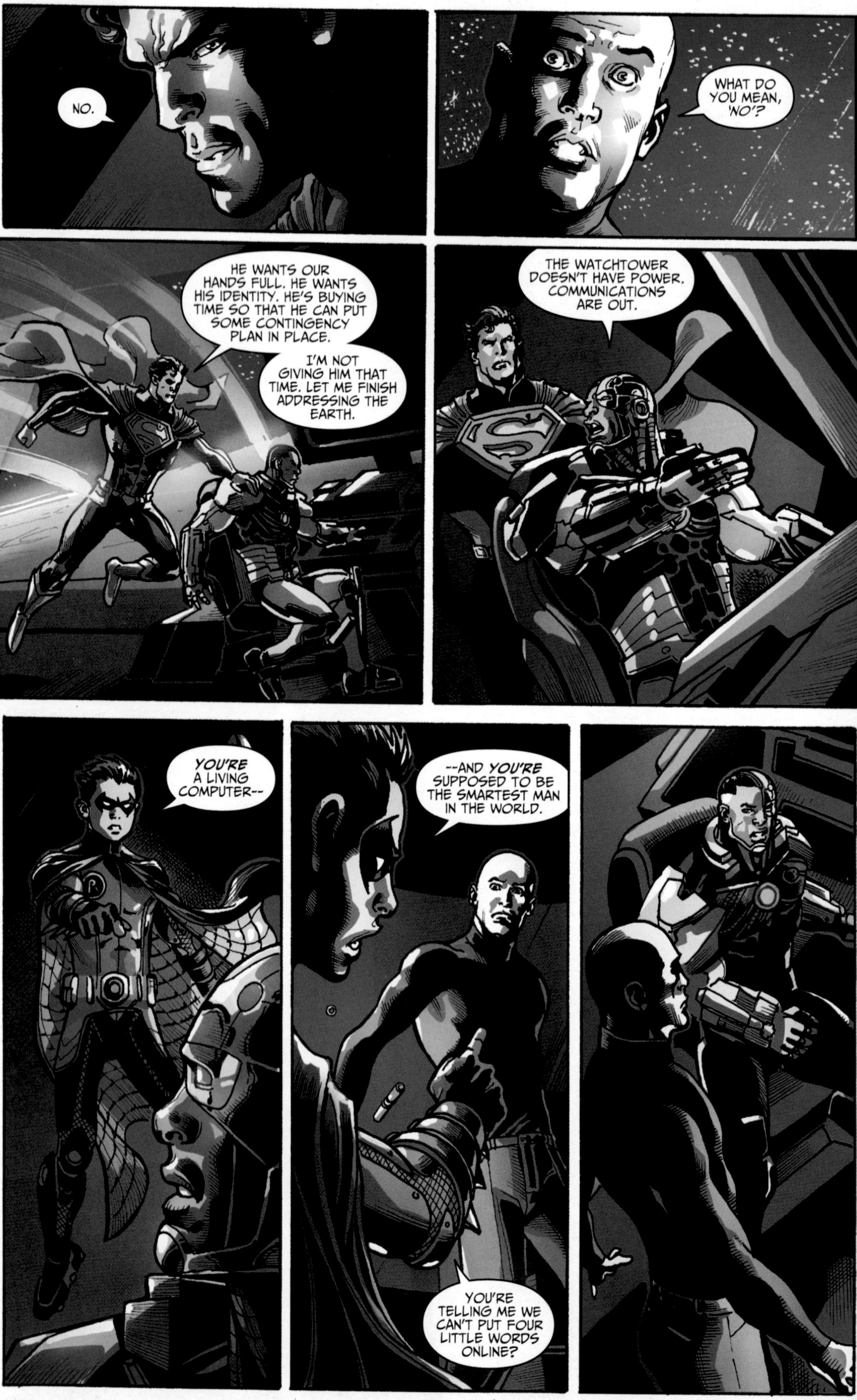
NO.
WHAT DO YOU MEAN, 'NO'?
HE WANTS OUR HANDS FULL. HE WANTS HIS IDENTITY. HE'S BUYING TIME SO THAT HE CAN PUT SOME CONTINGENCY PLAN IN PLACE.
I'M NOT GIVING HIM THAT TIME. LET ME FINISH ADDRESSING THE EARTH.
THE WATCHTOWER DOESN'T HAVE POWER. COMMUNICATIONS ARE OUT.
YOU'RE A LIVING COMPUTER--
--AND YOU'RE SUPPOSED TO BE THE SMARTEST MAN IN THE WORLD.
YOU'RE TELLING ME WE CAN'T PUT FOUR LITTLE WORDS ONLINE?

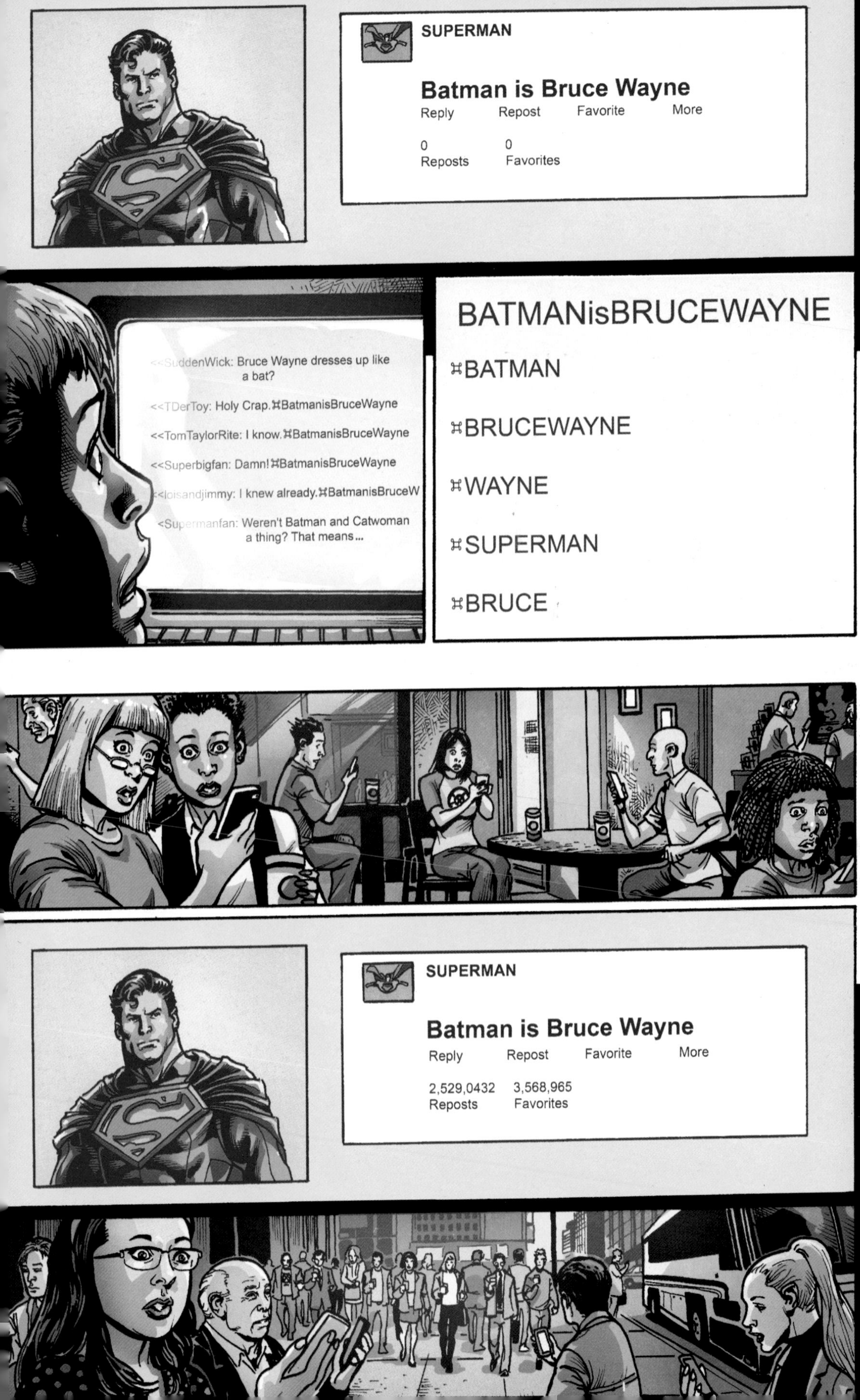

SUPERMAN
Batman is Bruce Wayne
Reply Repost Favorite More
0 Reposts 0 Favorites
<<SuddenWick: Bruce Wayne dresses up like a bat?
<<TDerToy: Holy Crap.⌘BatmanisBruceWayne
<<TomTaylorRite: I know.⌘BatmanisBruceWayne
<<Superbigfan: Damn!⌘BatmanisBruceWayne
<<loisandjimmy: I knew already.⌘BatmanisBruceW
<Supermanfan: Weren't Batman and Catwoman a thing? That means...
BATMANisBRUCEWAYNE
⌘BATMAN
⌘BRUCEWAYNE
⌘WAYNE
⌘SUPERMAN
⌘BRUCE
SUPERMAN
Batman is Bruce Wayne
Reply Repost Favorite More
2,529,0432 Reposts 3,568,965 Favorites

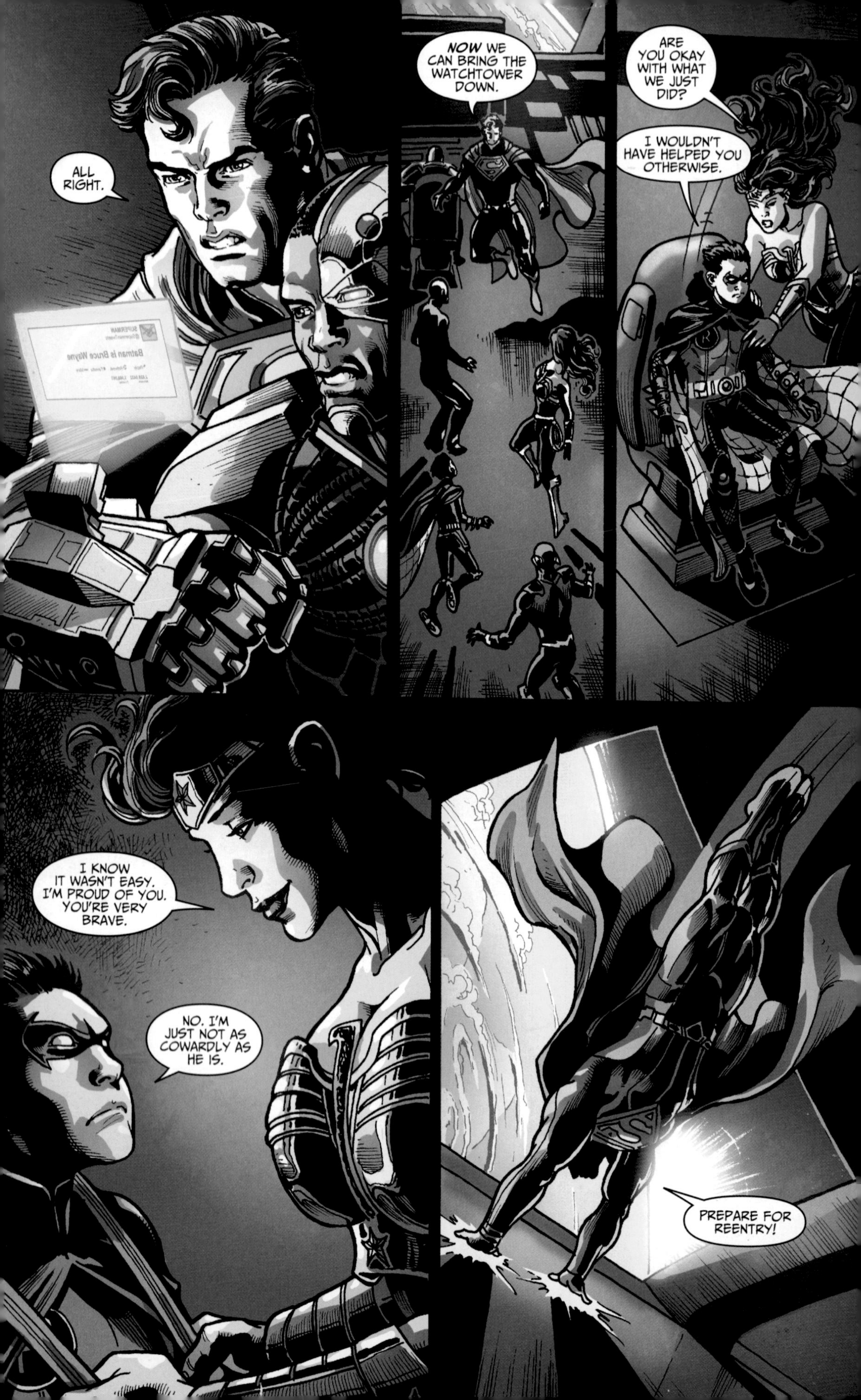
ALL RIGHT.
NOW WE CAN BRING THE WATCHTOWER DOWN.
ARE YOU OKAY WITH WHAT WE JUST DID?
I WOULDN'T HAVE HELPED YOU OTHERWISE.
I KNOW IT WASN'T EASY. I'M PROUD OF YOU. YOU'RE VERY BRAVE.
NO. I'M JUST NOT AS COWARDLY AS HE IS.
PREPARE FOR REENTRY!

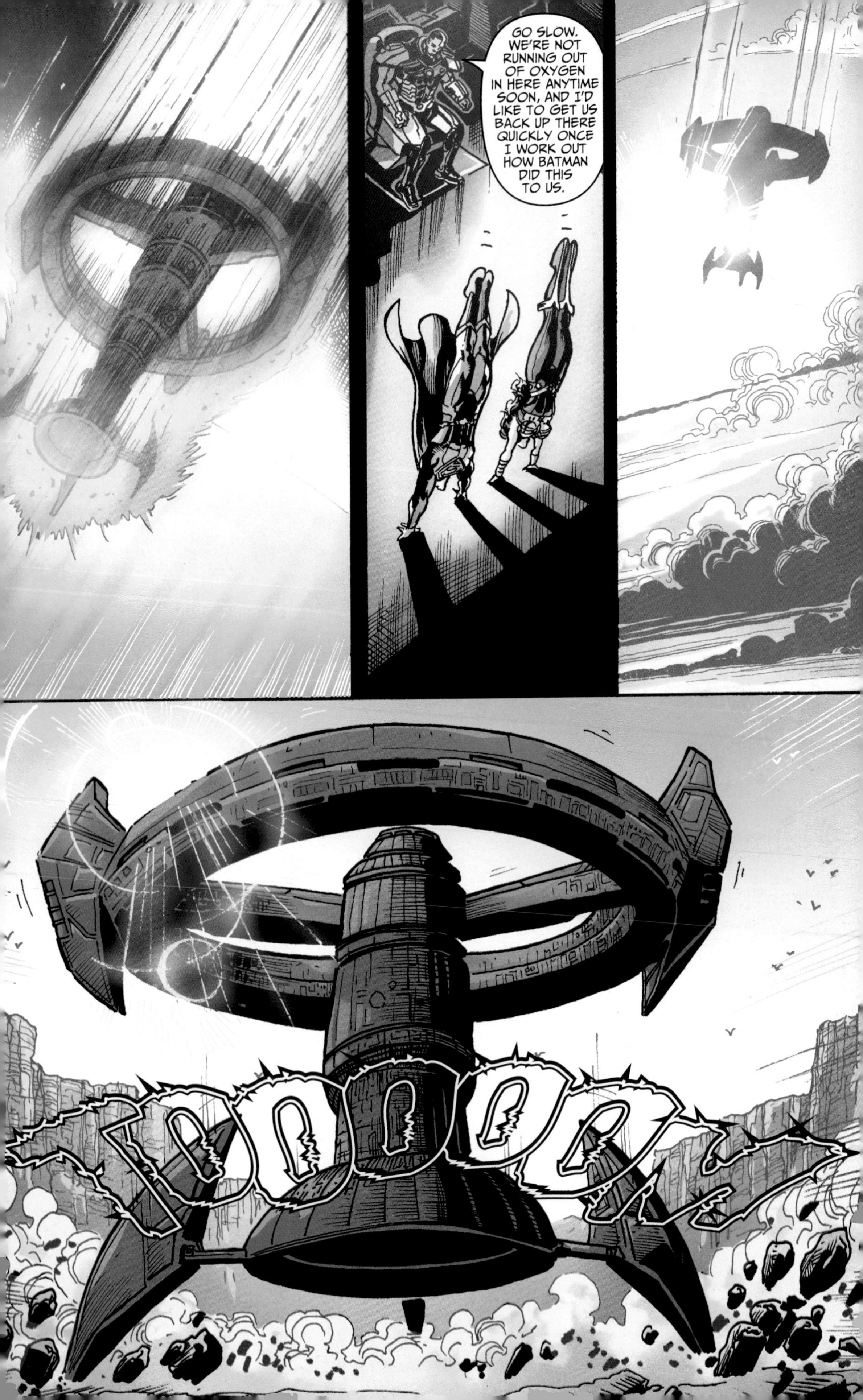
GO SLOW. WE'RE NOT RUNNING OUT OF OXYGEN IN HERE ANYTIME SOON, AND I'D LIKE TO GET US BACK UP THERE QUICKLY ONCE I WORK OUT HOW BATMAN DID THIS TO US.

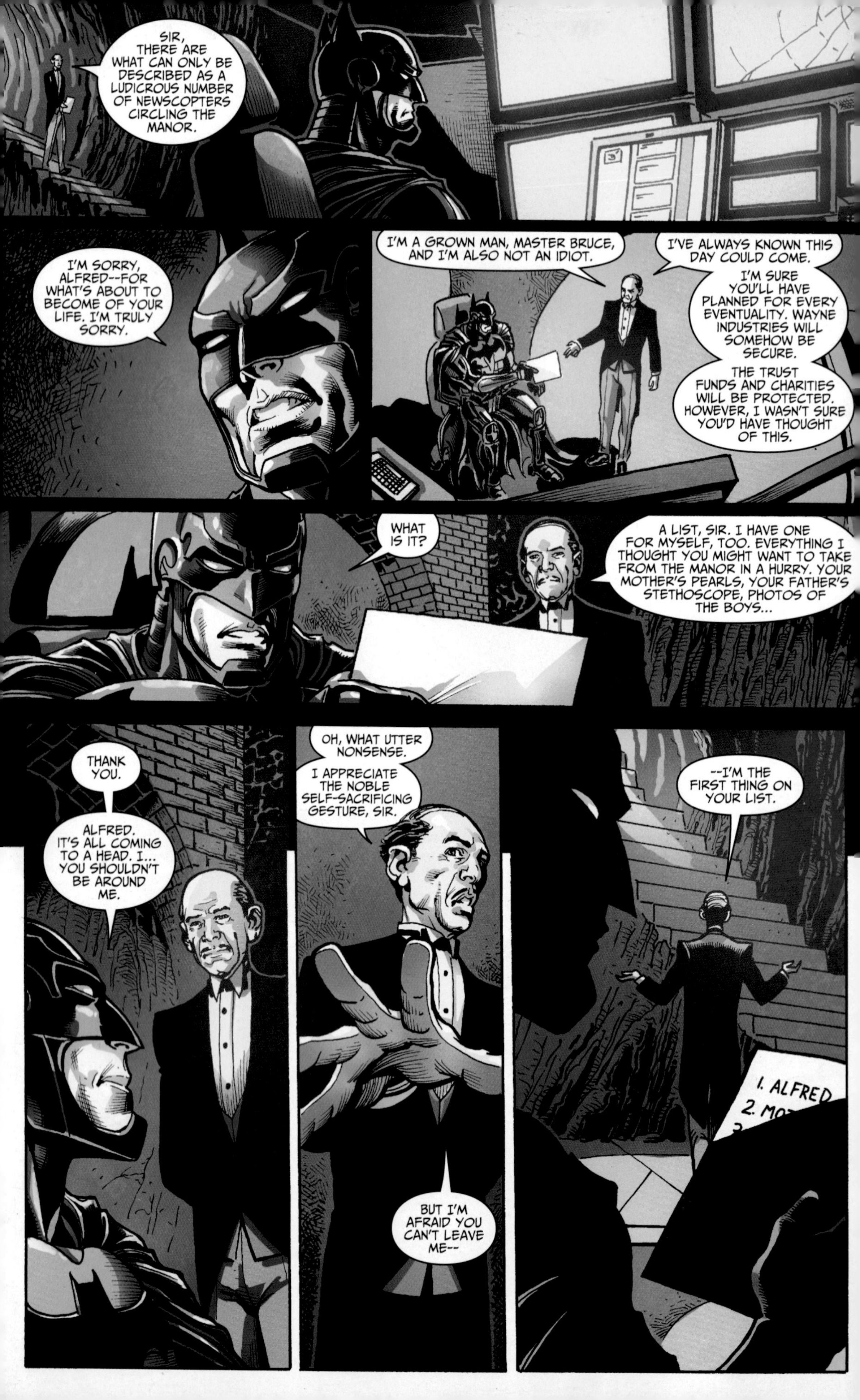
SIR, THERE ARE WHAT CAN ONLY BE DESCRIBED AS A LUDICROUS NUMBER OF NEWSCOPTERS CIRCLING THE MANOR.
I'M SORRY, ALFRED--FOR WHAT'S ABOUT TO BECOME OF YOUR LIFE. I'M TRULY SORRY.
I'M A GROWN MAN, MASTER BRUCE, AND I'M ALSO NOT AN IDIOT.
I'VE ALWAYS KNOWN THIS DAY COULD COME.
I'M SURE YOU'LL HAVE PLANNED FOR EVERY EVENTUALITY. WAYNE INDUSTRIES WILL SOMEHOW BE SECURE.
THE TRUST FUNDS AND CHARITIES WILL BE PROTECTED. HOWEVER, I WASN'T SURE YOU'D HAVE THOUGHT OF THIS.
WHAT IS IT?
A LIST, SIR. I HAVE ONE FOR MYSELF, TOO. EVERYTHING I THOUGHT YOU MIGHT WANT TO TAKE FROM THE MANOR IN A HURRY. YOUR MOTHER'S PEARLS, YOUR FATHER'S STETHOSCOPE, PHOTOS OF THE BOYS...
THANK YOU.
ALFRED. IT'S ALL COMING TO A HEAD. I... YOU SHOULDN'T BE AROUND ME.
OH, WHAT UTTER NONSENSE.
I APPRECIATE THE NOBLE SELF-SACRIFICING GESTURE, SIR.
BUT I'M AFRAID YOU CAN'T LEAVE ME--
--I'M THE FIRST THING ON YOUR LIST.
1. ALFRED

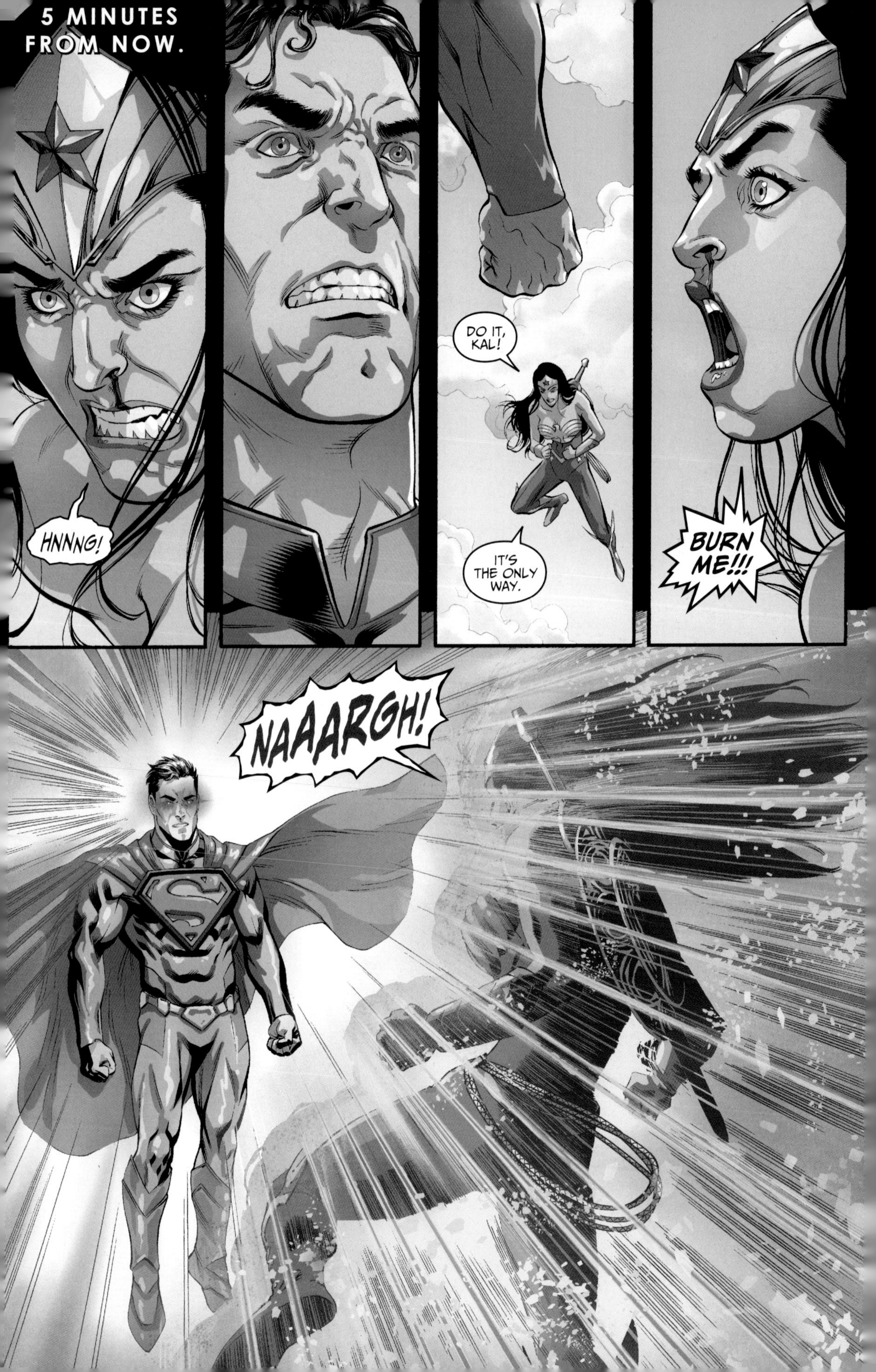
5 MINUTES FROM NOW.
HNNNG!
DO IT, KAL!
IT'S THE ONLY WAY.
BURN ME!!!
NAAARGH!

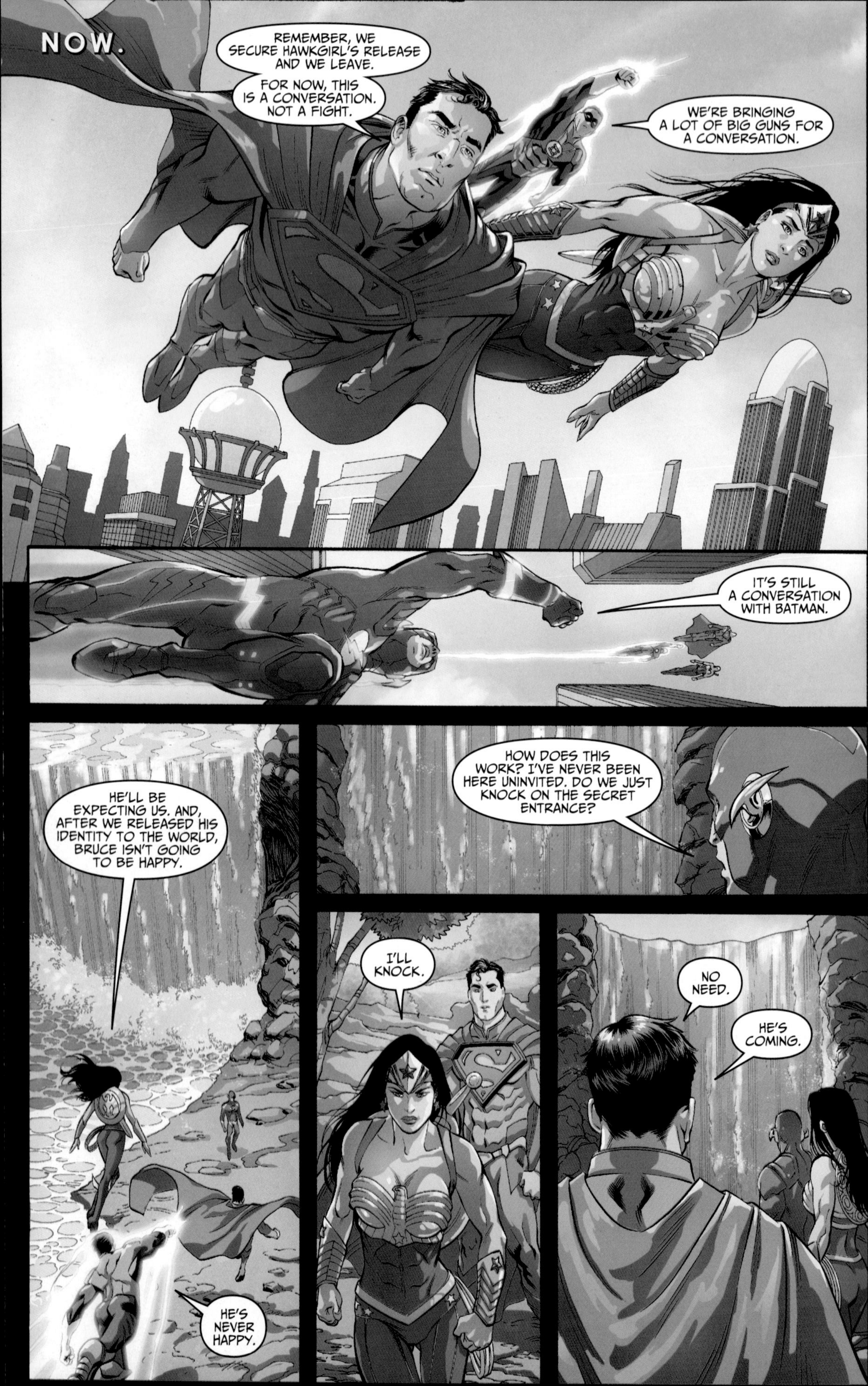
NOW.
REMEMBER, WE SECURE HAWKGIRL'S RELEASE AND WE LEAVE.
FOR NOW, THIS IS A CONVERSATION. NOT A FIGHT.
WE'RE BRINGING A LOT OF BIG GUNS FOR A CONVERSATION.
IT'S STILL A CONVERSATION WITH BATMAN.
HE'LL BE EXPECTING US. AND, AFTER WE RELEASED HIS IDENTITY TO THE WORLD, BRUCE ISN'T GOING TO BE HAPPY.
HE'S NEVER HAPPY.
HOW DOES THIS WORK? I'VE NEVER BEEN HERE UNINVITED. DO WE JUST KNOCK ON THE SECRET ENTRANCE?
I'LL KNOCK.
NO NEED.
HE'S COMING.

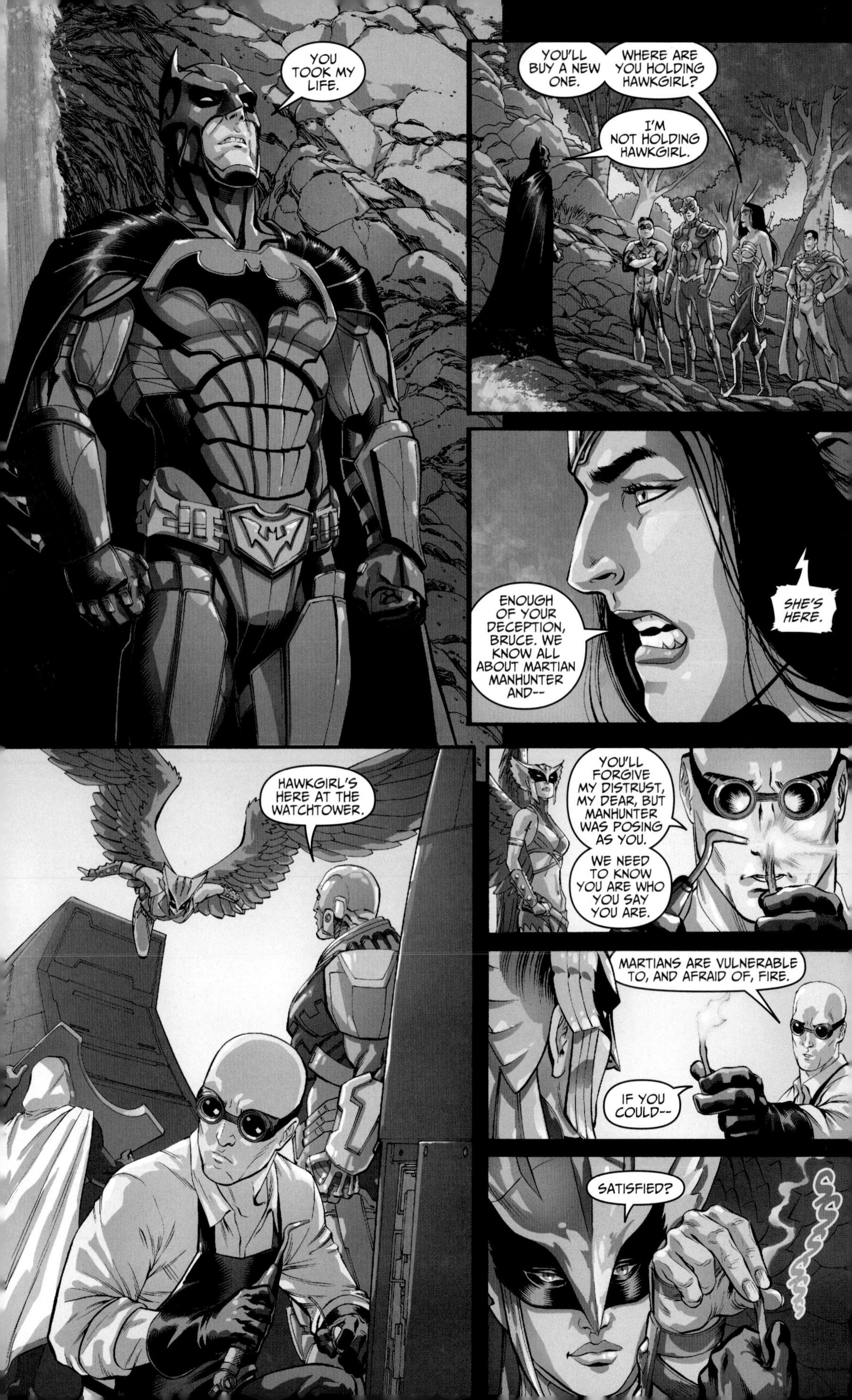
YOU TOOK MY LIFE.
YOU'LL BUY A NEW ONE.
WHERE ARE YOU HOLDING HAWKGIRL?
I'M NOT HOLDING HAWKGIRL.
ENOUGH OF YOUR DECEPTION, BRUCE. WE KNOW ALL ABOUT MARTIAN MANHUNTER AND--
SHE'S HERE.
HAWKGIRL'S HERE AT THE WATCHTOWER.
YOU'LL FORGIVE MY DISTRUST, MY DEAR, BUT MANHUNTER WAS POSING AS YOU.
WE NEED TO KNOW YOU ARE WHO YOU SAY YOU ARE.
MARTIANS ARE VULNERABLE TO, AND AFRAID OF, FIRE.
IF YOU COULD--
SATISFIED?

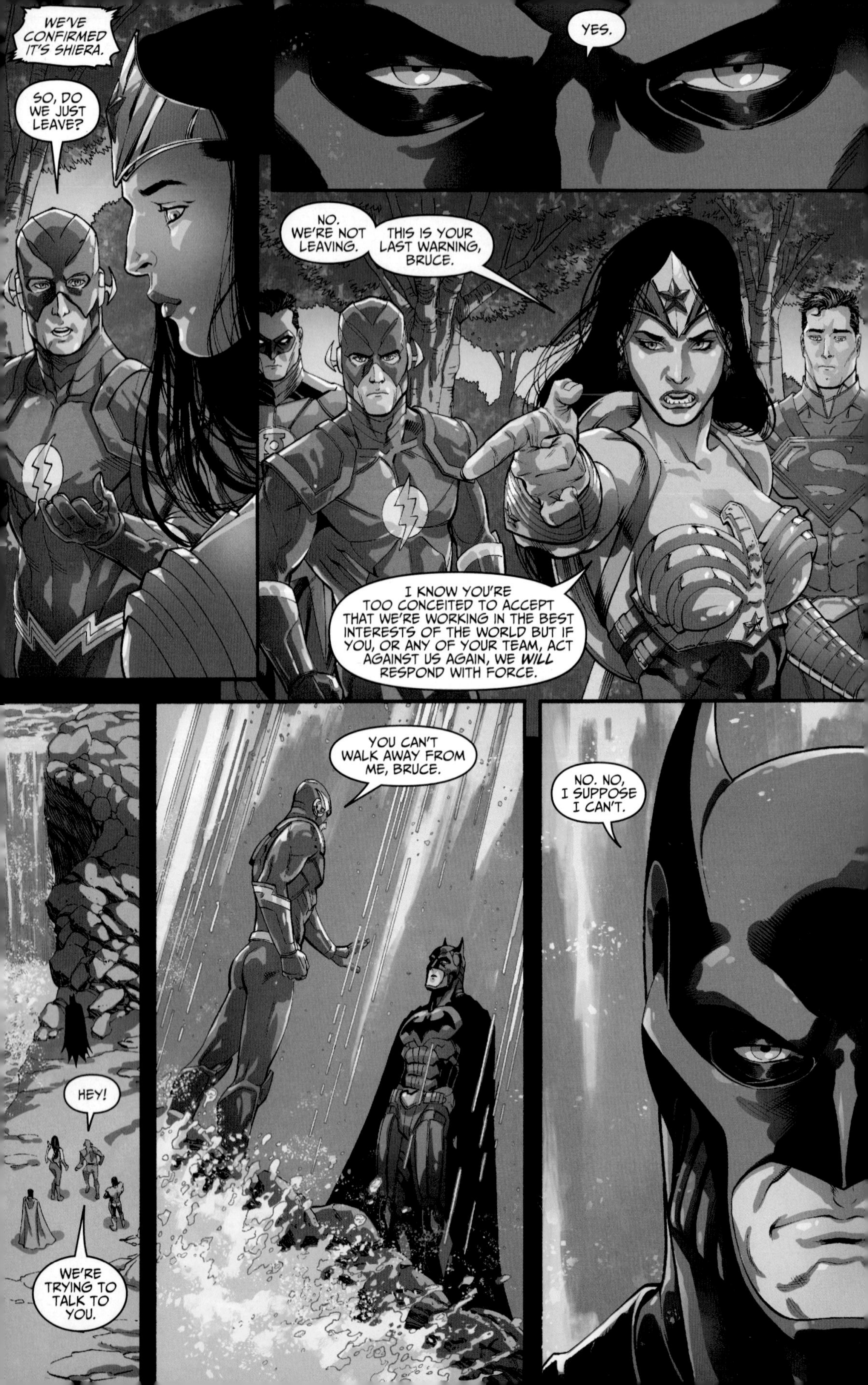
WE'VE CONFIRMED IT'S SHIERA.
SO, DO WE JUST LEAVE?
YES.
NO. WE'RE NOT LEAVING.
THIS IS YOUR LAST WARNING, BRUCE.
I KNOW YOU'RE TOO CONCEITED TO ACCEPT THAT WE'RE WORKING IN THE BEST INTERESTS OF THE WORLD BUT IF YOU, OR ANY OF YOUR TEAM, ACT AGAINST US AGAIN, WE WILL RESPOND WITH FORCE.
HEY!
WE'RE TRYING TO TALK TO YOU.
YOU CAN'T WALK AWAY FROM ME, BRUCE.
NO. NO, I SUPPOSE I CAN'T.

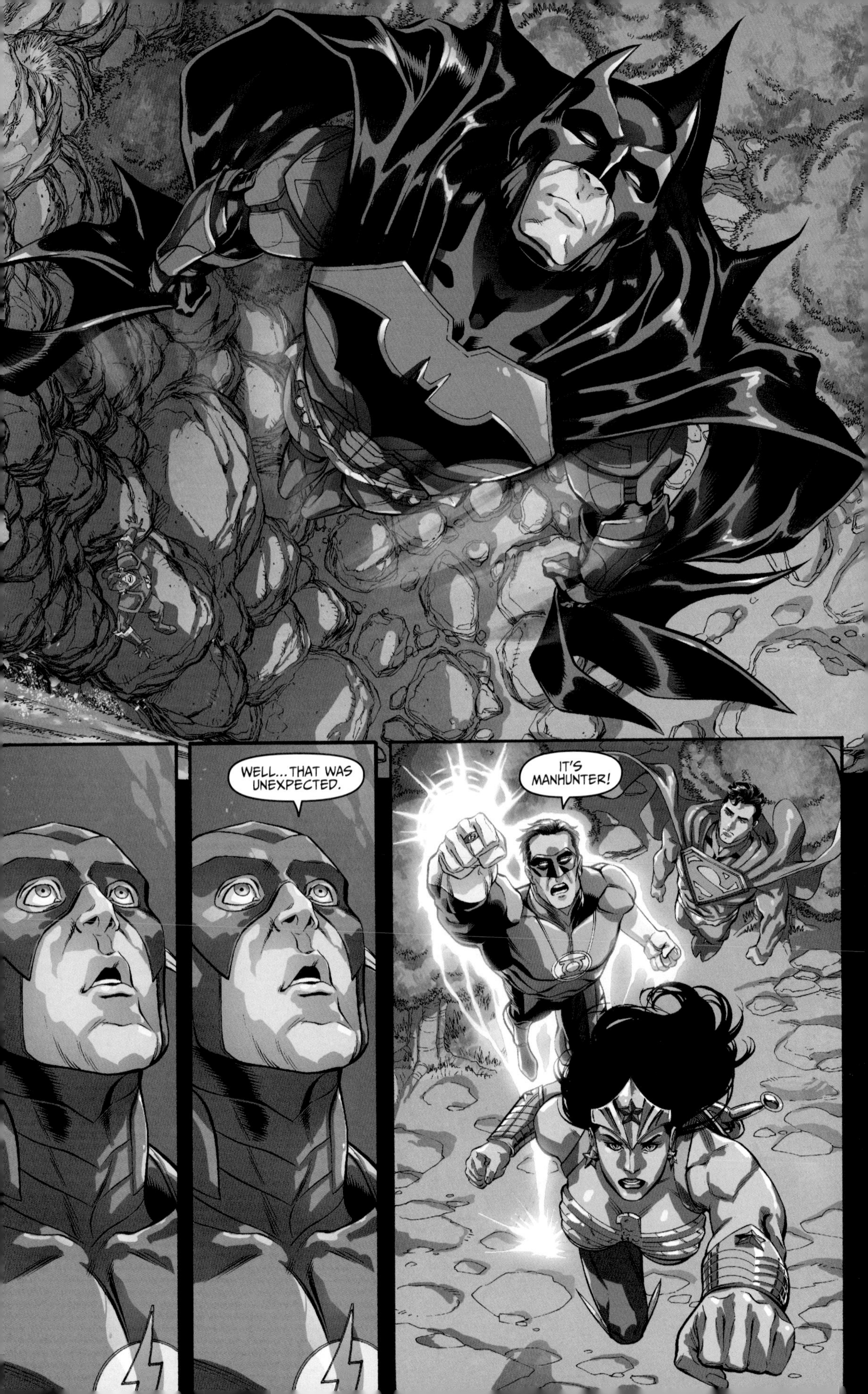
WELL...THAT WAS UNEXPECTED.
IT'S MANHUNTER!

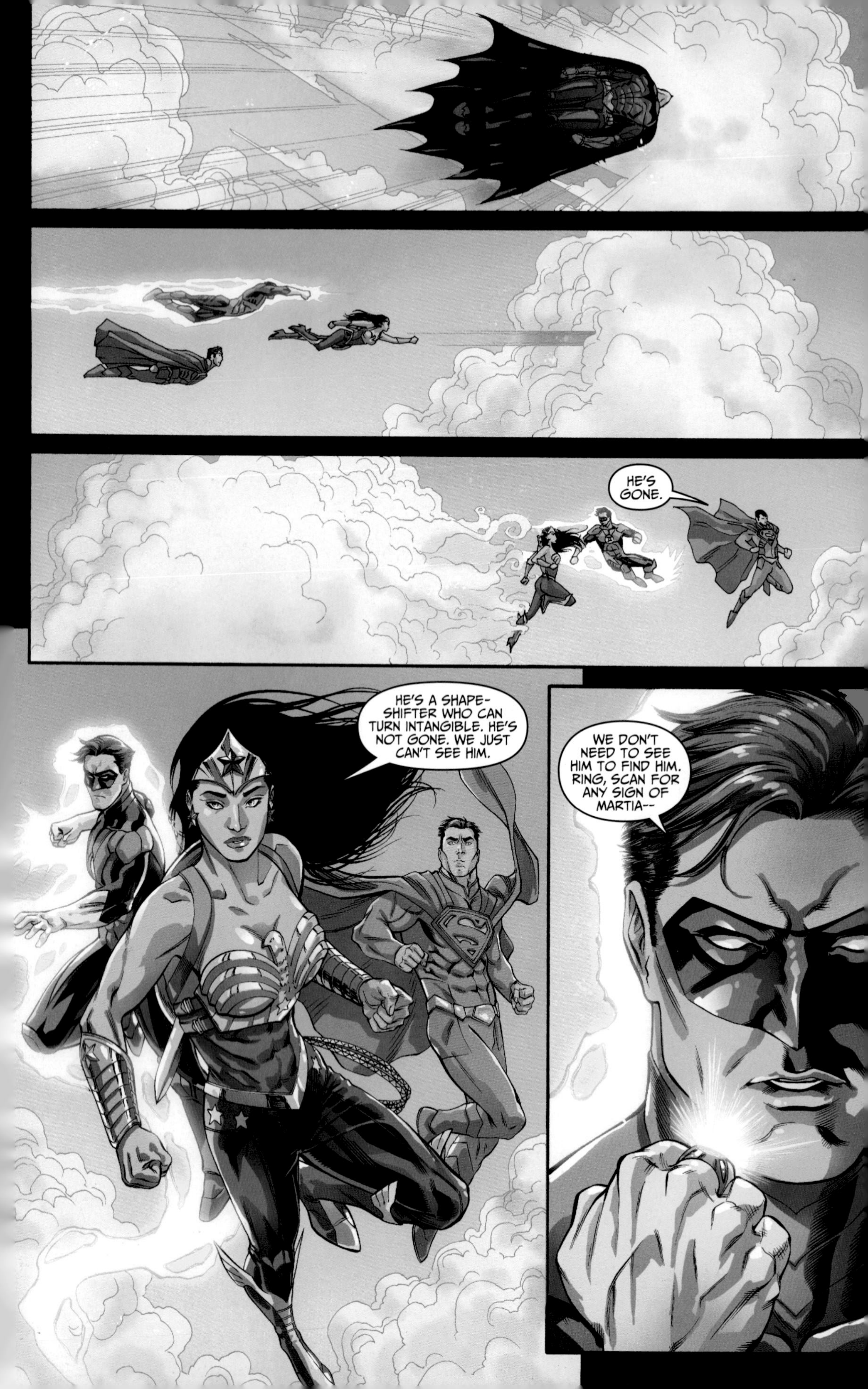
HE'S GONE.
HE'S A SHAPE-SHIFTER WHO CAN TURN INTANGIBLE. HE'S NOT GONE. WE JUST CAN'T SEE HIM.
WE DON'T NEED TO SEE HIM TO FIND HIM. RING, SCAN FOR ANY SIGN OF MARTIA--

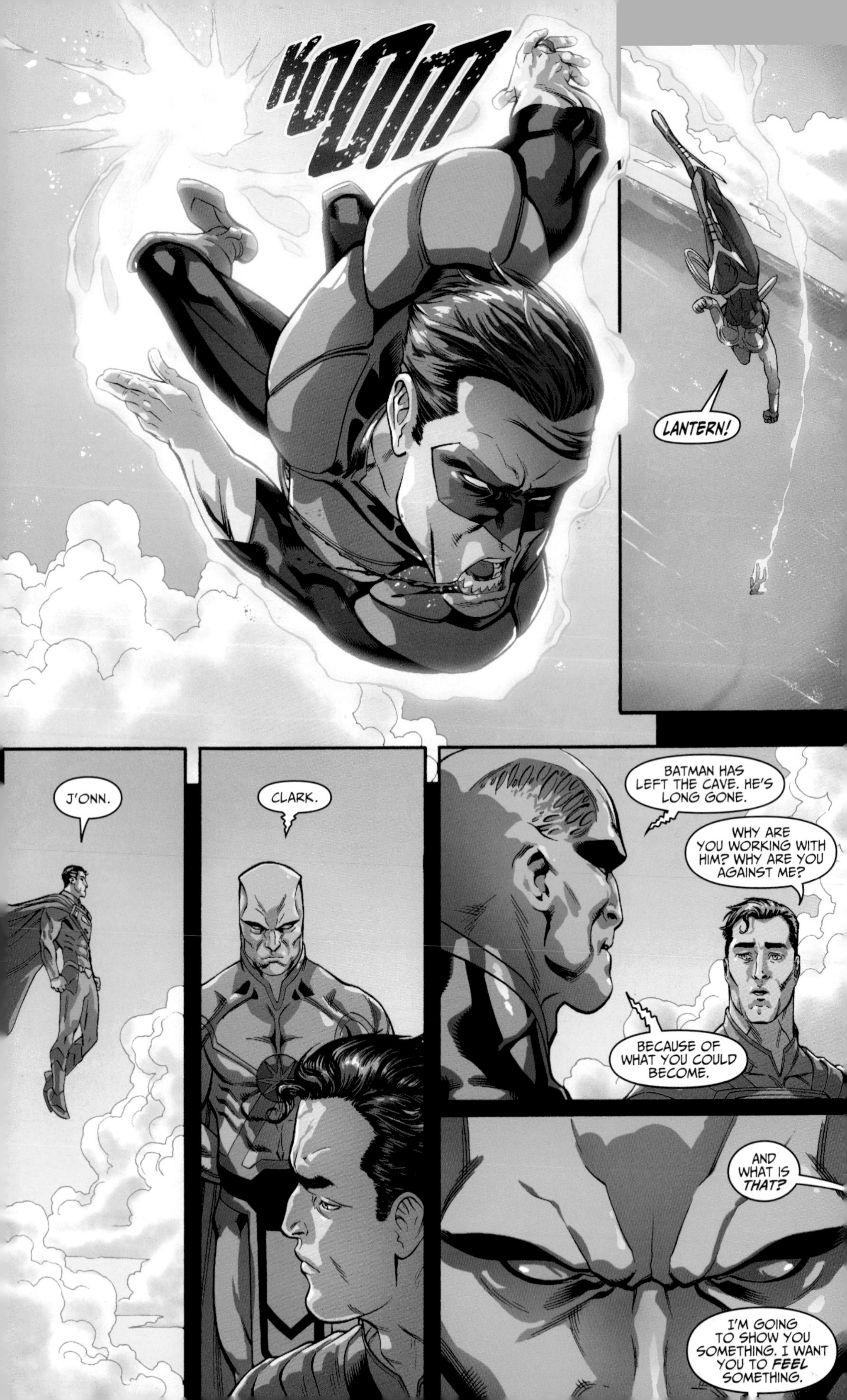
KOOM
LANTERN!
J'ONN.
CLARK.
BATMAN HAS LEFT THE CAVE. HE'S LONG GONE.
WHY ARE YOU WORKING WITH HIM? WHY ARE YOU AGAINST ME?
BECAUSE OF WHAT YOU COULD BECOME.
AND WHAT IS *THAT?*
I'M GOING TO SHOW YOU SOMETHING. I WANT YOU TO *FEEL* SOMETHING.

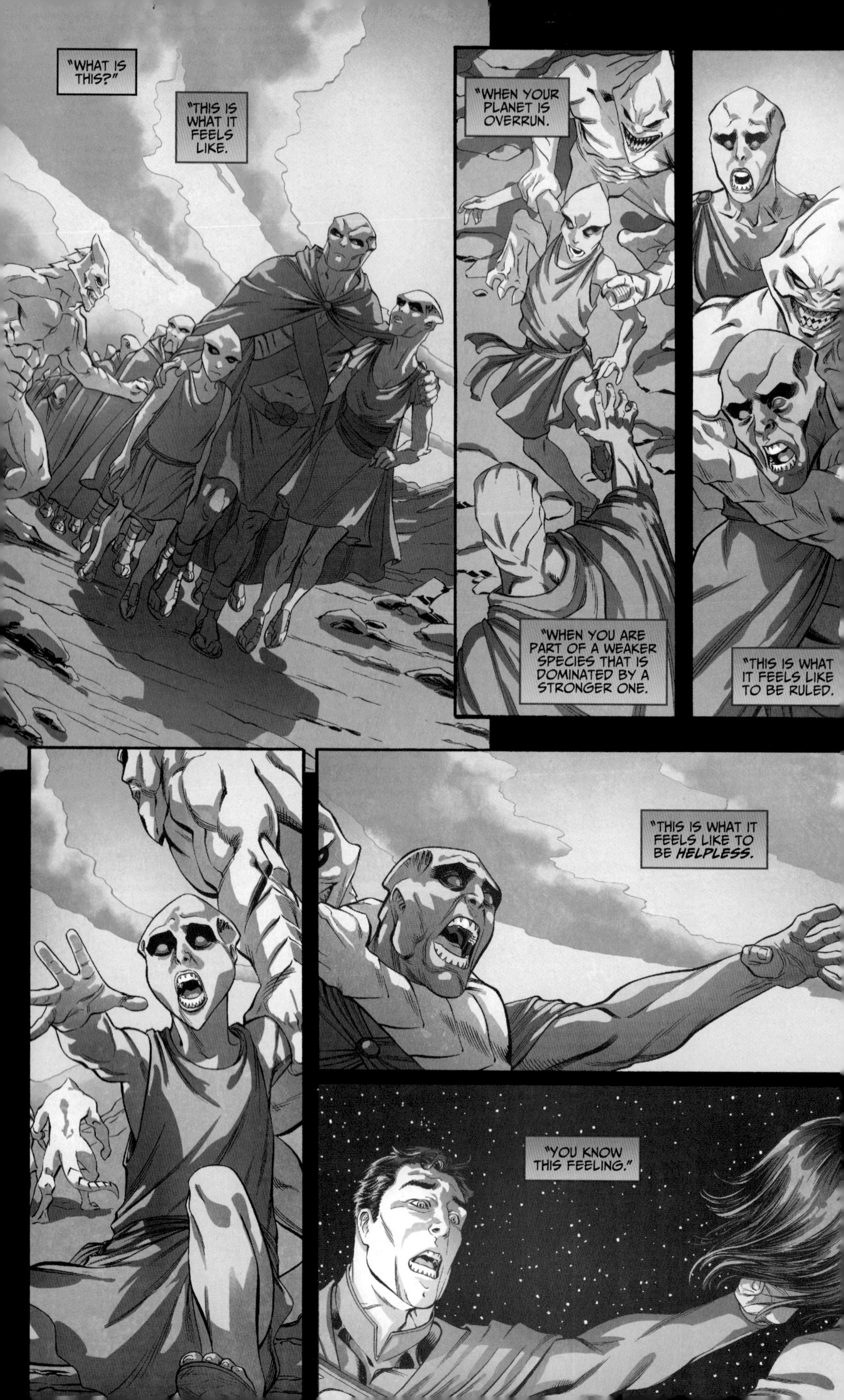
"WHAT IS THIS?"
"THIS IS WHAT IT FEELS LIKE.
"WHEN YOUR PLANET IS OVERRUN.
"WHEN YOU ARE PART OF A WEAKER SPECIES THAT IS DOMINATED BY A STRONGER ONE.
"THIS IS WHAT IT FEELS LIKE TO BE RULED.
"THIS IS WHAT IT FEELS LIKE TO BE *HELPLESS*.
"YOU KNOW THIS FEELING."

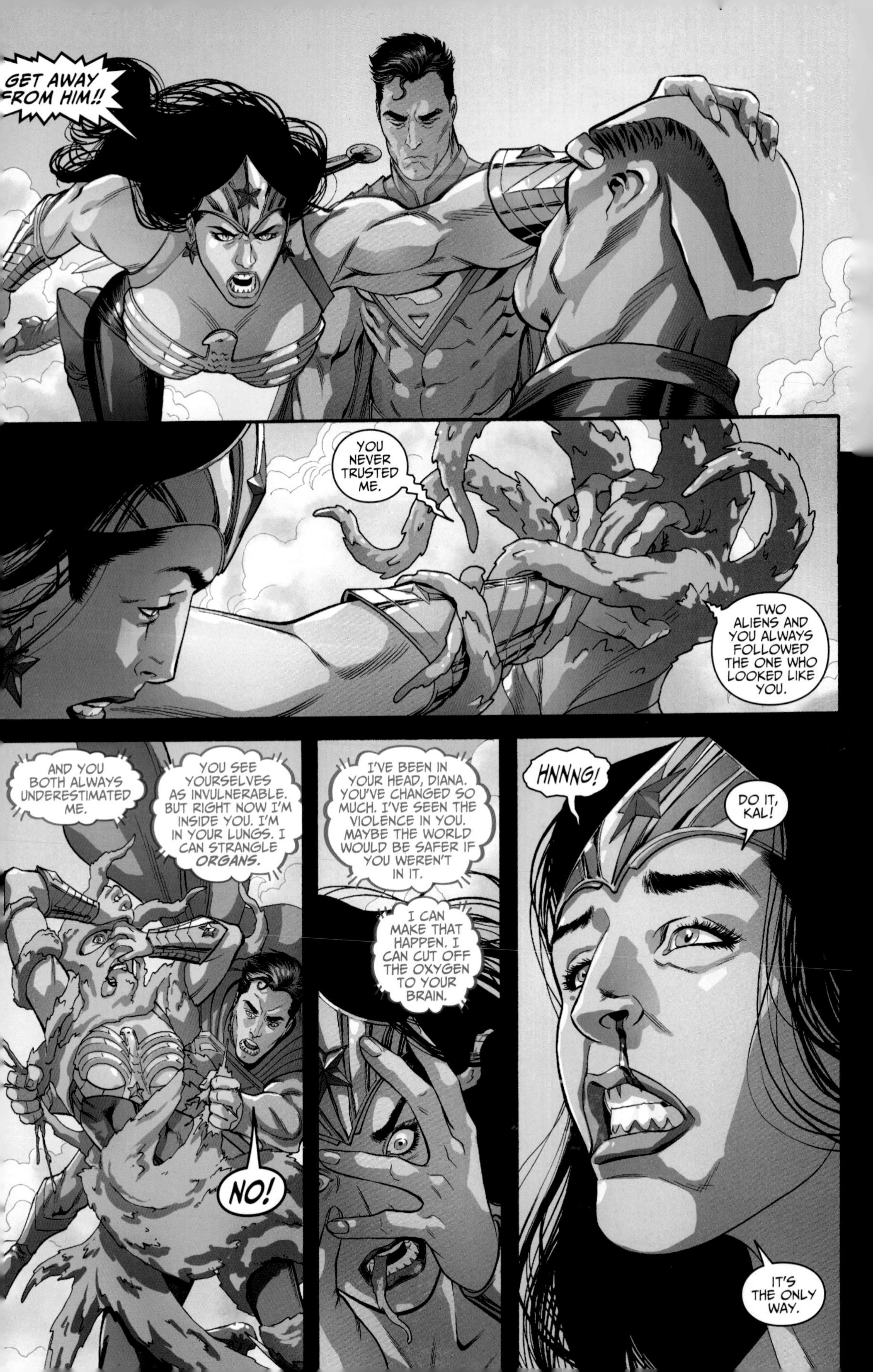
GET AWAY FROM HIM!!
YOU NEVER TRUSTED ME.
TWO ALIENS AND YOU ALWAYS FOLLOWED THE ONE WHO LOOKED LIKE YOU.
AND YOU BOTH ALWAYS UNDERESTIMATED ME.
YOU SEE YOURSELVES AS INVULNERABLE. BUT RIGHT NOW I'M INSIDE YOU. I'M IN YOUR LUNGS. I CAN STRANGLE ORGANS.
NO!
I'VE BEEN IN YOUR HEAD, DIANA. YOU'VE CHANGED SO MUCH. I'VE SEEN THE VIOLENCE IN YOU. MAYBE THE WORLD WOULD BE SAFER IF YOU WEREN'T IN IT.
I CAN MAKE THAT HAPPEN. I CAN CUT OFF THE OXYGEN TO YOUR BRAIN.
HNNNG!
DO IT, KAL!
IT'S THE ONLY WAY.

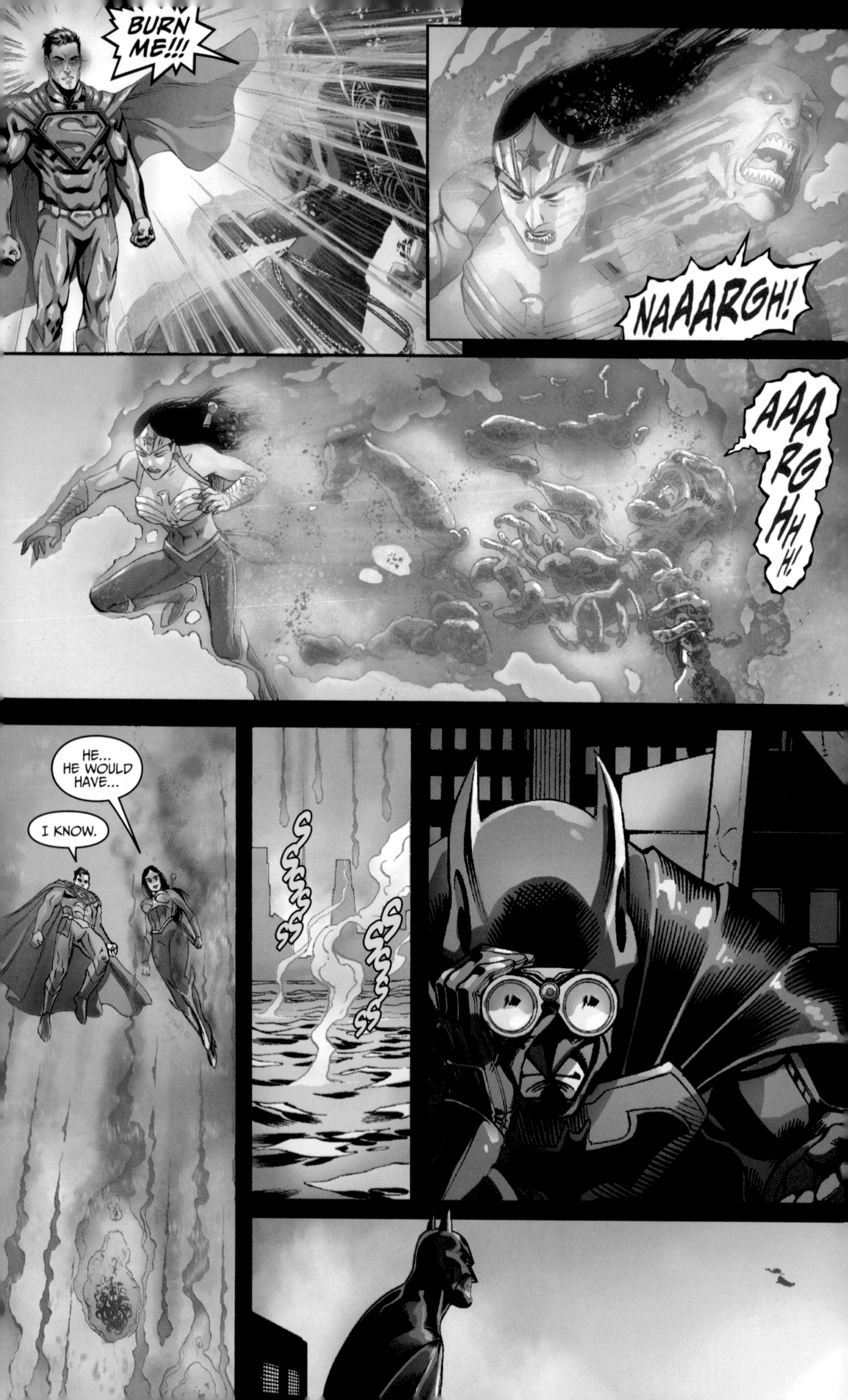

BURN ME!!!
NAAARGH!
AAAARGHHH!
HE... HE WOULD HAVE...
I KNOW.
SSSSSS
SSSSSS

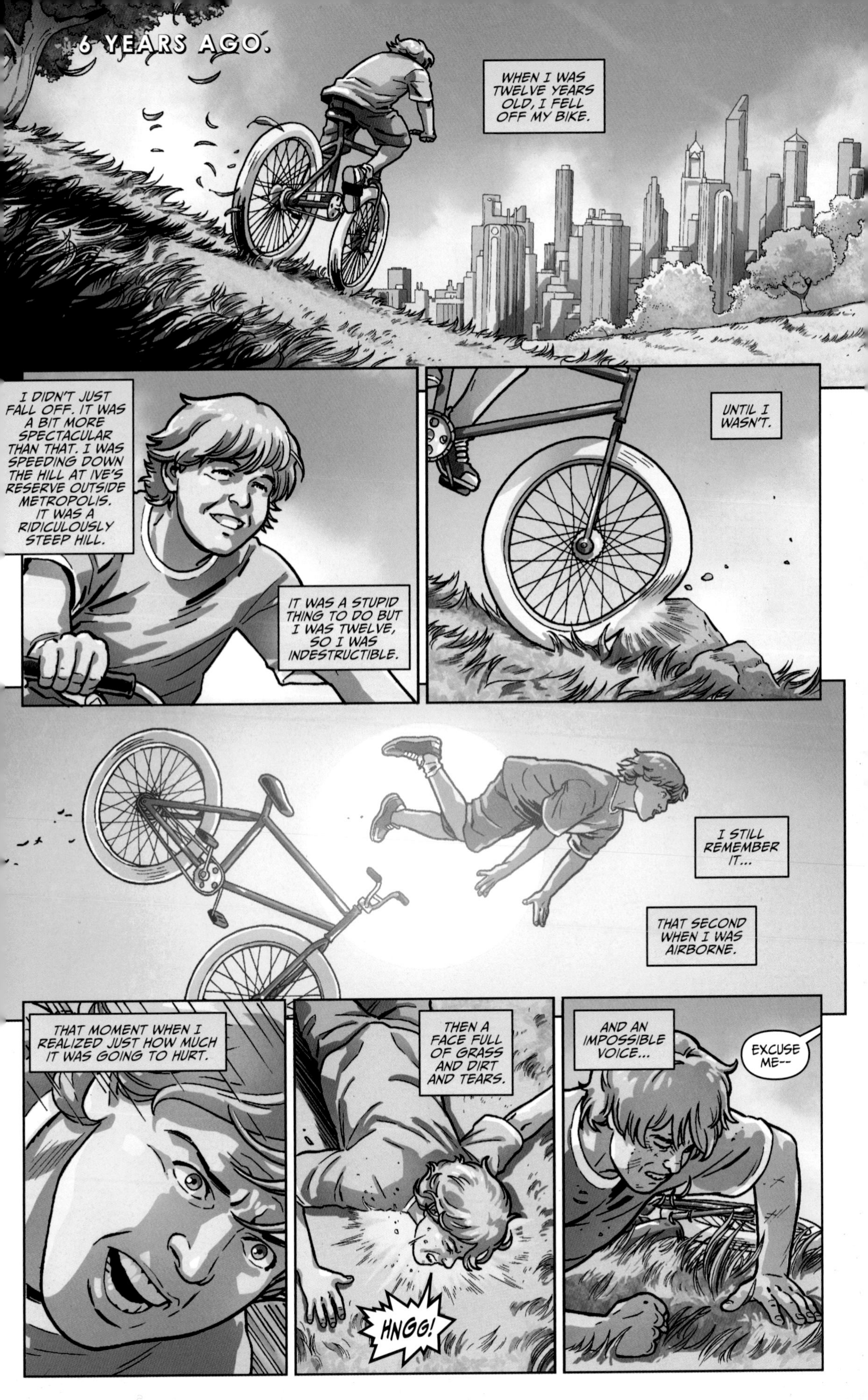
6 YEARS AGO.
WHEN I WAS TWELVE YEARS OLD, I FELL OFF MY BIKE.
I DIDN'T JUST FALL OFF. IT WAS A BIT MORE SPECTACULAR THAN THAT. I WAS SPEEDING DOWN THE HILL AT IVE'S RESERVE OUTSIDE METROPOLIS. IT WAS A RIDICULOUSLY STEEP HILL.
IT WAS A STUPID THING TO DO BUT I WAS TWELVE, SO I WAS INDESTRUCTIBLE.
UNTIL I WASN'T.
I STILL REMEMBER IT...
THAT SECOND WHEN I WAS AIRBORNE.
THAT MOMENT WHEN I REALIZED JUST HOW MUCH IT WAS GOING TO HURT.
THEN A FACE FULL OF GRASS AND DIRT AND TEARS.
HNGG!
AND AN IMPOSSIBLE VOICE...
EXCUSE ME--

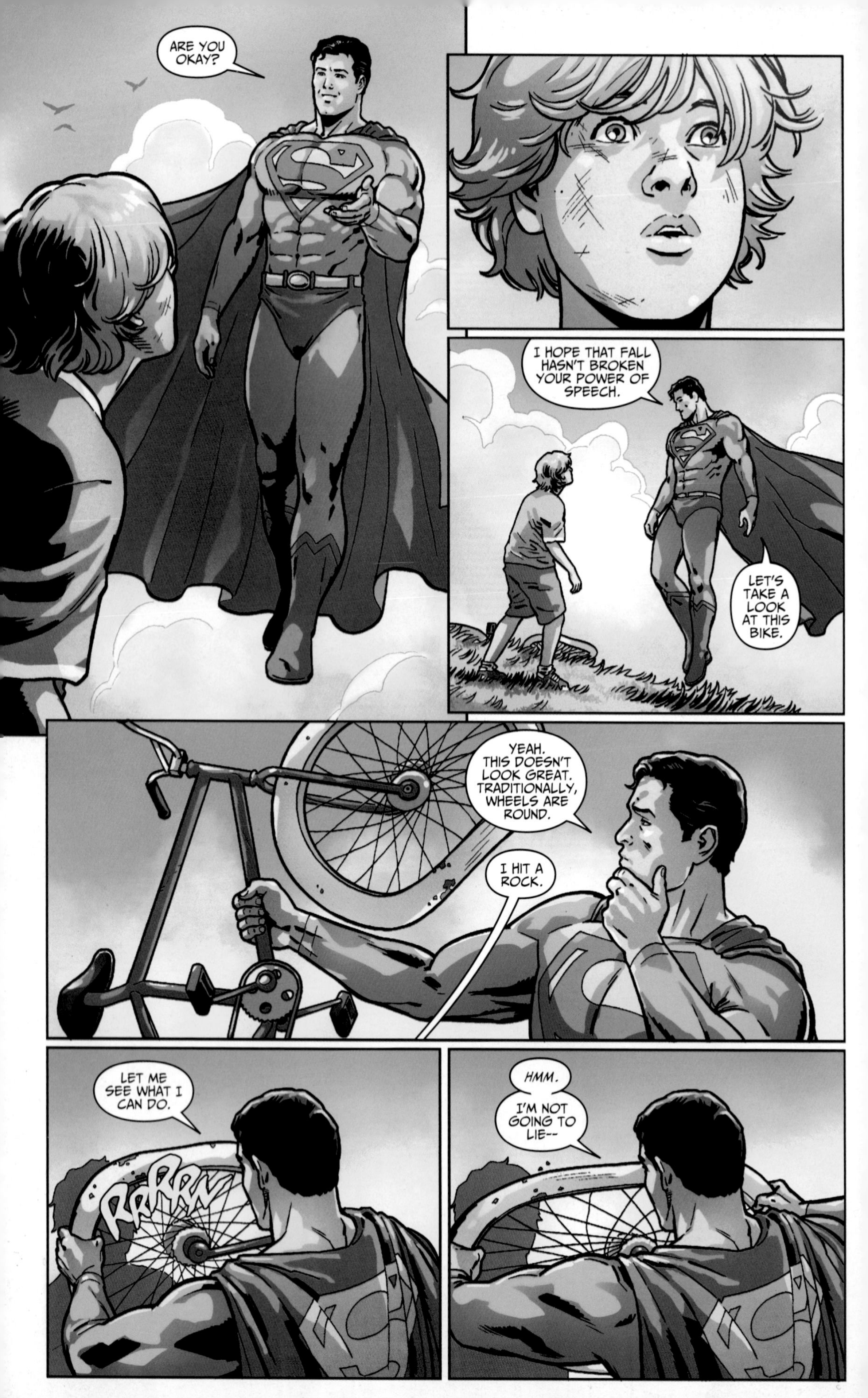
ARE YOU OKAY?
I HOPE THAT FALL HASN'T BROKEN YOUR POWER OF SPEECH.
LET'S TAKE A LOOK AT THIS BIKE.
YEAH. THIS DOESN'T LOOK GREAT. TRADITIONALLY, WHEELS ARE ROUND.
I HIT A ROCK.
LET ME SEE WHAT I CAN DO.
RRRRN
HMM.
I'M NOT GOING TO LIE--

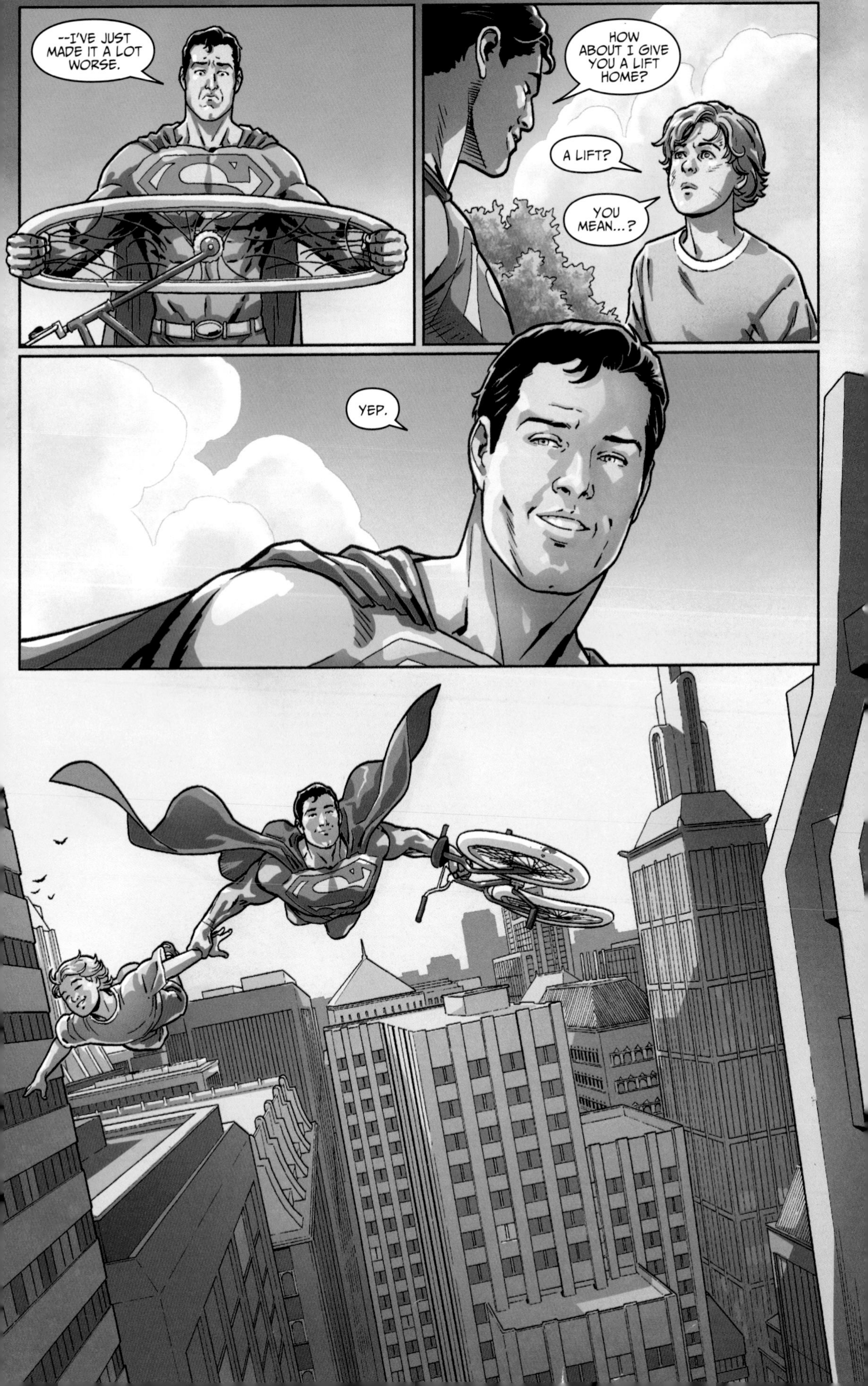
--I'VE JUST MADE IT A LOT WORSE.
HOW ABOUT I GIVE YOU A LIFT HOME?
A LIFT?
YOU MEAN...?
YEP.

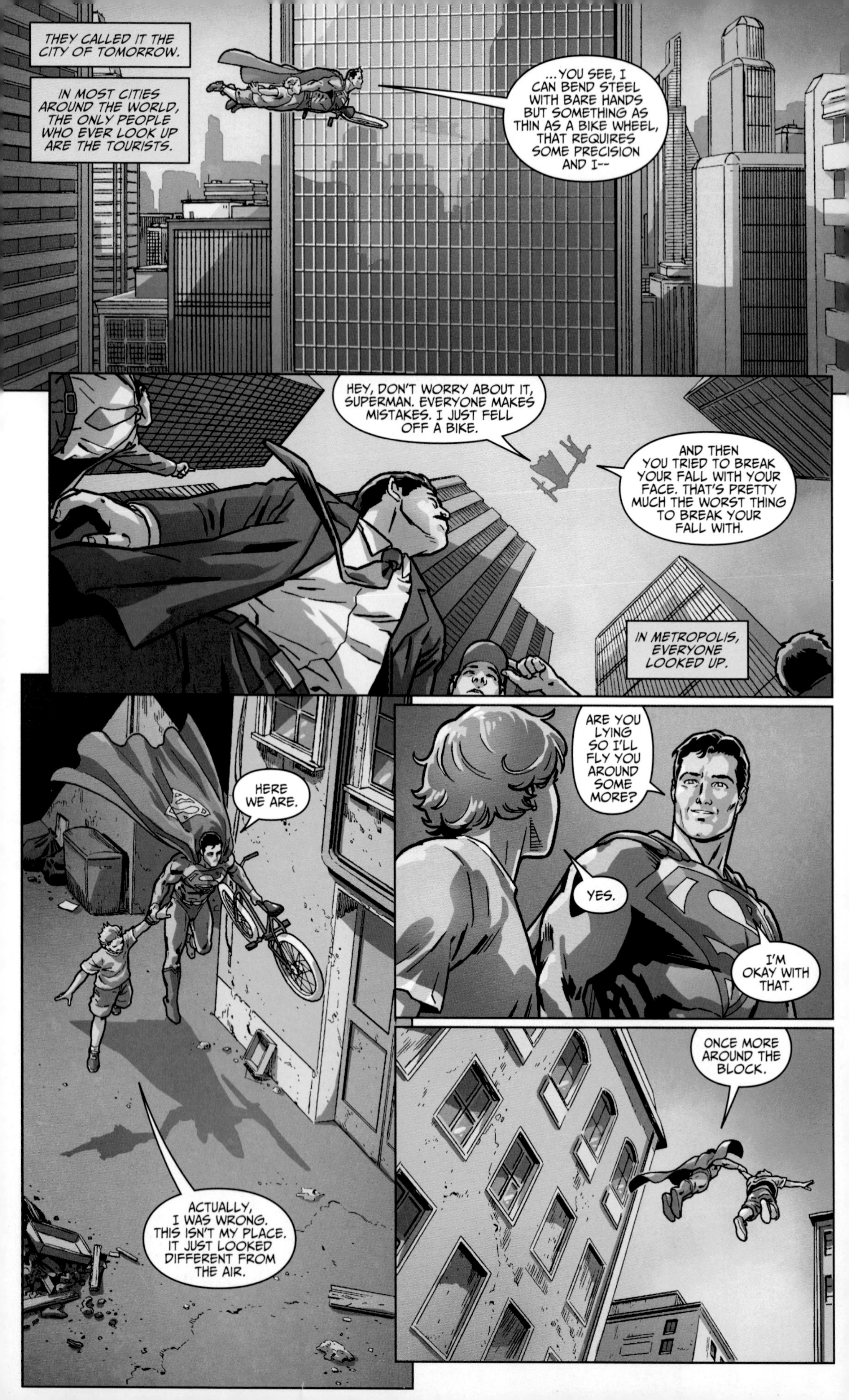

THEY CALLED IT THE CITY OF TOMORROW.
IN MOST CITIES AROUND THE WORLD, THE ONLY PEOPLE WHO EVER LOOK UP ARE THE TOURISTS.
...YOU SEE, I CAN BEND STEEL WITH BARE HANDS BUT SOMETHING AS THIN AS A BIKE WHEEL, THAT REQUIRES SOME PRECISION AND I--
HEY, DON'T WORRY ABOUT IT, SUPERMAN. EVERYONE MAKES MISTAKES. I JUST FELL OFF A BIKE.
AND THEN YOU TRIED TO BREAK YOUR FALL WITH YOUR FACE. THAT'S PRETTY MUCH THE WORST THING TO BREAK YOUR FALL WITH.
IN METROPOLIS, EVERYONE LOOKED UP.
HERE WE ARE.
ACTUALLY, I WAS WRONG. THIS ISN'T MY PLACE. IT JUST LOOKED DIFFERENT FROM THE AIR.
ARE YOU LYING SO I'LL FLY YOU AROUND SOME MORE?
YES.
I'M OKAY WITH THAT.
ONCE MORE AROUND THE BLOCK.

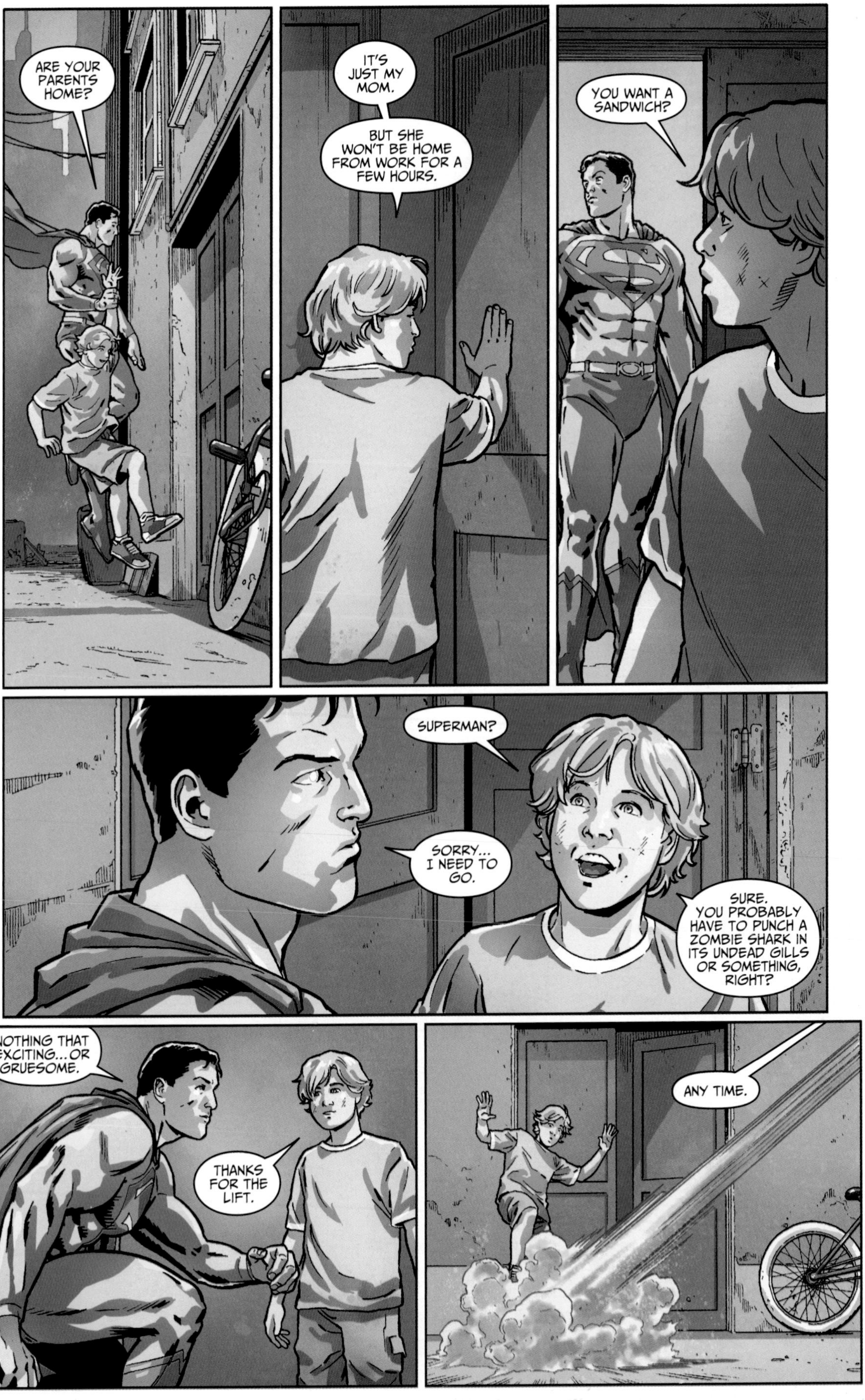
ARE YOUR PARENTS HOME?
IT'S JUST MY MOM.
BUT SHE WON'T BE HOME FROM WORK FOR A FEW HOURS.
YOU WANT A SANDWICH?
SUPERMAN?
SORRY... I NEED TO GO.
SURE. YOU PROBABLY HAVE TO PUNCH A ZOMBIE SHARK IN ITS UNDEAD GILLS OR SOMETHING, RIGHT?
NOTHING THAT EXCITING...OR GRUESOME.
THANKS FOR THE LIFT.
ANY TIME.

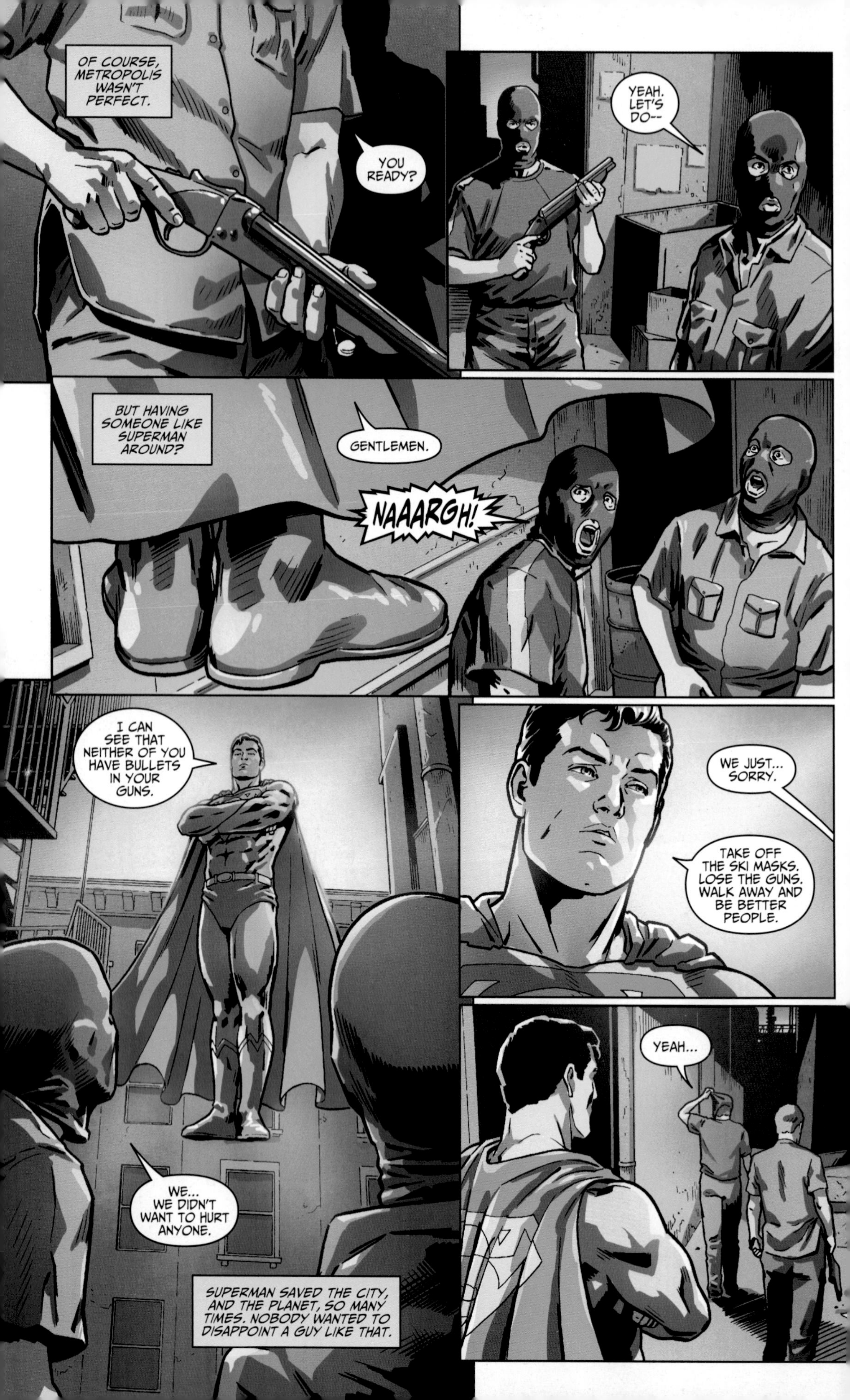
OF COURSE, METROPOLIS WASN'T PERFECT.
YOU READY?
YEAH. LET'S DO--
BUT HAVING SOMEONE LIKE SUPERMAN AROUND?
GENTLEMEN.
NAAARGH!
I CAN SEE THAT NEITHER OF YOU HAVE BULLETS IN YOUR GUNS.
WE... WE DIDN'T WANT TO HURT ANYONE.
SUPERMAN SAVED THE CITY, AND THE PLANET, SO MANY TIMES. NOBODY WANTED TO DISAPPOINT A GUY LIKE THAT.
WE JUST... SORRY.
TAKE OFF THE SKI MASKS. LOSE THE GUNS. WALK AWAY AND BE BETTER PEOPLE.
YEAH...

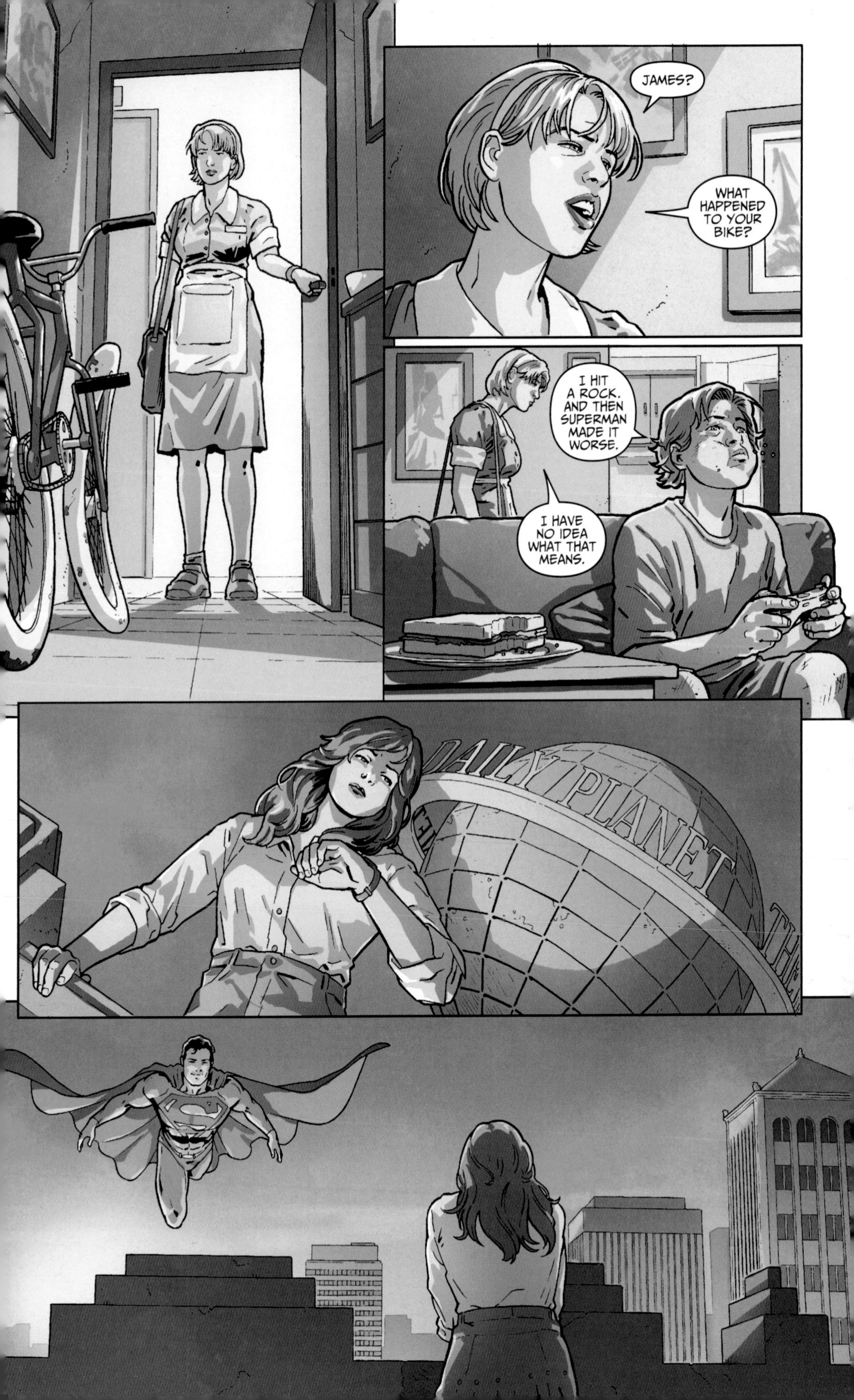
JAMES?
WHAT HAPPENED TO YOUR BIKE?
I HIT A ROCK. AND THEN SUPERMAN MADE IT WORSE.
I HAVE NO IDEA WHAT THAT MEANS.
DAILY PLANET

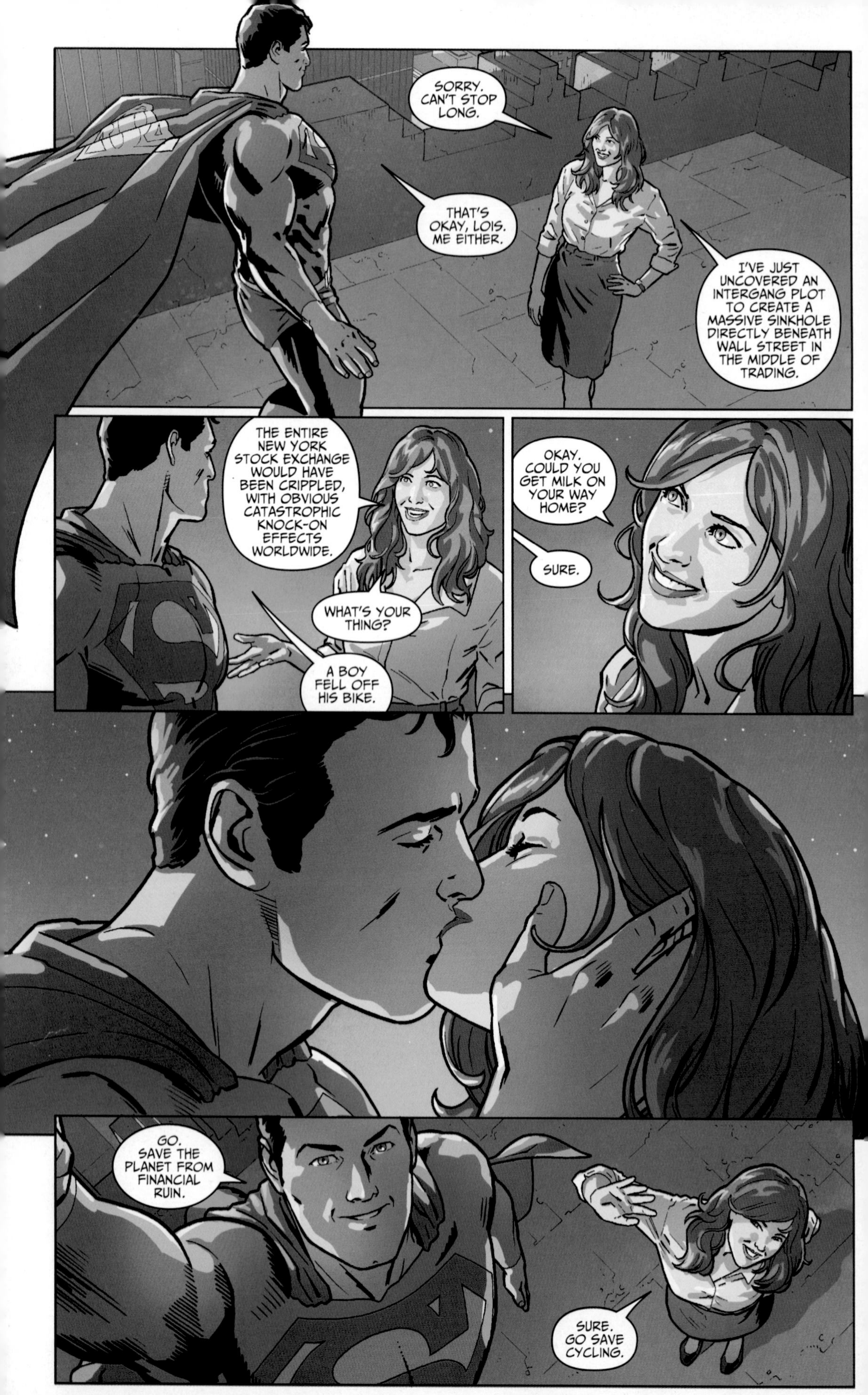
SORRY. CAN'T STOP LONG.
THAT'S OKAY, LOIS. ME EITHER.
I'VE JUST UNCOVERED AN INTERGANG PLOT TO CREATE A MASSIVE SINKHOLE DIRECTLY BENEATH WALL STREET IN THE MIDDLE OF TRADING.
THE ENTIRE NEW YORK STOCK EXCHANGE WOULD HAVE BEEN CRIPPLED, WITH OBVIOUS CATASTROPHIC KNOCK-ON EFFECTS WORLDWIDE.
WHAT'S YOUR THING?
A BOY FELL OFF HIS BIKE.
OKAY. COULD YOU GET MILK ON YOUR WAY HOME?
SURE.
GO. SAVE THE PLANET FROM FINANCIAL RUIN.
SURE. GO SAVE CYCLING.

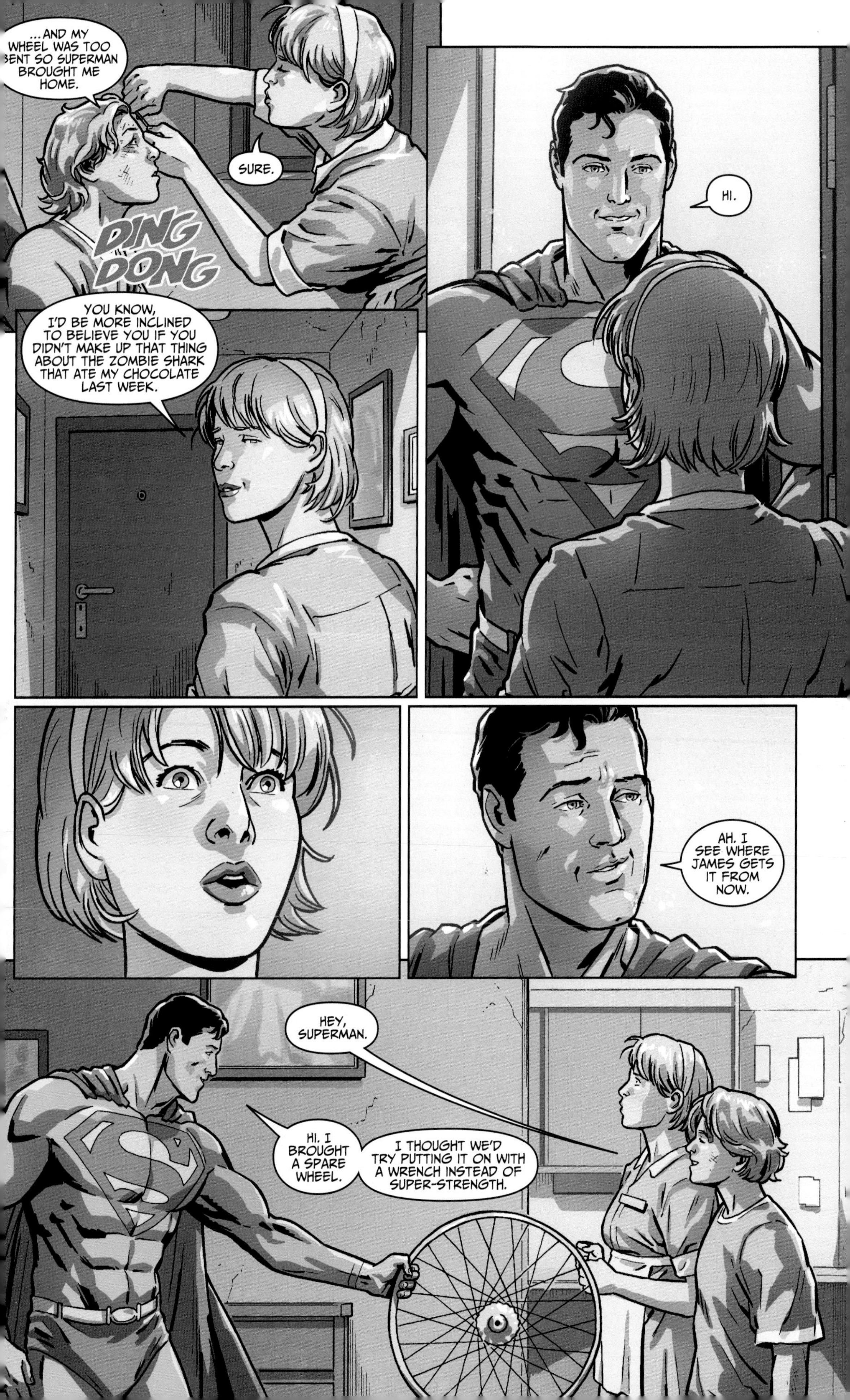
...AND MY WHEEL WAS TOO BENT SO SUPERMAN BROUGHT ME HOME.
SURE.
DING DONG
HI.
YOU KNOW, I'D BE MORE INCLINED TO BELIEVE YOU IF YOU DIDN'T MAKE UP THAT THING ABOUT THE ZOMBIE SHARK THAT ATE MY CHOCOLATE LAST WEEK.
AH. I SEE WHERE JAMES GETS IT FROM NOW.
HEY, SUPERMAN.
HI. I BROUGHT A SPARE WHEEL.
I THOUGHT WE'D TRY PUTTING IT ON WITH A WRENCH INSTEAD OF SUPER-STRENGTH.

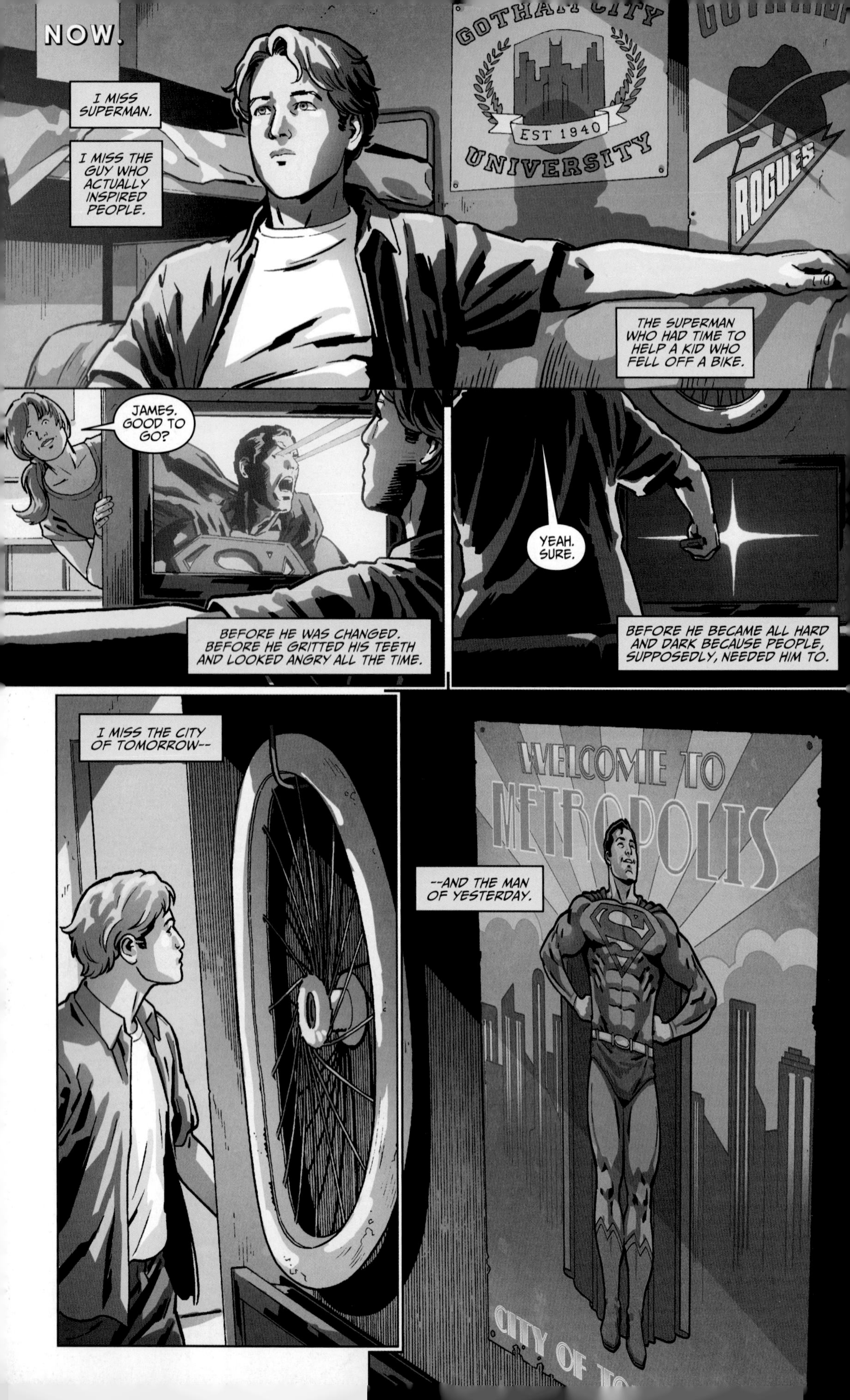
NOW.
I MISS SUPERMAN.
I MISS THE GUY WHO ACTUALLY INSPIRED PEOPLE.
GOTHAM CITY EST 1940 UNIVERSITY
ROGUES
THE SUPERMAN WHO HAD TIME TO HELP A KID WHO FELL OFF A BIKE.
JAMES. GOOD TO GO?
BEFORE HE WAS CHANGED. BEFORE HE GRITTED HIS TEETH AND LOOKED ANGRY ALL THE TIME.
YEAH. SURE.
BEFORE HE BECAME ALL HARD AND DARK BECAUSE PEOPLE, SUPPOSEDLY, NEEDED HIM TO.
I MISS THE CITY OF TOMORROW--
WELCOME TO METROPOLIS
--AND THE MAN OF YESTERDAY.

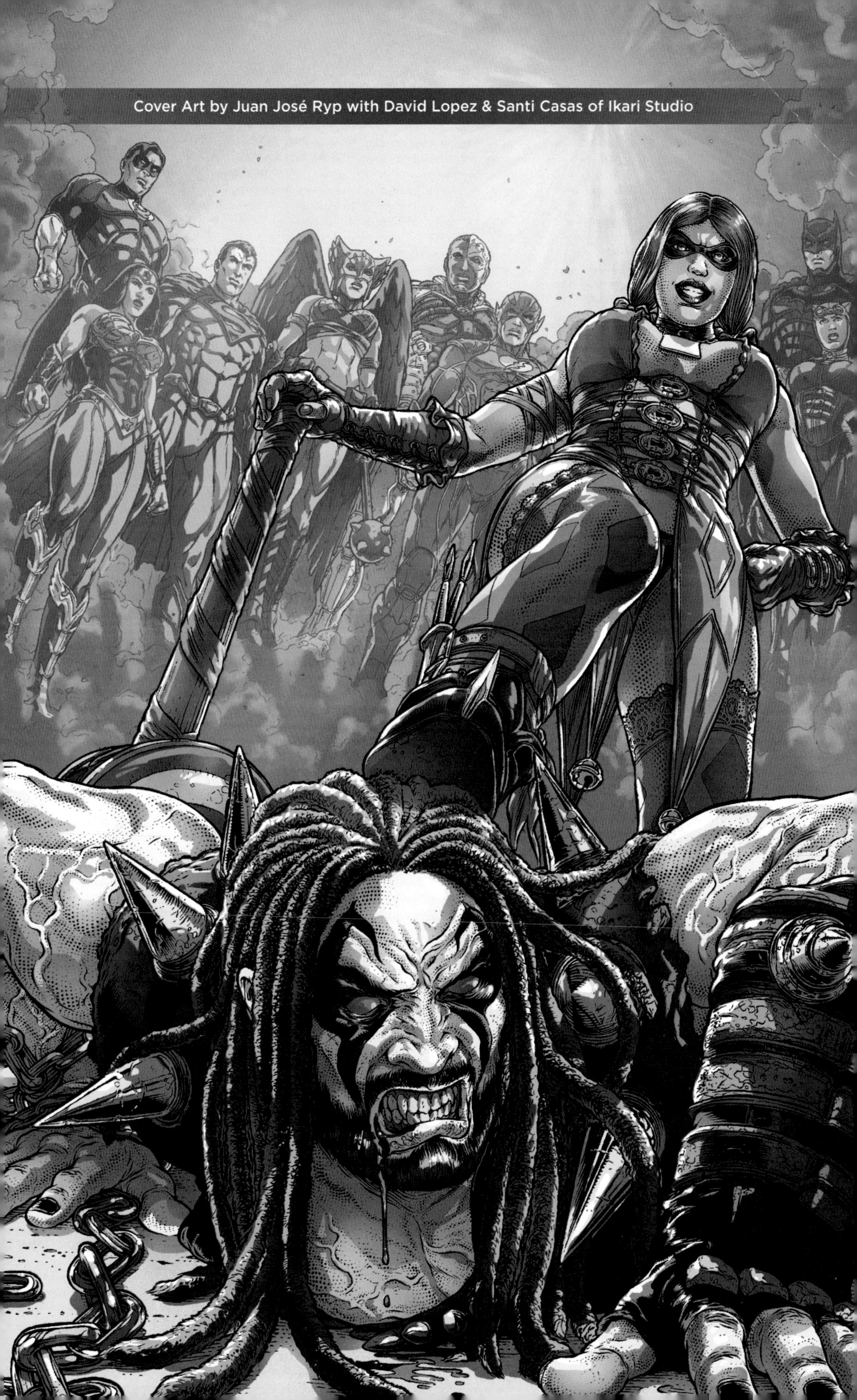

Cover Art by Juan José Ryp with David Lopez & Santi Casas of Ikari Studio

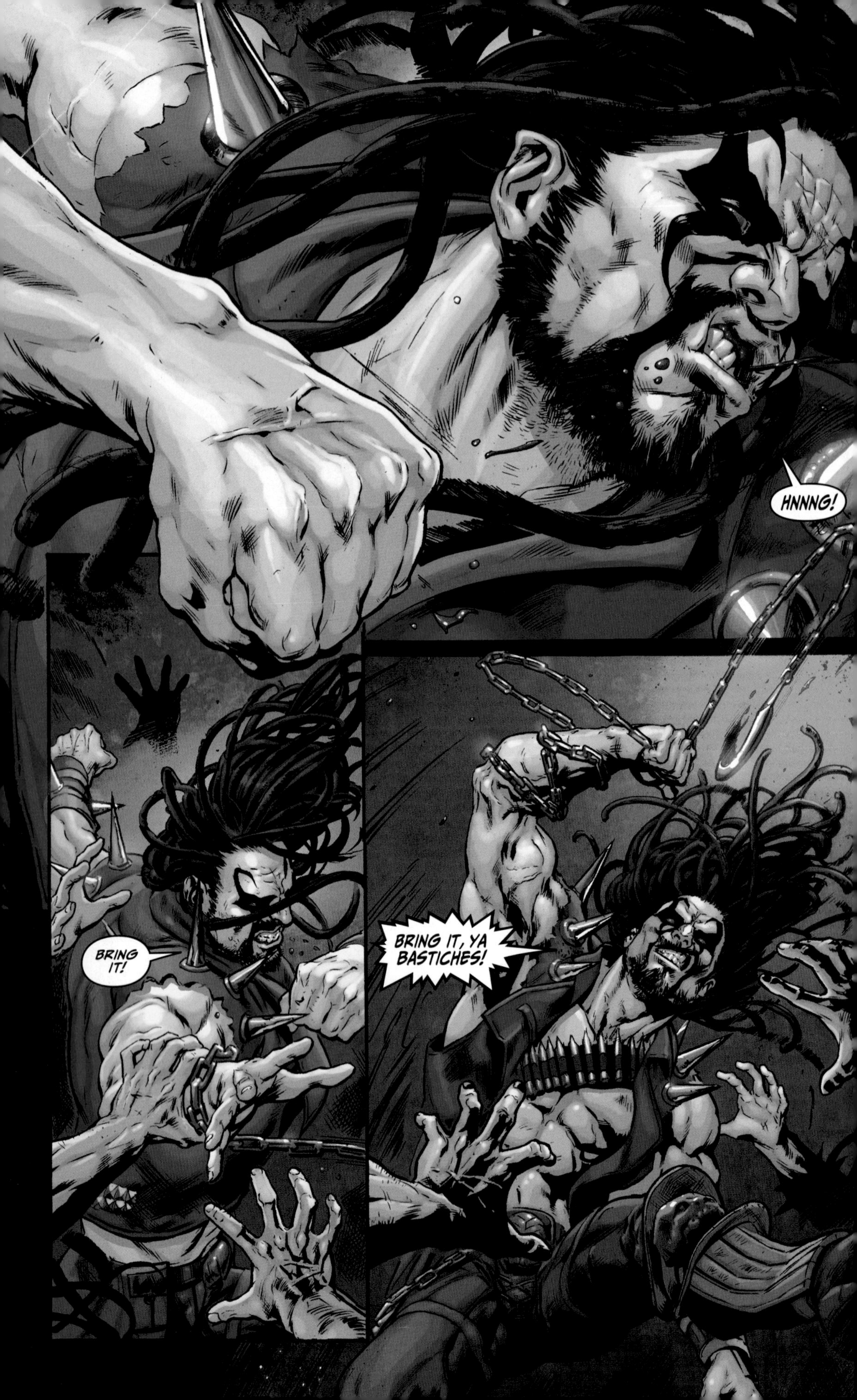
HNNNG!
BRING IT!
BRING IT, YA BASTICHES!

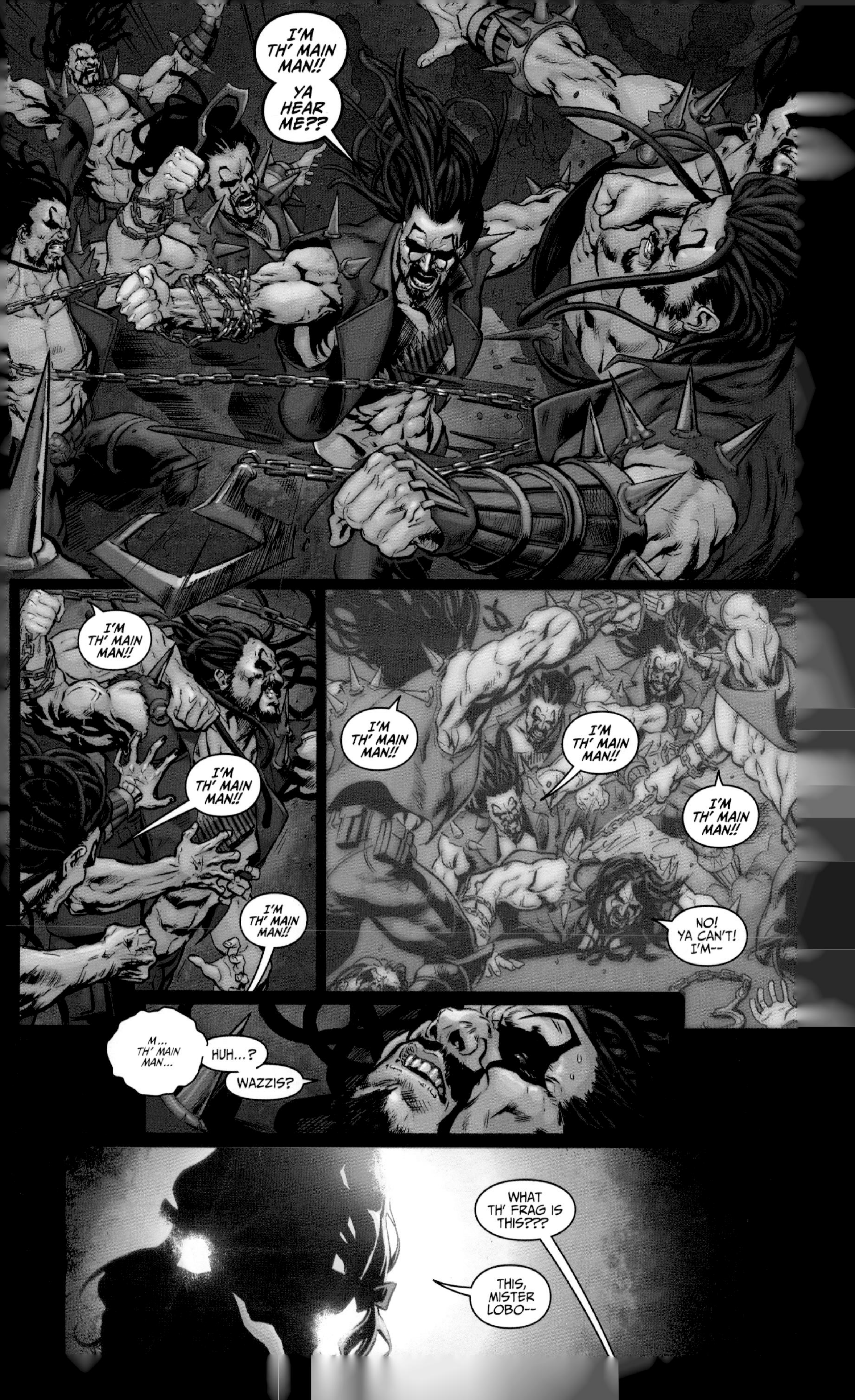
I'M TH' MAIN MAN!!
YA HEAR ME??
I'M TH' MAIN MAN!!
I'M TH' MAIN MAN!!
I'M TH' MAIN MAN!!
I'M TH' MAIN MAN!!
I'M TH' MAIN MAN!!
I'M TH' MAIN MAN!!
NO! YA CAN'T! I'M--
M... TH' MAIN MAN...
HUH...?
WAZZIS?
WHAT TH' FRAG IS THIS???
THIS, MISTER LOBO--

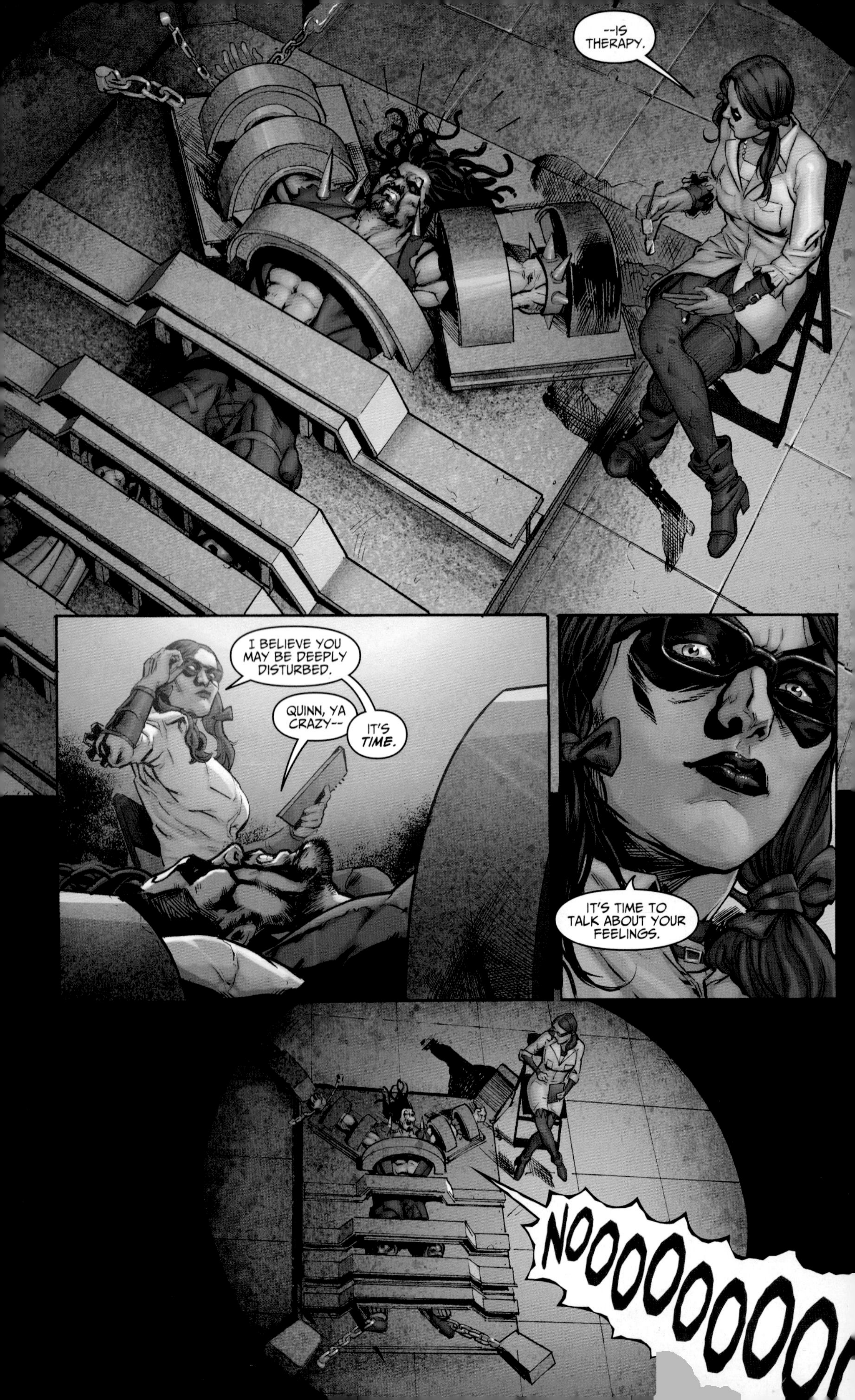
--IS THERAPY.
I BELIEVE YOU MAY BE DEEPLY DISTURBED.
QUINN, YA CRAZY--
IT'S *TIME.*
IT'S TIME TO TALK ABOUT YOUR FEELINGS.
NOOOOOOOOO

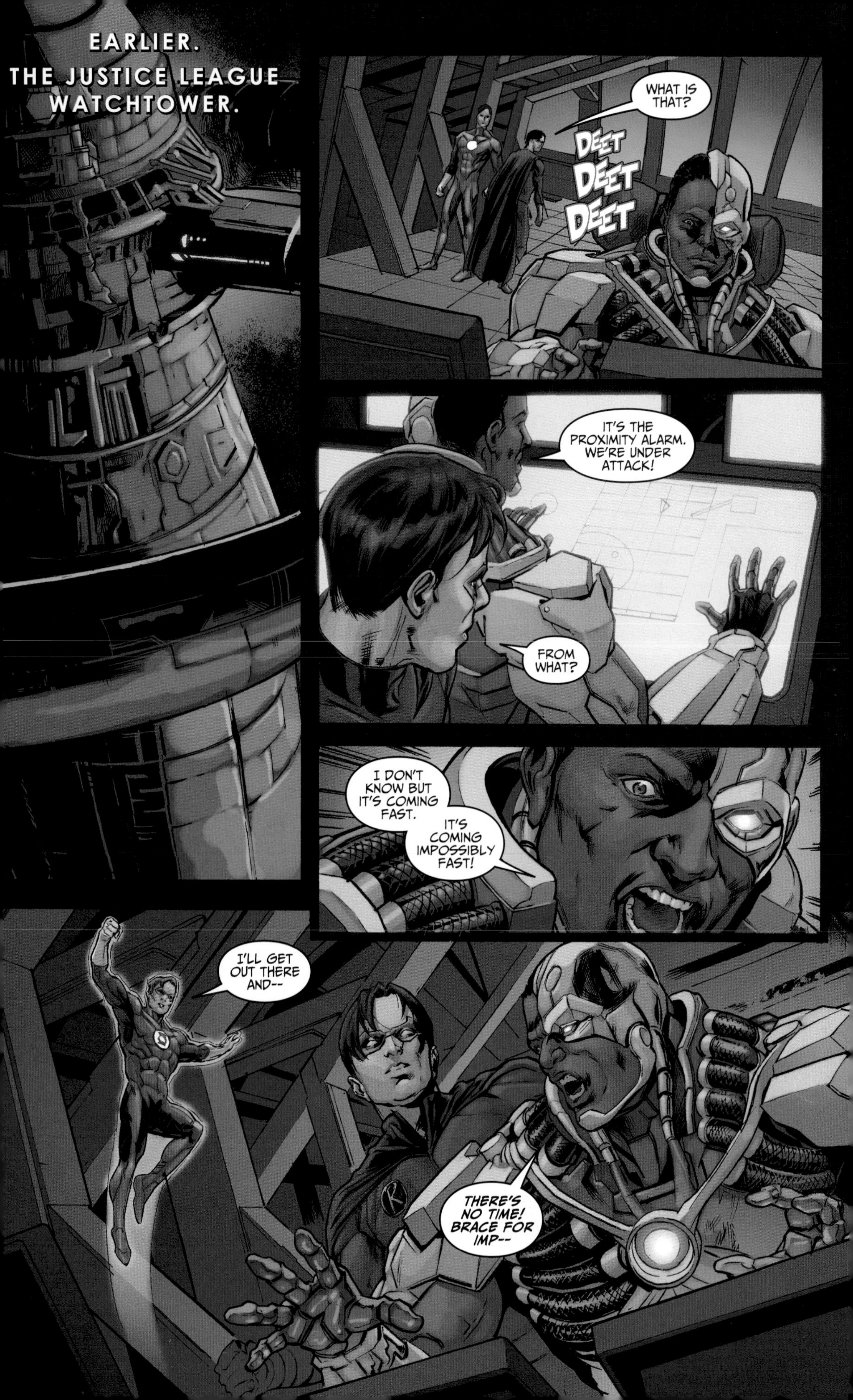
EARLIER.
THE JUSTICE LEAGUE WATCHTOWER.
WHAT IS THAT?
DEET DEET DEET
IT'S THE PROXIMITY ALARM. WE'RE UNDER ATTACK!
FROM WHAT?
I DON'T KNOW BUT IT'S COMING FAST.
IT'S COMING IMPOSSIBLY FAST!
I'LL GET OUT THERE AND--
THERE'S NO TIME! BRACE FOR IMP--

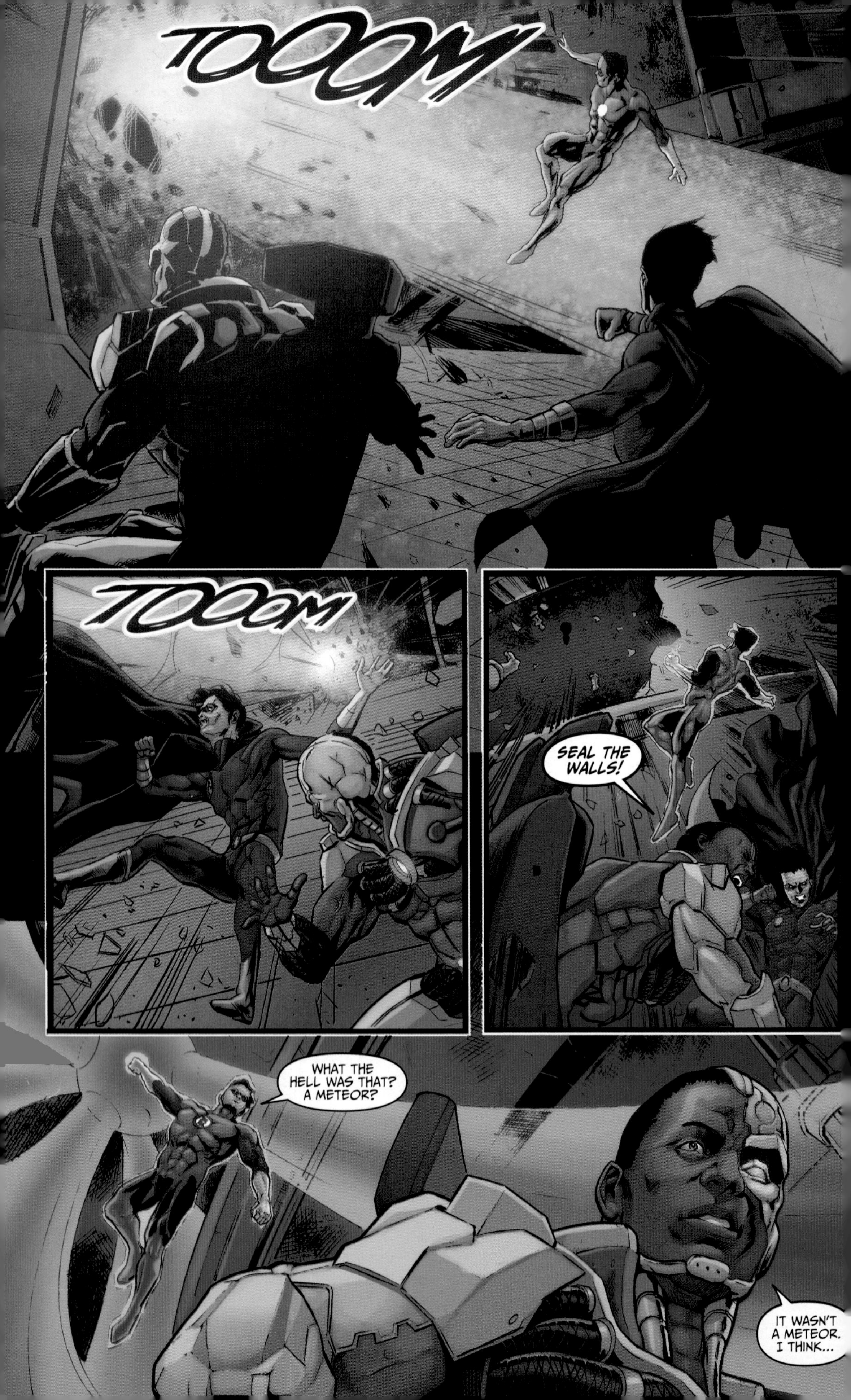
TOOOM
TOOOM
SEAL THE WALLS!
WHAT THE HELL WAS THAT? A METEOR?
IT WASN'T A METEOR. I THINK...

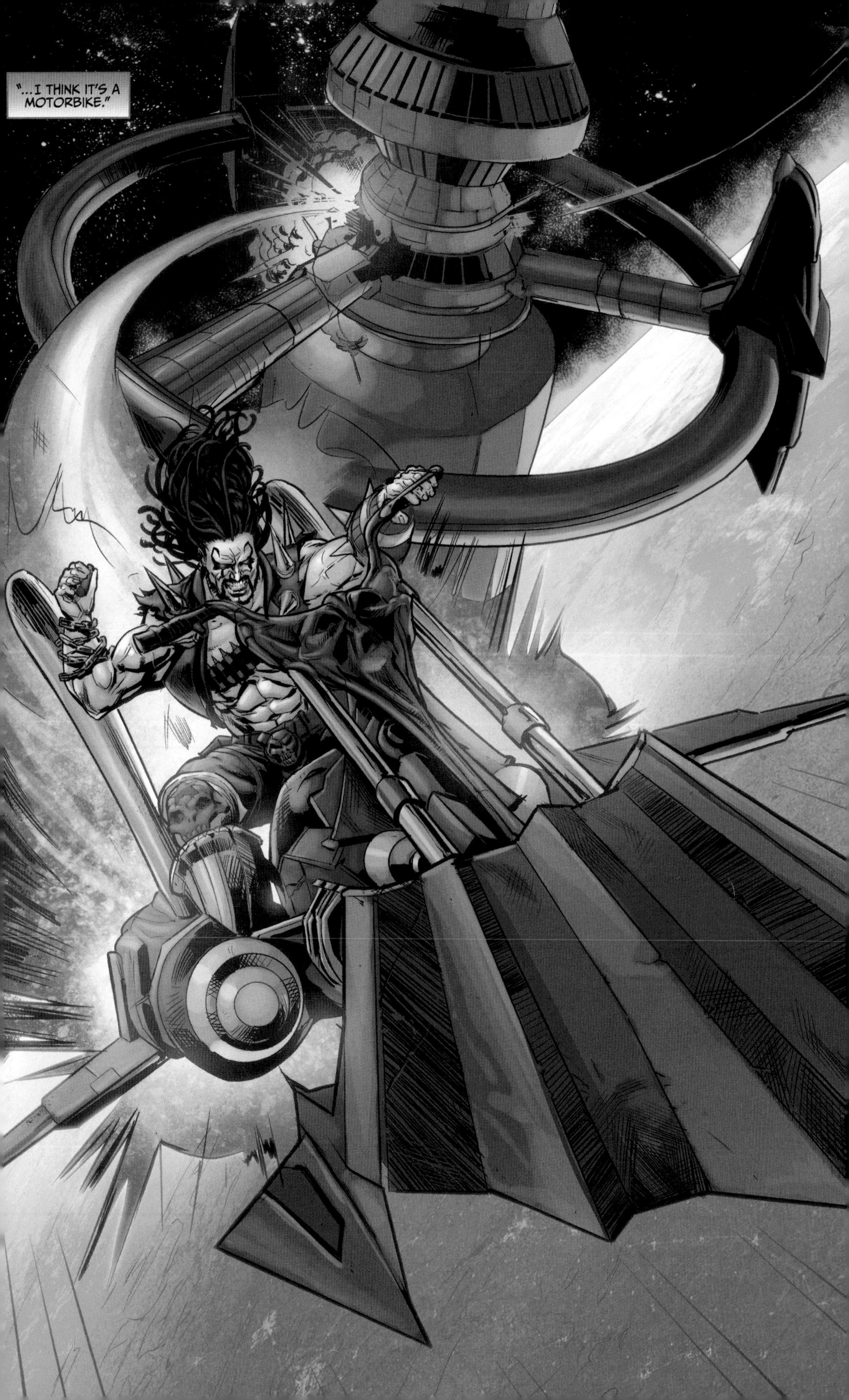
"...I THINK IT'S A MOTORBIKE."

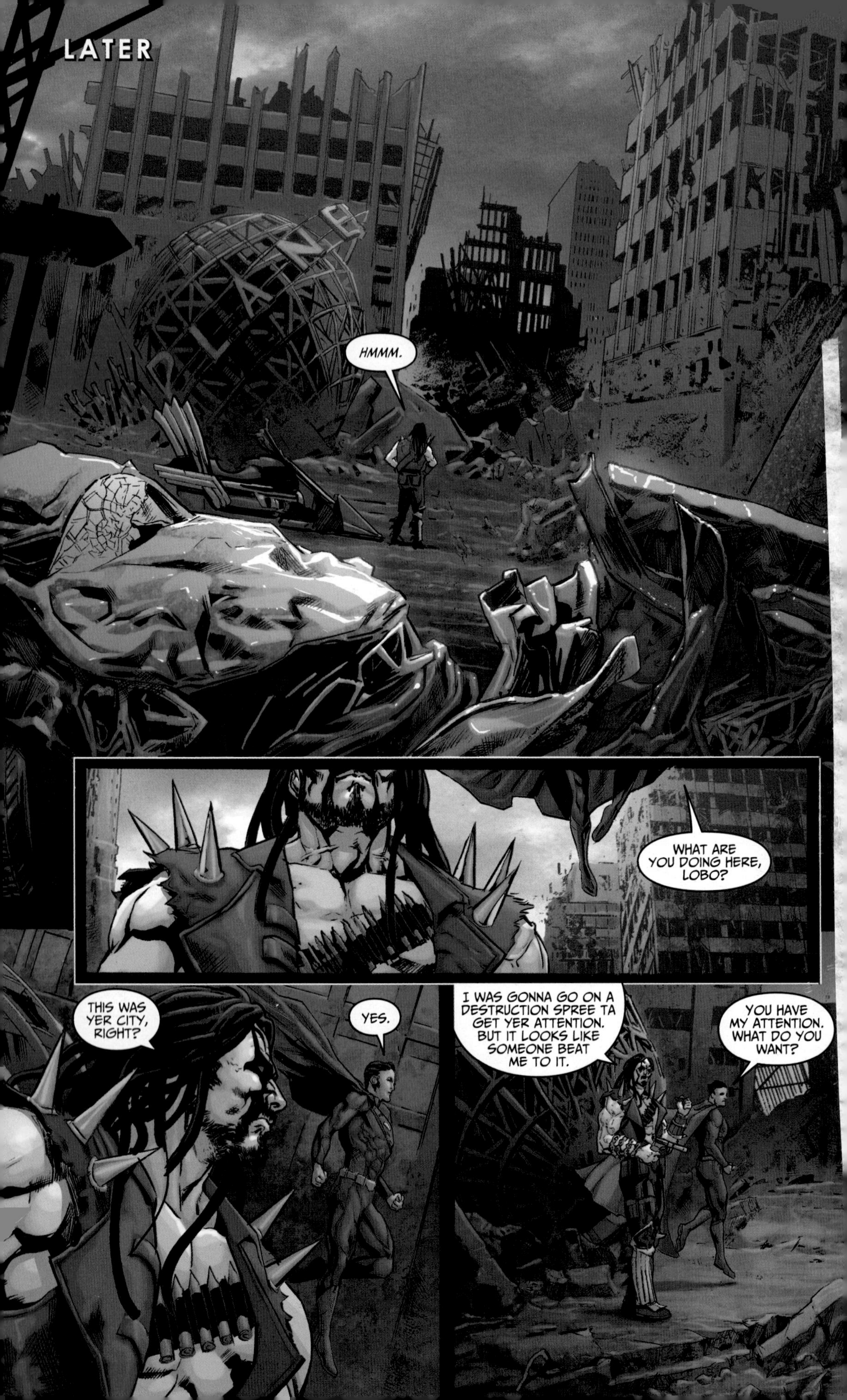
LATER
HMMM.
WHAT ARE YOU DOING HERE, LOBO?
THIS WAS YER CITY, RIGHT?
YES.
I WAS GONNA GO ON A DESTRUCTION SPREE TA GET YER ATTENTION. BUT IT LOOKS LIKE SOMEONE BEAT ME TO IT.
YOU HAVE MY ATTENTION. WHAT DO YOU WANT?

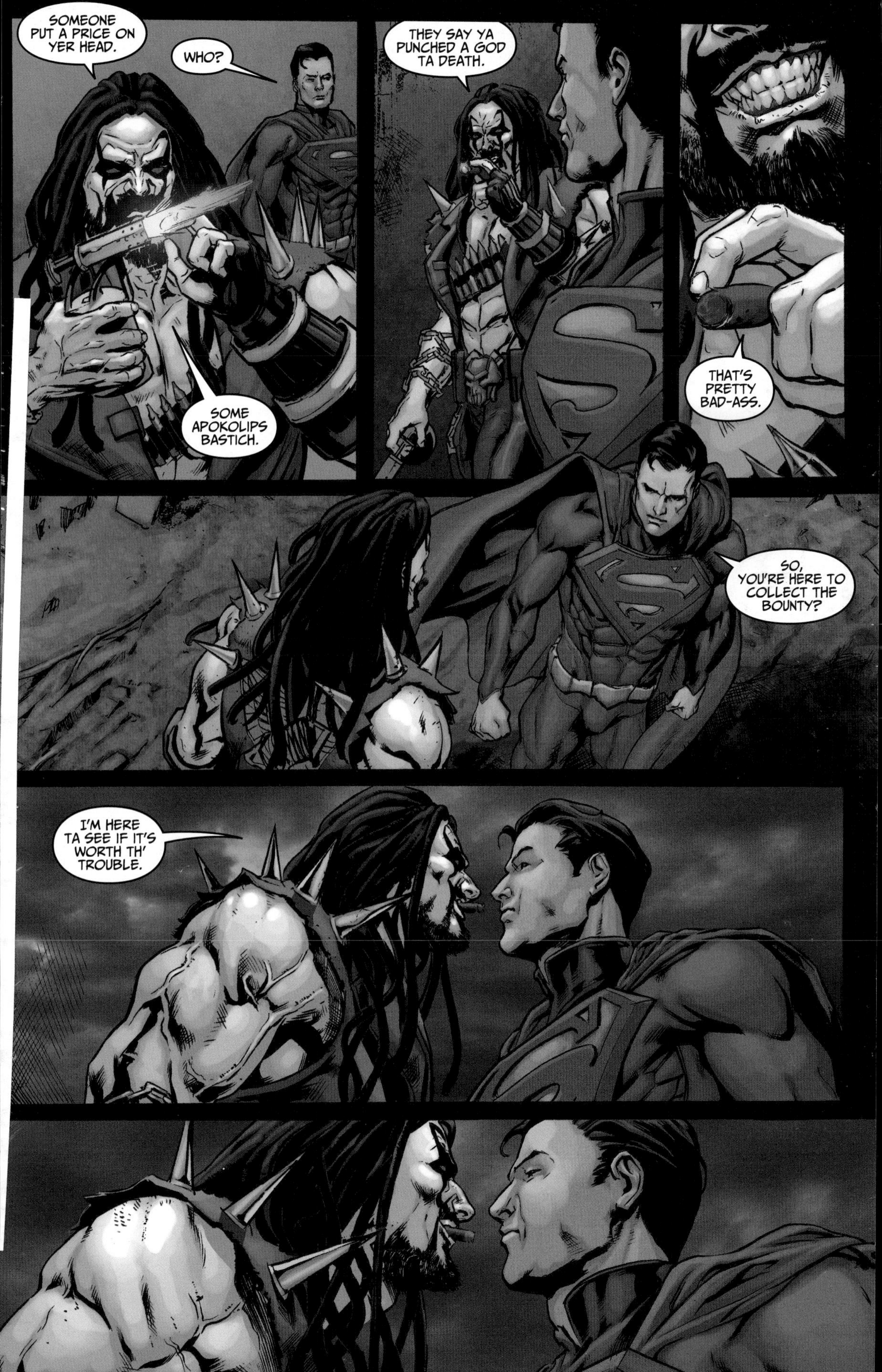
SOMEONE PUT A PRICE ON YER HEAD.
WHO?
SOME APOKOLIPS BASTICH.
THEY SAY YA PUNCHED A GOD TA DEATH.
THAT'S PRETTY BAD-ASS.
SO, YOU'RE HERE TO COLLECT THE BOUNTY?
I'M HERE TA SEE IF IT'S WORTH TH' TROUBLE.

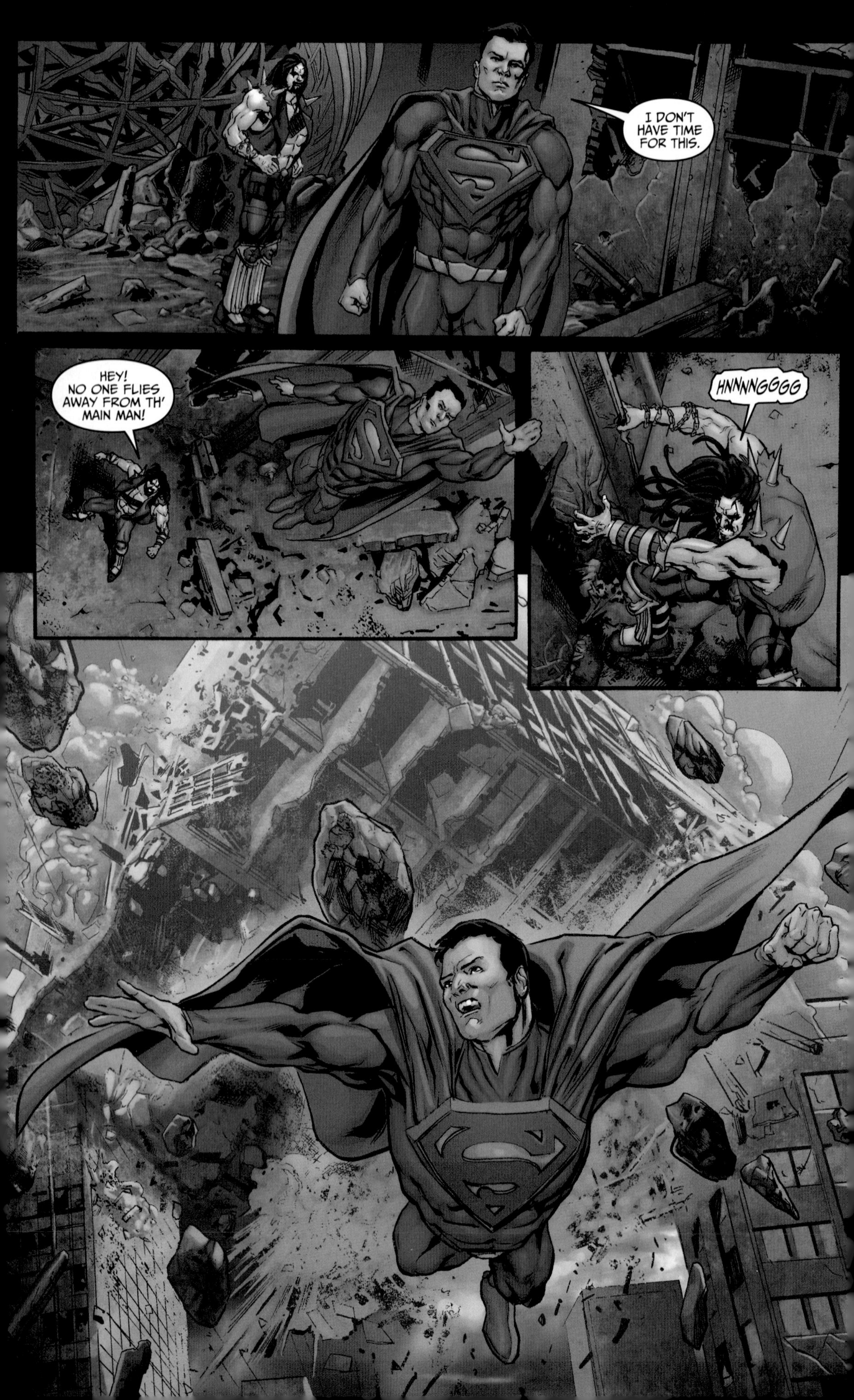
I DON'T HAVE TIME FOR THIS.
HEY! NO ONE FLIES AWAY FROM TH' MAIN MAN!
HNNNNGGGG

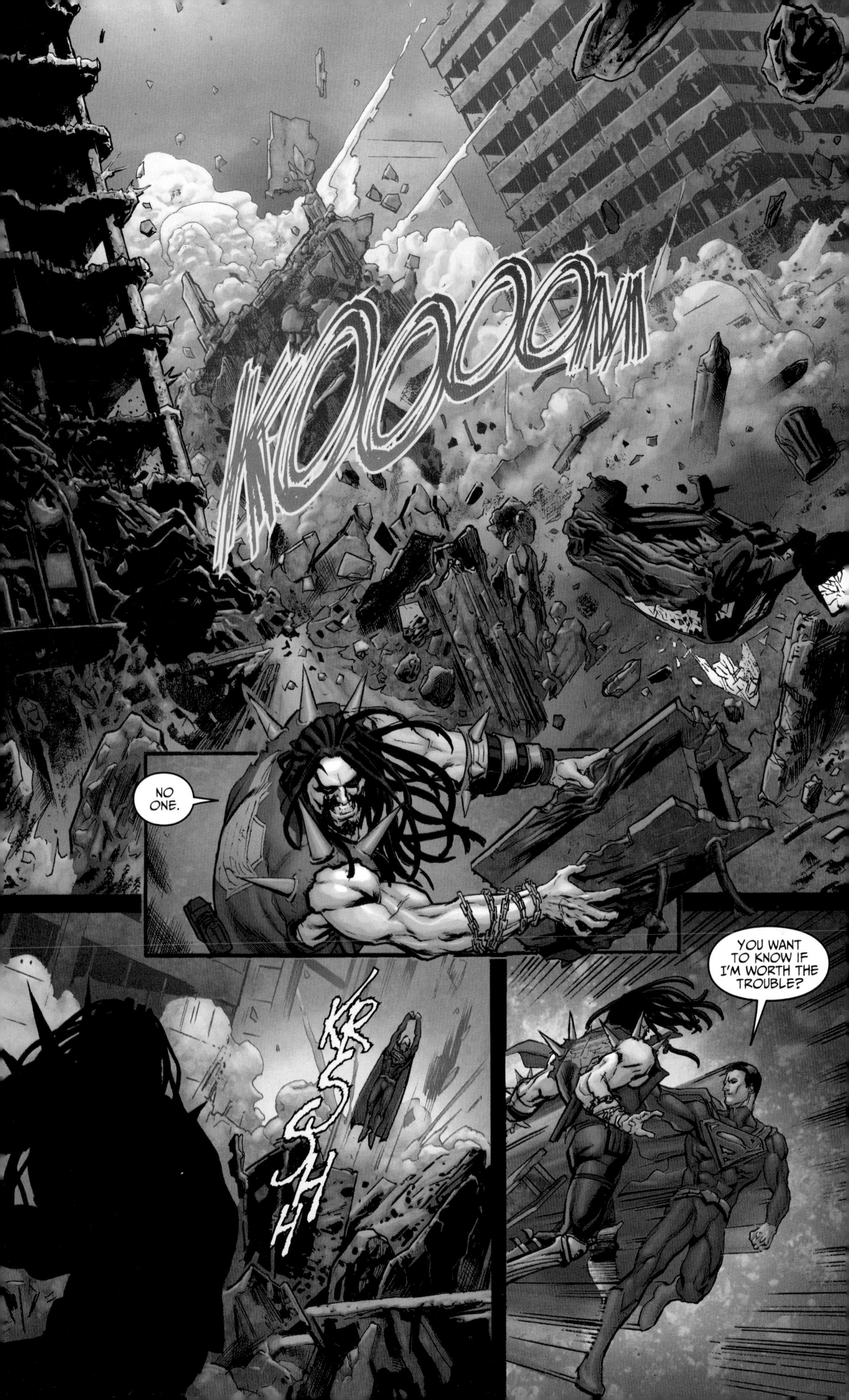
KOOOOM
NO ONE.
KRSSHH
YOU WANT TO KNOW IF I'M WORTH THE TROUBLE?

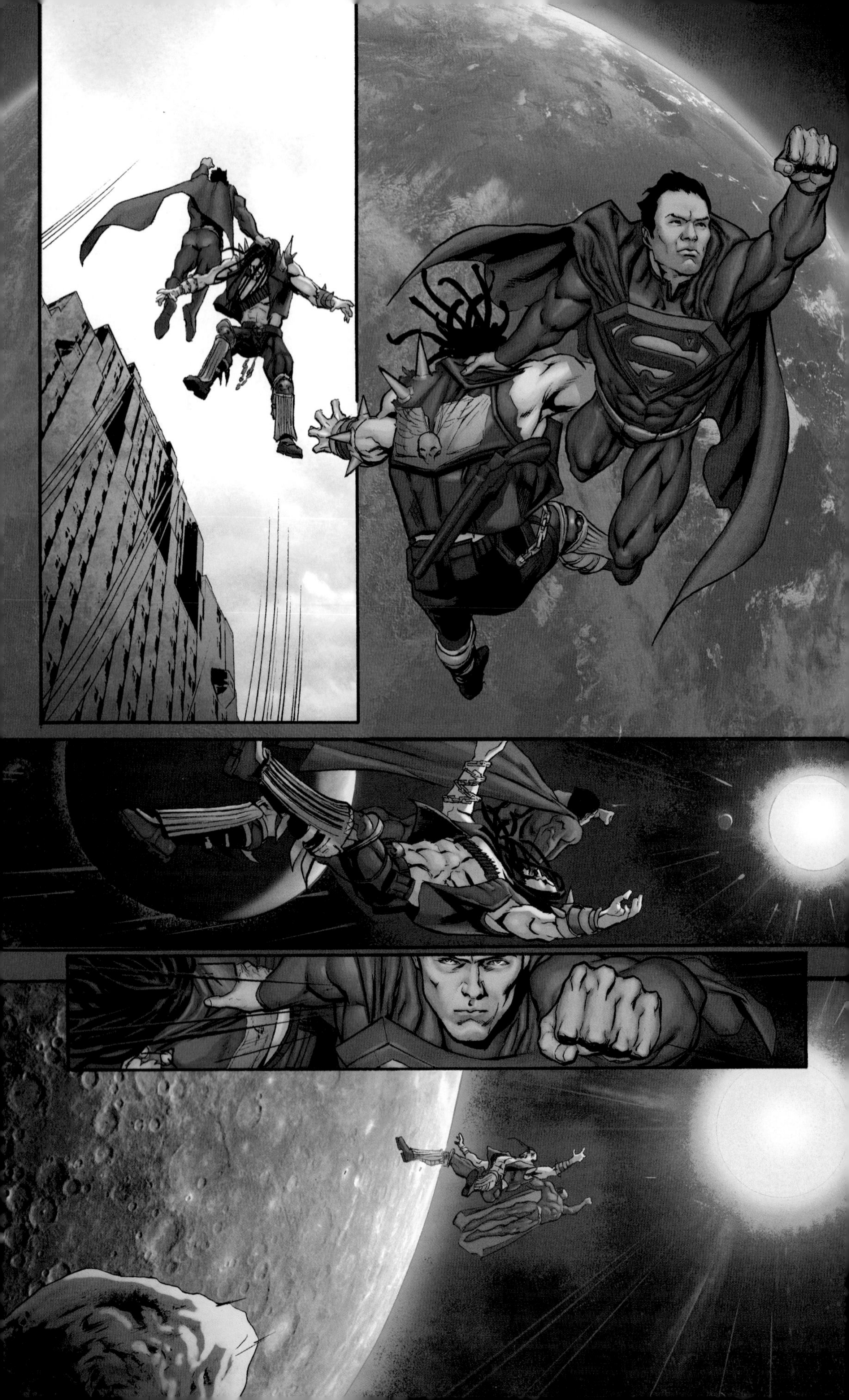

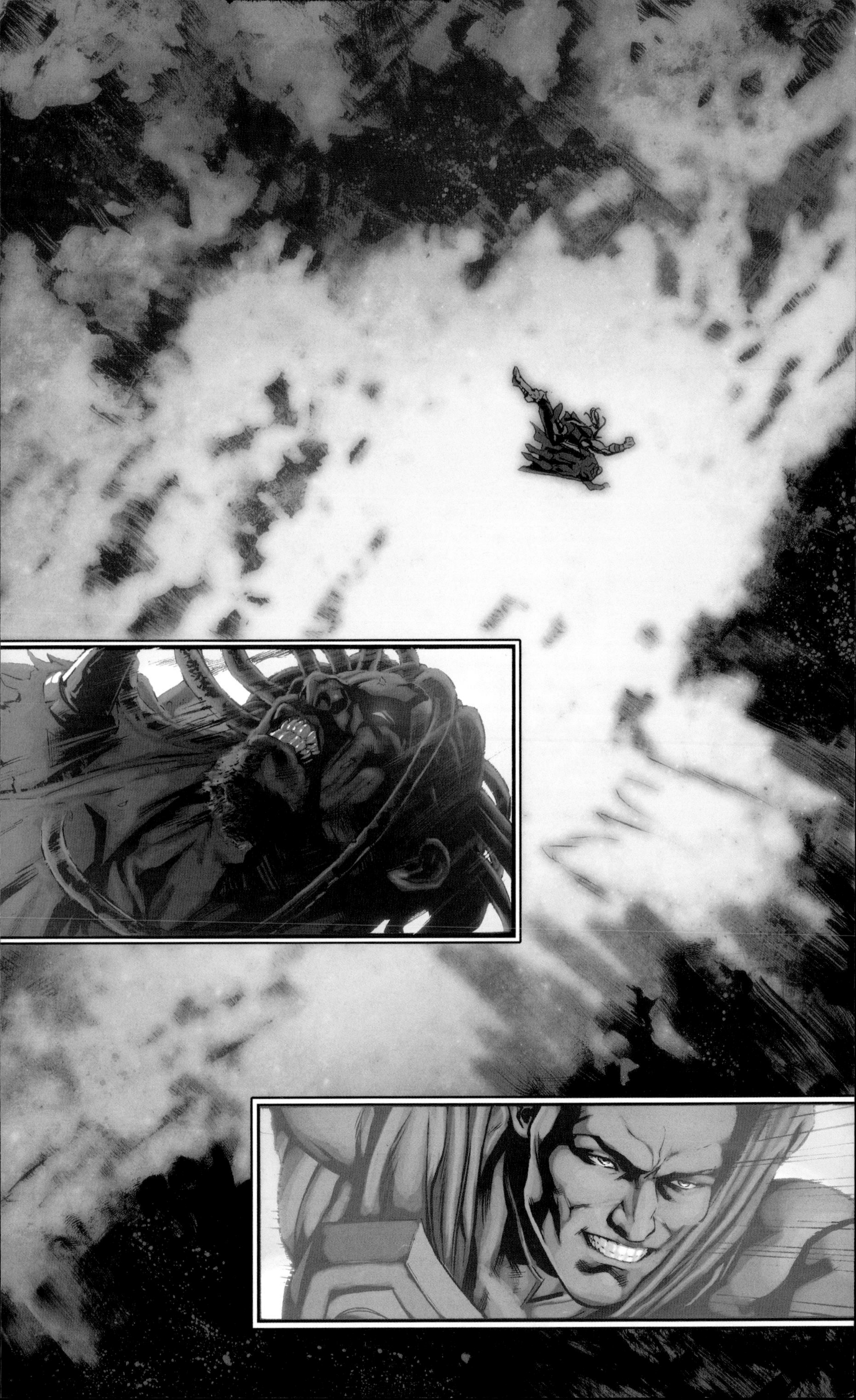

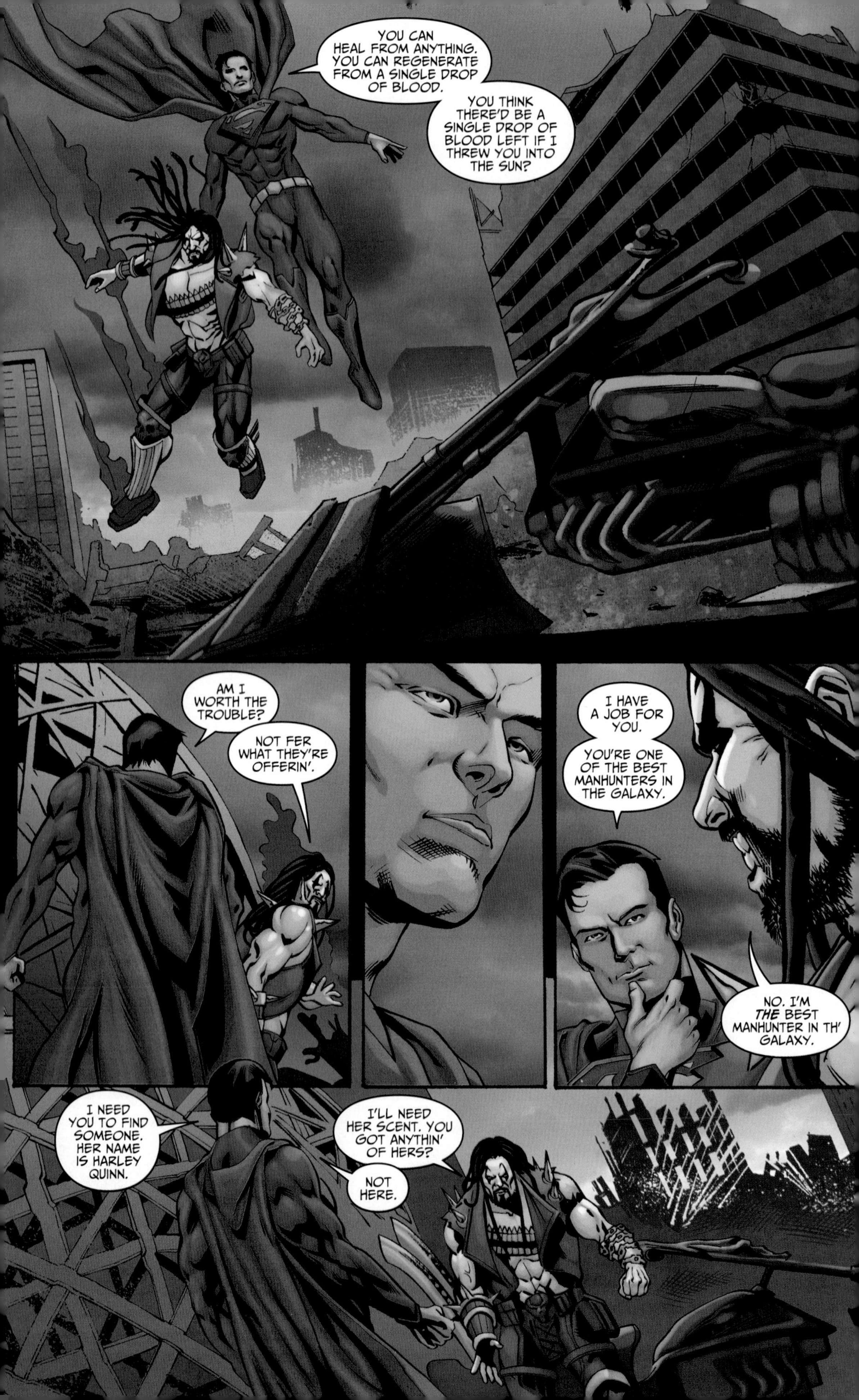
YOU CAN HEAL FROM ANYTHING. YOU CAN REGENERATE FROM A SINGLE DROP OF BLOOD.
YOU THINK THERE'D BE A SINGLE DROP OF BLOOD LEFT IF I THREW YOU INTO THE SUN?
AM I WORTH THE TROUBLE?
NOT FER WHAT THEY'RE OFFERIN'.
I HAVE A JOB FOR YOU.
YOU'RE ONE OF THE BEST MANHUNTERS IN THE GALAXY.
NO. I'M *THE* BEST MANHUNTER IN TH' GALAXY.
I NEED YOU TO FIND SOMEONE. HER NAME IS HARLEY QUINN.
I'LL NEED HER SCENT. YOU GOT ANYTHIN' OF HERS?
NOT HERE.

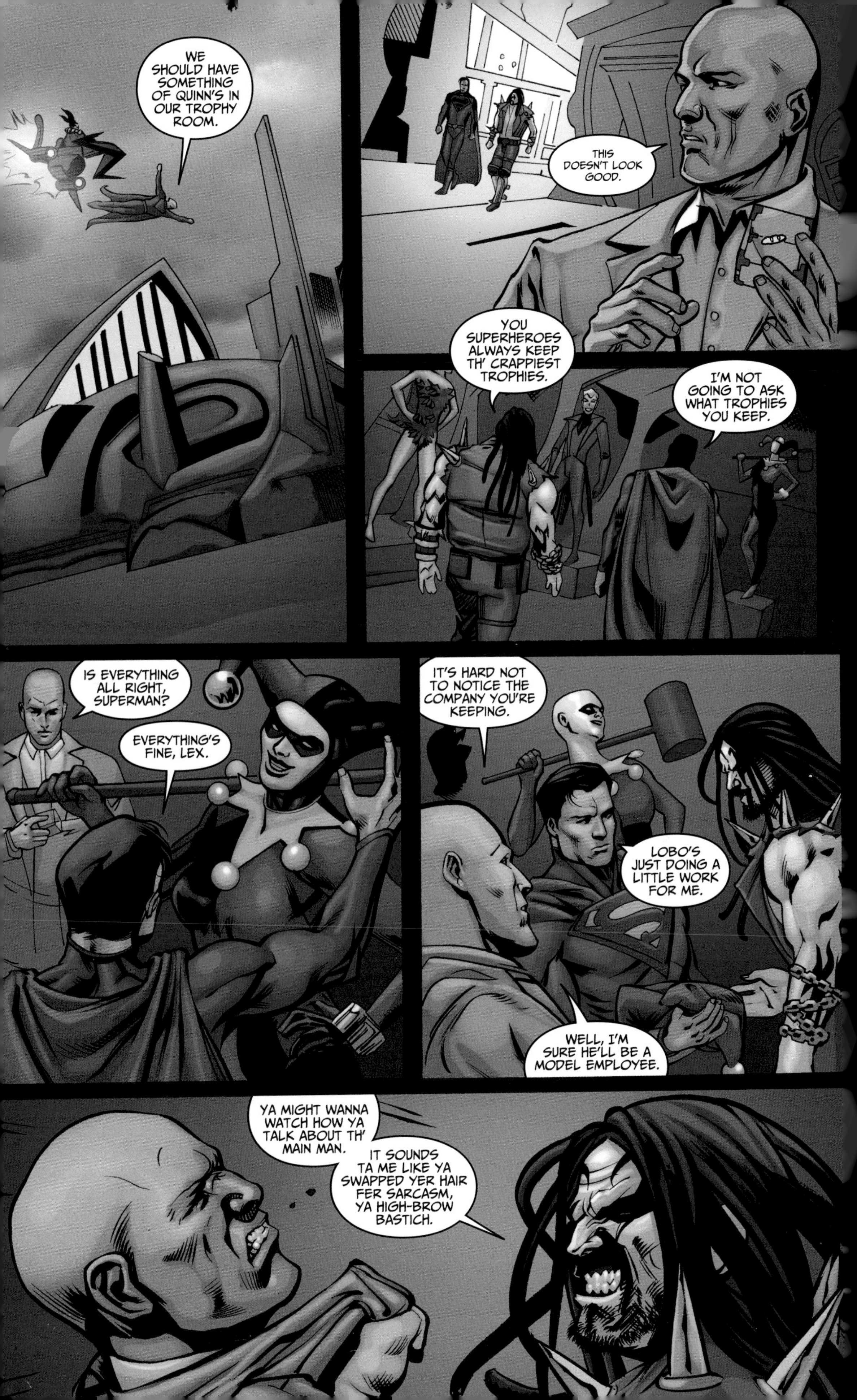
WE SHOULD HAVE SOMETHING OF QUINN'S IN OUR TROPHY ROOM.
THIS DOESN'T LOOK GOOD.
YOU SUPERHEROES ALWAYS KEEP TH' CRAPPIEST TROPHIES.
I'M NOT GOING TO ASK WHAT TROPHIES YOU KEEP.
IS EVERYTHING ALL RIGHT, SUPERMAN?
EVERYTHING'S FINE, LEX.
IT'S HARD NOT TO NOTICE THE COMPANY YOU'RE KEEPING.
LOBO'S JUST DOING A LITTLE WORK FOR ME.
WELL, I'M SURE HE'LL BE A MODEL EMPLOYEE.
YA MIGHT WANNA WATCH HOW YA TALK ABOUT TH' MAIN MAN.
IT SOUNDS TA ME LIKE YA SWAPPED YER HAIR FER SARCASM, YA HIGH-BROW BASTICH.

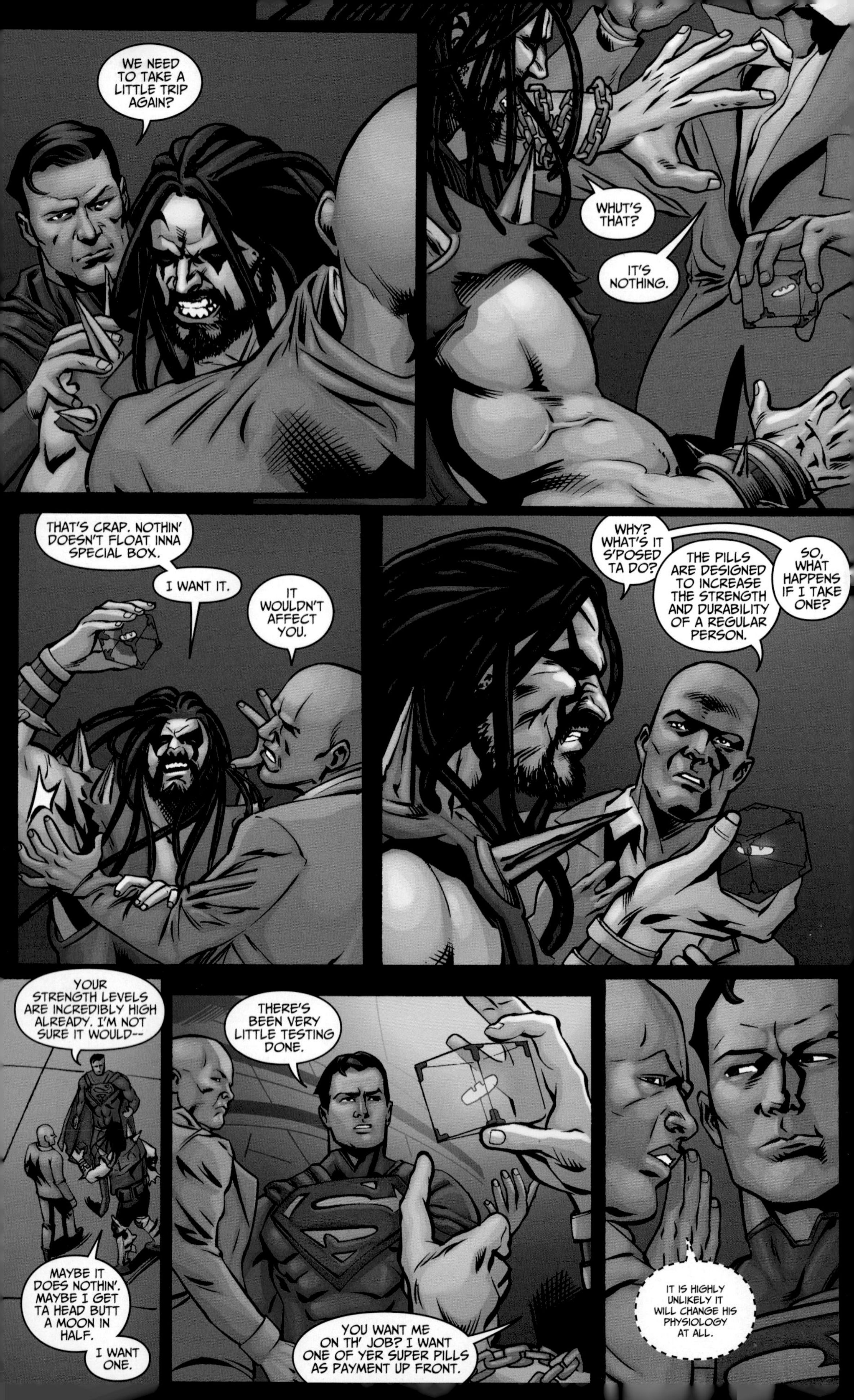
WE NEED TO TAKE A LITTLE TRIP AGAIN?
WHUT'S THAT?
IT'S NOTHING.
THAT'S CRAP. NOTHIN' DOESN'T FLOAT INNA SPECIAL BOX.
I WANT IT.
IT WOULDN'T AFFECT YOU.
WHY? WHAT'S IT S'POSED TA DO?
THE PILLS ARE DESIGNED TO INCREASE THE STRENGTH AND DURABILITY OF A REGULAR PERSON.
SO, WHAT HAPPENS IF I TAKE ONE?
YOUR STRENGTH LEVELS ARE INCREDIBLY HIGH ALREADY. I'M NOT SURE IT WOULD--
MAYBE IT DOES NOTHIN'. MAYBE I GET TA HEAD BUTT A MOON IN HALF.
I WANT ONE.
THERE'S BEEN VERY LITTLE TESTING DONE.
YOU WANT ME ON TH' JOB? I WANT ONE OF YER SUPER PILLS AS PAYMENT UP FRONT.
IT IS HIGHLY UNLIKELY IT WILL CHANGE HIS PHYSIOLOGY AT ALL.

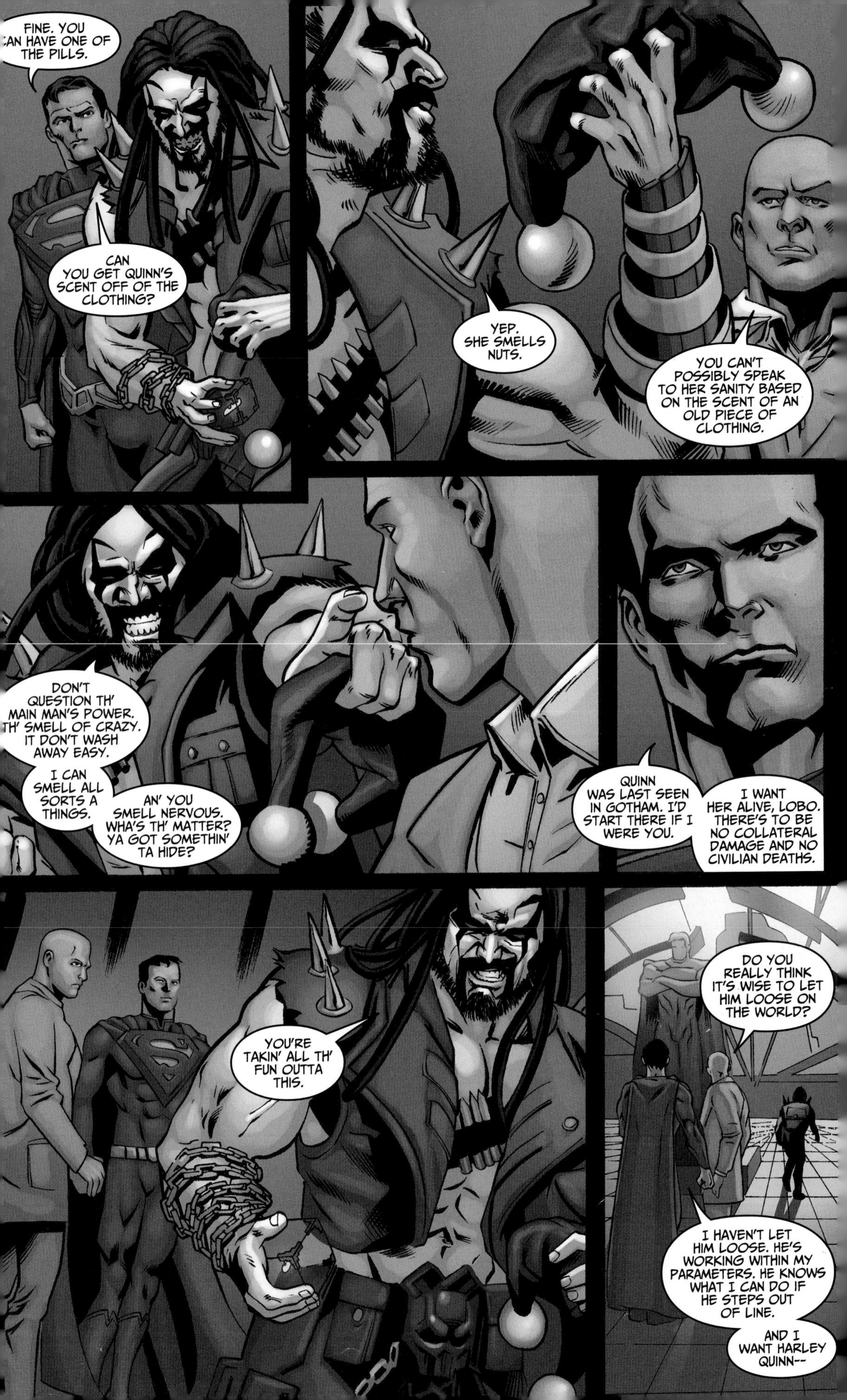

FINE. YOU CAN HAVE ONE OF THE PILLS.
CAN YOU GET QUINN'S SCENT OFF OF THE CLOTHING?
YEP. SHE SMELLS NUTS.
YOU CAN'T POSSIBLY SPEAK TO HER SANITY BASED ON THE SCENT OF AN OLD PIECE OF CLOTHING.
DON'T QUESTION TH' MAIN MAN'S POWER. TH' SMELL OF CRAZY. IT DON'T WASH AWAY EASY.
I CAN SMELL ALL SORTS A THINGS.
AN' YOU SMELL NERVOUS. WHA'S TH' MATTER? YA GOT SOMETHIN' TA HIDE?
QUINN WAS LAST SEEN IN GOTHAM. I'D START THERE IF I WERE YOU.
I WANT HER ALIVE, LOBO. THERE'S TO BE NO COLLATERAL DAMAGE AND NO CIVILIAN DEATHS.
YOU'RE TAKIN' ALL TH' FUN OUTTA THIS.
DO YOU REALLY THINK IT'S WISE TO LET HIM LOOSE ON THE WORLD?
I HAVEN'T LET HIM LOOSE. HE'S WORKING WITHIN MY PARAMETERS. HE KNOWS WHAT I CAN DO IF HE STEPS OUT OF LINE.
AND I WANT HARLEY QUINN--

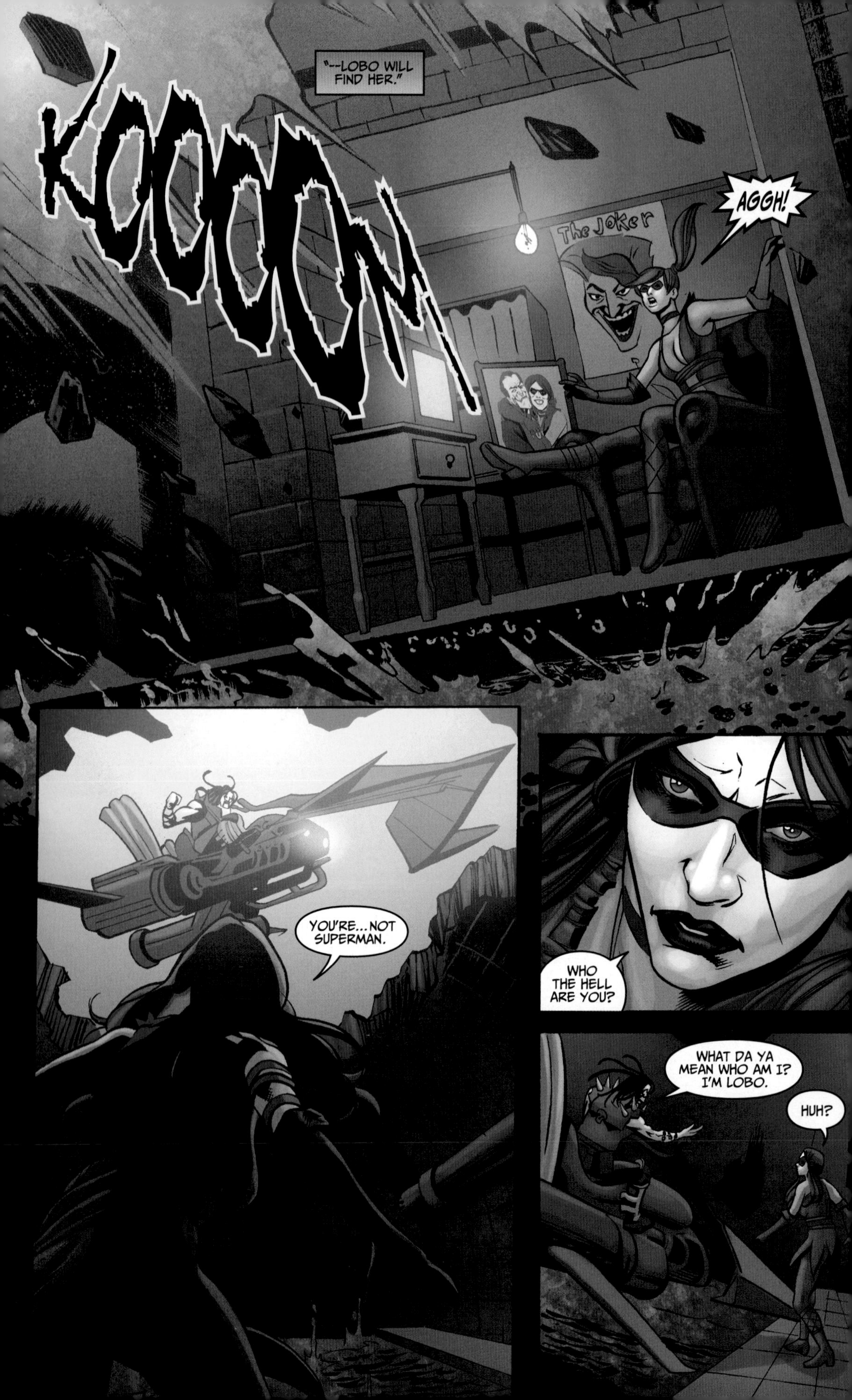
"--LOBO WILL FIND HER."
KOOOOOM
AGGH!
The Joker
YOU'RE...NOT SUPERMAN.
WHO THE HELL ARE YOU?
WHAT DA YA MEAN WHO AM I? I'M LOBO.
HUH?

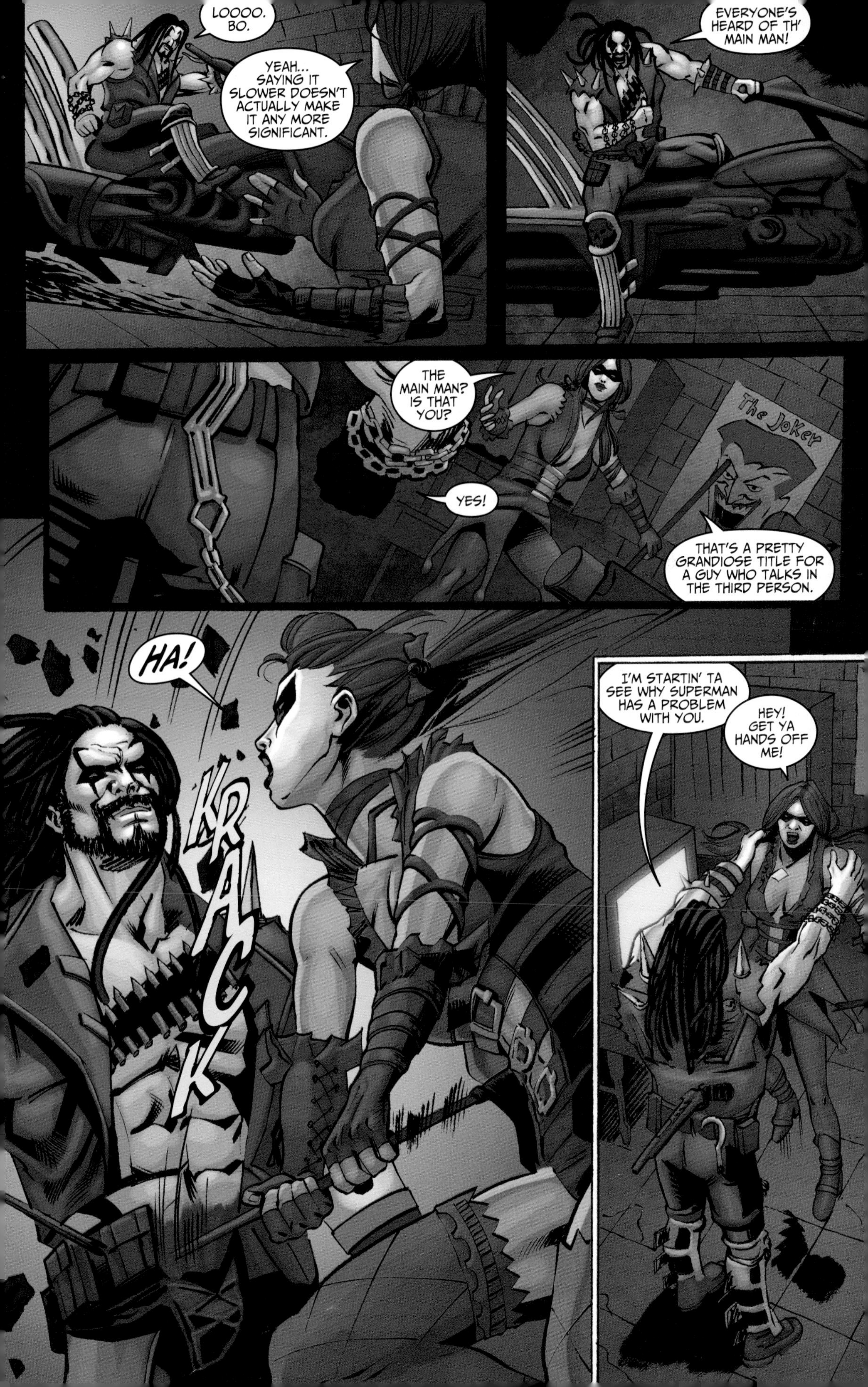
LOOOO.
BO.
YEAH... SAYING IT SLOWER DOESN'T ACTUALLY MAKE IT ANY MORE SIGNIFICANT.
EVERYONE'S HEARD OF TH' MAIN MAN!
THE MAIN MAN? IS THAT YOU?
YES!
THAT'S A PRETTY GRANDIOSE TITLE FOR A GUY WHO TALKS IN THE THIRD PERSON.
HA!
KRACK
I'M STARTIN' TA SEE WHY SUPERMAN HAS A PROBLEM WITH YOU.
HEY! GET YA HANDS OFF ME!

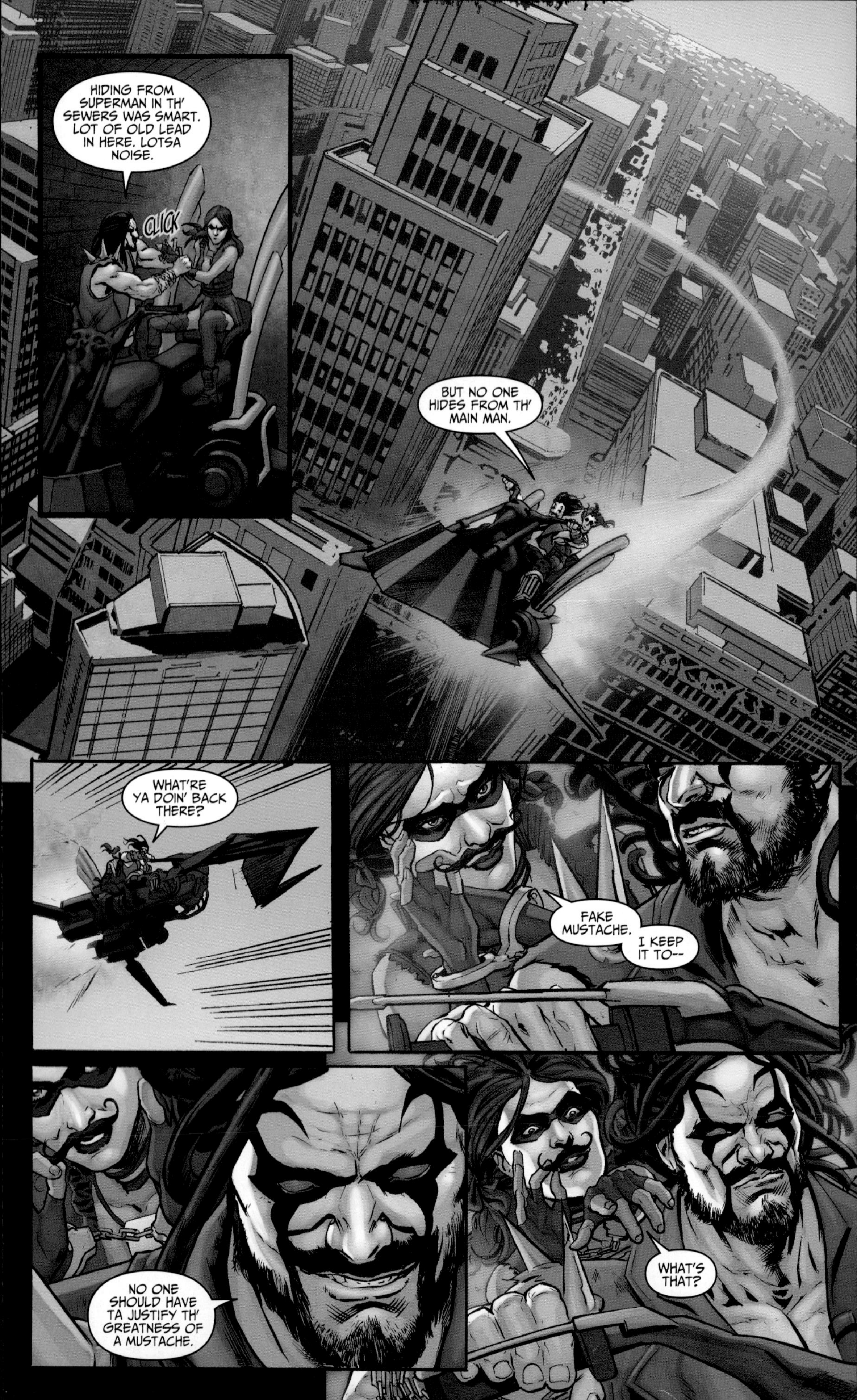
HIDING FROM SUPERMAN IN TH' SEWERS WAS SMART. LOT OF OLD LEAD IN HERE. LOTSA NOISE.
CLICK
BUT NO ONE HIDES FROM TH' MAIN MAN.
WHAT'RE YA DOIN' BACK THERE?
FAKE MUSTACHE.
I KEEP IT TO--
NO ONE SHOULD HAVE TA JUSTIFY TH' GREATNESS OF A MUSTACHE.
WHAT'S THAT?

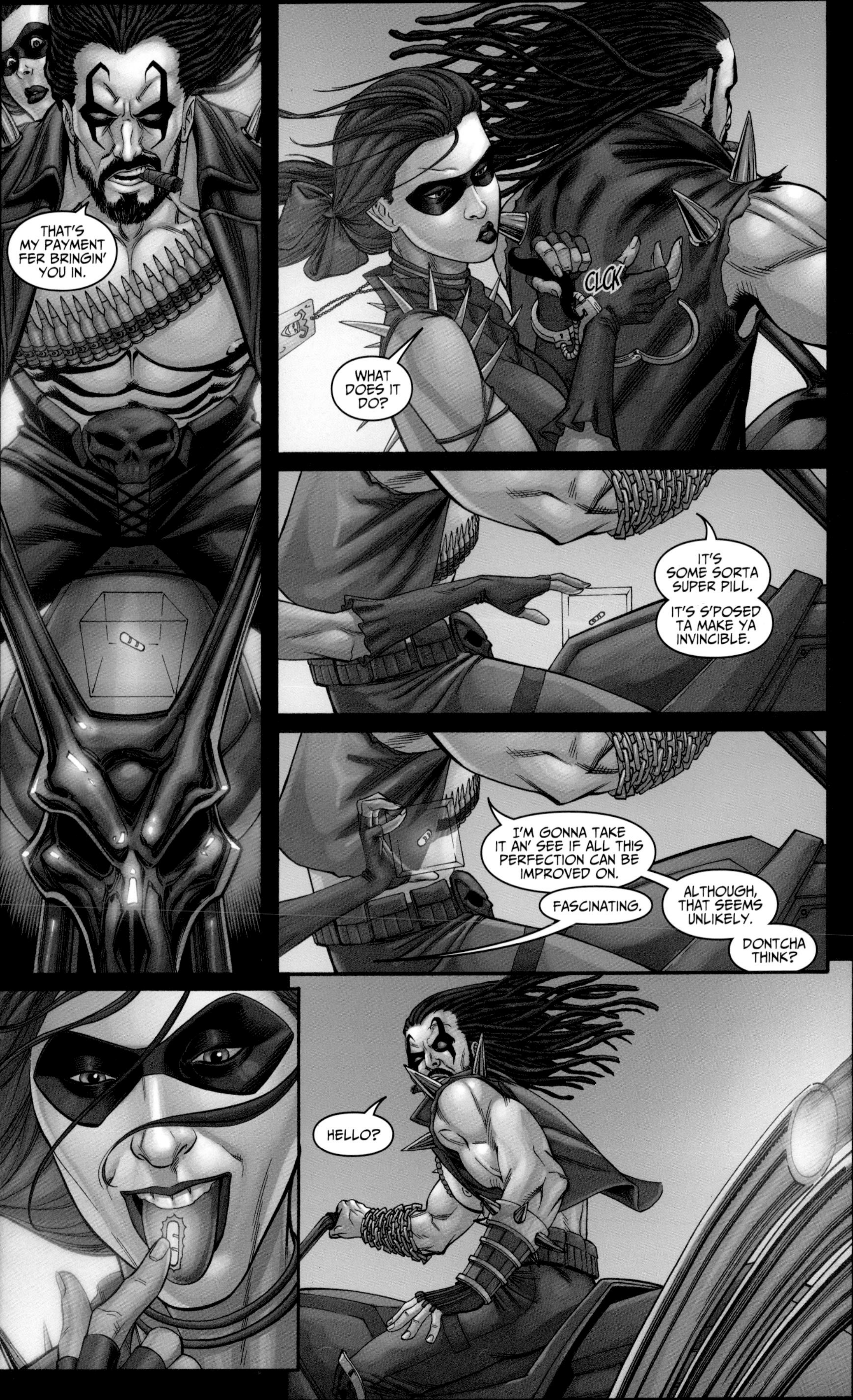
THAT'S MY PAYMENT FER BRINGIN' YOU IN.
CLCK
WHAT DOES IT DO?
IT'S SOME SORTA SUPER PILL.
IT'S S'POSED TA MAKE YA INVINCIBLE.
I'M GONNA TAKE IT AN' SEE IF ALL THIS PERFECTION CAN BE IMPROVED ON.
FASCINATING.
ALTHOUGH, THAT SEEMS UNLIKELY.
DONTCHA THINK?
HELLO?

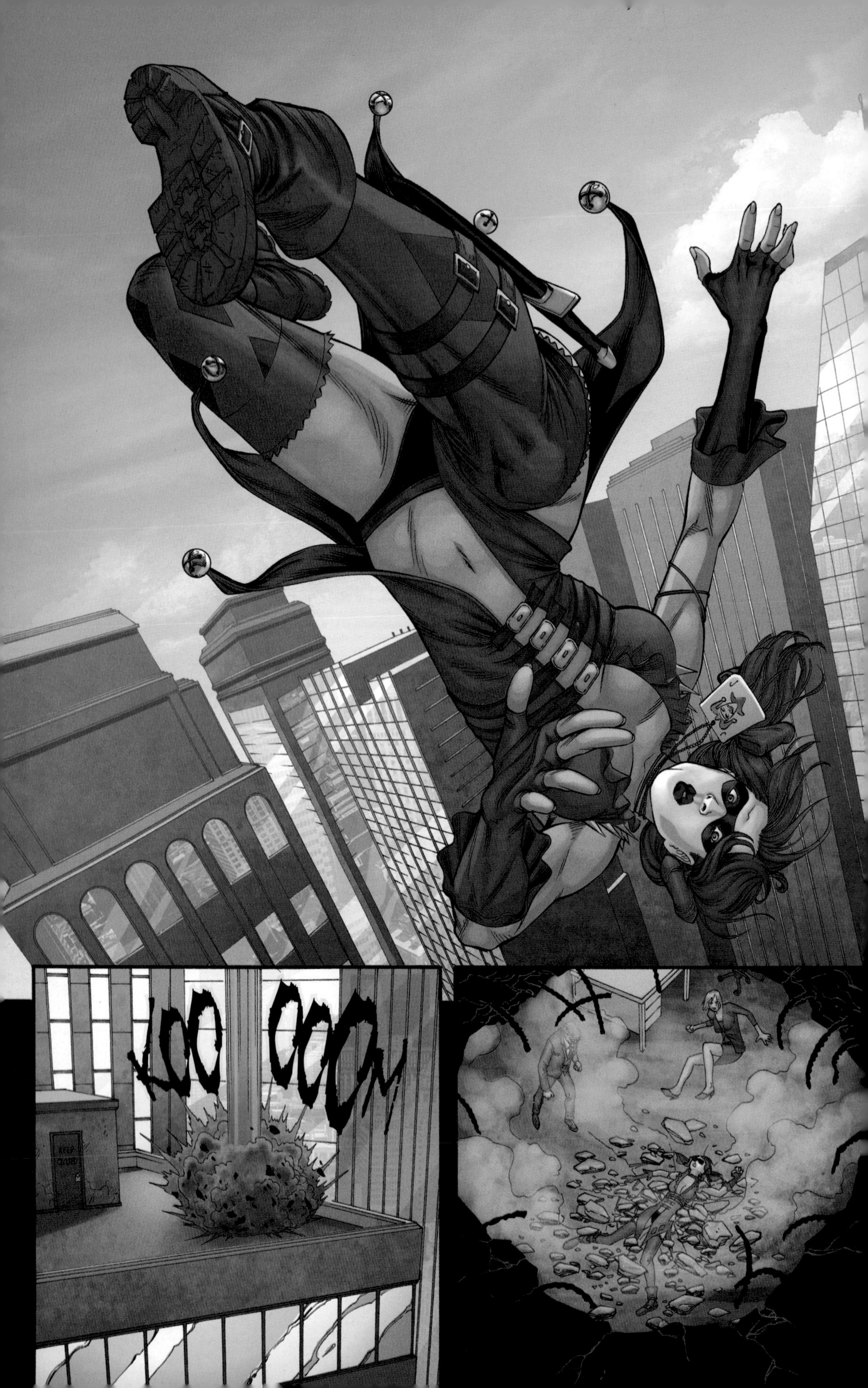
KOO OOOM
KEEP CLOSED

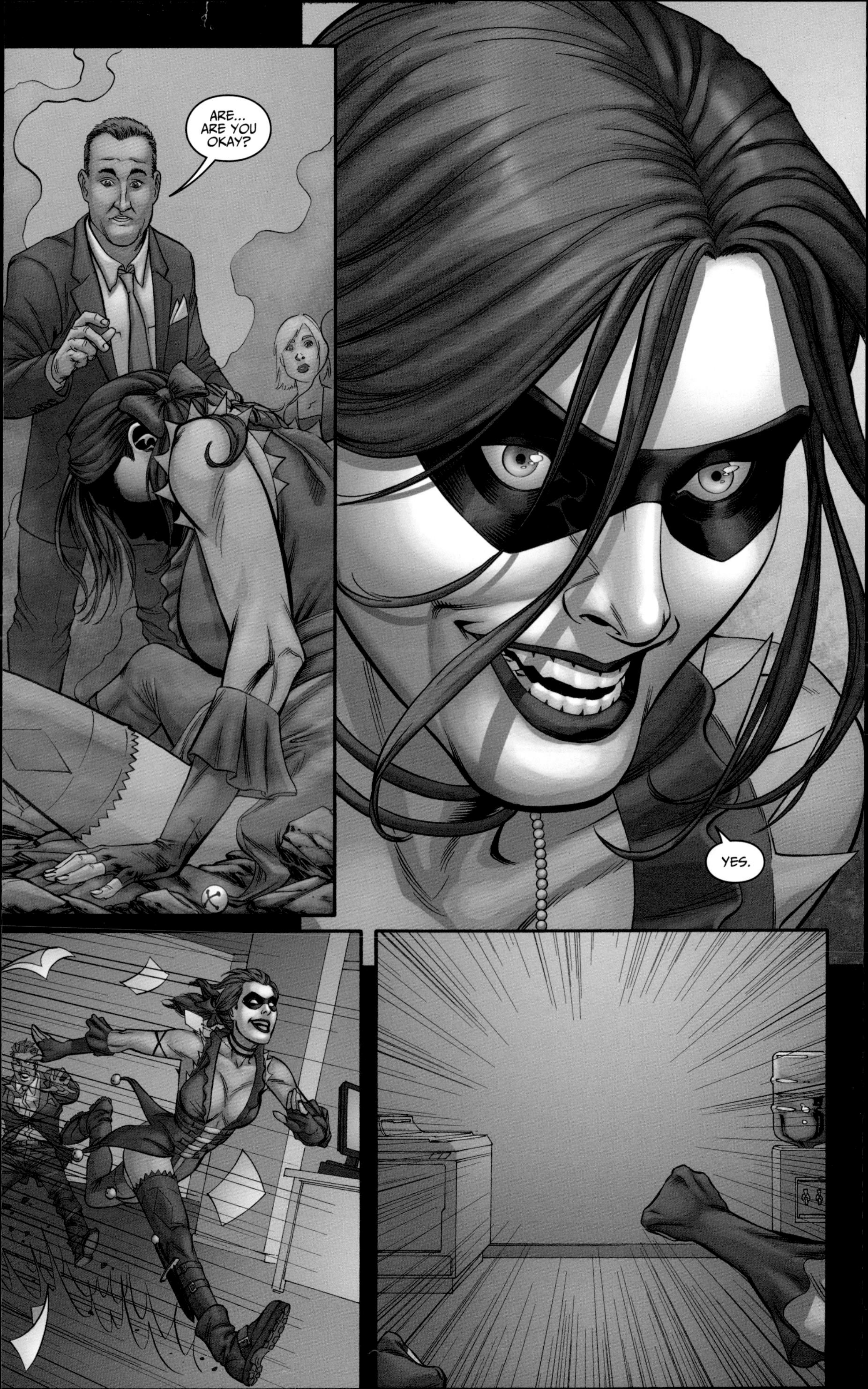
ARE... ARE YOU OKAY?
YES.

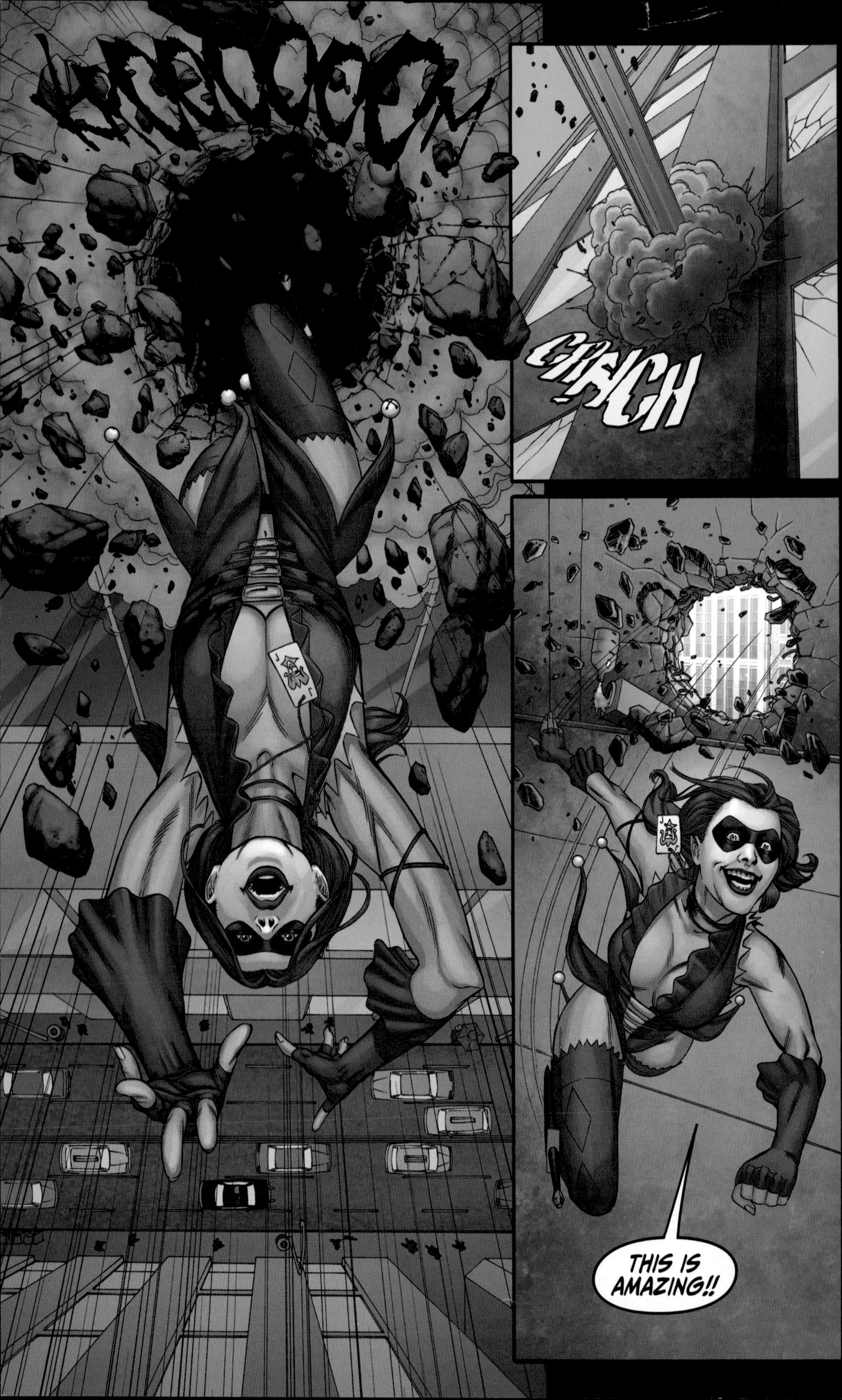
THIS IS AMAZING!!

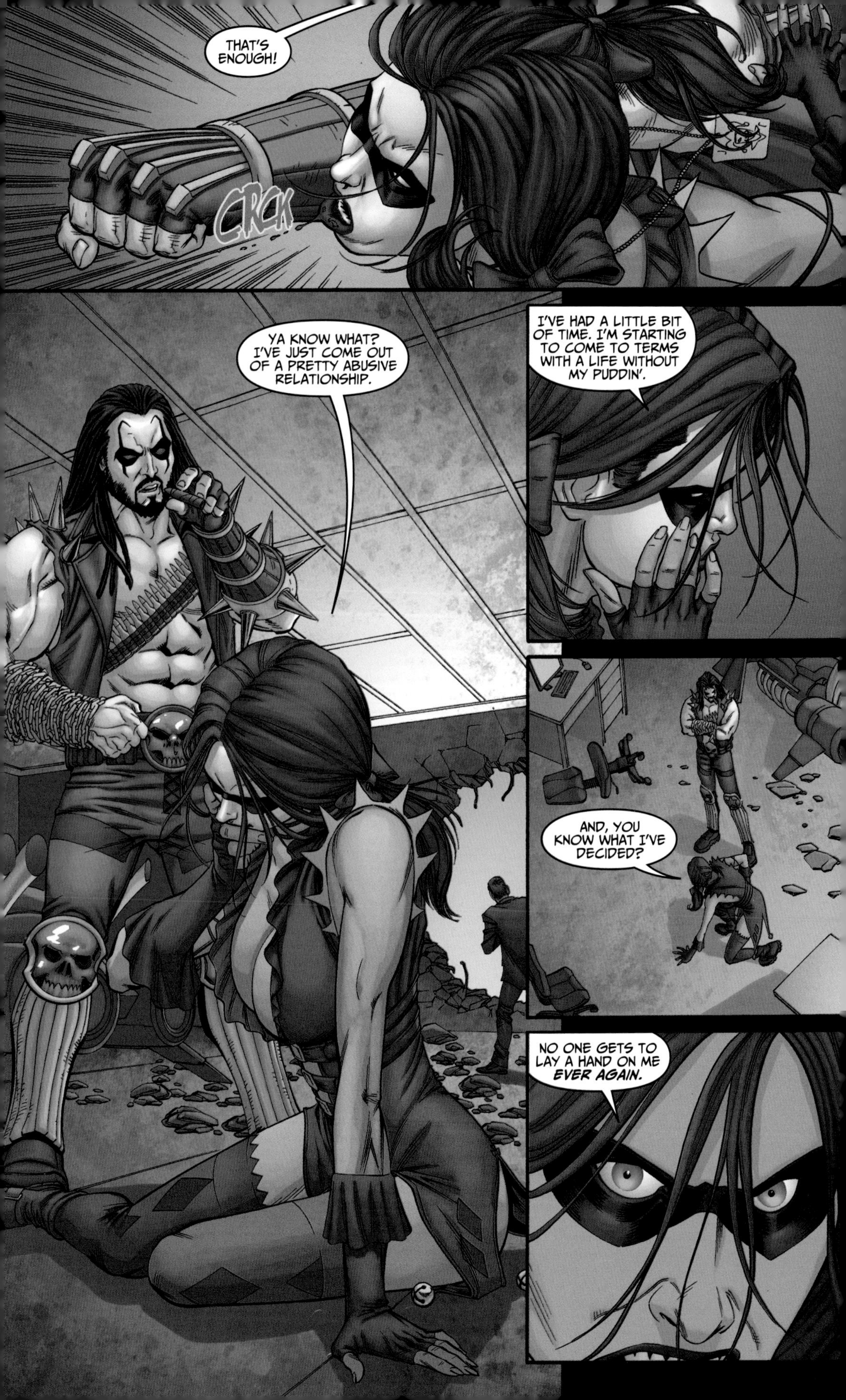
THAT'S ENOUGH!
CRCK
YA KNOW WHAT? I'VE JUST COME OUT OF A PRETTY ABUSIVE RELATIONSHIP.
I'VE HAD A LITTLE BIT OF TIME. I'M STARTING TO COME TO TERMS WITH A LIFE WITHOUT MY PUDDIN'.
AND, YOU KNOW WHAT I'VE DECIDED?
NO ONE GETS TO LAY A HAND ON ME *EVER AGAIN.*

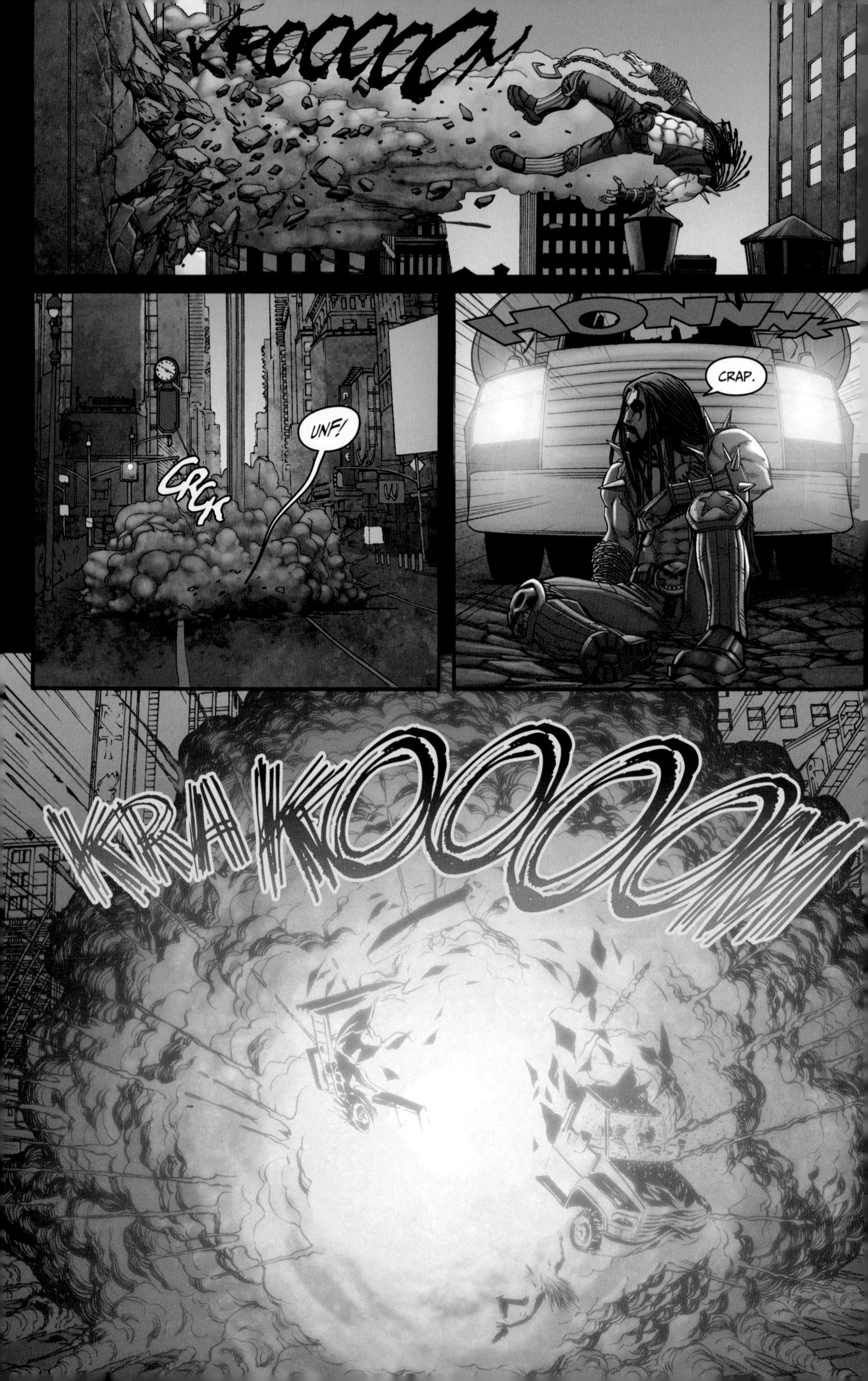
KROOOOOM
CRCK
UNF!
HONNNK
CRAP.
KRAKOOOOOM

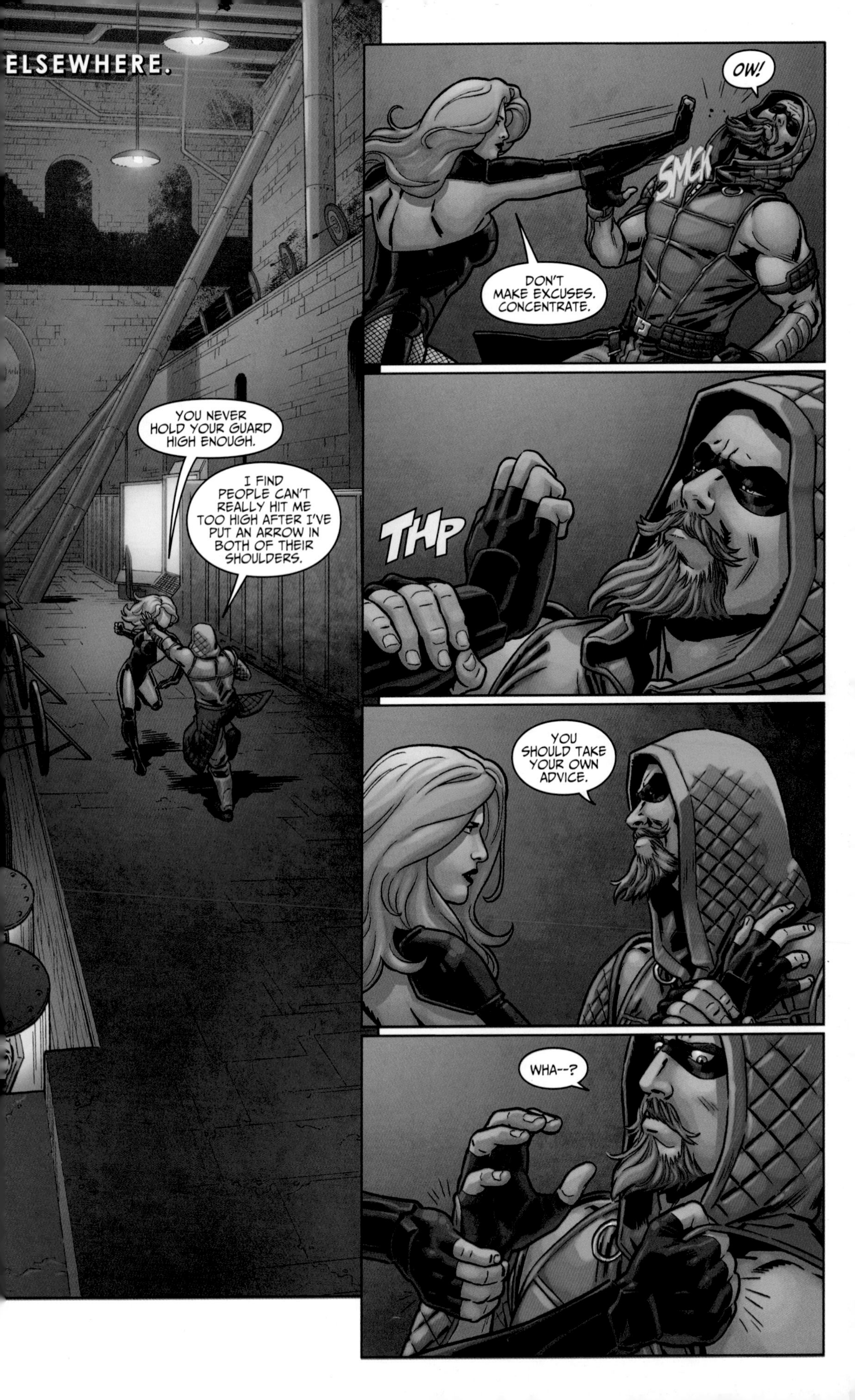
ELSEWHERE.
YOU NEVER HOLD YOUR GUARD HIGH ENOUGH.
I FIND PEOPLE CAN'T REALLY HIT ME TOO HIGH AFTER I'VE PUT AN ARROW IN BOTH OF THEIR SHOULDERS.
OW!
SMCK
DON'T MAKE EXCUSES. CONCENTRATE.
THP
YOU SHOULD TAKE YOUR OWN ADVICE.
WHA--?

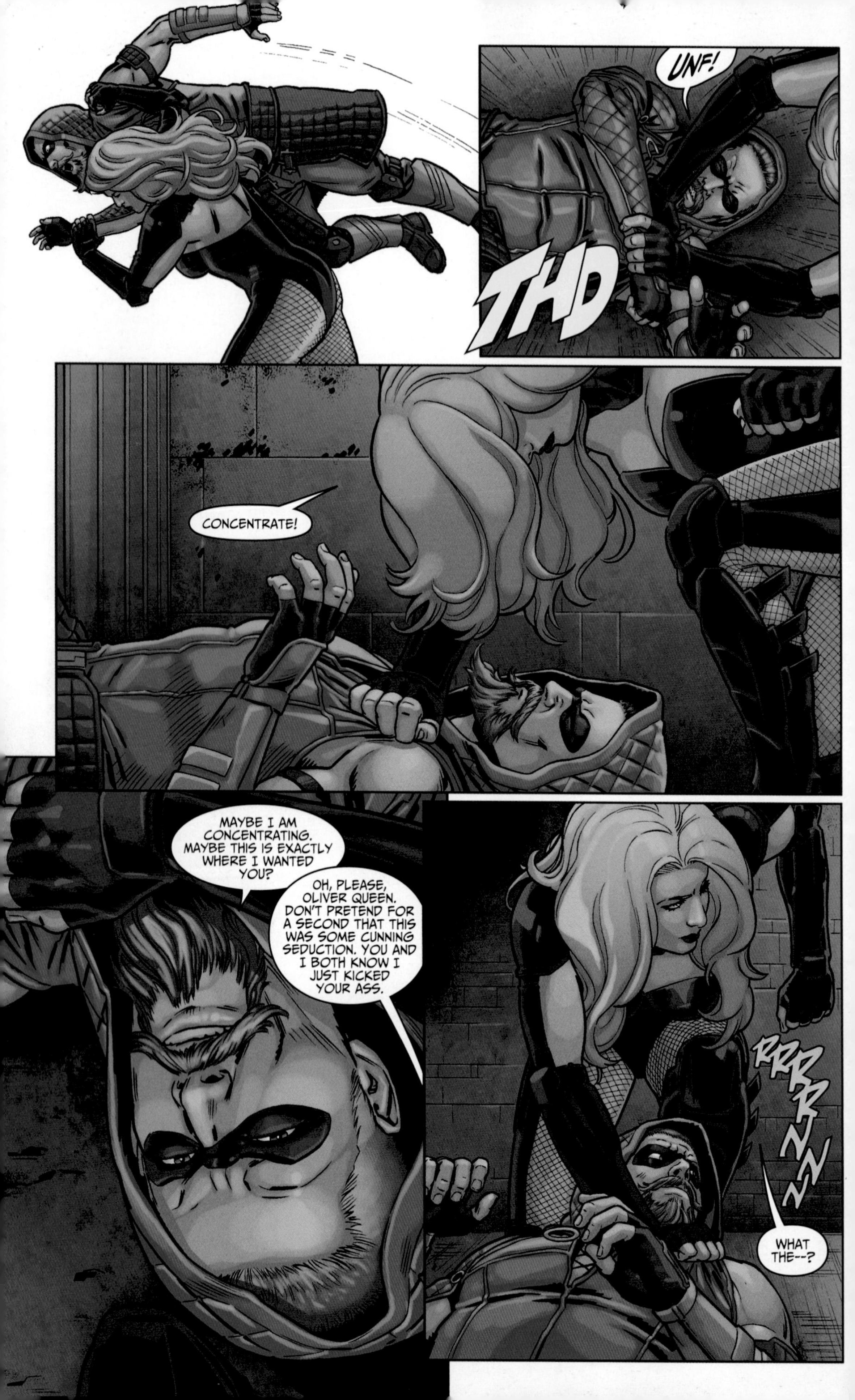
UNF!
THD
CONCENTRATE!
MAYBE I AM CONCENTRATING. MAYBE THIS IS EXACTLY WHERE I WANTED YOU?
OH, PLEASE, OLIVER QUEEN. DON'T PRETEND FOR A SECOND THAT THIS WAS SOME CUNNING SEDUCTION. YOU AND I BOTH KNOW I JUST KICKED YOUR ASS.
RRRRRNNN
WHAT THE--?

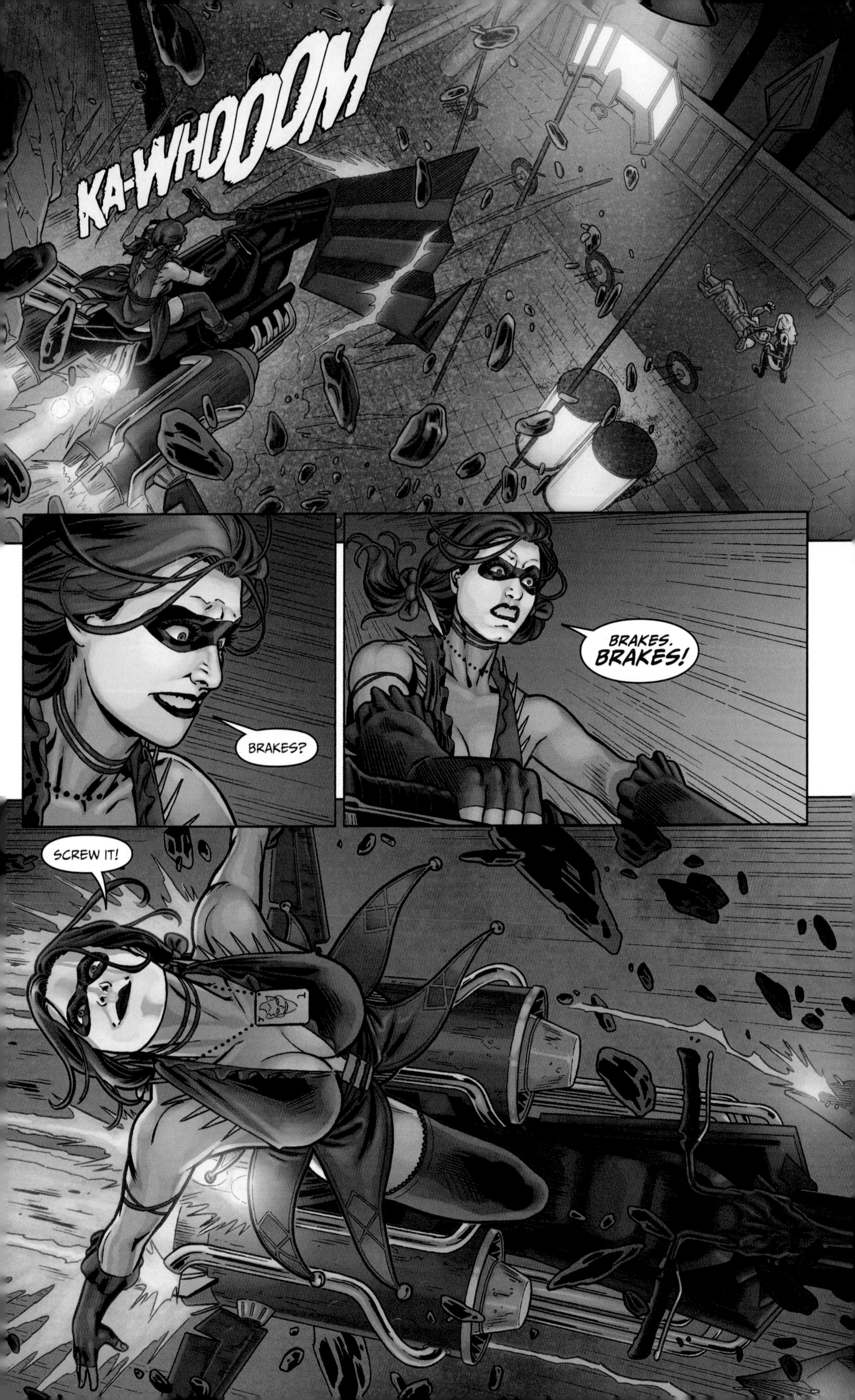
KA-WHOOOOM
BRAKES?
BRAKES.
BRAKES!
SCREW IT!

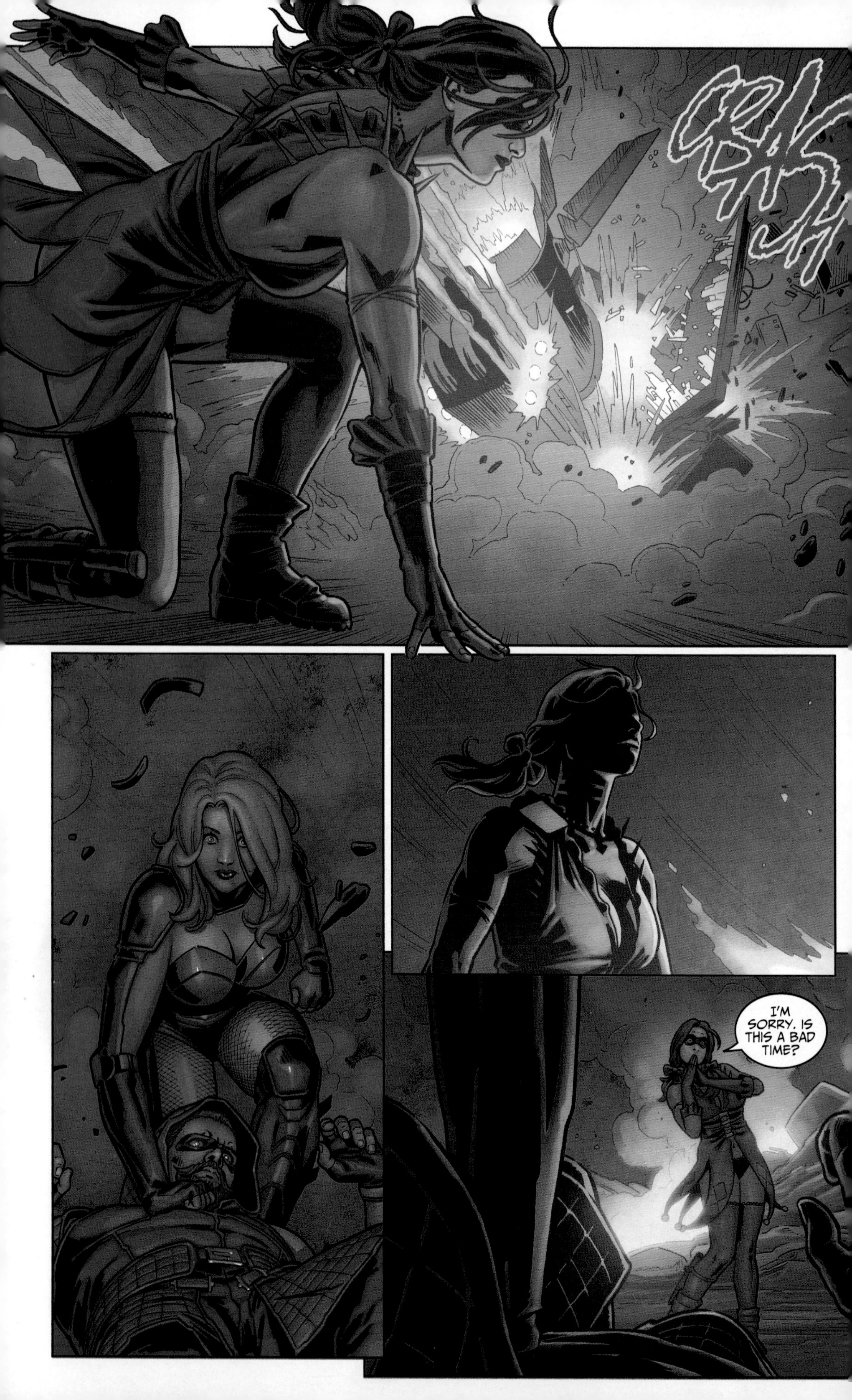
CRASH
I'M SORRY. IS THIS A BAD TIME?

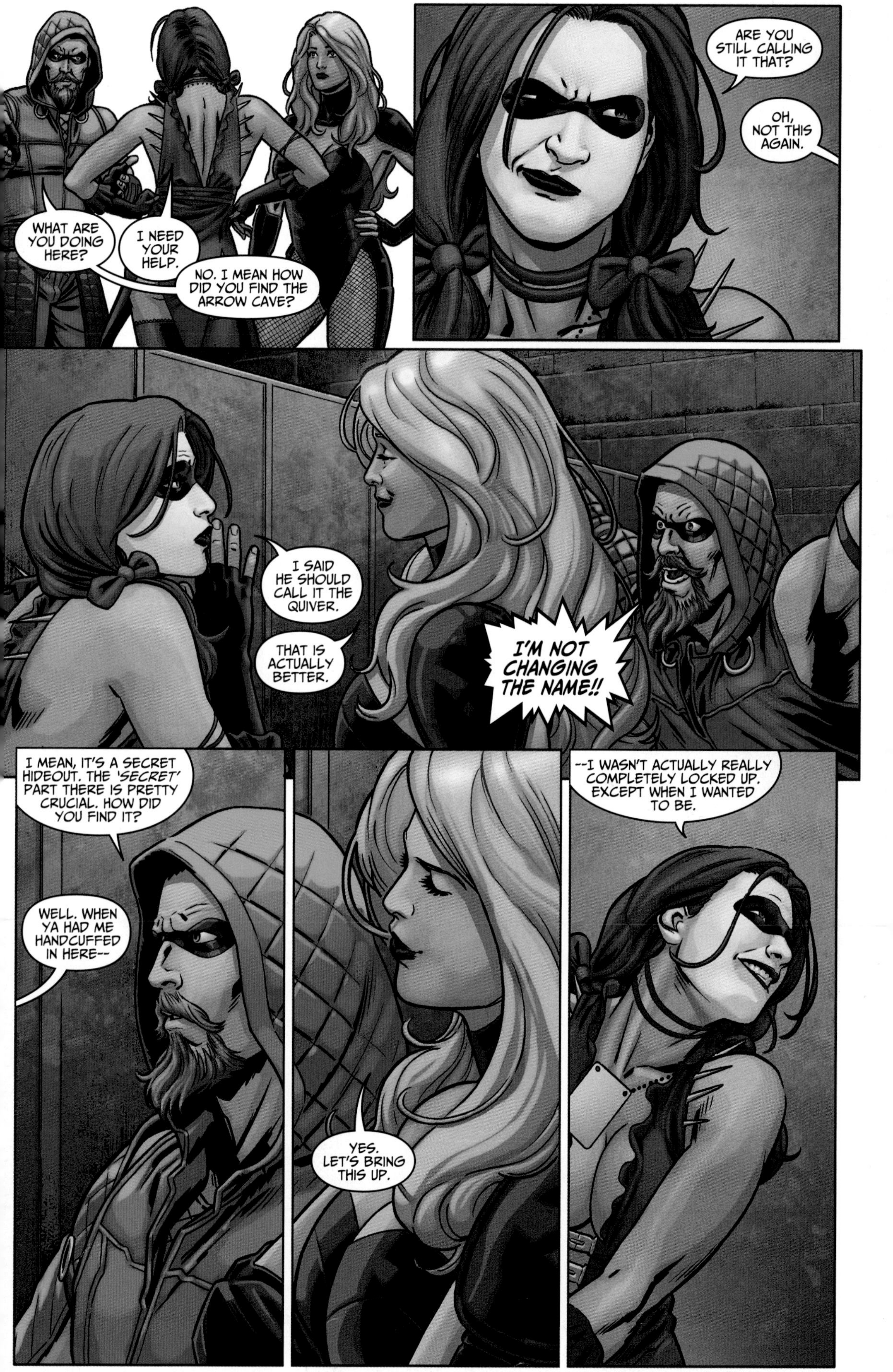
WHAT ARE YOU DOING HERE?
I NEED YOUR HELP.
NO. I MEAN HOW DID YOU FIND THE ARROW CAVE?
ARE YOU STILL CALLING IT THAT?
OH, NOT THIS AGAIN.
I SAID HE SHOULD CALL IT THE QUIVER.
THAT IS ACTUALLY BETTER.
I'M NOT CHANGING THE NAME!!
I MEAN, IT'S A SECRET HIDEOUT. THE 'SECRET' PART THERE IS PRETTY CRUCIAL. HOW DID YOU FIND IT?
WELL. WHEN YA HAD ME HANDCUFFED IN HERE--
YES. LET'S BRING THIS UP.
--I WASN'T ACTUALLY REALLY COMPLETELY LOCKED UP. EXCEPT WHEN I WANTED TO BE.

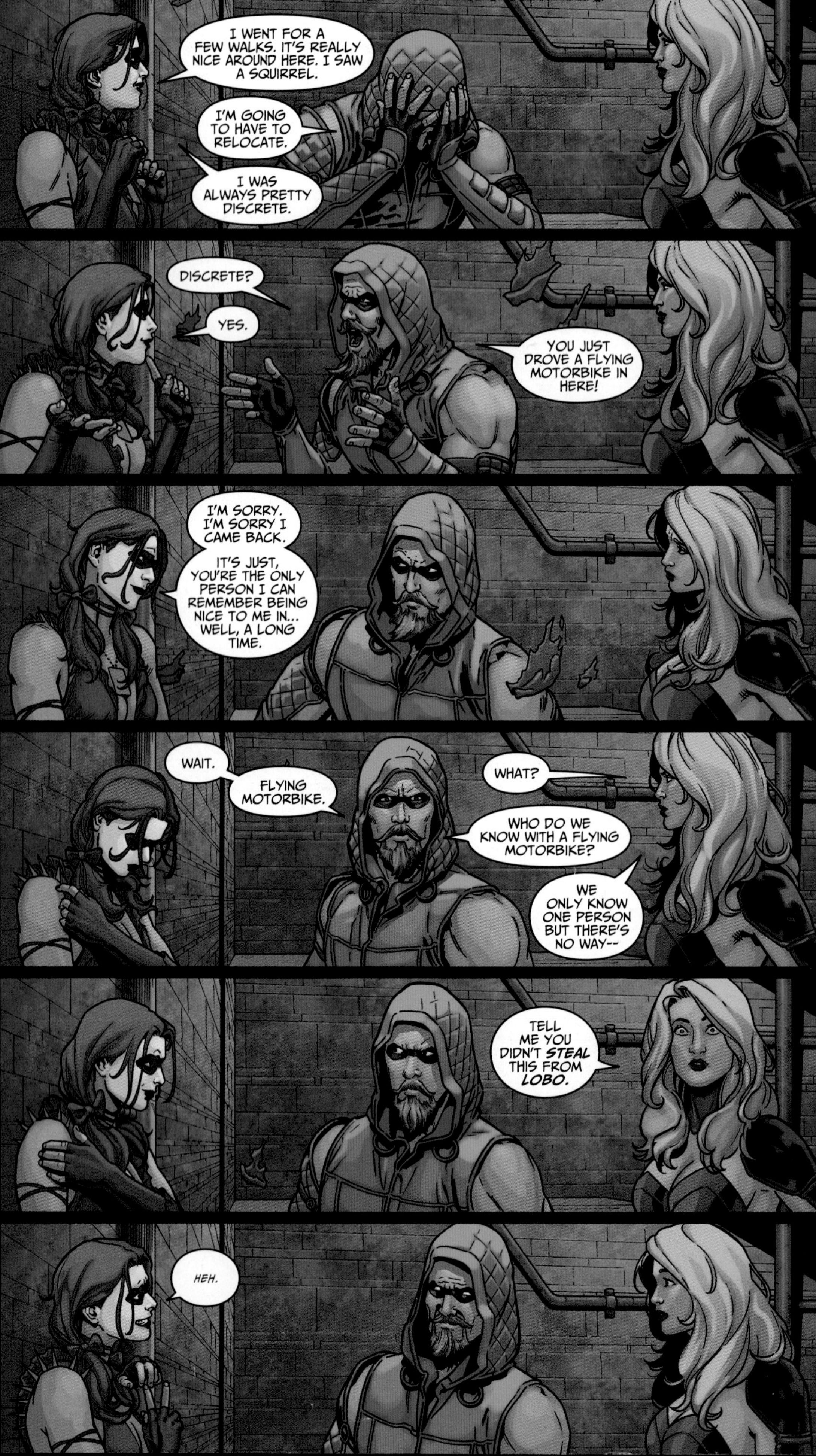

I WENT FOR A FEW WALKS. IT'S REALLY NICE AROUND HERE. I SAW A SQUIRREL.
I'M GOING TO HAVE TO RELOCATE.
I WAS ALWAYS PRETTY DISCRETE.
DISCRETE?
YES.
YOU JUST DROVE A FLYING MOTORBIKE IN HERE!
I'M SORRY. I'M SORRY I CAME BACK.
IT'S JUST, YOU'RE THE ONLY PERSON I CAN REMEMBER BEING NICE TO ME IN... WELL, A LONG TIME.
WAIT.
FLYING MOTORBIKE.
WHAT?
WHO DO WE KNOW WITH A FLYING MOTORBIKE?
WE ONLY KNOW ONE PERSON BUT THERE'S NO WAY--
TELL ME YOU DIDN'T *STEAL* THIS FROM *LOBO.*
HEH.

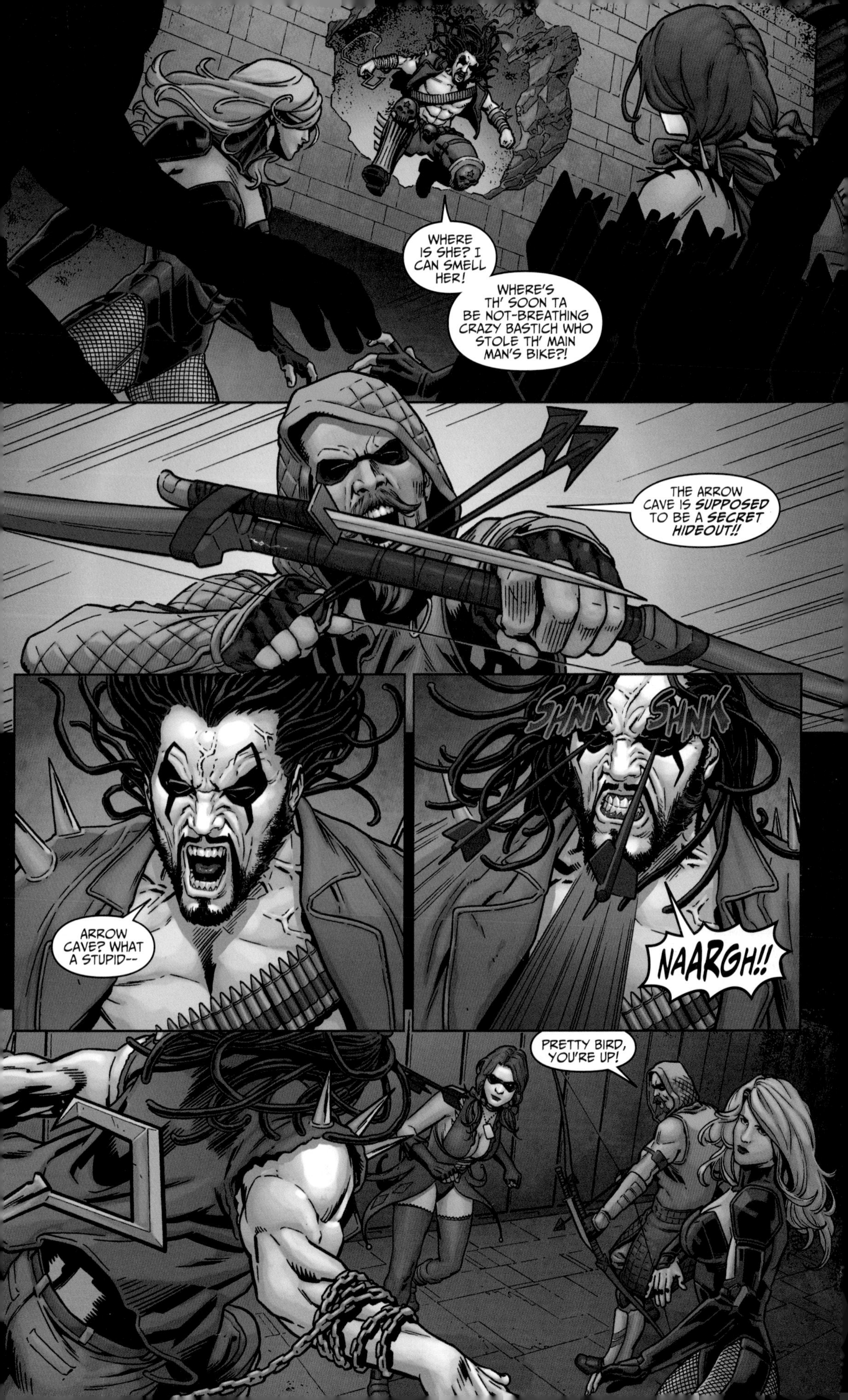
WHERE IS SHE? I CAN SMELL HER!
WHERE'S TH' SOON TA BE NOT-BREATHING CRAZY BASTICH WHO STOLE TH' MAIN MAN'S BIKE?!
THE ARROW CAVE IS *SUPPOSED* TO BE A *SECRET HIDEOUT!!*
ARROW CAVE? WHAT A STUPID--
SHNK SHNK
NAARGH!!
PRETTY BIRD, YOU'RE UP!

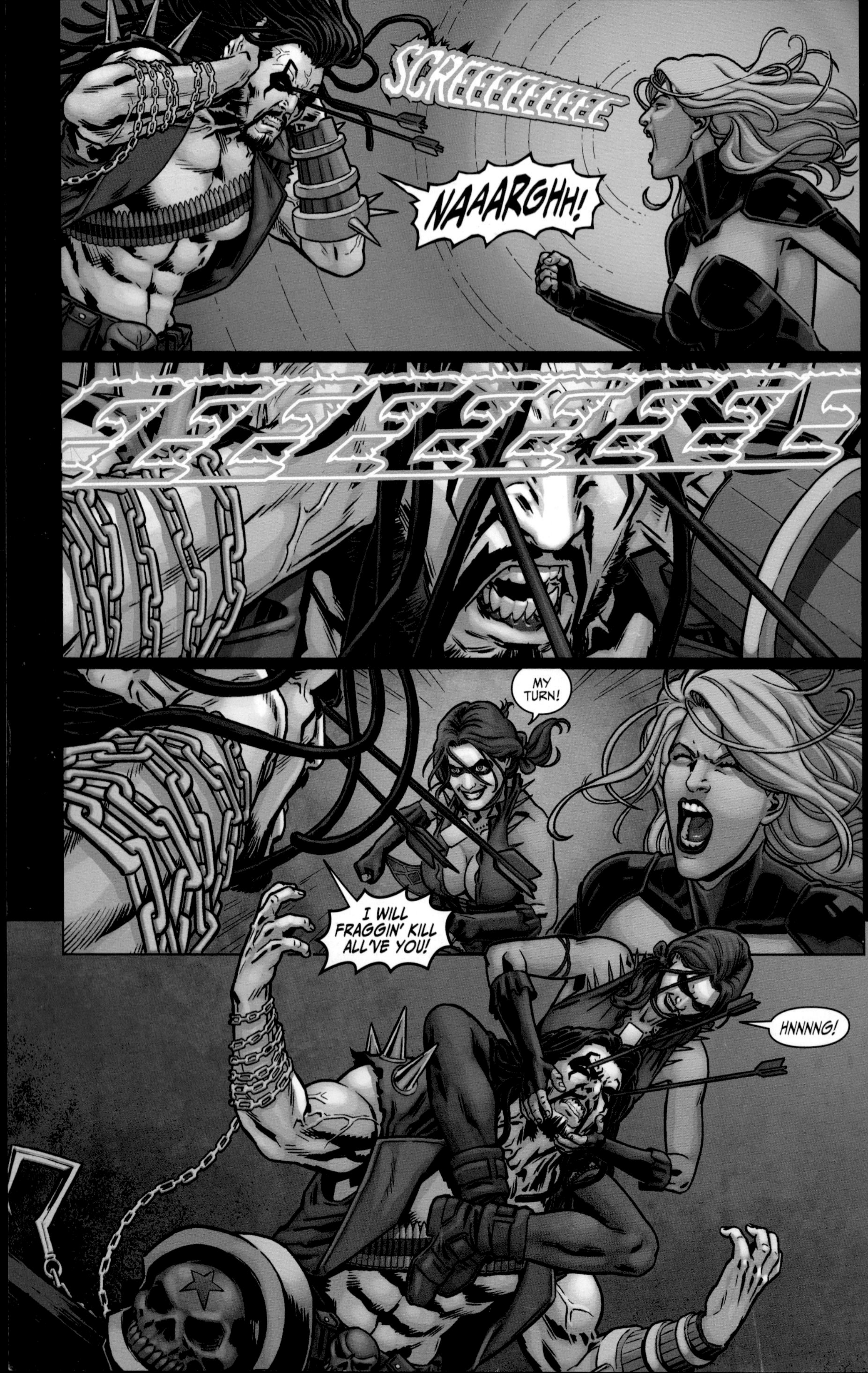
SCREEEEEEEEEE
NAAARGHH!
MY TURN!
I WILL FRAGGIN' KILL ALL'VE YOU!
HNNNNG!

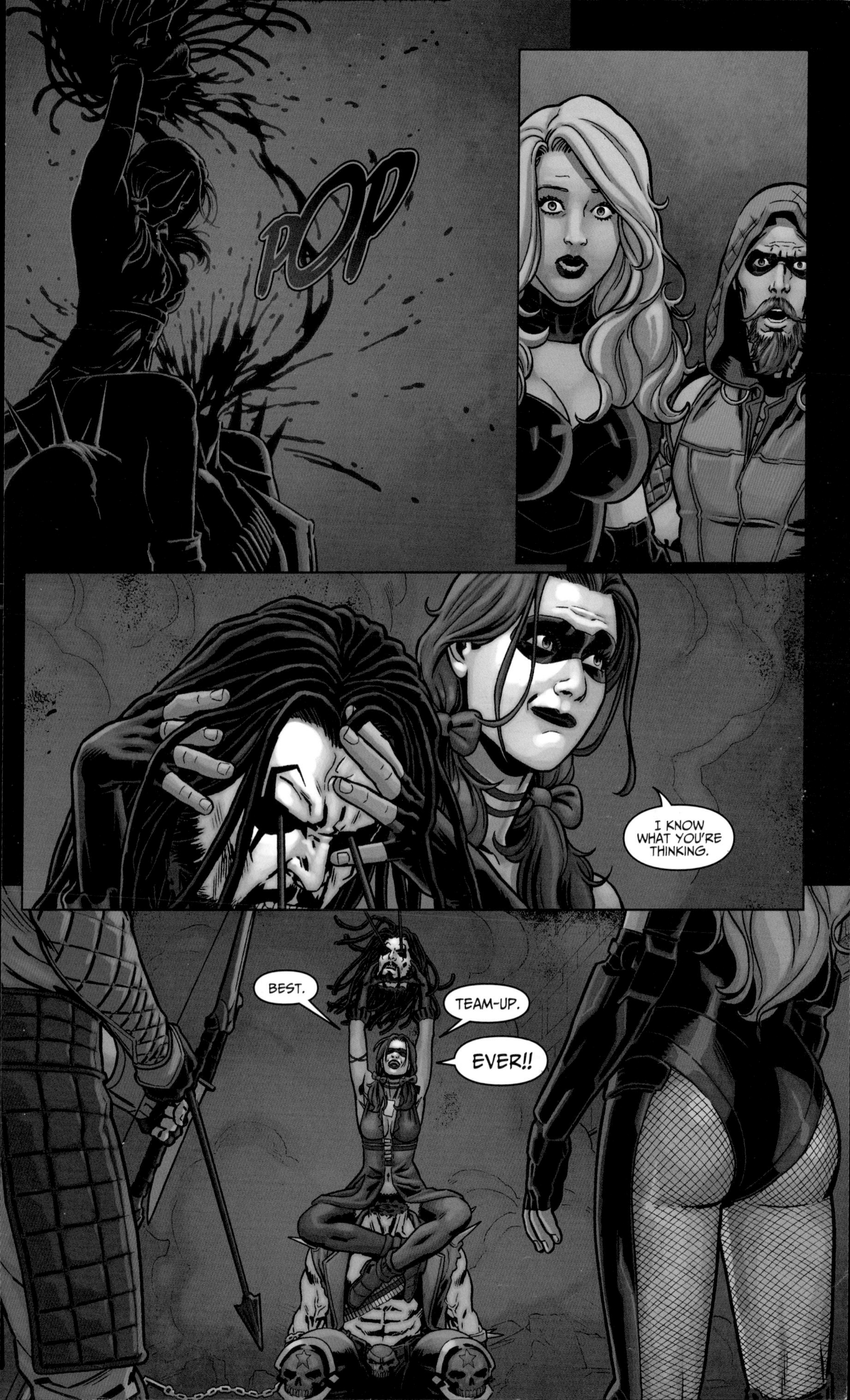
POP
I KNOW WHAT YOU'RE THINKING.
BEST.
TEAM-UP.
EVER!!

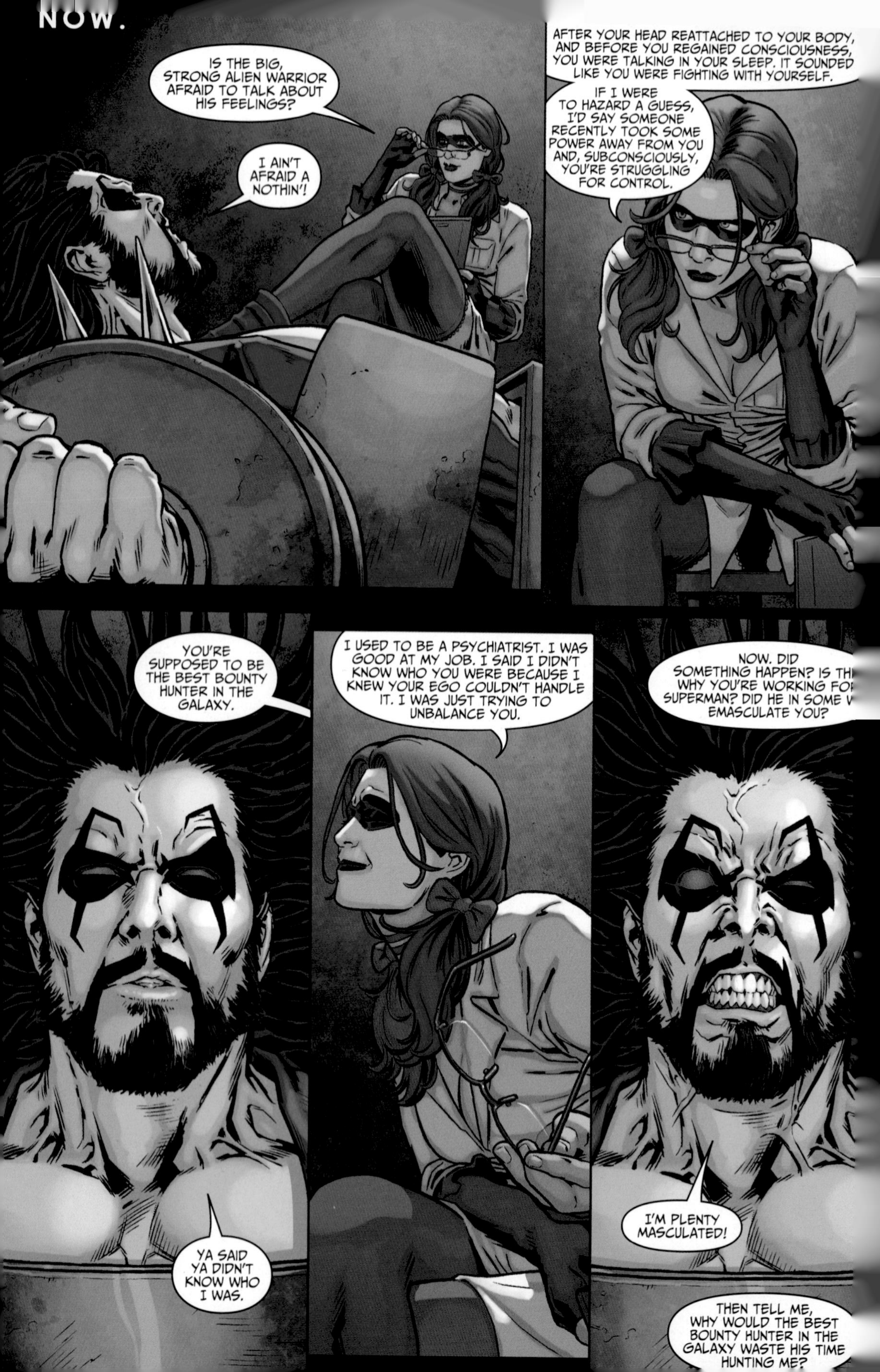
NOW.
IS THE BIG, STRONG ALIEN WARRIOR AFRAID TO TALK ABOUT HIS FEELINGS?
I AIN'T AFRAID A NOTHIN'!
AFTER YOUR HEAD REATTACHED TO YOUR BODY, AND BEFORE YOU REGAINED CONSCIOUSNESS, YOU WERE TALKING IN YOUR SLEEP. IT SOUNDED LIKE YOU WERE FIGHTING WITH YOURSELF.
IF I WERE TO HAZARD A GUESS, I'D SAY SOMEONE RECENTLY TOOK SOME POWER AWAY FROM YOU AND, SUBCONSCIOUSLY, YOU'RE STRUGGLING FOR CONTROL.
YOU'RE SUPPOSED TO BE THE BEST BOUNTY HUNTER IN THE GALAXY.
YA SAID YA DIDN'T KNOW WHO I WAS.
I USED TO BE A PSYCHIATRIST. I WAS GOOD AT MY JOB. I SAID I DIDN'T KNOW WHO YOU WERE BECAUSE I KNEW YOUR EGO COULDN'T HANDLE IT. I WAS JUST TRYING TO UNBALANCE YOU.
NOW. DID SOMETHING HAPPEN? IS TH WHY YOU'RE WORKING FOR SUPERMAN? DID HE IN SOME EMASCULATE YOU?
I'M PLENTY MASCULATED!
THEN TELL ME, WHY WOULD THE BEST BOUNTY HUNTER IN THE GALAXY WASTE HIS TIME HUNTING ME?

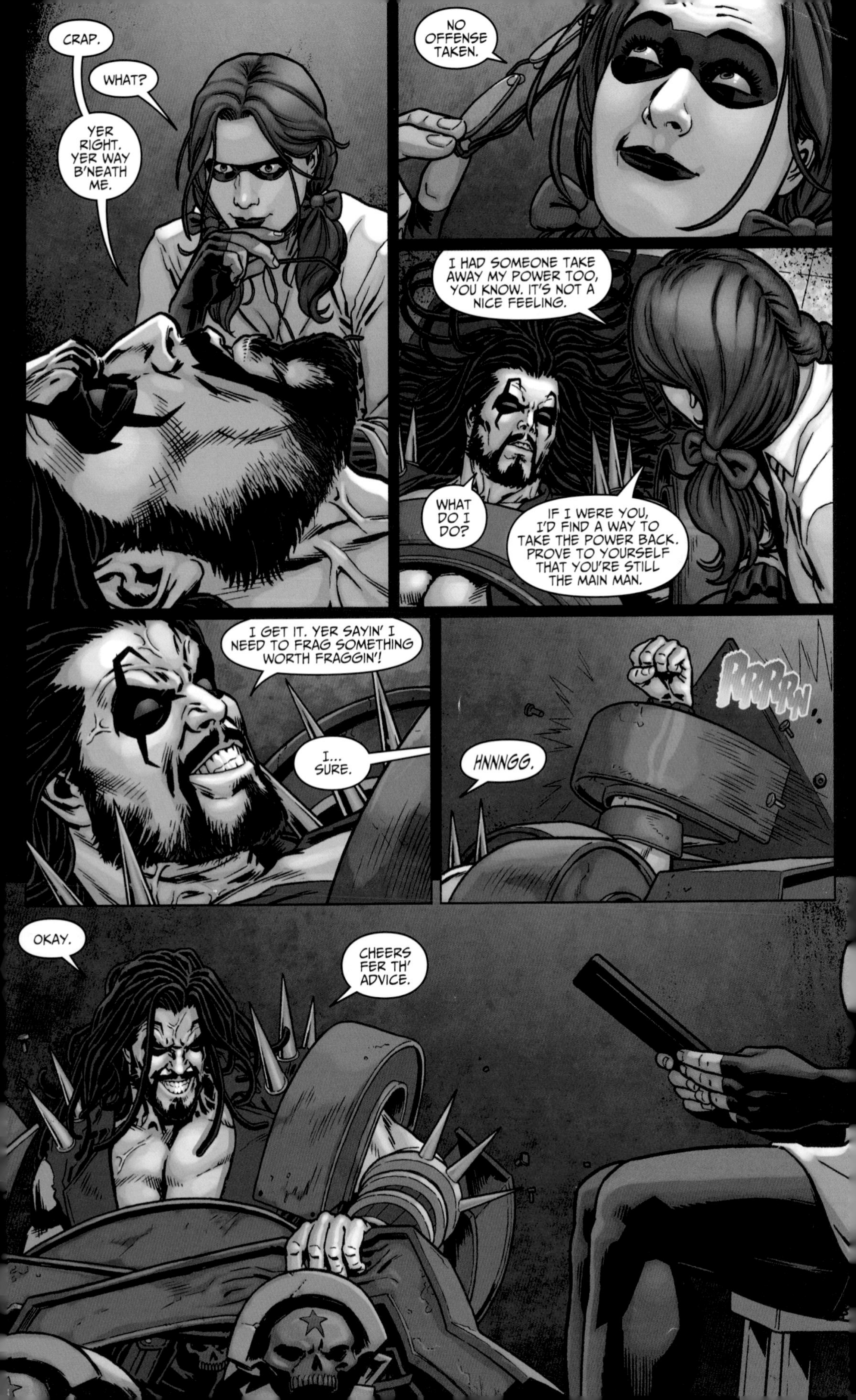
CRAP.
WHAT?
YER RIGHT. YER WAY B'NEATH ME.
NO OFFENSE TAKEN.
I HAD SOMEONE TAKE AWAY MY POWER TOO, YOU KNOW. IT'S NOT A NICE FEELING.
WHAT DO I DO?
IF I WERE YOU, I'D FIND A WAY TO TAKE THE POWER BACK. PROVE TO YOURSELF THAT YOU'RE STILL THE MAIN MAN.
I GET IT. YER SAYIN' I NEED TO FRAG SOMETHING WORTH FRAGGIN'!
I... SURE.
RRRRRN
HNNNGG.
OKAY.
CHEERS FER TH' ADVICE.

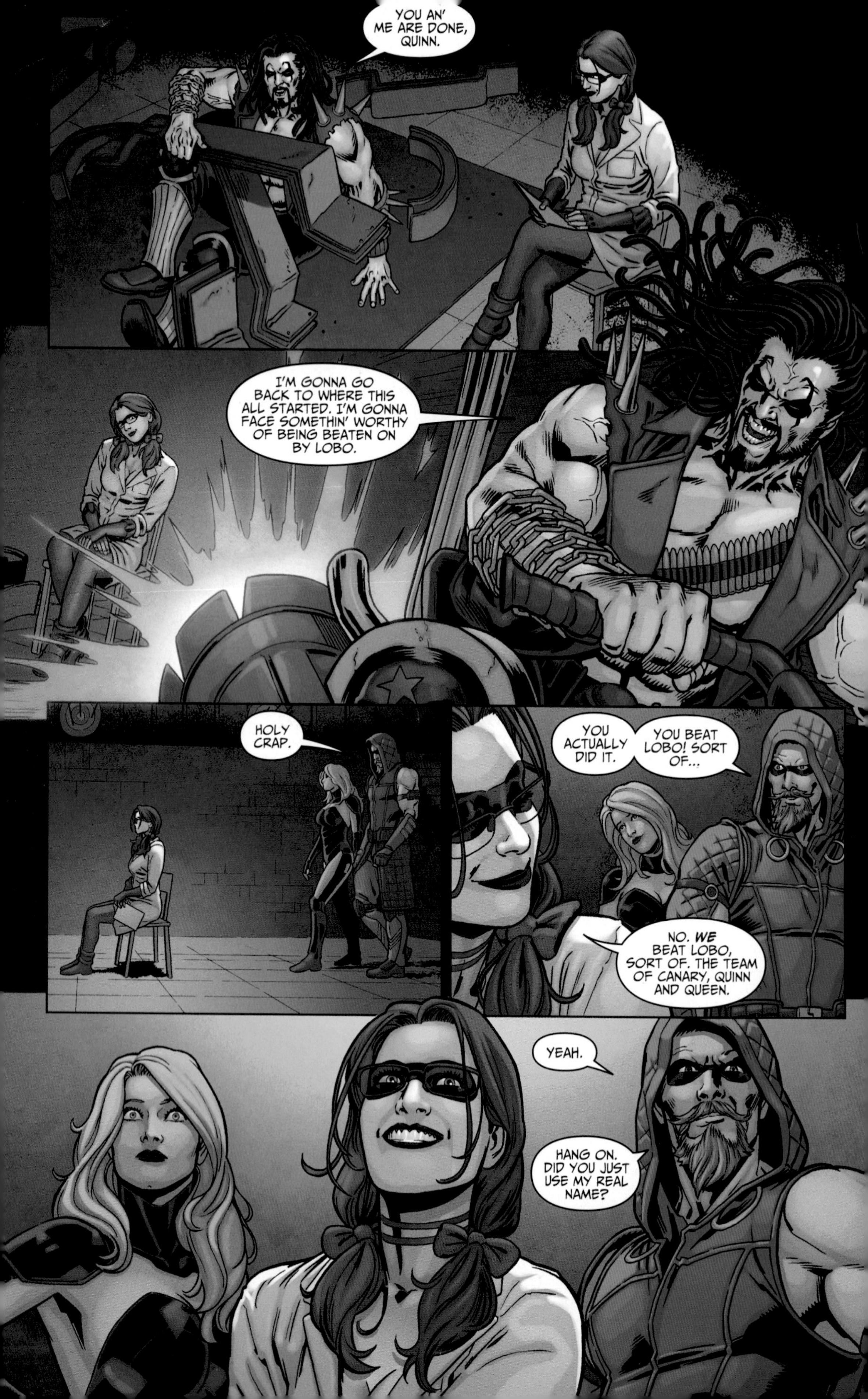
YOU AN' ME ARE DONE, QUINN.
I'M GONNA GO BACK TO WHERE THIS ALL STARTED. I'M GONNA FACE SOMETHIN' WORTHY OF BEING BEATEN ON BY LOBO.
HOLY CRAP.
YOU ACTUALLY DID IT.
YOU BEAT LOBO! SORT OF...
NO. WE BEAT LOBO, SORT OF. THE TEAM OF CANARY, QUINN AND QUEEN.
YEAH.
HANG ON. DID YOU JUST USE MY REAL NAME?

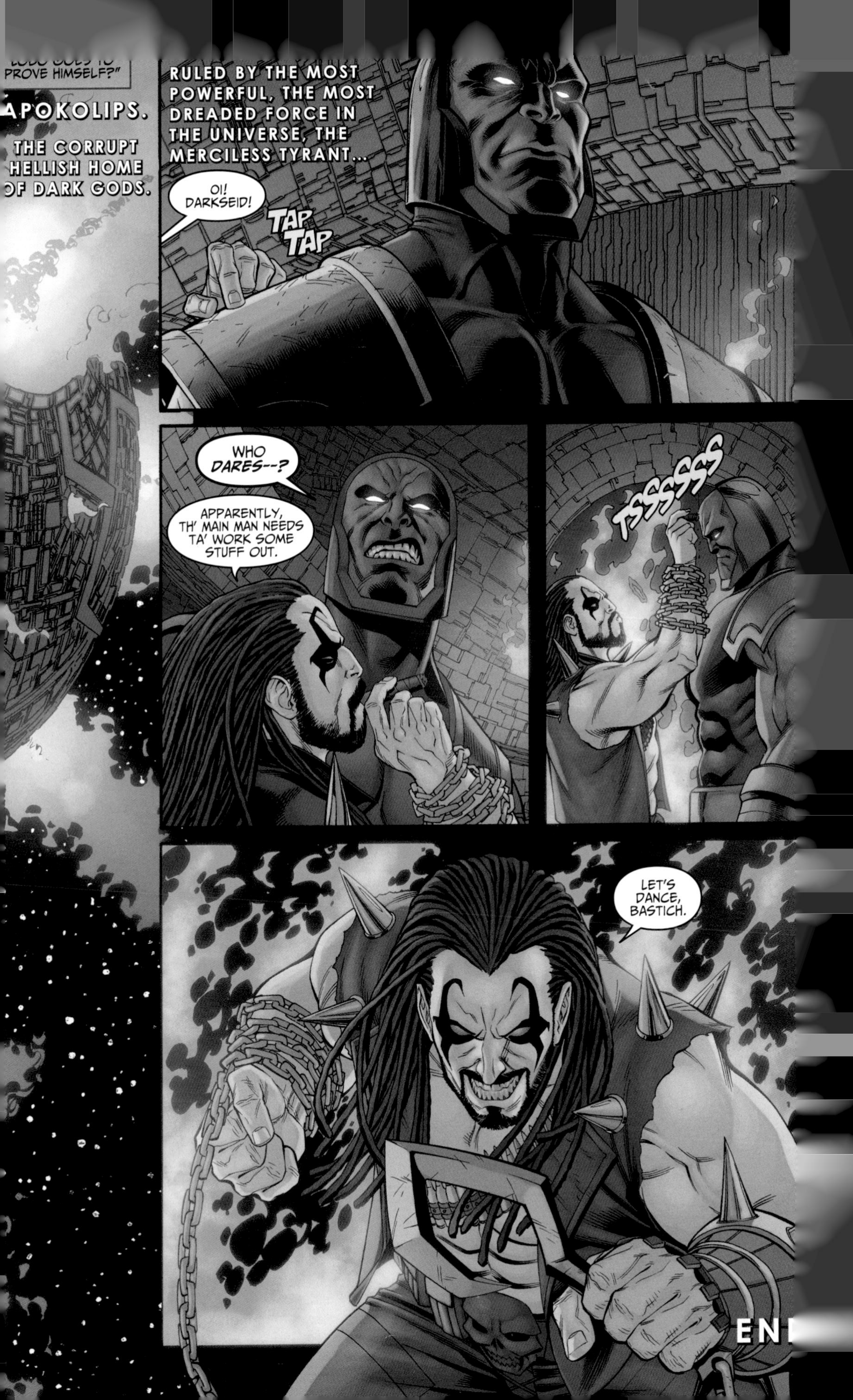

PROVE HIMSELF?"
APOKOLIPS.
THE CORRUPT HELLISH HOME OF DARK GODS.
RULED BY THE MOST POWERFUL, THE MOST DREADED FORCE IN THE UNIVERSE, THE MERCILESS TYRANT...
OI! DARKSEID!
TAP TAP
WHO DARES--?
APPARENTLY, TH' MAIN MAN NEEDS TA' WORK SOME STUFF OUT.
TSSSSSS
LET'S DANCE, BASTICH.

Cover Art by Mico Suayan with David Lopez & Santi Casas of Ikari Studio

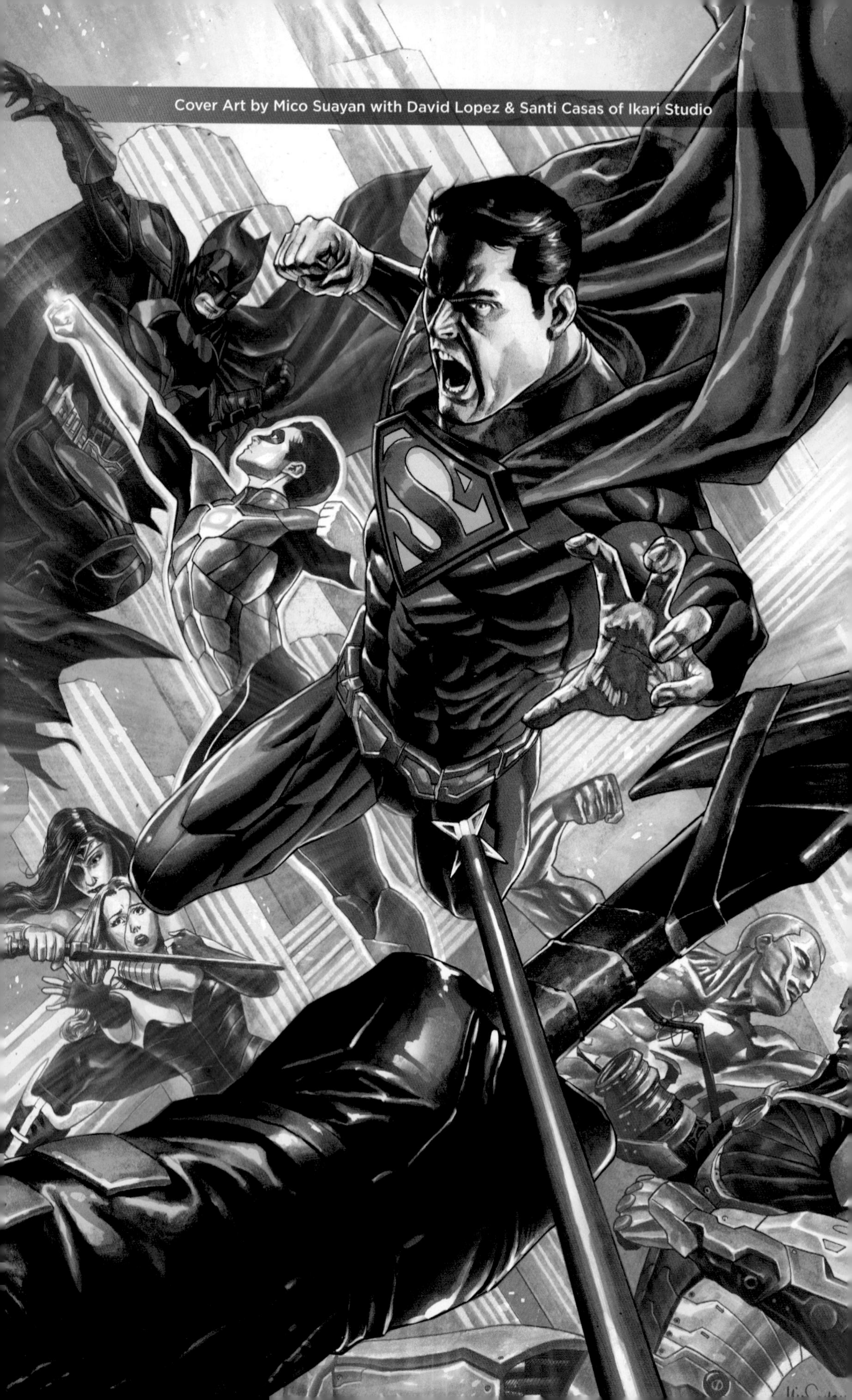

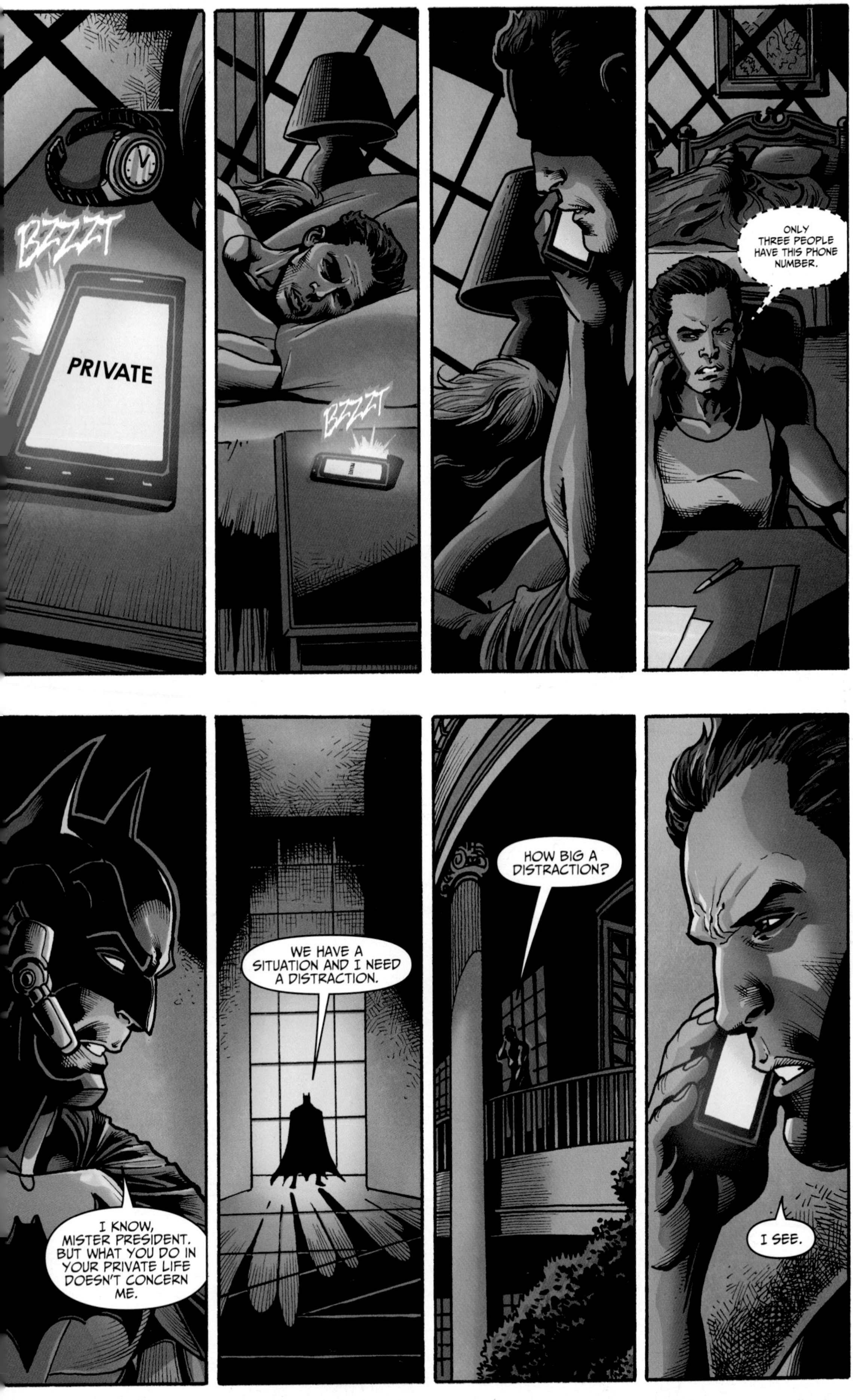
BZZT
PRIVATE
BZZT
ONLY THREE PEOPLE HAVE THIS PHONE NUMBER.
I KNOW, MISTER PRESIDENT. BUT WHAT YOU DO IN YOUR PRIVATE LIFE DOESN'T CONCERN ME.
WE HAVE A SITUATION AND I NEED A DISTRACTION.
HOW BIG A DISTRACTION?
I SEE.

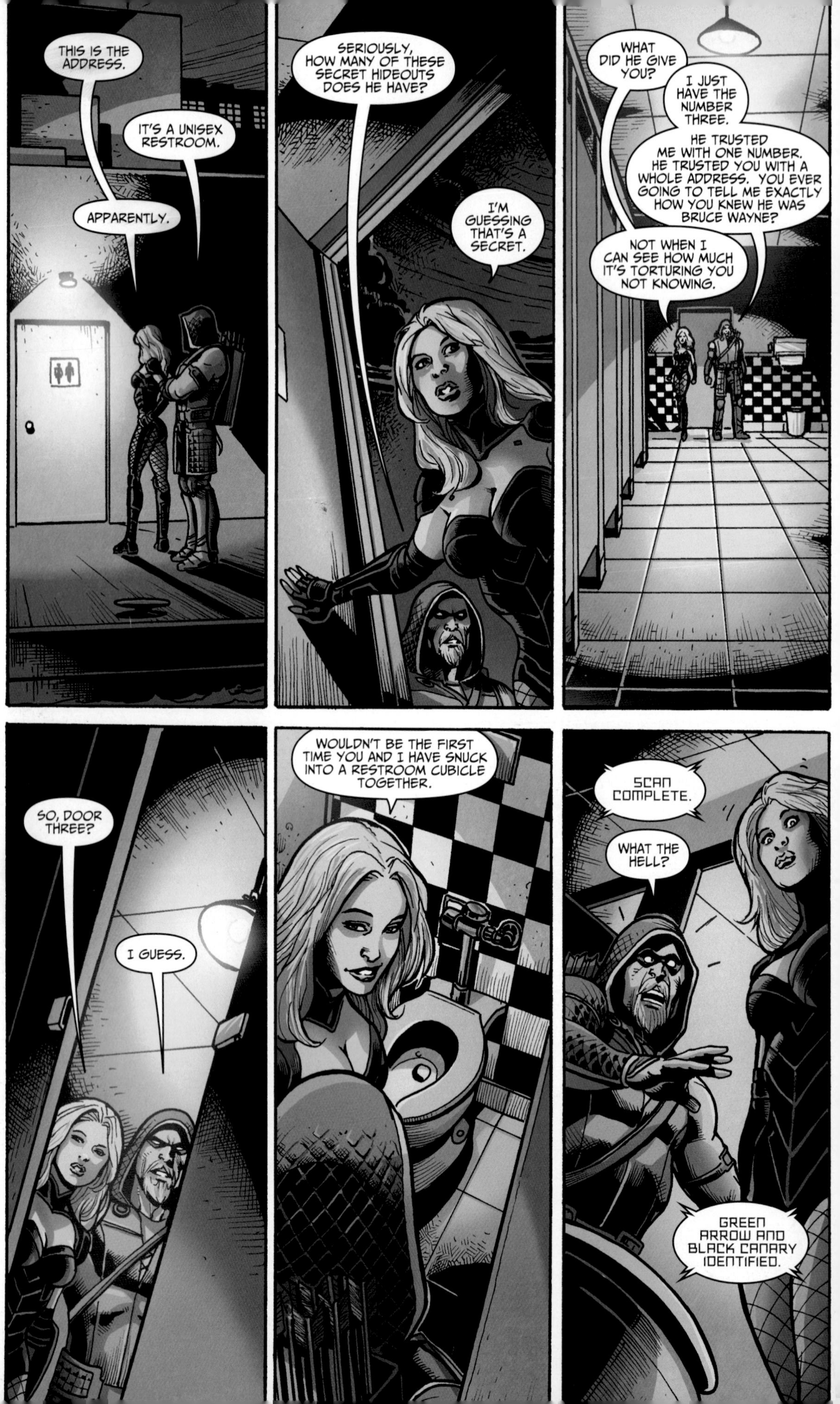

THIS IS THE ADDRESS.
IT'S A UNISEX RESTROOM.
APPARENTLY.
SERIOUSLY, HOW MANY OF THESE SECRET HIDEOUTS DOES HE HAVE?
I'M GUESSING THAT'S A SECRET.
WHAT DID HE GIVE YOU?
I JUST HAVE THE NUMBER THREE.
HE TRUSTED ME WITH ONE NUMBER. HE TRUSTED YOU WITH A WHOLE ADDRESS. YOU EVER GOING TO TELL ME EXACTLY HOW YOU KNEW HE WAS BRUCE WAYNE?
NOT WHEN I CAN SEE HOW MUCH IT'S TORTURING YOU NOT KNOWING.
SO, DOOR THREE?
I GUESS.
WOULDN'T BE THE FIRST TIME YOU AND I HAVE SNUCK INTO A RESTROOM CUBICLE TOGETHER.
SCAN COMPLETE.
WHAT THE HELL?
GREEN ARROW AND BLACK CANARY IDENTIFIED.

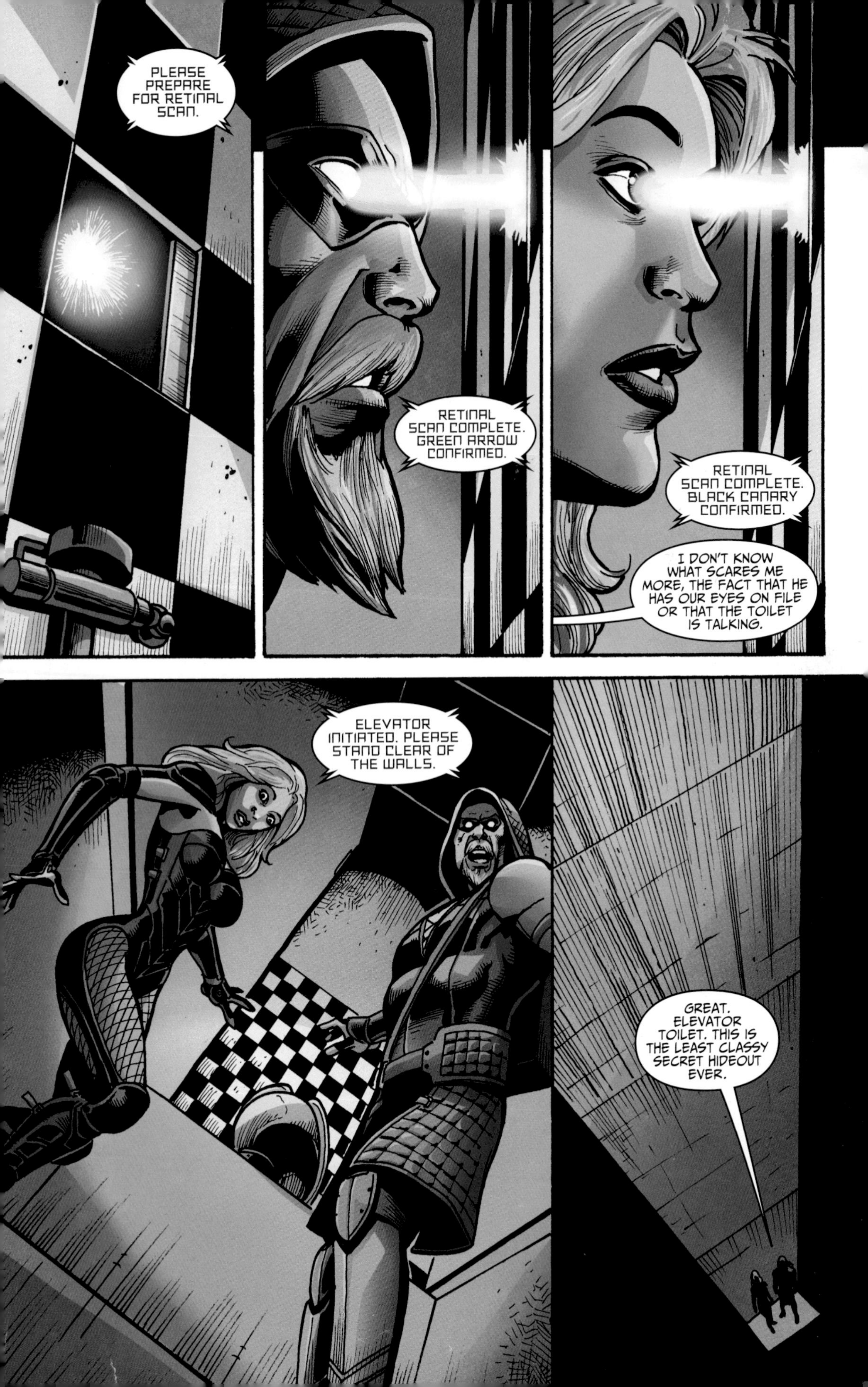
PLEASE PREPARE FOR RETINAL SCAN.
RETINAL SCAN COMPLETE. GREEN ARROW CONFIRMED.
RETINAL SCAN COMPLETE. BLACK CANARY CONFIRMED.
I DON'T KNOW WHAT SCARES ME MORE, THE FACT THAT HE HAS OUR EYES ON FILE OR THAT THE TOILET IS TALKING.
ELEVATOR INITIATED. PLEASE STAND CLEAR OF THE WALLS.
GREAT. ELEVATOR TOILET. THIS IS THE LEAST CLASSY SECRET HIDEOUT EVER.

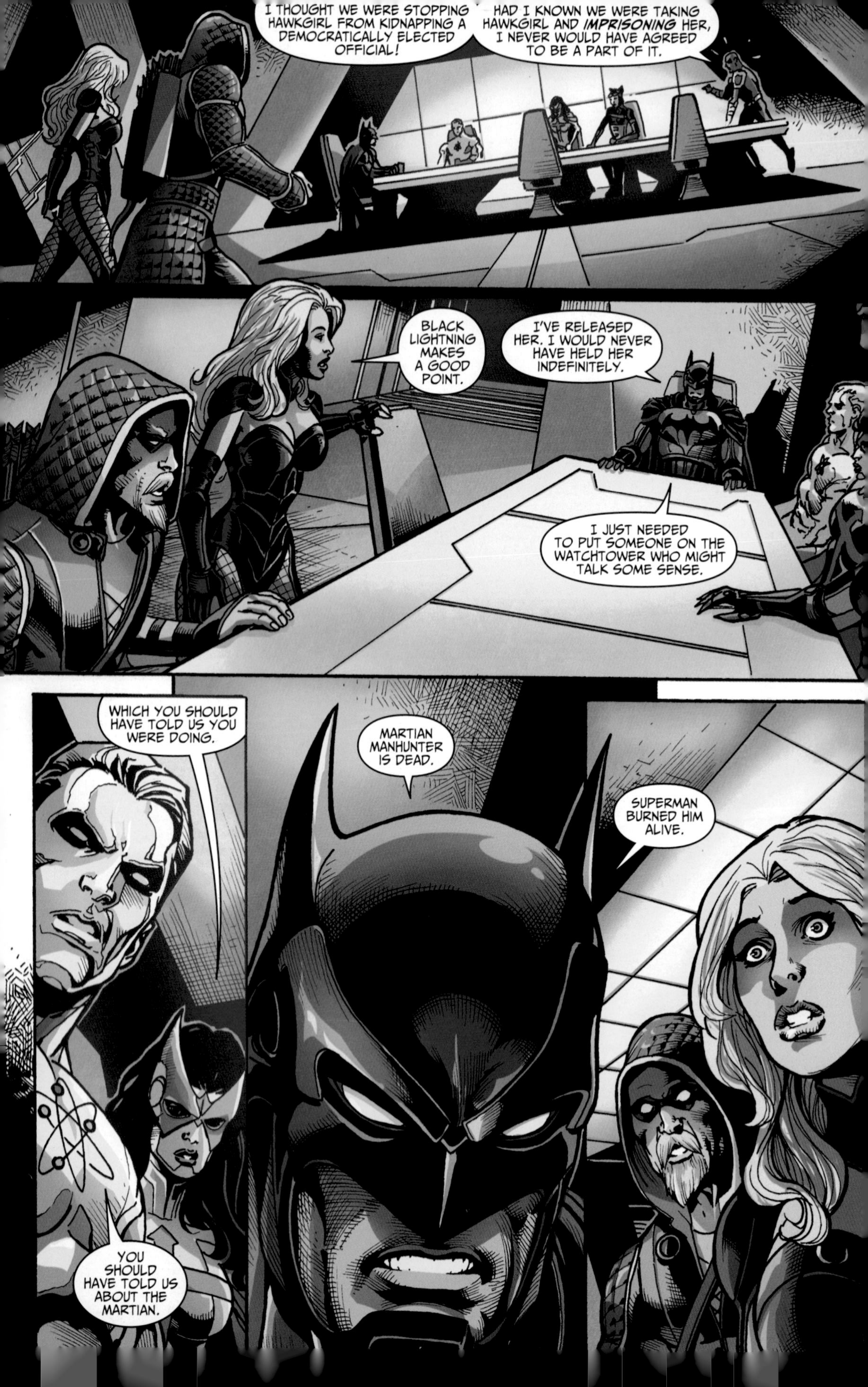
I THOUGHT WE WERE STOPPING HAWKGIRL FROM KIDNAPPING A DEMOCRATICALLY ELECTED OFFICIAL!
HAD I KNOWN WE WERE TAKING HAWKGIRL AND *IMPRISONING* HER, I NEVER WOULD HAVE AGREED TO BE A PART OF IT.
BLACK LIGHTNING MAKES A GOOD POINT.
I'VE RELEASED HER. I WOULD NEVER HAVE HELD HER INDEFINITELY.
I JUST NEEDED TO PUT SOMEONE ON THE WATCHTOWER WHO MIGHT TALK SOME SENSE.
WHICH YOU SHOULD HAVE TOLD US YOU WERE DOING.
YOU SHOULD HAVE TOLD US ABOUT THE MARTIAN.
MARTIAN MANHUNTER IS DEAD.
SUPERMAN BURNED HIM ALIVE.

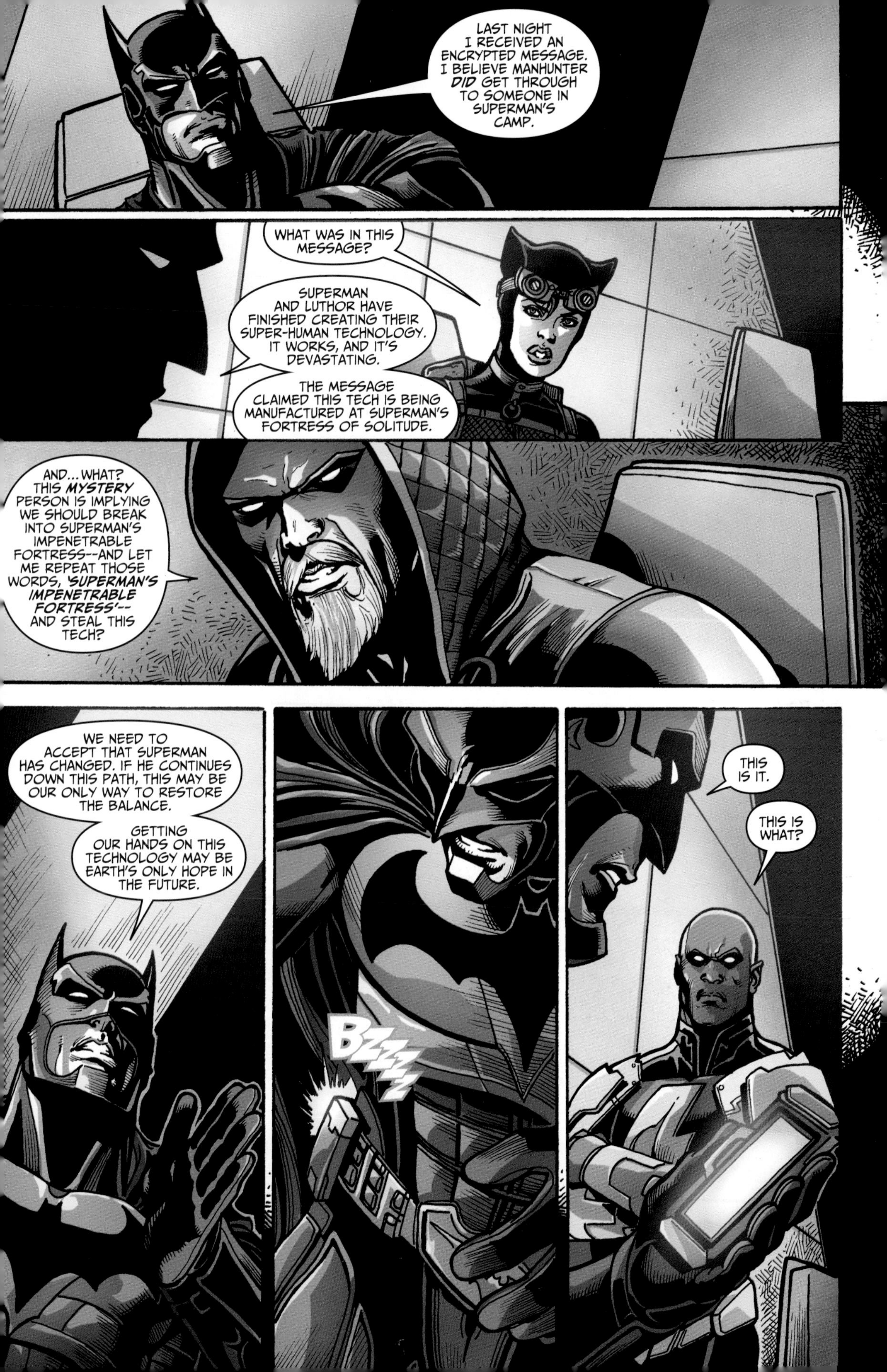
LAST NIGHT I RECEIVED AN ENCRYPTED MESSAGE. I BELIEVE MANHUNTER *DID* GET THROUGH TO SOMEONE IN SUPERMAN'S CAMP.
WHAT WAS IN THIS MESSAGE?
SUPERMAN AND LUTHOR HAVE FINISHED CREATING THEIR SUPER-HUMAN TECHNOLOGY. IT WORKS, AND IT'S DEVASTATING.
THE MESSAGE CLAIMED THIS TECH IS BEING MANUFACTURED AT SUPERMAN'S FORTRESS OF SOLITUDE.
AND...WHAT? THIS ***MYSTERY*** PERSON IS IMPLYING WE SHOULD BREAK INTO SUPERMAN'S IMPENETRABLE FORTRESS--AND LET ME REPEAT THOSE WORDS, ***'SUPERMAN'S IMPENETRABLE FORTRESS'***-- AND STEAL THIS TECH?
WE NEED TO ACCEPT THAT SUPERMAN HAS CHANGED. IF HE CONTINUES DOWN THIS PATH, THIS MAY BE OUR ONLY WAY TO RESTORE THE BALANCE.
GETTING OUR HANDS ON THIS TECHNOLOGY MAY BE EARTH'S ONLY HOPE IN THE FUTURE.
BZZZZ
THIS IS IT.
THIS IS WHAT?

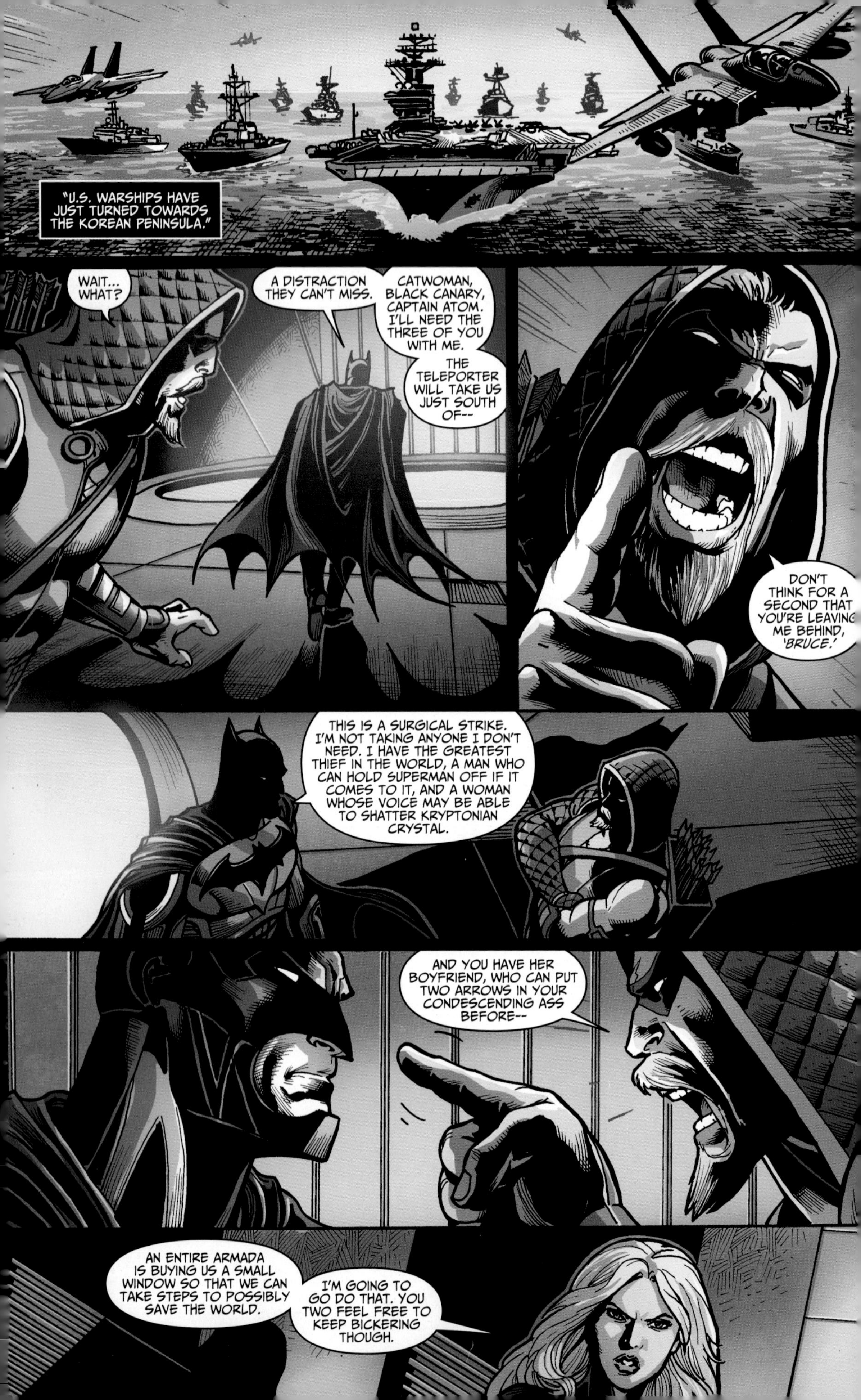
"U.S. WARSHIPS HAVE JUST TURNED TOWARDS THE KOREAN PENINSULA."
WAIT... WHAT?
A DISTRACTION THEY CAN'T MISS.
CATWOMAN, BLACK CANARY, CAPTAIN ATOM. I'LL NEED THE THREE OF YOU WITH ME.
THE TELEPORTER WILL TAKE US JUST SOUTH OF--
DON'T THINK FOR A SECOND THAT YOU'RE LEAVING ME BEHIND, *'BRUCE.'*
THIS IS A SURGICAL STRIKE. I'M NOT TAKING ANYONE I DON'T NEED. I HAVE THE GREATEST THIEF IN THE WORLD, A MAN WHO CAN HOLD SUPERMAN OFF IF IT COMES TO IT, AND A WOMAN WHOSE VOICE MAY BE ABLE TO SHATTER KRYPTONIAN CRYSTAL.
AND YOU HAVE HER BOYFRIEND, WHO CAN PUT TWO ARROWS IN YOUR CONDESCENDING ASS BEFORE--
AN ENTIRE ARMADA IS BUYING US A SMALL WINDOW SO THAT WE CAN TAKE STEPS TO POSSIBLY SAVE THE WORLD.
I'M GOING TO GO DO THAT. YOU TWO FEEL FREE TO KEEP BICKERING THOUGH.

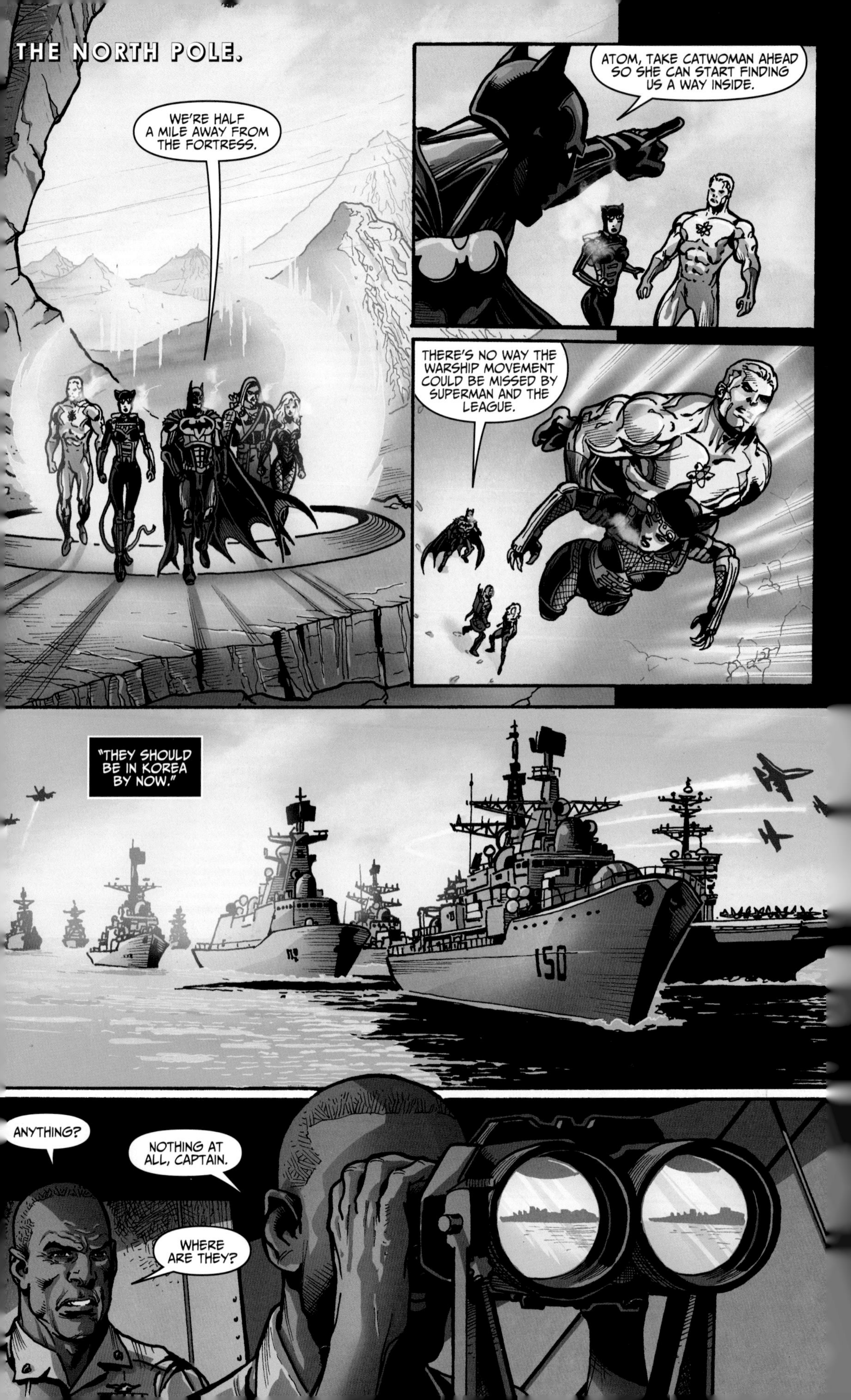
THE NORTH POLE.
WE'RE HALF A MILE AWAY FROM THE FORTRESS.
ATOM, TAKE CATWOMAN AHEAD SO SHE CAN START FINDING US A WAY INSIDE.
THERE'S NO WAY THE WARSHIP MOVEMENT COULD BE MISSED BY SUPERMAN AND THE LEAGUE.
"THEY SHOULD BE IN KOREA BY NOW."
150
ANYTHING?
NOTHING AT ALL, CAPTAIN.
WHERE ARE THEY?

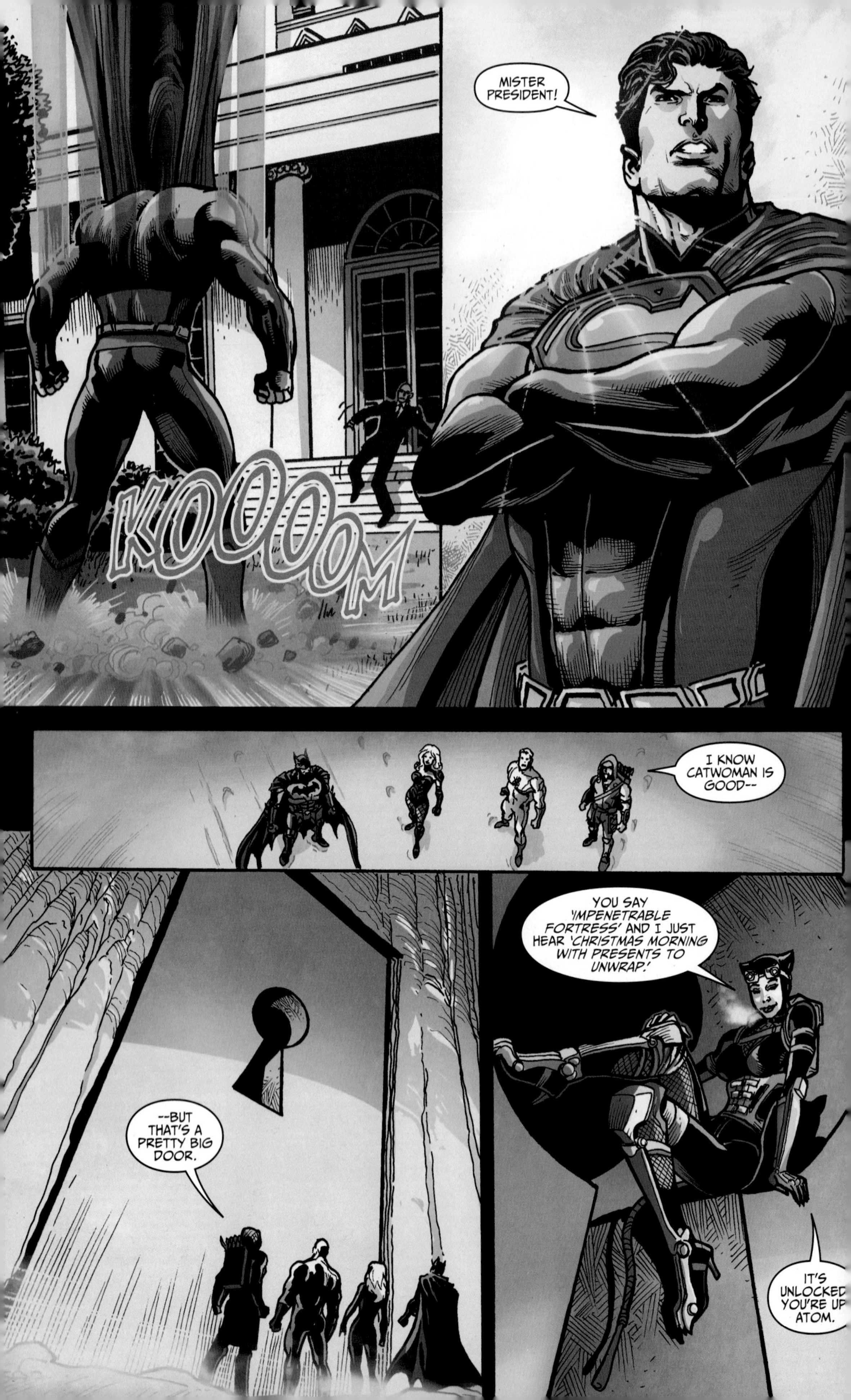
KOOOOM
MISTER PRESIDENT!
I KNOW CATWOMAN IS GOOD--
--BUT THAT'S A PRETTY BIG DOOR.
YOU SAY 'IMPENETRABLE FORTRESS' AND I JUST HEAR 'CHRISTMAS MORNING WITH PRESENTS TO UNWRAP.'
IT'S UNLOCKED. YOU'RE UP, ATOM.

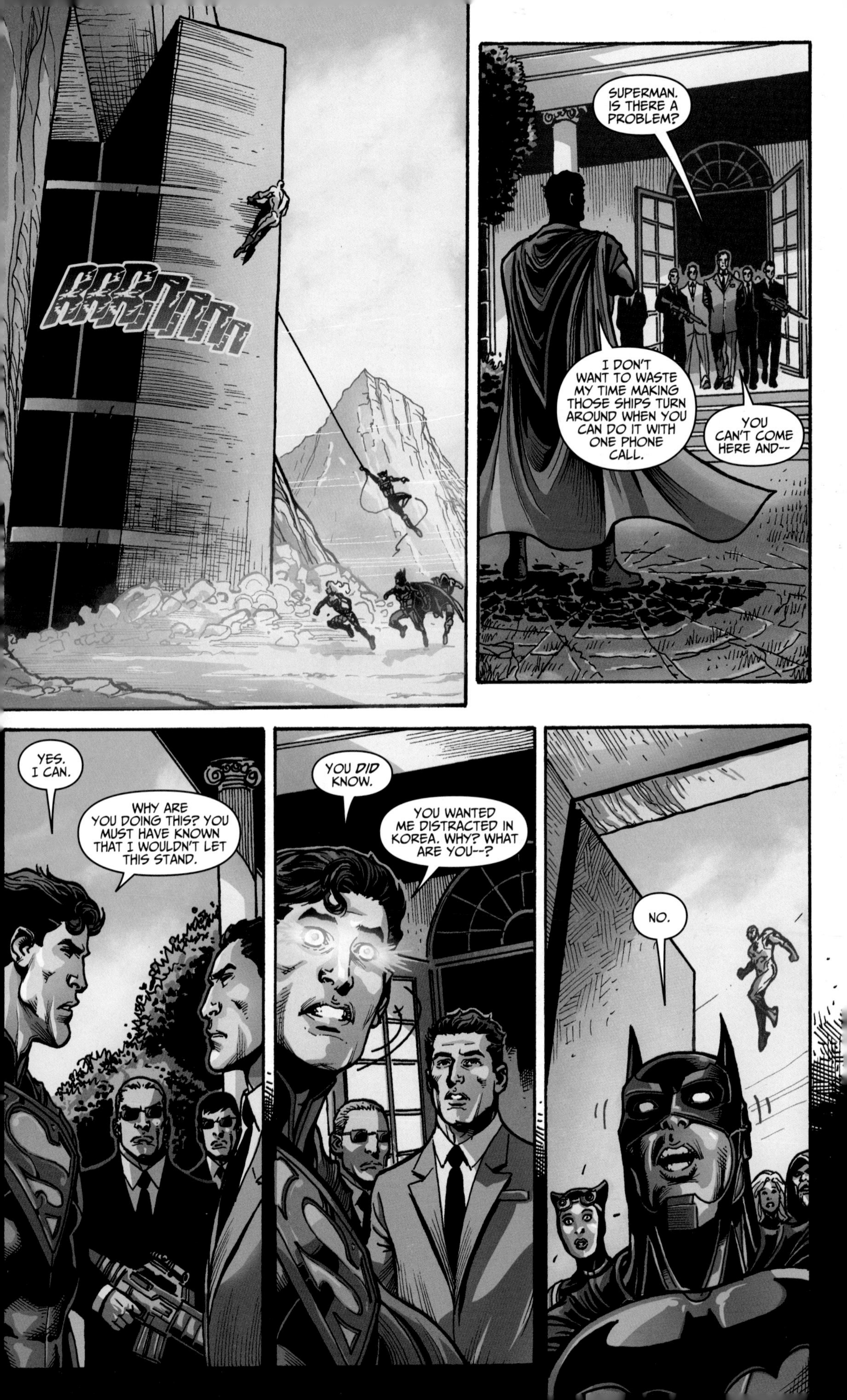
SUPERMAN. IS THERE A PROBLEM?
I DON'T WANT TO WASTE MY TIME MAKING THOSE SHIPS TURN AROUND WHEN YOU CAN DO IT WITH ONE PHONE CALL.
YOU CAN'T COME HERE AND--
YES. I CAN.
WHY ARE YOU DOING THIS? YOU MUST HAVE KNOWN THAT I WOULDN'T LET THIS STAND.
YOU *DID* KNOW.
YOU WANTED ME DISTRACTED IN KOREA. WHY? WHAT ARE YOU--?
NO.

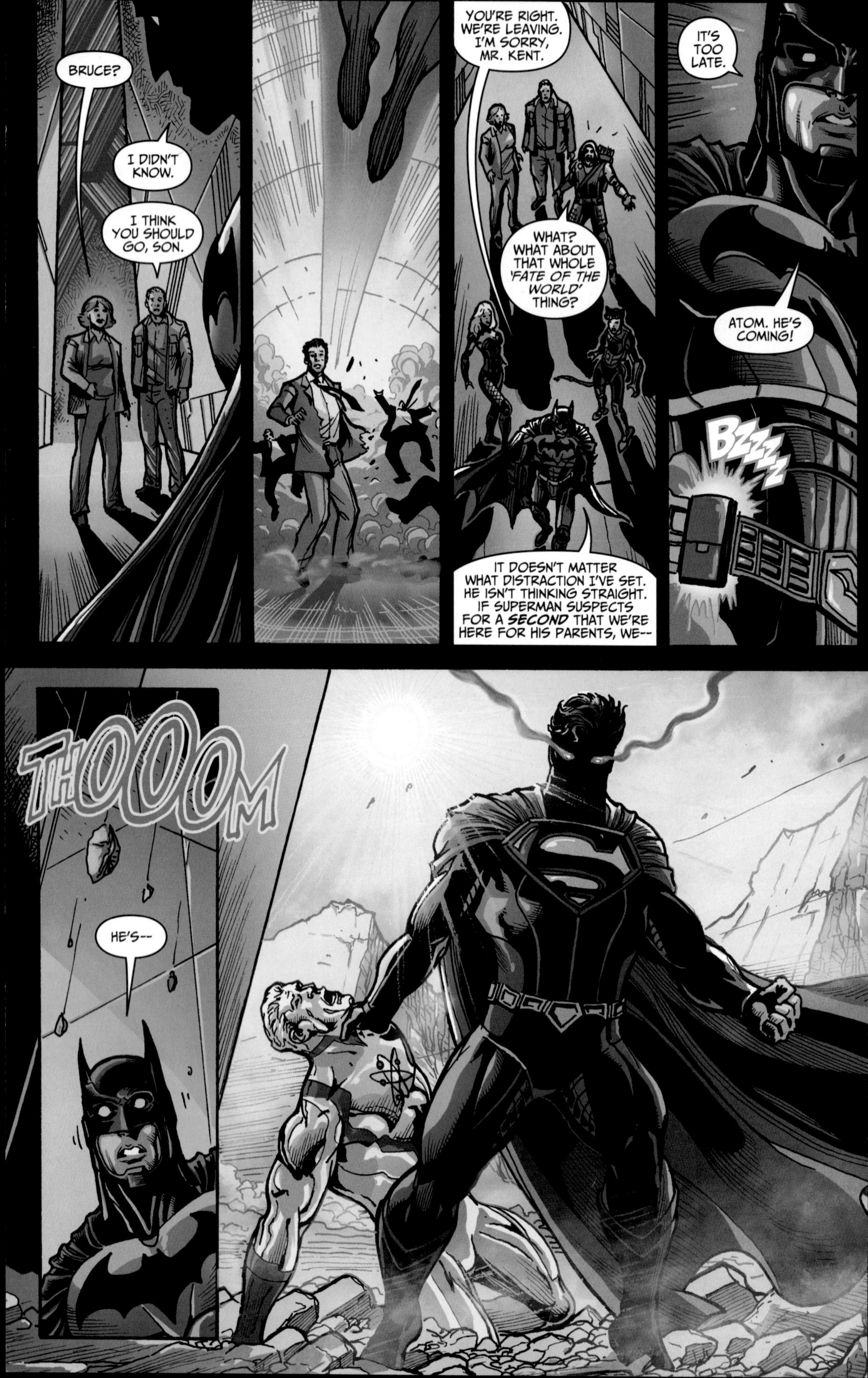
BRUCE?
I DIDN'T KNOW.
I THINK YOU SHOULD GO, SON.
YOU'RE RIGHT. WE'RE LEAVING. I'M SORRY, MR. KENT.
WHAT? WHAT ABOUT THAT WHOLE 'FATE OF THE WORLD' THING?
IT DOESN'T MATTER WHAT DISTRACTION I'VE SET. HE ISN'T THINKING STRAIGHT. IF SUPERMAN SUSPECTS FOR A SECOND THAT WE'RE HERE FOR HIS PARENTS, WE--
IT'S TOO LATE.
ATOM. HE'S COMING!
BZZZZ
THOOOM
HE'S--

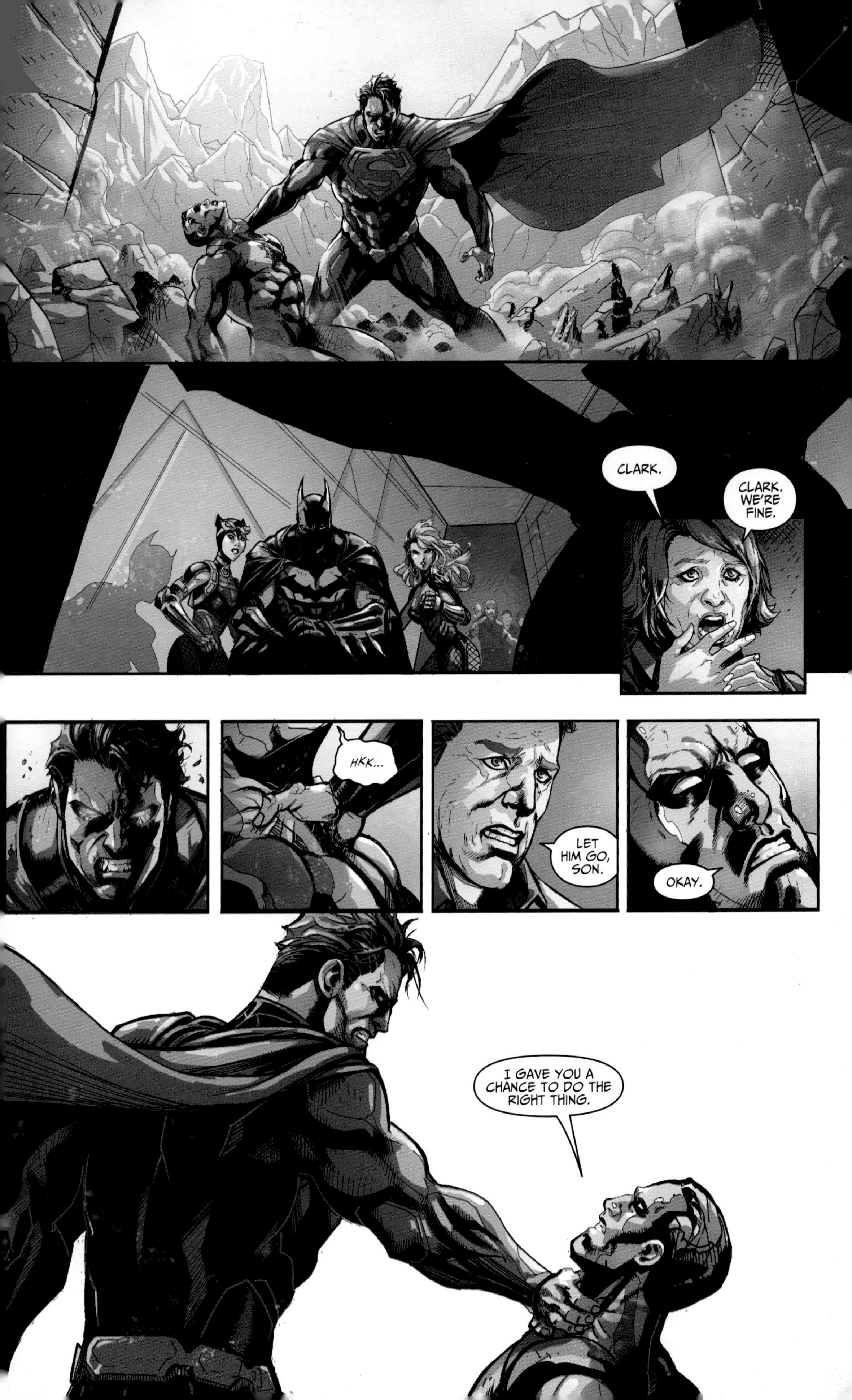
CLARK.
CLARK. WE'RE FINE.
HKK...
LET HIM GO, SON.
OKAY.
I GAVE YOU A CHANCE TO DO THE RIGHT THING.

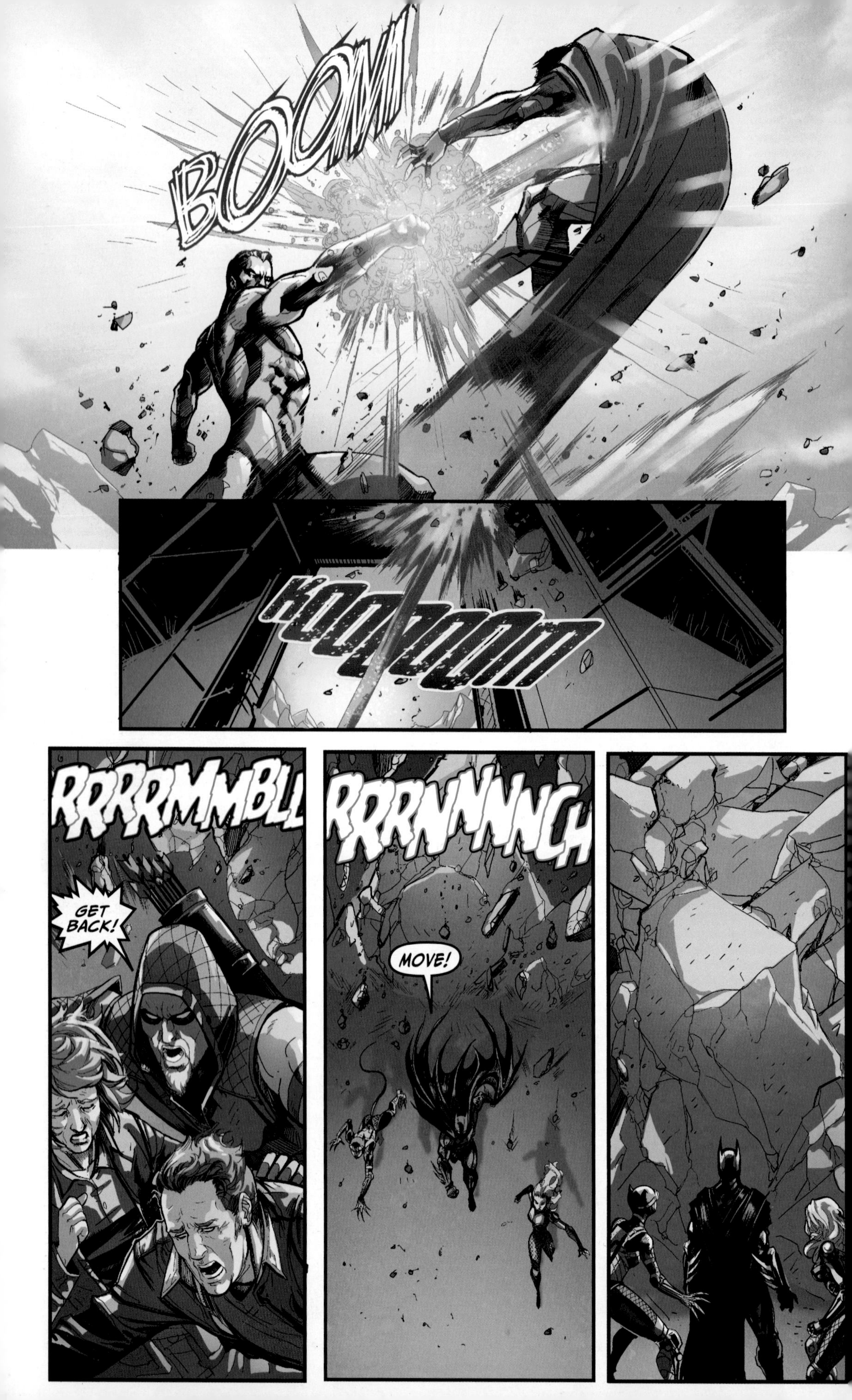
BOOM!
KOOOOOM
RRRRMMBLE
GET BACK!
RRRNNNNCH
MOVE!

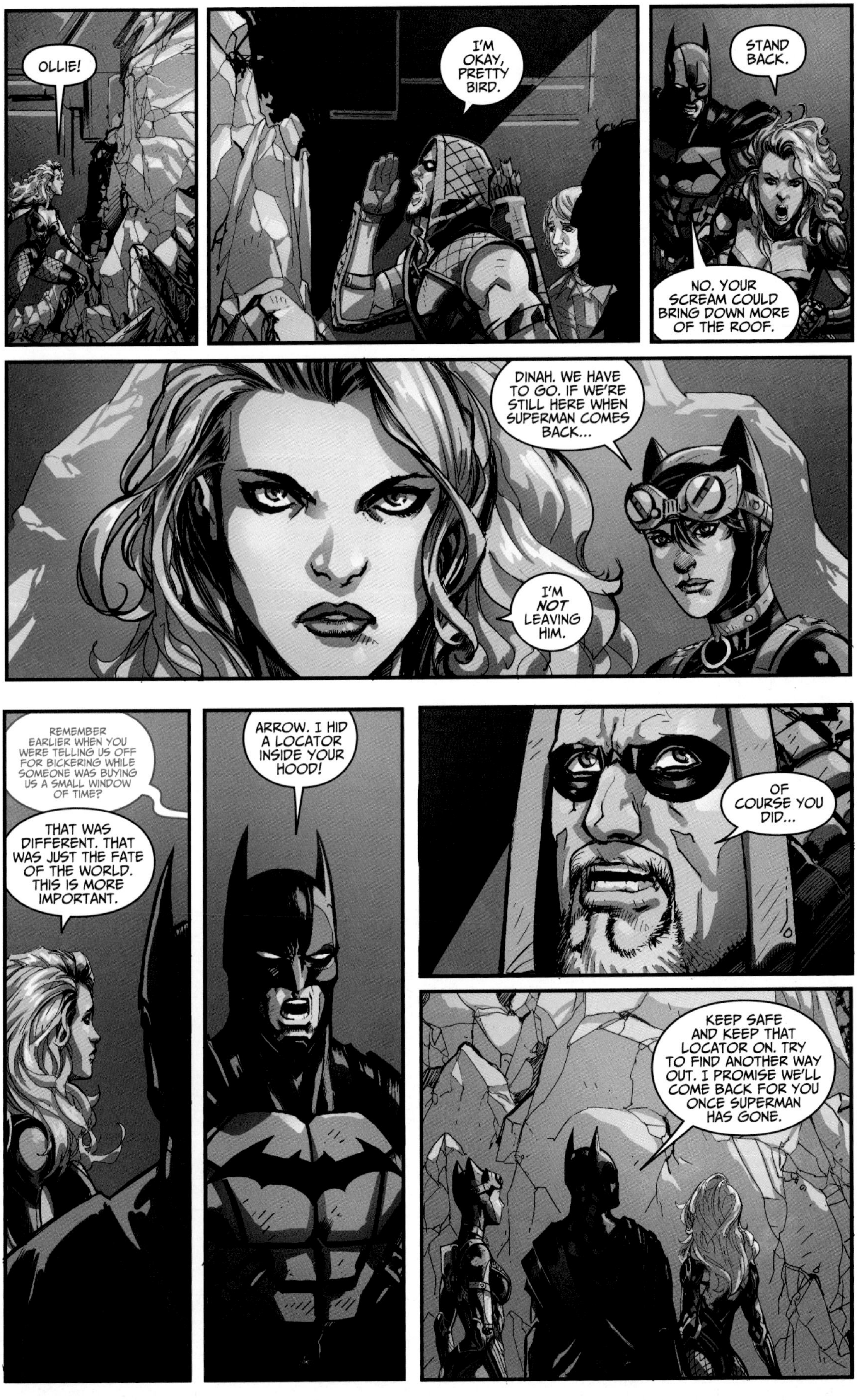
OLLIE!
I'M OKAY, PRETTY BIRD.
STAND BACK.
NO. YOUR SCREAM COULD BRING DOWN MORE OF THE ROOF.
DINAH. WE HAVE TO GO. IF WE'RE STILL HERE WHEN SUPERMAN COMES BACK...
I'M NOT LEAVING HIM.
REMEMBER EARLIER WHEN YOU WERE TELLING US OFF FOR BICKERING WHILE SOMEONE WAS BUYING US A SMALL WINDOW OF TIME?
THAT WAS DIFFERENT. THAT WAS JUST THE FATE OF THE WORLD. THIS IS MORE IMPORTANT.
ARROW. I HID A LOCATOR INSIDE YOUR HOOD!
OF COURSE YOU DID...
KEEP SAFE AND KEEP THAT LOCATOR ON. TRY TO FIND ANOTHER WAY OUT. I PROMISE WE'LL COME BACK FOR YOU ONCE SUPERMAN HAS GONE.

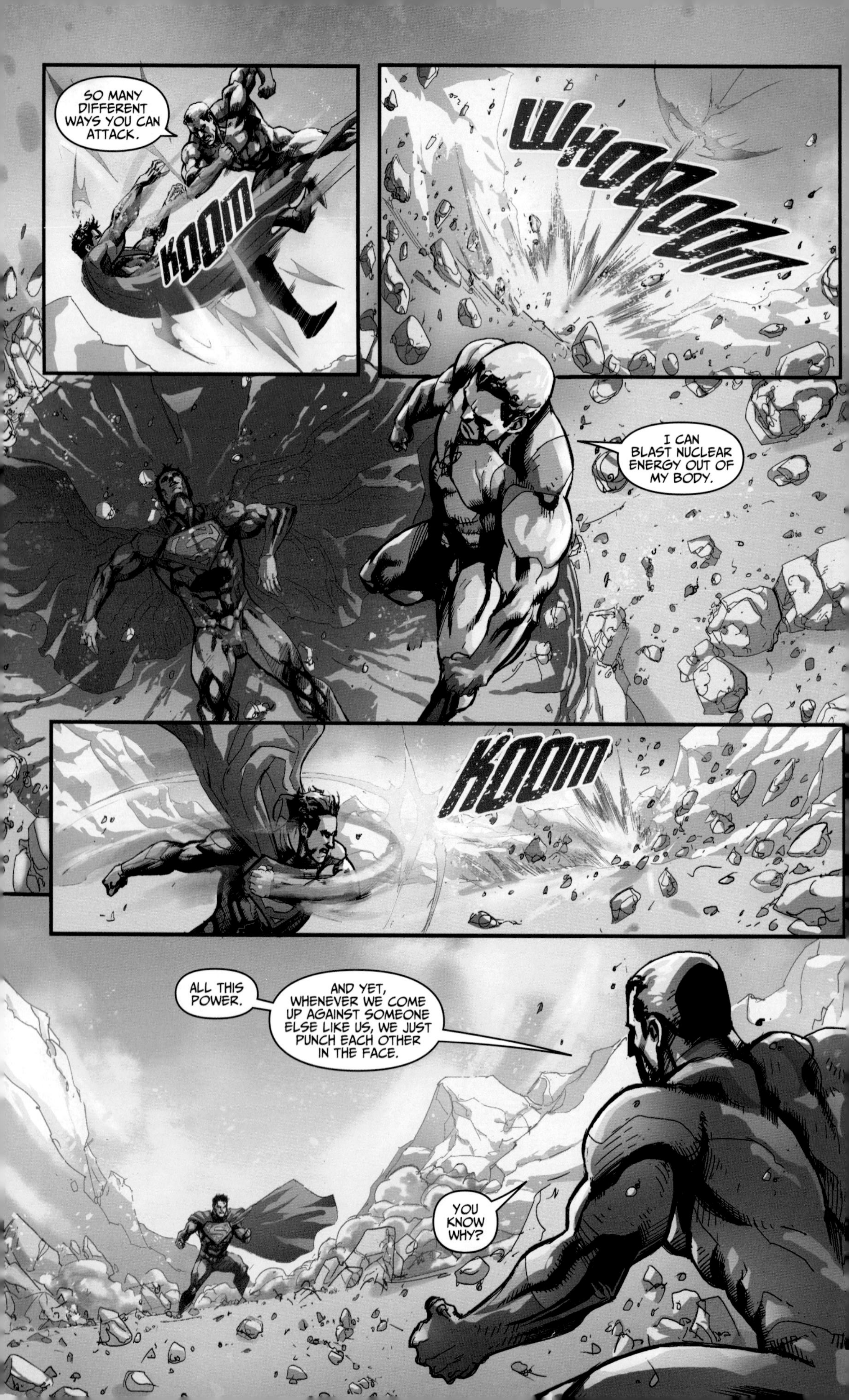
SO MANY DIFFERENT WAYS YOU CAN ATTACK.
KOOM
WHOOOOM
I CAN BLAST NUCLEAR ENERGY OUT OF MY BODY.
KOOM
ALL THIS POWER.
AND YET, WHENEVER WE COME UP AGAINST SOMEONE ELSE LIKE US, WE JUST PUNCH EACH OTHER IN THE FACE.
YOU KNOW WHY?

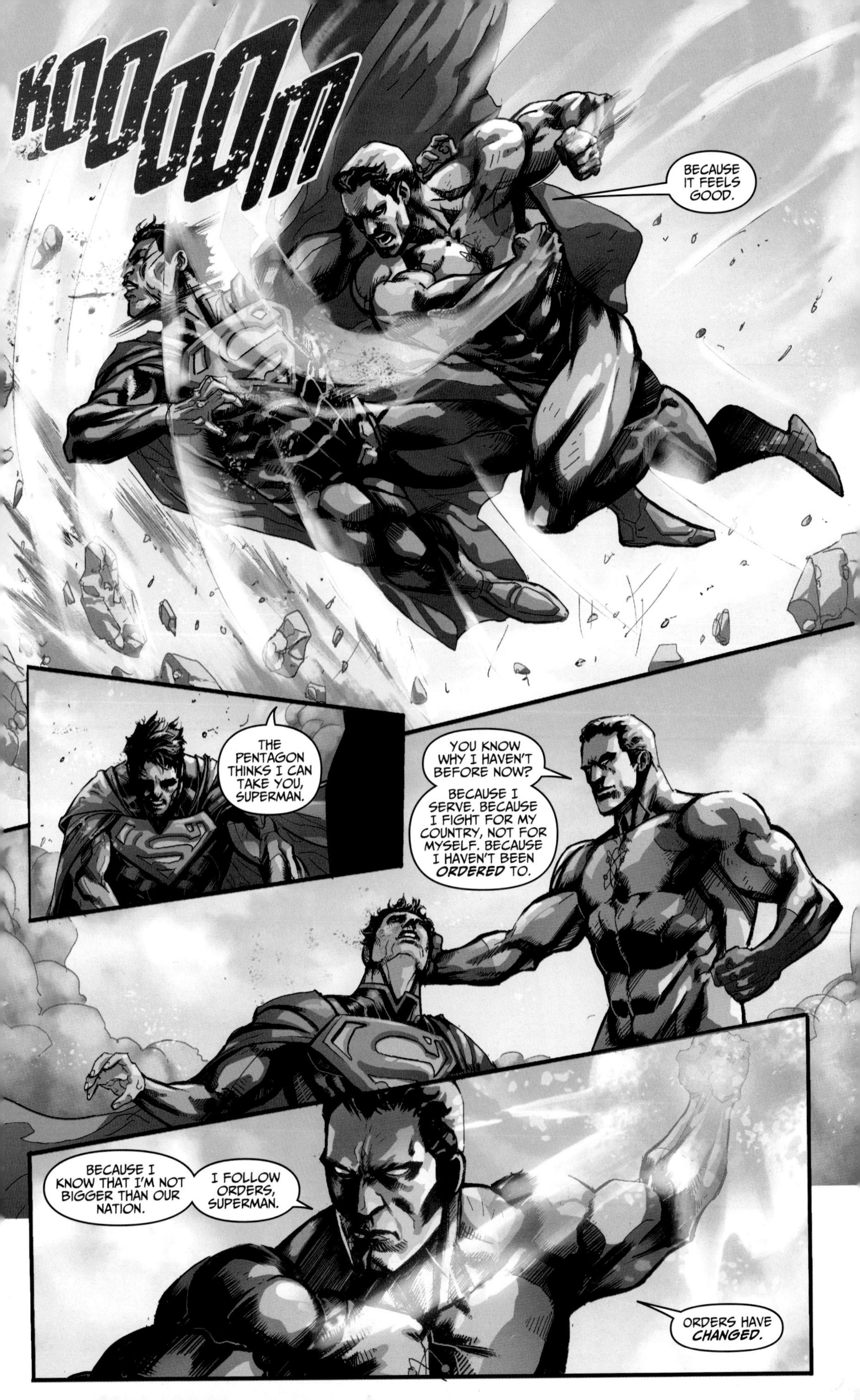
KOOOOM
BECAUSE IT FEELS GOOD.
THE PENTAGON THINKS I CAN TAKE YOU, SUPERMAN.
YOU KNOW WHY I HAVEN'T BEFORE NOW?
BECAUSE I SERVE. BECAUSE I FIGHT FOR MY COUNTRY, NOT FOR MYSELF. BECAUSE I HAVEN'T BEEN ORDERED TO.
BECAUSE I KNOW THAT I'M NOT BIGGER THAN OUR NATION.
I FOLLOW ORDERS, SUPERMAN.
ORDERS HAVE CHANGED.

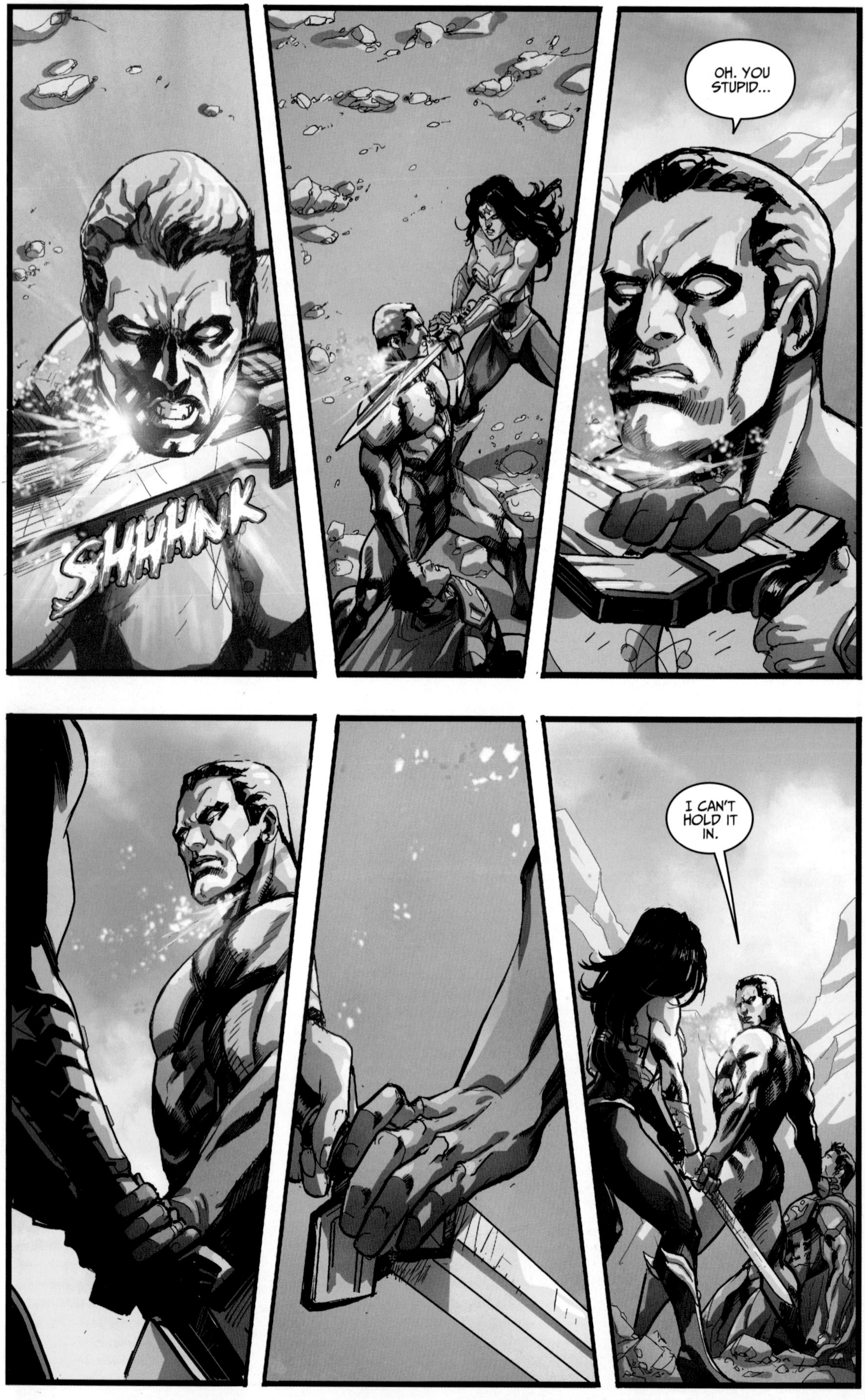
SHHHNK
OH. YOU STUPID...
I CAN'T HOLD IT IN.

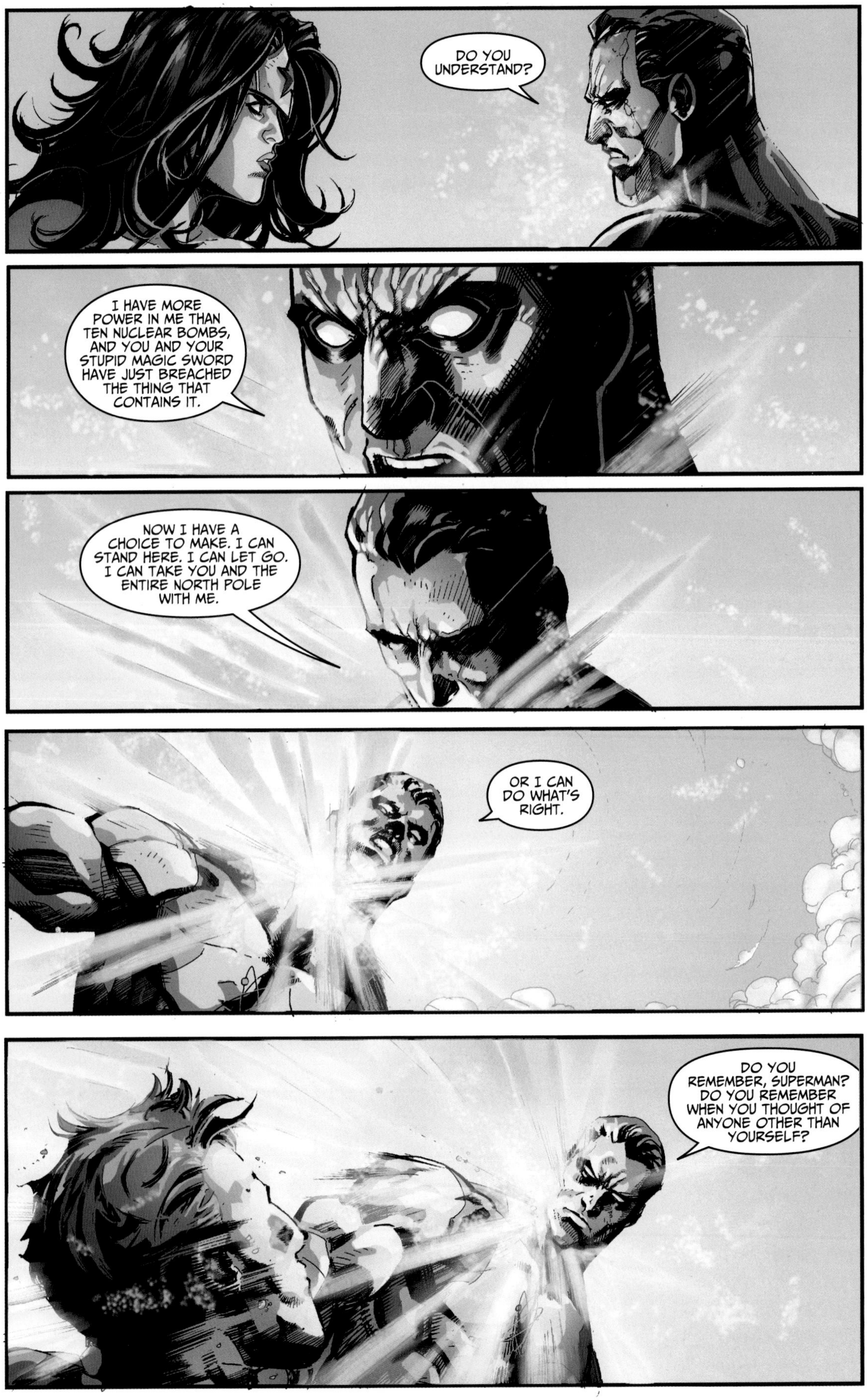
DO YOU UNDERSTAND?
I HAVE MORE POWER IN ME THAN TEN NUCLEAR BOMBS, AND YOU AND YOUR STUPID MAGIC SWORD HAVE JUST BREACHED THE THING THAT CONTAINS IT.
NOW I HAVE A CHOICE TO MAKE. I CAN STAND HERE. I CAN LET GO. I CAN TAKE YOU AND THE ENTIRE NORTH POLE WITH ME.
OR I CAN DO WHAT'S RIGHT.
DO YOU REMEMBER, SUPERMAN? DO YOU REMEMBER WHEN YOU THOUGHT OF ANYONE OTHER THAN YOURSELF?

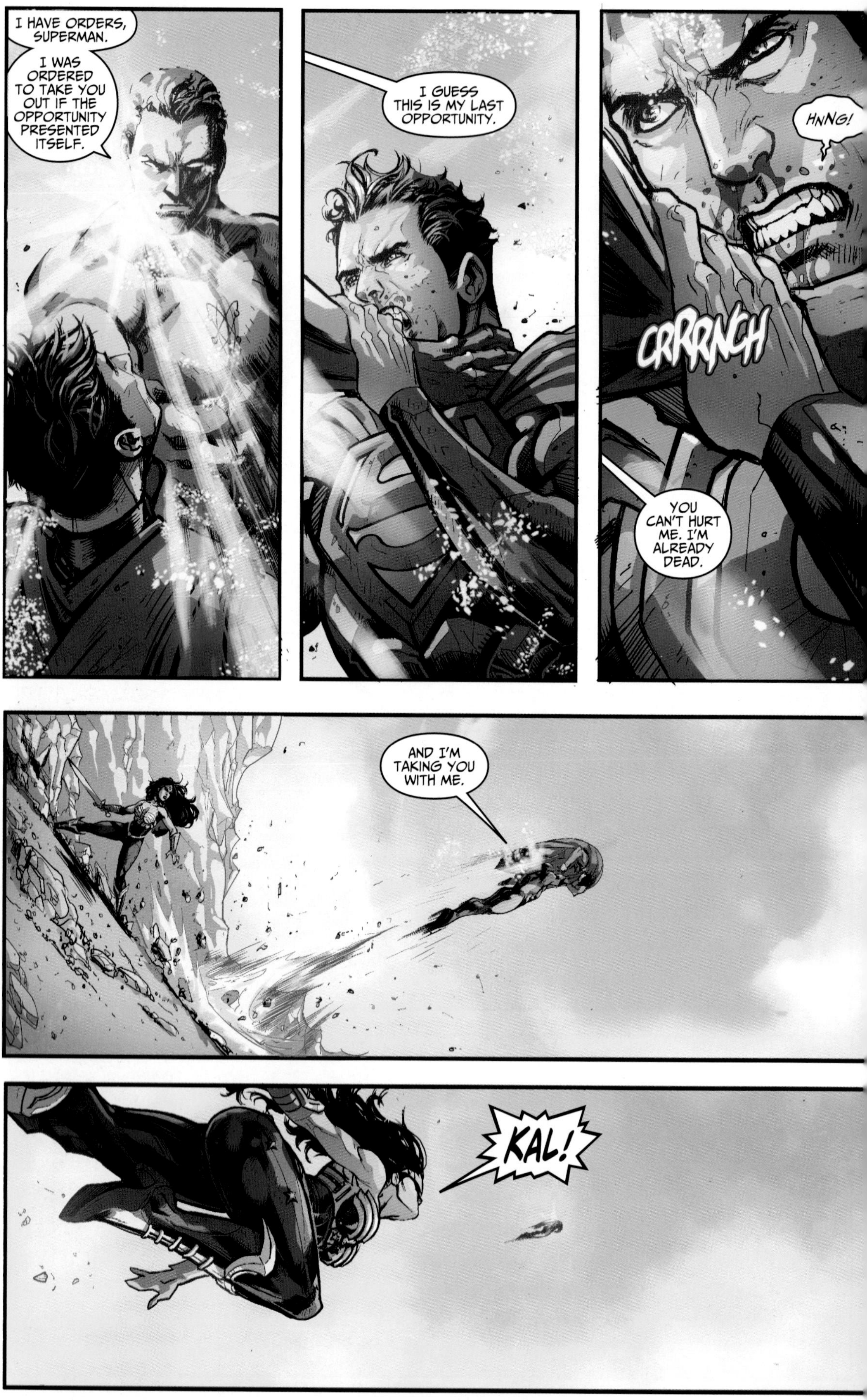
I HAVE ORDERS, SUPERMAN.
I WAS ORDERED TO TAKE YOU OUT IF THE OPPORTUNITY PRESENTED ITSELF.
I GUESS THIS IS MY LAST OPPORTUNITY.
HNNG!
CRRRNCH
YOU CAN'T HURT ME. I'M ALREADY DEAD.
AND I'M TAKING YOU WITH ME.
KAL!

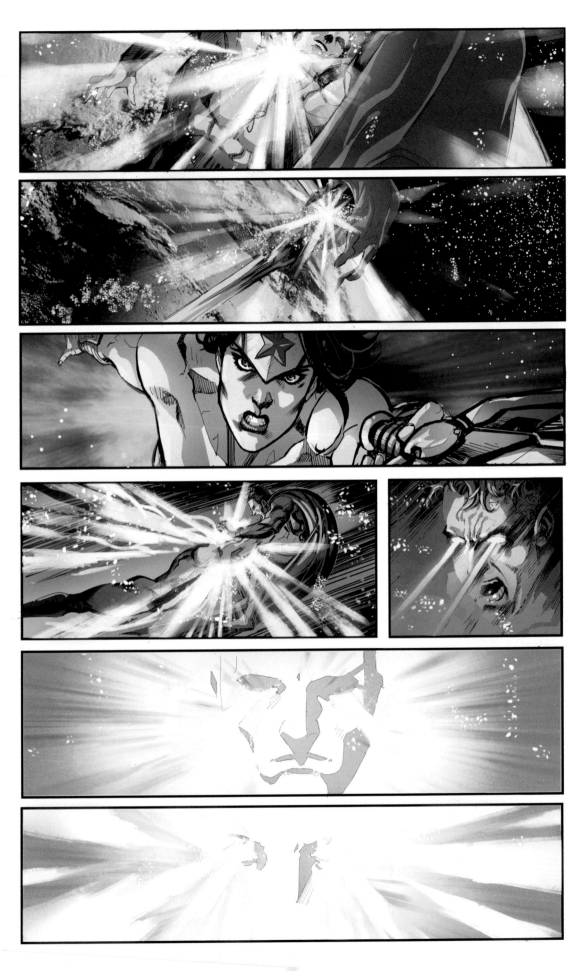

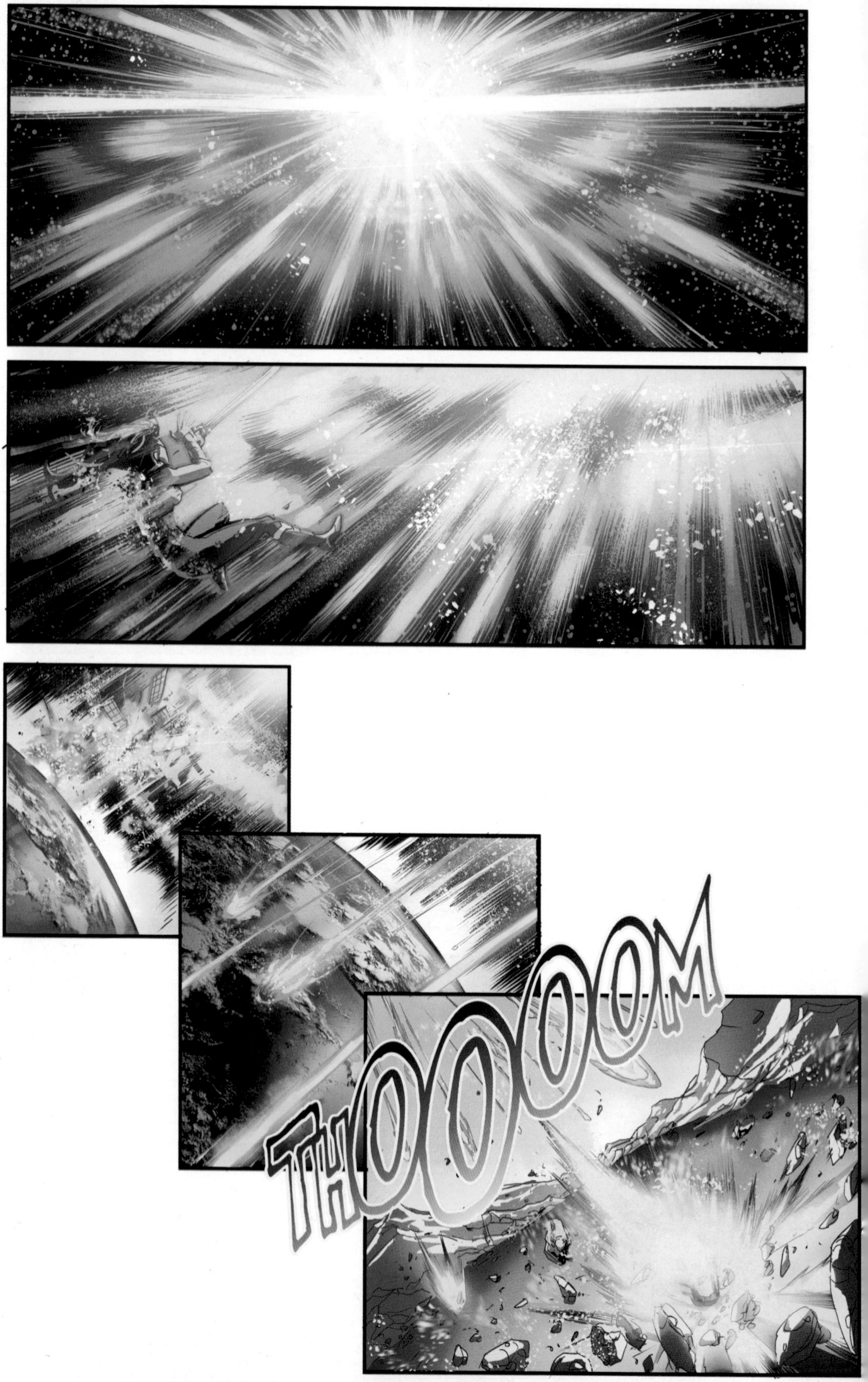
THOOOOOM

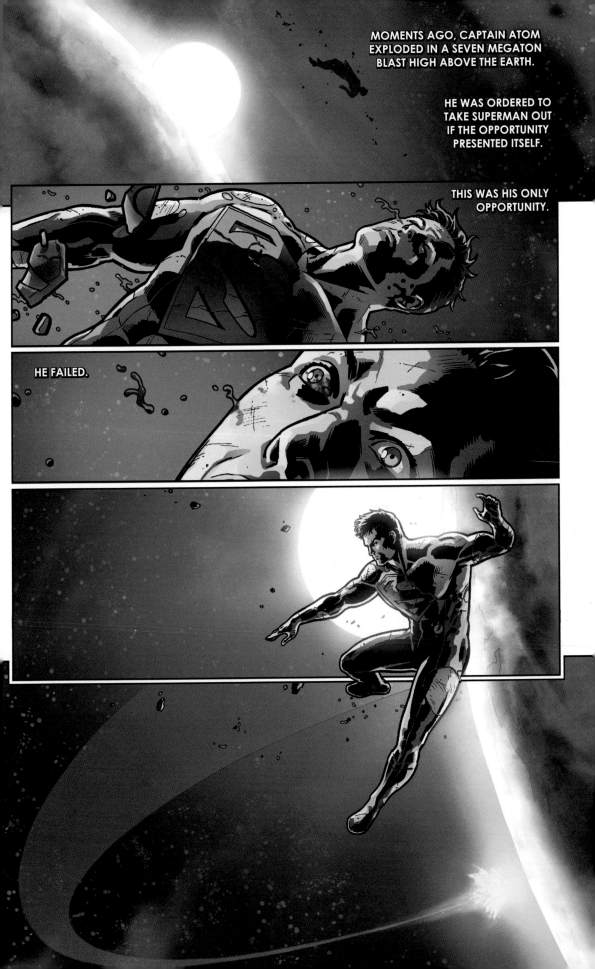

MOMENTS AGO, CAPTAIN ATOM EXPLODED IN A SEVEN MEGATON BLAST HIGH ABOVE THE EARTH.

HE WAS ORDERED TO TAKE SUPERMAN OUT IF THE OPPORTUNITY PRESENTED ITSELF.

THIS WAS HIS ONLY OPPORTUNITY.

HE FAILED.

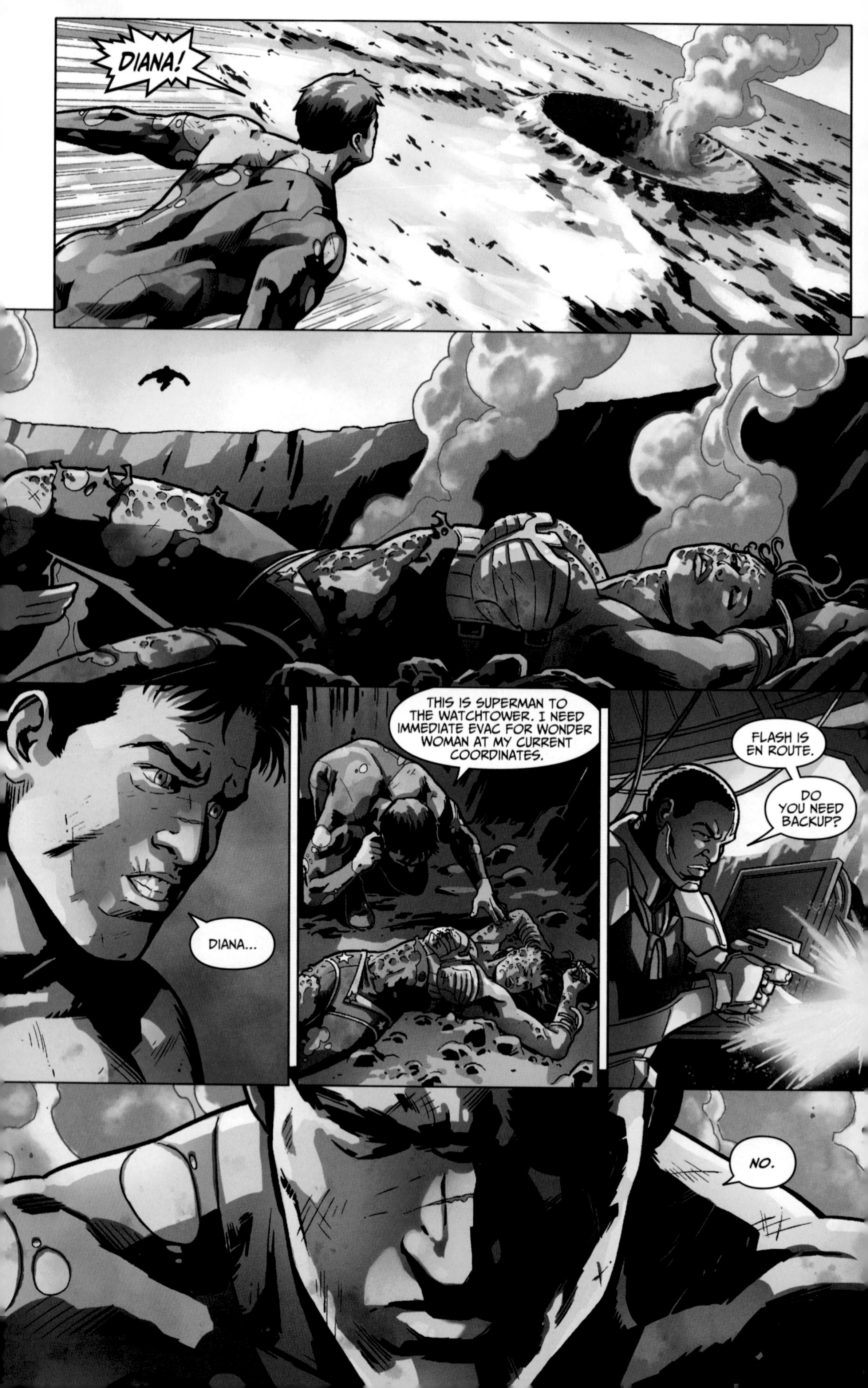
DIANA!
THIS IS SUPERMAN TO THE WATCHTOWER. I NEED IMMEDIATE EVAC FOR WONDER WOMAN AT MY CURRENT COORDINATES.
FLASH IS EN ROUTE.
DO YOU NEED BACKUP?
DIANA...
NO.

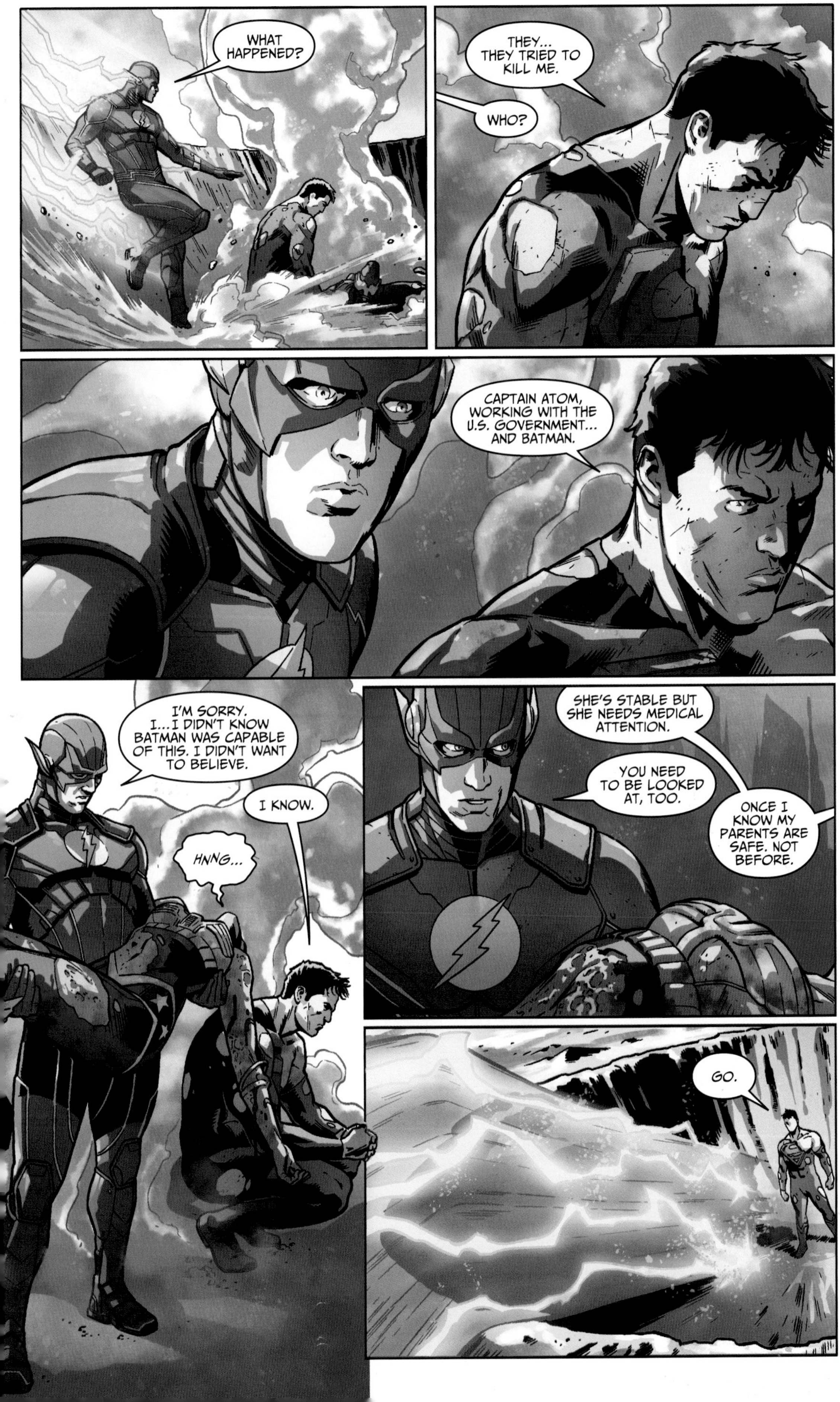
WHAT HAPPENED?
THEY... THEY TRIED TO KILL ME.
WHO?
CAPTAIN ATOM, WORKING WITH THE U.S. GOVERNMENT... AND BATMAN.
I'M SORRY. I...I DIDN'T KNOW BATMAN WAS CAPABLE OF THIS. I DIDN'T WANT TO BELIEVE.
I KNOW.
HNNG...
SHE'S STABLE BUT SHE NEEDS MEDICAL ATTENTION.
YOU NEED TO BE LOOKED AT, TOO.
ONCE I KNOW MY PARENTS ARE SAFE. NOT BEFORE.
GO.

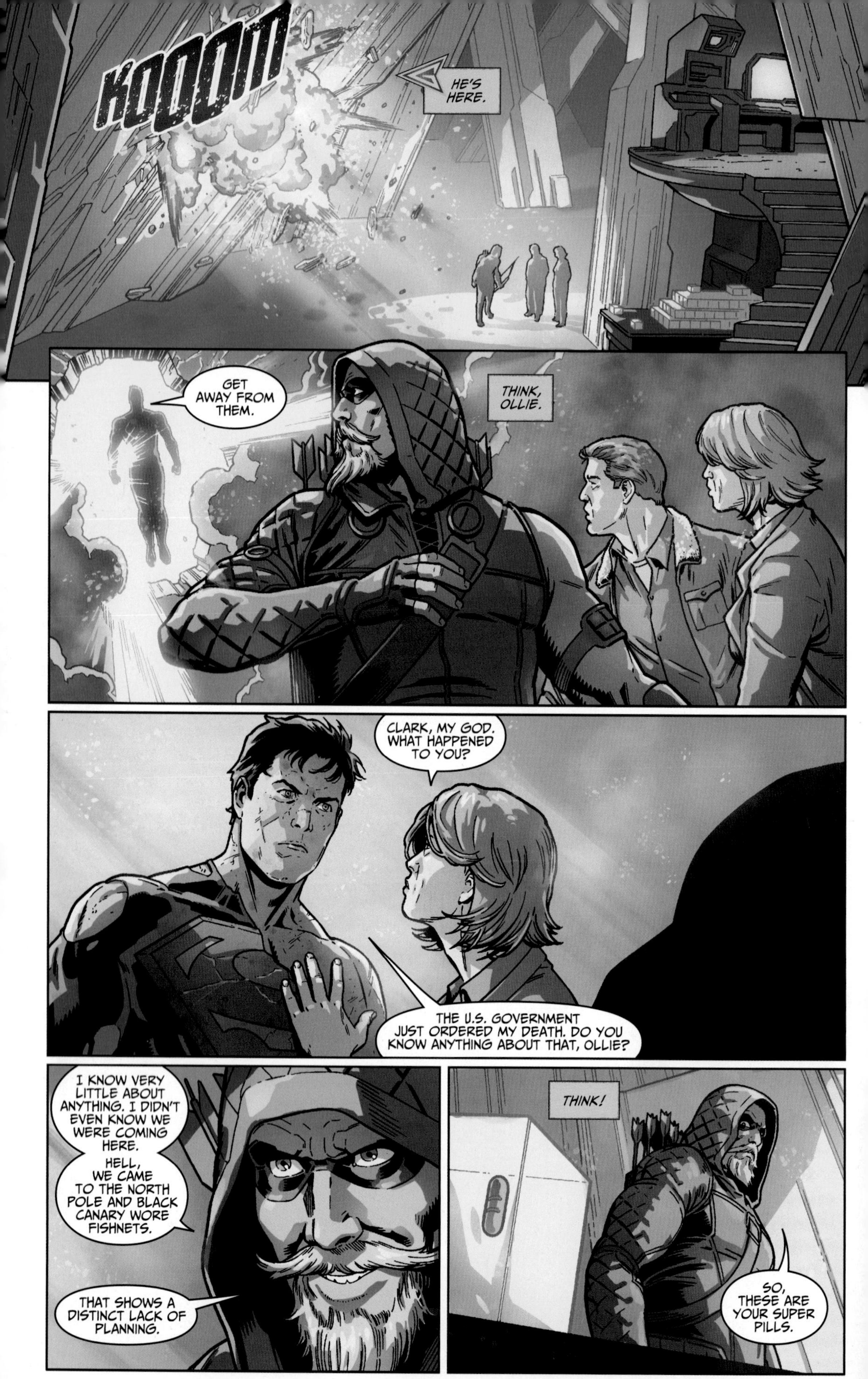
KOOOM
HE'S HERE.
GET AWAY FROM THEM.
THINK, OLLIE.
CLARK, MY GOD. WHAT HAPPENED TO YOU?
THE U.S. GOVERNMENT JUST ORDERED MY DEATH. DO YOU KNOW ANYTHING ABOUT THAT, OLLIE?
I KNOW VERY LITTLE ABOUT ANYTHING. I DIDN'T EVEN KNOW WE WERE COMING HERE.
HELL, WE CAME TO THE NORTH POLE AND BLACK CANARY WORE FISHNETS.
THAT SHOWS A DISTINCT LACK OF PLANNING.
THINK!
SO, THESE ARE YOUR SUPER PILLS.

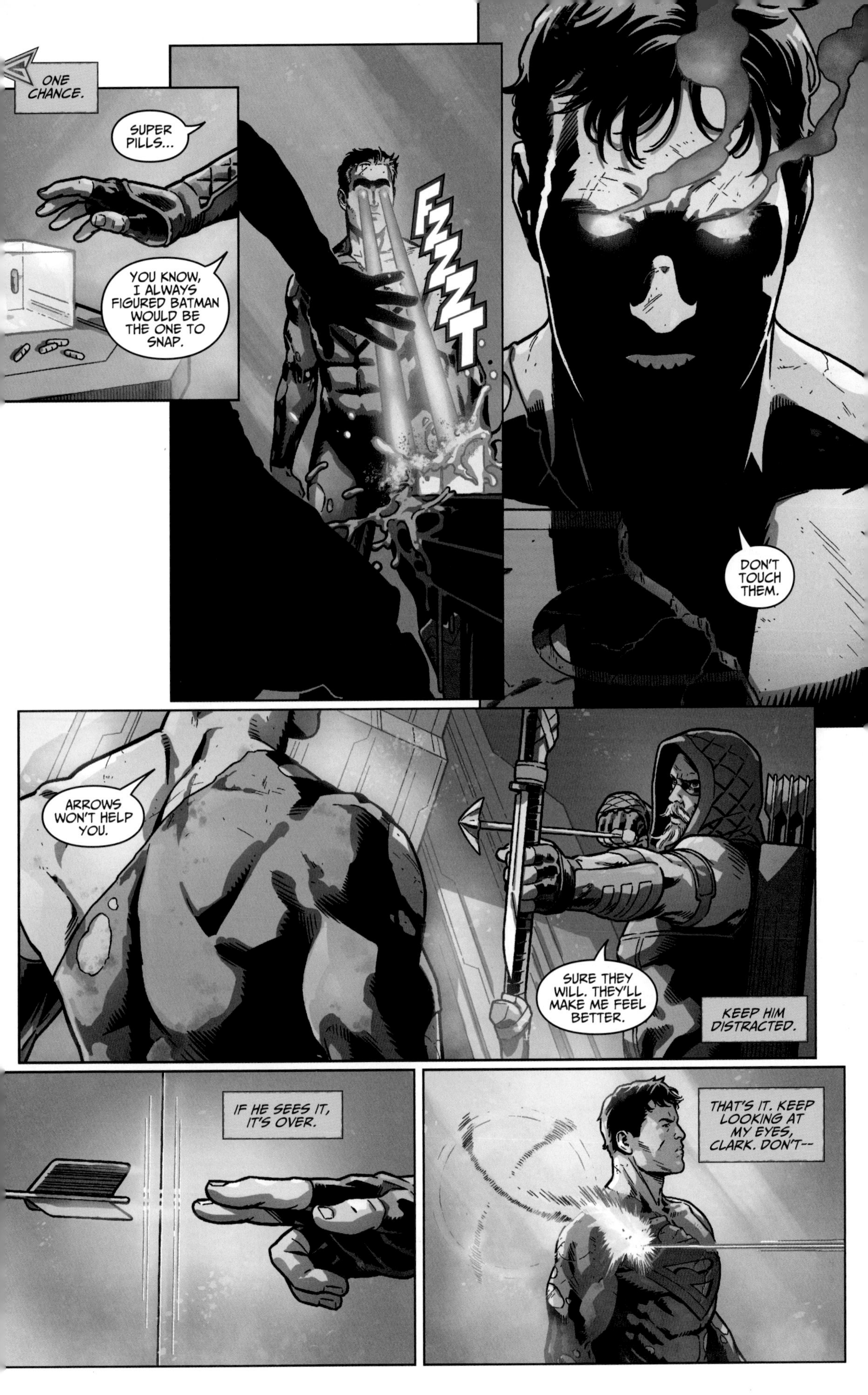
ONE CHANCE.
SUPER PILLS...
YOU KNOW, I ALWAYS FIGURED BATMAN WOULD BE THE ONE TO SNAP.
FZZZZT
DON'T TOUCH THEM.
ARROWS WON'T HELP YOU.
SURE THEY WILL. THEY'LL MAKE ME FEEL BETTER.
KEEP HIM DISTRACTED.
IF HE SEES IT, IT'S OVER.
THAT'S IT. KEEP LOOKING AT MY EYES, CLARK. DON'T--

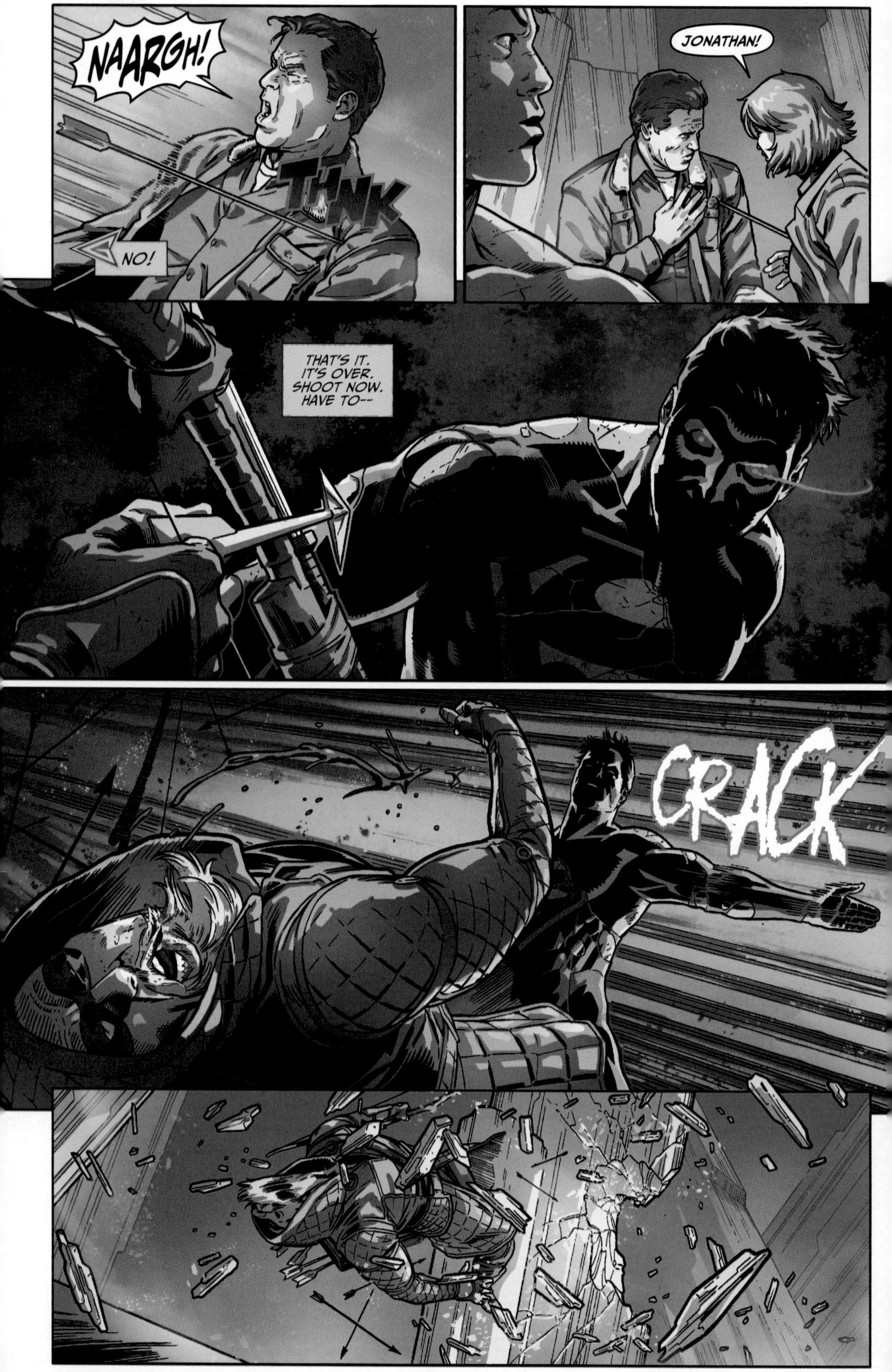
NAARGH!
THNK
NO!
JONATHAN!
THAT'S IT. IT'S OVER. SHOOT NOW. HAVE TO--
CRACK

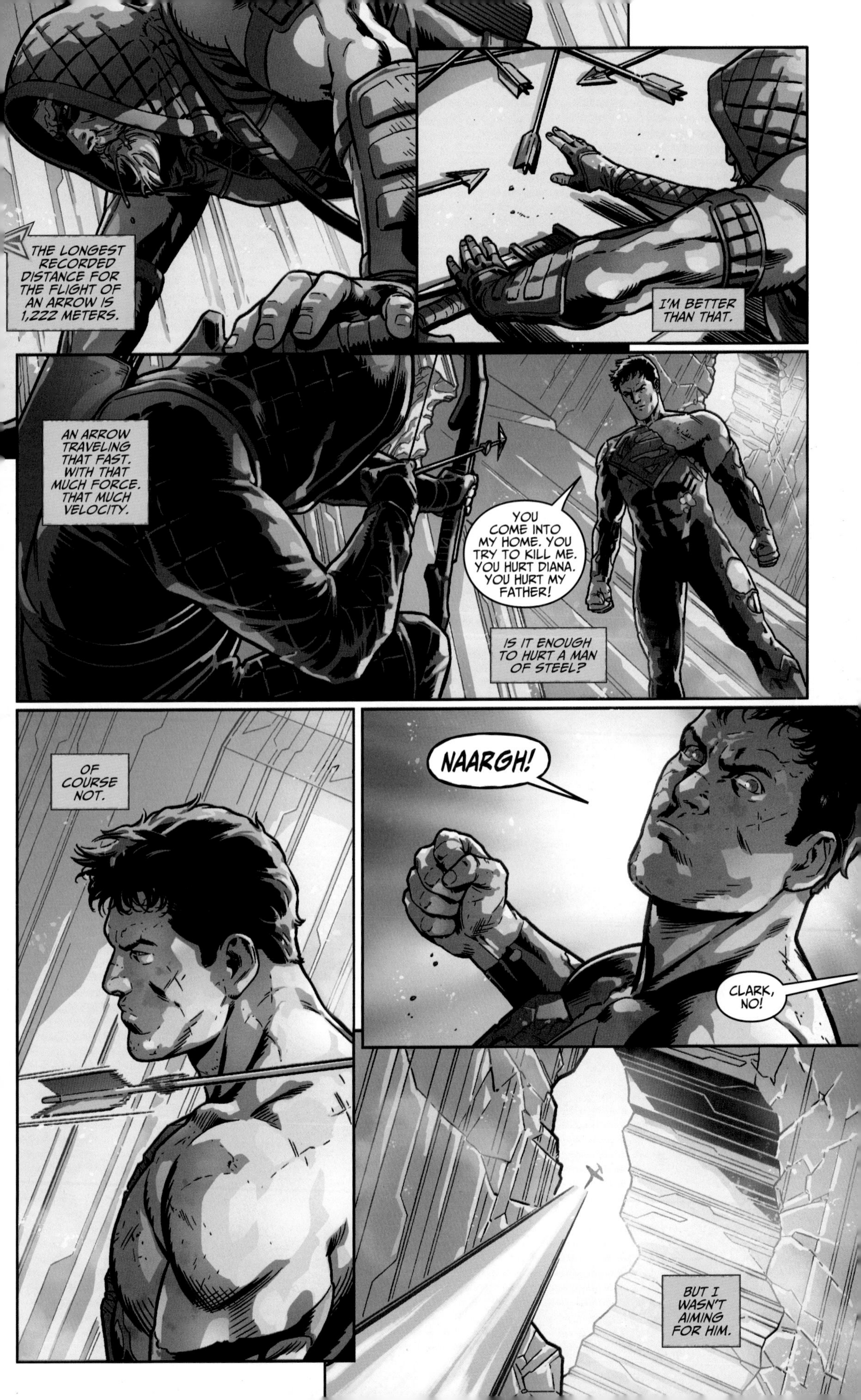
THE LONGEST RECORDED DISTANCE FOR THE FLIGHT OF AN ARROW IS 1,222 METERS.
I'M BETTER THAN THAT.
AN ARROW TRAVELING THAT FAST. WITH THAT MUCH FORCE. THAT MUCH VELOCITY.
YOU COME INTO MY HOME. YOU TRY TO KILL ME. YOU HURT DIANA. YOU HURT MY FATHER!
IS IT ENOUGH TO HURT A MAN OF STEEL?
OF COURSE NOT.
NAARGH!
CLARK, NO!
BUT I WASN'T AIMING FOR HIM.

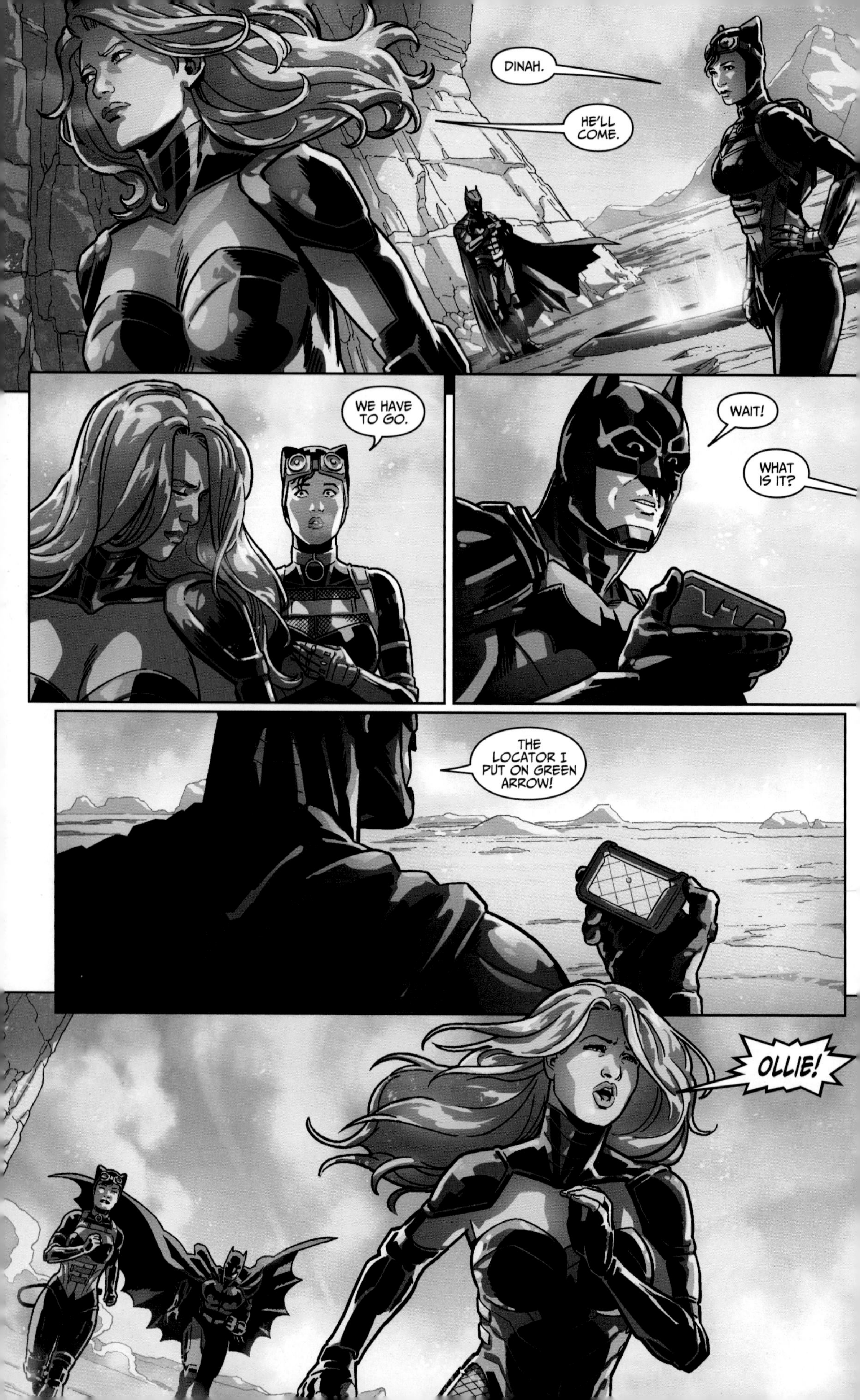
DINAH.
HE'LL COME.
WE HAVE TO GO.
WAIT!
WHAT IS IT?
THE LOCATOR I PUT ON GREEN ARROW!
OLLIE!

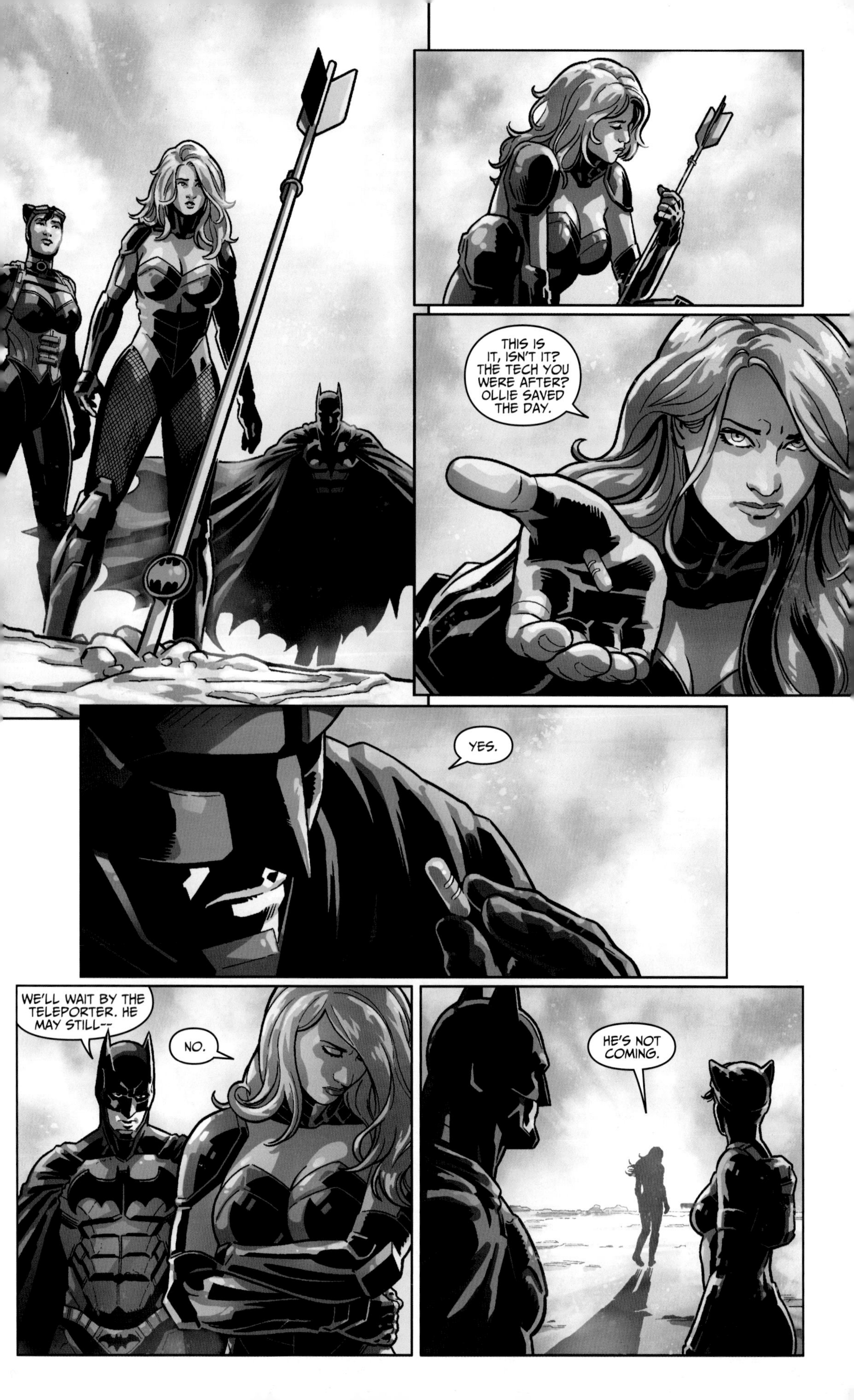
THIS IS IT, ISN'T IT? THE TECH YOU WERE AFTER? OLLIE SAVED THE DAY.
YES.
WE'LL WAIT BY THE TELEPORTER. HE MAY STILL--
NO.
HE'S NOT COMING.

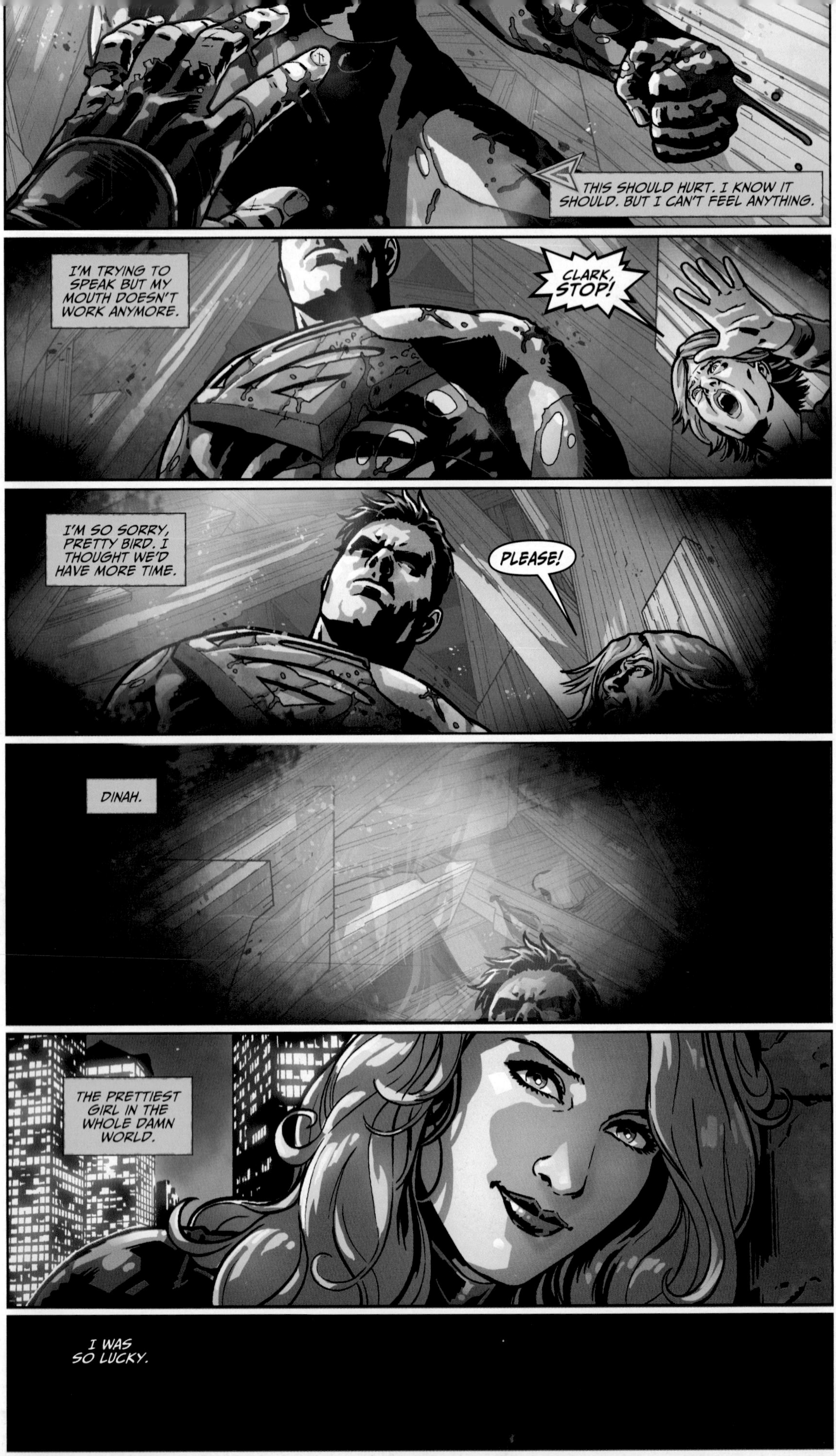
THIS SHOULD HURT. I KNOW IT SHOULD. BUT I CAN'T FEEL ANYTHING.
I'M TRYING TO SPEAK BUT MY MOUTH DOESN'T WORK ANYMORE.
CLARK, STOP!
I'M SO SORRY, PRETTY BIRD. I THOUGHT WE'D HAVE MORE TIME.
PLEASE!
DINAH.
THE PRETTIEST GIRL IN THE WHOLE DAMN WORLD.
I WAS SO LUCKY.

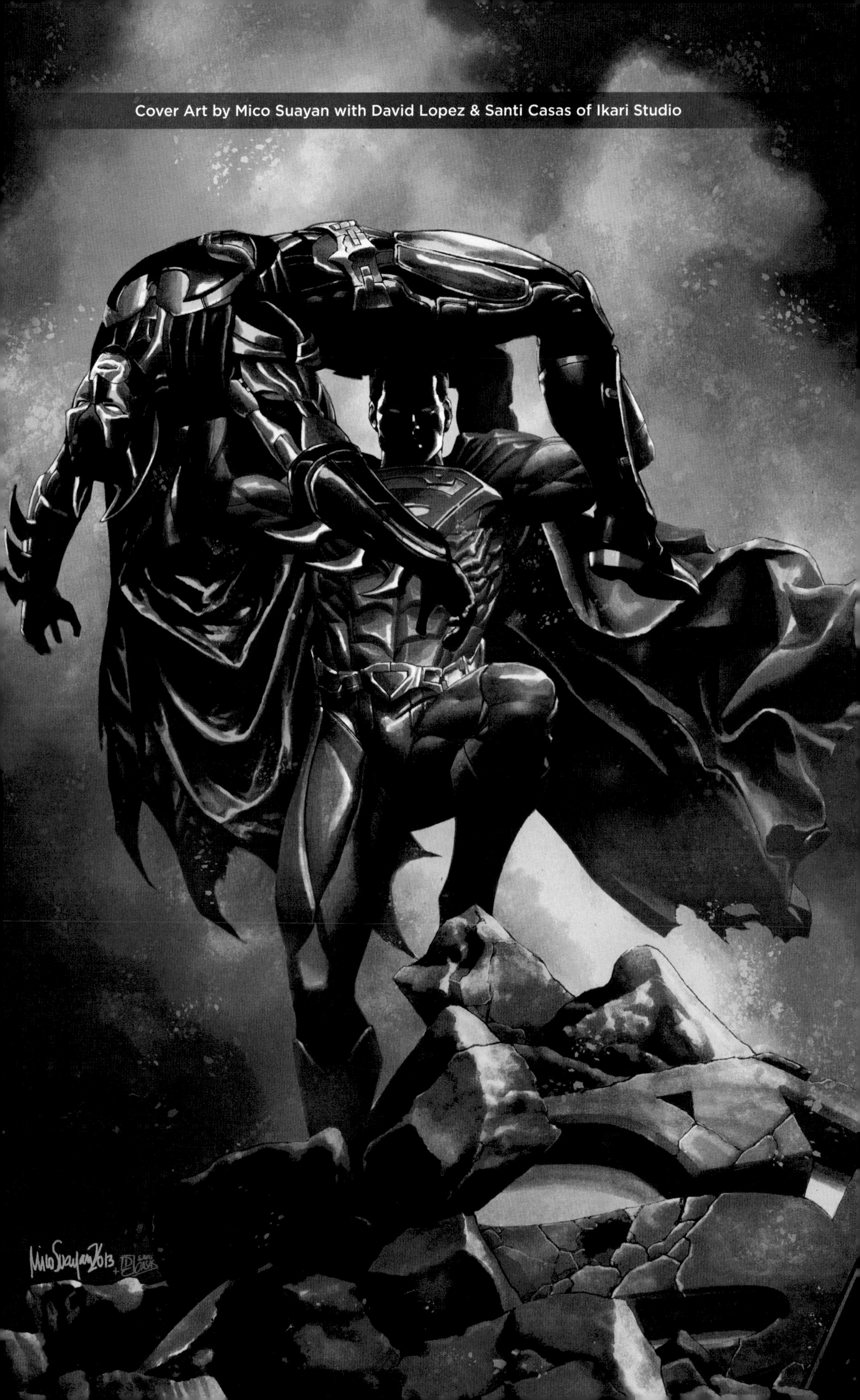

Cover Art by Mico Suayan with David Lopez & Santi Casas of Ikari Studio

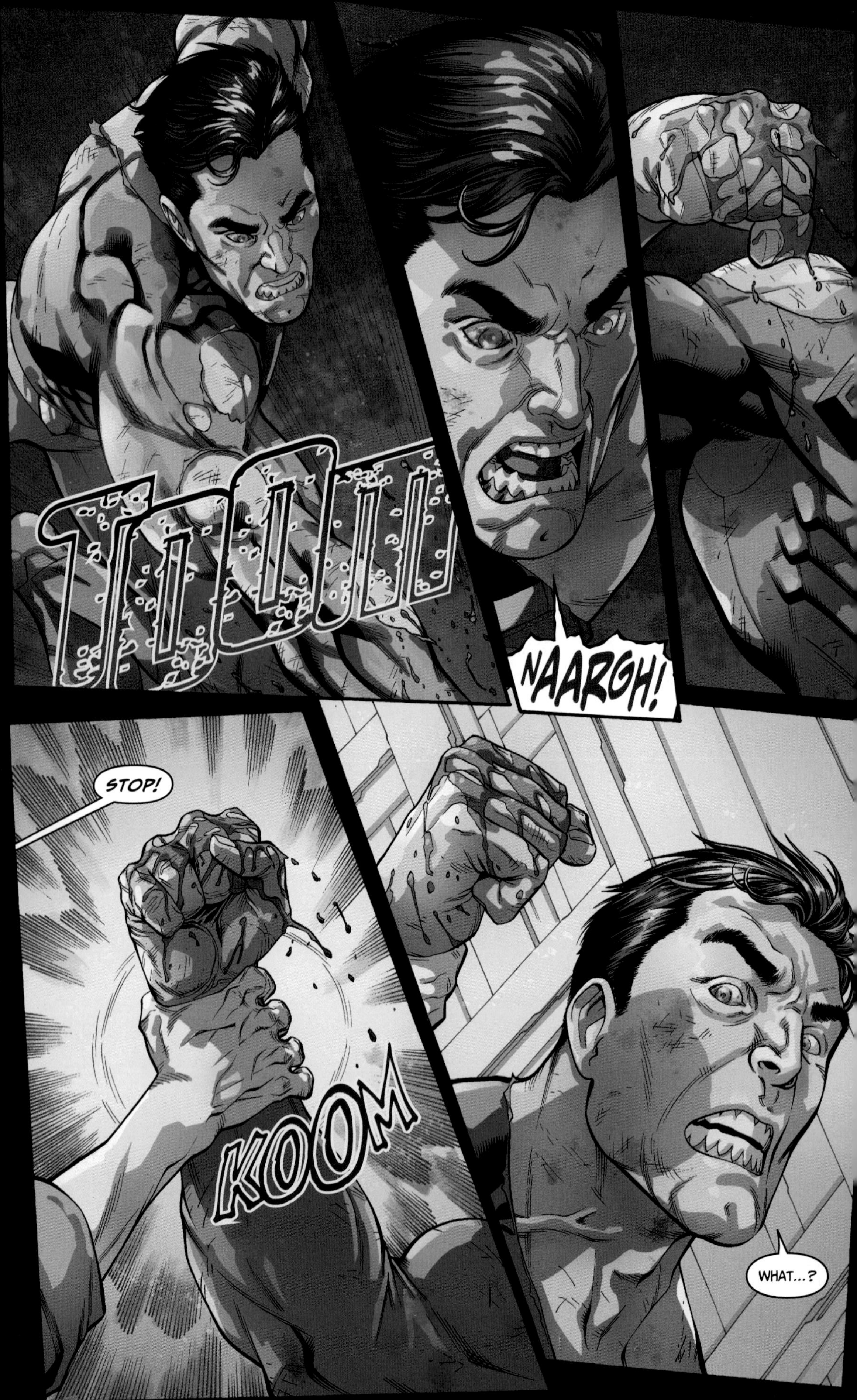
NAARGH!
STOP!
KOOM
WHAT...?

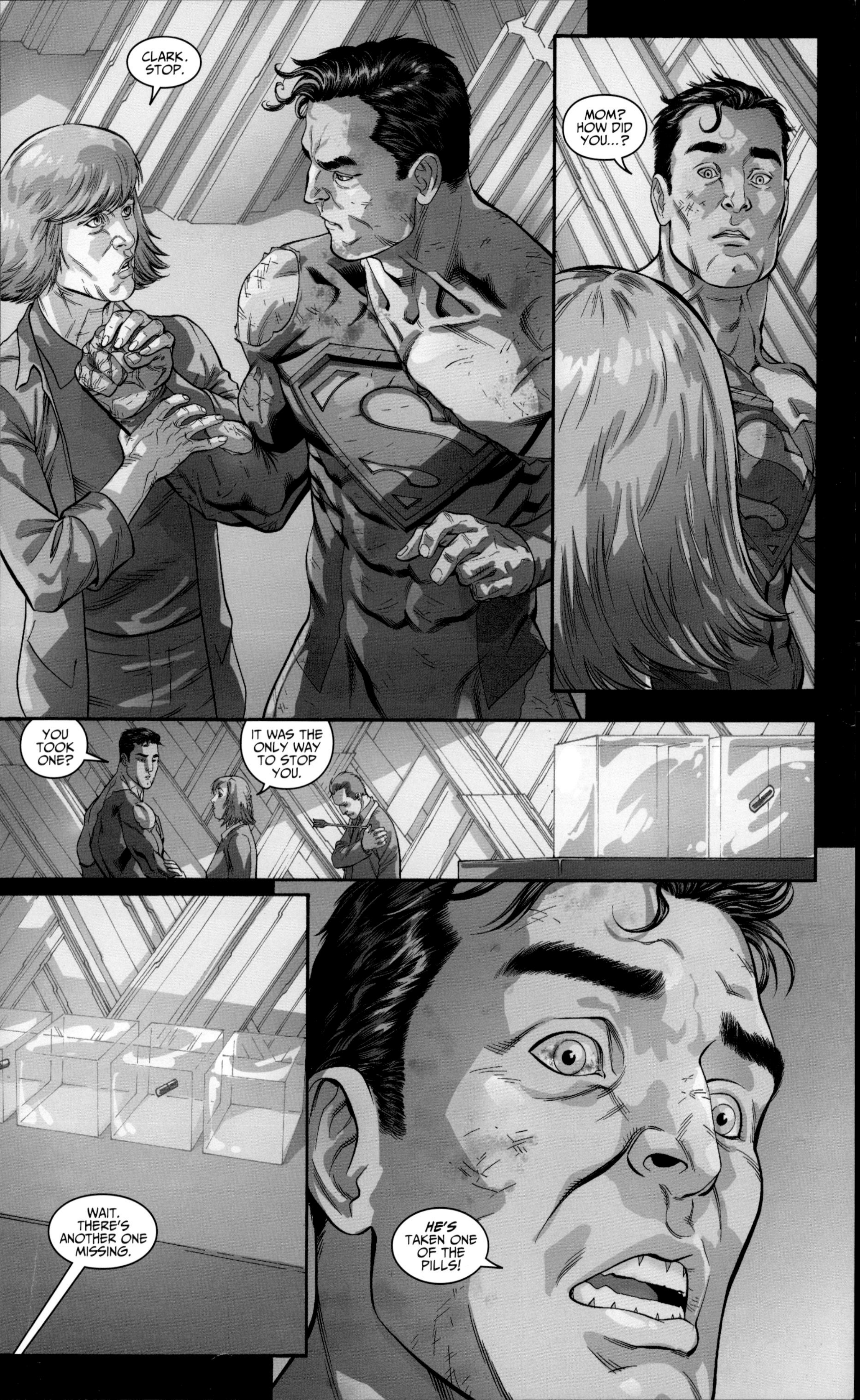
CLARK. STOP.
MOM? HOW DID YOU...?
YOU TOOK ONE?
IT WAS THE ONLY WAY TO STOP YOU.
WAIT. THERE'S ANOTHER ONE MISSING.
HE'S TAKEN ONE OF THE PILLS!

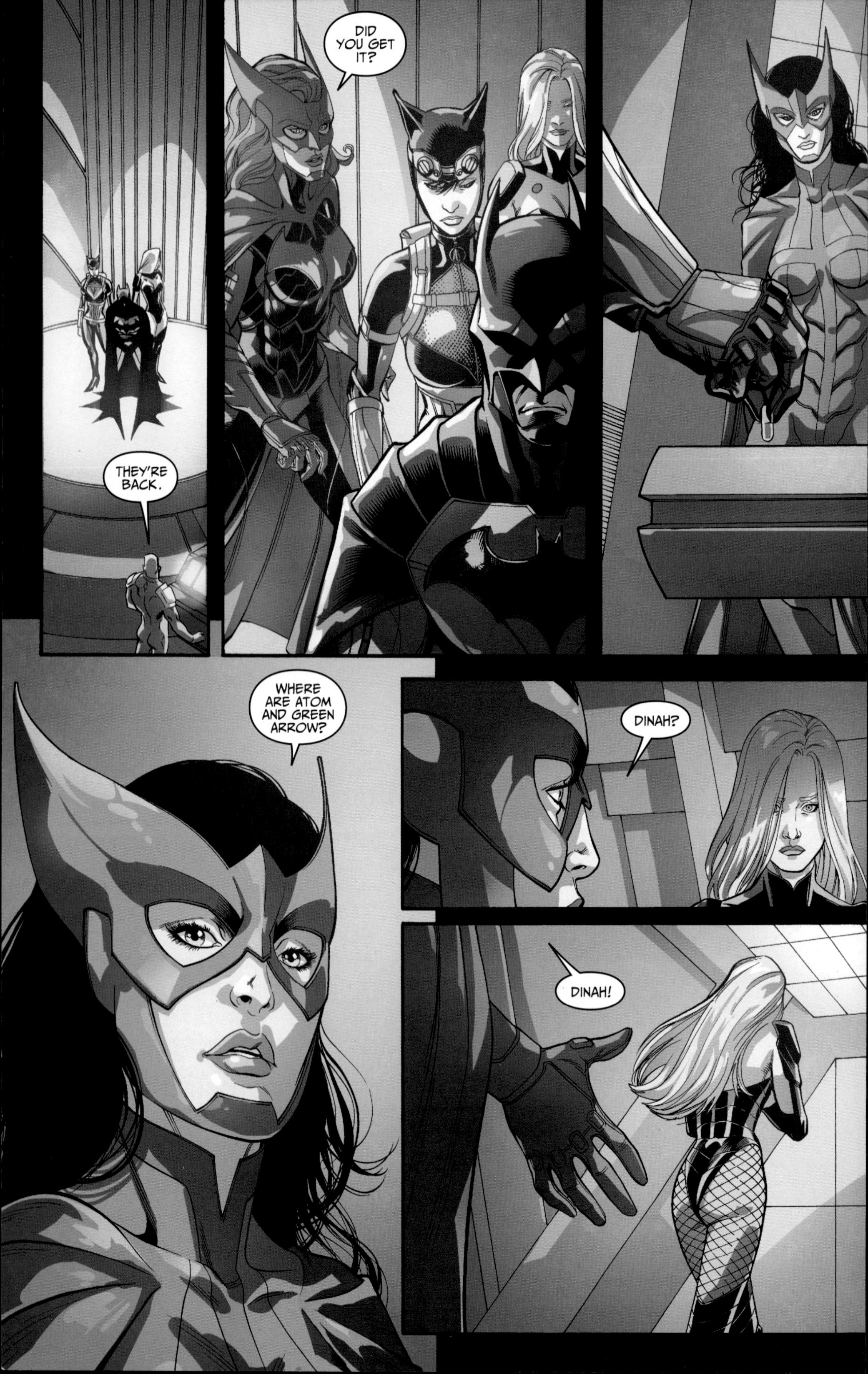
THEY'RE BACK.
DID YOU GET IT?
WHERE ARE ATOM AND GREEN ARROW?
DINAH?
DINAH!

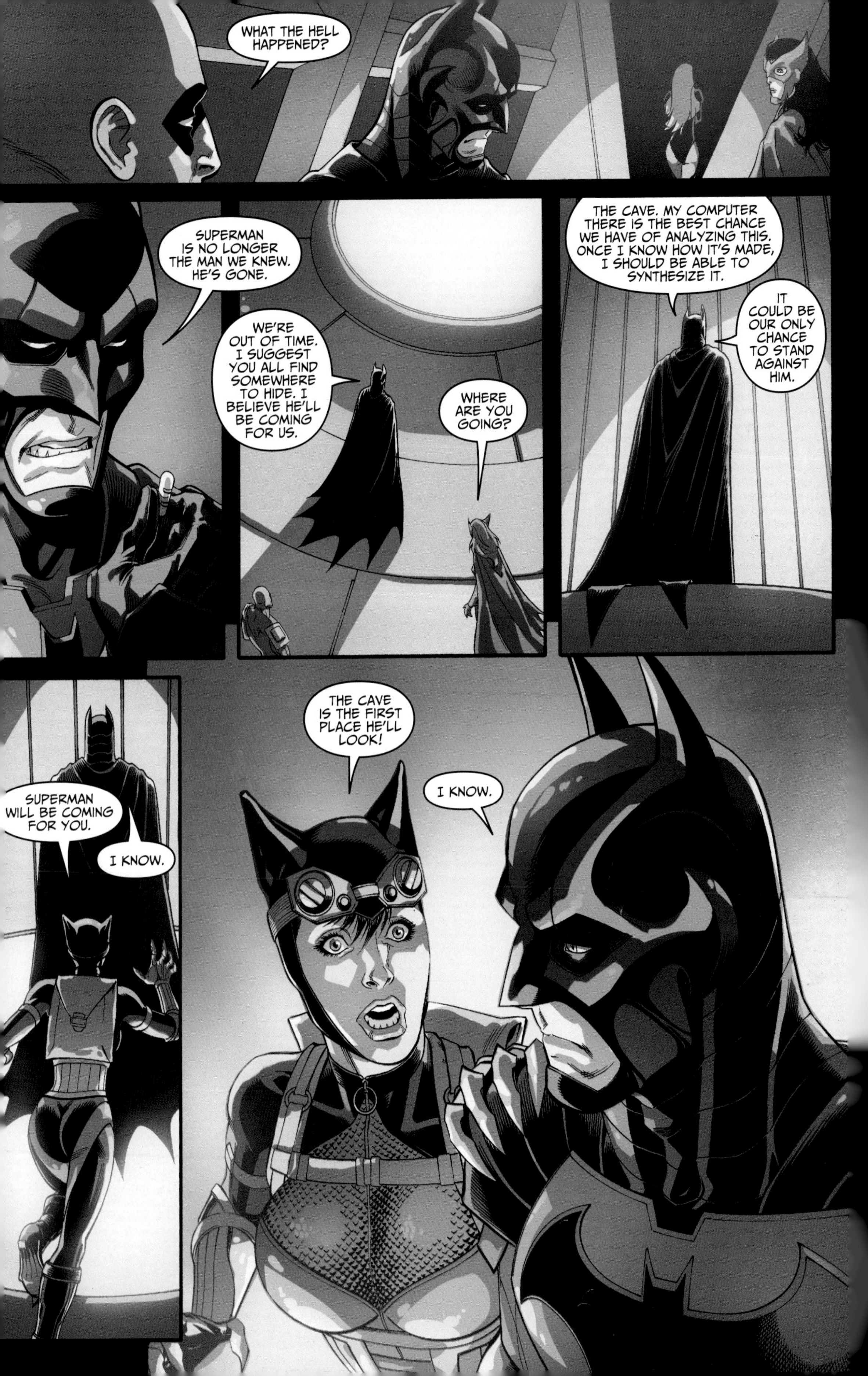
WHAT THE HELL HAPPENED?
SUPERMAN IS NO LONGER THE MAN WE KNEW. HE'S GONE.
WE'RE OUT OF TIME. I SUGGEST YOU ALL FIND SOMEWHERE TO HIDE. I BELIEVE HE'LL BE COMING FOR US.
WHERE ARE YOU GOING?
THE CAVE. MY COMPUTER THERE IS THE BEST CHANCE WE HAVE OF ANALYZING THIS. ONCE I KNOW HOW IT'S MADE, I SHOULD BE ABLE TO SYNTHESIZE IT.
IT COULD BE OUR ONLY CHANCE TO STAND AGAINST HIM.
SUPERMAN WILL BE COMING FOR YOU.
I KNOW.
THE CAVE IS THE FIRST PLACE HE'LL LOOK!
I KNOW.

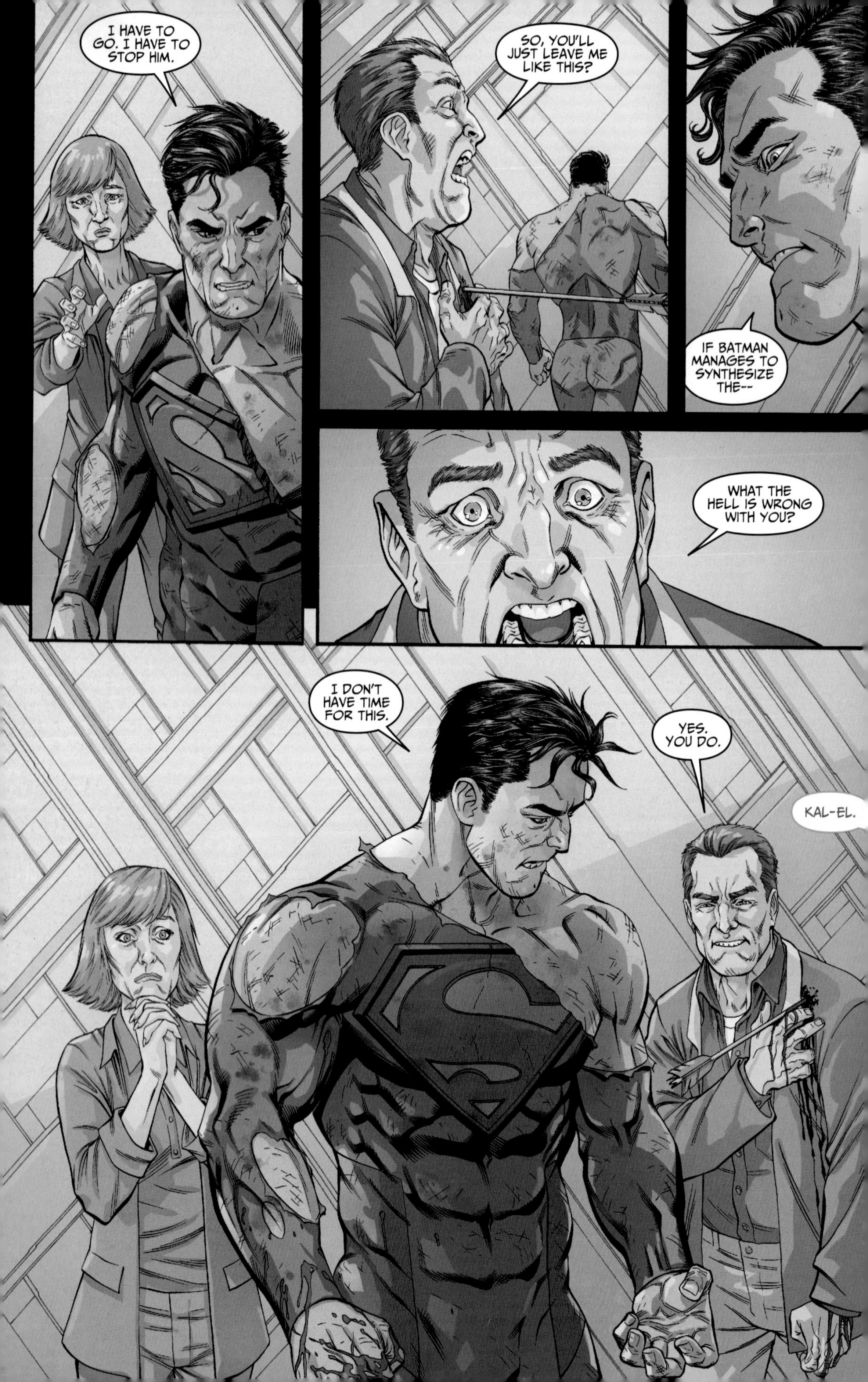
I HAVE TO GO. I HAVE TO STOP HIM.
SO, YOU'LL JUST LEAVE ME LIKE THIS?
IF BATMAN MANAGES TO SYNTHESIZE THE--
WHAT THE HELL IS WRONG WITH YOU?
I DON'T HAVE TIME FOR THIS.
YES. YOU DO.
KAL-EL.

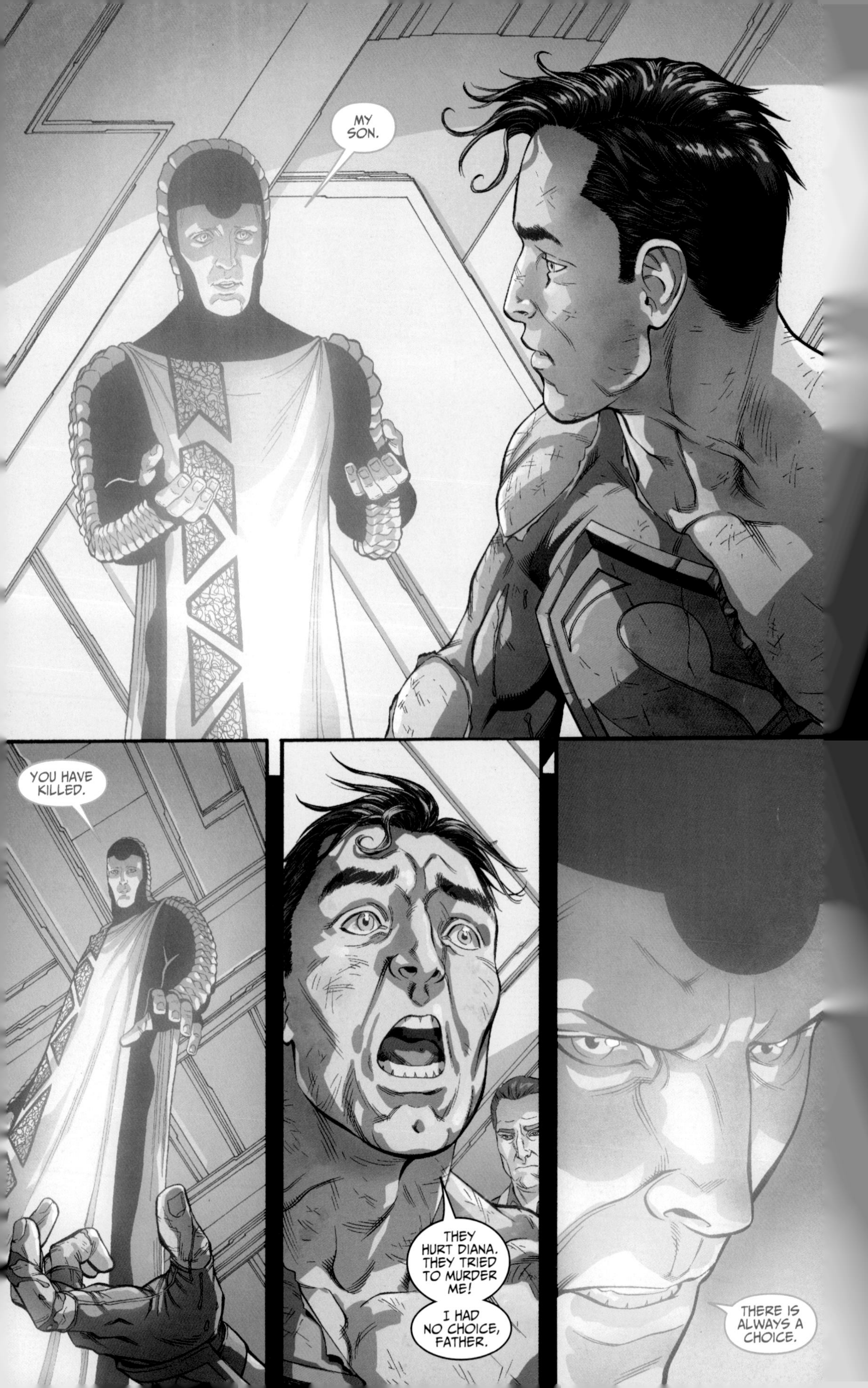
MY SON.
YOU HAVE KILLED.
THEY HURT DIANA. THEY TRIED TO MURDER ME!
I HAD NO CHOICE, FATHER.
THERE IS ALWAYS A CHOICE.

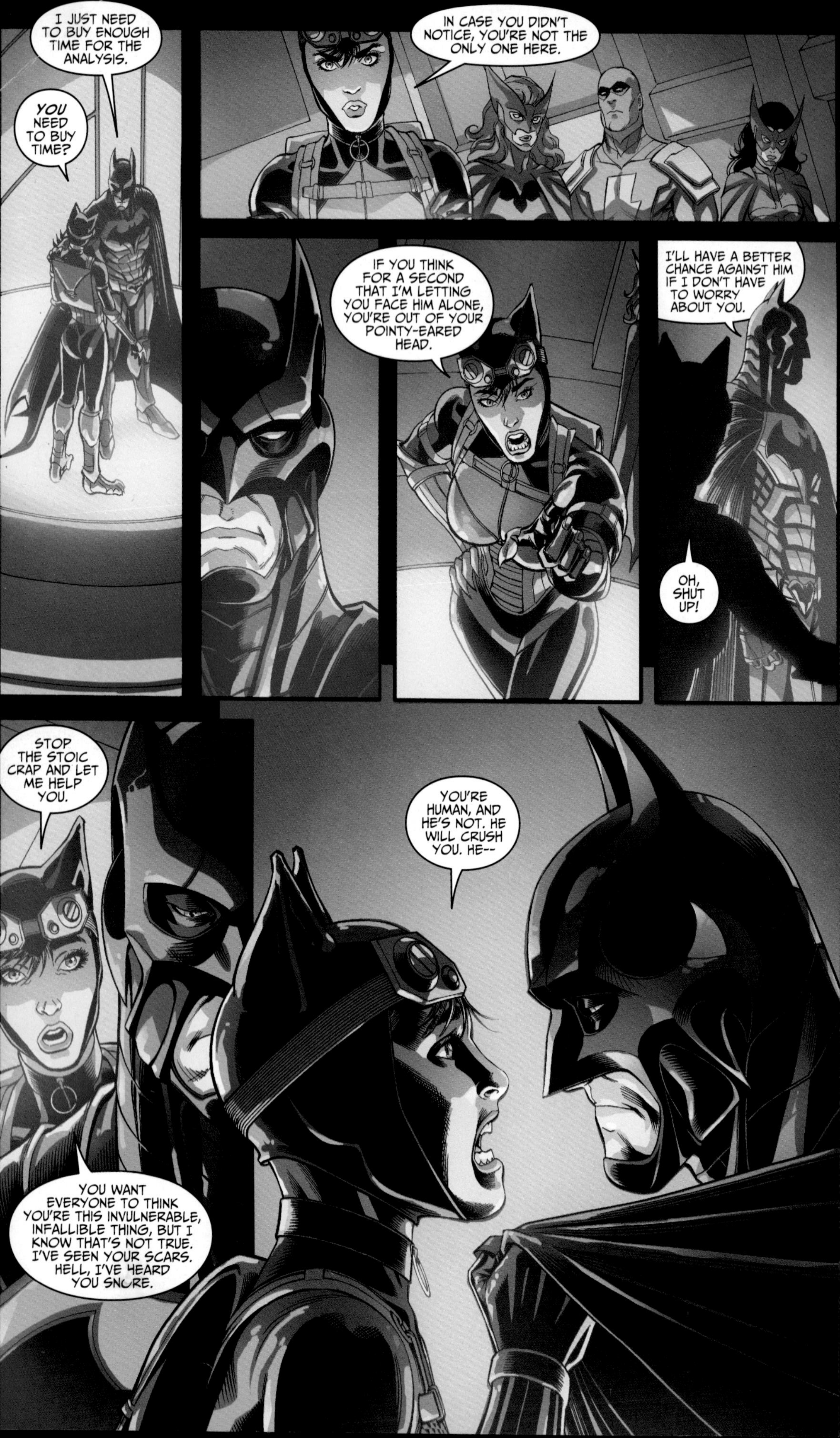
I JUST NEED TO BUY ENOUGH TIME FOR THE ANALYSIS.
YOU NEED TO BUY TIME?
IN CASE YOU DIDN'T NOTICE, YOU'RE NOT THE ONLY ONE HERE.
IF YOU THINK FOR A SECOND THAT I'M LETTING YOU FACE HIM ALONE, YOU'RE OUT OF YOUR POINTY-EARED HEAD.
I'LL HAVE A BETTER CHANCE AGAINST HIM IF I DON'T HAVE TO WORRY ABOUT YOU.
OH, SHUT UP!
STOP THE STOIC CRAP AND LET ME HELP YOU.
YOU'RE HUMAN, AND HE'S NOT. HE WILL CRUSH YOU. HE--
YOU WANT EVERYONE TO THINK YOU'RE THIS INVULNERABLE, INFALLIBLE THING, BUT I KNOW THAT'S NOT TRUE. I'VE SEEN YOUR SCARS. HELL, I'VE HEARD YOU SNORE.

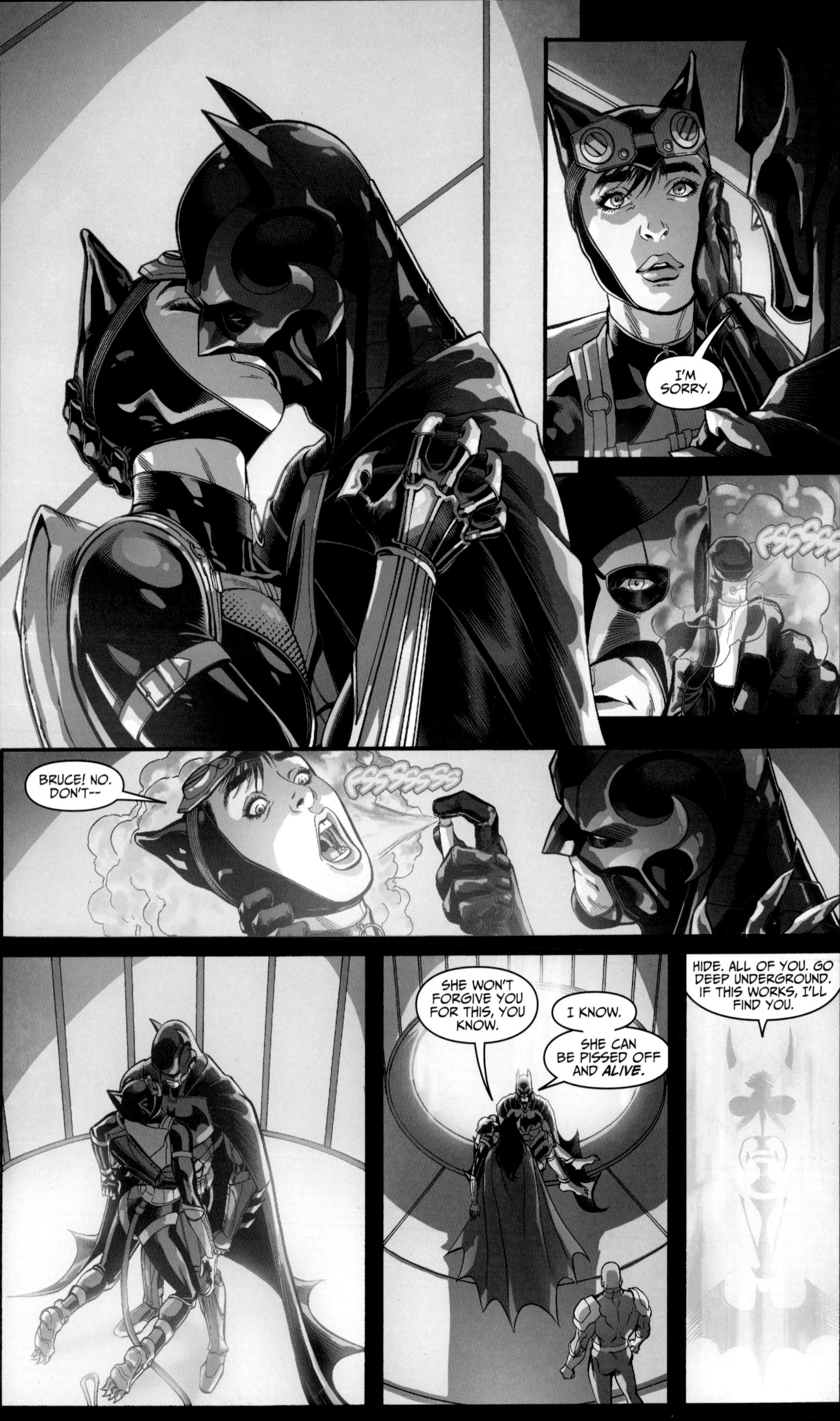
I'M SORRY.
FSSSSSS
BRUCE! NO. DON'T--
FSSSSSSS
SHE WON'T FORGIVE YOU FOR THIS, YOU KNOW.
I KNOW.
SHE CAN BE PISSED OFF AND *ALIVE.*
HIDE. ALL OF YOU. GO DEEP UNDERGROUND. IF THIS WORKS, I'LL FIND YOU.

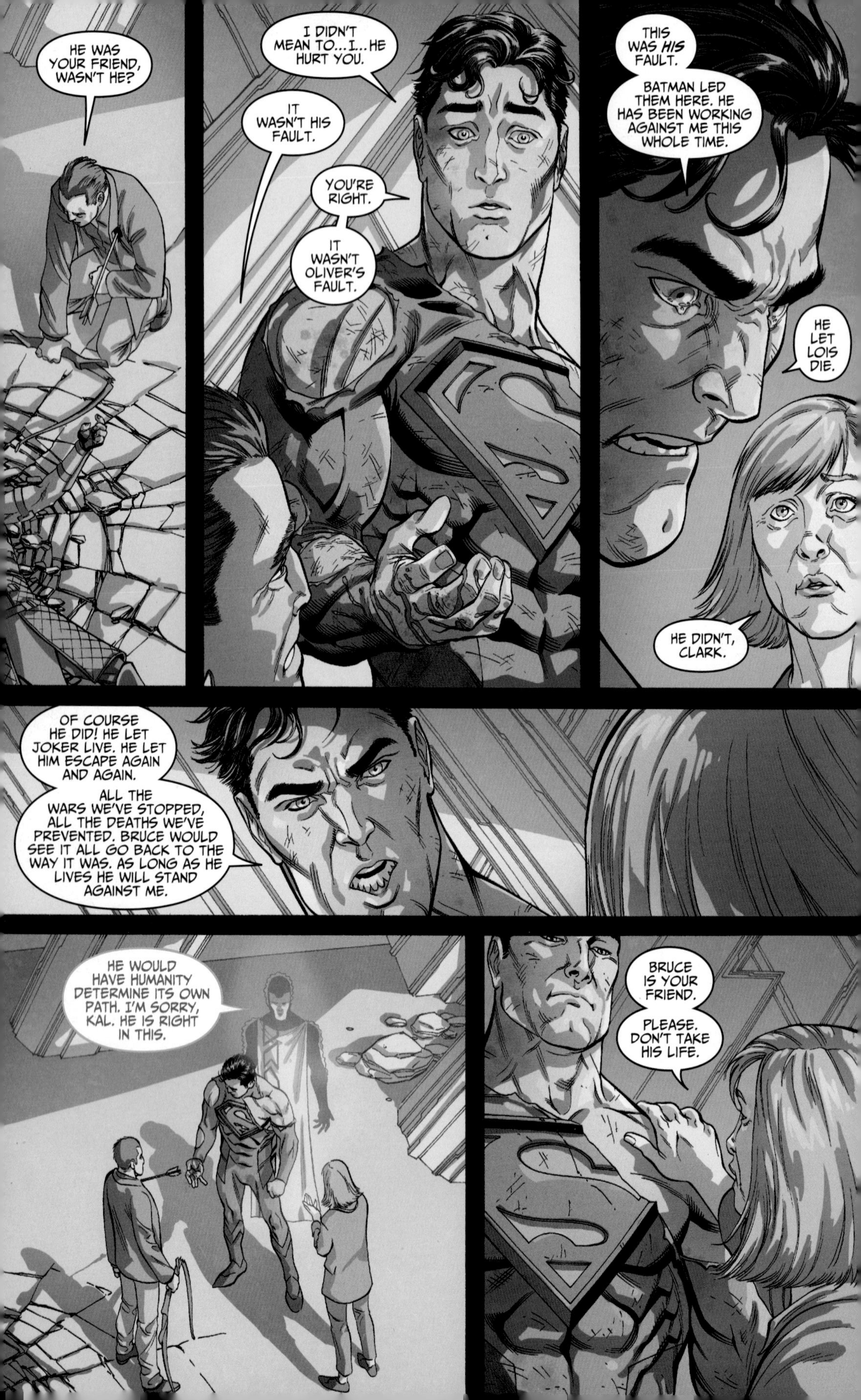
HE WAS YOUR FRIEND, WASN'T HE?
I DIDN'T MEAN TO... I... HE HURT YOU.
IT WASN'T HIS FAULT.
YOU'RE RIGHT.
IT WASN'T OLIVER'S FAULT.
THIS WAS *HIS* FAULT.
BATMAN LED THEM HERE. HE HAS BEEN WORKING AGAINST ME THIS WHOLE TIME.
HE LET LOIS DIE.
HE DIDN'T, CLARK.
OF COURSE HE DID! HE LET JOKER LIVE. HE LET HIM ESCAPE AGAIN AND AGAIN.
ALL THE WARS WE'VE STOPPED, ALL THE DEATHS WE'VE PREVENTED. BRUCE WOULD SEE IT ALL GO BACK TO THE WAY IT WAS. AS LONG AS HE LIVES HE WILL STAND AGAINST ME.
HE WOULD HAVE HUMANITY DETERMINE ITS OWN PATH. I'M SORRY, KAL. HE IS RIGHT IN THIS.
BRUCE IS YOUR FRIEND.
PLEASE. DON'T TAKE HIS LIFE.

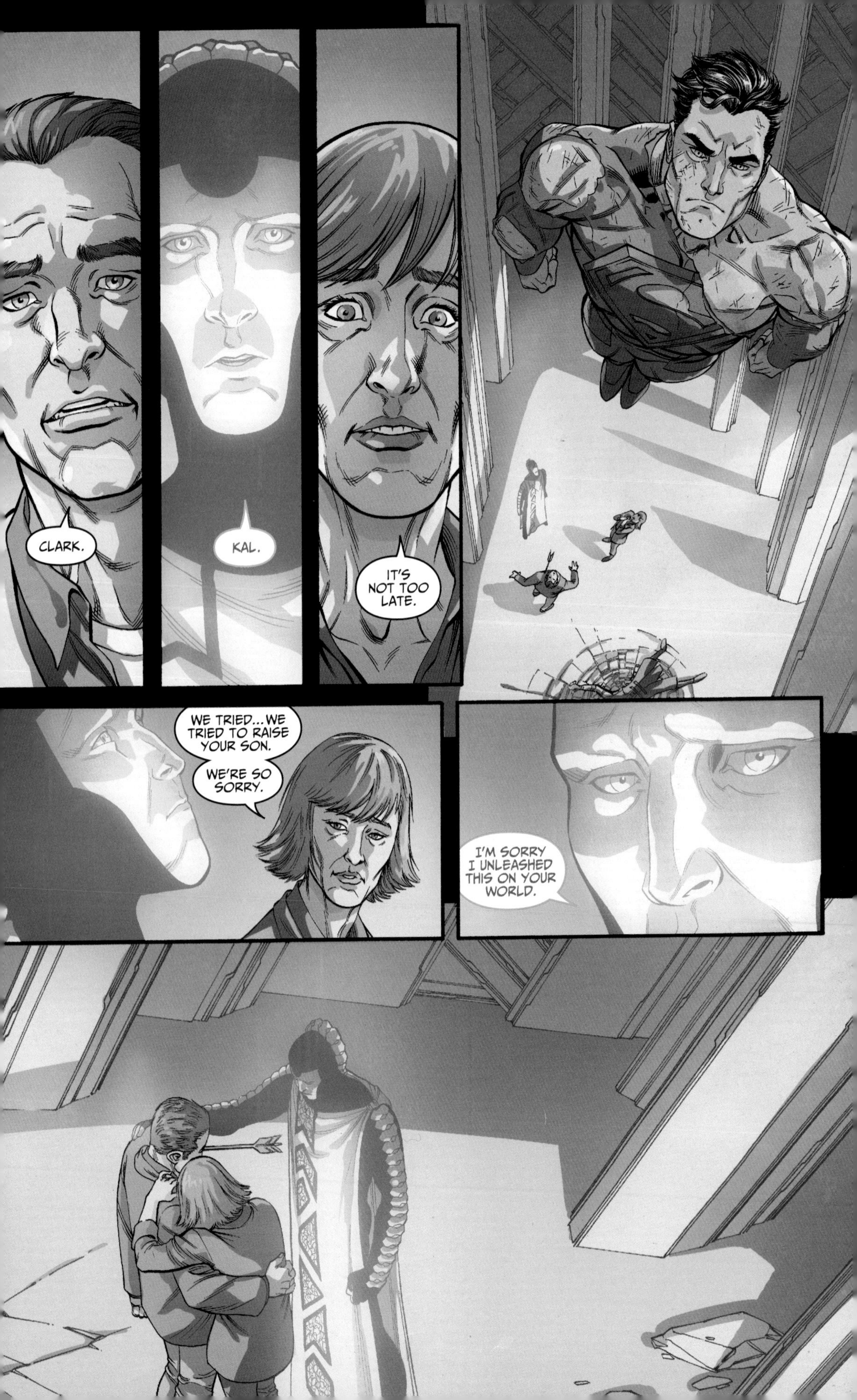
CLARK.
KAL.
IT'S NOT TOO LATE.
WE TRIED...WE TRIED TO RAISE YOUR SON.
WE'RE SO SORRY.
I'M SORRY I UNLEASHED THIS ON YOUR WORLD.

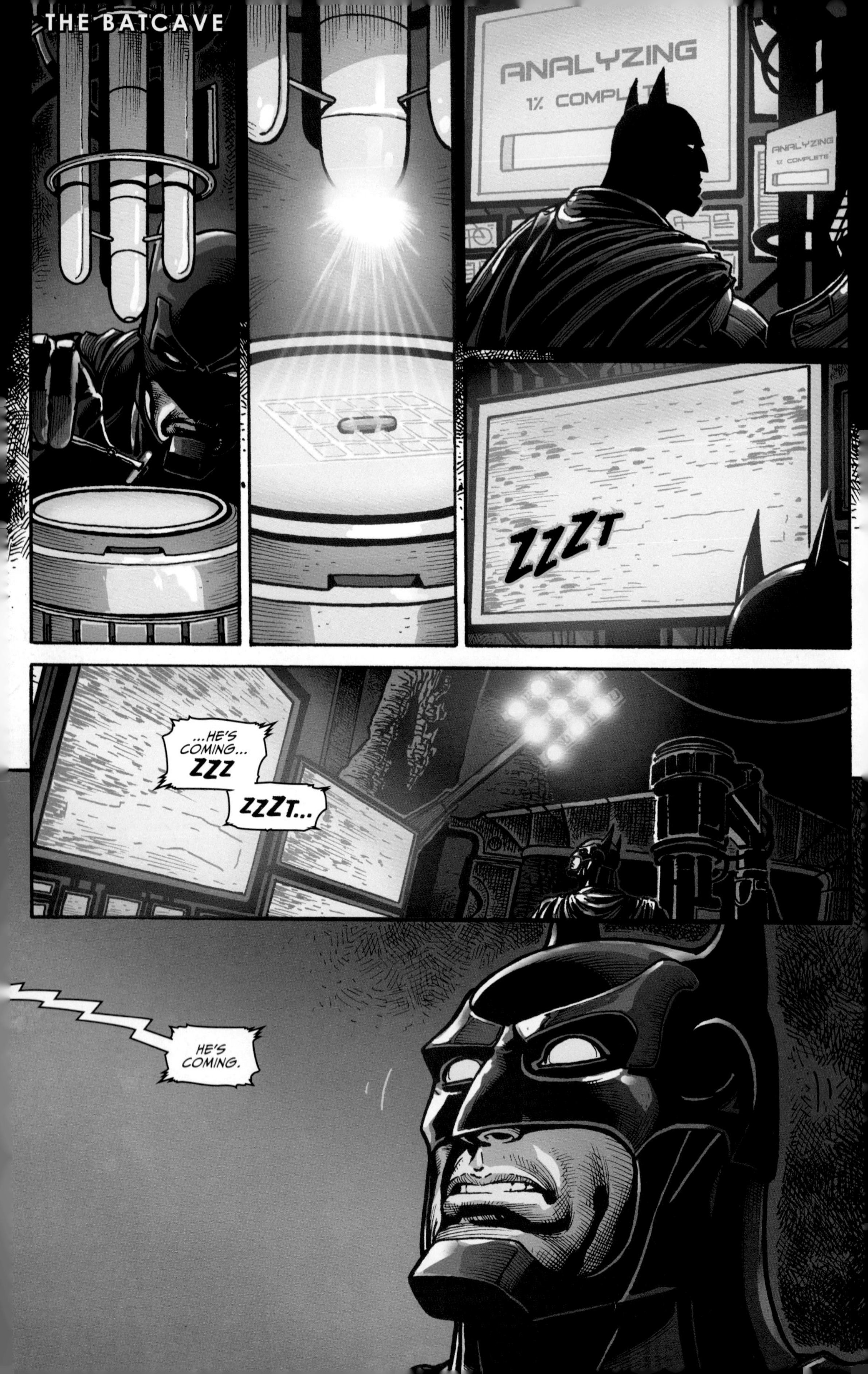
THE BATCAVE
ANALYZING
1% COMPLETE
ANALYZING
1% COMPLETE
ZZZT
...HE'S COMING... ZZZ
ZZZT...
HE'S COMING.

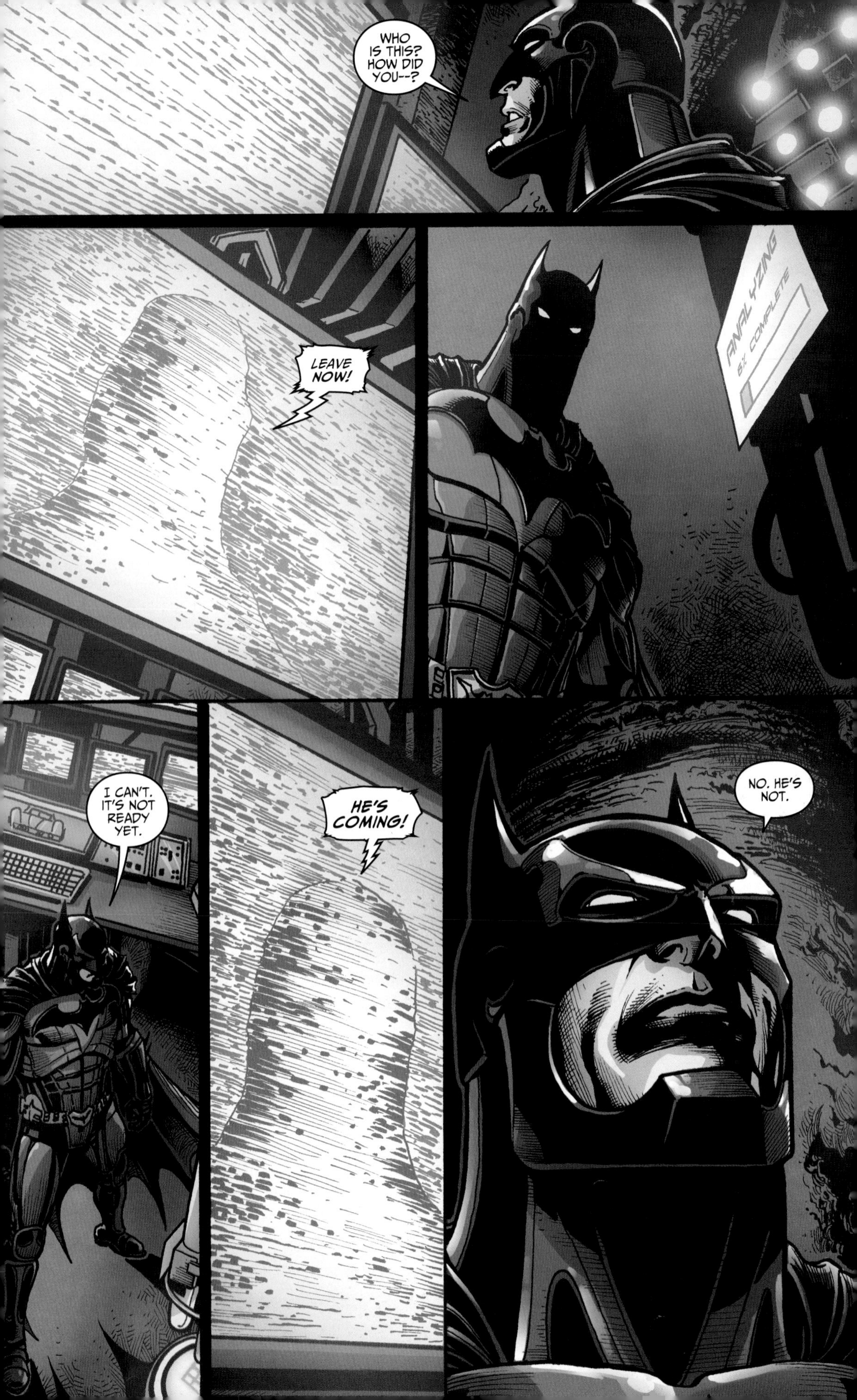
WHO IS THIS? HOW DID YOU--?
LEAVE NOW!
ANALYZING
6% COMPLETE
I CAN'T. IT'S NOT READY YET.
HE'S COMING!
NO. HE'S NOT.

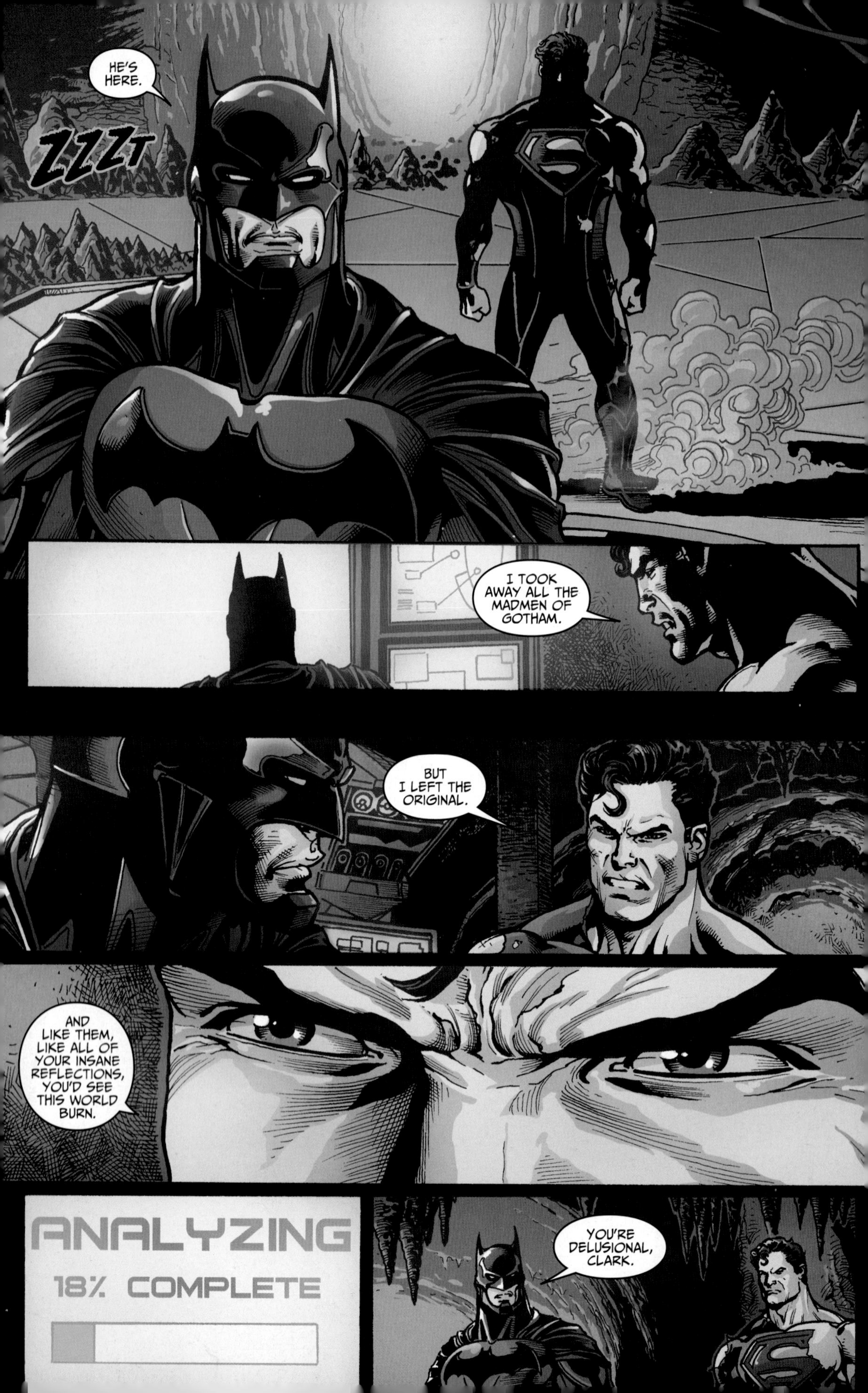
HE'S HERE.
ZZZT
I TOOK AWAY ALL THE MADMEN OF GOTHAM.
BUT I LEFT THE ORIGINAL.
AND LIKE THEM, LIKE ALL OF YOUR INSANE REFLECTIONS, YOU'D SEE THIS WORLD BURN.
ANALYZING
18% COMPLETE
YOU'RE DELUSIONAL, CLARK.

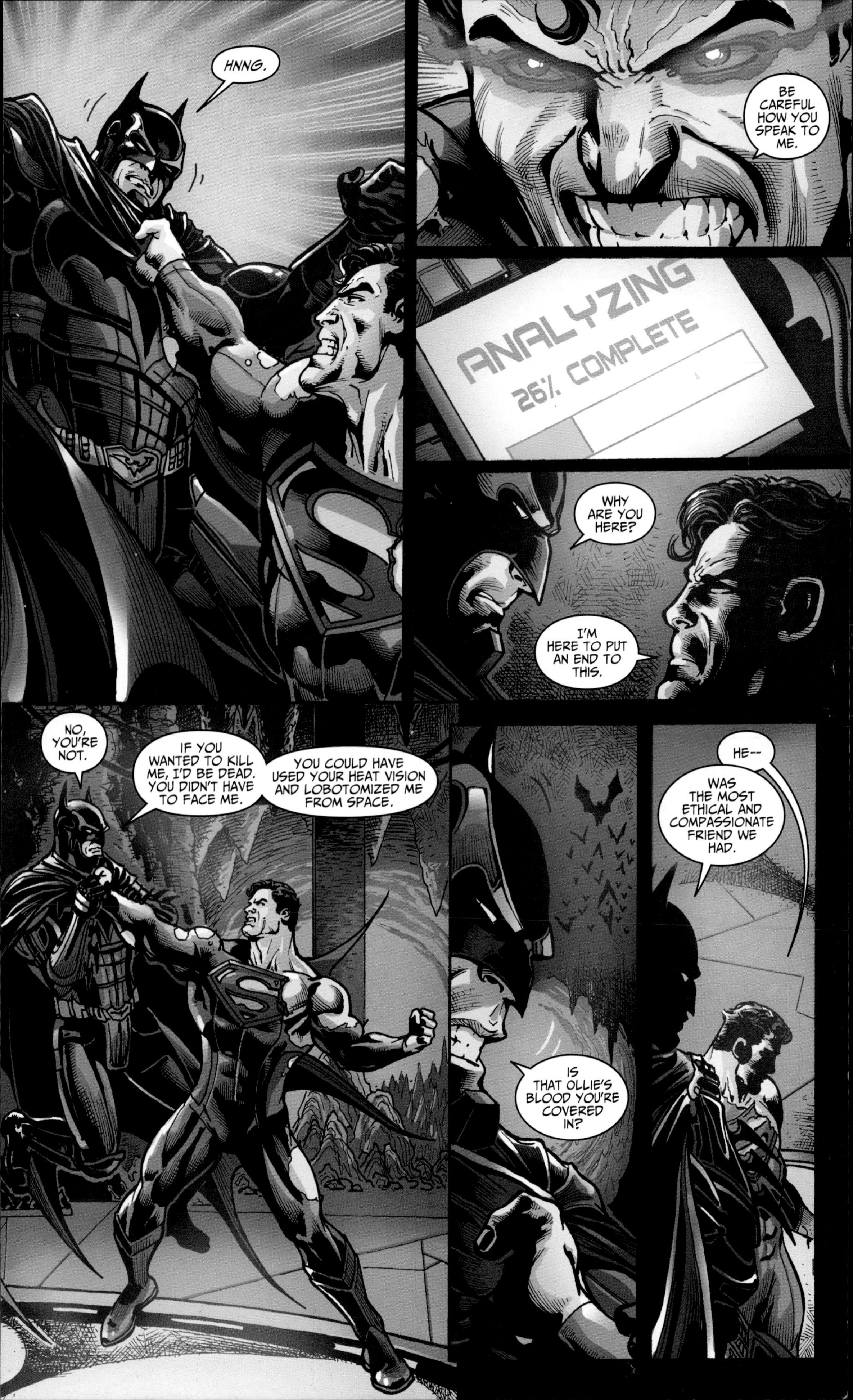
HNNG.
BE CAREFUL HOW YOU SPEAK TO ME.
ANALYZING
26% COMPLETE
WHY ARE YOU HERE?
I'M HERE TO PUT AN END TO THIS.
NO, YOU'RE NOT.
IF YOU WANTED TO KILL ME, I'D BE DEAD. YOU DIDN'T HAVE TO FACE ME.
YOU COULD HAVE USED YOUR HEAT VISION AND LOBOTOMIZED ME FROM SPACE.
IS THAT OLLIE'S BLOOD YOU'RE COVERED IN?
HE--
WAS THE MOST ETHICAL AND COMPASSIONATE FRIEND WE HAD.

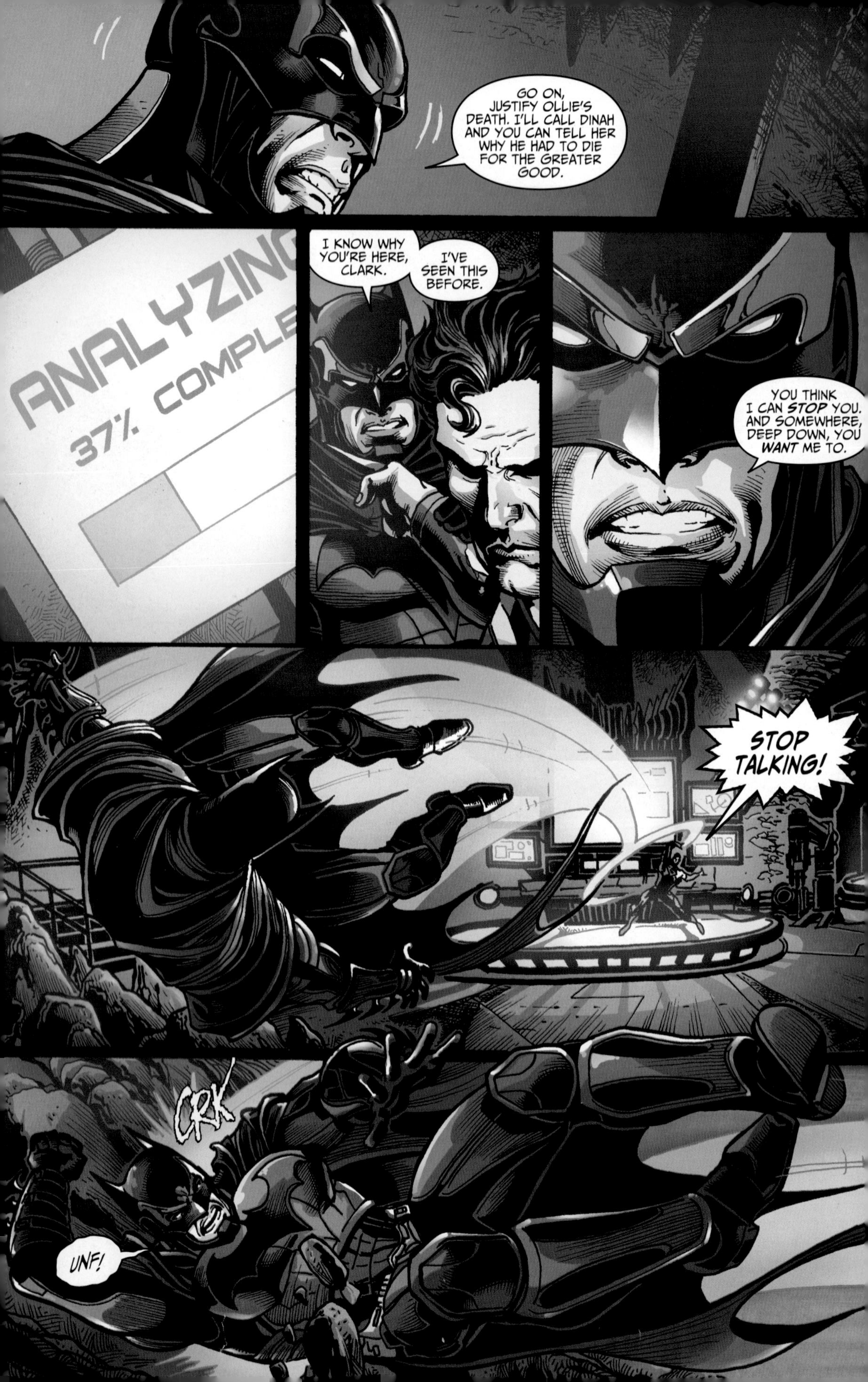
GO ON, JUSTIFY OLLIE'S DEATH. I'LL CALL DINAH AND YOU CAN TELL HER WHY HE HAD TO DIE FOR THE GREATER GOOD.
ANALYZING
37% COMPLE
I KNOW WHY YOU'RE HERE, CLARK.
I'VE SEEN THIS BEFORE.
YOU THINK I CAN STOP YOU. AND SOMEWHERE, DEEP DOWN, YOU WANT ME TO.
STOP TALKING!
CRK
UNF!

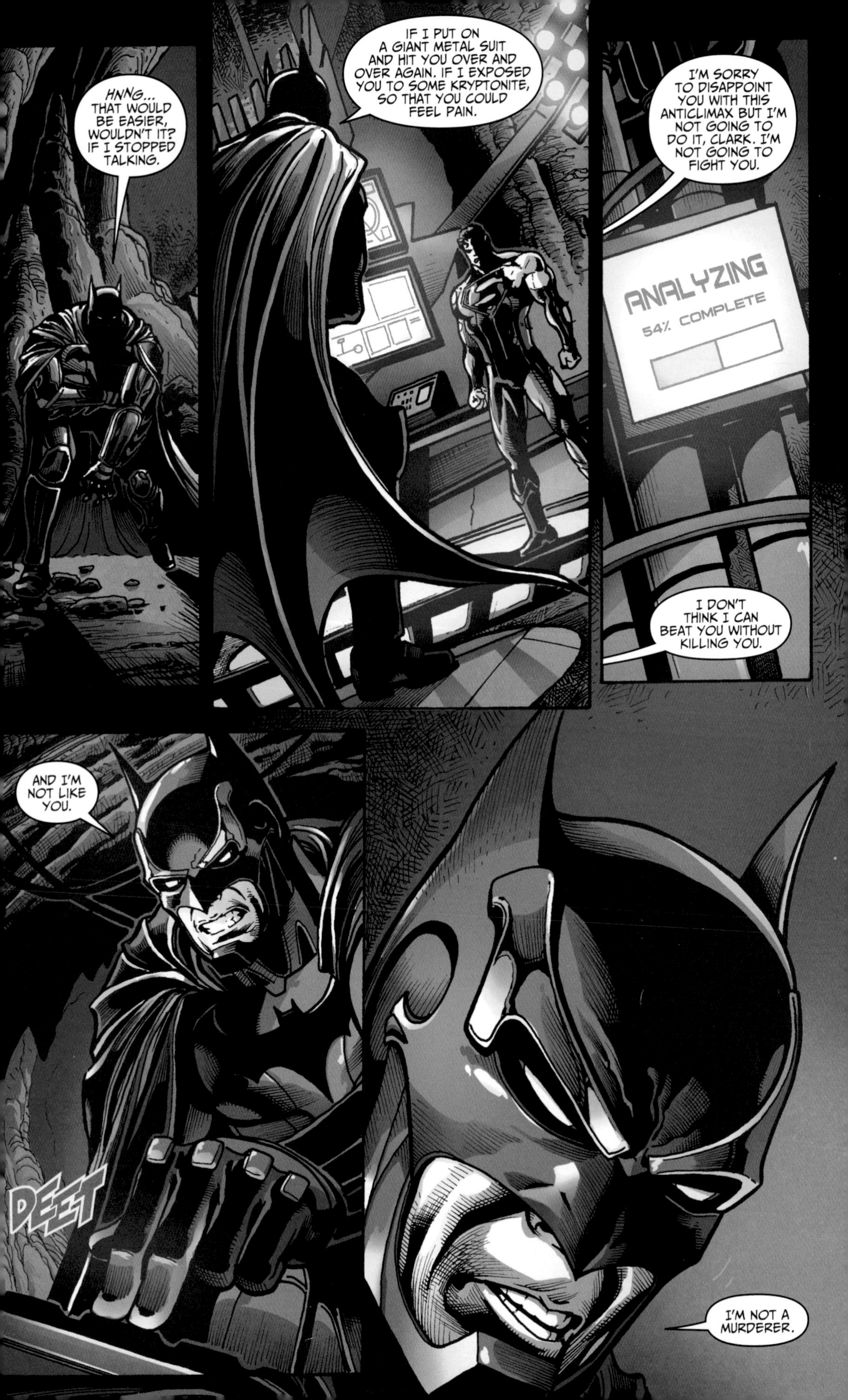
HNNG... THAT WOULD BE EASIER, WOULDN'T IT? IF I STOPPED TALKING.
IF I PUT ON A GIANT METAL SUIT AND HIT YOU OVER AND OVER AGAIN. IF I EXPOSED YOU TO SOME KRYPTONITE, SO THAT YOU COULD FEEL PAIN.
I'M SORRY TO DISAPPOINT YOU WITH THIS ANTICLIMAX BUT I'M NOT GOING TO DO IT, CLARK. I'M NOT GOING TO FIGHT YOU.
ANALYZING
54% COMPLETE
I DON'T THINK I CAN BEAT YOU WITHOUT KILLING YOU.
AND I'M NOT LIKE YOU.
DEET
I'M NOT A MURDERER.

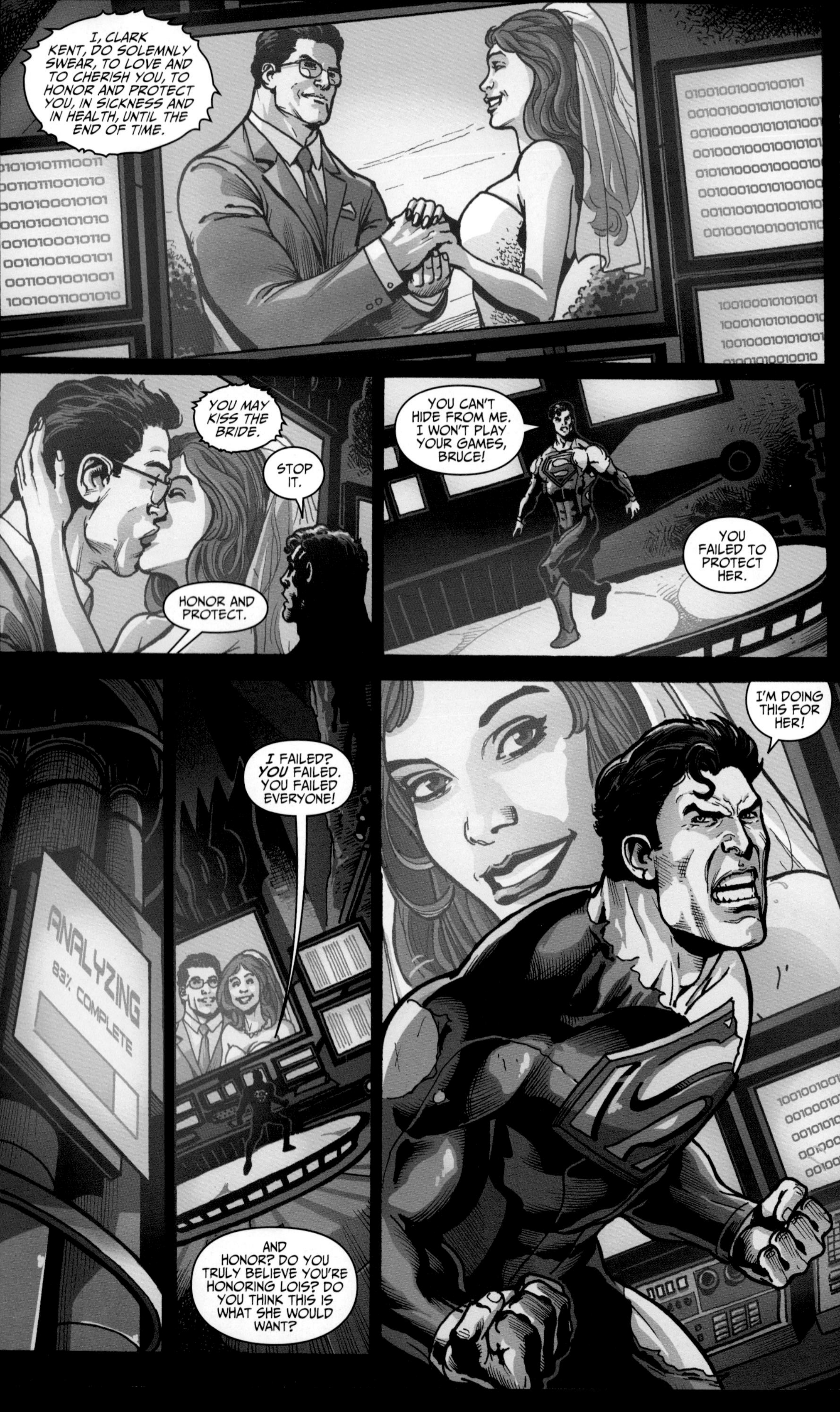

I, CLARK KENT, DO SOLEMNLY SWEAR, TO LOVE AND TO CHERISH YOU, TO HONOR AND PROTECT YOU, IN SICKNESS AND IN HEALTH, UNTIL THE END OF TIME.
YOU MAY KISS THE BRIDE.
STOP IT.
HONOR AND PROTECT.
YOU CAN'T HIDE FROM ME. I WON'T PLAY YOUR GAMES, BRUCE!
YOU FAILED TO PROTECT HER.
ANALYZING
83% COMPLETE
I FAILED? YOU FAILED. YOU FAILED EVERYONE!
AND HONOR? DO YOU TRULY BELIEVE YOU'RE HONORING LOIS? DO YOU THINK THIS IS WHAT SHE WOULD WANT?
I'M DOING THIS FOR HER!

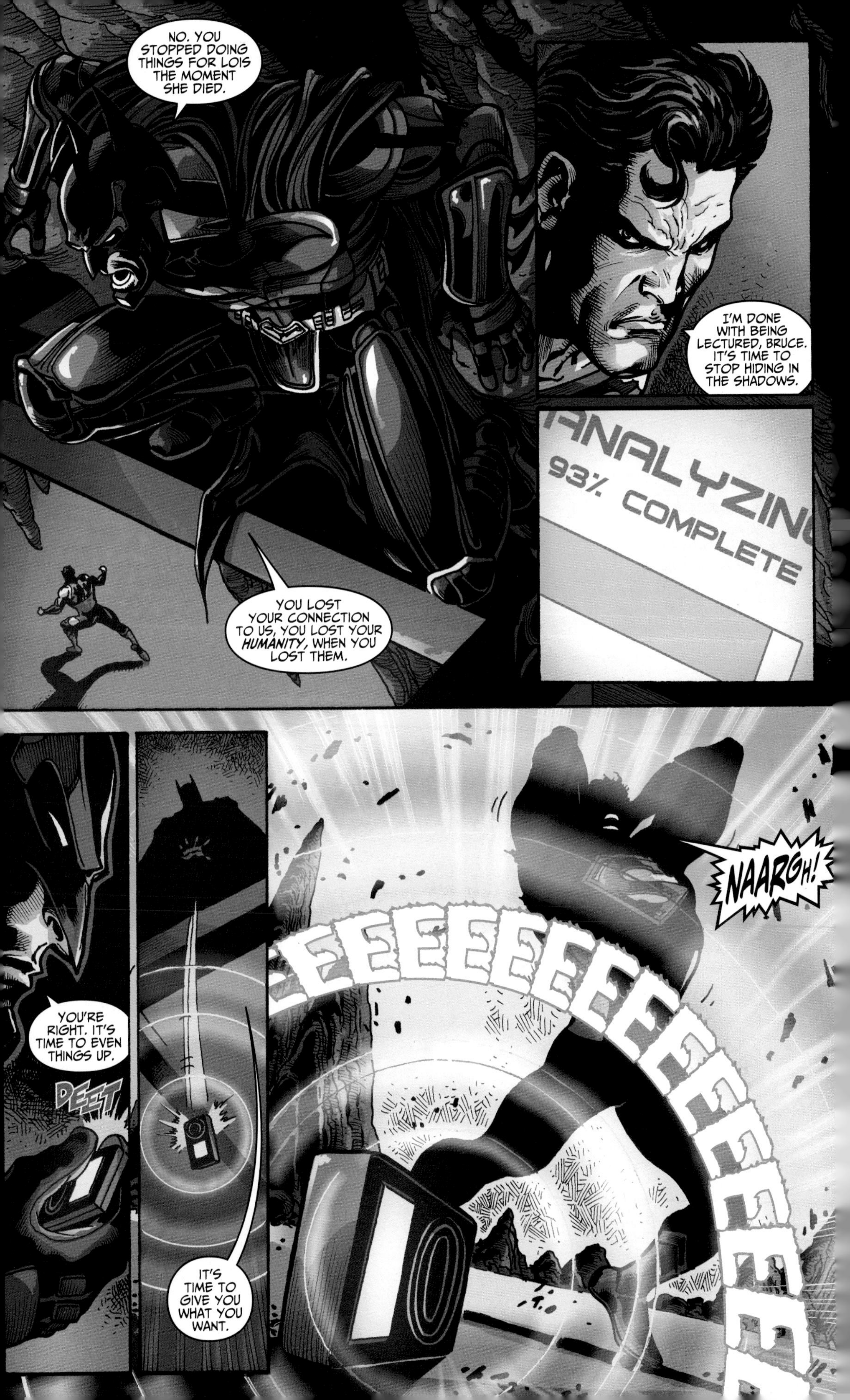
NO. YOU STOPPED DOING THINGS FOR LOIS THE MOMENT SHE DIED.
I'M DONE WITH BEING LECTURED, BRUCE. IT'S TIME TO STOP HIDING IN THE SHADOWS.
ANALYZING 93% COMPLETE
YOU LOST YOUR CONNECTION TO US, YOU LOST YOUR *HUMANITY*, WHEN YOU LOST THEM.
YOU'RE RIGHT. IT'S TIME TO EVEN THINGS UP.
DEET
IT'S TIME TO GIVE YOU WHAT YOU WANT.
EEEEEEEEEEEEEEEE
NAARGH!

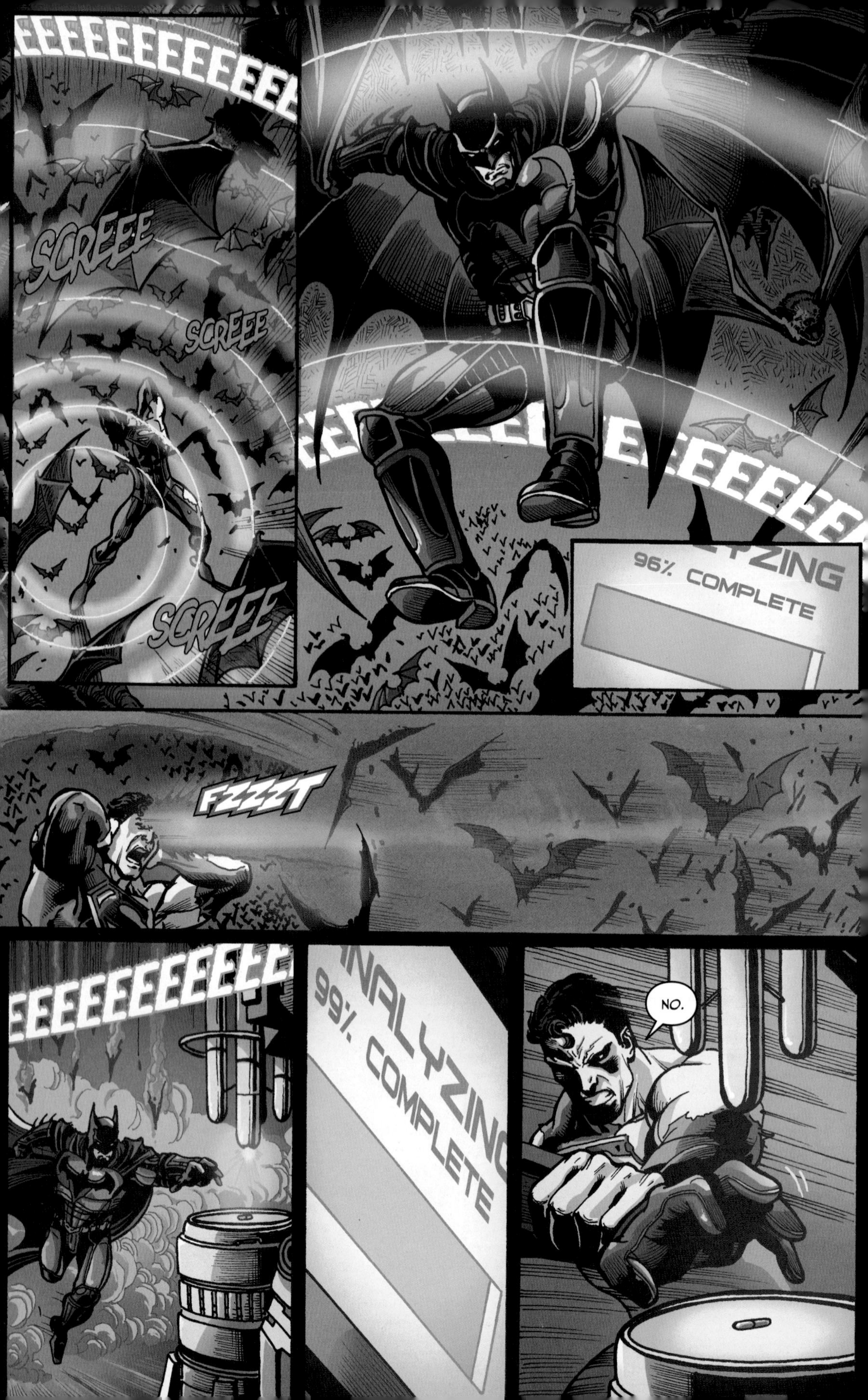
EEEEEEEEEEEE
SCREEE
SCREEE
SCREEE
EEEEEEEEEEE
96% COMPLETE
FZZZT
EEEEEEEEEEE
ANALYZING
99% COMPLETE
NO.

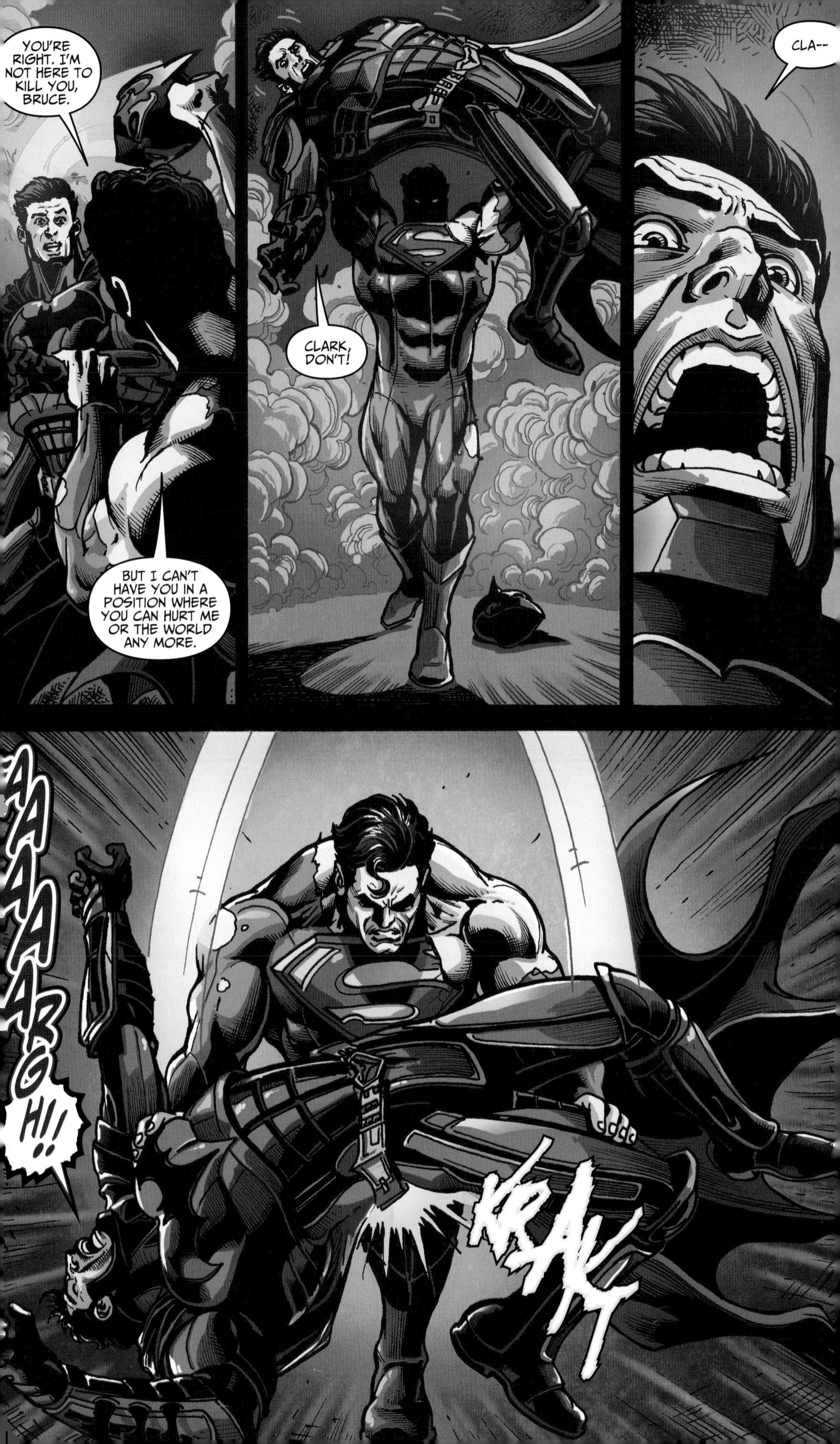
YOU'RE RIGHT. I'M NOT HERE TO KILL YOU, BRUCE.
BUT I CAN'T HAVE YOU IN A POSITION WHERE YOU CAN HURT ME OR THE WORLD ANY MORE.
CLARK, DON'T!
CLA--
AAAAAARRGH!!
KRAK

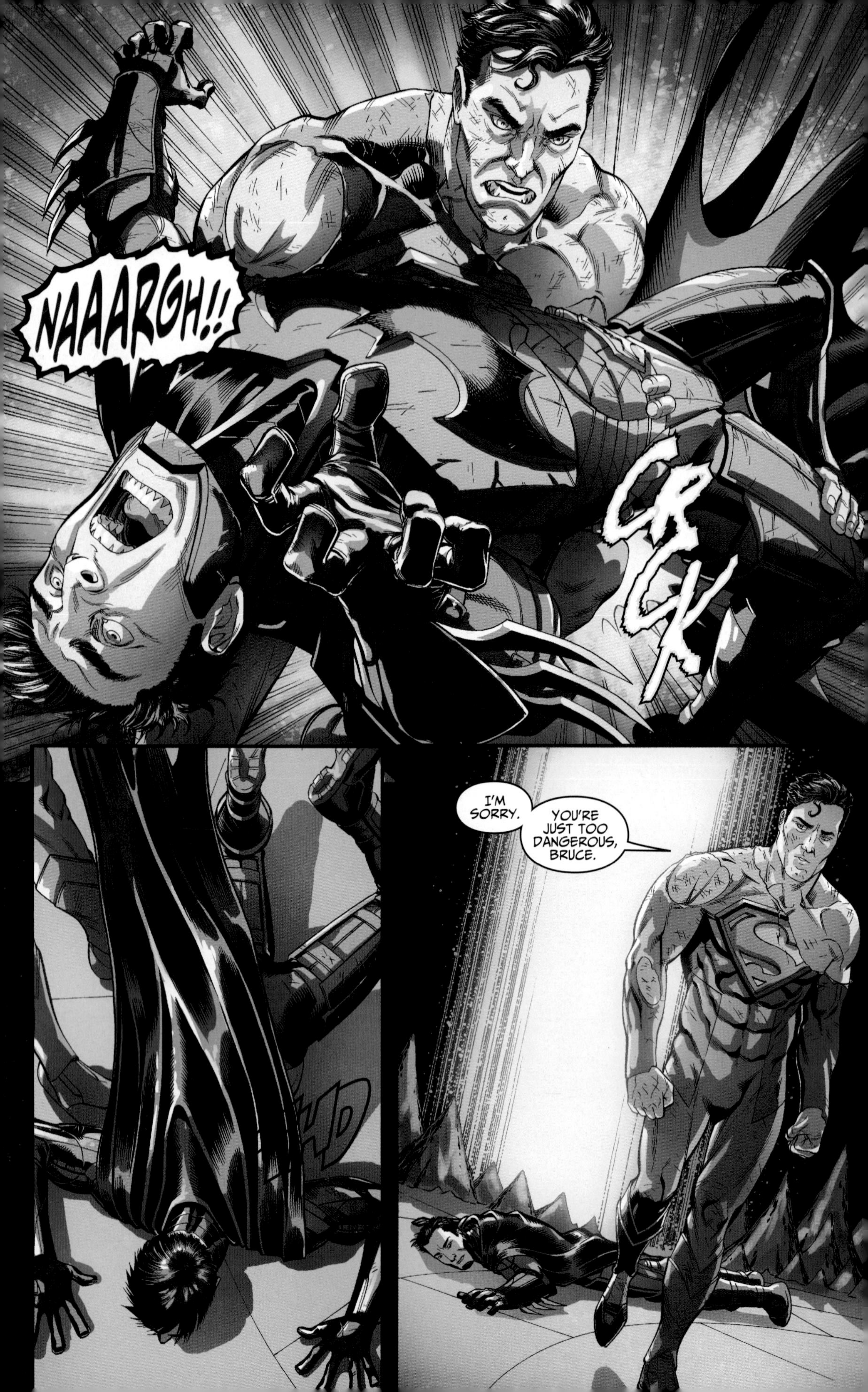
NAAARGH!!
CRCK
I'M SORRY.
YOU'RE JUST TOO DANGEROUS, BRUCE.

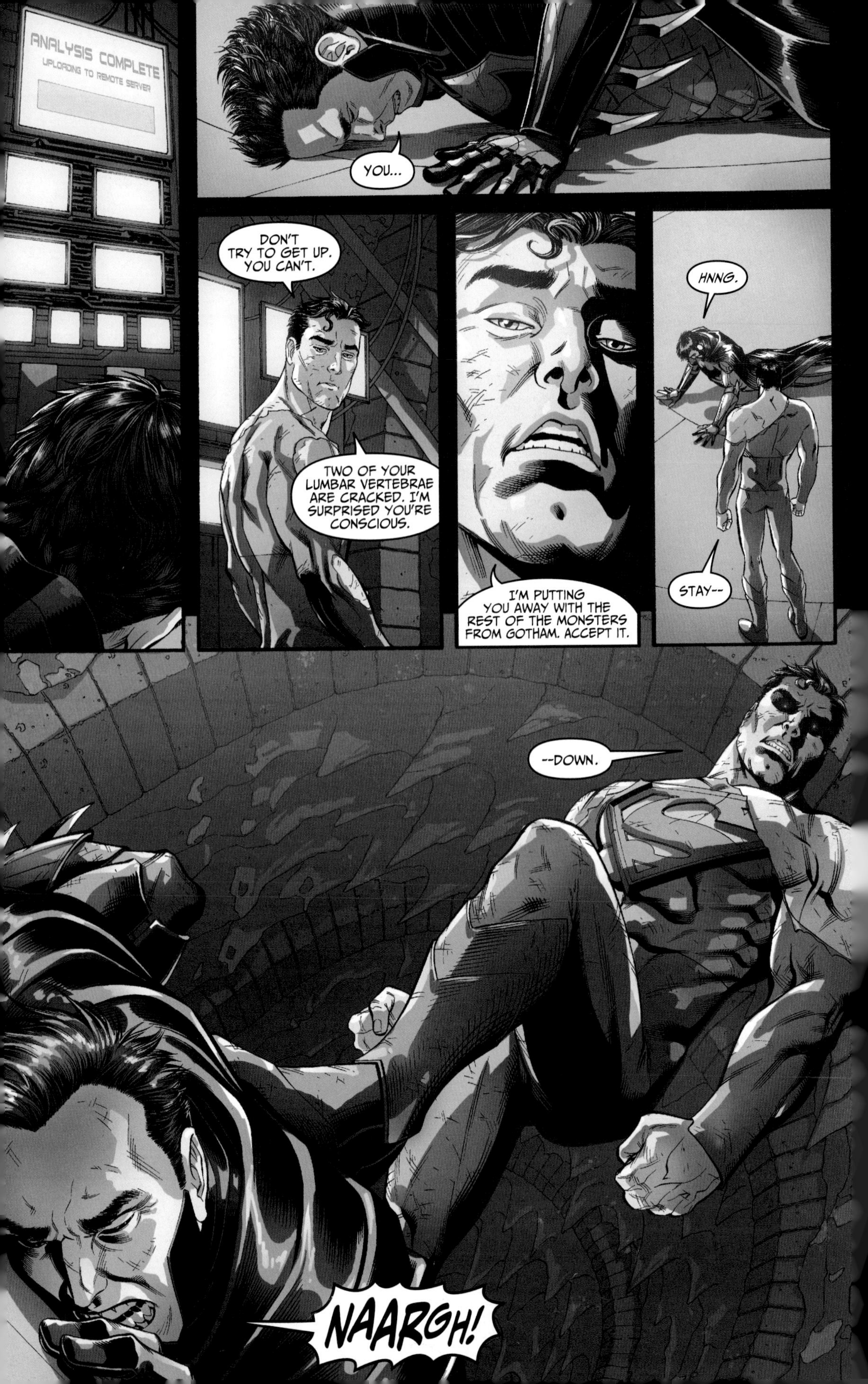
ANALYSIS COMPLETE
UPLOADING TO REMOTE SERVER
YOU...
DON'T TRY TO GET UP. YOU CAN'T.
TWO OF YOUR LUMBAR VERTEBRAE ARE CRACKED. I'M SURPRISED YOU'RE CONSCIOUS.
I'M PUTTING YOU AWAY WITH THE REST OF THE MONSTERS FROM GOTHAM. ACCEPT IT.
HNNG.
STAY--
--DOWN.
NAARGH!

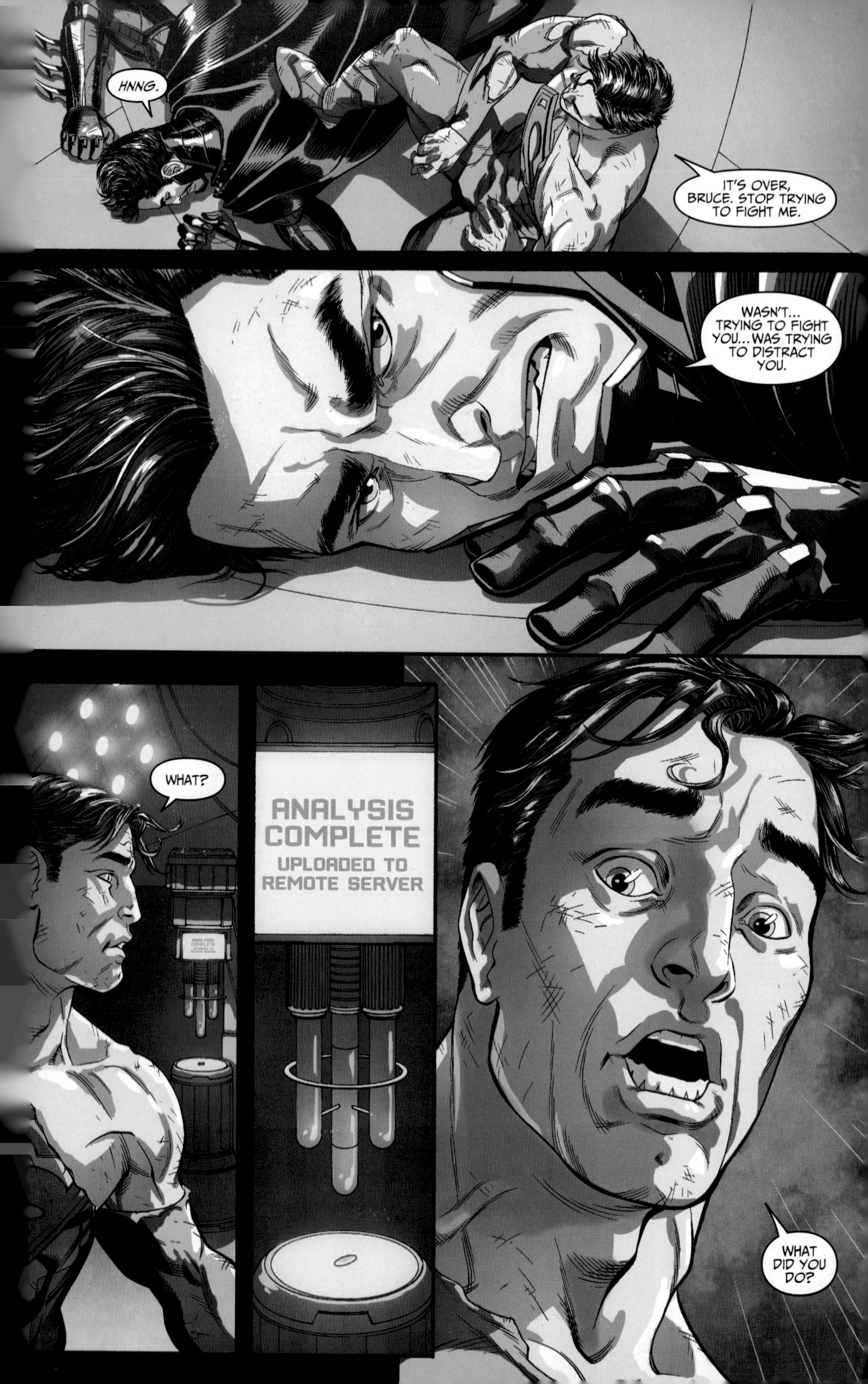
HNNG.
IT'S OVER, BRUCE. STOP TRYING TO FIGHT ME.
WASN'T... TRYING TO FIGHT YOU... WAS TRYING TO DISTRACT YOU.
WHAT?
ANALYSIS COMPLETE
UPLOADED TO REMOTE SERVER
WHAT DID YOU DO?

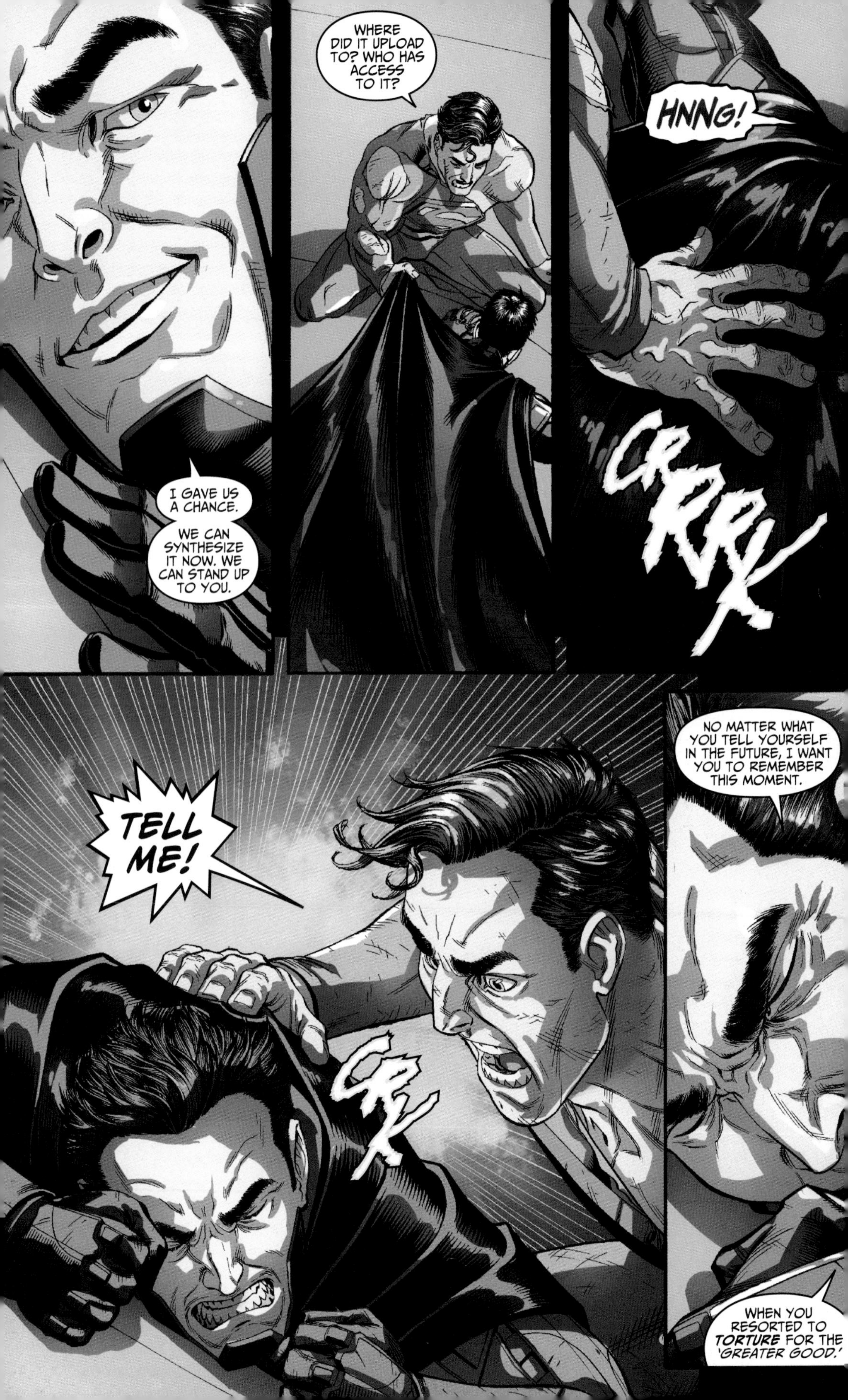
I GAVE US A CHANCE.
WE CAN SYNTHESIZE IT NOW. WE CAN STAND UP TO YOU.
WHERE DID IT UPLOAD TO? WHO HAS ACCESS TO IT?
HNNG!
CRRRK
TELL ME!
CRK
NO MATTER WHAT YOU TELL YOURSELF IN THE FUTURE, I WANT YOU TO REMEMBER THIS MOMENT.
WHEN YOU RESORTED TO *TORTURE* FOR THE *'GREATER GOOD.'*

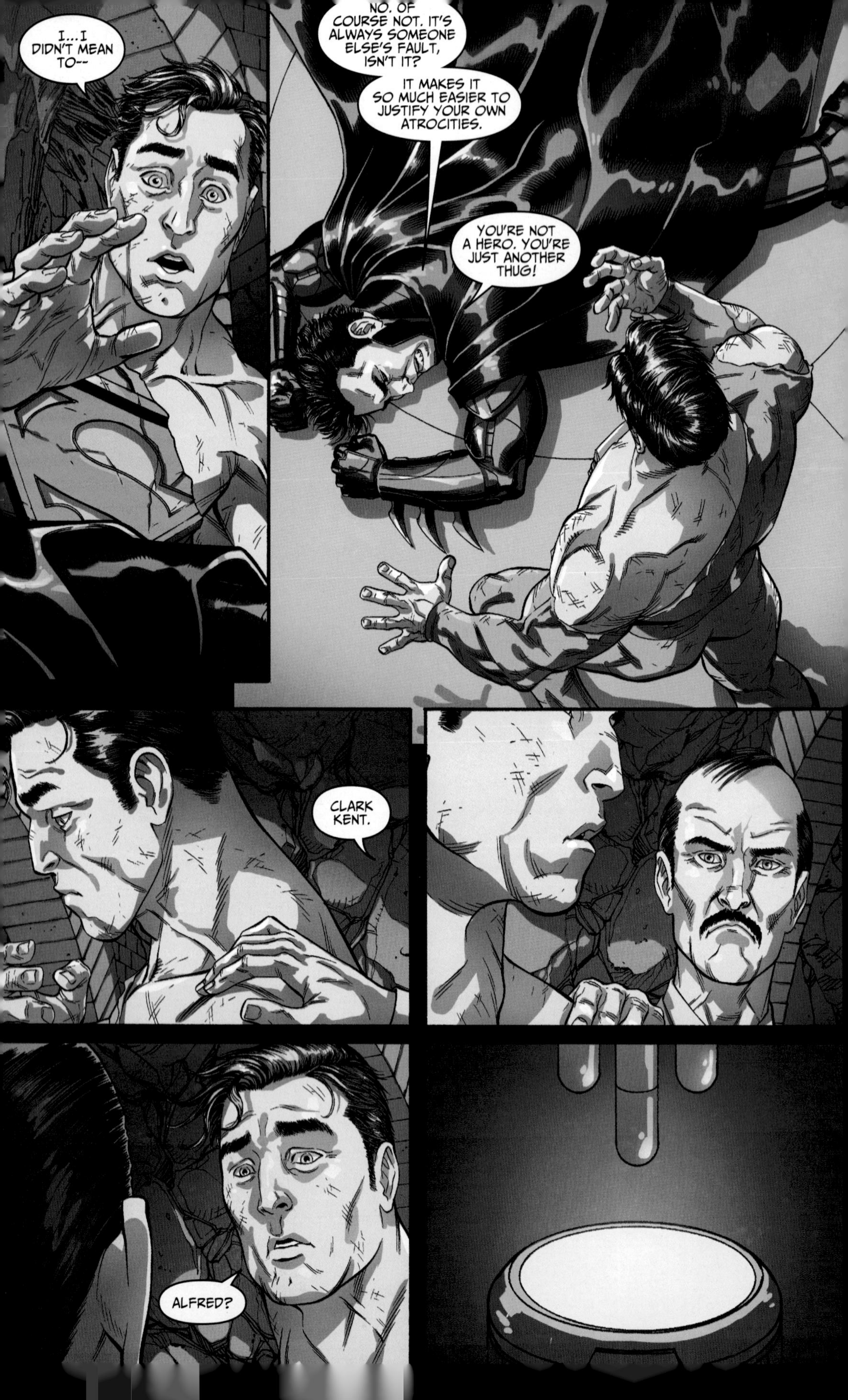
I...I DIDN'T MEAN TO--
NO. OF COURSE NOT. IT'S ALWAYS SOMEONE ELSE'S FAULT, ISN'T IT?
IT MAKES IT SO MUCH EASIER TO JUSTIFY YOUR OWN ATROCITIES.
YOU'RE NOT A HERO. YOU'RE JUST ANOTHER THUG!
CLARK KENT.
ALFRED?

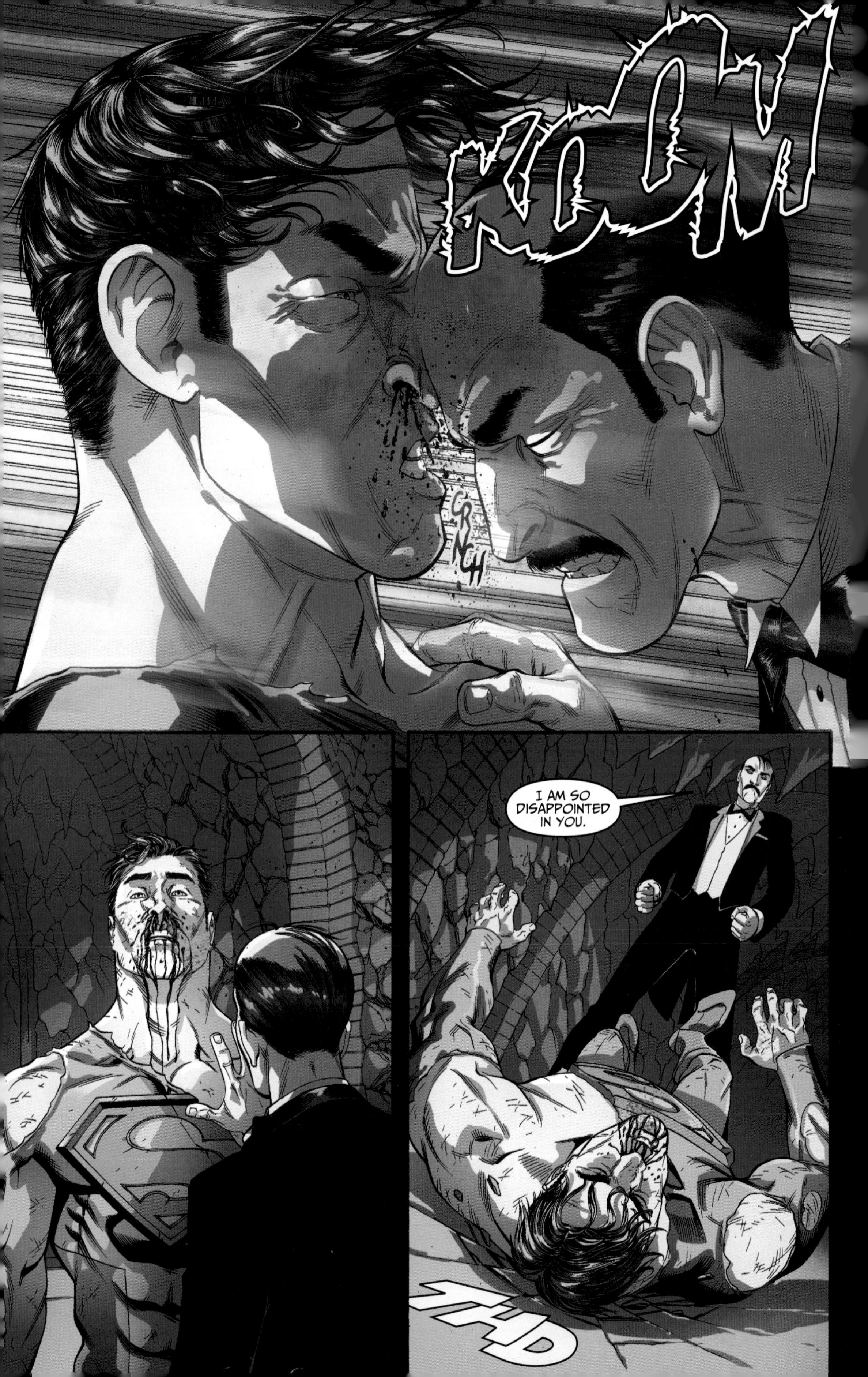
KOOM
CRNCH
I AM SO DISAPPOINTED IN YOU.
THD

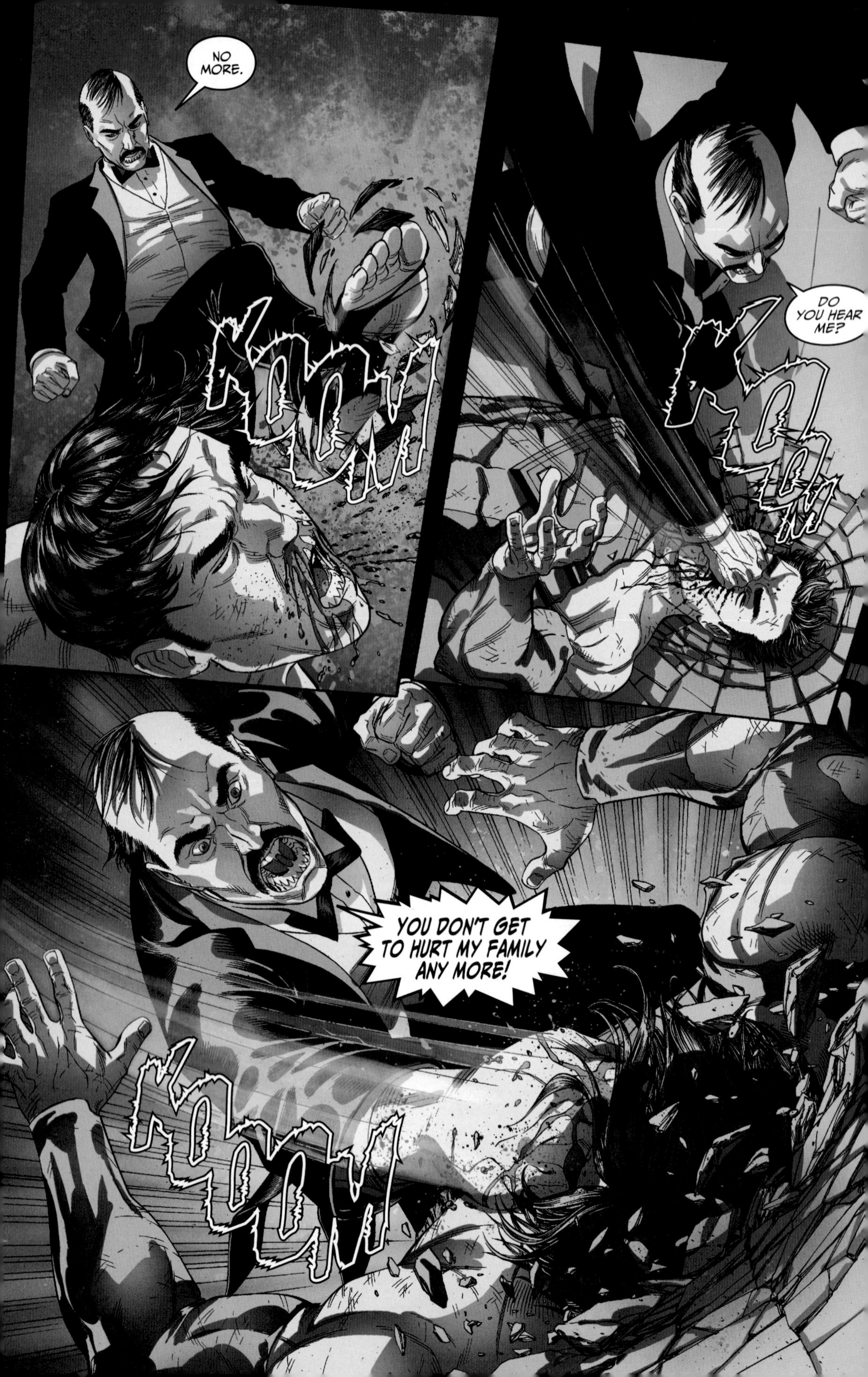
NO MORE.
DO YOU HEAR ME?
YOU DON'T GET TO HURT MY FAMILY ANY MORE!

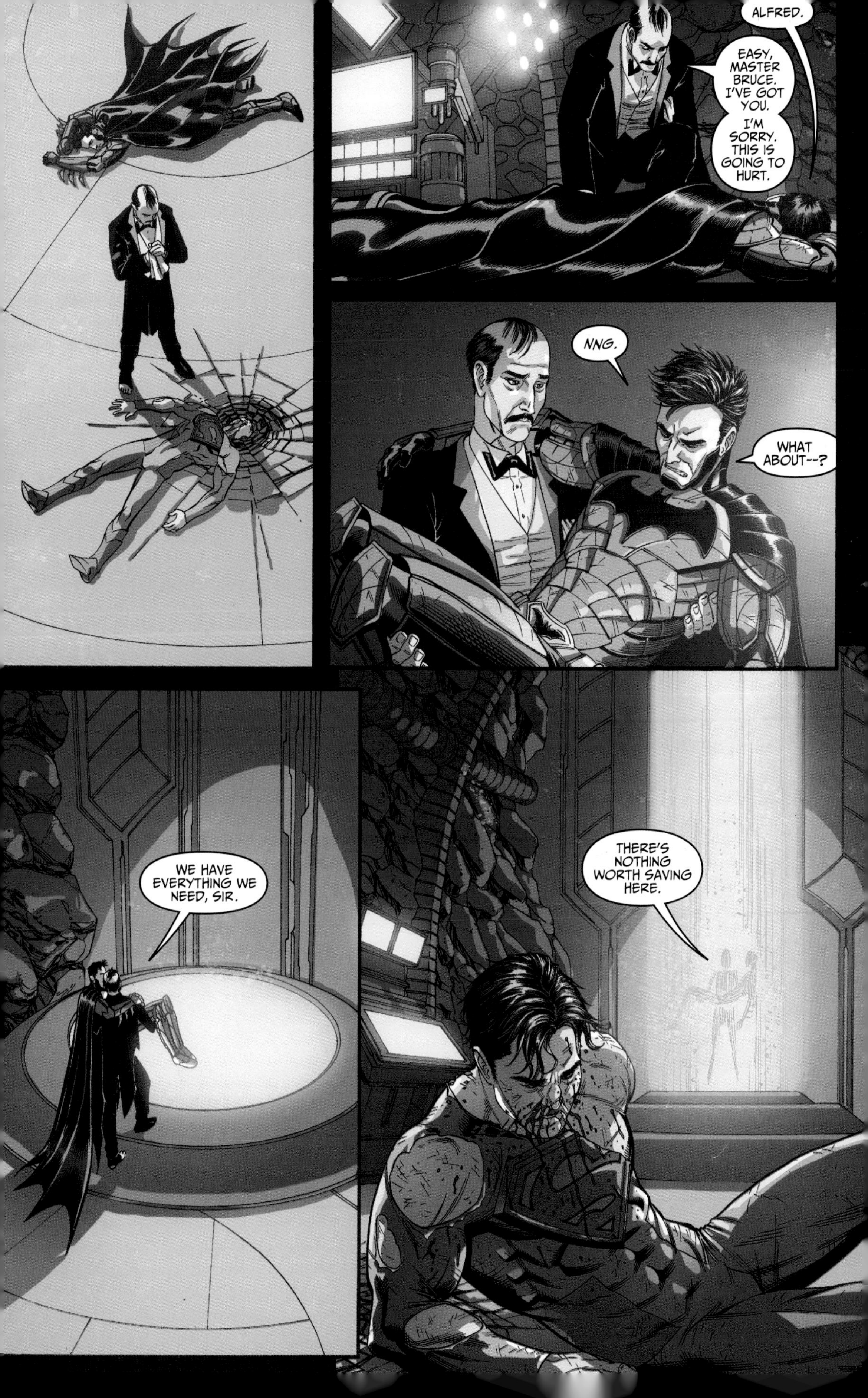
ALFRED.
EASY, MASTER BRUCE. I'VE GOT YOU.
I'M SORRY. THIS IS GOING TO HURT.
NNG.
WHAT ABOUT--?
WE HAVE EVERYTHING WE NEED, SIR.
THERE'S NOTHING WORTH SAVING HERE.

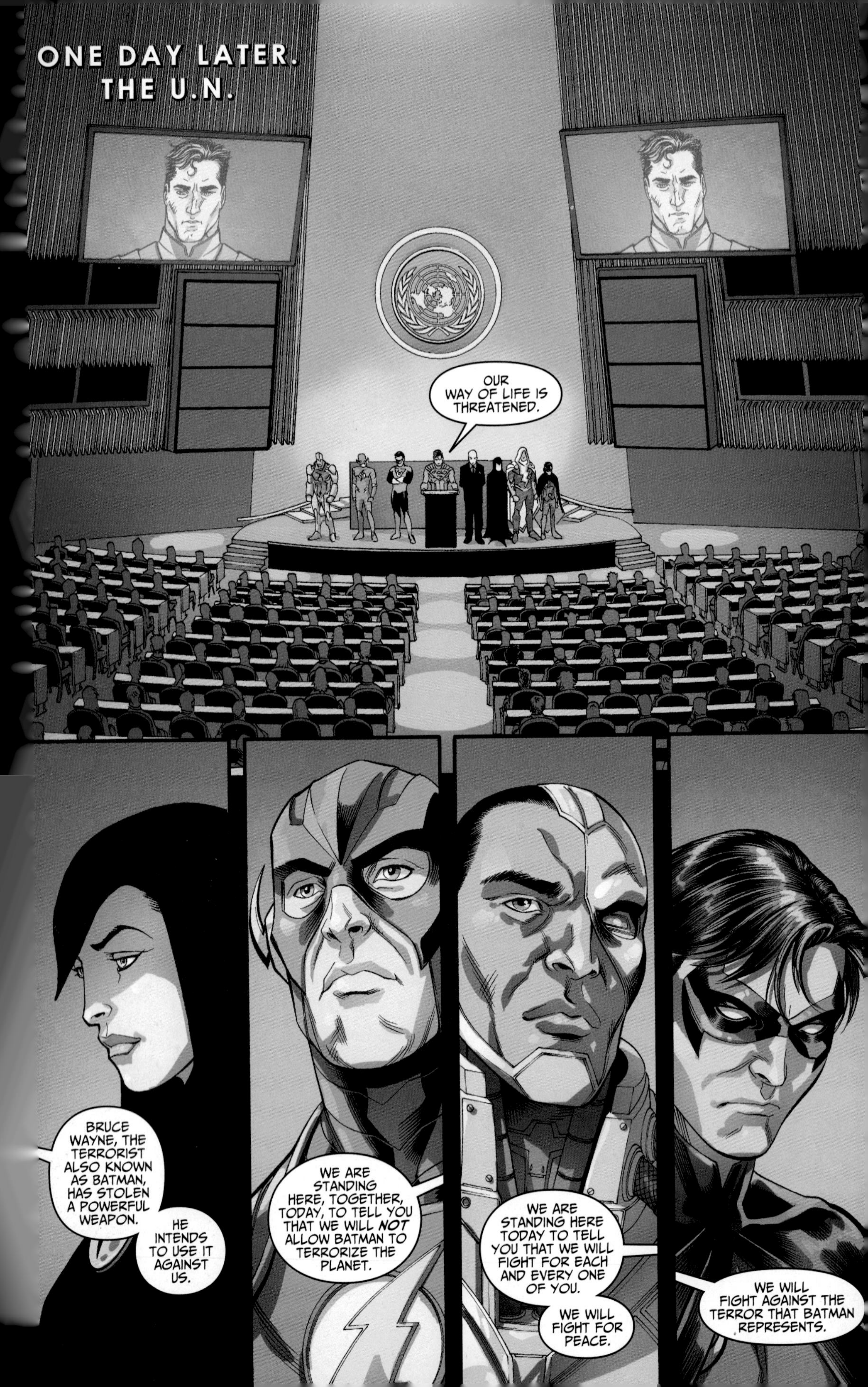
ONE DAY LATER. THE U.N.
OUR WAY OF LIFE IS THREATENED.
BRUCE WAYNE, THE TERRORIST ALSO KNOWN AS BATMAN, HAS STOLEN A POWERFUL WEAPON.
HE INTENDS TO USE IT AGAINST US.
WE ARE STANDING HERE, TOGETHER, TODAY, TO TELL YOU THAT WE WILL *NOT* ALLOW BATMAN TO TERRORIZE THE PLANET.
WE ARE STANDING HERE TODAY TO TELL YOU THAT WE WILL FIGHT FOR EACH AND EVERY ONE OF YOU.
WE WILL FIGHT FOR PEACE.
WE WILL FIGHT AGAINST THE TERROR THAT BATMAN REPRESENTS.

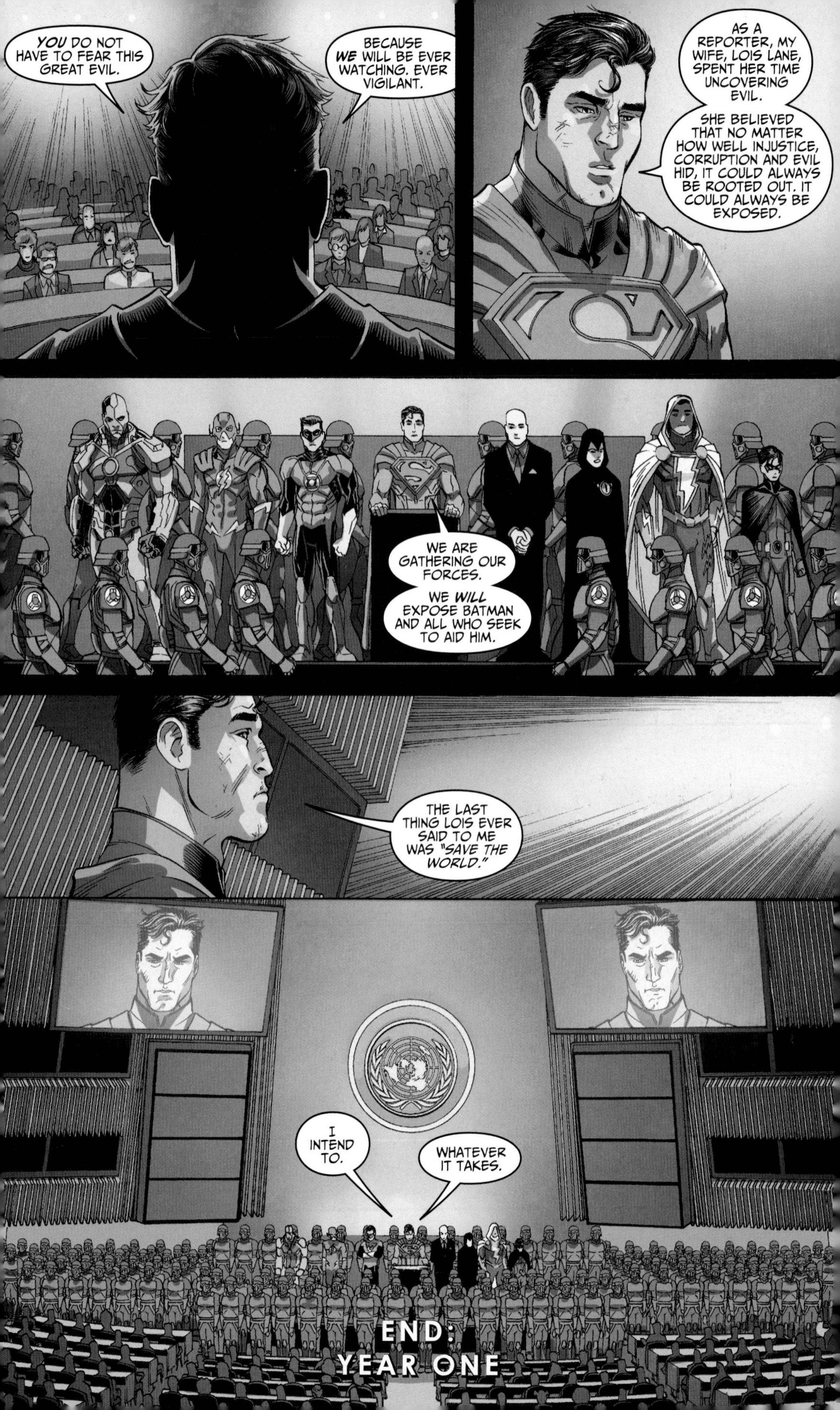
YOU DO NOT HAVE TO FEAR THIS GREAT EVIL.
BECAUSE WE WILL BE EVER WATCHING. EVER VIGILANT.
AS A REPORTER, MY WIFE, LOIS LANE, SPENT HER TIME UNCOVERING EVIL.
SHE BELIEVED THAT NO MATTER HOW WELL INJUSTICE, CORRUPTION AND EVIL HID, IT COULD ALWAYS BE ROOTED OUT. IT COULD ALWAYS BE EXPOSED.
WE ARE GATHERING OUR FORCES.
WE WILL EXPOSE BATMAN AND ALL WHO SEEK TO AID HIM.
THE LAST THING LOIS EVER SAID TO ME WAS "SAVE THE WORLD."
I INTEND TO.
WHATEVER IT TAKES.
END: YEAR ONE

Injustice #10 DC Collectibles Variant Cover

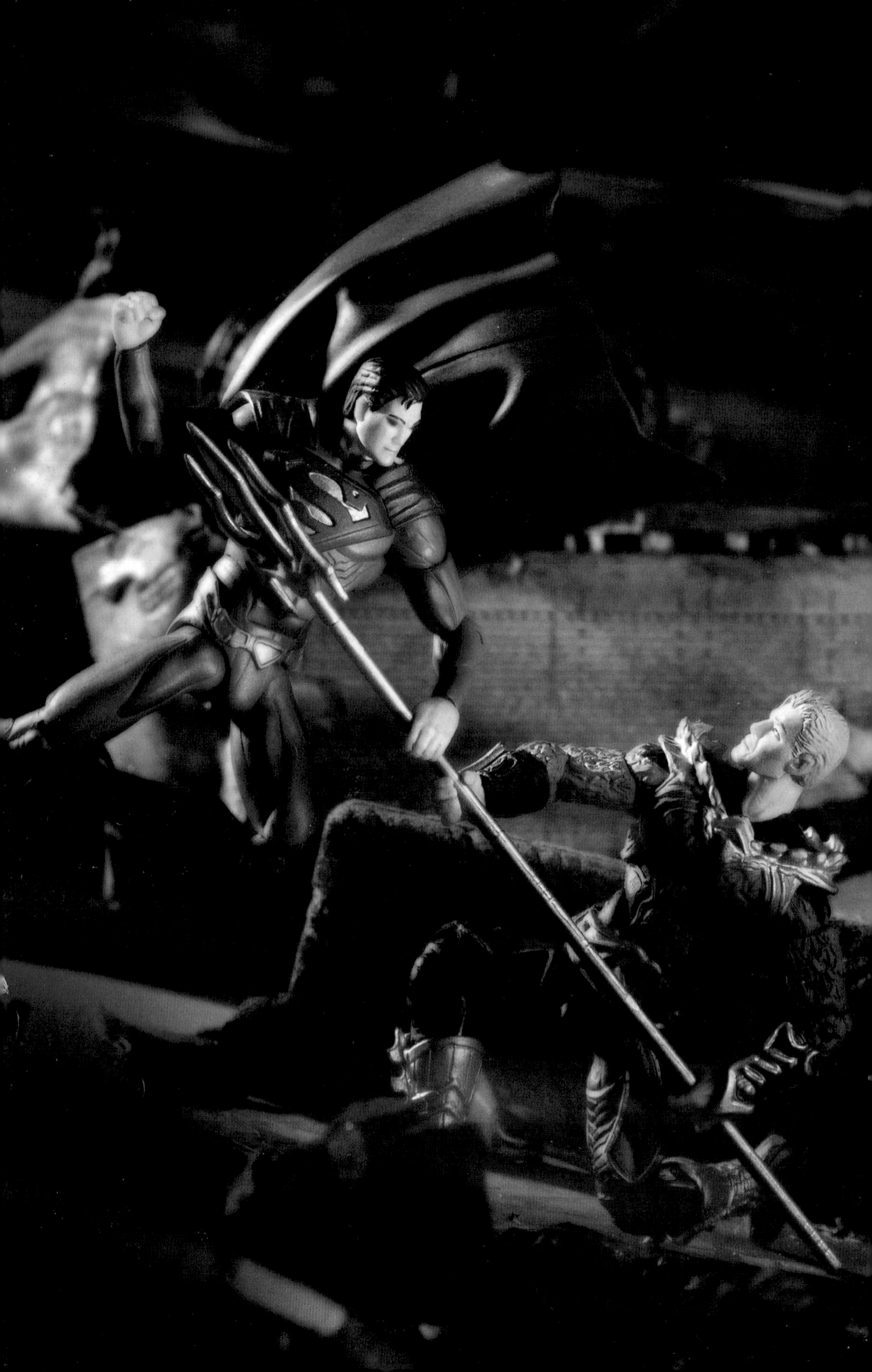

Injustice #11 DC Collectibles Variant Cover

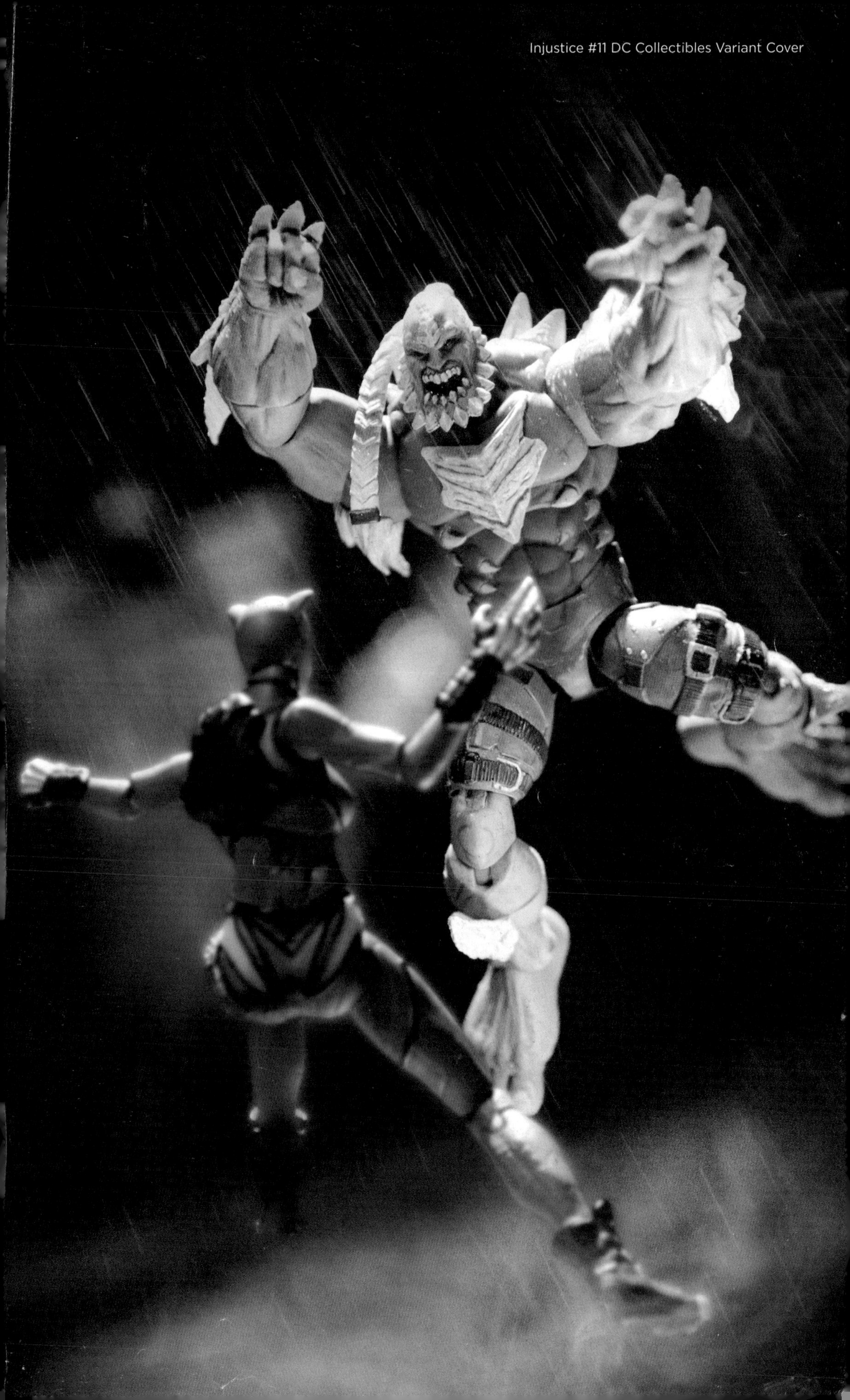

Injustice #12 DC Collectibles Variant Cover

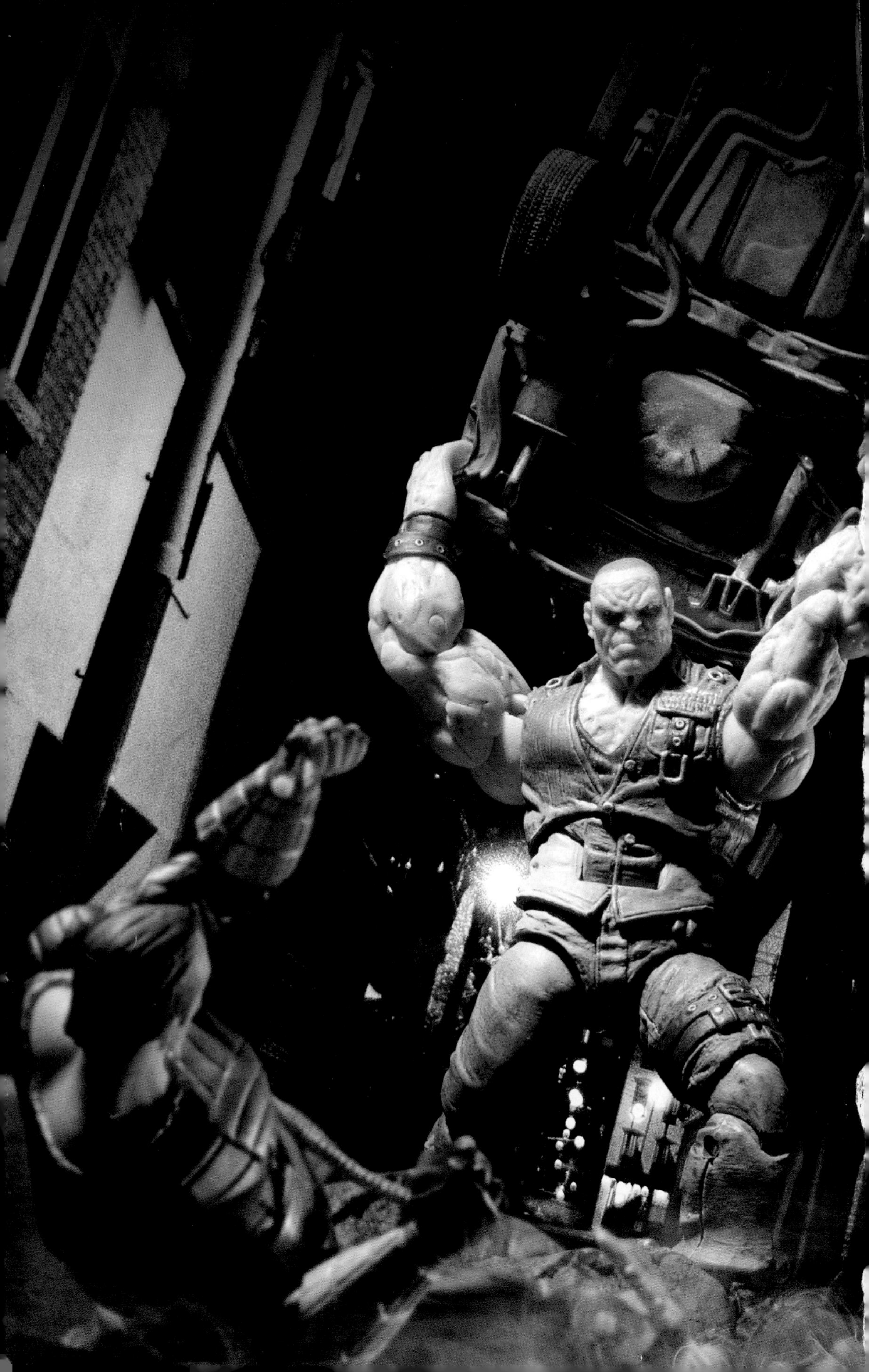

Check Out Receipt

Thomas Branch
(219) 926-7696

Thursday, May 17, 2018 11:39:05 AM

Title: Injustice : gods among us : year
one : the complete collection
Due: 06/14/2018

Title: Injustice : gods among us. Volume
2
Due: 06/14/2018

Items must be returned to the library
and checked in before closing on the
date(s) due.
Thank you!